HALTING DEGRADATION OF NATURAL RESOURCES

Halting Degradation of Natural Resources

Is there a Role for Rural Communities?

JEAN-MARIE BALAND
and
JEAN-PHILIPPE PLATTEAU

Foreword by Mancur Olson

Published by the
FOOD AND AGRICULTURE ORGANIZATION
OF THE UNITED NATIONS

and

OXFORD
UNIVERSITY PRESS

OXFORD
UNIVERSITY PRESS

Great Clarendon Street, Oxford OX2 6DP
Oxford University Press is a department of the University of Oxford.
It furthers the University's objective of excellence in research, scholarship,
and education by publishing worldwide in

Oxford New York

Athens Auckland Bangkok Bogotá Buenos Aires Calcutta
Cape Town Chennai Dar es Salaam Delhi Florence Hong Kong Istanbul
Karachi Kuala Lumpur Madrid Melbourne Mexico City Mumbai
Nairobi Paris São Paulo Taipei Tokyo Toronto Warsaw

Oxford is a registered trade mark of Oxford University Press
in the UK and certain other countries

Published in the United States
by Oxford University Press Inc., New York

The designations employed and the presentation of material in this publication do not imply the expression of any opinion whatsoever on the part of the Food and Agriculture Organization of the United Nations concerning the legal status of any country, territory, city or area or of its authorities, or concerning the delimitation of its frontiers or boundaries

The designations 'developed' and 'developing' economies are intended for statistical convenience and do not necessarily express a judgement about the state reached by a particular country, territory or area in the development process.

First published 1996
New as paperback edition 2000

Library of Congress Cataloging in Publication Data

Baland, Jean-Marie.

Halting degradation of natural resources: is there a role for
rural communities? / Jean-Marie Baland and Jean-Philippe Platteau;
foreword by Mancur Olson.
Includes bibliographical references
1. Natural resources—Management 2 Natural resources,
Communal—Management. 3. Commons I Platteau, J. P.
(Jean-Philippe), 1947- II. Title.
HC59.15.B35 1995 95-20282
333.7'2—dc20
ISBN 0-19-828921-9
ISBN 0-19-829061-6 (pbk.)

3 5 7 9 10 8 6 4 2

Typeset by Best-set Typesetter Ltd , Hong Kong
Printed in Great Britain
on acid-free paper by
Biddles Ltd., King's Lynn, Norfolk

This book is dedicated to our wives, Madeleine and Marie-Christine, who have renounced so many hours of our company to let this book come to fruition.

Foreword

This rich, balanced, and wide-ranging book will interest readers of a number of different backgrounds and interests. My guess is that each of these categories of reader would emphasize different features of the book: partisans on one side will find strong arguments and evidence to support their position, but their opponents will also find ammunition they can use in this fair-minded account. Those who like economic logic or game theory will probably emphasize the sound theoretical reasoning that inspires the book, while those who are inclined to inductive or anthropological work will tend to emphasize the way the book is guided by evidence and observation.

My emphasis is on what the book says about the relationship between the number of those who use or control a given common property and the likelihood that it will be protected—and especially on the question of whether a central government, on the one hand, or a small rural community, on the other, will be more likely to protect their environments and natural resources.

As I personally see the matter, several different factors have tended to make most of us assume that small rural communities in the Third World have relatively little to contribute to either economic development or environmental protection—the better and modern practices will come from the urbanized élites, the capital city, or from international organizations or aid-giving foreign countries. It is mainly regulation and constraints imposed from above upon the peasant communities that will make things better, and especially limit the degradation of the natural environment.

At the same time, a famous and marvellously simple theoretical idea—the prisoner's dilemma game—has tended to push in the same direction. Though it might seem utterly unrelated, the beguiling metaphor of the two prisoners has also, I think, worked to make many people assume that small groups, such as the families that make up a peasant village, would be at least as likely to despoil their environments as large or national populations would be.

Some neglected special characteristics of the classical illustration of the prisoner's dilemma game can help us see this from a new angle. In the canonical prisoner's dilemma example, the two men who were the only witnesses to the major crime they committed cannot be convicted of this crime unless at least one of them confesses and implicates the other, but the authorities have the evidence to convict them for another, lesser offence. The police put each man in a separate cell, and privately tell each that, if he does not turn State's evidence and the other does, he will be convicted and given an especially long sentence, but the sentence he receives will not be as severe if he confesses and implicates his partner. Most notably, the authorities make the bargain to each such that the rational strategy for each prisoner is to defect from the criminal partnership by turning State's evidence, irrespective of what each thinks the other will do. Therefore, each rational prisoner confesses, even though both prisoners would have been better off if neither confessed and they had thereby both been spared conviction for the major offence. To put the same point in another way, the criminal partnership does not obtain the collective good, for them, of keeping their participation in the major crime secret.

So, the story goes, just as the two prisoners do not serve their common interests by co-operation, so each of us individually has an incentive to take no account of the collective good of a wholesome environment, with the result that we jointly despoil our habitats and make ourselves worse off. It is, indeed, true that each individual in a large city has no incentive to limit his driving to curb air pollution, even when everyone would be made better off if all were induced to cut back their polluting behaviour. More generally, *laissez-faire* fails to prevent a population or large group from generating unjustifiably high levels of pollution.

And just as the two prisoners failed to serve their common interest, so the small number of families in a small community, such as in a Third World village, must also neglect their environment and their other collective interests. Right?

Wrong. The two rational prisoners failed to serve their common interest in avoiding conviction for the serious offence only because they were kept from communicating and making enforceable commitments to each other not to turn State's evidence. If they were allowed to communicate and work out an enforceable agreement not to give evidence to the police (mafioso do this all the time), they would have had an incentive to make a credible agreement to remain silent and both would have been spared conviction. It is only the very special circumstance that the two prisoners are kept in separate cells and are unable to communicate and make an enforceable agreement that prevents them from obtaining the gains from co-operation.

Thus it is no accident that the main metaphor that seems to show that even a group so small that it contains only two individuals will fail to serve its common interest—will fail to co-operate to achieve a collective good—is drawn from the realm of crime and punishment. If the two individuals in the prisoner's dilemma had not committed crimes, they would have been able to communicate freely and to make credible agreements, and even to make a contract enforceable by the courts. But for the very special circumstances that rule out communication and credible agreements, there would have been no dilemma in the first place.

Unfortunately, the textbooks ordinarily do not make clear what extraordinarily special circumstances are required to keep a group as small as two parties from providing themselves with a collective good.

In fact, when there are only a small number of parties that would gain from co-operation to provide a collective good, they will usually obtain at least much of the gains from co-operation. If, say, there are only three similar families who benefit from a local feature of the natural environment, each family will receive about a third of the benefits of whatever it does to protect this triadic collective good. Even though each family must bear the whole costs of whatever it does in the interest of the group of three, it may find it advantageous unilaterally to talk some account of the common interest of the three families. Most important, so long as there is nothing akin to the police that kept the prisoners in separate cells, they will be able to communicate and often make credible agreements to co-operate. Each family has an incentive to propose to the others that they will share the burden of providing the collective good if the others do and thereby achieve an ideal or group-optimal level of co-operation. All three may, for example, agree not to dump garbage on their common lot or to share the costs of planting the trees they need.

By contrast, in a population of a million, a representative individual will obtain only one-millionth of the benefits of whatever he or she does to provide or protect any collective good, yet bear all of the costs of whatever expenditure or forbearance is required for that collective good. The individual in a city of a million who drives less to prevent air pollution will bear the whole burden of this sacrifice but obtains only about a millionth of the benefits. So, as is well known, in large groups like nations we cannot depend upon Adam Smith's invisible hand to protect the environment.

In short, small groups, such as the few families in some rural communities in the Third World, will sometimes, through voluntary co-operation and traditional social organization, be able to do something to protect environmental assets that are important to them, whereas the large populations in huge cities can never rely on voluntary or *laissez-faire* mechanisms to protect their environments.

As I see it, this crucial importance of numbers for collective action, whether to protect the environment or for other purposes, has all too often not been understood. In part, I believe this because the very special 'prohibition of communication' that drives the two-person prisoner's dilemma tends to have been overlooked. At this point the reader who knows my own work may say that I am here revealing my partiality for my own analysis of the logic of collective action, which brings out the crucial role of numbers, over the prisoner's dilemma metaphor, which often leaves the impression that the likelihood of defection is not affected by the number involved, and wonder what I have just said has to do with this book by Baland and Platteau?

I think a great deal. The title of their book is *Halting Degradation of Natural Resources: Is there a Role for Rural Communities?* The foregoing argument suggests that the question in their subtitle should be answered in the affirmative. In a balanced way, Baland and Platteau go into both the strengths and weaknesses of traditional rural communities as custodians of natural resources. They point out that traditional rural communities in the least developed countries do suffer from lack of education and knowledge, and have still other weaknesses as guardians of natural resources.

None the less, both the examples and the reasoning they present, on balance, reinforce my belief that the question in their title should be answered with a 'yes'. They point to the 'upsurge of in-depth field studies pointing to the considerable collective action potential of rural communities'. Moreover, the central role of group size for collective action is one of the central themes running through the book. One of the authors' merits in this regard is to have referred to a variety of advantages of small groups beyond the incentive dilution argument underlined above. Also, they have clearly distinguished the issue of group size from that of group homogeneity/heterogeneity, providing us with a rich discussion of the various possible dimensions of social heterogeneity and their differentiated impact upon a society's collective action potential (see Chapters 5 and 12). In addition, Baland and Platteau have laid much emphasis on the role of inter-agent communication for fostering co-operation, more particularly in Chapter 7 where they review some salient results of experimental social psychology. A noteworthy feature of their discussion is that problems of commitment are brought into the picture, thus drawing attention to the crucial issue of the reliability of the promises made during the communication process.

Finally, their 'game theoretical analysis suggests that problems of the commons are not necessarily well depicted by the classic prisoner's dilemma'. As they show, important situations involve problems of trust, co-ordination, leadership, heterogeneity, etc., and one of the main contributions of their book is to have offered a precise theoretical characterization of such situations (in Chapter 5) and to have simultaneously illustrated and discussed them in the light of a host of socio-anthropological studies (in Chapter 12).

Admittedly, some readers may prefer to emphasize the value of other features of the book, and it is good that readers with different leanings should also find value in it. But I believe that, in view of the absolutely appalling record of most of the national governments of the poorest countries, the potentials of the smaller rural communities in these societies cannot be ignored. All too often these small communities are oppressed and repressed by the autocratic leaders and kleptocratic civil and military officers of these countries. These small communities have many disadvantages and they may often need help. That is one reason why the co-management approach discussed at the end of the book (in Chapter 13) deserves the attention of policy-makers: it underlines the case for institutionalizing co-operation between the State and the user communities by using their comparative strengths at different levels in a complementary way. Baland and Platteau realize that co-management is not, however, a magic word—that it should take on a variety of forms and that it is up to each country to find the most suitable one by taking due account of the specific characteristics of the resources and the users involved. I commend their balanced argument to readers.

Mancur Olson

Contents

List of Figures

List of Tables

Introduction

The present work is concerned with the topical issue of natural resource management. It does not deal, however, with broad-spectrum environmental concerns such as protection of wilderness areas (for example, the south pole), air or water pollution, etc., but focuses on local ecosystems. What distinguishes local-level resources from larger ecosystems is that (1) they are susceptible of appropriation by relatively small units (including individuals) and (2) they can lead to rivalry in consumption in so far as yields of these resources are clearly perceived as subtractable. This book thus addresses the question as to how these local or village-level natural resources (as contrasted with global commons) can be most efficiently and equitably managed. In other words, can we find guidelines or sound theoretical principles for an optimal long-term exploitation of local resources (forests, irrigation water, pastures, lakes and rivers, sea areas, etc.)? Disturbing evidence highlighting rapid processes of resource depletion, particularly so in developing countries, has stimulated a lot of theoretical and empirical works during the last decades. Moreover, relevant theoretical tools (such as game theory) have been developed independently of environmental concerns which have potential applications to this field. The present attempt aims essentially at making a pause in order to take stock of the achievements attained so far. We believe this step is necessary in view not only of the considerable body of literature which has accumulated on the subject under concern, but also of the multidisciplinary nature of the works involved. Due to these two characteristics, there are many gaps to be bridged between various strands of thinking or contributions to the field.

It is our conviction that the time has come to weave together or to otherwise compare and confront different kinds of works around well-defined questions and hypotheses so as to better structure and assess the available body of knowledge. It is striking that economic theorists ignore most of the results obtained by applied researchers, and therefore remain unable to make a valid judgement on the empirical relevance of their analytical propositions. And, on the other hand, applied researchers often ignore the contribution of theorists and, owing to this lacuna, their formulation of the problem and of the hypotheses being tested tends to be imprecise while the concepts used are not always sufficiently tight or rigorous. The field is very complex, indeed, and that is why, to repeat, it is an urgent task to bring some order and to shed some light on where we stand today, taking a broad view of what has been achieved by scholars belonging to different disciplines. Only then can we make a sound assessment of where we ought to direct our attention in future research efforts.

When tackling the question as how best to manage local commons or village-level resources, it has become common practice in many writings to distinguish between three modes of management: private, public (or state), and community management.

This typology is clearly of a legal type in the sense that the underlying criterion is the nature of ownership (is the owner of the resource a private individual, the State, or a group or community?). When various modes of management have to be compared on the field, this is undoubtedly a useful distinction although it is much too crude in so far as it rules out any intermediary mode mixing up elements of two or three of the above 'ideal' modes.

Economists tend to adopt another analytical grid which is particularly appropriate to raise pertinent theoretical questions. Here, the distinction is between open access (which is equivalent to a no-property or *res nullius* regime under the above legal typology), unregulated common property (access rules prevail that define insiders as against outsiders), regulated common property (not only is access delimited but rules of use are also defined), and private property. It must be emphasized that the regulating agency under regulated common property can take various concrete forms ranging from a small community to a state apparatus. Yet, when the State does not actually regulate, a regime of nationalized commons is akin to open access even though the State is the legal owner. As for private property, it differs from regulated common property only in so far as the rule-defining agent is also the unique user of the resource. As a result, what distinguishes fundamentally these two regimes is the fact that private property as opposed to regulated common property cannot give rise to collective action problems. Note again that, if we follow the analytical logic of the economists' perspective, private property where the owner is absent and careless about the resource is tantamount to open access because formal or legal ownership rights are not actually exercised.

The second above perspective—that of the economists—provides a framework for the analysis conducted in Part I of this work. In the first chapter, an attempt is made at defining properly what is meant by the optimal use of a natural resource. As will be seen, even though such an optimal pattern does not imply of necessity that a conservationist strategy is being followed, good grounds still exist to support the conservationist claim that natural resources should be safeguarded even at the cost of some production losses. Moreover, in the real world many resources are clearly over-exploited in ways incompatible with any optimality criterion. The main source of this mismanagement of natural resources is widely known in the literature as 'the tragedy of the commons', which attributes the inefficiency in resource use to the absence of well-defined property rights. Chapter 2 is devoted to an in-depth analysis of this issue.

It has often been claimed that the tragedy of the commons could be easily solved by simply establishing private property rights on the resource. In Chapter 3, a balanced view is proposed of the various implications of privatization of the commons. It is argued that, even on the basis of the strict criterion of efficiency, privatization of natural resources is not always an appropriate solution.

In Chapter 4, we call into question the pessimistic view according to which uncoordinated human behaviour inexorably leads to the destruction of the commons, as implied by the tragedy of the commons. It is argued that decentralized mechanisms may possibly prompt agents to avoid the collectively irrational outcome that such destruction amounts to. First, as suggested by Ronald Coase, agents may get involved in voluntary exchanges of their rights to impose externalities on the others. If they abstain from doing so, it is necessarily because these exchanges (including the establishment of private property rights) are not socially efficient. The limitations of the Coasian solution are nevertheless serious and will be duly emphasized. Second, the possibility of spontaneous co-operative behaviour in a strategic framework is examined in the light of recent developments of non-co-operative game theory. This analysis points to the importance of repeated interactions between actors and, therefore, to the advantages of small groups for the efficient use of local commons.

Contrary to what the tragedy of the commons' story suggests, many of the problems encountered in unregulated common property are problems of co-ordination and leadership and are, therefore, not adequately represented by the prisoner's dilemma. Chapter 5 first examines the contribution that game theory can make to the understanding of these two problems. In a second step, special attention is paid to heterogeneous situations in which different types of actors interact. In particular, we try to assess the threat to the stability of co-ordinated solutions that may be caused by a minority of opportunistic actors, both in small and large groups.

In Chapter 6, we relax the assumption of non-socialized individuals implicit in economic theorizing. More precisely, we envisage the role of moral norms as a possible way of shaping individual preferences and expectations in a way conducive to co-operation. The difficult issue as to how such norms emerge is also addressed in this chapter.

Chapter 7 confronts many of the results of non-co-operative game theory reviewed in the previous chapters with the findings of social experimental psychology. This exercise shows that often people tend to behave in ways that do not support the universal free-riding hypothesis, even when interactions are not repeated. More importantly, the function of communication, which is to facilitate promise-making and to build trust among strangers, is brought to light.

Chapter 8 is devoted to the detailed analysis of the possibility of collective regulation of the use of local resources. In theory, efficient use of these resources can be achieved through appropriate regulations. There are however two kinds of problems that may make regulation less attractive than it appears at first sight. First, regulation may be costly to achieve and carry out, especially in contexts of high uncertainties, pervasive market imperfections, and informational asymmetries. Second, regulation may seriously affect income distribution, and, for this reason, it is liable to generate strong opposition from some users.

Chapter 9 offers some concluding reflections on the privatization of common property resources.

In Part II, the main lessons drawn from Part I are confronted with the evidence accumulated in field settings, mainly pertaining to traditional village societies in developing countries. More precisely, the following questions are addressed in the light of the socio-anthropological empirical material available:

1. Do we find in these societies mechanisms or behaviours that have the effect of regulating use of common property resources? Do such mechanisms or schemes hinge upon the purposeful and unremitting intervention of a local authority or, on the contrary, are they the spontaneous outcome of completely decentralized initiatives? Are these mechanisms and behaviours aimed at an efficient use of the resources or do they serve other social purposes, particularly that of ensuring fair access to these resources (Chapter 10)?
2. How can we assess and explain the degree of effectiveness of state intervention in village-level resources (Chapter 11, sect. 1)?
3. Has the ability of traditional village societies in designing and enforcing effective regulatory schemes been affected by recent changes in the broad technological, demographic, social, and political environment in which these societies operate (Chapter 11, sect. 2)?
4. What are the main factors conditioning success of collective action with respect to local-level management of common property resources (Chapter 12)?
5. Do we find intermediary regimes at work that go beyond the conventional distinction between private, state, and community management? How can we assess their potential (Chapter 13)?

As is evident from the above presentation, this study has a clearly multidisciplinary character even though it uses essentially economic concepts that reflect the authors' basic training. This is especially obvious in Part I in which the arguments developed are understandable only to a reader with a fair background in economics. For those who do not meet this requirement or feel repelled by 'pure' economic arguments, the reading of Part II can still prove rewarding since it is conceived as a self-contained whole which can be read independently of Part I.

The above project was originally commissioned by the Food and Agriculture Organization of the United Nations (FAO) and, without the strong encouragements and continuous support of Apostolos Condos from the Policy Analysis Division, it would not have come to fruition. This book is actually based on a largely rewritten version of the report submitted to the FAO at the beginning of 1993. To carry out this revision of the original work, the authors have benefited from the observations and critiques of a number of scholars to whom they want to express their gratitude. In particular, thanks are due to Pranab Bardhan (University of California, Berkeley), K. P. Cannan and John Kurien (Centre of Development Studies, Trivandrum), Robert Cassen (University of Oxford), Partha Dasgupta (University of Cambridge), Robert Allen, Patrick François and Ashok Kotwal (University of British Columbia, Vancouver), François Maniquet (University of Namur), Sebastian Mathew (International Collective in Support of Fishworkers, Madras), Jeffrey Nugent (University of Southern California, Los Angeles), Mancur Olson (University of Maryland, Washington), Elinor Ostrom (Indiana University, Bloomington), Maurice Schiff (the World Bank), and Rolf Willmann (FAO). Moreover, the authors have been greatly stimulated by the thorough discussions that took place during a series of five seminars organized at the universities of Stanford and Berkeley, California. They feel especially indebted to Marcel Fafchamps, Carl Gotsch, and Albert Park (from Stanford University) and to Alain de Janvry and Elisabeth Sadoulet (from the University of California, Berkeley). The views expressed in the book are, however, the entire responsibility of the authors and, in particular, they do not necessarily reflect the position of the FAO. Finally, thanks are due to Anne Patigny for her helpful assistance in typing the text at various stages of the work.

PART I

Rationale and Scope of Local-Level Resource Management: Lessons from Economic Theory

1

Natural Resources and Economic Growth: Towards a Definition of Sustainability

That the limited availability of natural resources may threaten economic growth has preoccupied economists since the birth of the discipline. Thomas Malthus, David Ricardo, John Stuart Mill, and other classical economists have paid so much attention to the limits to growth caused by finite natural resources that they have given these limits a central role in their analysis of the long-term dynamic evolution of market economies towards a stationary state. The gloomy conclusions reached by those early economists have received a modern formulation and further support in recent years with the works of G. Hardin and Baden, 1977; J. W. Forrester, 1971; and H. S. D. Cole *et al.*, 1973.

1.1 Production and Exhaustibility

Modern economic theory allows us to distinguish between different characteristics of natural resources which are directly relevant to the problem in question. A resource is said to be *exhaustible* if one can find a pattern of use for this resource such that it will be depleted in finite time. Clearly, almost any natural resource, with perhaps the exception of solar energy, is exhaustible. A resource is said to be *renewable* if one can find a pattern of positive use such that its stock does not shrink over time. One can think of a fishery or of soil fertility as good illustrations of a renewable resource. Of course, if concern is about the issue of economic development and the possible constraints which natural resources may place on it, interest will naturally focus on the analysis of exhaustible and non-renewable resources which are *essential*. The definition of the latter concept is intuitive, though, as we shall see, it is not very useful: a resource is essential in production if 'the output of final goods is nil in the absence of the resource' (Dasgupta and Heal, 1974: 4). A similar definition can be used for a resource essential in consumption.

As pointed out by Stiglitz (1974), there are at least three ways to counterbalance the negative effects of essential resources on production: technical progress, increasing returns to scale, and substitution. The third factor needs to be examined in detail. Three different situations may again arise when one analyses the possibilities for substituting a reproducible input, say capital, to an increasingly scarce essential resource. The natural economic concept for measuring substitution possibilities is the elasticity of substitution (for a detailed exposition of what follows, see Dasgupta and Heal, 1974, 1979: 196–200). Let us focus on the class of CES production functions such as:

$$F(K,R,L) = (\alpha_1 K^{(\sigma-1)/\sigma} + \alpha_2 R^{(\sigma-1)/\sigma} + (1 - \alpha_1 - \alpha_2)L^{(\sigma-1)/\sigma})^{\sigma/(\sigma-1)}$$

where α_1, α_2, $1-\alpha_1-\alpha_2 > 0$, and $\sigma > 0$, $\sigma \neq 1$, K stands for reproducible capital, R for the flow of resources used in production, L for the labour force, and F for the final net output. If $\sigma > 1$, $F(K,0,L) > 0$: the resource is not essential for production. If $\sigma < 1$, the average product of the resource is bounded from above owing to the low degree of substitutability between R and K or L; therefore, if the resource stock is finite, it can only support a finite amount of output and, for infinite time, the only *sustainable* level of consumption is zero. In a way, the resource considered is trivially essential: no substitution allows the economy to escape the final doom. The really interesting case to analyse is that where $\sigma = 1$. In such a case, as is well known, the above production function reduces to a Cobb–Douglas:

$$Y = K^{\alpha_1} R^{\alpha_2} L^{1-\alpha_1-\alpha_2} \tag{2}$$

The question which arises is: does there exist a positive level of consumption which can be sustained for infinite time in this economy, assuming that there is no technical progress nor population growth?[1] The answer is 'yes', if the elasticity of output with respect to capital, α_1, exceeds that with respect to exhaustible resources, α_2. We normalize by setting $L = 1$, and assume that there is no depreciation of the capital stock. S_0, the initial stock of resources, and K_0, the initial stock of capital being given, the maximum constant consumption flow, C^*, is given by:

$$C^* = (\alpha_2^{\alpha_1/(1-\alpha_2)} - \alpha_2^{1/(1-\alpha_2)})((\alpha_1 - \alpha_2)/\alpha_2)^{\alpha_2/(1-\alpha_2)} S_0^{\alpha_2/(1-\alpha_2)} K_0^{(\alpha_1-\alpha_2)/(1-\alpha_2)} \tag{3}$$

Such a consumption programme can be sustained for infinite time, with the saving rate being set at α_2. It implies the following:

$$K_t = K_0 + mt \text{ and} \tag{4}$$

$$R_t = m((\alpha_1 - \alpha_2)/\alpha_2) S_0 K_0^{(\alpha_1-\alpha_2)/\alpha_2}(K_0 + mt)^{-\alpha_1/\alpha_2} \tag{5}$$

$$m = \alpha_2^{1-\alpha_2}((\alpha_1 - \alpha_2)/\alpha_2)^{\alpha_2/(1-\alpha_2)} S_0^{\alpha_2/(1-\alpha_2)} K_0^{(\alpha_1-\alpha_2)/(1-\alpha_2)} \tag{6}$$

where t stands for time, starting at time zero. The programme defined by equations (3) to (6) above is worth examining in detail:

1. The amount of resources used at time t, R_t, declines over time which does not cause the consumption flow to fall owing to the possibility of substituting the growing capital stock for the shrinking resources. In infinite time, the entire stock, S_0, is depleted.

2. As noted above, α_1 must be higher than α_2. Indeed, it can be shown that, if $\alpha_2 > \alpha_1$—the elasticity of output with respect to capital is low compared to that with respect to natural resources—output will eventually decline to zero. As is the case when the elasticity of substitution is smaller than one, the resource is trivially essential: substitution possibilities do not allow a positive consumption flow to be sustained in infinite time.

[1] As noted by Solow, the assumption of exponential growth of population is not very realistic on a time-scale appropriate to finite resources (Solow, 1974: 36–7).

3. The programme defined above is intertemporally efficient: it can indeed be proved that there is no feasible programme which gives at least as much consumption in every period and strictly more in some (see Dasgupta and Heal, 1979: ch. 7).

4. As shown by Solow (1974), it is also an optimal programme if the resource-managing authority follows the Rawlsian welfare approach to the intergenerational problem of optimal resource utilization by applying the maximin principle. Indeed, the interests of each succeeding generation are met when the minimum welfare which can be guaranteed to all of them is maximized.

5. The amount of the resource used at time zero, R_0, varies positively with S_0 and negatively with K_0. Comparing two economies, A and B, with the same amount of natural resources but where one of them, A, has a lower capital stock than the other, it can be shown that, to sustain the maximum constant consumption flow through time, A exhibits a higher initial rate of resource exploitation than B. Since both extraction paths must exhaust the resource stock over infinite time, the rate of extraction falls more rapidly in A than in B, and the extraction path curves cross once in the plane (R_t, t). Note also that, since A is poorer, the constant consumption flow it may enjoy is also lower. Finally, as given by equations (4) and (6), the accumulation of capital proceeds at a quicker pace in the capital-rich economy B. Diagramatically, these processes can be depicted as in Figure 1.1. It is therefore evident that high initial

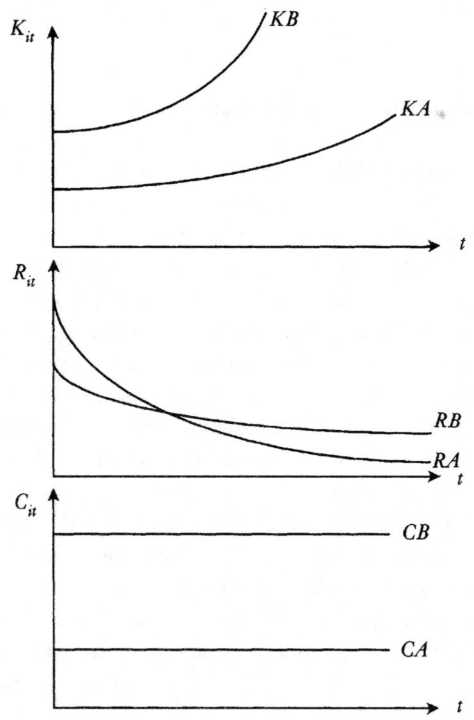

FIG. 1.1. Constant consumption flows and extraction paths of a capital-rich economy, B, and a capital-poor economy, A

rates of resource exploitation are not incompatible with a development process characterized by a sustainable consumption flow. For LDCs which are comparatively resource-rich economies, high rates of extraction of environmental resources may be part of a sustainable development strategy, and should not necessarily be confused with destructive overexploitation.[2]

6. If disembodied technical progress takes place, for instance at a constant rate λ, the exhaustible resource, though essential, does not prevent a positive sustainable level of consumption, even if $\alpha_2 > \alpha_1$: one can always find a pattern of extraction R_t such that $e^{\lambda t/\alpha_2}R_t$ does not fall to zero. The same argument evidently holds for any production function if resource-augmenting technical progress is assumed to operate at a constant rate.

7. We have not yet considered the possibility of an ever-growing level of consumption in the economy under concern. In the above model, it can be shown that such a growth path is actually possible if a constant level of consumption is feasible (that is, if $\alpha_1 > \alpha_2$): it just requires that capital is accumulated at a sufficiently high rate in the initial periods (see Dasgupta and Heal, 1979: ch. 10). To say that growing consumption is possible does not imply that it is optimal: 'A positive rate of impatience, no matter how small, implies that it is judged optimal to allow the economy to decay in the long run, even although it is feasible to avoid decay' (Dasgupta and Heal, 1979: 299).

1.2 Justifying a Conservationist Strategy

Up to now, we have examined the possibility for an economy to maintain a constant level of consumption over an infinite horizon with a given stock of a non-renewable resource which is essential in production. We have seen that, if a constant level of consumption is sustainable, then it requires that the resource stock is depleted at a decreasing rate. *A fortiori*, this also holds for a renewable resource: *here, sustainability does not require the resource base to be preserved.* Furthermore, it must be emphasized that in all the cases where the resource is *not* essential (in production), *optimality* may require its complete exhaustion in finite time. In other words, when technical conditions exist that render a resource (eventually) dispensable or superfluous, it may be quite sensible for a society to destroy it since, by doing so, it does not threaten future consumption and production possibilities.

Therefore, the conservationist view, following which the resource base is to be maintained, must be grounded elsewhere. There are at least four assumptions made in the model presented above which leave some space for a conservationist strategy to be vindicated. The first one is that of perfect information at the disposal of the decision-maker: anything relevant to the problem is known with certainty at the time of the decision. In the real world, however, information on natural resources is far from

[2] Summers, in a provocative World Bank internal memo, went so far as suggesting that 'underpopulated countries in Africa are vastly underpolluted, their air quality is probably vastly, inefficiently high compared to Los Angeles or Mexico City' (*The Economist*, 9 May 1992).

perfect. It is not at all clear, for example, that all future possible uses of the resource are correctly perceived today by the decision-maker: for instance, non-anticipated uses of the resource may be discovered some time in the future which will make its disappearance extremely prejudicial to the society. Under these conditions, it may be advisable to keep a minimum amount of a resource:[3] in the words of Henry, 'the mere prospect of getting fuller information, combined with the irreversibility of the non-preservation alternative, brings forth a positive *option value* in favour of preservation' (Henry, 1974*a*: 90).

The argument about incomplete information may however be turned the other way round: at the time of decision-making, information is not necessarily available on the possible appearance of perfect substitutes for the resource or on the exact size of the resource stock, which may render too conservationist a strategy uneconomical. For instance, from 1907 to 1957, the services rendered by a ton of coal have increased tenfold because of reductions in the energy required for mining, transport, and electricity generation and transmission (Fisher, 1981: 95). Or, from 1947 to 1972, the estimated world oil reserves[4] have also increased tenfold (see Fisher, 1981: 93). The effect of uncertainty may therefore be ambiguous. However, it is clear that irreplaceable assets, for which no close substitute exists, should be given some value *per se*, so as to prevent their complete destruction when this outcome can be avoided (see e.g. Krutilla, 1967; Henry, 1974*a*, *b*). This is probably the argument which underlies propositions to classify as world patrimony geographical zones of particular ecological interest (for instance, the Antarctic and, presumably, in the near future, part of the Amazonian forest) or to maintain a minimal biodiversity by protecting endangered biological species.

The second assumption made in the above model is that the resource in question is of no value except as a productive input. Exhaustible resources, such as places of natural beauty, pure air, or unpolluted rivers, may however be directly valuable to the consumer. As expressed by John Stuart Mill:

> A world from which solitude is extirpated, is a very poor ideal. Solitude, in the sense of being often alone, is essential to any depth or meditation of character; and solitude in the presence of natural beauty and grandeur, is the cradle of thoughts and aspirations which are not only good for the individual, but which society can ill do without. Nor is there much satisfaction in contemplating a world with nothing left to the spontaneous activity of nature; with every rood of land brought into cultivation, which is capable of growing food for human beings; every flowery waste or natural pasture ploughed up, all quadrupeds or birds which are not domesticated for man's use exterminated as his rivals for food, every hedgerow or superfluous tree rooted out, and scarcely a place left where a wild shrub or flower could grow without being eradicated as a weed in the name of improved agriculture. . . . If the earth must lose that great portion of its pleasantness which it owes to things that the unlimited increase in wealth and population would extirpate from it, for the mere purpose of enabling it to support a large, but

[3] This argument holds even if it is irreversibility itself which is uncertain, as long as there is a non-zero probability that the current move is irreversible (for more details, see Viscusi, 1985).

[4] Note that 'reserves are defined as the known amounts of mineral that can be profitably produced at current prices using current technology' (Fisher, 1981: 94).

not a better or happier population, I sincerely hope, for the sake of posterity, that they will content to be stationary, long before necessity compels them to it. (Mill, 1848: 115–16).

At some point therefore, it makes sense also to consider natural resources as consumer goods, a positive utility being associated with their mere presence, or their degree of purity. There is therefore a possible trade-off between their contribution as a productive input and the utility they bring when left unused. By analogy with a resource essential in production, exhaustion of a resource essential in consumption will never be optimal. Note also that it has been repeatedly suggested in the literature that environmental resources, as consumer goods, are superior goods: their demand is likely to have a very high income elasticity. Therefore, one may expect that, with the growth in income following from economic development, a demand for higher environmental standards will also develop. This must be taken into account in the decision process when, for instance, irreversible changes are to be brought about in the natural environment. Of course, if one does not know with certainty how preferences will be shaped in the future, then, as explained above, an option value must be given to the resource, that is, conservation is to be favoured. For instance, some may think that, in the future, environmental resources will be highly valued, while others may argue that people in the future will be satisfied with an almost entirely artificial world. Irreversibility implies that, in current decisions, more attention should be given to the former than to the latter possibility, even if one may think that both scenarios are equally likely: for the choice to be optimal, it must be *biased* towards preservation by taking into account the option value of the natural resources (for more details and a formal proof, see Henry, 1974*a*).

A third assumption made in the above models is that one can always substitute capital for environmental resources in the production functions. In the real world, technical conditions do not involve such possibilities for smooth substitution between these two factors, making unlimited growth in the presence of exhaustible resources a less likely outcome.

As for the fourth assumption, it lies in the smoothness of technical processes: it is indeed assumed that changes brought about by an optimal exploitation of the resource are slowly cumulative (there is no discontinuity). Though such an assumption may appear reasonable when it concerns resources such as fossil energy, it is hardly appropriate for natural resources involving ecological processes: just think of land, forests, pure air, or clean water. For these types of resources, there may well be threshold levels of 'exploitation' beyond which the whole system moves in a discontinuous way from one equilibrium to another.

One of the problems is that we do not know what lies ahead. Our knowledge of the real processes at work is simply too poor. As expressed by Broeker, 'we play Russian roulette . . . [and] no one knows what lies in the active chamber of the gun' (quoted in Chakravarty, 1990: 70). To take an example, the global warming-up resulting from the greenhouse effect will cause an increase in the mean global temperature estimated from 1.5 °C to 5 °C in the next fifty years (and from 3 °C to 10 °C for the next ninety years) (Schokkaert, 1992). In the present state of our knowledge, we are not able to predict more accurately the global warming-up, not to speak of its global consequences, even though it is clearly an issue to which an impressive amount of scientific work and a lot of attention from political authorities have been devoted in recent years. In general, one can surmise that, if there exists a threshold level beyond which complete disaster is a possibility, it is never optimal to go beyond it.

1.3 Sustainability and Reproducibility

The aforementioned arguments in favour of conservation rest on the idea of *irreversibility*: irreversibility is indeed at the heart of the problem. That the use of a mineral or of fossil energy in a production process is irreversible is quite obvious, total recycling never being possible (according to the second law of thermodynamics). The same holds true when there are use thresholds beyond which a global and irreversible change occurs in the ecosystem (e.g. desertification of the Sahelian area) or when destruction of a place of natural beauty (e.g. Hells Canyon—see Krutilla and Cicchetti, 1972; Fisher, 1981: 139–63—the Forest of Fontainebleau, or the Garibaldi pine tree in Rome) is contemplated. It nevertheless bears emphasis that many natural resources are, within given limits, renewable. Pure air or clean water are renewable resources and their use does not necessarily bring about irreversible changes.

Every ecosystem is characterized by a *carrying capacity*, a notion which can be defined in the present context as the amount of the natural resource that can be exploited without endangering the reproduction of the ecosystem. *Reproducibility* or *conservation* are directly related to the notion of carrying capacity: a level of production making use of a natural resource is reproducible if it lies within the upper limit set by the carrying capacity of the ecosystem within which it takes place. In other words, reproducibility refers to 'the ability of a system to maintain its productivity when subject to stress and shock, where the former is "a regular, sometimes continuous, small and predictable disturbance, for example the effect of growing soil salinity" . . . and the latter is "an irregular, infrequent, relatively large and unpredictable disturbance, such as is caused by a rare drought or flood or a new pest". The key is to reduce resource degradation and the associated stresses and shocks to a level where the natural processes and functions of the agro-ecosystem can counteract them' (Barbier, 1989: 441).

This concept of reproducibility or conservation should be carefully distinguished from the concept of sustainability:[5] as shown above, sustainability (of a consumption level, or of a development process) may require the ultimate destruction of a resource or a change in the ecosystem. Reproducibility is a more stringent criterion in that it requires the resource base to be preserved. When using the concept of sustainability, we are concerned about whether a level of well-being (or of production, or of con-

[5] In the literature, these two notions are often confused and both labelled 'sustainability'. Of course, the basic idea, that something has to be 'maintained', is identical. In one case, it is a level of well-being or a growth process (flows) that is to be maintained—this is the definition we have adopted—in the other, it is a 'resource base' (a stock). However, especially when the discussion bears upon 'sustainable development', the distinction between these two notions (which goes beyond a simple stock/flow dichotomy) will prove useful.

sumption) can be maintained over an infinite horizon, whereas, when referring to reproducibility, we are not only concerned with the possibility of sustaining a level of well-being but also with the way this can be done since we require the *stability* of the ecosystem within which human intervention takes place. The concept of reproducibility has a definite advantage over that of sustainability, namely that, in some instances, it has an operational content (the resource base cannot be destroyed) which is lacking in the concept of sustainability: whether a development process is 'sustainable' or not is, in general, unverifiable. On the other hand, though the concept of reproducibility helps to characterize human intervention in an ecosystem, it says nothing about its desirability (or optimality), except under ultraconservationist views considering the current *status quo* as preferable to anything else. The weakness of the latter concept is clear enough when the current ecosystem is itself the result of former non-reproducible human interventions, such as the conversion of wild forests into arable land, or when the resource base would disappear in the absence of direct human intervention to sustain it. In the words of Brookfield, 'it does no violence to sustainability to point out that conversion of a forest into well-managed agricultural land is not degradation if the product of the new use is of greater total utility to people, and can be maintained through time' (Brookfield, 1991: 48).

Management of renewable resources, such as animal population and forests, and the concept of reproducibility can be illustrated with the help of a well-known diagram first developed to analyse fisheries (see Dasgupta and Heal, 1979: 113–17; Fisher, 1981: 79–86). The crucial feature of a renewable resource is the natural growth law according to which the growth of a resource is a function of its stock. For the sake of simplicity, we shall assume that the latter is the only variable affecting the growth of the resource. Furthermore, the relation between growth and stock is not monotonic. Indeed, the environment has a carrying capacity for the resource, a maximum level of population beyond which the growth of the resource is negative. Before this point, however, the growth–population curve takes on the form of a logistic curve. The relation can be represented as in Figure 1.2.

In this diagram, X_c represents the maximum population the environment can

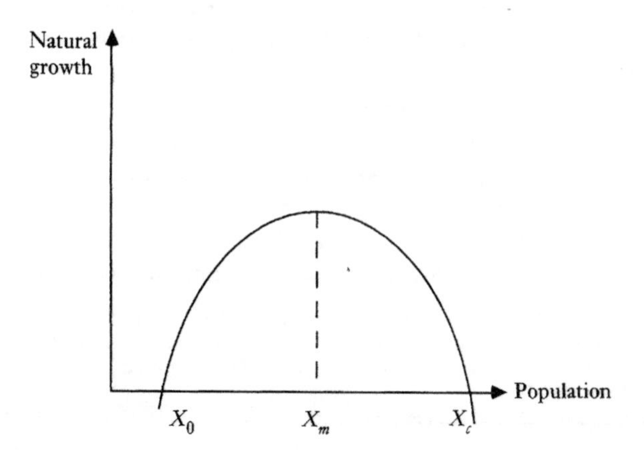

FIG. 1.2. Biological growth law

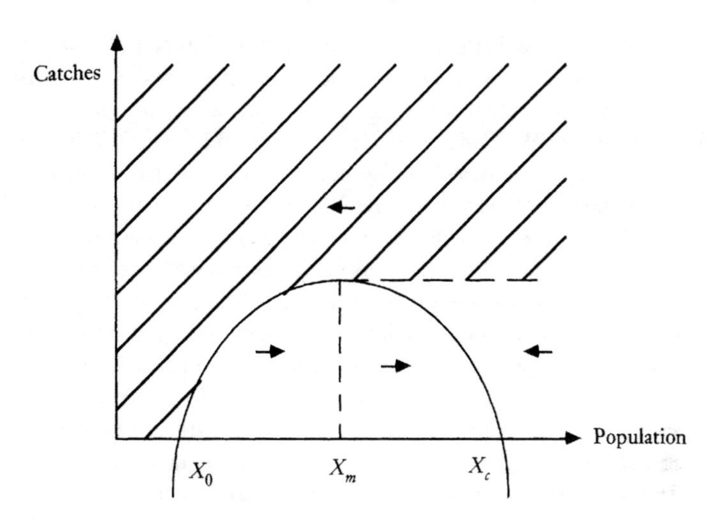

FIG. 1.3. Catches and biological growth

sustain, i.e. the carrying capacity. X_0 represents the minimum population size below which the growth of the population is negative: the population dies out. For many natural resources, $X_0 = 0$. However, for some animal species, X_0 can be strictly positive, either because, below this level, the population is too scattered to assure its reproduction (whales or elephants might be examples), or because it lacks the necessary genetic diversity. Between X_0 and X_C, the growth curve takes on a bell-shape, with a maximum in X_m. This level is often called 'maximum biological yield'. Let us now introduce human intervention in the form of fishing efforts resulting in fish catches. Since it has the effect of changing the population size, it is measured on the vertical axis as shown in Figure 1.3.

The curve can be straightforwardly derived from the growth–population curve. It represents the relation between the stock of population and the maximum amount of fish which can be caught while keeping this stock constant. We shall refer to this level of catches as the equilibrium level. A given level of catches is *compatible with a conservationist objective* and is called reproducible if it is located on the catch–population curve: any level of fishing effort or catches in that area allows the population stock to be maintained. An amount of catches located below the curve allows the population stock to grow (as indicated by the arrows) and is also compatible with a conservationist objective. A given level of catches is called *sustainable* if it lies beneath the shaded area: despite the changes in population that it may bring about, the level of catches can be maintained for ever. Note also that, as soon as there is human intervention, the equilibrium stock is lower than it would have been if the level of catches were nil (see X_C in Figure 1.3).[6]

[6] It is worth noting that only the decreasing part of the curve (in the positive quadrant) is stable. If, at one point of time, a slight, temporary, deviation from the equilibrium level of effort occurs, the population stock will return to its previous level in the long run. This does not hold true for the rising portion of the curve: a slight deviation from the equilibrium level implies that, when the previous level of effort is restored, the population stock either falls to zero or rises up to the corresponding point on the decreasing part of the curve.

A last application of the distinction between reproducibility and sustainability can be found in the recent proposals for the reform of conventional methods of national accounting. In the recent literature on environmental economics (see e.g. Dasgupta and Heal, 1979: 245–6; Weitzmann, 1976; Dasgupta and Mäler, 1990; Chakravarty, 1990), it has indeed been repeatedly suggested that conventional national accounting approaches should be modified to better reflect the environmental costs brought about by the processes of income creation. The basic idea is to extend conventional measures of net national income by adding measures of changes in the stock of natural resources. 'In the simplest of cases, where current well-being depends solely on current consumption, real net national product reduces to the *sum* of the social (or shadow) price of an economy's consumptions and the social (or shadow) price of the changes in its stocks of real capital assets' (Dasgupta and Mäler, 1990: 9), it being understood that capital assets include manufactured capital as well as natural resources. The most important implication of the approach adopted by Dasgupta and Mäler is that, if an economy simply exchanges natural resources against consumer goods on foreign markets but does not produce anything, it will exhibit a net national product equal to zero. This is because the increased consumption flow is bought at the price of a proportionate reduction of the nation's nature-made capital. Such a result is in total contrast with the conventionally measured national income which may be quite high and even grow if resources are depleted at an increasing rate. The measure gives a more sensible description of the real income generated by oil exports or destruction of tropical forests, when the proceeds of the sales involved are not invested in building up national productive capital. To take another example, compare two economies where the sole production sector is fishing. The first economy 'produces' (at no cost) and consumes the sustainable yield from its resource base while the second economy 'produces' and consumes in one period the entire stock of its resource. According to conventional national accounting practice, the NNP of the second economy in that period would of course be much greater than that of the first economy. According to the practice advocated by Dasgupta and Mäler, however, the reverse would hold true since the NNP of the second economy would just be nil.

The relevance of the new accounting method is particularly evident in the case of developing countries, as suggested by Chakravarty:

> a look at the world at large would suggest that for the majority of inhabitants on the earth the precariousness of their daily existence has not been significantly reduced by the development process even where there have been increases in per capita GNP. . . . Neither new technology nor investment in material capital have enabled them to substitute for the loss of their environmental capital stock which has been substantially eroded. The situation has been rendered more difficult by the imitation of an alien life-style especially by the élite in these countries. (Chakravarty, 1990: 70)

1.4 Sustainability and Individual Rationality

So far, we have essentially described the conditions under which the resource base of an economy can be physically preserved and the social rationale for a conservationist policy. We have therefore ignored the conditions under which environmental reproducibility is optimal for an individual agent.

In actual fact, there are frequent circumstances in which it is individually rational to degrade a natural resource. This may or may not run counter to collective rationality. For instance, agents who live close to their subsistence level and have no alternative income-earning opportunities, are concerned that the income they derive from the exploitation of the resource meets their subsistence requirement *in each period*. If the conservation of the resource involves costly investments that have a long gestation period (think of many agro-forestry practices), it may happen that they are not able to bear such a sacrifice. Subsistence constraints may therefore drive people to draw down the resource to a shut-down point. Note carefully that there are two conditions for this proposition to hold true. First, capital markets must be imperfect with the effect that the agents are not able to obtain loans which would help them to undertake the necessary investments. Second, the market for the resource must also be imperfect since, otherwise, the agents under a binding subsistence constraint would be better off by selling immediately their resource to a new owner who would make a better use of it.

Another important circumstance in which agents may be individually led to degrade a resource occurs when the rate of return on a conservation investment falls below the return achievable by allocating production factors to alternative uses. Striking illustrations of this situation are easy to find in the forestry and the fishery sectors where some species are long-maturing. Thus, there are some species of fish whose rate of growth is so slow that it is bound to be below the ruling rate of interest in any economy. For instance, the *Orange Ruffy* which are exploited in depth ranging from 700 to 1,400 metres (e.g. in New Zealand and Australian waters) reach maturity only at age 20 to 25 years and may live above one hundred years. Any private owner of such a resource has therefore an incentive to deplete it. Most sharks, to take a less exotic example, are also low-reproducing and there are few, if any, commercial shark fisheries which have not depleted the stocks (personal communication of Rolf Willmann). Resource depletion leading to extinction is an undesirable outcome if preservation of the resource produces positive external effects (biodiversity is a public good, of unknown and uncertain return, for which it is clear that no market exists) or if there are market imperfections that distort prices (for more details, see also Sect. 3.2 below).

From the above discussion, it should be evident that rational agents can have an incentive to degrade natural resources even when these resources are under private property. Following Pagiola (1993), let us consider the problem of soil conservation (in the same vein, see also Perrings, 1989). A producer cultivates a soil which has initially a given level of productivity and the higher the soil level the greater the output per unit of land area. A production input is applied to this soil and generates output according to a determinate production function describing the prevailing technology: the function has standard properties, including diminishing returns to the production input. Yet, applying this input causes damage to the soil, reducing its future level. Soil degradation and the consequent future losses of output are not inevitable, however, since a conservation input can also be applied with the effect of mitigating damage to soil. Use of the conservation input does not contribute to immediate production and, in fact, it even reduces it by diverting resources from directly productive activities. To put it in another way, conservation is costly in terms of both conservation expenditures and forgone revenues from production since production input use must be kept low. Finally, as there are diminishing returns to the conservation input, the soil level cannot be built up beyond a certain level.

If the farmer's strategy is such that damage caused to soil by using the production input is exactly offset by the mitigating effect of the conservation input, production can continue indefinitely: in this case, the optimal path converges to a long-run steady state. Conversely, as suggested above, it is also possible that the optimal path might lead the farmer to draw down his soil to the point that he is forced to shut down production: the resource is not conserved either because the farmer does not deem it worth while to do so or because he cannot bear the necessary cost. In the former case, the farmer has available to him alternative uses of his labour resource in the form of migration possibilities. If there is no market where to sell his land,[7] he would then prefer to degrade it in order to reap the high returns from overexploitation and, thereafter, to switch to his off-farm alternative activity.[8] In the latter case, he is confronted by a subsistence constraint and he cannot borrow or insure himself to meet basic consumption needs when his agricultural output falls short of these needs in any period. If the conservation strategy entails current (investment) expenditures or a less intensive use of the soil so that his subsistence constraint is violated, he cannot adopt this strategy even though it may be very profitable in the long run.

Let us represent graphically the two possible paths that have just been characterized. The vertical axis of Figure 1.4 measures discounted profits and, therefore, the area under the paths described can be interpreted as the net present value of returns from following the corresponding path. Note that, as drawn in this figure, the non-conservation path is initially more profitable than the conservation path. This may result from the fact that adoption of conservation practices requires an initial investment or use of less productive practices. Under the assumption that β stands for the alternative annual migration income (the alternative path is therefore calculated as $e^{-rt}\beta$, where r represents the discount rate), the net present value of returns from

[7] Indeed, if rights of access to natural resources could be traded in a market, users would be concerned with the residual (sale) value of their assets after exploitation. Yet, for obvious reasons, this is not the case for many village-level CPRs.

[8] Imagine that a farmer can earn an income of y units by migrating while his return from the land at the productivity level that ensures indefinite conservation is z units, with $z < y$. Moreover, by exploiting his land too intensively to maintain its fertility in the long run, he can earn incomes higher than y till a certain time-period, T^*, when the land's productivity falls below y units. In these conditions, the farmer has an incentive to overexploit his land during T^* periods and, thereafter, to shut down and switch to his alternative (labour migration) activity, which will bring him a regular income of y units. It is worth noting that it will be optimal for the farmer to degrade his land even if $z = y$. In this case, indeed, he would be no worse off after shutting down than if he had remained at the long-run steady state, yet, during the time that he was drawing down his soil, he would have enjoyed a higher income level (Pagiola, 1993: 76). In the above illustration, we have assumed that only the farmer's labour has alternative uses. It is of course easy to construct an example in which the land itself can be put to several competing uses—for instance, it can be cleared for agriculture or kept as a forest area—that yield different ecological effects. The conclusion may well be that the villager has an incentive to fell the forest to sell the wood and, once it is destroyed, to start cultivating the land thereby cleared on a sustainable basis.

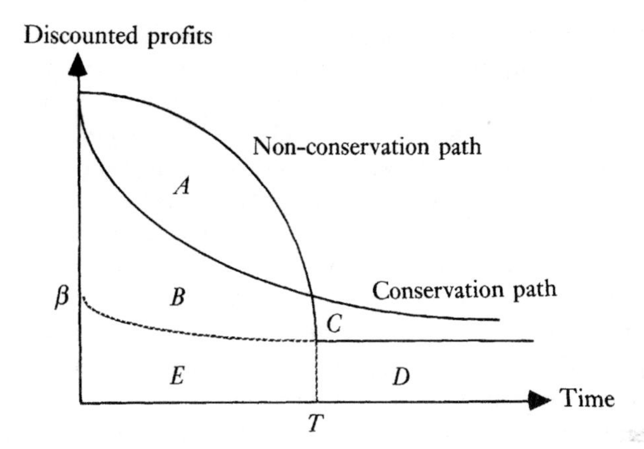

FIG. 1.4. Comparison of returns under conservation and non-conservation paths

following the conservation path is given by $(B + E + C + D)$ while that achievable by following the path under which the resource is gradually destroyed is $(A + B + E + D)$. T represents the shut-down point of the latter strategy. Whether the conservation or the non-conservation path is preferable from a net present value perspective therefore depends on whether A is greater or smaller than C.

As is evident from the above comparison, the role of β is crucial to determine whether the resource will be conserved or degraded: for example, if β is higher, the area C is reduced and, consequently, the probability that A exceeds C increases. This is an important implication of the present analysis: the higher the return on alternative uses of production factors, the more likely it is that the resource will not be conserved. Note, however, if the $e^{-rt}\beta$ curve is so high that it lies wholly above the non-conservation path, cultivation of the land will be given up from the very beginning and, consequently, the soil resource will not actually be degraded (the shut-down point coincides with the vertical axis). In such circumstances, the incomes from migration are so high that it is not even worth exploiting the land to the utmost until it is eventually depleted. Alternatively, β can be interpreted as the subsistence income of a farmer who has no alternative income-earning opportunities. In that case, the path $e^{-rt}\beta$ becomes a constraint. In the situation described in the diagram, the conservation path is clearly possible since it satisfies this constraint, and it is obviously preferred to the non-conservation strategy which destroys the resource on which the farmer crucially depends. This need not be so, though. Thus, if population increases, the subsistence requirement, β, rises in proportion to the number of dependants in the farmer's family and higher returns need to be extracted from each unit of land to maintain subsistence levels: the whole path $e^{-rt}\beta$ shifts upwards. At a certain point, it will move above the conservation path and destruction of the resource becomes inevitable: in this case, by adopting a shut-down practice that mines their available soil in order to obtain current consumption, poor farmers can at least postpone the inevitable (Pagiola, 1993: 87).

A rather unexpected result which emerges from a more formal analysis of the conservation issue (for more details, see Pagiola, 1993: ch. 5) is that the effect of a rise in output prices on conservation practices is ambiguous. True, such a rise enhances the future value of production, thereby encouraging conservation. Yet, on the other hand, it increases the value of the forgone production resulting from use of the conservation input and, consequently, it tends to induce the farmers to reallocate inputs from conservation to production purposes in the current period. Which effect dominates depends on how easily soil is damaged as a result of increased exploitation, what is the consequent effect on productivity, the cost of additional conservation, and the discount rate. Depending on site-specific biophysical conditions, price movements may either increase or decrease the incentives to degrade the soil (ibid. 83). A policy that aims at furthering conservation by supporting output prices is not, therefore, necessarily justified. By contrast, such uncertainty vanishes when the government chooses to subsidize the prices of conservation inputs.

Finally, Pagiola proposes a dynamic analysis in which the choice of the soil level by the farmer is explicitly modelled. An important result is the following: *the resource exploitation strategy chosen by the farmer crucially depends on the initial conditions.* More precisely, if initially the soil level is very low, adoption of a conservation strategy implies that the soil will first have to be built up to a level compatible with such a strategy in the long run. If this is not done, the soil will be inexorably degraded under the impact of continuous production operations. As long as returns at the steady state are sufficiently high that the conservation investment can be repaid, the adoption of the conservation strategy should not cause any problems. If farmers are facing a minimum subsistence constraint, however, the need to meet this constraint *in every period* may prevent them from following the conservation path. In the words of Pagiola, 'the need to meet a subsistence constraint in every period might prevent farmers from adopting sustainable practices even though these practices would ensure that farmers could meet their constraint in the long run' (Pagiola, 1993: 90). In these circumstances, public intervention is clearly required to support poor farmers in order that they can increase the quality of their soil and escape the aforedescribed low-level equilibrium trap. Towards this end, the State may have recourse to temporary income support policies, selective subsidies, and also measures aimed at improving poor farmers' access to credit markets.

On the other hand, the initial level of the soil may be so high (above the steady-state level) that it is not optimal for the farmer to maintain it. In other words, the optimal path may consist of allowing some degradation to occur since conservation, especially at such high levels of productivity, may entail high costs (not only direct costs but also costs that interfere with production efforts). In these circumstances, the short-term benefits from use of more degrading practices exceed the long-term costs resulting from a lower steady-state income level. As already pointed out in sect. 1, 'observing agricultural practices that degrade soil does not, therefore, necessarily imply that farmers have adopted unsustainable practices; they may simply be drawing down their soil stocks to their optimal long-run level' (Pagiola, 1993: 73).

Clearly, the conservationist attitude which claims that the stocks of natural resources ought to be maintained at their *present* level is hard to justify as a matter of principle. A *conservation* strategy does not imply adherence to such a rigid, *conser-*

vationist policy which arbitrarily rests upon the assumption that the existing stocks are optimal in some sense. As stressed by Pagiola, the optimal solution for the farmer 'will not necessarily be the solution with the highest long-run resource stock; nor will it necessarily meet or exceed any arbitrarily set level of the resource stock' (Pagiola, 1993: 46).

We have seen above that poor users may be *unable* to bear the cost of profitable conservation investments. It must now be added that in general they have much greater *incentives* to seek to conserve their resource base, since they have limited alternative income sources. In other words, the short-term returns from drawing down the resource to a shut-down point are unlikely to offset the long-run penalties from doing so. It is only if the short-term benefits from mining the resource are sufficiently high, if the future penalty from non-conservative behaviour is sufficiently distant, and if the discount rate is sufficiently high that subsistence-constrained users might still prefer the shut-down strategy (ibid. 88).

On the other hand, it cannot be taken for granted that the initial productivity level of a resource is sufficiently high that it can be actually built up to the steady-state level, possibly with the financial support of the State: the biophysical environment may be so degraded and so fragile that production is not and *will never be* sustainable however important the conservation investments undertaken. These investments may be too costly or ineffective for the initial ecological imbalance to be redressed. Clearly, the biophysical characteristics of the resource matter and they interact with the economic parameters to determine whether conservation is a profitable strategy. Thus, the more fragile or the lower the quality of the resource base, the more sensitive production is to resource degradation, and the less effective conservation investments are, the more likely it is that adoption of shut-down practices will be optimal for the users, and the lower the long-run (steady-state) stock of the resource will be even under conservation practices (ibid. 85–6).

1.5 Conclusion

The following points deserve to be singled out for special emphasis at this concluding stage of the analysis.

First, high rates of resource exploitation, when resources are exhaustible, are not incompatible with a development process characterized by a sustainable consumption flow. At least, this is so under the realistic assumption of sufficient substitutability between these resources and capital assets.

Second, there are a number of serious reasons which may justify a conservationist policy. In particular, information on natural resources including future possible uses for them may be highly imperfect, a worrying feature given that their destruction is irreversible. Also, natural resources may have a utility as consumer goods, an argument which, perhaps, applies better to richer countries.

Third, it does not follow from the fact that certain natural resources are renewable that they should actually be preserved. The conservationist argument in favour of maintaining the stock of these resources at its present level is particularly hard to justify. It is not even certain that maintaining them at some positive stock level is optimal from the users' standpoint. There is indeed the possibility that the rate of return on maintaining the resource for indefinite use is lower than the value of the users' fixed assets in their best alternative use. And even if it is actually higher, this still does not guarantee that conservation is more profitable than drawing down the resource to a shut-down point since conservation may involve high costs while yielding benefits only in the distant future. In other words, the availability of conservation techniques or practices does not ensure that resource users will actually adopt them since it can be presumed that users are typically sensitive to whether the long-term benefits of adopting conservation practices make the cost worth bearing.

Four, the more fragile is the resource base, the more sensitive production is to resource degradation, and the less effective conservation investments are, the more likely it is that adoption of shut-down practices will be optimal for resource users, and the lower the long-run (steady-state) stock of the resource will be even under conservation practices.

Five, in general, subsistence-constrained users have much greater *incentives* than more well-off users to seek to conserve their resource base, since they have limited alternative income sources. Nevertheless, if the resource base is *initially* degraded, they may be unable, owing to the low level of their wealth and to severe credit market imperfections, to build it up to the level where it can be optimally maintained. In such circumstances, there is good ground for state interventions that enable these poor users to overcome the initial barrier presented by conservation investments. Another, more well-known, rationale for such interventions is the presence of externalities.

2

The Tragedy of the Commons

2.1 A Preliminary Statement of the Problem

Though, as demonstrated in the preceding chapter, high rates of resource exploitation in LDCs may be part of a welfare-maximizing programme, it is often claimed that the rates currently observed in those countries are exceedingly high and that the resulting pattern of management of natural resources is patently inefficient. This observation is the starting-point of an abundant literature which identifies the main source of inefficiency in the management of natural resources with the absence of well-defined property rights and the regime of open access which characterizes them. As early as 1833, William Foster Lloyd (who was concerned with the check on population growth imposed by limited employment opportunities) identified the problem which later on came to be known as 'the tragedy of the commons':

Why are the cattle in a common so puny and stunted? Why is the common itself so bare-worn and cropped differently from the adjoining enclosures? No inequality, in respect of natural or acquired fertility, will account for the phenomenon. The difference depends on the difference of the way in which an increase of stock in the two cases affects the circumstances of the author of the increase. If a person puts more cattle into his own field, the amount of subsistence which they consume will be deducted from that which was at the command of his original stock; and, if, before, there was no more than a sufficiency of pasture, he reaps no benefits from the additional cattle, what is gained in one way being lost in another. But if he puts more cattle on a common, the food which they consume forms a deduction which is shared between all the cattle, as well as that of others as his own, in proportion to their number, and only a small part of it is taken from his own cattle. In an enclosed pasture, there is a point of saturation, if I may so call it, (by which, I mean a barrier depending on considerations of interest), beyond which no prudent man will add to his stock. In a common, also, there is in like manner a point of saturation. But the position of the point in the two cases is obviously different. Were a number of adjoining pastures, already fully stocked, to be at once thrown open, and converted into one vast common, the position of the point of saturation would immediately be changed. The stock would be increased, and would be made to press much more forcibly against the means of subsistence. (Lloyd, 1833, in Hardin and Baden, 1977: 11)

In a more recent neo-Malthusian pamphlet, this position has been restated by Garett Hardin under the expression 'the tragedy of the commons' in the following way:

The tragedy of the commons develops in the following way. Picture a pasture open to all. It is to be expected that each herdsman will try to keep as many cattle as possible on the commons. Such an arrangement may work reasonably satisfactorily for centuries because tribal wars, poaching and disease keep the numbers of both man and beast well below the carrying capacity of the land. Finally, however, comes the day of reckoning, that is, the day when the long desired goal of social stability becomes a reality. At this point, the inherent logic of the commons remorselessly generates tragedy. As a rational being, each herdsman seeks to maximize his gain. Explicitly or implicitly, more or less consciously, he asks: 'What is the utility to *me* of adding one more animal to my herd?' This utility has one negative and one positive component.

1. The positive component is a function of the increment of one animal. Since the herdsman receives all the proceeds from the sale of the additional animal, the positive utility is nearly +1.
2. The negative component is a function of the additional overgrazing created by one more animal. Since however, the effects of overgrazing are shared by all the herdsman, the negative utility for any particular decision-making herdsman is only a fraction of −1.

Adding together the component partial utilities, the rational herdsman concludes that the only sensible course for him to pursue is to add another animal to his herd. And another. . . . But this is the conclusion reached by each and every rational herdsman sharing a commons. Therein is the tragedy. Each man is locked into a system that compels him to increase his herd without limit—in a world that is limited. Ruin is the destination toward which all men rush, each pursuing his own best interest in a society that believes in the freedom of the commons. Freedom in a commons brings ruin to all. (Hardin, 1968: 20)

2.2 The Problem of Open Access

Two different sets of issues must be distinguished in the above statements: the problem of open access and the problem of common property. Let us first analyse the question of open access. When a given resource is in open access, the agents have to decide whether or not they should 'enter' and start exploiting the resource. Their choice is based on the comparison between the price of entry which they have to bear and the expected income they will get. As long as the net expected benefit is positive, they decide to enter and exploit the resource. The problem is that their private evaluation of the expected benefits does not take into account the fall in the others' incomes which is caused by their entry: by their action, they impose an externality on the other agents. Since they do not allow for it, the resulting situation will be typically inefficient.

Let us take the example of a fishery, and assume that the entire stock of fish, S, could be caught by one fisherman alone (we abstract momentarily from the kind of dynamic considerations which we have made in Chapter 1 regarding the management of a renewable resource). The fishing technology is such that the entire stock is divided equally among n active fishermen. Consider the choice facing the nth fisherman. The cost of renting a boat is given and equal to p. He chooses between not to hire a boat and catch nothing, or to hire a boat at a price p and catch S/n units of fish. As we assume that all other costs are negligible, he will decide to hire a boat iff: $p < S/n$ (the price of fish is assumed to be unity). Since all agents have access to the fishing activity (anybody has a right to fish) and there are many agents in this economy, they will enter as long as the average product of fishing exceeds the price of entry, i.e. the rental price of a boat. The equilibrium number of fishermen, n_0, is such that: $n_0 = S/p$. In equilibrium, the rent is totally dissipated. If a second fisherman enters the fishery, the first fisherman's profit will be reduced from $(S - p)$ to $(S/2 - p)$ and, if there are n_0

fishermen eventually active in the fishery, his profit, like that of all other operators, will become nil ($S/n_0 - p = 0$). It is clear that such an equilibrium will typically be inefficient (for instance, in our example, efficiency requires only one fisherman on the fishing-ground). The problem addressed here is actually analogous to that of sharing a pie where, to have access to a share of the pie, agents have to pay an entry fee at some positive cost. The source of inefficiency in open-access situations clearly lies in the fact that people must mobilize non-free production factors (factors carrying a positive opportunity cost) where they are not required for production purposes.

Let us now consider another example of a fishery where the total amount of catches depends on the number of fishing boats. Let Y stand for total catches and n for the number of boats operated. For the sake of simplicity, let us assume that, in the relevant range, $Y = F(n)$ can be approximated by the following functional form: $Y = an - bn^2$. In this situation, the open-access equilibrium will be such that Y/n, the *average* catch per boat, is equal to p, the rental price of a boat. In other words, open access is characterized by n_0 boats, with n_0 such that:

$$n_0 = (a - p)/b.$$

On the other hand, if the whole fishery was efficiently managed so as to maximize profits, the marginal catch per boat would be equal to the boat's rental price. Standard calculus yields:

$$n^* = (a - p)/2b$$

with n^* standing for the profit-maximizing number of boats. It is immediately evident that $n^* < n_0$: as a matter of fact, $n_0 = 2n^*$. In other words, in this example, the impact of open access is to double the number of boats operating in the fishery, thereby leading to the complete dissipation of the total rent. The mechanics of determination of both the open access and the efficient equilibria is portrayed graphically in Figure 2.1 (where it happens that n_0 is much more than twice as high as n^*).

That the magnitude of inefficiencies thus generated in fisheries can be considerable is attested by the following recent estimates: Iceland and the EEC could cut their fleets

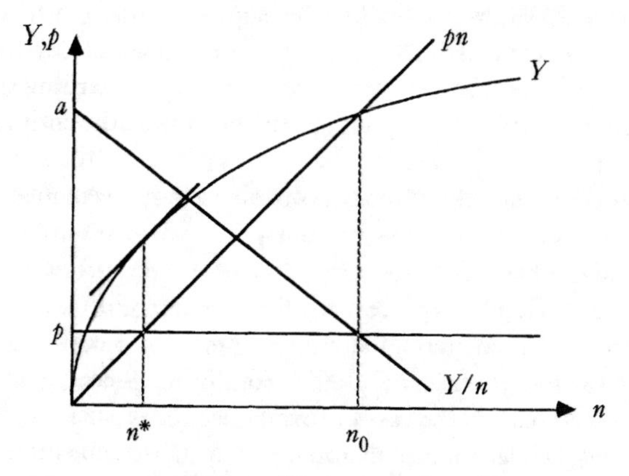

FIG. 2.1. Impact of open access on the equilibrium number of boats

by 40 per cent, Norway by two-thirds, and all three would still catch as much fish as they do today (*The Economist*, 19 March 1994: 23).

We have so far disregarded the dynamic considerations which were at the centre of the model of fishery presented in the preceding chapter. In the simple case where there are no costs of production and where the price of fish is constant, the optimal catch policy obtains when the stock of fish grows at the same rate as the rate of interest. This rule is widely known in the literature as the Hotelling rule. When there are costs of production, one can show that, in most cases, intertemporal profit maximization entails a long-run *stationary* catch programme as well as a long-run equilibrium level in the stock of fish. To make matters more complicated, there is in fact a multiplicity of such optimal programmes (for more details, see Spence and Starett, 1977). What bears emphasis is that this equilibrium level does not in general correspond to the maximum biological yield.

Under open access, however, the dynamic consequences of the current catch policy are completely disregarded. What matters for potential entrants is the average catch per boat and its rental price: there is no way in which, by refraining from fishing today, the agents can be assured that, in the next period, they will receive the amount of fish they have left untouched, augmented by its natural growth. As a result, in an open-access situation, every fisherman is forced to follow the myopic rule (by comparing average instantaneous returns to the rental price of a boat) even though he may well be aware that he thereby contributes to reduce the future stock. The problem is simply that there is no way in which he can reap the future benefits of restraint in the present: the total amount of fish currently caught is independent of the individual decisions taken by the participants. As should be clear from Chapter 1, a sequence of open-access equilibria may lead to a stationary long-run stock, depending on the particular form of the cost curve and of the natural growth law.

It is in the light of the perverse logic of open access (since fisheries' management has miserably failed in Europe and America, and threatens to fail in developing countries, too) that the following distressing facts must be understood. Almost all the world's 200 fisheries monitored by the FAO are today fully exploited. One in three is depleted or heavily overexploited, almost all in the developed countries. On the other hand, American fishery managers estimate that the US catch is only half as valuable as it could be if fish stocks in federal waters were allowed to recover. The FAO has estimated the annual loss world-wide at $15–30 billion worth of fish (*The Economist*, 19 March 1994: 23–4; FAO, 1993: 31–2).

It is also a well-documented fact that the open-access status of many tropical forests in Latin America has contributed significantly to deforestation under demographic pressure. Since no one has a clear right to the income associated with forest conservation (land-clearing is actually a prerequisite for formal tenure), everyone has a strong incentive to respond immediately to any opportunity to capture the rents generated by land-use conversion (Southgate, 1990; Southgate, Sierra, and Brown, 1991). Binswanger has noted that, in the case of Brazil, incentives to degrade forests are even more perverse since 'a claimant is allocated two to three times the amount of land cleared of forests'. Many people therefore clear land 'simply for purposes of solidifying land claims and increasing the size of allocations' (Binswanger, 1991: 827–8).

2.3 The Problem of Common Property

Common property and open access have often been confused in the literature, as is attested by the following quotation from an article by Cornes and Sandler: 'Traditionally common property analyses demonstrate the overexploitation of the scarce fixed resource; the *average product* of the variable input, not its *marginal product*, is equated to the input's rental rate when access is free and the number of exploiters is large' (Cornes and Sandler, 1983: 787). These two situations are however essentially different in so far as, in a common property, the community has the right to exclude non-members from the use of the resource. Under common property, the *right of exclusion* is assigned to a well-defined group. Under open access, a *right of inclusion* is granted to anyone who wants to use the resource. As a consequence, common property and open access are also analytically distinct: because the very concept of common property supposes the existence of a well-defined group, the agents are now allowed to *interact strategically* with each other. In other words, the agents do not any more think that the final outcome is independent of their own individual decisions, as was the case under open access. They actually *expect* that their action will induce a particular reaction from the other agents and, thereby, affect the collective result.[1]

The problems raised by common property are usually represented by the formal framework of the popular 'prisoner's dilemma'. Let us consider two herdsmen who must decide on the number of animals to let pasture on a 'common' land (belonging to both). To further simplify the presentation, let us assume that the choice facing each herdsman is between letting one or two animals on the common land. If each herdsman chooses to have one animal each, each of them gain $5. If, however, they both choose to have two animals each on the common land, these animals will be underfed and will lose much of their economic value. As a result, the total gain each herdsman may expect for having two animals pasturing is $4. Finally, if one herdsman has only one animal on the common field, and the other has two, their total gains are $3 and $6 respectively. This situation can be summarized by entering the different gains, also called *payoffs*, in a double-entry matrix, called the *payoff matrix*, as in Figure 2.2. Note

		Herdsman 1	
	No. of animals	1	2
Herdsman 2	1	5, 5	6, 3
	2	3, 6	4, 4

FIG. 2.2. The herdsmen game as a prisoner's dilemma game

[1] In the words of Bentham 'The idea of property consists in an established expectation' (Bentham, quoted in Runge, 1984: 808).

that the first number in each cell is the payoff accruing to the row player, while the second number refers to the column player.

A player's (pure) *strategy* is 'a statement that specifies an action at each of the decision nodes at which it would be player i's duty to make a decision if that node were actually reached' (Binmore, 1992: 30). In the herdsmen game presented above, there is only one decision node for each player, and two possible strategies. Comparing the payoffs associated with each strategy, it is easy to see that each herdsman will choose the strategy '*put two animals*'. Such a strategy is called a *dominant strategy*, since the optimal action for one player does not depend on the strategy followed by the other player: whatever the other does, the action chosen is the one which maximizes his payoff.

A pair of strategies is a *Nash equilibrium* if each player's strategy is optimal, i.e. maximizes his payoffs, given the strategy of the other player. In the present context, each player has a dominant strategy so that the Nash equilibrium of the game comes out naturally as the one where each player chooses to put two animals on the common field. Here lies the tragedy of the commons: even though it would be better for both herdsmen to put only one animal on the commons, it is individually rational for each of them to put two animals, and the Pareto-dominated outcome obtains. In the words of Roemer: 'Everyone's welfare can be improved by exercising a restraint that no one has any interest to exercise in the state of nature' (Roemer, 1988: 2).

The representation of the commons problem as a prisoner's dilemma (PD) game (Sen, 1967; Dasgupta and Heal, 1979) is not without problem, however. Indeed, if the prisoner's dilemma game may be useful as a first approximation of the problem at work in the 'tragedy of the commons', it is not strictly speaking an appropriate representation of the commons problem. Indeed, such a problem is in general not characterized by the existence of dominant strategies for each agent. To show this, let us return to the example of the fishery presented above, where Y stands for total catches, n_i, for the number of boats operated by player i, and p, for the initial price of a boat. Assume furthermore that, within the relevant range:

$$Y = a\left(\sum_i n_i\right) - b\left(\sum_i n_i\right)^2$$

Let us consider the case where access to the lake is restricted to two fishermen. Their individual profit function can be written as:

$$P_i = (a(n_i + n_j) - b(n_i + n_j)^2)\frac{n_i}{(n_i + n_j)} - pn_i$$

Given n_j, the profit-maximizing number of boats for fisherman i is:

$$n_i^N = \frac{a - p - bn_j}{2b}$$

His optimal strategy, n_i^N, depends on the number of boats the other fisherman operates. He has therefore no dominant strategy. The Nash equilibrium of this game is characterized by each fisherman operating $(a - p)/(3b)$ boats. The total number of boats operated in this case is equal to two-thirds of the number of boats operated under open access (i.e.

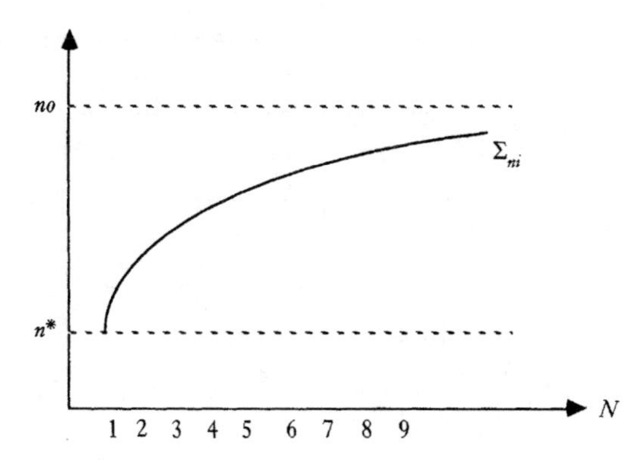

FIG. 2.3. Common property, open access and social optimum in a fishery

$(a - p)/b$) and to four-thirds the socially optimal number (i.e. $(a - p)/2b$). It is interesting to note that, if more fishermen are admitted on the common fishery, the total number of boats as well as the total catches will increase and gradually approach the open-access situation. As a matter of fact, if we let N stand for the number of fishermen allowed into the fishery, it is easy to show that the ratio of the total number of boats operated to the social optimum, n^*, increases with N as follows:

$$\sum_{i}^{N} \frac{n_i^N}{n^*} = \frac{2N}{N+1}$$

The open-access situation obtains when $N \rightarrow \infty$ and the value of the above ratio then equals 2. This is portrayed in Figure 2.3. As is illustrated, the degree of inefficiency resulting from common ownership depends crucially on the number of agents operating on the commons: the lower the number of agents, the greater the extent to which they can take into account the negative consequences of their actions on the productivity of the common property.

2.4 Co-ordination Failure under Common Property[2]

The Pareto-inefficiency of the Nash equilibrium under common property also holds when the production function exhibits increasing returns to scale (and not only under decreasing returns to scale).[3] In that case indeed, the agents will typically underexploit the common property, leaving productive opportunities unused in the absence of any commitment or contractual arrangement. One may even find situations where two Nash equilibria coexist, one supporting the collectively rational outcome and the other yielding the increasing-returns-to-scale equivalent of the tragedy of the commons.

[2] In the present chapter, we shall illustrate only part of the problem with the help of a simple model. A thorough and more systematic analysis of the problems of collective action will be provided in Chs. 4 and 5.

[3] Under constant returns to scale, there is no tragedy of the commons.

		Agent B	
		X	Y
Agent A	X	2, 2	0.5, 0
	Y	0, 0.5	3, 3

FIG. 2.4. Co-ordination failure under common property

When such a situation obtains, the problem is not so much that the collectively rational outcome cannot be supported by utility-maximizing agents without a change in their economic environment but that it will not materialize because the agents fail to communicate and co-ordinate their actions.

Let us at this stage present a very simple example derived from that model with a view to highlighting what is meant by 'co-ordination failure'. Suppose a CPR exploited by two agents, agent A and agent B. They have to choose between two different techniques, X and Y, where X is inefficient compared to Y but where, for technique Y to be advantageous, it must be used by both agents simultaneously. In other words, the two techniques are interdependent in such a way that Y appears as a superior technique to an agent only if the other already uses it. Otherwise, X is chosen. By co-ordination failure, we mean the case where both agents do not choose the superior technique Y because they fail to communicate and co-ordinate. They are both stuck into an inferior Nash equilibrium, while another Pareto-dominating Nash equilibrium exists.

For the sake of illustration, we may have the payoff matrix (note the difference with a PD game structure) depicted in Figure 2.4.

Both agents may choose the inferior equilibrium (X,X), with a payoff (2,2) and have no interest in a unilateral change while they could be much better off if they both chose (Y,Y) with a payoff (3,3). In the game structure given above, we cannot tell a priori whether an equilibrium will be chosen, nor which one. What is interesting, however, is to consider that X is the old technique used since ages by both agents, and Y is a new technique which has just been made available. What the example above then shows is that it is likely that, by 'failing to co-ordinate', both agents will not switch to this new opportunity but will choose to keep the old technique at work and thus maintain the *status quo*.

Such a problem would of course not appear were the resource privately owned, since, in that case, the private owner would immediately choose the more efficient technique. In other words, a private owner, by being alone to exploit a given share of the resource, would internalize the externalities involved in his own choice of techniques.

2.5 The Conjectural Variations Approach

We have so far identified two sources of inefficiency for the unregulated common: first, in a common property game, where technology is such that the production function exhibits decreasing or increasing returns to the variable[4] factor, the Nash equilibrium of the game is Pareto-inefficient, and second, people may fail to co-ordinate their action. In recent years, the very idea of applying the concept of Nash equilibrium—which implies that, when deciding on their actions, the agents assume that the other players don't change their decisions—to analyse the former type of issues has been questioned by R. Cornes and T. Sandler in a paper entitled 'Commons and Tragedies'. They propose that, instead of applying the concept of Nash equilibrium, we should allow players of a 'common ownership game' to hold 'non-zero conjectural variations regarding what one exploiter thinks will be the effect of his exploitation on the exploitation efforts of the others' (Cornes and Sandler, 1983: 787). In other words, when maximizing his payoffs, the agent should anticipate that the others will 'react' to his own action, and take into account these reactions in his private calculus. It is clear that, when the conjectural variations are nil, that is when the player does not expect the other players to react, the Nash equilibrium obtains. Similarly, the Pareto-optimal outcome results when each player expects the others to behave exactly in the same way he does (in the case of identical players).

Since there is virtually an infinity of conjectural variations which may be assigned to the players, it is desirable to restrict the set of possible conjectures by requiring that they should have a particular property, namely that they are *consistent*:[5] 'a conjectural variation is consistent if it is identical to the optimal (actual) response of the other agent(s) in a neighborhood of the equilibrium based upon this conjecture . . . at the equilibrium, the slope of each firm's reaction path equals the corresponding conjectural variation held by the other firms.' In other words, 'conjectures are consistent when they conform to reality' (Cornes and Sandler, 1983: 791).

In the context of a simple model of a fishery (similar to that presented above), the authors show that, in general, *there is no consistent conjectural equilibrium*. It is only in the particular case where the industry's profits are equal to zero that a consistent conjectural equilibrium exists. The required conjecture is that 'an individual firm expects the rest of the industry to reduce its input by one unit in response to a one unit increase in the firm's input, so that industry output will remain unchanged' (Cornes and Sandler, 1983: 792).

Our problem with conjectural variations is that, in general, they correspond to *ad hoc* theorizing. Furthermore, economic theory provides a much more rigorous alternative to that approach under the form of repeated games: indeed, in the latter framework, the analyst is forced to clearly specify the structure of the game, and by doing so and making use of the appropriate equilibrium concept, he (she) is led to

[4] One of the differences between the common property game and the model analysed above is that, in the latter, the input (i.e. the investment decision) is not 'variable' in a continuous way but takes the form of a lump sum.

[5] For a less stringent criterion of consistency, see Kreps, 1990: 329–30.

investigate how players interact in a dynamic setting, why players can reasonably expect a particular behaviour from the other players, and how the system evolves from its initial to its final position . . . Irrationality is not called for in the latter setting. Let us see more precisely what kind of irrationality underlies the conjectural variation approach.

First, in the case where conjectures are non-consistent, players do not anticipate correctly the optimal response of the other players. Irrationality prevails because, knowing that the other players expect you to behave in a certain sub-optimal way, you may, and in general you will, take advantage of this situation by undertaking actions which do not correspond to what the other players expect, nor to the 'optimal' behaviour under conjectural variations. Therefore, adherence by the players to non-consistent conjectural variations is simply irrational. Second, one does not know where the 'conjectures' come from: do they originate in past experience (in which case the learning process and the original conjecture ought to be defined and specified), do they come from the institutional setting, from pre-play discussions between players? All this should be made explicit. Nor can one see why they should be continuous. Third, the use of the consistent conjectural variations hypothesis is of no use in understanding how the consistent equilibrium emerges: what are the forces driving the system towards this particular equilibrium? The problem is particularly serious since, in the example chosen by Cornes and Sandler, the consistent conjectural equilibrium corresponds to the zero-profit situation. One cannot find any reason why (nor how) this particular equilibrium will be chosen or attained by the players.

To conclude, we do not consider the conjectural variation approach as a fruitful method to analyse the commons problem: it is not an alternative to the Nash equilibrium concept. As a matter of fact, a well-defined game can be developed to analyse any question raised by the partisans of conjectural variations.

2.6 The Lindahl Equilibrium

By definition, the concept of externality, of which the tragedy of the commons provides a particular illustration, refers to a missing market. In the words of S. Cheung, 'externalities . . . are thus attributable to the absence of the right to contract' (Cheung, 1970: 50). In the commons problem, if a competitive market could be established for the externality which i imposes on j by putting one more animal on the common field or by putting one more boat at sea, the externality and the resulting inefficiency would simply disappear. This is the basic idea underlying the Lindahl equilibrium.

It can be shown that, by creating competitive markets for 'named goods', the 'good' exchanged being the externality agent j imposes on agent i, the competitive path of exploitation of the resource is optimal. In this respect, a Lindahl equilibrium is a simple generalization of the competitive equilibrium, and the traditional welfare theorems apply. The generalization consists in regarding the externality i imposes on j as a private good which can be exchanged on a competitive market.

Does this efficiency result imply that it is desirable to create and develop markets on which agents sell and buy rights to generate externalities? In the case of the commons, the general answer is 'no' (the discussion provided below is directly based on Dasgupta and Heal, 1976: ch. 3). Indeed, the problem with the Lindahl equilibrium is that one cannot see clearly how to implement it. First, private property rights in externalities may be impossible to define and enforce since, in principle, one must be able *to exclude* non-buyers from consuming the commodities purchased by someone else. Second, the markets supporting the Lindahl equilibrium typically involve one buyer and one seller: the market structure is that of bilateral monopoly. One cannot see clearly the driving forces leading to a competitive equilibrium in this framework. The problem is made even more complicated if one admits that many externality problems are characterized by private information (this issue will be analysed in more detail in Chapter 8).

Finally, in many commons problems, the Lindahl equilibrium fails to exist. To illustrate this, let us consider, in the fishery problem, the market where agent i buys from agent j the right to generate externalities on j by putting fishing boats to sea. Let us call this commodity x_{ij}, and its price, p_{ij}. If p_{ij} is positive, then j can close down and sell an unlimited quantity of these rights x_{ij}, while i asks only for a limited amount of them: demand and supply will not match and $p_{ij} > 0$ is not an equilibrium. But, if p_{ij} is negative (or nil), j does not supply any positive amount of x_{ij}, while i asks for an infinite (or positive) amount of it: again, supply and demand for the named commodity do not match. As a result, a competitive market for the externality does not exist (the technical reason thereof is that, as long as the resource is common property, the production possibility set is not a convex set). The source of the problem, however, is that property rights so defined are not appropriate: if the fishing ground could be divided into parcels privately appropriated by the fishermen, the inefficiency problem simply would not arise. In other words, the non-convexity of the production possibilities set, in this particular case, originates in the absence of well-defined property rights (this, however, is not always the case: a good illustration of this point, for the case of pollution, is given in Dasgupta and Heal, 1979: 78–92). It is to the definition of such rights that we shall now turn our attention.

3

The Property Rights School Solution: The Privatization Programme

3.1 The Position of the Property Rights School

We have so far shown that open access and unregulated CPRs were likely to be exploited in an inefficient way. In other words, if a costless system of transfers could be established, a pattern of resource exploitation can be found which makes everyone strictly better off. The core problem is that open access and unregulated common property do not give individuals the proper incentives to act in a socially efficient way. In other words, such property systems are likely to generate externalities.

The property rights school argues that private property is the most appropriate way to make the individuals internalize the externalities. In the words of Demsetz, 'A primary function of property rights is that of guiding incentives to achieve a greater internalization of externalities' (Demsetz, 1967: 348). The incentive effect of a private property regime has long been recognized, as is attested by the following excerpt from Lloyd: 'The common reasons for the establishment of private property in land are deduced from the necessity of offering to individuals sufficient motives for cultivating the ground, and of preventing the wasteful destruction of the immature products of the earth' (Lloyd, 1833: 14). Or, in the emphatic style adopted by Garett Hardin, 'An alternative to the commons need not be perfectly just to be preferable. With real estate and other material goods, the alternative we have chosen is the institution of private property coupled with legal inheritance. . . . we are not convinced, at the moment, that anyone has invented a better system. The alternative of the commons is too horrifying to contemplate. Injustice is preferable to total ruin' (Hardin, 1967: 27–8).

The ultimate superiority of private property rights has been expressed by R. Posner as follows:

> The proper incentives [for economic efficiency] are created by the parceling out among the members of society of mutually exclusive rights to the exclusive use of particular resources. If every piece of land is owned by someone, in the sense that there is always an individual who can exclude all others from access to any given area, then individuals will endeavor by cultivation or other improvements to maximize the value of land. . . . The foregoing discussion suggests three criteria of an efficient system of property rights. The first is universality. Ideally, all resources should be owned or ownable by someone, except resources so plentiful that everybody can consume as much of them as he wants without reducing consumption by everyone else. . . . The second criterion is exclusivity. . . . The third criterion of an efficient system of property rights is transferability. If a property right cannot be transferred, there is no way of shifting a resource from a less productive to a more productive use through voluntary exchange. (Posner, 1977: 10–13, as quoted in Bromley, 1989*a*: 13)

In short, private property rights should be established. The property rights school does not however limit itself to bringing out the static gains in efficiency which may be engendered by private property. It also makes the contention that the institution of private property will spontaneously emerge in reality whenever a cost-benefit comparison makes it appear as more desirable than any other system.

If the main allocative function of property rights is the internalisation of beneficial and harmful effects, then the emergence of property rights can be understood best by the association with the emergence of new or different beneficial or harmful effects.

Changes in knowledge result in changes in production functions, market values, and aspirations. New techniques, new ways of doing the same thing, and doing new things—all invoke harmful and beneficial effects to which society has not been accustomed. It is my thesis in this part of the paper that the emergence of new property rights takes place in response to the desires of interacting persons for adjustment to new benefit-cost possibilities.

The thesis can be restated in a slightly different fashion: property rights develop to internalise externalities when the gains of internalisation become larger that the cost of internalisation. Increased internalisation, in the main, results from changes in economic values, changes which stem from the development of new technology and the opening of new markets, changes to which old property rights are poorly attuned. (Demsetz, 1967: 350)

In short, efficiency considerations dominate the property rights school arguments. In this respect, private property rights are alleged to be superior. Furthermore, it is claimed that changes in property rights systematically achieve greater efficiency.

3.2 The Efficiency of the Privatization Programme

Let us assume that private property rights can be defined and enforced *costlessly* over a resource in an open access or unregulated common property regime. Then it is standard economic wisdom that, under the new definition of property rights and *perfect* markets, a *competitive* equilibrium is efficient. This proposition rests upon four central assumptions: (*a*) enforcement costs are nil, (*b*) property rights are well defined, (*c*) markets are competitive, and, (*d*) markets are perfect, each of which we shall now examine in detail.

Enforcement costs are nil

First, in most instances, defining and enforcing private property rights entail the physical costs of defining a 'territory'. For some resources, property rights simply cannot be established because the costs involved are prohibitive (or, even, infinite): migratory fish species or clean air provide well-known examples. For instance, in the case of lobster fishing territories in Maine, 'it would be very difficult or impossible to divide the entire coast into small territories owned by single individuals. If a person is going to fish year-round or even most of the year, he needs access to a large and diverse area. The costs of defending such a territory would be prohibitive' (Acheson, 1978: 61). However, some groups of fishermen were able to secure an exclusive access to some fishing territories where the topological conditions significantly lower the costs of defending them. Such a situation characterizes the 'islands that have been in the hands of one or more of the old-established families for generations' (Acheson, 1989: 367).

We are told that private property in land in the American Great Plains did not develop fully before the 1870s because the cost of fencing was too high, making it impossible to prevent livestock from crossing range boundaries. 'The introduction of barbed wire greatly reduced the cost of enclosing one's land. To the homesteader whose land was invaded by cowboys and their herds which trampled down crops, barbed wire defined the prairie farmer's private property. . . . In 1882, the Frying Pan Ranch, in the Panhandle, spent $39,000 erecting a four-wire fence around a pasture of 250,000 acres' (Anderson and Hill, 1977: 207–8). Among the Indians of the American south-western plains, property rights on hunting-grounds were absent: 'animals of the plain are primarily grazing species whose habit is to wander over wide tracts of land. The value of establishing boundaries to private hunting territories is thus reduced by the relatively high cost of preventing the animals from moving to adjacent parcels' (Demsetz, 1967: 353).

In general, the costs of enforcing private property rights are likely to be smaller when the resource is concentrated. For instance, in the tropical forests of East Kalimantan (Borneo), the great diversity of species of trees, of which only some are economically valuable, and the fact that they are largely dispersed throughout the forest prohibited their privatization. However, birds'-nests caves which are concentrated and therefore more easily watched and guarded, are 'often controlled as private property by individuals and families' (Jessup and Peluso, 1986: 510). 'In Tripolitania, for example, potentially lucrative almond trees are reported to have been forsaken for cattle raising owing to the "common ownership" of land. This can be explained by the fact that the costs of policing investment in a tree, perenially "attached" to the common land, is high, whereas cattle are driven home at night' (Cheung, 1970: 53).

Enforcement costs are also likely to be high where the new distribution of property rights tends to hurt the former users. In most historical cases, indeed, privatization initially took the form of expropriation and was achieved through violence. The Far West conquest and the expropriation of the native Indians in North America is an interesting example in this perspective. The genocide which accompanied this process has had such a traumatic impact on the North American society that its members felt the need to mythify these events by resorting to all cultural means, particularly cinematographic production, in some ritual of exorcism. The enclosure movement in the plains of North America and in England were also accomplished by force. In the latter case, 'early enclosures, especially those before the mid-sixteenth century, frequently involved the destruction of villages and the expulsion of their inhabitants as lords seized peasant land. . . . Before 1450 and 1525, about one-tenth of the villages in the midlands were destroyed' (Allen, 1982: 14). The current privatization process of the Amazonian forest in Brazil gives rise to many armed conflicts which will ultimately lead to the genocide of the native Indians. In India, the nationalization of forests led to violent reactions and, in some instances, to the complete destruction of the commons by dispossessed former users (for further details, see Chapter 11, sect. 1).

In other words, the costs of enforcing exclusive property rights partly depend on the way distribution of wealth is affected and also on the perceived legitimacy of the new legal system and authorities by the dispossessed former users. Violence is likely to be resorted to when perceived legitimacy is low. One might apparently argue that transfers can be made from the new owner to the former users to compensate for their loss, *as if the latter were to sell their informal right of use*. We analyse this issue in detail at the end of this chapter. At this stage, let us note that, *historically, such transfers seldom took place, and the rights of the former users were seldom recognized*. As an additional example, in the case of English enclosures, we are told that, 'during the parliamentary enclosures less than seven per cent of enclosed land went to peasants holding a total of 25 acres of land or less. In the earlier enclosures, not regulated by parliamentary acts, the allotment was presumably even more disproportionate. . . . If a tenant was able to demonstrate to the satisfaction of a court that he had good title to land (if his family has worked it for time out of mind), his tenure was secure, although this didn't necessarily mean that he ended up "owning it". If he was unable to do this, he was at the mercy of the enclosing lord. For the most part, good title to the land was difficult to establish for a copy-holder and insecurity was widespread where enclosures were extensive' (Cohen and Weitzman, 1975: 324; see also Allen, 1992).

In some cases, the appropriation is made by a minority of traditional users at the expense of the remaining ones. For instance, we are told by Karanth in his analysis of a village in Karnataka:

> From the point of view of some elders in the village, such greed for land resulted in the poor maintenance of the village tank, garden, manure pit and what remained of the pastures. Those owning land around a pasture began to encroach it with a hope that sooner or later they would regularise the unauthorised occupation. Likewise the dry bed of the tank, the garden and the manure pit were also being encroached. Given the increased politicisation of village factions, there had been several signed and anonymous complaints of encroachment. Officials of the revenue department had made several visits to the village for a 'spot' inspection and after a customary meal in the houses of leading families reports were made to state that the complaints were not found to be true. The consequence was that the village garden, the extent of which was 1.13 acres has now been reduced to less than 0.40 acres. Although the index of land states that there were several varieties of fruit-bearing trees, there are hardly any left now. (Karanth, 1992: 1685)

Equally important to emphasize are the two following problems: (1) *private information problems may make compensation of the former users infeasible,* and (2) *the private value attached by former users to their access to the resource* (a plot of land, a hunting-ground or a fishing territory) *may be very high* and exceed by far its economic value on the market.[1] This is particularly evident when their ancestors have been buried on or

[1] For this argument to be really relevant, we should add that traditional users are not able to pay for the full economic value of the resource usually because they are denied access to the capital market (see below) and, in some instances, because their use of the resource is not identical to the one which the market would dictate to a profit-maximizing landowner.

near the land to be privatized and when magical beliefs or historical considerations impart a highly emotional value to the same (see Chapter 10 for more details). For instance, in Sub-Saharan Africa, we are told that 'Land was held communally by clan or lineage. A *sacred* trust, it was essentially in the holding of the ancestors. It was the only area from which rituals to the ancestors could be effectively performed and hence where one should be buried' (Caldwell and Caldwell, 1987: 422). One may also think of the symbolic role of the 'sacred islands' among aboriginal fishing and hunting communities such as the Bijagos in Guinea-Bissau. Commercial exploitation of these islands following assignment by the State of private landleases to business interests (for touristic development) or even temporary occupation by outsiders (migrant small-scale fishermen from Senegal) have aroused indignant feelings and violent reactions (in the form of poisoning of some intruders) among the Bijagos (personal field observation of Platteau).

The importance of this last point should not be underemphasized: indeed, many conflicts accompanying a privatization process develop because the new arrivals and the legal authorities did not recognize the symbolic value attached to the resource by the former users. For example, a recent CIDA (Canadian International Development Agency)-supported project of establishing seven 4,000-hectare highly mechanized wheat farms in Northern Tanzania is strongly opposed by the Barabaig herders. About 30,000 Barabaig live in that area and have for more than 100 years moved their livestock on a rotational basis around the territory. Five Barabaig elders, supported by Charles Lane, a British anthropologist of the IDS (Sussex), sent a letter to the Canadian authorities, in which they claimed that 40,000 hectares of land, some of their best grazing land, had been taken with *inadequate compensation* and *without their consent*. They also claimed that they had been personally beaten and robbed by farm employees, that their houses and possessions had been burned out, and their access to traditional water sources and pastures prohibited. 'Many of the *graves of our elders* have been ploughed up and are no longer recognizable', said the letter. 'These sacred sites are very important to us as places of worship. It is there that we make offerings and call on God's blessings through the medium of our ancestors' (as quoted by the *Globe and Mail*, 8 May 1989). By 1987, already 57 Barabaig burial sites had been destroyed and others were either surrounded by cultivated fields or rendered inaccessible because of threats from new settlers or project staff.

Another example of the same discrepancy between the private and market values that can be attributed to a resource is given implicitly in the following judgment rendered in 1493 by an English Court condemning Henry Smith, who seized a domain traditionally used as cultivated land by eighty customary tenants in order to convert it into pastures for his sheep. The persons who were formerly

> occupied in the same cultivation . . . were compelled to depart tearfully against their will. Since then, they have remained idle and thus lead a miserable existence, and indeed they die wretched. What is more to be lamented is [that] the church of Stretton on that occasion fell into ruin and decay, so that the Christian congregation, which used to gather there to hear the divine offices, is no longer held there and the worship of God is almost at an end. In the church animals are sheltered from the storms of the air and brute animals feed among the tombs of Christian bodies

in the churchyard. In all things *the church and burial places are profaned to the evil example of others* inclined to act in such a manner (Leadan, 1897: 432, emphasis added).

What the above analysis tends to show is that, due to the intervention of equity considerations, costs of enforcing private property may be much higher than usually thought. They might even be so high that we cannot be sure that establishing this new system of rights will actually reduce transaction costs (including litigation costs) as predicted by the property rights school. This is all the more true if allowance is made not only for transaction costs resulting from land-market imperfections, but also for those arising from labour-market imperfections. As a matter of fact, moral hazard problems on the labour-market (absenteeism, labour-shirking, input-pilfering, asset mismanagement, etc.) may increase owing to the resistance or vengefulness of dispossessed resource users (for a more elaborate analysis of these and related points, see Platteau, 1992).

Property rights are well defined

The second point we would like to draw attention to is the following: to be efficient, *the privatization process must be perfect*, in the sense that it has to eliminate all the externalities involved in exploitation of the resource. First, it must lead to 'the internalization of the good externality'. In his analysis of fur trade in Labrador, Demsetz notes that private property rights on land developed with the development of the commercial fur trade (Demsetz, 1967: 351–3). This is a typical illustration of the case where privatization is imperfect. Since exclusive property rights could not be enforced at a reasonable cost in the game itself, they were created around hunting-territories with the consequence that externalities were not all removed. The importance of remaining externalities obviously depended upon the mobility of the game and the size of the territories. Exclusive fishing rights in well-defined territories provide another well-known illustration. In many cases, the resource itself (migratory species of fish) can hardly be privatized so that exclusive rights bear upon the (fishing) area where the resource is living. The importance of the residual externality should not be underestimated.

Second, *privatization must be complete*: exclusive rights have to be defined on the whole resource. Otherwise, perverse effects are bound to develop and to lead to a worsening of the situation. For example, Gilles and Jamtgaard report that 'the decline of the English commons may have resulted from the exclusion of animals from agricultural lands. In the English open-field system, animals grazed on the commons during the summer months and fed on stubble and hay during the rest of the year. As fields became privately owned, animals had to spend longer periods on the commons. The result was overgrazing' (Gilles and Jamtgaard, 1981: 138). Migration of workers from newly enclosed to unenclosed areas also contributed to the degradation of the commons system. 'The . . . effect was to be seen in the so far unenclosed towns and villages where some of the dispossessed tenants moved. The overcrowded squatter settlements set up on the border of these towns were a direct result of enclosures.

Chambers notes that Nottingham, by its decision not to enclose, left itself no choice but to grow within its ancient manorial boundaries, and before the end of the eighteenth century, there were complaints of severe overcrowding. 'By turning its face against enclosures, it had condemned itself to a period of unparalleled overcrowding and squalor' (Cohen and Weitzman, 1975: 326). In the Karnataki village analysed by Karanth, 'the consequences of privatisation of CPRs in land was that there was a gradual depletion of village pasture. Farmers became increasingly dependent upon the forests for grazing, which in turn led to depletion of forest resources too' (Karanth, 1992: 1687).

Also worth stressing is the fact that reforming customary property right arrangements is likely to create serious uncertainties about the future use rights of former resource users. For instance, not infrequently, enforcement costs are either so high that the State is unable to establish the new property right arrangements, or of such a nature that the change can only be carried out at a slow pace, thus lengthening the transitory phase. This is bound to lead to conflicting claims over these ill-specified rights and there is no assurance that the newly emerging situation will be superior, in efficiency terms, to the previously obtained arrangement. In the worst case, a genuine open-access situation might arise as a result of the complete breakdown of traditional norms and codes of behaviour.

Third, *privatization may create new externalities*. For example, in his analysis of the green revolution in Gujarat (India), B. Bhatia (1992) demonstrates convincingly how the privatization of the irrigation system through the development of private tube-wells led to such an overexploitation of underground water that tube-well irrigation is doomed to come to an end in the coming decades. Note in passing that this is of course related to the fact that private property rights in underground water are too costly to define. To take another example, the privatization of forests in Scotland may cause 'the siltation of salmon streams caused by logging' (Hardin, 1977: 223); in semi-arid areas, it may induce users of firewood to overexploit a close substitute (young trees from adjacent bushes); in Belgium, it has actually fostered the extension of pine forests (a quick-maturing species) with the result that soils became increasingly acid and that biodiversity and game stock were drastically curtailed.

Markets are competitive

The third point we would like to make is closely related to the second. In many cases, such as when the resource can be detained by only one owner or when there are increasing returns to scale, the correct internalization of the externality implies the creation of a local monopoly,[2] a classical cause of inefficiency.

In a static framework, an oligopolistic producer tends to exploit too little, and unregulated common property too much of the resource. Therefore, unregulated common property with respect to a resource for which the community considered is

[2] This monopoly can moreover be compounded by a monopsony on the labour-market to the extent that all former users of the resource are likely to offer their labour services to the new resource owner.

the only seller on the corresponding goods market may be the most efficient (Pareto optimal) pattern of resource management. Indeed, Cornes *et al.* (1986) have shown that, when the n agents who exploit a resource collectively are the only sellers of that resource on the market, there exists an optimal number n^* of these agents, with $n^* > 1$, such that the non-co-operative pattern of resource exploitation (the 'tragedy of the commons') is Pareto-efficient.

There are actually many instances where privatization of the resource involves the creation of a monopoly. For example, we are told by Bromley that, in Switzerland, 'the several farmers who jointly own a summer pasture are able to share the cost of a single herder to move the animals around to water, and to select those areas for grazing where the vegetation is particularly lush. If the summer pastures were owned in severalty, it might then be possible for one strategically located owner to prevent all others from gaining access to water—a potentially serious issue for the welfare of the group' (Bromley, 1989*a*: 16).

This is not a marginal example. As a matter of fact, the problem of access to water wells in many arid and semi-arid areas in the developing world is so critical that the consequences of replacement of communal by (monopolistic) private ownership for herders and other nomadic people cannot be underestimated.

Protection of underground water against overexploitation, of the Sahelian area against desertification, or of a lake against overfishing may therefore require the whole underground water, the Sahelian pastures, or the lake to be owned by a single agent. The inefficiencies likely to be involved in such schemes, if feasible, may render them unacceptable to many. It must also be stressed that, in many cases, it is the former users of the resource who will bear the whole burden of the inefficiency thus created: here is another reason why enforcement costs of privatization may turn out eventually to be unbearable.

Markets are perfect

A basic assumption underlying the proposition according to which development of private property rights in a resource will lead to efficiency is that all other markets are perfect and competitive. Indeed, it is only under this assumption that costless establishment of private property rights will increase efficiency. If other markets are absent or imperfect, the reform of traditional property arrangements may cause inefficiencies and paradoxically lead in some instances to the overexploitation of the resource. For instance, 'roughly 75 per cent of the publicly held rangeland and 60 per cent of the privately held ranges in the United States are in fair to poor conditions as a result of over-grazing' (Gilles and Jamtgaard, 1981: 129).[3] What are the reasons which lead us to surmise that 'market failures' are an important source of concern when it comes to privatizing natural resources?

[3] One may argue that such overgrazing may be the efficient path of exploitation of the resource. However, considering the extent of the phenomenon, the validity of such an argument appears doubtful.

Absent markets

Standard economic arguments show that a necessary condition for the efficiency of private exploitation of an *exhaustible resource* is the existence of *a complete (infinite) set of forward markets*. In fact, a sequence of momentary equilibria such that, at each period, the market for the flow of the resource clears and the rate of return to holding the resource stock is equal to the rate of interest (the Hotelling rule) is not sufficient to guarantee that the resource will be exhausted over an infinite horizon. This is due to the fact that complete forward markets do not exist to determine the correct initial price of the resource, p_0, so as to ensure that the stock will be just depleted in infinite time. Given the absence of these markets, p_0 may be either too high or too low. If too high, although competitive momentary markets always equilibrate, some portion of the resource stock will never be extracted. If too low, the stock will be exhausted in finite time (prematurely), assuming again that the agents cling to their myopic rule (i.e. the Hotelling rule). Presumably, however, the latter process will not persist, and traders will realize that the resource, at the current rates of exploitation, will be exhausted in finite time: they will buy up stocks and the spot price of the resource will jump. This argument can be generalized to exclude the possibility that any path for which the initial price, p_0, is lower than the optimal price will be followed up to the point of exhaustion of the resource in finite time. This however does not remove inefficiency in resource use: indeed, exploitation goes too fast initially and too slow thereafter when compared to the optimal path. The following conclusion emerges: in the absence of a complete set of forward markets or, under uncertainty, in the absence of a complete set of forward contingent markets, a competitive private economy will be inefficient.[4]

The problem is that, in real economic life, there do not exist many complete sets of forward markets for a resource (not to speak of contingent markets). As pointed out by Dasgupta and Heal, for *exhaustible resources*, 'the problems associated with the non-existence of a suitable set of forward markets may well be more important and less tractable than those arising from externalities' (Dasgupta and Heal, 1979: 472). Moreover, it is not clear that the setting up of such markets, no matter how difficult it can be, necessarily leads to an increase in social welfare if other market imperfections remain.

The second point we would like to make is that many environmental resources exhibit characteristics for which no market exists. In other words, part of the social valuation given to such a resource cannot be reflected in competitive market prices. This is so because some of the features displayed by environmental resources, such as the recycling of CO_2 by the forests or the beauty of a natural site, are *public goods*, a well-known source of market failure.[5] It implies that, though everybody enjoys clean

[4] It has been suggested (see Dasgupta and Heal, 1979: 163) that a planning board announcing 'notional' prices may help in removing the inefficiencies by providing traders with reliable signals. Though this may be right in principle, it is hard to see why a state agency should necessarily have access to better information than private traders, particularly for that type of commodity. As we shall see below, the existence of such information problems actually provides a powerful economic argument in favour of the local management for local commons (see in particular Dasgupta, 1993: ch. 10).

[5] Of course, to say that there are characteristics of the environmental resources whose value is not

air or the beauties of an unspoilt Antarctica, if asked to, nobody would be ready to pay for it. Therefore, by neglecting some important roles played by environmental resources, markets fail to give the correct signals to private traders in the absence of state intervention. This argument is important, and has been repeatedly used by conservationists to support their claim for a better protection of environmental resources, notably in the form of state-protected areas. For instance, it is very unlikely that the world market for forestry products correctly reflects their role in recycling CO_2, and that current deforestations in Amazonia, Sub-Saharan Africa, South-East Asia (Sarawak forests are currently being irreversibly destroyed), or Siberia (the forests of which represent 25 per cent of the world total resources, but are currently being destroyed at the rate of 4 million hectares per year) correspond to an optimal utilization of forest resources.

Seabright (1993) makes essentially the same point in connection with local commons. He indeed stresses the implicit contracting aspects of traditional CPRs: the users' entitlements and obligations are too complex and interlinked to be written in a formal contract and, moreover, they require reasonably long time-horizons to work effectively. And yet, implicit aspects are important because they induce informal co-operation among the users. According to him, therefore, privatization with tradability of private property rights may undermine the reliability of those co-operation arrangements. This is not only because 'it is difficult to frame formal contractual rights so as to safeguard traditional entitlements', but also because privatization weakens the credibility of long-term contracts and suppresses the kind of interdependence and reputation effects that are conducive to informal co-operation practices. In particular, if sale of assets is possible, the incentive of customary users to invest in a personal relationship and to co-operate with the new private owner is dampened since there is no way the latter can credibly commit himself to sustain these 'relationship-specific' arrangements (Seabright, 1993: 124–9).

Imperfect markets

A second type of reason why one may suspect that private property does not necessarily increase efficiency is that some markets, and particularly the *capital market*, are imperfect. First, due to informational asymmetries (and the resulting problem of moral hazard), access to credit may be restricted to those having sufficient collateral. If the resource is sold by the State, those having a privileged access to capital are more likely to become private owners. Therefore, in the absence of state support, traditional users of the resource are likely to be denied access to it in the course of privatization. Though this is basically a distributive issue, it is important to see that efficiency may be impaired for at least three reasons: (*a*) if the legitimate interests of the former users are hurt, their passive or active resistance may cause enforcement costs to increase; (*b*)

correctly reflected in market prices is formally identical to saying that the privatization process has been incomplete by not achieving the internalization of these residual externalities. The reason why we think it nevertheless constitutes a separate point is that the characteristics of the resource we are concerned with here cannot be privatized: they are public goods, and it is this last aspect that we want to investigate here.

traditional users of the resource are likely to have developed particular skills and acquired a detailed knowledge of the resource which renders them more efficient to exploit the resource than outsiders (and markets for those skills and knowledge are bound to fail due to informational asymmetries), and (*c*) the market for private rights in the resource may become too thin and oligopsonistic practices, such as collusive arrangements, are likely to distort it. For instance, from a detailed study of the rope-making industry in the Himalayan foothills (Johri and Krishnamukar, 1991), we learn that raw material for making ropes is a wild grass, locally known as *bhabhar*, which grows on the Shivalite hills. It was a common property resource until British rule. Nowadays, the State has established state property over the grass which it sells during summer at an auction. Access of poor rope-makers to capital is so restricted that, in effect, 'the auction is attended by a handful of local traders who collude to keep their price hovering around the price first quoted' (ibid. 2898), and secure a net rate of return of about 50 per cent per year by selling the grass to the rope-makers. In recent years, credit co-operatives have started to appear to allow rope-makers to buy *bhabhar* at the auctions and circumvent the traders.

Furthermore, when access to sources of credit is imperfect, the extreme poverty of the agent who exploits the resource (be it a traditional user or a private owner) may have deleterious consequences since 'poverty may be expected to drive up their rate of time preference to the point where all that matters is consumption today' (Perrings, 1989: 20). In the case of US rangeland referred to at the beginning of this section, poor people are led to 'stock their pastures at higher rates than do their larger more conservative neighbors. A result of this strategy can be overgrazing and environmental degradation' (Gilles and Jamtgaard, 1981: 132). In some cases, traditional users themselves may sell out their common assets to industrial concerns in order to get cash to meet immediate needs (more about this in Chapter 11).

The general line of the argument presented here is also applicable at a world-wide level. Given difficult access to international credit to pay off past debts and/or finance economic development, governments of capital-hungry developing countries may not resist the temptation to sell or to lease national resources. This may give rise to at least two kinds of serious problem. First, being under stress, governments may easily be led to sell their natural assets or rights of exploitation at abnormally low prices (as is evidenced in the case of fishing rights conceded to foreign fleets by governments of poor African coastal countries). Second, the new owners or users of the resources may be induced to overexploit them because they strongly doubt the ability of governments to make credible commitments on such touchy issues as those pertaining to the nation's natural patrimony. Their fear is actually that the agreements involved might well be soon rescinded if the economic situation of the host country improves or if political change brings to power a new government with a more nationalistic outlook.[6]

The second reason why imperfect capital markets may lead to an inefficient exploitation of the privatized resource is that, in the presence of those imperfections, the interest rate fails to represent correctly the social rate of discount (see also Fisher,

[6] The problem of resource extraction in indebted developing countries has recently begun to be studied by economic theorists (see Rauscher, 1990; Strand, 1992, 1994*a*, 1994*b*).

1981: 68–71). It is often suggested that the *market rate of interest* is too high. It may result in the excessive exploitation of the natural resources and even in their destruction in those cases where the natural rate of growth of a renewable resource remains below the market rate of interest when its stock approaches zero.

3.3 The Distributive Impact of Privatization

We have argued so far that the privatization programme advocated by the property rights school does not necessarily promote efficiency. We would like at this point to evaluate the impact of such a programme on income distribution. Let us assume that it can be achieved costlessly, and that the markets are perfect and competitive. Since, under these conditions, we have already shown that the unregulated common property equilibrium was Pareto-dominated by the competitive (private property) equilibrium, we know that, through an appropriate set of transfers, everybody can be made better off under the competitive equilibrium: *everybody can gain from privatization.* The above statement holds true only in those situations where the former users of the resource get their rights recognized and get compensated for the loss in income which they incur when privatization is carried out.[7] This is clearly the case when traditional users of a resource are made private owners, or when the proceeds from the sale of property rights in the resource are remitted to the former users. In many circumstances, unfortunately, traditional communities do not get their user rights recognized and are simply excluded from the use of the resource with no compensation.[8] In those situations, an interesting issue emerges: since the resource is now efficiently managed, is it possible that the marginal productivity of labour increases in such proportions that the former users, now working as wage-earners, actually gain from privatization? The question applies to two situations of particular interest:

1. The resource is now privately owned by an outsider who manages it competitively and hires former users as wage labour.
2. The rights in the resource are sold competitively by the State and the former users become the private owners of the resource. The proceeds of the sale (which represent the discounted sum of the rents which an efficient use of the resource will yield over time) are siphoned off by the State.

In these two situations, will the former users necessarily lose? This is the question raised by Weitzman (1974) in a celebrated article (see also Cohen and Weitzman, 1975: 311–13), and the answer given is 'yes'. Unfortunately, the proof provided seems to be unnecessarily complicated. As a matter of fact, the underlying argument can be easily formulated with the help of a standard diagram (Figure 3.1). Assume that the average product, *AP*, is decreasing in the variable factor, *L* (this is indeed the classical situation

[7] Bear in mind that, owing to private information problems, transfers may simply be impossible (see also Ch. 4, sect. 1).

[8] As we shall in Ch. 4, sect. 3, even the case where the rights of the former users are fully recognized, that is where the former users are simply turned into full owners of private property rights, can be problematic, but for other reasons than the one analysed here.

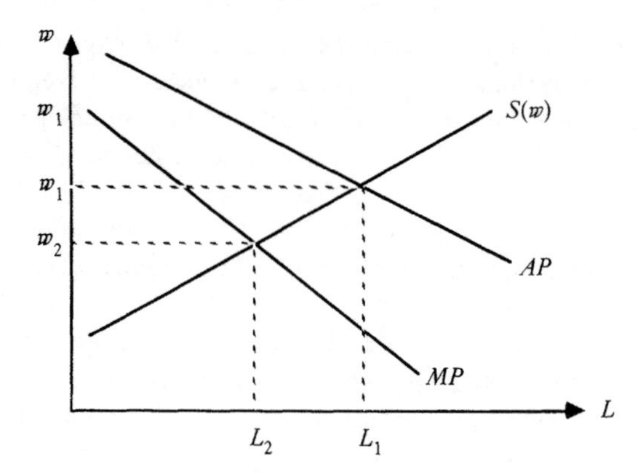

FIG. 3.1. The welfare impact of privatization, Weitzman (1974)

where the tragedy of the commons arises). Thus the marginal product of the variable factor, *MP*, is also decreasing and, for each level of *L*, $MP(L) < AP(L)$. Let us draw the supply curve of the variable factor, $S(w)$, where w stands for its market price, and assume that $S'(w) > 0$. Then we can draw the diagram depicted in Figure 3.1.

In an open-access situation, we know that the variable factor is remunerated at its average product, w_1, while, in the competitive situation, it is remunerated at its marginal product, w_2. It is evident from the graphical analysis above that $w_2 < w_1$, $L_2 < L_1$, and $w_2L_2 < w_1L_1$. This is precisely the conclusion reached by Weitzman (1974): the remuneration of the variable factor falls.

It must nevertheless be noted that Weitzman actually compares open access (OA) to private property (PP), i.e., the no-rent to the maximum-rent situation. Using the same diagram, it is a simple matter to extend the argument to unregulated common property (CP). Indeed, we already know that $w(\text{CP}) \geq w(\text{OA})$. From the above, we also know that $w(\text{OA}) > w(\text{PP})$. Therefore, $w(\text{CP}) > w(\text{PP})$. As for the amount of labour spent under unregulated common property, it is of course smaller than that obtained under open access (since output is restricted and labour is the only production factor considered), yet larger than that achieved under private property. As a result, it is certain that the wage bill is greater under common (unregulated) than under private property.

The practical implication of this analysis is, in the words of Weitzman, that 'there may be a good reason for propertyless variable factor units to be against efficiency improving moves . . . like the introduction of property rights . . . unless they get a specific kickback in one form or another' (Weitzman, 1974: 234). It is indeed striking from Weitzman's proof that former resource users lose not only in terms of employment but also on account of reduced individual labour earnings.

4

The Unregulated Common Property: The Prisoner's Dilemma Revisited

Theoretical arguments can be put forward to show that the tragedy of the commons is an unduly pessimistic story. They all rest on the idea that purely decentralized mechanisms exist which allow agents to escape perverse equilibria leading to the gradual destruction of local CPRs. Essentially, these arguments call into question Hardin's representation of the pattern of resource exploitation by a one-shot static PD game. To that effect, different theoretical approaches can be followed. First, decentralized contracting processes around use rights may bring about a Pareto-optimal pattern of exploitation through side payments that transform the payoff structure of the original PD game. Second, co-operation may be shown to emerge even within the framework of the PD game provided, however, that allowance is made for repeated interaction over time between different individuals' choices. Third, the payoff structure of the game being played may not be that of the PD, and in these new types of games, collectively rational outcomes become more likely. In the following, an extensive discussion of these different approaches will be undertaken and, in the process, the role of such variables as group size, group homogeneity, trust among agents, and moral norms will be highlighted. Given the magnitude of the task, this discussion will take place in two steps corresponding to two distinct chapters: the first two aforementioned approaches will be the focus of this chapter while the third one will be the object of the next chapter.

4.1 The Role of Private Contracting: Lessons from the Coase Theorem

A simple exposition of the Coase theorem

In a celebrated article, Coase argues that, provided rights are well defined, agents will negotiate so as to achieve Pareto-efficiency. The starting-point of his analysis is the reciprocal nature of the damages related to an externality and its correction: 'We are dealing with a problem of reciprocal nature. To avoid harm on B would inflict harm on A. The real question that has to be decided is: should A be allowed to harm B or should B be allowed to harm A? The problem is to avoid the more serious harm' (Coase, 1960: 2). For instance, if, by his activities, a polluter imposes an externality on someone, by asking him to reduce his emission of pollutants, the pollutee also causes a damage to the polluter. Provided that either the polluter's or the pollutee's rights are recognized, they will negotiate and, by comparing their respective costs, choose the efficient course of action. State intervention is not necessary to achieve efficiency. 'It is necessary to know whether the damaging business is liable or not for damage caused since without the establishment of this initial delimitation of rights, there can be no market transactions to transfer and recombine them. But the ultimate result (which maximizes the value of production) is independent of the legal position if the pricing system is assumed to work without costs.' Indeed, 'It is always possible to modify by transactions on the market the initial delimitation of rights. And, of course, if such market transactions are costless, such rearrangements of rights will always take place if it would lead to an increase in the value of production' (ibid. 8, 15).

Coase's work on 'the problem of social cost' has been interpreted in various ways in the literature. We concentrate below on one particular version of what has come to be known as the Coase theorem. According to this interpretation, '*voluntary negotiation will lead to a fully efficient outcome*' (Farrell, 1987: 115, our emphasis) provided: (*a*) rights are well defined, (*b*) transactions are costless, and (*c*) there are no income effects. The implications of this proposition are far-reaching:

1. if markets are incomplete, people will negotiate and the efficient outcome will result;
2. there is no need for government intervention; and
3. the outcome is independent of the initial assignment of rights.

Let us illustrate this with the help of a simple example. Assume that, in a fishery, there are three fishermen, say A, B, and C, each of whom operates only one boat. The production conditions in the fishery are such that the net profits per boat are determined as follows:

Number of boats	1	2	3
Net profit per boat	\$3	\$2	\$1

In such a fishery, there is one Pareto optimum, where only two boats are operated. First consider the situation of an unregulated common property, where each fisherman has a right to fish. In the absence of any transaction, each of them will enter the fishery and the tragedy of the commons results. However, such a result is unlikely if transactions are costless. Indeed, A and B (or B and C, or A and C) are ready to pay C (or A, or B) up to \$2 if C renounces to make use of his right of access to the fishery. C is ready to sell his right provided he is paid at least \$1. The precise amount which will be decided depends in general on the bargaining strength of the partners. In the symmetric game examined here, one may argue that they will agree on \$1.33 (that is, the maximum total catch of \$4 divided by the number of potential fishermen) so that each fisherman will be indifferent between fishing or not. In any case, by negotiating, the three fishermen achieve Pareto-efficiency.

If, however, instead of being an unregulated common property, the fishery considered above was the exclusive property of A who is able to operate only one boat, the fishery would be underexploited. Fisherman B, or C, would be ready to pay A as much as \$2 to have a right of access to the fishing-ground. Once again, if transactions are costless, an agreement will be reached by which agent A will sell to another agent the right to fish on his territory. In other words, provided property rights are well defined, the fishery will always be exploited efficiently. Variation in the system of property rights (private or common property) has the only effect of altering the distribution of income.

The Coase theorem can be applied to a variety of cases where externalities are involved, and in most of the problems we are concerned with it merely *implies that collective action (through regulation) is not needed*: through negotiation, agents will make up for missing markets. As evident from the foregoing example, an immediate application of the Coase theorem—and one that, strangely enough, is never mentioned in the literature—is that, in an unregulated common property resource, no tragedy of the commons can ever occur: people will always be able to negotiate to avoid this inefficient outcome. *There is no need for any central intervention, whether for the purposes of taxation or of privatization* of the whole resource domain. This being said, as will be argued in the following, the Coase theorem suffers from a number of serious limitations which considerably restrict its practical relevance.

The problem of the existence of a solution to bargaining

Though in many cases bargaining may lead to efficiency, there is at least one important class of problem where it does not. More precisely, Shapley and Shubik (1969), with the help of the 'garbage game', have shown that, if there are more than two parties, 'the economy can fail to possess a core allocation if there are polluters' rights over *private bads*, such as household garbage' (Dasgupta and Mäler, 1990: 15–16). Let us consider a modified version of Shapley and Shubik's pollution example: assume there are three herdsmen, A, B, C who also possess their own plot of land L_A, L_B, L_C. The pastures are common property but lie next to these plots. When a herd grazes, it causes damage to the adjoining cultivated field. However, there is one field, L_C, less intensively cultivated, for which the damage caused by a herd is less important, equal to a, while the damage caused on each of the other two plots, L_A and L_B, is equal to b, with $b > a$.

Let us first consider the case where each herdsman has the right to let his herd graze close to any of the cultivated fields, L_A, L_B, L_C, and suppose that side-payments are authorized. If no agreement is reached, a herdsman, say A, lets his herd graze close to one of the two plots belonging to the others, L_B or L_C, causing a damage of b or a. However, he can also negotiate, say, with C, to the effect that both of them locate their herds close to L_B. At most, they risk a loss of b (if B chooses to place his herd close to L_A), that they share together, C paying e to compensate A. The resulting payoffs to (A,B,C) are then $(-b+e,-2b,-e)$. However, in this situation, B is ready to accept from C a compensation smaller than e, say d, so that they can both form a coalition against A. The resulting payoffs are $(-2b,-b+d,-d)$. But A can make a counter-offer, for example to B. . . . It is easy to verify in this example that no agreement can satisfy every (group of) herdsmen 'to the point where they cannot, by violating it, be sure of doing better' (Shapley and Shubik, 1969: 541). In other words, though there does exist an efficient solution in this game, players will not be able to reach it through bargaining. As a matter of fact, the core is empty.

Things are however different if, instead of giving to the herdsmen the right to graze their herds wherever they wish, the agriculturalists' exclusive rights to an undamaged harvest are recognized. In that case indeed, it is clear that all three herdsmen will locate their herds close to the field L_C. A and B each pay to C a sum between a and b, since otherwise either C will not tolerate that their herds graze close to his field or A and B will find it more interesting to let their animals graze close to their own fields. When the rights are given to the agriculturalists, decentralized bargaining thus results in an efficient solution.

The conclusion is clear: in games involving more than two parties, whether or not an efficient solution will be reached through decentralized bargaining may depend on the initial assignments or rights: as it stands, the Coase theorem is not valid.

Another crucial difficulty with the Coase theorem is its implicit requirement that all parties concerned are in a position to negotiate. However, in many environmental problems, it is the future generations who bear the costs of the externality. It is not at all clear how their interests may be systematically taken into account in the bargaining process.

The importance of transaction costs

There is no doubt that Coase was well aware of the importance of transaction costs for the validity of his theorem.

> But this assumed costless market transactions. Once the costs of carrying out market transactions are taken into account it is clear that such a rearrangement of rights will only be undertaken when the increase in the value of production consequent upon the rearrangement is greater than the cost which would be involved in bringing it about. . . . In those conditions, the initial delimitation of legal rights does have an effect on efficiency with which the economic system operates. One rearrangement of rights may bring about a greater value of production than any other. But unless this is the arrangement of rights established by the legal system, the costs of reaching the same result by altering and combining rights through the market may be so great that the optimal arrangement of rights, and the greater value of production which it would bring, may never be achieved. (Coase, 1960: 15–16)

This argument is particularly important in the case where there are many parties affected by the externality, such as stream pollution by a firm.[1] Assume that no pollution is the optimal situation. If the potential pollutees have a right to clean water, the firm will take measures not to pollute the river: there are no transaction costs in this case. However, if the firm has a right to pollute, the costs of having all the pollutees organized and prepared to contribute financially to the firm's efforts to reduce pollution may simply be prohibitive, and the sub-optimal situation of pollution will obtain and persist.

As noted by Fisher, Demsetz's argument that 'where transaction costs block a

[1] Even in relatively small groups, as experimental tests have revealed, people seem to be rather reluctant to trade as much as predicted by the Coase theorem (Kahneman *et al.*, 1990).

private bargaining solution . . . the status quo must be optimal in the sense that the benefits from moving are less than the costs, including the transaction costs' (Fisher, 1981: 182) is not valid. Indeed, in many cases, such as in the pollution example given above, state intervention to the effect of redesigning the allocation of rights may be optimal, even when the transaction costs of such intervention are taken into account. By contrast, the private bargaining solution is not optimal.

In short, the importance and size of transaction costs in private bargaining agreements depend upon the initial delimitation of rights and the number of agents concerned. The State has an important role to play in this respect. First, in designing the initial allocation of rights, it has to take account of the transaction costs which such an allocation will entail in private bargaining. Second, given an initial allocation of rights, public intervention may incur lower transaction costs than private agreements.

The distributive effects

As our statement of the Coase theorem has made clear, the theorem bears only upon the issue of efficiency. The distributive effects of private bargaining are completely disregarded, though they may be the most important issue in practice. They may also have an important impact on the outcome of the private bargaining process itself. Indeed, 'when the damaged party is a consumer . . . willingness to pay may differ from required compensation because the former is constrained by the consumer's income.' When income effects are thus taken into account, 'the assignment of property rights will affect resource use' (Fisher, 1981: 184).

Private information

The validity of the Coase theorem is seriously challenged when allowance is made for the fact that, in many private bargaining processes, information is not perfect.[2] When there are informational asymmetries, the parties to the bargain often have an incentive to cheat and to give false information in order to manipulate the outcome of the process. In these cases, bargaining is typically inefficient. For instance, 'a potential buyer may value a house more than its prospective seller does, but less than the seller believes "most" buyers do. He would then have trouble persuading the seller to lower the price enough to make the deal' (Farrell, 1987: 115). A well-known problem in the negotiation of self-imposed catch restrictions (or quotas) is the incomplete information about others' past harvesting performances. Depending upon the chosen mechanism for setting individual quotas (that is, for sharing the burden of restrictions), fishermen may be incited to over- or under-report their past records so as to bear the smallest possible burden of restriction. Moreover, as this is common knowledge, everybody becomes suspicious of all statements made by others.[3]

[2] This part draws heavily upon the insightful analysis by Farrell (1987). For more details, see also Myerson and Satterthwaite (1983) and d'Aspremont and Gerard-Varet (1979).

[3] In point of fact, manipulation of information may be aimed not only at minimizing one's own share in the collective restriction effort within a given sharing mechanism but also at bringing about the mechanism most congenial to one's own interests.

The question which arises is whether it is possible for a central authority, when deciding about a project, to induce people to release the true information, even though they know that this information will be used to decide (*a*) whether the project is worth undertaking and (*b*) the amount of the contributions each beneficiary will be required to pay. In the case of the commons, the 'project' may typically consist in determining the extent of reduction in total use of the variable factor (fishing effort, size of the herd) to be imposed on the users and the 'contribution' is the reduction each individual agent may be required to accept. It can be shown (see d'Aspremont and Gerard-Varet, 1976, 1979) that there indeed exists such a scheme or 'mechanism' which can be proposed to the players by a mediator and such that these players will be induced to reveal the truth (even though they fully anticipate that such information will be used to decide on their contribution). The following conditions are sufficient to ensure that result:

1. there are at least three players, or,
2. each player can be of only two possible 'types', a type being determined by the extent of interest an individual agent has in a particular project, or,
3. the individual types are independently distributed.

This approach nevertheless suffers from two important limitations. First, the agents are not free to decide whether they will participate or not, even though their participation may actually hurt them. If we require furthermore that each player must be willing to participate in the scheme (the scheme must be 'individually rational'), then it can be shown that, for a whole class of bargaining problems, efficiency cannot be achieved. This fundamental result is due to Myerson and Satterthwaite (1983) and is to be ascribed to the fact that there are almost always losers who are reluctant to join the scheme. To achieve efficiency, a central authority is therefore needed for the purpose of coercing each player to participate. Its role is obviously much more compelling than that of a mediator who is content with centralizing and processing the information dispersed throughout the resource users.

Second, the central authority must commit itself to carrying out the scheme proposed, and this commitment must be credible to all participants, even though they all know that, in some instances, it may not want to carry out the scheme. For instance, the State may offer freedom to a convict who is ready to denounce his accomplices and later regret this move of forgiveness. In other words, the central authority is bound to its promise, and is not free to reconsider its decisions.

Even when these two conditions are satisfied, the Coase theorem loses much as a decentralization result when there is private information. Indeed, *a central authority is needed to achieve efficiency in order to commit itself to an incentive scheme and to make participation in the scheme compulsory*.

In a remarkable paper, Joseph Farrell, arguing first that people may not trust the State's commitment to an incentive scheme and, second, that doubts can be expressed about the actual ability of the State to collect and process such information flows, suggests that the comparison to be made is perhaps between the inefficient outcome of a private bargaining process and the inefficient outcome of an uninformed central authority. In other words, a second-best comparison may be what is called for: 'perhaps the Coase theorem should be viewed as a second-best result: property rights are more efficient than some reasonable alternative' (Farrell, 1987: 122).

Let us examine a simple example proposed by Farrell in which an inefficient state outcome is compared to an inefficient private bargaining outcome. The problem is the following: two people, A and B, care about a decision x: x can take on any positive value, but A would prefer it to equal a value a, and B, a value b, with $a < b$ by assumption (think of x as the (unidimensional) location of a collective good, such as an irrigation canal, the timing of a collective action, or the number of boats each fisherman will be allowed to operate). Suppose that the payoffs to A and B in monetary units can be expressed as follows:

A's payoffs: $u(x,a) = -\alpha(x - a)^2$
B's payoffs: $v(x,b) = -\beta(x - b)^2$.

These functions reflect the fact that A and B receive a negative payoff when x is different from their preferred value (a for A and b for B) and, the more x deviates from this value, the higher the disutility.

A problem arises because a and b are private information: only A knows a and only B knows b. However, to the outside world, a is uniformly distributed on $[a_-,a_+]$, and b on $[b_-,b_+]$, with $a_+<b_-$ (the latter assumption means that people are aware that there are two distinct types of players: even if they are not sure about the exact value ascribed by each type to the decision variable, they know that the possible range of such values for one type is strictly above the possible range for the other type). If a and b were public information, the Pareto-efficient decision would be the one which maximizes $u(x,a) + v(x,b)$:

$$x^* = (\beta b + \alpha a)/(\beta + \alpha).$$

Let us now consider a 'bumbling bureaucrat' who is not able to design an incentive scheme, and must base his decision on public information. His best choice is to set

$$x^B = (\alpha E(a) + \beta E(b))/(\beta + \alpha),$$

where E(.) refers to the expected value of (.). This achieves a good compromise, but one cannot expect a and b to be equal to their expected value. The expected loss can be estimated at $(\alpha^2\sigma_a^2 + \beta^2\sigma_b^2)$, where $\sigma^2(.)$ refers to the variance of (.).

If, however, A has the right to choose x, in the absence of any side-payment, she will set $x = a$. B expects to lose $E(-\beta(a - b)^2)$. Yet, he can also offer bribes to A so as to induce A to change his choice of x. In other words, B can offer a contract to A specifying for each choice of x a price B will pay to A.

A will always choose the efficient level of x, x^*, if she is offered a contract which allows her to internalize all the positive externality such a choice is bound to create. Such a contract specifies that B must pay to A: $p(x) = \beta((a_- - b)^2 - (x - b)^2)$, if A chooses x (for proof, see Farrell, 1987). However, with such a contract, B looses $(-\beta(a_- - b)^2)$, which is worse than if A sets $x = a$. Therefore, B will never propose such a contract.

One can show that, if B maximizes his payoffs, B will propose a particular contract to A (see Farrell, 1987: 126–8), such that, for very low values of a, A will ignore B's bribe and set $x = a$, and for high values of a, A will set $x = x^* - \alpha(a_+ - a)$, which is above a but below x^*. The expected welfare loss resulting from this situation is $4\alpha^2\sigma_a^2$, to be compared with the loss that can be attributed to the bumbling bureaucrat, that is, $(\alpha^2\sigma_a^2 + \beta^2\sigma_b^2)$. If the right to choose x was given to B, the resulting expected welfare loss would amount to $4\beta^2\sigma_b^2$. Therefore, for many values of the parameters, '*the bumbling bureaucrat outperforms both allocations of rights*' (ibid. 128).[4] This important result, unfortunately demonstrated only in the context of a limited example, sheds a new light on the validity of the Coase theorem in the presence of private information. What comes out is that this theorem is invalid, *even as a second-best theorem: an inefficient centralized decision-making process yields a better outcome than private bargaining.*

To summarize, in this section, we have analysed in detail the claim made by Coase following which a centralized intervention is not needed in situations involving externalities since the efficient solution will emerge from private bargaining. This claim is an important one since it applies to any externality, including that which causes the tragedy of the commons: it implies in particular that no policy intervention is required in the situation of unregulated common property, since the agents are free to sell or buy their rights to use the commons. Although the Coase theorem is helpful in calling attention of policy-makers to the potentialities of private bargaining to enhance efficiency, it suffers from a number of severe limitations. In particular, it does not apply, even as a second-best result, to problems involving private information, that is, paradoxically enough, to problems for which a centralized intervention is the most delicate to design and to carry out. Moreover, the negotiation processes involved are likely to be so costly as to be infeasible except when the number of agents concerned is small.

4.2 The Role of Decentralized Punishment: Spontaneous Co-operation in Repeated PD Games

A survey of prominent results in two-player games

As a unique model of strategic behaviour, the PD poses an obvious problem, all the more so as non-co-operation appears as a stable outcome in this game. Even if one player offers in advance a commitment that he will co-operate (which, given the

[4] We are not convinced that the best choice of the bumbling bureaucrat is to set arbitrarily $x^B = \alpha E(a) + \beta E(b)$. Indeed, there are cases (P $(a > x^B) > 0$) where both A and B would simultaneously prefer $x > x^B$, it is then more interesting to give A the right to set x under the condition that $x \geq x^B$ (or to B, with $x \leq x^B$). Whether the right should be given to A or to B depends on an a priori analysis of the expected welfare losses in both cases. Note that this remark however strengthens Farrell's conclusions. As he himself suggested, the most interesting arrangement may be to combine inefficient bargaining with a bumbling bureaucracy. In particular, the above remark suggests that one may give to A the right to set x, under the condition that $x \geq x^B$, and then let the two parties negotiate privately on any x, $x \geq x^B$. To investigate this issue is however beyond the scope of the present analysis.

		Period 1				Period 2	
		Player B				Player B	
		C	D			C	D
Player A	C	5, 5	−1, 10	Player A	C	5, 5	−1, 10
	D	10, −1	0, 0		D	10, −1	0, 0

FIG. 4.1. A repeated PD game

structure of the payoffs in the PD game, can only be the result of irrational behaviour), the other player will stick to a free-riding strategy. Likewise, if both players agree to co-operate, they both have an incentive to violate such a (non-binding) agreement. Precisely because they have found such a result too limiting, game theorists have worked hard to determine analytical conditions under which the mutual defection outcome would cease to be a unique possible equilibrium *even within the basic framework of the PD game*. In other words, they have set about demonstrating the possibility of co-operation without giving up the payoff structure characteristic of the PD.

As pointed out above, it is by assuming that the PD game is repeated, thereby creating what is called a (PD) supergame, that the co-operative equilibrium can be generated.[5] The fundamental reason why co-operation—understood as a high occurrence of (C,C) outcomes—may then be consistent with self-interested behaviour is that the repetition of the game opens the door to the possibility of conditional co-operation and punishment, a possibility which was precluded as long as the PD was deemed to operate within a single-period framework (see above). More precisely, to show that co-operation is possible, the assumption must be made that the game is repeated infinitely or that information is incomplete—there is some uncertainty about the others' strategies (either because their payoffs or the degree of their rationality are imperfectly known) or about the length of the game (the game horizon is finite but indefinite). In the following, we explain these results in three distinct steps.

1. Repetition of the PD game is not by itself sufficient to make co-operation a possible outcome. Indeed, when the game has a finite length (players know for sure when the process of their interactions will end), non-co-operation is the unique equilibrium outcome. Let us illustrate this important result with the help of a simple example. Consider two players who have to choose whether to co-operate or defect on two successive occasions. In particular, they face at each period the same payoff structure as given in Figure 4.1.

Each player when choosing his own strategy, has to decide whether to co-operate or to defect at the first period *and* at the second period. A strategy is now somewhat more complicated to devise than in a one-shot PD game. Indeed, the move in the second period can now be conditioned by the outcome of the first period (that is, by the history of the game till the second stage is reached), and this implies that a strategy is

[5] Note incidentally that, in general, repetition of the game does not necessarily yield higher average payoffs to the players than the corresponding one-shot game (for an example, see Myerson, 199: 331).

a complete plan of action over the whole game: 'it specifies a feasible action for the player in every contingency in which the player might be called upon to act' (Gibbons, 1992: 93). For instance, a possible strategy for player A, called a 'strategy of brave co-operation', could be to start by co-operating in the first period, to co-operate in the second period if player B has co-operated in the first period and to defect otherwise. In such a strategy, the fact that player B has acted 'co-operatively' in the first period is interpreted as an act of 'goodwill' which must be reciprocated in the second period. Can such a strategy be an equilibrium strategy?

To answer this question, one has to look at what happens in the second period. If, in the second period, player A co-operates, clearly, player B should defect, since such a move yields a payoff of 10 to player B instead of 5 if he co-operates. But, then, it cannot be part of an equilibrium strategy for A to co-operate since, if B always chooses to defect in the second period, he would be better off defecting in the second period (which would bring him a payoff of 0 instead of a negative payoff of −1): co-operation in the second period is not the best response to unconditional defection of player B in that period. Therefore, in such a framework, a strategy of brave reciprocation cannot be an equilibrium strategy. It is also clear that, if player A defects in the second period, it is always better for player B to also defect in period 2, as a result of which unconditional defection is a dominant move for both players in the second period. Reasoning backwards, it is now easy to understand why *co-operation cannot be an equilibrium move even in the first period, since it cannot help establish co-operation in the second period*. Unconditional defection in both periods is a dominant strategy for both players and corresponds to the unique equilibrium of this repeated game.

The same reasoning, known as the backwards induction argument, can be applied to any PD game repeated a finite number of times, T: the players anticipate that co-operation in period $T-1$ cannot trigger co-operation in period T (since defection is a dominant move in that period), and therefore choose to also defect in period $T-1$. Similarly, a co-operative move in period $T-2$ will not help establish co-operation in the following two periods, and defection is a dominant strategy. Obviously, this is equally true of any period t with respect to the $T-t$ rounds still to be played. Unconditional defection at all periods is the equilibrium strategy of this game. Since this argument applies irrespective of the length of the game, it is moreover evident that, even as the number of rounds increases, co-operation does not become an equilibrium behaviour in a finitely repeated game.[5]

2. What deserves to be emphasized is that, in the above example, the number of rounds (stages) in the game is finite and certain. If the length of the game is infinite, co-operation becomes possible. This is because there is no more any last period from which to reason in the way described above. In this case, it *may* be worth while giving co-operation a try. A similar possibility obtains when the length of the game is finite but indefinite. It is useful to elaborate on this case in order to show more precisely why and under which conditions co-operation may arise. Consider the simple strategy known as 'tit for tat', based on the following principles:

(1) Start by choosing to co-operate;

		Player B	
		C	D
Player A	C	$b-c, b-c$	$-c, b$
	D	$b, -c$	0, 0

FIG. 4.2. A 2×2 symmetrical PD game

(2) Thereafter in period n choose the action that the other player chose in period $n-1$.

We will now demonstrate that 'tit for tat' is an equilibrium strategy under certain conditions. Consider the version of the PD game given in Figure 4.2.

In this game, c is therefore the utility which one player loses when he (she) co-operates while the other free-rides; b is the utility he (she) gains when the situation is reversed ($b > 0$, $c > 0$). If both players co-operate, they receive $b - c$ while if both defect they get zero. It is assumed that $b > c$: players derive more utility from joint co-operation than from joint defection. Furthermore, individuals play the above game repeatedly *and* non-anonymously: each player accumulates experience of the behaviour of his (her) opponent since he (she) meets him (her) personally at each round of the game and is able to recall his (her) past moves. The game horizon is finite but the players do not know the end of the game. In other words, whenever they meet, the players ignore whether they are encountering for the last time. Let π be the probability that, after each round, the (extended) game is carried over into the next period. These assumptions, it would appear, offer a valid description of the way human interaction works in many small group settings.

In the foregoing context, a strategy is a plan for playing the whole extended (or repeated) game. Two possible strategies are unconditional co-operation—co-operating in every round, irrespective of the opponent's behaviour—and unconditional defection—defecting in every round. It is manifest that the former cannot be an equilibrium strategy: if A knows that B is always going to co-operate whatever he himself (or she herself) does, he (she) will have no interest ever to co-operate with B and B would be an eternal sucker (hence the label S given by Sugden to such a strategy of unconditional co-operation). Clearly, S is not a best reply to itself: the only strategies that are best replies to S are those that reply to S by defecting in every round, among which is the strategy of unconditional defection denoted by N (for nasty).

The strategy N, by contrast, is evidently an equilibrium strategy: the only strategies that are best replies to N are those that reply to N by defecting in every round and, since N is such a strategy, it is a best reply to itself (Sugden, 1986: 109). Indeed, if A knows that B will always freeride, there is no point in his (her) ever co-operating with B.

Another equilibrium strategy is precisely the simple tit-for-tat strategy (T for short). As we know, this is a strategy of conditional co-operation or reciprocity (to use Sugden's term). It may be noted that if two T-players meet, they co-operate in every round (since they both start by co-operating and then continue forever to co-operate). If, however, a T-player meets an N-player, the T-player will co-operate only in the first round; thereafter he will defect. This is because T-players are not altruists: they are prepared to co-operate only with people like themselves and they wish to avoid being suckers.

For the sake of illustration, let us now consider three (among many other) possible replies to T: T itself, N, and a new strategy, A (for alternation) which consists of defecting in odd-numbered rounds and co-operating in even-numbered ones. It can be shown that one of these three strategies must be a best reply to T (see Axelrod, 1981, 1984 or Sugden, 1986: 110–11 for proof). The expected utility derived from playing each of these strategies against T is as follows:

$$E(T,T) = (b-c) + \pi(b-c) + \pi^2(b-c) + \cdots$$

$$= \frac{b-c}{1-\pi}$$

$$E(N,T) = b + 0 + 0 + \cdots = b$$

$$E(A,T) = b - \pi c + \pi^2 b - \pi^3 c + \pi^4 b \cdots$$

$$= \frac{b - \pi c}{1-\pi^2}.$$

It is then easy to see that if $\pi > c/b$, we have $E(T,T) > E(N,T)$ and $E(T,T) > E(A,T)$. Thus, if $\pi > c/b$, T is better than N or A as a reply to T and, since one of these strategies is a best reply to T, T must necessarily be a best reply to itself. In other words, tit-for-tat is an equilibrium strategy: if player A knows that player B follows the tit-for-tat strategy, the most rational thing for player A to do is to adopt the same strategy.

Let us look at the condition $\pi > c/b$ more closely. If the game is certain to end after one round, so that $\pi = 0$, this condition is violated. We are brought back to the one-shot PD game where each player's interest is to defect. Conversely, if the game horizon is infinite, $\pi = 1$ and the condition for T to be an equilibrium strategy is automatically satisfied (since c/b is smaller than one by assumption). In other words, when the players are assured that the game will be played forever, they will follow a strategy of conditional co-operation when they know that their opponents have chosen that strategy, and this they will do irrespective of the particular values taken by b and c. Moreover, it is worth noticing that the condition $\pi > c/b$ does not imply that the game must be very long: for example, if $b = 2$ and $c = 1$, the condition is satisfied if $\pi > 1/2$, that is, if the average number of rounds played per game is greater than 2.0.

Notice carefully that it is only when B plays T that A has also an interest in playing T: T is a best reply to itself, that is a Nash equilibrium strategy, but not necessarily a best reply to any other strategy. Contrary to defection in the one-shot PD game, T is thus not a dominant strategy. If, for example, B plays N (the 'nasty' strategy of defecting in every round), A's best reply to B cannot be to play a simple tit-for-tat strategy: if B plays N, A would lose c units (since his payoff would be $-c$ in the first round and 0 in all the subsequent rounds), and would obviously be better off defecting from the beginning. In other words, N is also a best reply to itself and therefore also supports a Nash equilibrium. As a matter of fact, there are many possible equilibrium strategies.

The tit-for-tat strategy is clearly a useful pedagogical device to illustrate how a punishment mechanism can be embodied in the strategy itself and thereby allow co-operation to emerge. Bear in mind that this is only possible if the time-horizon is infinite so as to ensure that any player can *always* be punished for long enough to prevent any deviation from being worth while. This being said, it is important to stress that the tit-for-tat strategy suffers from a fundamental drawback inasmuch as, being myopic and mechanical, it cannot 'absorb' mistakes understood as unintended deviations from the chosen strategy. In other words, whenever a mistake occurs, blind adoption of this strategy inescapably leads to the considerable social losses that result from repeated mutual defections. To see this, suppose A knows that B is a T-player. Yet, in one round, say round i, A makes a mistake and defects (even though B has co-operated in round i–1). A expects B to defect in round i+1 in response to his occasional lapse. If A follows the strict principles of tit for tat, he will respond by defecting in round i+2 which, in turn, would cause B to defect in round i+3, and so on. An endless chain of retaliation and counter-retaliation is thereby initiated which really looks absurd given the fact that the triggering factor was a simple mistake.

In actual fact, this absurd outcome is to do with the fact that such a blind strategy is not subgame-perfect because it relies on an out-of-equilibrium threat that is not credible. Indeed, how can a player believe that, if he deviates, the other player will be ready to carry out a punishment threat that everybody knows unmistakably leads to definitive partial defection? Given that, after a 'mistake' has occurred, a player is known to defect at a particular stage, clearly, the other player should also defect at that stage, instead of co-operating and being a 'sucker'.

In game-theoretical terms, this idea is captured by the concept of subgame-perfectness. A Nash equilibrium is *subgame-perfect* if the players' strategies constitute a Nash equilibrium in every subgame. A subgame is the piece of a game 'that remains to be played beginning at any point at which the complete history of the game thus far is common knowledge among the players' (Gibbons, 1992: 94–5). In the two-stage PD, for instance, there are four subgames, corresponding to the second-stage games that follow the four possible first-stage outcomes, namely (C,D), (D,C), (D,D), (C,C) [ibid.]. In equilibrium, of course, punishment strategies are devised in such a way that they are never actually implemented. But, to be effective, those punishments must be credible in the sense that each player must find it optimal to carry them out if needed, that is in all the possible subgames whether or not on the equilibrium path.

As shown above, there are many possible Nash equilibria in the infinitely repeated PD game. Such a result is known as the folk theorem, which states that almost any outcome that on average yields at least the mutual defection payoff (i.e. the minimax outcome) to each player can be sustained as a Nash equilibrium. As pointed out by Kreps, 'a good way to interpret the folk theorem, when the players can engage in explicit pre-play negotiation, is that it shows how repetition can greatly expand the set of self-enforcing agreements to which the players might come' (Kreps, 1990: 512). A stronger version of the *folk theorem* is couched in terms of subgame-perfect Nash equilibrium strategies: it shows that it is possible to find a pair of subgame-perfect equilibrium strategies to support any possible sequence of outcomes (provided it yields on average at least the minimax outcome to each player). In other words, in the infinite version of the prisoner's dilemma, any (finite) succession of actions can be shown to belong to a subgame-perfect equilibrium strategy.

As Abreu (1988) has shown, such strategies need not be particularly complex. More precisely, any subgame-perfect outcome of an infinitely repeated game can be supported by a 'simple' strategy profile which is history-independent, that is it specifies the *same* punishment for *any* deviation, after any previous history, by a particular player.[6]

Now, for the folk theorem to hold true, players must be especially induced to punish those who deviate, even if it is costly to them. This is achieved by resorting to what Axelrod (1986) has called 'metanorms', that is, strategies that punish players who fail to play their part in punishing free–riders (Myerson, 1991: 335–7; Seabright, 1993: 120). Interestingly, Axelrod has shown with the help of a computer-based simulation, that co-operation can be sustained provided that the players start with a sufficiently high level of 'vengefulness', vengefulness being defined as the probability that a player will punish someone who is seen non-punishing (Axelrod, 1986; see also Elster, 1989*a*: 132–3 and Dasgupta and Mäler, 1990: 16).

3. One of the most surprising results of repeated game theory is the following: in a game of finite duration, a suspicion by one party that the other may practise a tit-for-tat strategy induces the other to adopt the same and both have then an incentive to co-operate till near the end of the game (Kreps and Wilson, 1982; Kreps *et al.*, 1982; Kreps, 1990: 536–43; see also Friedman, 1990: 190–4). This indicates that the set of Nash equilibria is not robust to slight perturbations. Thus, 'A one-in-one-thousand chance that one's opponent is generous, or that one's opponent assesses a substantial probability that oneself is benevolent, isn't much of a "change" in the game. Yet it completely changes the theoretical prediction', implying that we must be very wary of the theoretical prediction (Kreps, 1990: 542). This agnostic conclusion can be actually tied back to reputation in the following sense:

In the finitely repeated prisoners' dilemma, suppose one player assesses a small probability that the second will 'irrationally' play the strategy of tit-for-tat. . . . In a long-enough (but still finite) repetition of the game, if you think your opponent plays tit-for-tat, you will want to give

[6] The result obtained by Abreu is especially powerful since it makes it possible to overcome the potential complexities of plans of actions outside the equilibrium path. 'For instance a player who is being punished for a deviation may have "myopic" incentives to cheat (i.e. the action stipulated by the equilibrium may not be a single-period best response, in one or more stages of the punishment (path)). If so, perfection requires that he be deterred from cheating by the threat of a *further* punishment. This problem reappears at the next level and one is led into a *hierarchy* of punishments. Reflecting this complexity, an arbitrary strategy profile may be contingent on history in essential and elaborate ways. It may involve an infinity of punishments and a complicated rule specifying which punishment is imposed for any particular deviation from the initial path or from an ongoing punishment. Much of this potential complexity is in fact redundant' (Abreu, 1988: 348).

cooperation a try. And even if your opponent isn't irrational in this fashion, the 'rational' thing for her to do is to mimic this sort of behavior to keep cooperation alive. . . . We can think of these effects as 'reputation' in the sense that a player will act 'irrationally' to keep alive the possibility that she is irrational, if being thought of as irrational will later be to that player's benefit through its influence on how others play. That is, in this sort of situation, players must weigh against the short-run benefits of certain actions the long-run consequences of their actions. (Kreps, 1990: 542–3)

It is important to emphasize that, for co-operation to succeed in this kind of game, the following assumption is crucial: if the player with the uncertain type (that is, the player for whom there is a doubt that he could follow a tit-for-tat strategy) ever deviates from that strategy, then he would be immediately considered as being rational by the other player(s) and non-co-operation would ensue.

The above conclusion may also be reached if the number of rounds in the game is rather small. Yet, the probability that the other player can play only the tit-for-tat strategy must be large enough if co-operation is to occur in a game that is not long repeated. If this requirement is met, there exists an equilibrium in which both players co-operate in all but the last two stages of the game.[7] It thus appears that co-operation can be sustained if a sufficiently high suspicion that the opponent plays only tit for tat makes up for a low number of game stages (for more details and proof, see Gibbons, 1992: 224–32).

Two last remarks are in order (see Myerson, 1991: 342). First, not every way of modifying the game with small initial doubt will lead to the co-operative outcome. Perhaps paradoxically, a suspicion that the other player is still more inclined to co-operate than in tit for tat may actually make co-operation impossible. This happens in so far as his strategy entails too much tolerance regarding the other's 'accidental' defection. For instance, if the first player assigns a small positive probability that the other player always co-operates (a 'generous' strategy), then the unique subgame-perfect equilibrium would be for each player always to defect. The best response to the generous strategy is indeed always to defect so that no player has any incentive to cultivate the other's belief that he is going to be always generous. Second, as shown by Fudenberg and Maskin (1986), any payoff allocation that is achievable in an infinitely repeated game may also be approximately achieved in a long finite version of the game with small-probability perturbations.

Co-operation in N-player PD games

So far, attention has been limited to games involving only two players. An interesting question arises as to what extent the reported results can be extended to situations involving more than two players. To answer this question, it is necessary to focus on the decision problem of a given player interacting with the $(n - 1)$ other players. Consider, for instance, a PD game where the collective output Y to be divided equally

[7] More exactly, the player who is uncertain about the strategy played by the other will co-operate till the last stage of the game while the latter about whom doubts are entertained will co-operate till the penultimate stage.

Pay-off to player i if the number of other players contributing is

		$N-1$	$N-2$	$N-3$	. . .	0
Player i	contributes	$\frac{f(N)}{N}-c$	$\frac{f(N-1)}{N}-c$	$\frac{f(N-2)}{N}-c$		$\frac{f(1)}{N}-c$
	does not contribute	$\frac{f(N-1)}{N}$	$\frac{f(N-2)}{N}$	$\frac{f(N-3)}{N}$		$\frac{f(0)}{N}$

FIG. 4.3. N-person prisoner's dilemma

among the N players is a concave function, $f(n_i)$ of the number of voluntary contributors n_i, and where each contributor has to bear a fixed cost, c. Figure 4.3 illustrates this case.

We assume that $f(n_i) - f(n_i - 1) < N.c$, for all values of n_i between 0 and N, which implies that the 'marginal' productivity of an additional contribution is everywhere strictly smaller than N times the fixed cost incurred by one contributor. If such were not the case, then it would mean that the marginal productivity of the contributions is so high as to induce everyone to contribute even though he would internalize only a tiny fraction ($1/N$) of the benefits: in this case, the problem of public good provision would have obviously vanished. If the above condition holds true, as a comparison of corresponding entries in the figure's two rows indicates, the non-contributing strategy dominates regardless of the number of contributors.

If the above game is repeated a finite and certain number of times, then the backwards induction argument applies, and the dominant strategy of every player is to free–ride at every stage of the game. Conversely, if the length of the game is finite and uncertain or if it is infinite, the results obtained for a two-player game continue to hold provided that the tit-for-tat strategy of conditional co-operation (or the corresponding T_1 strategy, defined below) is properly redefined. Indeed, in N-player games, it is not a priori clear what playing tit for tat means since one does not know what number of defections is needed to make one player following the tit-for-tat strategy defect. For the sake of illustration, it can easily be seen that the following is an equilibrium stratcgy: (i) start co-operating, (ii) defect if at least one other player has defected in the previous round, (iii) otherwise co-operate.

Such a generalized tit-for-tat strategy is a best response to itself and, if followed by everybody, universal co-operation will get established: it is therefore a Nash equilibrium.

Consider now the situation in which all players but one follow a modified strategy where the component (ii) above becomes 'defect if at least two other players have defected in the previous round'. It is then obvious that the last player will choose to start by defecting and continue to do so. The above modified tit-for-tat strategy is therefore not a best reply to itself, yet it is a Nash equilibrium strategy for the $(N - 1)$ remaining players. At equilibrium, co-operation is almost universal since there is an unrepentant free–rider. Similarly, if component (ii) above is replaced by 'defect if at least M other players have defected in the previous round', there is a partial co-operation equilibrium in which $(M - 1)$ players defect while $(N - M + 1)$ players co-operate (as long as M remains relatively small).

Notice carefully that the above equilibria are not subgame-perfect. This should not trouble us too much since the stronger version of the folk theorem has been generalized for N-player-games (see, e.g., Myerson, 1991: 331–7), thereby ensuring that other, more sophisticated, strategies exist which support the co-operative outcome as a subgame-perfect equilibrium.

Co-operation and imperfect monitorability

So far, we have assumed that any defection can without cost be unfailingly attributed to the real culprit. In actual fact, this assumption is not as crucial as it may appear at first sight because in an N-player repeated PD game framework, most punishing strategies carry out a threat of *collective punishment*: this means that, as long as the adverse consequences of defection can be detected by the players, *anonymous* retaliatory strategies (that is, strategies which are not explicitly directed at the culprits) can be effective in discouraging defection. Just consider the trigger strategy which consists of co-operating as long as *no other player* has defected, and otherwise defect. It is evident that if everyone follows that strategy, an equilibrium can be sustained in which no defection occurs. Yet, off equilibrium, any lapse into defection would cause a collective reaction which blindly harms everyone's interests. (This does not prevent this strategy from being subgame-perfect.)

Now, it is not at all certain that, as has been assumed above, the adverse consequences of defection can easily be detected. Indeed, if there are exogenous risks (by which we mean uncertainties that are beyond man's control), the players may not be able to ascertain whether a given reduction in the productivity of a resource is due to natural factors or to a malevolent human act. This gives rise to more complex problems as it is more difficult to relate punishment to actual defection given that punishment may be carried out even though exogenous factors are entirely responsible for the disappointing results. For example, in marine fisheries, the complexity of the ecological system is such that it may be difficult to determine whether a drop in total catches is to be ascribed to a sudden change in marine environment (e.g. in marine currents), to overfishing, or to any other potentially harmful human practice (e.g. the use of destructive fishing gears). To take another example, in water management systems, not only may water losses result from stealing by a few participants but also from technical deficiencies that are not directly imputable to the user group. Likewise, in forestry management schemes in which exclusion is imperfectly enforced, participants may be unable to ascertain whether violation of a rule of access to the forest is to be assigned to someone from the user community or to an outsider. Note that this problem is also very common in fisheries and has actually become more serious with the introduction of mechanized, highly mobile boats.

As underlined above, imperfect observability of the aforementioned kind implies that punishment threats that deter opportunistic behaviour may actually have to be carried out with positive probability in equilibrium (since one may misleadingly believe that defection has occurred). As a result, threats in an equilibrium may have a positive expected cost (they may have to be carried out even though nobody defected) and the expected benefit of deterring opportunistic behaviour. In such circumstances, finding the best equilibria for the players 'may require a trade-off or balancing between these costs and benefits' (Myerson, 1991: 343).

In theory, one can envision a kind of punishment mechanism similar to that in the perfect information PD game which is susceptible of deterring defection even though observability of the players' actions is imperfect. Such a mechanism has been illustrated in the case of a class of infinitely repeated PD games by Abreu *et al.* (1991).[8] Consider five players who are working independently to prevent some damage to a common infrastructure (one could think here of a water management system) from occurring by choosing an appropriate level of supervision and maintenance effort. For instance, assume that (1) in a period of time of length ε, the cost to player i of exerting effort at level e_i (where $0 < e_i < 1$) is $\varepsilon(e_i + (e_i)^2)/2$, (2) the probability of the damage occurring is $\varepsilon(6 - \Sigma_{i \in N} e_i)$, and (3) the damage, if occurring, costs one unit of payoff to each player. The players cannot observe one another's effort levels but everyone can observe the damage whenever it occurs. At each period of time, the expected net payoff to each player is maximized over his own level of effort by letting $e_i = 1/2$. This is of course far below the social optimum which would require each player to exert an effort level equal to one. There is however a way of getting out of this awkward equilibrium. In the words of Myerson:

> Because the players can observe accidents but cannot observe one another's effort, the only way to give one another an incentive to increase his or her effort is to threaten that some punishment may occur when there is an accident. Notice that the probability of an accident depends symmetrically on everyone's effort and is positive even when everyone chooses the maximum effort level 1. So when an accident occurs, there is no way to tell who, if anyone, was not exerting enough effort. Furthermore, the only way to punish (or reward) anyone in this game is by reducing (or increasing) effort to change the probability of accidents, which affects everyone equally. (Myerson, 1991: 344).

It can be shown that there exists another equilibrium, which actually maximizes the average expected payoff of each player and, in this equilibrium, high efforts are most effectively encouraged if the players plan to punish only if there is an accident. Similarly, for punishment to be most effective, it is important that all players reduce their effort levels as much as possible and this can be achieved if they return to their 'co-operative' effort levels only when another accident occurs. Such a result may perhaps appear surprising, yet it is perfectly in the logic of punishment strategies that are generated *within the PD game itself.* It is precisely because such a sanctioning system may be quite costly and complex to carry out that people usually prefer to devise *external* mechanisms to deter opportunistic behaviour (see below, Chapters 8 and 12).

[8] Our presentation follows Myerson, 1991: 342–9.

Co-operation and limited rationality

The complexity involved in the analysis of the repeated play of such a simple game as the PD game is considerable. First, there are innumerable possible strategies.[9] As a matter of fact, a repeated game is characterized by the fact that the players may devise strategies which make their actions in a given round conditional on their opponents' actions in previous rounds. Given this possibility, the number of conceivable strategies increases explosively with the number of rounds that may be played (Sugden, 1986: 107–8).

Second, related to the above feature is the aforementioned fact that repeated games are characterized by a 'profusion' (to use Kreps's word) of possible (Nash) equilibria. As has been shown, non-co-operative equilibria are as likely as co-operative ones: for instance, unconditional defection is an equilibrium strategy. Moreover, as long as everyone follows cautious strategies of one kind or another ('start by defecting, and thereafter co-operate if your opponent has co-operated in some previous rounds'), these strategies produce the same result: no one ever co-operates. An obvious consequence of this profusion of equilibria is that the predictive power of game theory is very much restricted when agents interact frequently and repeatedly. This is in stark contrast to its predictive power in one-period situations such as that described by the one-shot PD game.

Third, underlying repeated game theory is two strong assumptions about human behaviour. On the one hand, agents are supposed to be hyper-rational since they must be able to conceive, implement, and choose among numerous and complex strategies. In particular, they must be able to anticipate all the possible reactions of the other players, even in a distant future, and to decide their current moves accordingly. If such requirements of computerizability were met in reality, in any chess contest, the whites would never lose. On the other hand, once they have identified the best strategy, agents never make mistakes, in the sense that they unremittingly act according to this strategy.

It is in view of these difficulties that some authors have chosen to develop alternative approaches to strategic interactions that take into account explicitly the possibility of mistakes and the limitations of the human brain's computational ability. The latter constraint is reflected in the fact that human beings can only devise a restricted number of rather simple or basic strategies.

One strategy which has drawn a lot of attention in this respect is the aforementioned tit-for-tat strategy which emerged as a winner from computer tournaments conducted by Axelrod. In these simulation experiments, the participants, among which were many game theorists, were invited to propose strategies without there being any arbitrary limit imposed by the analyst on the players' possible strategic choices. These strategies were then compared against each other in pairwise encounters with repeated

[9] Strategies may of course be much more complex and less myopic than the tit-for-tat strategy. Think, for example, of the following strategy: (1) start by choosing to co-operate; (2) thereafter, in period t co-operate if the other player has co-operated during the previous three rounds, and if he has not defected more than once during the thirty rounds preceding the last five rounds, otherwise defect.

plays. (The median length of games was 200 rounds.) On average, tit for tat yielded the highest payoff and further analysis suggested that, in repeated tournaments, 'tit for tat would continue to thrive, and that eventually it might be used by virtually everyone' (Axelrod, 1984: 55). Moreover, it appeared that tit for tat is 'a very robust rule', that does very well over a wide range of environments (ibid. 53).

It has been shown earlier that the tit-for-tat strategy is defective in the sense that it relies upon non-credible threats (it is not subgame-perfect) so that a mistake triggers off an endless chain of retaliation and counter-retaliation. A reasonable way of cutting short the above chain would be for A, who defected in round i, to refrain from retaliating in round i + 2, that is, to admit that B's defection in i + 1 was somehow justified and therefore to agree to co-operate in i + 1 and i + 2 without regard to B's (understandable) defection in i + 1 (which is another way of showing that tit for tat is not subgame-perfect). This is precisely the intuition behind the subgame-perfect variant of tit for tat denoted T_1 by Sugden (1986) or called 'getting even' by Myerson (Myerson, 1991: 326–7):

> T_1 starts from a concept of being in good standing. The essential idea is that a player who is in good standing is entitled to the co-operation of his opponent. At the start of the game both players are treated as being in good standing. A player remains in good standing provided that he always co-operates when T_1 prescribes that he should. If in any round a player defects when T_1 prescribes that he should co-operate, he loses his good standing; he regains his good standing after he has co-operated in *one* subsequent round. (This is why I call this strategy T_1; if it took two rounds of co-operation to regain good standing, the strategy would be T_2, and so on.) Given all this, T_1 can be formulated as follows: 'Co-operate if your opponent is in good standing, or if you are not. Otherwise, defect'. (Sugden, 1986: 112)

As expected, T and T_1 are perfectly equivalent strategies in a game where players never make mistakes. The only difference between these two strategies concerns the moves of a player after he has defected by mistake. Such an event makes him lose his good standing: in accordance with T_1, he should co-operate in the subsequent round i + 1 while his opponent may defect *without losing his good standing*. Whatever the opponent does in round i + 1, T_1 therefore requires that the first player (the one who made the mistake) co-operates in round i + 2 also (Sugden, 1986: 113).

T_1 is clearly a strategy of reciprocity since a person's co-operation is conditional on the others' co-operation. But it is also a strategy of punishment. As a matter of fact, when T_1 is followed by two players, the reversal of the combination of moves from (D,C)—the first player defects, by mistake, and the second one co-operates—to (C,D) (the first player co-operates while the second one defects) may be interpreted as a punishment for the faulty player. This player suffers the worst possible outcome in the 'punishing' round i + 1 and, in so far as he has chosen to follow T_1, it may be said that he accepts punishment (with a view to preventing the adverse long-term consequences of his mistake from arising). Of course, there is the other side of the story. In the 'punishing' round, the other player receives the best possible outcome (even better than the outcome of a round of mutual co-operation). So not only punishment but also reparation take place: strategy T_1 prescribes that to regain his entitlement to the co-operation of others, the faulty player must perform an act of reparation during one round following his defection (Sugden, 1986: 114–15).

Now, the question may be raised as to why reparation ought to be confined to one round. After all, as pointed out by Sugden, 'this reparation is insufficient to compensate the injured party fully for the losses he has suffered from the other players' breach of the convention' (1986: 115). Indeed, using the utility indices of Figure 4.2, the breach imposes a cost of b on the injured party whereas the act of reparation in the subsequent round allows him to save c. Since b is greater than c and since, in addition, the cost saving c must be discounted to allow for the possibility that the round following the breach will never be played, the injured party receives only partial compensation for the mistake of his opponent.

The answer provided by Sugden is that the extent of reparation is a matter of convention: 'the injured party demands just as much reparation as he expects his opponent to concede, and his opponent offers just as much as he expects the first player to insist on' (Sugden, 1986). A strategy T_2 can thus be imagined that prescribes two rounds of reparation for each unjustified defection or, alternatively, a strategy T_3 prescribing three rounds of reparation (or any strategy T_r prescribing r rounds of reparation). The more r increases, the more vengeful are the people who have been 'suckers' during one round and the less forgiving the reciprocity strategy. Quite evidently, there is a limit to how forgiving such a strategy may be if it is to be an equilibrium: 'reparations must be sufficiently burdensome to deter deliberate defections' (ibid.). Yet, on the other hand, there is also a danger in being too vengeful: after having made a mistake, a player is under no compulsion to accept punishment since he may possibly resign himself to the loss of his good standing and continue to defect. It is clear that the less forgiving the opponents' strategy, the more attractive this second option becomes. Moreover, it will also be all the more attractive as the value of π is lower: 'the sooner the game is likely to end, the less there is to gain from being in good standing' (ibid.).

In actual fact, tit-for-tat strategies—whether of the T or of the T_r types—are members of a much larger class which Sugden has called strategies of brave reciprocity. These strategies have two defining characteristics. In the words of Sugden:

> First, against an opponent who defects in every round, these strategies defect in every round except the first (provided no mistakes are made). Second, if two players following strategies of brave reciprocity meet, they both co-operate in every round (again, provided no mistakes are made). Notice that the two players need not be following the *same* strategy. (Sugden, 1986: 116)

As emphasized by Sugden, strategies can satisfy the second condition above only if they prescribe co-operation in the initial round. This is precisely why such strategies are *brave*: players are ready to co-operate in advance of any evidence that the other will reciprocate, thereby exposing themselves to the risk of being exploited by freeriders. It must be noted, however, that 'brave reciprocators' cannot be thus exploited during more than one round. The danger of exploitation appears as the necessary price to be paid for ensuring the possibility of repeated co-operation amongst players. Indeed, if both players are cautious (they will not co-operate until the other has already done so),

		Player B	
		R (Brave reciprocity)	N (Unconditional defection)
Player A	R	$\frac{b-c}{1-\pi}, \frac{b-c}{1-\pi}$	$-c, b$
	N	$b, -c$	0, 0

FIG. 4.4. The extended PD game where players are unconditional defectors or 'brave reciprocators'

they will never co-operate at all. Therefore, if a strategy is to co-operate with itself—that is, if it is such that when both players follow it they will jointly co-operate—it must be willing to co-operate at a positive risk for the players.

Evolution of co-operation and limited rationality

Pairwise interactions in an evolutionary framework

Keeping with the assumption of limited rationality, Sugden considers an extended PD game in which people have available to them only two kinds of strategies—strategies of brave reciprocity (henceforth denoted by R), and the 'nasty' strategy of unconditional defection (N).[10] The issue which he then addresses is whether, in repeated pairwise encounters, we can expect *spontaneous evolution* to favour reciprocity. Three possibilities of encounter arise. First, two N-players meet. This can only lead to repeated joint defections from the very first round of the game: both players will therefore derive a utility of zero from the game. Second, an N-player meets an R-player (a 'brave reciprocator'). Clearly, the result is that in the first round the R-player co-operates and the N-player defects while in all the subsequent rounds both players defect. There is thus an asymmetry in the payoffs received by the players over the whole game: the N-player gets b and the R-player gets $-c$. Third, two R-players meet. They co-operate in every round, obtaining $(b - c)$ in each round: over the whole game, the expected value of their utility stream is equal to $(b - c)/(1 - \pi)$.

These results are displayed in Figure 4.4.

We know (see above) that N is the best reply to N and that, provided $\pi > c/b$, R is the best reply to R. Consequently, the choice of strategy by each player will hinge upon the probability that his opponent will choose one strategy rather than the other. Let then p be the probability that a random opponent will follow strategy R. There is then some critical value of p, say p^*, such that when p is greater than, or equal to, p^*, the strategy R will prove more rewarding than, or just as rewarding as, the strategy N. This critical value is easily derived from

[10] It is worth noting that it does not matter whether all R-players follow the same strategy or not; all that matters is that they all adopt some kind of strategy of brave reciprocity (Sugden, 1986: 116).

$$p^*\frac{b-c}{1-\pi}-(1-p^*)c = p^*b, \text{ so that}$$
$$p^* = \frac{c(1-\pi)}{\pi(b-c)}.$$

It is immediately apparent that $dp^*/d\pi < 0$: if the probability of meeting an opponent again is high, the critical value of p can be quite low (for example, if $b = 2$, $c = 1$, and $\pi = 0.98$, so that the average game has fifty rounds, p^* equals 0.02 only). In other words, if one player assesses even a small probability that the other will be a 'brave reciprocator', he will be induced to choose to play the same strategy instead of following the 'nasty' strategy, provided that the game comprises a sufficient number of rounds. Sugden's interpretation of his result is that playing R is a kind of risky investment: by incurring the risk of being exploited by an N-player in the *first* round, a player is able to co-operate with an R-player in *every* round. Therefore, 'the longer the game is likely to last, the more time there is to recoup on a successful investment' (Sugden, 1986: 117).

Adopting an evolutionary perspective in which patterns of behaviour that have proved relatively successful in the past are more likely to survive and reproduce,[11] Sugden reaches the conclusion that *evolution (in repeated pairwise encounters) tends to favour co-operation*: in games which on average have many rounds, 'a convention of brave reciprocity has a good chance of evolving' (Sugden, 1986: 116–20). In particular, when the probability of meeting an opponent again is fairly high, even if initially the great majority of players defect, the latter may do less well than the small minority who are following strategies of brave reciprocity, and there may then be a self-reinforcing tendency for the minority group to grow (ibid.).

Sugden obtains an even stronger support for his thesis that evolution favours co-operation by allowing the players to choose between three strategies: brave reciprocity, the 'nasty' strategy, and the strategy of cautious reciprocity. The result arrived at can be formulated as follows: even if initially *almost everyone defects*, cautious reciprocators will gradually emerge and their presence will help to bring about conditions causing brave reciprocators eventually to invade and take over (Sugden, 1986: 118–20). It is noteworthy that, to obtain this result, Sugden had to assume that cautious strategies are tailored to the reparation rules which prevail among the 'brave reciprocators'. Thus, if the latter follow T_1 (there is only one round of reparation for each unjustified defection), a cautious player's best plan is to co-operate for the next two rounds which

[11] In the human world, the evolutionary approach implies that a deviant play, if successful (that is, if it brings a relatively high payoff), tends to be repeated and imitated (Sugden, 1989: 92). For a short description of the way biological evolutionary models work, see Rasmusen, 1989: 123. Binmore has contrasted in a vivid way the behavioural assumptions underlying classical game theory, on the one hand, and evolutionary game theory, on the other hand. According to him, the model of man present in evolutionary stories is not *homo economicus* but *homo behavioralis*. The latter is 'a piece of hardware that Nature can program as she chooses—unlike *homo economicus*, whom Nature can manipulate only via his preferences. The program that she writes for him will determine his *disposition*. It is important to bear in mind that *homo behavioralis* does not choose his own disposition. He has no preferences or beliefs. After being programmed, he just carries out his instructions' (Binmore, 1994: 187).

follow his initial defection, and then play tit for tat. Mutual co-operation can thus emerge from the third round onwards, because the cautious player's defection in the first round is treated as though it had been a mistake. If, on the other hand, 'brave reciprocators' follow the strategy T_2 (there are, by convention, two rounds of reparation), a cautious player must co-operate during rounds 2, 3, and 4 to make his strategy successful (mutual co-operation would then start in round 4). In a more general way, if R-players follow T_j, a cautious player must co-operate during $j + 1$ successive rounds after his initial defection, and thereafter play the simple tit-for-tat strategy.

However, as pointed out by Binmore, these results obtain only in so far as attention is restricted to a few strategies (see Binmore, 1992: 434). Strictly speaking, the strategy of brave reciprocity is not evolutionarily stable, that is, it is *not* 'a pattern of behaviour such that if it is generally followed by the population, any small number of people who deviate from it will do less well than the others' (Bardhan, 1993*b*: 635): in other words, it is not true to say that no 'mutant' strategy can 'invade' the population. For instance, if the mutant strategy is 'always co-operate' (or any other strategy of conditional co-operation, for example, a strategy with several rounds of reparation), this strategy played against brave reciprocators does as well as the latter's strategy. Note moreover that it is important to distinguish between the evolutionary stability and the viability of a strategy. While the former concept refers to the capacity of a strategy to defend itself against invasion, the latter means that it can invade a large population of non-co-operators. So far, we have contended that the strategy of brave reciprocity is not, strictly speaking evolutionarily stable, yet it is a best reply to itself (it is 'collectively stable' to use Axelrod's terminology). Now, it has to be added that, for such a strategy to be *viable*, the assumption that agents are randomly paired for contests has to be given up: for instance, we have to allow for the fact that agents are more likely to be paired with others adopting the same strategy (Axelrod and Hamilton, 1981; Bardhan, 1993*b*: 635). This result can be interpreted as implying that the chance of success of conditional co-operation is all the greater as more encounters take place between homogeneous agents.

It also bears emphasis that the kind of analysis proposed by Axelrod and Sugden is somewhat misleading in so far as it suggests that the possibility of co-operation depends on the presence in the population of at least a small number of players who start by co-operating. That this is not true can easily be seen by considering the so-called tat-for-tit strategy (Binmore, 1992: 434) which does not satisfy this requirement and yet leads to co-operation in the long run if adopted by the two players. This strategy is: (i) start by defecting, (ii) co-operate if both players have co-operated or if they have both defected in the previous round, (iii) and otherwise defect.

This strategy leads to a Nash equilibrium in which both players defect in the first round and then co-operate forever. If the component (i) of the above strategy is replaced by (i′) 'defect for n periods and then, follow rules (ii)–(iii)', the resulting strategy when chosen by both players supports a Nash equilibrium in which co-operation follows n rounds of defection.

Multiple interactions in a learning model of strategy revision

While in most evolutionary models (including the above model of Sugden) pairs of players are selected randomly from a 'large' population to play the given game once, and are thereafter returned to the population, in learning models, each player is assumed to interact with many varying opponents with a fixed strategy, modifying his strategy thereafter based on the cumulative experience (Bendor *et al.*, 1994: 2). What deserves to be noted is that in both classes of models, 'the "fitness" of a given strategy at any stage of the game depends on its average payoff, achieved against the rest of the population'. This implies that 'a strategy revision by any single player evokes no response from the other players, as it does not appreciably affect their average payoffs' (ibid.).

Recently, however, economists have paid increasing attention to learning models where the strategy revisions of a given player generate substantial feedback effects by affecting the other players' payoffs, thereby inducing the latter also to revise their strategies subsequently. Models of strategy learning embodying such feedback effects differ according to the degree of rationality assumed for the players. On the one hand, we find the 'myopic best-response' models (such as 'fictitious play') that Selten (1991) considers under the heading of 'belief learning': this class of models presumes that each player observes the past moves of other players, forms beliefs about their strategies in the next iteration of the game, and then calculates a best response. On the other hand, we have the models belonging to the so-called 'stimulus learning' approach. They are much less requiring in terms of rationality assumptions since they presume a rather high level of bounded rationality characterized by severe limits on information gathering or cognitive abilities. They actually apply to players ignorant of payoff functions and of opponents' past choices, and, moreover, they do not require them to solve maximization problems (Bendor *et al.*, 1994: 4–5; see also Fudenberg and Kreps, 1992; Kalai and Lehrer, 1993 for recent surveys of learning game-theoretical models).

One particular model based on the latter approach is grounded in the 'satisficing' principle and has been proposed by Bendor *et al.* (1994). In this model, the strategy revisions made by the players after every interaction are based on a comparison between a given aspiration level and the payoff actually obtained in the current period. More precisely, the state of any player at any stage t is represented by a probability vector over his set of pure actions and these probabilities can be interpreted as reflecting his relative inclination to select different actions. Such a state is updated in the following manner: if the payoff realized from the action chosen at t exceeds an aspiration level, the weight on that action is increased at the following stage, with compensating adjustment in the weights on other available actions. And vice versa if the payoff falls short of the aspiration level. (Note that a player's state will remain unchanged if the achieved payoff exactly equals the aspiration level.)

In this framework, different players 'adapt without explicitly co-ordinating with one another and without devoting any cognitive effort to predicting the choices of others and choosing appropriate responses to such predictions' (Bendor *et al.*: 6). As Bendor *et al.* have shown, stable long-run outcomes (that is, equilibria with consistent aspirations) in such repeated games with feedback effects need not be Nash equilibria of the one-shot game. This is essentially because feedback effects operate in a manner that resembles 'punishments' imposed on unilateral deviations in repeated games.

For example, mutual co-operation in a PD game of the above kind is always an equilibrium outcome with consistent aspirations despite the fact that mutual defection is a dominant strategy equilibrium in the one-shot game. The interesting question is of course what prevents the players from 'learning' the payoff advantage to defection. Following the aforementioned study, let us start with aspirations near the (mutual) co-operative payoff (Bendor *et al.*, 1994: 6). Suppose that, in a two-player game, player 1 experiments with defection at stage t. Since player 2 continues to co-operate, player 1 obtains a payoff higher than his aspiration, thereby making him even more inclined to deviate at $t + 1$. As for player 2, he ended up with a payoff below his aspiration at t and this also makes him more inclined to deviate at $t + 1$, though for entirely different reasons. Then both players receive below-aspiration payoffs at $t + 1$, thus tending to induce both of them to return to co-operation at $t + 2$. In the words of Bendor *et al.*: 'once the players arrive at a state where both defect with substantial probability, both will indeed defect simultaneously, beginning the process of a simultaneous return to co-operation. Hence, the mutual co-operation outcome is stable with respect to periodic random switches to defection by either player' (ibid. 6). Clearly, assuming that players behave myopically, i.e. try to increase current payoffs, the degree of rationality that is conducive to co-operation is low in some well-defined sense (ibid. 26).

It is worth noting that, in the random matching framework of most evolutionary models, such an outcome could not survive in the long run since a deviation by a single player will not have an appreciable impact on the 'fitness' of any other strategy in the population, and therefore not evoke any feedback effect. To put it in another way, the initial benefits of the deviation are not 'undone' by the reactions of other players, and the player can sustain the benefits of the unilateral deviation, as a result of which the 'fitness' of the deviating strategy will be enhanced, at the eventual expense of other strategies in the population (Bendor *et al.*, 1994).

As is evident from the foregoing discussion, the main result achieved by the above kind of learning model, namely that the intrinsic structure of interactive play may prevent each player from choosing a best response to the other's strategy (non-Nash play can arise), pertains only to environments where current experience is paramount in determining current strategy *and* where there are only a small number of players. For one thing, in 'learning' games (even with a few players) where the past is given the same weight as the present but where play is otherwise myopic, the tendency to co-operate is weakened: 'A current deviation does not evoke a large reaction from the opponent, who considers his rival's entire history of play' (Bendor *et al.*, 1994: 26). For another thing, in games with many players, co-operation is more problematic for two reasons. First, 'in the event of a defection the co-ordination required to restore co-operation is of an order of magnitude that is exponential in the number of players' and, second, any single player's deviation has a smaller effect, thereby dampening the reactions of the other players. In particular, with a continuum of players co-operation is impossible: limit play must be Nash (ibid.).

All this being said, stress must be laid on the fact that 'there is scope for considerable multiplicity of equilibria' in the above 'satisficing' model of strategy learning, a feature that directly follows from the possibility of varying the initial aspiration level. Thus, if the agents' aspiration is near the (mutual) non-co-operative payoff instead of being near the (mutual) co-operative payoff as previously assumed, it is easy to see that, after a non-co-operative random move of one of them at stage t, they will both receive their aspiration payoff at $t + 1$. As a result, they will have no incentive to return to co-operation at later stages. There is evidently a 'self-fulfilling' property in the 'satisficing' model: if members of a given society have low aspirations to start with—say, because of a disappointing experience in a previous game—they will behave in such a way as to repeat this negative experience in the present.

Given the obvious importance of group size for the prospect of co-operation, as again illustrated above in the case of a 'stimulus-learning' model, it is useful to summarize the main sources of the advantage of small groups. This is done below by the way of a conclusion to this chapter.

Co-operation and group size: some reflections

1. As shown above, an important result of repeated PD game theory is the following: if individuals know one another well, can observe one another's behaviours, and are in continuous interaction with one another, then any pattern of collective behaviour, including co-operation, can be sustained, which will make each individual better off than under universal defection. This is because each player's plan of action can be made dependent on the others' past actions, given that they are all easily observable either directly or indirectly. Indirect observability is possible in as much as, even though individual actions are not directly observable, their impact on the collective performance can be unambiguously assessed so that the number of defections is easily inferred. Notice carefully that it is precisely because a co-operative move is observable that it can be interpreted as a sign of goodwill and purposefully used as such.

These particular conditions of perfect information and repeated interactions obviously correspond to small-group settings in the real world. When they are satisfied, individuals have a strong incentive to consider the more indirect and long-term consequences of their choices instead of paying exclusive attention to immediate costs and benefits. In other words, given the long time-horizon of the game and the easy observability of each other's actions, they are incited to care about their reputation. Over two centuries ago, Hume (and Adam Smith as well, who spoke about the 'discipline of continuous dealings') had already well understood that, in small-scale social settings, considerations of what is sometimes called reciprocal altruism but really amounts to selfishness with foresight, should lead people to co-operate. The same considerations help explain why they are quite reliable about keeping promises when no legal sanction requires them to do so and when keeping them is inconvenient or costly:

We can better satisfy our appetites in an oblique and artificial manner, than by their headlong and impetuous motion. Hence I learn to do a service to another, without bearing him any real kindness; because I forsee that he will return my service, in expectation of another of the same kind, and in order to maintain the same correspondence of good offices with me or with others. And accordingly, after I have serv'd him, and he is in possession of the advantage arising from my action, he is induc'd to perform his part, as foreseeing the consequences of his refusal. . . . After these signs [i.e. promises] are instituted, whoever uses them is immediately bound by his interest to execute his engagements, and must never expect to be trusted any more, if he refuse to perform what he promis'd. (Hume, 1740: Bk. III, pt. II, sect. V, 521–2)

2. Small groups or communities are generally characterized not only by the continuous, but also by the multiplex pattern of their members' interrelationships, a feature which follows from the socially 'embedded' nature of many micro-societies. This means that the sectors of social life in which individuals interact are numerous and can never be neatly separated in the minds of the people. If interests are so tightly intertwined, it becomes difficult to conceive of their interactions with respect to resource management as an isolated 'game'. The common property resource problem becomes part of a repeated multiple prisoners' dilemma corresponding to many social and economic activities at the village level (or even, as we shall see below, to an assurance game). Speaking of social life in a rural county in present-day California, Ellickson (1991) has recently captured this essential characteristic of village communities in a vivid manner. We cannot resist the temptation to quote him at some length:

Shasta County norms entitle a farmer in that situation to keep track of those minor losses in a mental account, and eventually to act to remedy the imbalance. A fundamental feature of rural society makes this enforcement system feasible: rural residents deal with one another on a large number of fronts, and most residents expect those interactions to continue far into the future. . . . They interact on water supply, controlled burns, fence repairs, social events, staffing the volunteer fire department, and so on. . . . Thus any trespass dispute with a neighbour is almost certain to be but one thread in the rich fabric of a continuing relationship. A person in a multiplex relationship can keep a rough mental account of the outstanding credits and debits in each aspect of that relationship. Should the aggregate account fall out of balance, tension may mount because the net creditor may begin to perceive the net debtor as an over-reacher. But as long as the aggregate account is in balance, neither party need be concerned that particular subaccounts are not. For example, if a rancher were to owe a farmer in the trespass subaccount, the farmer could be expected to remain content if that imbalance were to be offset by a debt he owed the rancher in, say, the water supply subaccount. (Ellickson, 1991: 55–6)

3. When a group is small, it is less vulnerable to the problem of incentive dilution. Indeed, free riding is a strategy whereby an individual trades a reduction in his own effort, from which he alone benefits, for reductions in the income of the whole group, which are shared among all members. Therefore, as the size of the group increases, the terms of this exchange become more and more favourable to the free rider (since shares are diluted), and vice versa when the size of the group decreases. This is why 'large groups are less able to act in their common interest than small ones' (Olson, 1982: 31).

In Chapter 2, we have shown in the framework of a one-shot fishing game that the Nash equilibrium outcome tends to move away from the collectively rational outcome as the number of fishermen increases. This relationship between group size and the chance of co-operation was actually discovered by David Hume as early as the first half of the eighteenth century:

Two neighbours may agree to drain a meadow, which they possess in common; because 'tis easy for them to know each others mind; and each must perceive, that the immediate consequence of his failing in his part, is the abandoning the whole project. But 'tis very difficult, and indeed impossible, that a thousand persons shou'd agree in any such action; it being difficult for them to concert so complicated a design, and still more difficult for them to execute it; while each seeks a pretext to free himself of the trouble and expence, and wou'd lay the whole burden on others. (Hume, 1740: Bk. III, pt. II, sect. VII: 538)

As is evident from the above excerpt, the advantage of small groups is not only that they prevent incentives from being excessively diluted, but also that they allow for agreements to be reached among the people concerned at low negotiation costs, which include the costs of communication and bargaining as well as, possibly, those of creating and maintaining a formal organization (Olson, 1965). However, it bears emphasis that this consideration takes us away from the non-co-operative game-theoretical framework, a point to which we shall return in Chapter 8.

4. A fundamental lesson of game theory is that, in a repeated PD game, there may exist a 'profusion' of equilibria. This means that, when interactions are repeated, many patterns of behaviour may get established and be stable. Unfortunately, perhaps, game theory has little to say about which equilibria will arise and in what manner. It is precisely with respect to this selection problem, which will be addressed at a later stage, that small groups may be at an advantage. As a matter of fact, by allowing individuals to reveal and signal their intended plans of action and to learn about others' intentions, pre-play communication in small-group settings may enable them to choose 'good' equilibria. Similarly, but in a less explicit way, shared experiences or beliefs and inherited patterns of behaviour may also play a role in such settings. For example, if there is a tradition of trust or a group-centred culture, members of a given community are more likely to give co-operative strategies a chance (more about this in Chapter 7).

Yet, at the same time, it must be stressed that small groups, precisely because the relationships among their members are highly personalized, are vulnerable to strong manifestations of envy and rivalry which may sometimes make co-operation very difficult. In other words, it is not because people can easily communicate within small groups that co-operative equilibria will necessarily emerge. An atmosphere of distrust can lead to 'bad equilibria' even within such groups. We shall return in Chapter 12 to this important but systematically neglected aspect of the issue under concern.

5. The feeling of sameness or togetherness which may permeate the culture of small groups may also promote co-operation in an unexpected, irrational way. Indeed, as pointed out by Elster on the basis of empirical evidence, people may be easily led into 'magical thinking', that is, they may believe (or act as though they believed) that their co-operation can cause others to co-operate *even though such causal relationship is*

evidently absent (Elster, 1989*a*: 195–200). In other words, people are sometimes prone to believe that everything turns upon their own behaviour so that whether joint co-operation or joint defection (the only two outcomes that are then considered to be possible) will occur is deemed to entirely depend on what decision they themselves choose to make. Consider a two-person PD where the agents make their decisions independently of each other. According to Elster, 'if they are sufficiently alike, each of them may reason in the following manner. "If I co-operate, there is a good chance that the other will co-operate too. Being like me, he will act like me. Let me, therefore, co-operate to bring it about that he does too"' (ibid. 197). Now, the smaller the group, the more other people are like oneself and the more plausibly (in a psychological rather than logical sense) one can infer that they will behave like oneself (ibid. 208). In the context of a small group, therefore, people's proclivity to think in magical terms—that is, upon the belief that by acting on the symptoms one can also change the cause—helps explain why they may start by co-operating, thereby providing an irrational basis for strategies of 'brave reciprocity'.[12]

[12] For Elster, moral behaviour actually rests on a form of magical thinking (Elster, 1989*a*: 195–6), an approach which we will not follow in Ch. 6.

5

Co-ordination and Leadership in the Unregulated Common Property: Some Lessons from Game Theory

In the previous chapter, describing the various advantages of small-group settings, we have drawn attention to the fact that the prisoner's dilemma is not necessarily an appropriate representation of the payoff structure obtaining in situations of unregulated common property. We now want to delve into this issue by discussing different game forms that may be more relevant in this respect, particularly the so-called chicken game, the co-ordination game, and heterogeneous games that combine the payoff structures of the PD and these two games. Note that so far, the analysis has been essentially focused on *appropriation* problems understood as collective action problems concerned with excluding potential beneficiaries and allocating the subtractable flow of an existing common property resource. Another category of collective action problems may arise: these are the *provision* problems which are to do with the process of creating a resource, maintaining or improving its production capabilities, or avoiding its destruction. The latter type of problems are obviously akin to the well-known *public goods* problems (Ostrom, 1990: 30–3; Ostrom *et al.*, 1993).

5.1 Unilateral Contribution

Let us first consider a kind of situation in which everybody agrees that something is to be done but the problem is who will actually do it. In the real world, indeed, one encounters many situations in which a collective problem is solved through unilateral action. Olson has clearly such situations in mind when he discusses the possibility of groups being *privileged*. A *privileged* group is defined as a group so small 'that each of its members, or at least some one of them, has an incentive to see that the collective good is provided, even if he has to bear the full burden of providing it himself' (Olson, 1965: 50). This happens when the collective good (or some quantity of it) can be obtained at a cost sufficiently low in relation to its benefit that it pays any individual in the relevant group to provide it all by himself. In other words, the total gain resulting from the production of a collective good or from the avoidance of a collective bad is so large in relation to the total cost that an individual's share of the aggregate gain would exceed the total cost. Such a situation may also obtain when the group is composed of individuals of unequal size or extent of interest in the collective good. According to Olson, in *heterogeneous* groups, the greater the interest in the collective good of any

		Player B	
		C	D
Player A	C	8, 8	6, 10
	D	10, 6	2, 2

FIG. 5.1. A 2×2 symmetrical chicken game

single member, the greater the likelihood that this 'large' member will get such a significant proportion of the total benefit from the collective good that he will gain from seeing that the good is provided, even if he has to pay all of the cost himself [ibid. 33–4]. As we shall see below, however, the case of heterogeneity may cover a wide variety of different situations which need to be carefully specified. Indeed, the meaning behind the notion of interest has to be clarified in order to be able to predict which type of resource user (the rich or the poor) is more likely to contribute.

Collective action in privileged groups

Let us begin by examining the situation obtaining in small homogeneous groups. This situation can be portrayed as a two-person chicken game, that is, as a game in which there are two (Nash) equilibria in pure strategy and in each of these one player co-operates while the other defects. Consider the game with the payoff structure described in Figure 5.1.

The following provision problem can serve as a first illustration. Assume that players A and B are two small-scale marine fishermen who stand threatened by the invasion of a fleet of foreign trawlers in their traditional fishing-zone. The incomes of A and B are presently 10 units. However, to maintain the level of their present catches, they need to have their inshore waters legally protected against the encroachments of the foreign boats. It is assumed that they can succeed in securing that protection from their government provided that they make lobbying efforts (which is the 'public good' to be produced) the total cost of which amounts to 4 units. If both players defect in the sense that they refuse to exercise pressure on their government until it agrees to act in their interests, the competition from the highly efficient foreign trawlers will soon bring their individual incomes down to a mere 2 units (D,D). The total benefit of the lobbying action—that is, the joint payoff (C,C) minus the joint payoff (D,D), or 16–4 = 12—is therefore much larger than its total cost (4). If A and B co-operate in the sense that they agree to share that cost equally between them (C,C), they will both be assured of receiving a payoff of 8 units. Moreover, the lobbying action is so rewarding that it can pay a single player to bear the entire cost of it (D,C, or C,D): the politically active player (the 'sucker') will then get 6 units while the passive player (the free-rider) will of course get more, 10 units in this instance.

From Figure 5.1, it is then easy to see that players have no dominant strategies in this game. What each will decide to do depends on what he expects the other to do. As in a PD game, each player prefers that the other undertakes the lobbying action while he refrains from moving since he will thereby get the maximum possible income (10 units). However, and contrary to the situation obtaining in a PD game, each is willing to take full responsibility for that action if the other refuses to do anything about it. In other words, the consequences of nobody doing the lobby are so disastrous that either of the players would undertake it if the other did not (it is better to be a 'sucker' and to get 6 units of net income than not to be a 'sucker' and get only 2 units).[1]

The problem in the above game is of course that the best symmetric payoff (8,8) cannot be achieved because (C,C) is not an equilibrium outcome: player A would choose to defect if he expected player B to choose to co-operate. However, *with communication*, the players can make a *self-enforcing* plan of action (in the sense that neither player could gain by unilaterally deviating from this plan) that gives them both higher expected utility than what they can get in the absence of communication. In other words, they can benefit, from co-ordinating their actions. Thus, they could agree to toss a coin and then choose (C,D) if it is heads and (D,C) if it is tails. As pointed out by Myerson, this plan of action is self-enforcing, even though the coin toss has no binding impact on the players: player A could not gain by choosing D after heads, since player B is then expected to choose D (Myerson, 1985: 254; 1991: 249–50). In game theory, this plan is known as a *correlated equilibrium*. In our example, it gives each player an expected utility of 8 ($0.5 \times 6 + 0.5 \times 10$). This is a better result than that achieved under the randomized or mixed-strategy equilibrium (7.33) where, in one-ninth of the cases, the worst outcome (D,D) will materialize.

Under a correlated equilibrium, agents endogenously and *non-co-operatively* generate a *co-ordinated* solution which gives them the assurance that collective action will take place: one of them will have to undertake it, but under a scenario agreed on by everybody.

There are many other applications of the chicken game to provision problems, such as maintenance and surveillance of common properties (irrigation systems, pastures, collective fields, hunting-grounds), in particular protection tasks aimed at enforcing exclusive rights against possible intrusion by outsiders, activities of lobbying and political representation, and initiation of collective action. The latter example actually refers to the problem of leadership and is noticeably present in all situations where the production of a public good is envisaged. It should nevertheless be borne in mind that not all the aforementioned activities can be described as chicken games. As we shall see below, this depends on the particular configuration of costs and benefits obtaining in each situation.

[1] There are actually three Nash equilibria of this game: not only (C,D) and (D,C), but also a randomized Nash equilibrium, called a 'mixed strategy' equilibrium in which each player plays his different strategies with a certain, predetermined probability. In the mixed equilibrium of the game considered here, each player co-operates with probability 2/3 and defects with probability 1/3. The expected utility for each is therefore equal to $2/3(2/3 \times 8 + 1/3 \times 6) + 1/3(2/3 \times 10 + 1/3 \times 2) = 7.33$.

		Fisherman B	
		enters	does not enter
Fisherman A	enters	–1, –1	10, 0
	does not enter	0, 10	0, 0

FIG. 5.2. Assignment problem as a 2×2 chicken game

Contrary to a widely held view, chicken games may also be suitable for depicting appropriation problems. Consider the case of fishing of lobsters or some other bottom-dwelling species. It is easy to find situations in which the number of (potential) fishermen exceeds the number of locations where enough lobsters can be caught to justify the effort involved. There then arises the problem as to how those fishing locations will be assigned so as to avoid the eruption of harsh conflicts (since two fishermen fishing on the same spot would be doing so at loss). In some fishing communities, such a problem is solved by recognizing the claim of the 'first entrant' into the fishing-ground (see Chapter 10, sect. 2). This solution clearly corresponds to a chicken game as illustrated in Figure 5.2.

Assigning exclusive rights to the first entrant is not the only possible solution to the problem concerned. Assignments by lottery are not infrequently practised which really amount to a correlated equilibrium as defined above (see also Chapter 10).

Extending the chicken game to *N*-player situations is quite straightforward: there are as many Nash equilibria in pure strategies as there are players and, in each of them, a single player contributes while the others freeride. In an infinitely repeated framework, the folk theorem also holds, implying the existence of a plethora of equilibria. Paradoxically perhaps, some of these equilibrium outcomes may be characterized by a large number of 'non-co-operative' rounds: indeed, a player may have an interest in building a reputation of being 'tough' so as induce another player to contribute.

It is noteworthy that, in the above two numerical examples, the equilibrium outcomes in pure strategies are Pareto-optimal. This is not necessarily so, at least in the one-shot game. For the sake of illustration, let us consider the case of two fishermen who must decide how many boats to put out at sea. If they put out one boat each, their payoffs are (4,4). If they put out two boats each, the catch per boat becomes so low that the net profit (payoff) is negative so that the outcome is (–1,–1). On the other hand, if one of the fishermen puts out two boats while the other puts only one boat, the former's payoff jumps to 6 while the latter's payoff is 1. The corresponding payoff matrix is given in Figure 5.3.

In the one-shot version of the above chicken game, there are two Nash equilibria in pure strategies {(1,6), (6,1)} and one in mixed strategy, where putting out one boat is played with a probability of 1/2, and putting out two boats, with a probability of 1/2, yielding an expected payoff of 2.5 to each fisherman. It is therefore evident that the

	no. of boats	Fisherman B 1	2
Fisherman A	1	4, 4	1, 6
	2	6, 1	–1, –1

FIG. 5.3. A chicken game with a non-(Pareto) optimal equilibrium

Pareto-optimum (4,4) cannot be achieved. In the long finitely repeated version of that game (and *a fortiori* in an infinitely repeated version), however, the Pareto-efficient allocation can be approximately reached if each player obeys the following equilibrium strategy as described in Myerson (1991: 338). Each fisherman puts out only one boat as long as both of them have done so, until the last two rounds. If the two fishermen have always abided by this plan of action, then, in the last two rounds, they both play the mixed equilibrium that yields expected payoffs (2.5, 2.5) at each round. On the other hand, if, in a round before the last two rounds, either fisherman ever deviates from the strategy of putting only one boat at sea, then the two fishermen thereafter play the equilibrium that, at each round, gives payoff 1 to the fisherman who deviated first and payoff 6 to the other one. (If both deviate first at the same round, then let us say that the fishermen act as if fisherman A deviated first). It is a subgame-perfect equilibrium for both fishermen to behave according to this scenario in the T-round finitely repeated game (for any positive integer T). Furthermore, this equilibrium gives an expected average payoff per round of $((T-2) \times 4 + 2 \times 2.5)/T$, which gets close to 4 when T is large.

It is important to note that there are also equilibria of such finitely repeated games that are worse for both players than any equilibrium of the one-shot game, but of course are not worse than the minimax value (for more details, see Myerson, 1991: 339). One can therefore conclude that, contrary to a widely held view, repetition does not always improve the average performance of the group.

The above results actually illustrate an important theorem of game theory which has been proved by Benoit and Krishna (1985) following which, if a strategic-form game has multiple equilibria (when it is not repeated) that give two or more different payoffs to each player, then, under general conditions, the average payoffs in subgame-perfect equilibria of long finitely repeated versions of this game are very close to *any* average payoffs attainable in the *infinitely* repeated versions of the game (Myerson, 1991: 338). (Bear in mind that the folk theorem applies in the latter case.) This theorem points up the essential difference that exists between prisoner's dilemmas and other game forms and the consequent danger, frequently encountered in the so-called 'collective action' literature, of confining the analysis to the former as though the theoretical propositions applying to it could be easily generalized to other games. More specifically, while in PD games, the results obtained under infinitely repeated

		Player B (poor)	
		C	D
Player A (rich)	C	15, 3	13, 5
	D	17, 1	2, 0

FIG. 5.4. A 2 × 2 asymmetrical chicken game

versions radically differ from those obtained in finite versions, this is not true of other game forms.

Collective action in heterogeneous groups

Let us now turn to situations where asymmetric payoffs prevail, reflecting economic inequalities within the small group. As pointed out above, Olson then predicts that the richer party will necessarily contribute because he has a higher stake. To examine the validity of this prediction, let us start by considering the chicken game presented in Figure 5.4 in which it is evident that player A (the richer player) has a lot to lose if (D,D) occurs.

As is typical of any 2 × 2 chicken game, there are two equilibria in pure strategies leading to an asymmetric outcome (D,C) or (C,D), and an equilibrium in mixed strategy where all outcomes have a positive probability of occurrence. It cannot therefore be taken for granted, as Olson seems to do, that the richer party necessarily plays C in equilibrium. This is all the more so if we assume that the richer party is superior not only in economic terms but also in terms of power. As a matter of fact, in the kind of situation contemplated here, one obvious form which the power of the rich can take on is his ability to make a move prior to the poorer and weaker party. If this is so, the appropriate tool for analysing the decision problems of both parties is no more the strategic form game used above but a two-step chicken game best described in extensive form. In a two-player extensive game, decision-making is sequential so that one player (the follower) can observe what the other (the leader) has done before deciding his own action. In Figure 5.5, we have translated the payoff matrix described in Figure 5.4 into such an extensive form.

Player B will make his decision to play C or D only after having observed what player A has done. His best strategy is clearly 'play C if A has played D, and play D if A has played C'. The strength of player A lies in the fact that, owing to his privileged position as the first mover, he is able to take into consideration B's best reactions while making his own decision in the first stage of this sequential game. In this case, it is obvious that he will choose to play D in the expectation that player B will choose C. The outcome (D,C) is therefore the unique subgame-perfect Nash equilibrium. Note carefully however that, for the above result to obtain, it is necessary that the first move

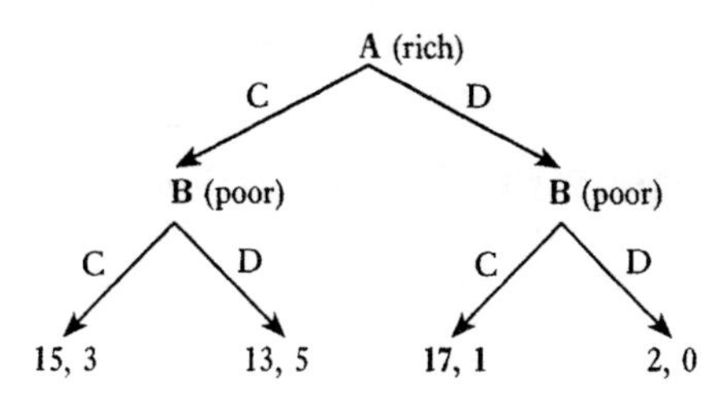

FIG. 5.5. A 2×2 asymmetrical chicken game with sequential moves

by the richer party is perceived by the poorer party as an unmistakable signal about the intention of the former. This is precisely the ability of the richer party to commit himself to a particular plan of action and to signal it in an unambiguous way to the weaker party that constitutes the source of his power. If such power imbalance did not exist, one could argue that the above representation is unsuitable to describe the decision problem under concern. This is because, if power is more or less evenly distributed, the position of the first mover cannot be clearly established: one player can give a signal to the other to which the latter may respond by a counter-signal, to which the former again responds, etc. The analysis of such games, which involve continuous time, lies beyond the scope of the present work.

Even in the absence of any explicit demonstration of power by the richer party, the sheer poverty of the poorer party may create a situation in which he is forced to contribute. This may most obviously happen when the latter's subsistence is threatened by, say, the neglect or the disappearance of a common property. Consider the following problem: a land area is being irrigated through a surface canal system and the proper maintenance of some water control infrastructure is crucial for the satisfactory performance of the system. The land in the command area is unequally distributed among two persons: the rich and the poor. Yet, contrary to the rich who possesses a large portfolio of assets including the irrigated parcels, the poor has no other wealth besides his tiny plots of irrigated land. In such circumstances, it is a serious possibility that the rich is less mindful of the proper maintenance of the irrigation system. We moreover assume that maintenance works can be effectively carried out by a single player alone. That this is not a completely unrealistic assumption is attested by the observation made by Yoder (1986) about the Thambesi irrigation system in Nepal. As a matter of fact, we are told that maintenance carried out prior to the monsoon rains requires 'only four to five hours of work with all the members participating', as a result of which it is possible for only a few farmers to keep the whole system going (Yoder (1986), quoted from Ostrom and Gardner, 1993: 97).

Fitting the above set of assumptions is the payoff matrix depicted in Figure 5.6.

Two Nash equilibria in pure strategies (and none in mixed strategy owing to the infinitely negative payoff accruing to the poor in case of universal neglect) characterize the above game. This being said, there is good ground to believe that, given the peculiar circumstances highlighted above, the two 'pure' Nash equilibria are not

		Poor	
		maintains	neglects
Rich	maintains	15, 3	13, 5
	neglects	17, 1	2, $-\infty$

FIG. 5.6. A 2×2 asymmetrical chicken game with a subsistence constraint

equally plausible. Indeed, one of them (neglects, maintains), is likely to emerge as a 'focal' point because, the poor, being subsistence-minded, is not ready to incur the least risk that the system ends up remaining unmaintained. In fact, what this means is that, given the binding nature of the subsistence constraint, the poor tends to adopt a maximin strategy which is justifiable in rational terms. In particular, if there is the slightest chance of the rich being irrational, mindless, or prone to making 'mistakes', the poor is eager to ensure his livelihood by choosing the safe outcome, which is personally to carry out the maintenance work. (In game-theoretical terms, the (neglects, maintains) outcome is the only trembling-hand equilibrium.)

In actual fact, it is not difficult to find, in the real world, situations in which the poorer segments of the population have a vital interest in the preservation of common properties, while the rich do not have that concern because they have available to them significant *exit* options. Here lies another source of power in the hands of the rich.

The array of possibilities may be further enlarged if we allow for the fact that the situation of the poor may be so desperate that he cannot be forced to contribute. Consider the following appropriation problem. There are two players who can choose between a conservationist strategy, C, or a more destructive strategy, D, regarding the exploitation of a common property resource. One of them is very poor, so that he cannot afford to follow *alone* the conservationist strategy, C. (For instance, his concern about sheer survival in the short run may lead him to heavily discount the future benefits of such a strategy and to overweigh the present costs, an issue which has already been addressed in Chapter 3.) Such is not the case, however, with the other player who, being richer, can safely adopt a more conservative use of the resource. This situation is depicted in Figure 5.7.

Evidently, the above game is not a chicken game. The poor has a dominant strategy, which is to defect, while the rich has a payoff structure characteristic of a chicken game. The only equilibrium outcome is (13,5), in which the poor, despite his weaker economic position, cannot be coerced into being the single contributor. Such a result (which is Pareto-inferior) also holds in any finitely repeated version of the game, as was observed with the PD game, with which it shares the feature of yielding a unique equilibrium. (The theorem of Benoit and Krishna (1986) does not apply.)

An important lesson to be drawn from the latter example is that a player does not enjoy a decisive advantage over another player who is hard-pressed by a survival

		Poor C	Poor D
Rich	C	15, 4	13, 5
	D	17, –1	2, 2

FIG. 5.7. A 2×2 asymmetrical heterogeneous game with a subsistence constraint

		Poor C	Poor D
Rich	C	15, 4	16, 2
	D	14, 2	2, 2

FIG. 5.8. A 2×2 asymmetrical game with a norm of participation

constraint. This arises from the fact that, in some circumstances in which he has actually no choice, the poor may credibly precommit himself to non-co-operation. In this case, power, understood as the ability to precommit to non-co-operation, appears to be on the unexpected side.

A last form of power is worth mentioning, which is perhaps more subtle or disguised than those analysed above. Under this form, the stronger party assumes a leadership role in devising and putting into effect a system of sanctions (in the form of payoff transfers) that punishes all free-riders, including himself. This allows him to bring pressure to bear on the weak party so as to make him share the burden of collective action even though the latter has much less interest than the former in the success of this action. In other words, the strong party agrees to bind himself to co-operation in order to bring the weak party to co-operate. One can think of a norm of participation according to which everybody, rich or poor, must join the collective action irrespective of whether there is much or little to gain from participating. By referring to such a norm, the rich and powerful can thus drive the poor and weak to take actions that entail large benefits for the former and small (or even negative, as in the game below) ones for the latter (for example, all landowners, both large and small, participate to an equal extent to the construction of an irrigation canal). This situation is illustrated by the game portrayed in Figure 5.8, which is actually a modified version of the game depicted in Figure 5.7 in which a player pays a fine of 3 units to the other player whenever he free-rides on the other's effort. (We return in Chapter 8 to the role of sanctions as a co-operation-enforcing mechanism.)

It is easy to verify that the game in Figure 5.8 is virtuous in the sense that universal co-operation is the only equilibrium outcome. What needs to be stressed is that in this instance such an outcome has been achieved through a subtle manipulation. As a matter of fact, the stronger party has resorted to a genuine strategy of delusion. By threatening himself with sanctions for any act of free–riding on the weaker party's effort, he conceals the fact that he has no interest in defecting: clearly, the threat is empty as far as he is concerned.

That power is effectively exercised in the above instance is evident from the fact that, were the poor allowed to do it, he would vote against establishing the aforedescribed norm of participation and the payoff transfers associated with it. As a matter of fact, he earns a payoff of 4 units after this norm has been laid down whereas he could earn 5 units in the initial situation. The rich will of course vote in the opposite way since the change in the payoff matrix brings him a payoff gain of 2 units (he earns 15 instead of 13 units).

Note carefully that the problem of whether or not to establish the norm of participation with the attendant payoff transfers is quite distinct from the question as to whether, once established, the punishment system involved is self-enforcing. It is easy to see that, if the right to punish is vested with either the rich or the poor, punishment will not be meted out whenever the agent (whether rich or poor) has to punish himself. If, however, the punishment mechanism is actuated by a neutral external agent or any kind of automatic device set for that purpose, it will be unfailingly enforced (provided that, whenever he punishes, the punisher gets a reward, say ε, from the guilty player). The corresponding game is the three-stage game described in Figure 5.9 in which we have assumed that the rich makes the first move and there are three players including the punishing agent. The latter must choose between two strategies: punish (denoted by P) and abstain from punishing (denoted by N).

Knowing that the punishing agent always punishes (he always plays P rather than N), the poor has an interest in co-operating if the rich has done so in the first round of the game whereas he is indifferent between co-operating and defecting if the rich has previously defected. Being aware of this optimal reaction of the poor conditional

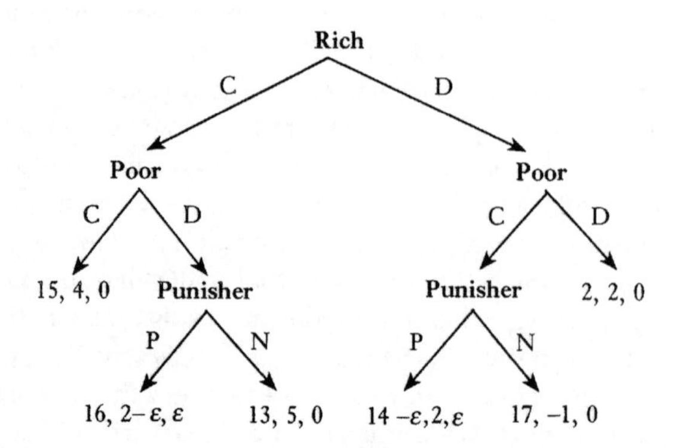

FIG. 5.9. A three-stage sequential asymmetrical game with a punishing player

on his own previous move, and knowing that he will be punished if the (D,C) outcome materializes, the rich will choose to co-operate, since he will thereby get 15 payoff units instead of either $(14 - \varepsilon)$ or 2 units. As a consequence, the co-operative outcome (C,C) is a subgame-perfect equilibrium.

Incentive dilution in a chicken game

As we have seen in the previous chapter, the size of the group may be an important determinant of the success of collective action. That the incentive for the members of a group to act in a collectively rational way tends to become thinner as the number of members increases is a proposition generally understood in the framework of the prisoner's dilemma. What we now want to argue is that, starting from a chicken game, the same dilution process may occur. As the size of the group increases, the structure of the game modifies itself from a chicken game into that of a prisoner's dilemma, and, as a result, the collectively rational outcome which was initially established degenerates into the Pareto-dominated non-co-operative outcome.

Let us illustrate this result with the help of a simple example. A group of n members can create a public good which yields a benefit of b to each of them at a collective cost of $c(n)$, where c is an increasing function of n, but $(c(n))/n$ is decreasing with n. Each member of the group is free to contribute or not. If he contributes, he shares the cost $c(n)$ with the m other willing contributors so that each of them incurs individually a cost of $(c(n))/(m + 1)$. If not, he simply free-rides on the public good produced by others, enjoying its benefits without incurring any cost. We assume that $b - (c(n))/n$ is always positive, so that creating the public good is collectively rational. However, we also assume that there exists n^*, with $n^* > 0$, such that, if $n < n^*$, $b - c(n) \geq 0$ and, if $n > n^*$, $b - c(n) \leq 0$. Figure 5.10 portrays the choice problem facing player i.

As can be readily seen from the figure, as long as n is relatively small ($n \leq n^*$ so that $b > c(n)$), the payoff structure given above defines an N-player version of a chicken game. However, when the size of the group increases, $c(n)$ rises up to a point where $b - c(n)$ becomes negative: the payoff structure of the above game turns into a PD and defecting becomes a dominant strategy. In other words, in the simple example described here, when the group is small, the cost of creating the public good is also small

Pay-off to player i if the number of other players contributing is

		$n-1$	$n-2$	$n-3$	. . .	0
Player i	contributes	$b-\dfrac{c(n)}{n}$	$b-\dfrac{c(n)}{n-1}$	$b-\dfrac{c(n)}{n-2}$		$b-c(n)$
	does not contribute	b	b	b		0

FIG. 5.10. Endogenous transformation of a chicken game into a PD game

so that everyone is ready to pay for it, even if he is alone to do so. However, as the size of the group increases, the cost involved also increases, while the individual benefits remain unchanged. Consequently, financing the public good on a voluntary basis becomes problematic when the group reaches a certain size. This is essentially the same argument as that put forward by Olson to underline the advantage of small ('privileged') over large groups, even though he presented it in the converse way (as the size of the group increases, the total cost of producing the public good is constant but the share of the benefits accruing to each individual declines).

5.2 Co-ordinated contributions

An important class of problems that arise in connection with the management of common property resources requires symmetric and co-ordinated actions to be overcome. Examples abound both in appropriation and in provision problems. For instance, in a fishery where the use of dynamite is an available technical option, it is obvious that self-restraint must be practised by everybody if the destruction of the fishing-ground is to be avoided. Protection of the breeding-grounds gives rise to the same problem. To quote examples from other sectors, restricted use of fire for the clearing of agricultural lands or management of water control infrastructures (including control of soil salinity and water-logging problems through sub-surface drainage) also require co-ordinated actions. Important issues of provision, such as steep-slope management and anti-erosion control in mountainous terrain, programmes of pest control, or certain surveillance actions requiring a critical amount of effort (e.g. guarding coastal fishing-grounds against the encroachments of mechanized boats) obviously belong to the above class of problems.

The one-shot assurance game

The game form suitable for representing this kind of situation is known as the assurance game (see Sen, 1967, 1973, 1985; Runge, 1981, 1984*b*, 1986; Dasgupta, 1988; Taylor, 1987; see also Ullmann-Margalit, 1977: 41; Collard, 1978: 12–13; 36–44, 80–9; Field, 1984: 699–700; Levi, 1988: ch. 3). In this game, a minimal effort must be contributed by all players if they are to receive any benefit from their own action.

To return to a familiar example, consider the case in which two fishermen must independently decide whether to put one or two boats at sea for the catching of fish. Let us assume that their payoffs for the various possible outcomes are as given in Figure 5.11.

The important point to note is that, contrary to what obtains in a PD game, the net payoff accruing to a player when he freerides on the public good provided by the other player (6 units) is smaller than the net payoff he would receive by co-operating (8 units). Nevertheless, if actors think it best to co-operate with each other, they still find it very unpleasant to be exploited by free-riders: contrary to what is observed in the chicken game, each player prefers mutual defection (where he gets a payoff of 2 units)

no. of boats	Fisherman B: 1	2
Fisherman A: 1	8, 8	1, 6
2	6, 1	2, 2

FIG. 5.11. A fishing assurance game

to being a 'sucker' (which causes him to receive a payoff of only 1 unit). In short, universal co-operation is the most preferred outcome. Then comes generalized free-riding. Least preferred are those outcomes in which a mismatch of actions occurs. This payoff structure actually determines three possible equilibria, two in pure strategies—each fisherman puts out one boat or each fisherman puts out two boats—and one in mixed strategy. The Pareto-optimal outcome (each fisherman puts one boat out to sea), is only one of the two equilibria in pure strategies. Which equilibrium will be selected actually depends on prior expectations regarding the other's intended action.

Clearly, therefore, the best policy for each party depends on what he thinks the other will do. In actual fact, optimal choice for each fisherman is to put out only one boat if the probability that the other fisherman will choose the same strategy is assessed by him to be in excess of 1/3, and his optimal choice is to put out two boats if this probability is less than 1/3. Denoting by p the probability that the other fisherman puts out one boat, the value of 1/3 is obtained by solving the following equation:

$$8p + 1(1 - p) = 6p + 2(1 - p)$$

which establishes the condition for each fisherman to be indifferent between putting out one boat and putting out two boats to sea. (As is implicit from the above equation, the equilibrium in mixed strategy is such that each fisherman puts out one boat with probability 1/3 and two boats with probability 2/3.)

Thus, there is no certainty that the game will equilibrate at the more favourable of the three (Nash) equilibrium points. It is noteworthy, however, that players need not have complete assurance that others will also co-operate to adopt the same strategy: probabilities significantly smaller than 1 may provide sufficient incentive for co-operation. Still, the possibility exists that the worst equilibrium outcome will emerge *even though* the assumption of common knowledge implies that *each player knows that the other also prefers the co-operative outcome.*[2] This is because there is a genuine trust

[2] Curiously, Taylor rules out this possibility on the grounds that, since both players prefer the co-operative outcome to the mutual defection outcome, 'neither will expect the latter to be the outcome, so the unique Pareto-optimal outcome will result'. The assurance game is consequently deemed to be 'unproblematic' (Taylor, 1987: 39–40). For the reason explained in the text, Taylor's argument is unacceptable. In effect, it comes down to denying the fundamental fact that the 2×2 AG comprises three (Nash) equilibria.

problem, that is, a problem of assurance regarding the other person's intended action. Thus, A may know that B would prefer joint co-operation, yet he entertains the fear that B, even though he has corresponding knowledge about his own preference, will choose the maximin strategy ('defect') due to mistrust in what he will himself eventually decide to do. And B can reason in the same way with respect to A's presumed behaviour. *The trust problem is clearly reciprocal since it is basically a problem of mutual expectations*: A may fear that B will abstain from co-operating not because B prefers to free-ride but because B's expectations about his own (A's) behaviour may be pessimistic, and vice versa for B *vis-à-vis* A.

Now, if some form of rudimentary co-ordination device such as pre-play communication (say, in the form of 'cheap talk') is allowed and if the signals sent by the players are interpretable in an unambiguous way, co-operation or joint contribution by both players is much more likely to arise because the players then have the opportunity to reassure one another and to form optimistic expectations about their mutual behaviours.[3] What is worth emphasizing is that the nature of interactions in small groups is highly conducive to pre-play communication and, therefore, if both players' profile is that of an AG player, the Pareto-superior outcome is very likely to be established even in this one-shot game. (Remember that we have reached the same conclusion, *but for repeated games*, when we analysed situations structured as PD.)

Leadership in co-ordination problems

The uncertainty surrounding the players' decisions in a co-ordination problem is overcome as soon as either of the two players can take the initiative in the game with a view to signalling to the other his intention to co-operate. In game-theoretical terms, a particular way of representing the possibility of leadership is by specifying a two-stage assurance game. When the game is played in such a fashion, co-operation by both players is certain to occur: indeed, knowing that the other player will follow suit, the leader has an incentive to make a co-operative move. In other words, by co-operating in the first stage of the game, the leader does not incur the least risk of being 'exploited' by the follower. The outcome (co-operate, co-operate) is clearly a subgame-perfect equilibrium. This is illustrated in Figure 5.12 in which the same payoffs as those assumed in Figure 5.11 have been represented in an extensive form.

If a pure problem of distrust (such as is implicit in the assurance game) can be easily surmounted as soon as one of the players can send a signal or make a first move to the effect that he is determined to co-operate, then, *a fortiori*, the same problem is solved when the game can be repeated. Assume, for instance, that one of the players follows a cautious strategy (start by defecting and, thereafter, co-operating only if the other player has co-operated in the previous round). The other player's best reply to that strategy is obviously not to replicate it but, instead, to start by co-operating (say,

[3] Note that this is precisely the crucial role which Runge ascribes to institutions: to co-ordinate individuals' expectations so as to enable them to co-operate (Runge, 1981, 1984*a*, 1984*b*, 1986).

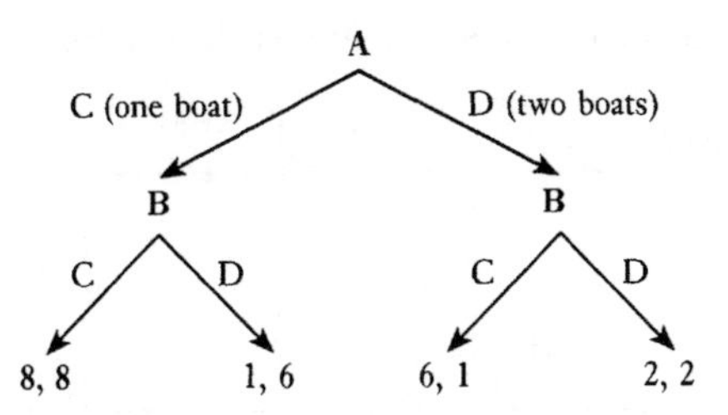

FIG. 5.12. A sequential assurance game

because he follows a strategy of unconditional co-operation) so as to trigger an uninterrupted chain of universal co-operation. Clearly, the cautious strategy is not a Nash equilibrium strategy. However, a 'bad' strategy such as one of unconditional defection is a best reply to itself and therefore supports a Nash equilibrium. (This obviously follows from the fact that, if AG players like best to co-operate, they do not want to be 'exploited'.) What needs to be stressed is that such a strategy is not subgame-perfect since, if by mistake a player co-operates, the other player's best response to that mistake is to co-operate, thus deviating from his Nash equilibrium path. To put it in another way, the commitment of one player to unconditional defection is not credible. Notice that the possibility of a co-operative outcome in such a repeated game is an application of the aforementioned folk theorem and its extension by Benoit and Krishna (1985). Just to give a simple example, a repeated assurance game underlies the observation that in lobster fisheries molesting another fisherman's trap is rarely done because by refraining from doing so a fisherman improves the chances that his own traps will not be molested (Sutinen, Rieser, and Gauvin, 1990: 341).

Threshold effects and freeriding in N*-player co-ordination games*

An interesting feature that arises in connection with co-ordination problems is the existence of threshold effects. As a matter of fact, in many cases, a collective action can bear fruit only if the number of contributors reaches a critical size. To analyse such kinds of situation, we need to consider an N-player assurance game. Let us assume that a given public good (say, the maintenance and management of an irrigation system) yields individual benefits to each member of a group equal to $b(m)$, where m stands for the number of voluntary contributors. Each contributor incurs a fixed cost of c units and, therefore, the total cost for the group is equal to $c \times m$. The choice facing player i can then be represented as in Figure 5.13.

First assume that both $(\partial b(m))/\partial m$ and $(\partial^2 b(m))/\partial m^2$ are positive, implying increasing returns to provision of the public good. Assume also that $b(1) - c < 0$, so that if no other player contributes to the public good, player i also chooses not to contribute. Yet, there exists a critical size m^* such that $b(m) - c > b(m^* - 1)$ or $c < b(m^*) - b(m^* - 1)$: once a certain number, m^*, of other players agree to contribute, player i

Pay-off to player i if the number of other players contributing is

		$n-1$	$n-2$	$n-3$	. . .	0
Player i	contributes	$b(n)-c$	$b(n-1)-c$	$b(n-2)-c$		$b(1)-c$
	does not contribute	$b(n-1)$	$b(n-2)$	$b(n-3)$		0

FIG. 5.13. A N-player assurance game

has an incentive to follow suit since the cost of individual contribution is less than the marginal individual benefit of that contribution. It is evident that, since $(\partial^2 b(m))/\partial m^2 > 0$, if $b(m^*) - c > b(m^* - 1)$, then $b(j) > b(j-1) + c$, $\forall j > m^*$. Therefore, as long as at least m^* other players contribute, player i prefers to co-operate rather than free ride.

In the above game, there are two Nash equilibria in pure strategies. The first equilibrium is characterized by universal defection: given that no one else contributes, player i has no incentive to undertake the collective action alone (we are therefore not in a chicken game). The second equilibrium is characterized by the fact that the collectively optimal level of the public good is provided: everybody contributes to that equilibrium. To avoid falling into the 'bad' equilibrium, a subgroup of players may decide to undertake the collective action in concert, regardless of what the others do. Here lies an important rationale for leadership and the function of the leader consists of mobilizing a sufficient number of contributors rather than showing the good example as assumed in the previous subsection.

It deserves to be noted that an interesting problem which can be raised within the framework of an N-player assurance game is actually a limit case of that analysed above, namely the case in which $b(j) = 0$, $\forall j < n$ and $b(n) > c$. In other words, the collective action can succeed or the public good can be provided only if everyone participates; if only a single agent defects, the public good disappears. The protection of an endangered species or of a breeding-ground illustrates such a possibility that perfectly fits with the description of what an assurance game is about.

Let us now consider the case where there are decreasing returns to scale in the provision of the public good: $(\partial^2 b(m))/\partial m^2$ is negative. In this case, there again exists a critical number of contributors, m^*, below which no individual player has any incentive to contribute. Yet, there now also exists an upper threshold number of contributors, say m^{**}, beyond which the individual marginal benefit of contributing falls short of cost c. The two Nash equilibria in pure strategies are easy to identify: the 'bad' equilibrium in which nobody contributes and a 'nice' equilibrium in which just m^{**} players contribute while the others defect. As long as the size of the group, n, is small (below m^{**}), everyone participates in the collective action under the 'nice' equilibrium. However, in large groups whose size exceeds the threshold m^{**}, the public good is only *partially* produced by a subgroup of players and the amount provided is not Pareto-optimal. It is actually less than the collectively rational amount which would require m° contributors, with $m^{\circ} = \text{argmax}(nb(m^{\circ}) - m^{\circ}c)$. The collectively rational (co-operative) outcome requires that the collective marginal benefit is equal to the marginal cost c, that is $n(\partial b(m^{\circ}))/\partial m^{\circ} = c$. It is to be compared to the individually rational (Nash) outcome, m^{**}, which is by definition such that $(\partial b(m^{**}))/\partial m^{**} = c$. Bearing in mind the assumption of decreasing returns to public-good provision, it is evident that $m^{\circ} > m^{**}$.

In the latter circumstances (the group is large and $n > m^{**}$), a fraction of the players does not contribute in equilibrium and freeride on the others' efforts. Of course, the wider the gap between the size of the group, n, and the equilibrium threshold number of contributors, m^{**}, the larger the proportion of freeriders. In actual fact, the problem facing the players resembles that of an N-player chicken game, in which the Nash equilibrium would be suboptimal.

In community settings, a large proportion of such freeriders may cause serious tensions to arise. The community may possibly overcome these tensions, however. Thus, it may resort to a co-ordinated solution which has the effect of rotating over time the burden of contributions among the various agents. One option here is to use a correlated equilibrium solution in which contributors are selected through a lottery mechanism. It may also, at a given point of time, ensure that contributors with respect to a given collective action are allowed to abstain from participating in other collective actions so as to distribute equally the costs of public-good provision over a series of different activities. If the above kind of solutions are not applied, an exclusionary process is likely to ensue. This is apparently the case referred to by Ostrom and Gardner (1993) when analysing the Thambesi irrigation system in Nepal. Here, as pointed out earlier, maintenance of the headworks can be carried out by a limited number of the water users and, in particular, the work can be done by head-enders alone. The implication of this situation is that tail-enders may find themselves in a low bargaining position whenever important matters are to be discussed (Ostrom and Gardner, 1993: 97–9).

5.3 Heterogeneous Situations with PD, AG, and CG Players

In real-world settings, groups may not be homogeneous as we have assumed so far. This certainly applies to communities with respect to the management of local-level natural resources. It is indeed often observed that members of a particular user group behave differently because they do not derive the same benefits from a given action. This may be due to a variety of reasons, including differential endowments, different characteristics in terms of the technique employed and the pattern of use of the resource concerned (think of nomadic herders and sedentary agriculturalists), different social identities, different exit possibilities, varying perceptions of the stake involved in resource preservation, etc.

In game-theoretical terms, we will say that, in this case, encounters are heterogeneous in the sense that different *types* of players have to deal with each other. The type of a player is characterized by a particular payoff vector, which may be known or not by the other players. In the following, attention will be focused on heterogeneous games in which players with a payoff structure characteristic of the assurance game face players with a payoff structure characteristic of the prisoner's dilemma. These games are especially interesting because they portray a situation that has much relevance in many human encounters, namely that in which people who do not like to 'exploit' others meet with opportunists. The question that arises in such games is theoretically rich, in so far as it is not a priori clear who among the 'fair' players and the opportunists will determine the final outcome. Before turning to these games, however, mention will be made of two other kinds of heterogeneous encounters. First, we will consider a game in which the two players have an AG payoff structure, yet the benefits accruing to them are not identical. Second, a game in which a player with a chicken game (CG) structure encounters a player with an AG structure will be analysed.

Encounters between two different AG players

Let us assume that the two players who meet in an one-shot game have an AG payoff structure, implying that both of them have no incentive to free–ride on the other's efforts. However, player A has a greater interest in joint co-operation than player B, as illustrated in Figure 5.14.

As usual, there are three Nash equilibria: (C,C), (D,D), and the mixed strategy in which the probability that A plays C is equal to 1/2 and the probability that B plays C is 1/4. Which of these equilibria will emerge depends on the expectations that the players hold about the likelihood that the other co-operates. Assuming that they both hold the same expectation, p, both players co-operate if $p > 1/2$ and defect if $p < 1/4$. Clearly, there exists a range, $1/4 < p < 1/2$, in which A co-operates while B abstains from doing so. Such an outcome, however, is not an equilibrium (player A will not accept to be 'exploited' by player B). If it may arise, it is actually because there exists an inverse relationship between the size of the payoff accruing to the player in case of joint co-operation and the degree of trust required to prompt the player to co-operate.

		Player B	
		C	D
Player A	C	8, 6	1, 5
	D	5, 1	2, 2

FIG. 5.14. A 2 × 2 asymmetrical assurance game

		AG player C	AG player D
CG player	C	10, 4	8, 4
	D	12, 0	0, 2

FIG. 5.15. A CG player meets an AG player

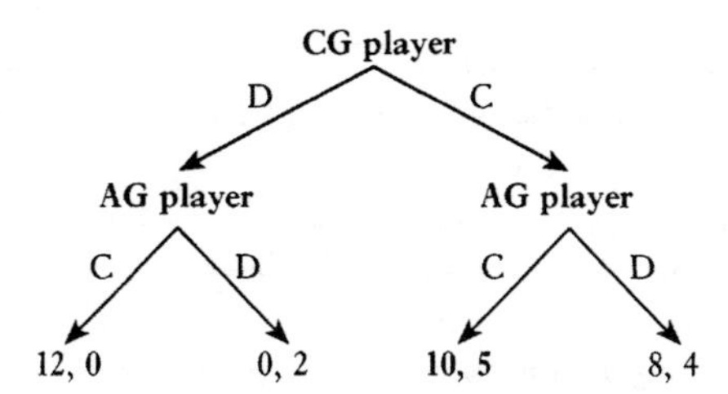

FIG. 5.16. A CG player meets an AG player and leads the sequential game

Encounters between AG and CG players

An interesting situation emerges when an AG player faces a CG player, since it allows us to realize the importance of leadership in determining the equilibrium outcome. To start with, consider the one-shot game with simultaneous moves represented in Figure 5.15.

It is easy to check that, in this game, no equilibrium in pure strategy exists. There is only one equilibrium in mixed strategy, where the probability of the CG player playing C is 2/3 and the probability of the AG player playing C is 4/5.

Equilibria in pure strategies are nevertheless possible as soon as the game is played sequentially. Yet, which equilibrium will arise depends on which player is in the first-mover position. Assume first that the CG player is the leader, as in the sequential game described in Figure 5.16.

It is immediately apparent from Figure 5.16 that joint co-operation will occur: it is in the interest of the CG player to start by co-operating so as to induce the AC player to follow suit. Indeed, if the CG player makes a non-co-operative first move, he is sure to bring about a situation of mutual defection, which he wants absolutely to avoid. In other words, when a party with a leadership role is keen that a collective action is undertaken, but preferably not by himself, whereas the other party tends to follow the leader's behaviour, but prefers bilateral co-operation to bilateral free–riding, joint co-operation will be established. This happy outcome entirely depends on the fact that the leader has a CG payoff structure. Indeed, had the leadership roles been inverted

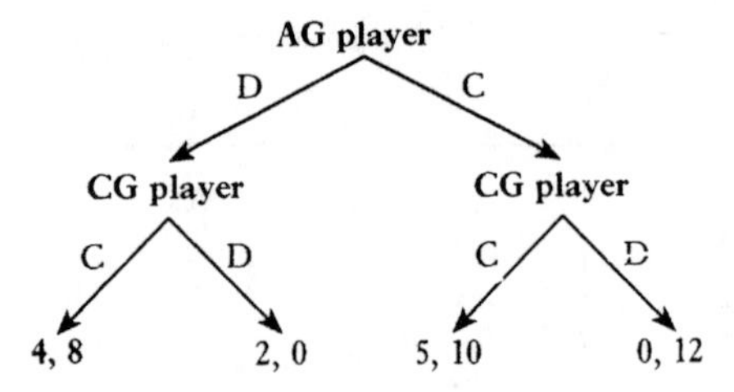

FIG. 5.17. An AG player meets a CG player and leads the game

(the leader is the AG player and the follower is the CG player), universal co-operation would be prevented from arising. This is a straightforward conclusion from Figure 5.17 where the game is led by the AG player.

As is evident from the figure, the collective action will also be undertaken but only by one of the players: having the right to the initial move, the AG player uses the advantage of knowing that the other player has a CG payoff structure to force him to bear the whole cost of this action. Notice carefully, however, that the AG player as a leader is unable to bring about the outcome which he best prefers (universal co-operation) since by co-operating he would incite the follower to defect. This frustration would not have occurred if both players had a CG payoff structure: forcing the other player to co-operate by defecting in the first place is then the ideal outcome which each player wishes for.

An interesting feature which emerges from any encounter between an AG player and a CG player is that both players have an interest in granting leadership to the latter: indeed, the outcome of the first game (Figure 5.16) dominates the outcome of the second game (Figure 5.17). This means that, in a more complex game in which the players would be invited to select the leader before deciding sequentially whether to co-operate or not, the unique subgame-perfect equilibrium path is as follows: the players select the CG player as the leader, thereafter this player co-operates and, in the final stage, the AG player responds by co-operating too. The lesson from such a three-stage game is that, by binding himself to the leadership position, the CG player commits himself to co-operation.

An example which illustrates the aforedescribed situation can again be borrowed from studies of irrigation management. Consider once more a situation in which water users are divided into two subgroups according to whether they are head-enders or tail-enders. Head-enders have a CG payoff structure since they are keen that maintenance of the water control infrastructure is undertaken, but would very much prefer that tail-enders do the work alone (something which may be technically possible, as we have pointed out in the case of the Thambesi irrigation system). On the other hand, tail-enders who are at a locational disadvantage entertain the fear that they may be excluded from decision processes that affect the flow of water reaching their fields (see above): this is why they are eager to participate in maintenance works alongside head-enders, yet would not like to be 'suckers' if head-enders refrain from such partici-

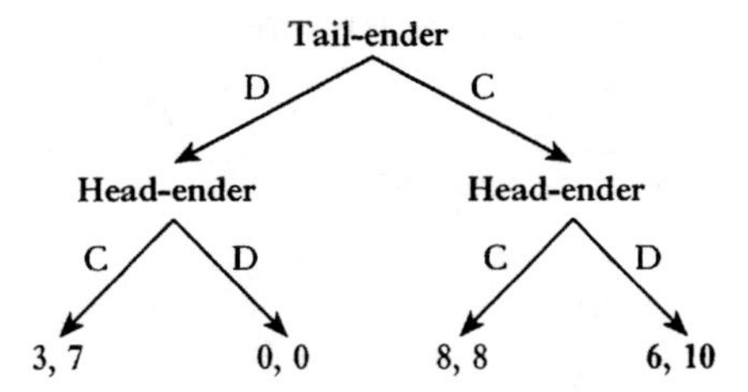

FIG. 5.18. Head-enders deal with tail-enders in a CG-AG encounter

pation (they have an AG payoff structure). In these circumstances, as argued above, head-enders have an incentive to take the leadership so as to associate tail-enders in the maintenance works. This situation seems to fit rather well with the experience of the Pithuwa irrigation project reviewed by Ostrom and Gardner (1993: 105–6).

Another, more plausible situation arises when tail-enders have a mixed CG–AG payoff structure in the following sense: if head-enders participate in the maintenance works, they want to join in order to avoid the aforementioned negative spillover effect but, if head-enders abstain from such participation, they prefer to undertake these works alone rather than leaving the system to fall into decay. If, moreover, as assumed in Figure 5.18, the tail-enders' payoff is higher when they are 'suckers' (6 units) than when they free–ride on the head-enders' maintenance efforts (3 units)—because the price to be paid in terms of loss of reliable access to water is high when participation in these efforts is shunned—the following result obtains: whether the game is played simultaneously or sequentially and whether, in the last case, leadership is exercised by tail-enders or head-enders, the equilibrium outcome is characterized by participation on the part of tail-enders and defection on the part of head-enders. In other words, even though they have the first move, the tail-enders are unable to take advantage of the chicken game structure of the head-ender' payoffs to make them co-operate, owing to the latter's critical control over the supply of water.

Note that, if the tail-ender's payoff when they are 'suckers' is 2 units instead of 6 units or, if their payoff while freeriding on the head-enders' efforts is 6.5 instead of 3 units, it is easy to see that what has just been said is no longer true: if they have the first move, they are now in a position to force head-enders to undertake (alone) the maintenance works. In other words, if the cost of free–riding on maintenance efforts in terms of loss of reliable access to water is not too high for the tail-enders and if they hold a leadership position (two rather implausible assumptions), their leverage allows them to impose the cost of maintenance on the head-enders.

Encounters between AG and PD players in small groups

Let us now turn to the important set of situations in which AG players encounter PD players. There are numerous relevant cases which are worth considering. In order to

		PD player	
		C	D
AG player	C	2, 2	13, 5
	D	1, −1	0, 0

FIG. 5.19. A PD player meets an AG player

help the reader to follow the arguments, these cases are presented in increasing order of complexity.

1. To start with, let us examine the simple one-shot two-player game with perfect information in which an AG player meets a PD player. That in this case co-operation cannot occur is immediately evident from the payoff matrix depicted in Figure 5.19.

The non-co-operative outcome (D,D) is the only Nash equilibrium in this game. Note that defection is a dominant strategy for the PD player as a result of which there is no equilibrium in mixed strategy.

2. What would happen if such a game were to be played in a sequential manner? The answer to that question is rather straightforward. If the AG player is in the first-mover position, he will be prompted to defect since he anticipates that the PD player defects in any event. In contrast, and rather unexpectedly, the reverse outcome obtains in the case where the PD player takes the lead: as a matter of fact, knowing that his opponent responds to co-operation by co-operation and to defection by defection, the PD leader has an incentive to start by co-operating. Because (D,D) is the subgame-perfect equilibrium of the former sequential game and (C,C) that of the latter, were both players allowed to choose their leader, both of them would concur in selecting the PD player. Note the similarity between this conclusion and that reached when analysing CG–AG player encounters.

3. If the game is (finitely) repeated rather than being played sequentially, mutual defection appears as the only possible equilibrium as observed in the finitely repeated PD game. Reasoning by backwards induction makes this result clear. As a matter of fact, since the AG player knows that his opponent has a PD payoff structure, he can infer that the latter will surely defect in the last round of the game. His best reply is therefore also to defect in this last round. Being aware that the AG player is going to defect, the PD player has no incentive to build a reputation of 'co-operator' in the round $(t - 1)$ and, as a consequence, he will also defect in that round. Since he knows that things will turn out that way, the AG player defects in the same round too. This reasoning can be pursued backwards till the very first round of the game.

4. If the game is played in infinite time (or if its length is finite but indeterminate), the folk theorem applies and joint co-operation is a possible (subgame-perfect) equilibrium.

AG against PD player

	C	D
C	2, 2	−1, 3
D	1, −1	0, 0

AG against AG player

	C	D
C	2, 2	−1, 1
D	1, −1	0, 0

FIG. 5.20. A 2 × 2 game with one-sided asymmetric information

5. By relaxing the assumption of perfect information, we can raise the question as to whether co-operation becomes a possible equilibrium outcome in a finitely repeated game. This question is worth raising bearing in mind the result achieved by Kreps and his associates in the framework of a finitely repeated PD game (see above). Let us first consider the case where uncertainty about the payoff structure of the other player is one-sided asymmetric. More precisely, we assume the first player has a PD payoff structure, and this is common knowledge, while the type of the second player is not known with certainty: the first player assigns probability p to the possibility of the second player being an AG player and probability $(l - p)$ to the possibility that he is a PD player. We know from Kreps *et al.* (1982: 251) that in these circumstances defection will occur throughout the whole game: indeed, if the other player is a PD player, we know that defection is the only possible equilibrium and we have just shown that, if a PD player meets repeatedly an AG player, defection also occurs. There is therefore no reason to expect that a co-operative equilibrium can be generated when there is a doubt about whether the second player has an AG or a PD payoff structure.

6. The next case to consider is that in which the first player is an AG player, and this is common knowledge, while there is doubt about the payoff structure of the second player. Is co-operation more likely to emerge in those more favourable conditions? The answer is a conditional 'yes'. More precisely, co-operation by both players till the last stage of the game may occur if the expectation held by the player with a certain AG payoff structure that the opponent is also an AG player exceeds a certain level. In case this expectation falls below that level, universal defection occurs throughout the game. To see this, consider a three-period game in standard form in which the Row player is known with certainty to be an AG player while there is doubt about whether the Column player is a PD or an AG player. The payoffs pertaining to the two possible kinds of encounters are given in Figure 5.20.

Thus, for instance, by defecting while his opponent co-operates, the PD player gets a payoff of 3 which is more than his payoff when both co-operate. By contrast, in the same circumstances, the AG player gets a payoff of only 1 which is less than his payoff when both co-operate. Let us now assume that an AG player follows the brave reciprocity strategy consisting of starting by co-operating and, thereafter, co-operating as long as the opponent is in 'good standing'. As for the PD player, he starts by co-operating, thereafter mimics what the opponent has done in the previous round till the last round where he defects. The question then is whether these two strategies are the best replies to one another, which would imply that mutual co-operation starts from the first round and continues till the last round when the Column player defects while the Row player co-operates till the very end of the game.

To begin with, consider which payoffs the Column player would earn, *if he is of the AG type*, by following various possible strategies in his encounters with the Row player who is known to be of the AG type and follows the aforedescribed strategy. If he plays a strategy of brave reciprocity (note that similar strategies such as tit for tat or unconditional co-operation also lead to the (C,C,C) sequence of actions), he gets a total payoff over the three periods equal to 6 (2 + 2 + 2). If he plays a strategy whereby, against the brave reciprocity strategy of Row, he co-operates in the first two rounds and defects in the last one, his payoff amounts to 5 (2 + 2 + 1). If he co-operates in the first round and defects in the last two rounds, he earns 3 (2 + 1 + 0) while, if he defects from beginning to end, he earns only 1 (1 + 0 + 0). It is therefore evident that unconditional co-operation dominates the other three strategies. In other words, if Column is of the AG type and Row is of the same type and follows a strategy which consists of starting by co-operating and, thereafter, mimicking what the opponent has done in the previous round, then Column's best reply to the latter is to co-operate throughout the whole game. Since the Row player has adopted the above strategy, he will also co-operate from the beginning to the end of the game. Mutual co-operation therefore occurs till the game ends. There is actually nothing surprising in this result which has already been accounted for at an earlier stage of our analysis.

If Column is of the PD type, his total payoffs while playing various possible strategies against Row are as follows: 6 (2 + 2 + 2) if he plays a co-operative strategy leading to the (C,C,C) sequence of actions; 7 (2 + 2 + 3) if he plays the *fake strategy* whereby he co-operates as his opponent co-operates, and defects in the last round, then revealing his true type; 5 (2 + 3 + 0) if his strategy leads to a (C,D,D) sequence of moves; and 3 (3 + 0 + 0) if he plays unconditional defection. The fake strategy dominates the other strategies available to Column.

Let us now turn to the Row player in order to check whether the brave reciprocity strategy can be a best reply to brave reciprocity (or similar strategies) played by Column if of the AG type and to the fake strategy if of the PD type. Let p be the probability Row assigns to the possibility that Column is of the AG type and $(1 - p)$ the probability that Column is of the PD type. If Row plays brave reciprocity, his payoff is 2 for the first period, 2 again for the second period, and $(p \times 2 + (1 - p)(-1))$ for the third period, amounting to a total payoff of $3p + 3$ for the three periods together. If, instead, he plays a *safe strategy* whereby he follows the strategy of brave reciprocity except in the last round when he ensures himself against being a 'sucker' by defecting, his payoff is $2 + 2 + (p \times 1 + (1 - p)0) = p + 4$. If he plays a strategy leading to the (C,D,D) sequence of actions, he earns $2 + 1 + 0 = 3$ while, if he plays unconditional defection, he gets only 1 $(1 + 0 + 0)$. Clearly, the latter two strategies are dominated by the first two. Whether the first strategy dominates the second strategy or is dominated by it hinges upon the value of p, that is, upon the expectation of Row regarding the payoff identity of Column. In more exact terms, brave reciprocity dominates the safe strategy if $p > 1/2$.

Row will therefore co-operate all throughout the game if he believes there is more than 50 per cent chance that Column is of the same type as himself, otherwise he will stop co-operating after two periods. Since p is common knowledge—Column knows Row's expectation regarding his own (Column's) payoff structure—if $p > 1/2$, Column will continue to co-operate till the very end of the game in case he is of the AG type, and till the last period in case he is of the PD type. If $p < 1/2$, on the other hand, Column knows that Row will defect in the last (third) round of the game and, as a result, he has no incentive to co-operate in the second round to maintain a reputation of 'co-operator'. Applying the argument backwards, it is easy to see that, in these conditions, co-operation unravels and universal defection occurs from beginning to end. To sum up, either Row's expectation regarding the chance that Column is of the AG type is sufficiently high, and universal co-operation is sure to occur till at least the last stage of the game, or this expectation is too low and universal defection occurs throughout the game.

Clearly, co-operation is not doomed to failure because groups are heterogeneous in the sense that there is a non-negligible proportion of potential opportunists. As we have seen above and will continue to see in the three following points, co-operation is a serious possibility when expectations are favourable to it.

7. In the two foregoing points, we have only considered situations of one-sided asymmetric information. It is tempting to examine now whether co-operation is a possible outcome when the imperfection of information is two-sided, that is, when the two players entertain mutual doubts about their respective payoff structure. An important—but largely neglected (see, however, Gibbons, 1992: 226)—result obtained by Kreps and his associates in their aforementioned, celebrated article (1982) is that extension of uncertainty about payoffs to the two players may increase the chance of co-operation. Remember that, as seen under point 4 above, co-operation is impossible when one player is of the PD type and doubts whether the other player is of the AG or the PD type. What Kreps *et al.* show, however, is that when the two players are of the PD type but believe that their opponent might perhaps be of the AG type, there can exist an equilibrium in which both players co-operate until the last few stages of the game (the end-game is rather complex). Yet, it deserves to be emphasized that this game admits (subgame-perfect Nash) equilibria in which long-run co-operation does not ensue. Co-operation actually requires a 'boot-strapping' operation (since there is obviously a trust problem): even if each side is certain that the other has an AG payoff structure, co-operation ensues only if each side hypothesizes that the other side will co-operate (Kreps *et al.*, 1982: 251).

To see this possibility of co-operation when there is two-sided uncertainty about payoff structures, let us again use our simple three-period framework. Pay-offs are assumed to be the same as in Figure 5.19. In the mind of Row, Column might be of the AG, rather than PD, type, an eventuality to which he assigns a probability p. On the other hand, Column entertains the hypothesis that Row is an AG player (with probability q) rather than a PD player (with probability $(1 - q)$). What we want to show is whether and under which conditions the two aforeprescribed strategies ('start by co-operating and thereafter mimic what the opponent has done in the previous round', till the last stage of the game for the PD player and till the end of the game for the AG player) can be best replies to each other.

In actual fact, part of the preparatory work required to answer that question has already been done in the previous point while considering the decision problem of Row. Bear in mind, indeed, that Row's best strategies, *when he is of the AG type*, are a strategy of brave reciprocity, which yields him a total payoff of $3p + 3$ over the three periods, and the safe strategy, which yields a payoff of $p + 4$. The former strategy dominates the latter if $p > 1/2$. *When Row is of the PD type*, on the other hand, his payoffs are as follows:

$2 + 2 + [p \times 2\,(1 - p)(-1)\,] = 3p + 3,$ if he plays brave reciprocity;

$2 + 2 + [p \times 3 + (1 - p)0] = 3p + 4,$ if he plays the fake strategy;

$2 + 3 + 0 = 5,$ if he plays the (C,D,D) sequence of moves;

$3 + 0 + 0 = 3,$ if he plays unconditional defection.

The strategies of unconditional defection and of brave reciprocity are clearly dominated. Whether the fake strategy is superior to the other (which leads to the (C,D,D) sequence of moves) depends on the value of p: the former dominates if $p > 1/3$. It is therefore apparent that, if Row expects with a probability higher than 1/3 that Column is of the AG type, he will co-operate till, at least, the last stage of the game. If this probability is higher than 1/2 and he is himself of the AG type, Row will even co-operate till the end of the game.

Exactly the same reasoning can be made with respect to Column. If Column expects with a probability higher than 1/3 ($q > 1/3$) that Row is of the AG type, he has an incentive to co-operate, at least till the last round of the game. We can conclude that, if expectations of both players regarding the chance that the opponent is of the AG type exceed 1/3, co-operation till at least the last stage of the game is an equilibrium outcome. If this expectation is higher than 1/2, both Row and Column will co-operate till the end of the game provided that they are of the AG type. If, say, the expectation of one player is more pessimistic and falls below the threshold level of 1/3, this is sufficient to destroy co-operation. Indeed, the opponent then knows that the pessimistic player is going to defect from as early as the second round—since the (C,D,D) sequence of moves then dominates the fake strategy—and, therefore, he himself has no incentive to co-operate in the second round nor actually in the first round (since it is of no use for him to build up a reputation of 'co-operator'). The pessimistic player, aware of this calculation made by his opponent, will also defect in the initial round. Universal defection occurs throughout the game.

8. We will now extend the above analysis to games with many players. To keep things as simple as possible, consider a three-player game that is played over only two periods. The three players are uncertain about the payoff structure of the other two

		C,C^1	C,D^2	D,D^3
Player 3	co-operates	**4** (4)	**3** (1)	**−1** (−1)
	defects	**2** (5)	**1** (3)	**0** (0)

FIG. 5.21. A three-player game with asymmetric information

players; more specifically they entertain doubts about whether the other players are of the AG or PD type.

Let us consider the decision problem faced by player 3 as it is depicted in Figure 5.21.

All players have a probability q of being AG and a probability $(1 - q)$ of being PD. If player 3 is of the AG type, he faces the payoff numbers written in bold characters. For instance, if he defects while at least another player co-operates, he is less well-off than if he co-operates. If both other players defect, he prefers to defect too because he does not want to be a 'sucker'. In contrast, if player 3 is of the PD type, his payoffs are those indicated between brackets: defection is then a dominant strategy.

(i) Let us first assume that, if of the AG type, a player adopts a *strategy of harsh punishment*. In this case, he starts by co-operating and thereafter defects if one of the other two players defected in the previous round. Otherwise, he co-operates. Now, if a player is of the PD type, he follows a *fake strategy* (he mimics being an AG player by co-operating in the first round, and continues to co-operate as long as the other two players co-operate till the last round when he defects). The question is: are these two strategies best replies to one another?

To proceed with the analysis, we begin by examining the situation in which player 3 is of the AG type. If he plays the harsh punishment strategy, his total payoff over the two periods is:

$$\underbrace{4}_{\textit{period 1}} + \underbrace{[q^2 4 + q(1-q)3 + (1-q)q3 + (1-q)^2(-1)]}_{\textit{period 2}} = -3q^2 + 8q + 3$$

This payoff is obviously identical to that which he would obtain were he to follow either an *unconditional co-operation strategy* or a *soft-punishment strategy*, since, in actual fact, he cannot know the other players' types by observing their first period's moves (since PD players fake till the last round). By *soft-punishment strategy*, we mean a strategy whereby he continues to co-operate as long as at least one other player has co-operated in the previous round (or, to put it in another way, he defects only if all other players have defected). We will return later to this particular strategy. To counter the difficulty that he will know the other players' types only in the last round, player 3 may choose to play a *safe strategy* (he starts by co-operating and defects in the last round):

$$\underset{period\ 1}{4} + \underbrace{[q^2 2 + q(1-q) + (1-q)q + (1-q)^2(0)]}_{period\ 2} = 2q + 4$$

If he plays other strategies (implying such sequences of actions as (D,D) or (D,C)), the payoffs will obviously be lower than when he plays the above two strategies. Whether the harsh-punishment strategy yields a higher payoff than the safe strategy obviously depends on the value of the probability q. More specifically, the former is superior to the latter if: $-3q^2 + 6q - 1 > 0$, implying that $q > 0.18$.

Consider now the alternative situation in which player 3 is of the PD type. If he plays the fake strategy, he gets the following total payoff:

$$\underset{period\ 1}{4} + \underbrace{[q^2 5 + q(1-q)3 + (1-q)q3 + (1-q)^2(0)]}_{period\ 2} = -q^2 + 6q + 4$$

If he, instead, plays *unconditional defection strategy*, he gets:

$$\underset{period\ 1}{5} + \underbrace{[q^2(0) + q(1-q)(0) + (1-q)q(0) + (1-q)^2(0)]}_{period\ 2} = 5$$

If he plays other strategies, implying in particular a co-operative move in the last round, his payoffs will obviously be lower than when he plays the above two strategies. Moreover, the fake strategy dominates unconditional defection if $-q^2 + 6q - 1 > 0$, implying that $q > 0.17$.

Note carefully that the critical value of q that induces an AG player to reject the safe strategy is actually greater than the value required to prompt a PD player to use the fake strategy, thereby making the latter condition redundant. We can therefore conclude that, if q, the probability that a player is of the AG type, is greater than 0.18, then the best reply to the harsh-punishment strategy adopted by AG players is faking for the PD player, and vice versa. This is an important result in so far as it shows that, even if in the one-period game the dominant strategy of a PD player is to defect, he may have an incentive, in a two-period game, to behave 'co-operatively', as though he were an AG player, till the second round of the game. This result can be extended to more periods: if his expectation that the other players are of the AG type is sufficiently high, the PD player has an incentive to start by co-operating and thereafter continue to co-operate as long as these other players co-operate, till the last round of the game when he defects. It is noteworthy that the critical values of q obtained in games that stretch over, say, three periods are precisely the same as those obtained in the two-period case. Finally, it should be emphasized that, as the above example shows, the critical values of q need not be very high. This obviously hinges upon the fact that, in this example, defection is not very rewarding for a PD player.

(ii) Let us now investigate the possibility of the AG players adopting a soft punishment strategy. In these circumstances, the PD players know that their defection may not necessarily be retaliated in the next round by a non-co-operative move of the AG players. This obviously depends on what the other PD players choose to do. Consider first the decision problem faced by player 3 if he is of the AG type. For a reason explained above, when opposed to a fake strategy, the payoffs associated with different strategies are exactly the same as those obtained under a harsh-punishment strategy. In particular, the soft-punishment strategy is superior to the safe strategy if $q > 0.18$. If player 3 is, instead, of the PD type, the fake strategy yields the following total payoff:

$$\underbrace{4}_{period\ 1} + \underbrace{[q^2 5 + q(1-q)3 + (1-q)q3 + (1-q)^2(0)]}_{period\ 2} = -q^2 + 6q + 4$$

The payoff resulting from unconditional defection is:

$$\underbrace{5}_{period\ 1} + \underbrace{[q^2 5 + q(1-q)3 + (1-q)q3 + (1-q)^2(0)]}_{period\ 2} = -q^2 + 6q + 5$$

Strategies that imply a co-operative move in the last round are clearly inferior. It is immediately apparent that playing unconditional defection is always more rewarding than playing the fake strategy. As a result, with a soft-punishment strategy, it is impossible that all types of players *always* co-operate in the first round. In the above, we have assumed that the other players, if of the PD type, start by co-operating and defect in the second round. We now have to check whether this is really the most sensible strategy for such players given that the third player, when PD, replies by always defecting. To carry out this check, let us examine whether unconditional defection is the best strategy for *all* the PD players simultaneously. The payoff obtained by player 3 when he always defects against the other players who, if of the PD type, are also unconditional defectors, is the following:

$$\underbrace{q^2(5+5)}_{2\ AG} + \underbrace{(1-q)^2(0+0)}_{2\ PD} + \underbrace{2q(1-q)(3+0)}_{1\ AG\ and\ 1\ PD} = 4q^2 + 6q$$

If, instead, he plays the fake strategy, he gets:

$$\underbrace{q^2(4+5)}_{2\ AG} + \underbrace{(1-q)^2(-1+0)}_{2\ PD} + \underbrace{2q(1-q)(1+3)}_{1\ AG\ and\ 1\ PD} = 10q - 1$$

As can easily by seen, unconditional defection always dominates the fake strategy. This, however, is a result that pertains to a border case since the quadratic equation, $4q^2 + 6q = 10q - 1$, has a unique root equal to 0.5. When q is just equal to 50 per cent, player 3 is thus indifferent between the two strategies whereas, for all other values of q, he prefers unconditional defection. By altering the payoffs given in Figure 5.21, it is possible to construct a more general case in which the fake strategy is the best reply of the third player, if PD, to unconditional defection by other PD players and the soft-punishment strategy by the AG players. (Presumably, there is an interval for q such that PD players will adopt a mixed strategy which consists of randomizing between the fake strategy and unconditional defection and such that AG players prefer soft punishment to harsh punishment.) To conclude the analysis based on the payoff matrix given in Figure 5.21, there still remains the question as to whether the soft-punishment strategy is the best reply of an AG player to the unconditional defection strategy adopted by the PD players. To see this, let us consider the payoffs which would accrue to an AG player when he, alternatively, chooses to play soft punishment, harsh punishment, or a strategy of cautious reciprocity (start by defecting and co-operate only if at least one other player has co-operated in the first round). The payoffs associated with these strategies are, respectively:

$$\underbrace{q^2(4+4)}_{2\text{ AG}} + \underbrace{(1-q)^2(-1+0)}_{2\text{ PD}} + \underbrace{2q(1-q)(3+3)}_{1\text{ AG and }1\text{ PD}} = -5q^2 + 14q - 1,$$

$$\underbrace{q^2(4+4)}_{2\text{ AG}} + \underbrace{(1-q)^2(-1+0)}_{2\text{ PD}} + \underbrace{2q(1-q)(3+1)}_{1\text{ AG and }1\text{ PD}} = -q^2 + 10q - 1,$$

$$\underbrace{q^2(2+4)}_{2\text{ AG}} + \underbrace{(1-q)^2(0+0)}_{2\text{ PD}} + \underbrace{2q(1-q)(1+(-1))}_{1\text{ AG and }1\text{ PD}} = 6q^2$$

From a comparison of the above payoffs, it is evident that the harsh-punishment strategy is dominated by the soft-punishment strategy. On the other hand, the strategy of cautious reciprocity is superior to the latter when the probability of meeting AG players is very low (below 0.08 approximately).

To conclude, there are plausible conditions, implying a sufficient probability of meeting other players of the AG type, under which AG players follow a strategy of soft punishment while PD players unconditionally defect.

Encounters between AG and PD players in large groups

Let us turn to another type of situation where the number of players is significantly large. In such a situation, members meet anonymously, they cannot remember the exact course of actions followed in the past by any particular player, yet past aggregate outcomes are observable and remembered. In these conditions, agents have no incentive to build up a 'good' reputation and, therefore, to play strategically has not the same meaning as when group size is restricted. To proceed with the analysis of such games, let us first consider the payoff matrices described in Figure 5.22: the first one gives the benefits accruing to an AG player, when the proportion of players who co-operate varies from 0 to 100 per cent while the second one gives the benefits accruing to a PD player in the same circumstances.

The argument behind this example is the following. In an *N*-person game, the gains from co-operation and defection for each actor obviously depend on the proportion of people who actually co-operate (or defect) in the entire group. The gains which both AG- and PD-type players derive from co-operation decrease when the proportion of co-operating members in the group declines. Yet such gains are higher for AG players than for PD players for any given proportion of co-operators in the group. On the contrary, the gains from defection are always smaller for AG players than for PD

Pay-offs for a AG-player	Proportion of co-operators in the group					
	100%	80%	60%	40%	20%	0%
C	20	13	6	–1	–8	–15
D	6	6	6	6	6	6

Pay-offs for a PD-player	Proportion of co-operators in the group					
	100%	80%	60%	40%	20%	0%
C	10	4	–2	–8	–14	–20
D	30	28	25	21	16	8

FIG. 5.22. Payoffs to AG- and PD-type players according to the proportion of co-operators in a large group

players. Moreover, the latter's gains from defection have a tendency to diminish with the proportion of co-operators in the group: it is more rewarding to free–ride when everyone else co-operates than when only a fraction of the other members co-operate, and the gains from free–riding are at their lowest when defection is generalized.

By contrast, the gains from defection accruing to AG players exhibit a constant pattern even when the proportion of co-operators in the group decreases. This is because two opposite effects are at work when these players defect. On the one hand, there is the above-noted fact that defection is all the less rewarding as the percentage of free–riders in the population increases. But, on the other hand, AG players 'feel bad' about defecting, especially so if they are amidst a large number of co-operating people. Or, to put it in the converse way, the higher the proportion of free–riders in the group, the more they are relieved of their 'bad feelings' since they can justify their 'opportunistic' acts by reference to the fact that many others behave in the same way as they do. Consequently, the net effect of an increase in the proportion of free–riders on the utility payoffs accruing to AG players when they defect cannot be determined on an a priori basis. Here, we have assumed that the two effects exactly counterbalance each other so that these payoffs are left unaffected by changes in the percentage of freeriders in the group.

Furthermore, it is worthy of note that the payoff to AG players when they co-operate and everybody else also co-operates (or when more than 60 per cent of all members co-operate) is higher than the payoff they receive when they are the only ones to defect in the group (6 units): this is a typical reflection of an AG-preference structure. The opposite is of course true of PD players who receive higher payoffs by defecting than by co-operating not only when all other members or a majority of them co-operate but also when few others or even nobody in the group co-operates. Another noteworthy feature is that the payoff received by PD players when they freeride jointly with everybody else (8 units) is smaller than that which they obtain by co-operating jointly with everybody else (10 units), a feature characteristic of a PD game. This, of course, holds *a fortiori* true for AG players.

It is immediately apparent from Figure 5.22 that PD players have a dominant strategy which is to defect. As for AG players, their preferred strategy will obviously depend on their expectations regarding the likely behaviour of the other players. They will choose to co-operate if they expect more than 60 per cent of the group members to co-operate, otherwise they will defect. Thus, for example, if AG players assess the proportion of co-operators in the group to be around one-half, generalized freeriding will take place as both types of players choose to defect. In this kind of situation, the meaningfulness of the concept of trust is evident. In the words of Dasgupta, trust here is to be understood 'in the sense of correct expectations about the *actions* of other people that have a bearing on one's own choice of action when that action must be chosen before one can *monitor* the actions of those others' (Dasgupta, 1988: 51).

The main conclusion that emerges from the above N-players game at this stage is the following: for co-operation to prevail on a large scale in an anonymous society or in a large group, it is not sufficient that a significant majority of people prefer universal co-operation but it must also be the case that these people feel confident enough that their willingness to co-operate is shared by many others too.

Now the question is not only how, or under what conditions, collective action can occur in a large group with the characteristics considered here; the question is also whether the co-operative outcome can be sustained on a large enough scale over time. To answer this last question, more information is needed about the dynamics of expectation formation. In a dynamic setting, indeed, decision by AG players whether or not to co-operate requires continual re-evaluation of the probability that others will also co-operate based on concrete experiences in past rounds. Not only do expectations affect co-operative behaviour but, over time, past co-operative outcomes affect expectations and future actions, though in a way that leaves no room for strategic considerations: a single player's co-operation cannot affect the proportion of co-operators in the group.

In accordance with what has been said above about the observability of past aggregate outcomes, the assumption is made that agents are broadly able to make out *ex post* whether and to what extent the collective action under concern has been successful. This is because they can observe the concrete results that collective action has produced: an irrigation canal has been more or less well maintained; foreign trawlers have been effectively deprived of access to inshore waters; the spawning area for fish has not been encroached upon; no felling of trees or cutting of wood has happened in the forest during forbidden times; little grazing occurred on the collective fields before the date fixed, etc. As is evident from these illustrations, the members of a large group may even be in a position to *approximately* assess the relative number of individuals who have co-operated or defected (yet they are not able to personally identify them).

Let us adopt the following conventions:

P^{AG}	denotes the proportion of AG players in the group;
$P^{PD} = 1 - P^{AG}$	denotes the proportion of PD players in the group;
P^*	denotes the minimum proportion of co-operators required to induce co-operative behaviour among AG players;
P^e_t	denotes the proportion of co-operators whom AG players expect to be present in the group at time $t + 1$; (P^e_0 is therefore the *initial* expectation of AG players which reflects their beliefs about the percentage of group members who will co-operate in the *first* round of the game)
P^a_t	denotes the actual proportion of co-operators in the group at time t.

We know that, if $P^e_0 \geq P^*$, AG players choose to co-operate at the beginning of the game and, as a result, the actual proportion of co-operators equals the proportion of AG players in the group: $P^a_1 = P^{AG}$. On the other hand, if $P^e_0 < P^*$, AG players choose to defect and $P^a_1 = 0$.

We are now ready for a discussion of the dynamics of collective action in a large group where there are two types of players with the preferences depicted in Figure 5.22. Four possibilities can be distinguished. Under the first possibility, we have $P^{AG} \geq P^e_0 \geq P^*$. The AG players co-operate from the beginning of the game, P^e_t is equal to P^{AG} for all t greater than zero, and their willingness to so behave is actually confirmed as more rounds are completed. If P^e_0 is strictly smaller than P^{AG}, these players realize after the first round that the actual proportion of co-operators in the group is higher than what they had initially expected (bear in mind that $P^a_1 = P^{AG}$ since $P^e_0 \geq P^*$). Consequently, their expectations are revised upwards and P^e_t becomes equal to P^{AG} at $t = 1$. If P^e_0 is equal to P^{AG}, AG players discover after the first round that their expectations are fully justified by experience and no change occurs in their expectations. In both cases, collective action is clearly a durable outcome.

The second possibility arises when the following conditions are satisfied: $P^e_0 > P^{AG} \geq P^*$. This is typically the case where AG players are overoptimistic about the likely behaviour of others, yet this does not prevent collective action from being established and sustained. The AG players participate in collective action but they are led to bring down their assessment of the likely proportion of co-operators in the light of the first round's experience.

Such is not the case under the third possibility where the overoptimism of AG players cannot avoid the collective action to suddenly collapse at the second round. This case obtains when we find $P^e_0 \geq P^* > P^{AG}$. The problem obviously arises from the fact that there are now in the group less AG players than required to induce *sustainable* co-operation ($P^{AG} < P^*$). After the first round, AG players choose to discontinue co-operation forever.

The fourth possibility is the most interesting one. It arises when the proportion of co-operators expected by AG players is smaller than the minimum required to induce co-operation among these players, that is, when $P^e_0 < P^* < P^{AG}$. In this case, nobody co-operates in the initial round and nobody will ever be incited to co-operate thereafter. In other words, even though there are actually enough willing co-operators in the (large) group to make co-operation possible, such co-operation fails to emerge because they do not have sufficient confidence in the group's inclination to co-operate. Because it cannot be corrected through a co-ordination mechanism, pessimism turns into a self-fulfilling prophecy. This case illustrates the critical importance of trust for co-operation to be possible in large groups.

Note that, even if there is one fully informed AG player who knows that there are actually enough players like him in the population to sustain co-operation, he will not choose to co-operate in the first round since, given the large size of the group, he is unable to persuade others to change their expectations and modify their behaviour. It would be wrong to think that such a result obtains because this individual player is alone to hold correct expectations. To see this, let us assume that, among AG players, there is a subgroup of players who hold optimistic expectations. These players are called subtype I AG players and are distinguished from another category called subtype II who are pessimistic. By optimists, we mean AG players who believe that the proportion of subtype I players in the population is at least equal to P^*. Pessimists are those AG players for whom the proportion of subtype I AG players is less than P^*.

Two different situations can arise. In a first case, the actual proportion of optimists in the population is higher than P^*. After one round, they realize that they are numerous enough to sustain co-operation, no matter what the pessimists do, and the latter are then led to revise their expectations upwards. From the second round onwards, the pessimists join the optimists in the collective action. The presence of the optimists, to paraphrase Elster, appears as a catalyst for co-operation while the pessimists act as a multiplier on the co-operation of the former (Elster, 1989*a*: 205). In the second case, the *actual* proportion of optimists in the population is lower than the critical level P^*. After one round when the optimists realize that they are not numerous enough to justify co-operation, and are unable to drive the pessimists in the collective action, they stop co-operating: universal defection ensues.

A richer picture of reality obtains when the assumption of two homogeneous subtypes of AG players is relaxed and replaced by the more realistic one that the *degree* of optimism of each player is different and unknown to the others. To put it in another way, the distribution of subtypes (i.e. optimism) among AG players is not known a priori. However, the analysis of such a situation lies beyond the scope of the present work. We shall here restrict ourselves to pointing out the main results which can be intuitively expected from such an analysis. The important point to note is that the revision of expectations now takes place in a gradual way after each round rather than in a discrete manner after the first round only. In a border case, all AG players start by co-operating and continue to co-operate forever since even the pessimists have high enough expectations to give co-operation a try. Experience confirms them in their behaviour. A more general case is when the most optimistic players start by co-operating but it turns out in the initial rounds that their number is too small to make co-operation worth while even for them. If those players are led to revise their expectations downwards, some initially pessimistic players may now be induced to co-operate. In such circumstances, it is impossible to say a priori whether co-operation will spread or gradually unravel. Note that in the latter, general case, the most favourable scenario occurs when co-operation is initiated by the most optimistic AG players, then, after subsequent rounds these players revise downwards their expectations yet still co-operate and they are joined by successive batches of players who were initially less optimistic than themselves.

Let us now return to the case where the AG players are divided between two subgroups. However, instead of assuming that members from subtypes I and II differ in terms of the more or less pessimistic character of their expectations, it is possible to differentiate them in terms of the intensity of their interest in co-operation. More precisely, we may assume that players from subtype I derive a higher payoff from co-operation than players from the other subtype, with the result that the threshold proportion for co-operation is lower for the more co-operation-interested players. Let us denote this assumption by writing $P^{*II} > P^{*I}$. Three interesting cases may be distinguished which lead to results analogous to those obtained in the above analysis of heterogeneous AG players. In a first situation, we have (assuming that players of the two subtypes have *similar expectations*):

$$P^{*I} < P_0^e < P^{*II} < P^{AGI},$$

where P^{AGI} stands for the proportion of subtype I AG players in the population. Under these conditions, all AG players participate in the collective action after the first round. Players I participate from the very beginning while players II first choose to defect but, as their expectations are being adjusted upwards, concrete experience from the first round gives them enough assurance of others' willingness to co-operate for themselves to join the collective action. This is the virtuous situation in which the more co-operation-inclined players succeed in *anonymously* persuading the less co-operation-inclined (but non-opportunistic) players to participate in collective action. Thanks to this demonstration effect, the former see their payoffs increase once the latter have joined them. *Ex post*, we can reinterpret the utility 'losses' incurred by players I during the first round as the necessary price to pay for dragging more prudent men of goodwill into the production of a public good, and thereby draw higher benefits from their own participation in this effort.

A second interesting situation obtains when the following conditions are satisfied:

$$P^{*I} < P_0^e < P^{AGI} < P^{*II}.$$

Here, the more co-operation-interested players continuously co-operate but, contrary to what we observed in the previous situation, they are not able to prevent the less co-operation-interested players from defecting. This is because, even though the latter's expectations are adjusted upwards, the threshold proportion P^{*II} will not be crossed. Such a situation is especially unfortunate if

$$P^{AG} > P^{*II},$$

that is, if the proportion of *all* AG players in the group actually exceeds that required to induce co-operation among the less co-operation-interested players.

There then remains the third, vicious case where even players I's willingness to co-operate unravels. This case is observed when

$$P^{AGI} < P^{*I} < P_0^e < P^{*II},$$

which conditions can also be satisfied when $P^{AG} > P^{*II}$. Players I start by co-operating but, as players II do not join hands with them, the actual proportion of co-operators (P^{AGI}) is too small to incite even the former to sustain their co-operative efforts.

5.4 Conclusion

Clearly, situations which can arise in field settings are of a much wider variety than what the tragedy of the commons implies. In the previous chapter, emphasis was laid on the fact that even within the PD framework repetition can possibly get people out of the non-co-operative equilibrium trap. In this chapter, it has been argued that this framework, although useful to account for many field situations which have really developed into the kind of tragedy envisioned by Hardin, is nevertheless too narrow to describe a whole range of other situations. Depending on the characteristics of the resource and the technique used as well as on various features of user groups (their size, their rate of discount of future income and the importance of their subsistence constraints, their exit possibilities, etc.), problems of resource exploitation may or may not be adequately described as PD games. Thus, such problems of resource management may well entail co-ordination or chicken game-like problems, or a mixture of different payoff structures. In this new perspective, the focus of the analysis is no more on the irresistible tendency of individuals to overexploit the commons. It is being shifted to human encounters involving problems of trust, leadership, co-ordination, group identity, and homogeneity or heterogeneity of group members.

A particularly striking result obtains in heterogeneous encounters with sequential moves in which the first agent has an AG payoff structure while the second agent has a CG, an AG, or even a PD payoff structure. If the second type of agent can assume leadership, co-operation will automatically ensue but the reverse is not true except in the case where both the leader and the follower happen to have an AG payoff structure. Clearly, the payoff profile of the leader matters a lot and, in a rather paradoxical way, co-operation is better ensured if 'nice' people do not occupy the leadership position.

Leadership does not necessarily refer to the ability to make the first move in a sequential decision-making process. It can also mean the ability to mobilize a sufficient number of people for enterprises requiring co-ordinated efforts. If such leadership is not present in these situations, collective action may not occur even though every agent would actually like to co-operate with the others.

The discussion about situations structured like asymmetric chicken games has shown the importance of precising the nature of power in order to be able to predict who, between the rich and the poor, are more likely to bear the cost of producing a public good (or preventing a public 'bad') in this kind of situation. Power can take various forms. It may be reflected in the ability to make a credible commitment to non-co-operation in the first stage of a sequential decision-making process. Or, it may have its source in exit possibilities that are not available to the other agents. Or again, it may express itself in the ability to lay down social norms that drive everybody to co-operate, irrespective of individual interests in the public good. Sheer poverty can, however, confer leverage upon the poor if the latter are so hard-pressed by subsistence constraints that they are not capable of producing the public good alone. Yet, even in this case, the third way of exercising power (imposing norms of participation) can enable the rich to transform the situation partly to their advantage. Note, moreover, that in situations involving co-ordination problems but where the efforts of the whole group are not required, power can manifest itself in the ability to exclude people from collective action, thereby preventing them from fully participating in the management of community affairs.

Regarding group size, it bears emphasis that the central conclusions reached at the end of Chapter 4 continue to hold true and are even reinforced when allowance is made for non-PD payoff structures. Thus, as the size of the group increases, due to incentive dilution a chicken game degenerates into a prisoners' dilemma with the result that no contribution, whether unilateral or universal, is made towards producing collective CPR infrastructures or no effort towards following use-restraining rules. Also, the fact that limited group size favours continuous interactions and easy observability and memorization of each other's actions proves to be a decisive factor in explaining the emergence of co-operation. In particular, when PD players coexist with AG players, it may be in the interest of the former to conceal their freerider type by co-operating till the last (few) stages of the game. This is not possible in large groups since the agents' co-operative moves cannot be interpreted by the others in a way conducive to universal co-operation. As a result, when numerous actors are involved, each of them tends to consider others' behaviour as a datum which he is unable to influence (Buchanan, 1975: 66).

In the previous chapter, the feasibility of pre-play communication in small-group settings has been emphasized. This aspect of the problem of collective action assumes special relevance when agents operate within an AG payoff structure. As a matter of fact, if such agents are able to signal to the others their predisposition to co-operate and their aversion to being 'exploited', the Pareto-superior equilibrium is very likely to be established and sustained. This is all the more true if the feeling of sameness or togetherness permeates the culture of the small group.

6

Moral Norms and Co-operation

So far we have focused our attention on the kind of predictions to which economic (game) theory can lead when interaction takes place between self-interested individuals with given preferences. This approach is not completely satisfactory in so far as it implicitly assumes an 'undersocialized' conception of human action (Granovetter, 1985). In the following, we would like to go beyond this rather narrow framework by allowing for the influence of social forces acting through moral norms. In all logic, we expect that the possibility of co-operation is enhanced in groups whose members are tied together through the sharing of a common ethos. Analytically, there are two different ways of addressing the issue of moral norms. In the first one, they are seen as a binding constraint limiting the choices of a maximizing self-interested individual while, in the second one, they play an important role in shaping individual preferences.

6.1 Norms as Constraints on the Pursuit of Self-Interest

Since the economists' paradigm of human choice is based on constrained individual maximization, a natural way for them to incorporate social phenomena such as moral norms is to consider them as additional constraints on human choice sets. This presumably avoids the pitfalls of treating norms as factors affecting individual utilities, an approach which easily gives way to *ad hoc* explanations (Becker, 1976). Two pioneering attempts at modelling norms as constraints have been proposed by Laffont (1975) and Sugden (1984). In the following, discussion is limited to the second contribution as it explicitly deals with the problem of the production of a public good (whereas the former contribution is concerned with the consumption of a good that gives rise to a macro-externality in consumption).

In Sugden's attempt, morality manifests itself as a *principle of reciprocity* that provides not that 'you must always contribute towards public goods, but that you must not take a free ride when other people are contributing'. Moreover, the principle of reciprocity never requires you to contribute more than other people in the group (Sugden, 1984: 775). Everyone accepts this principle as a morally binding constraint.

Let us assume that the production function for the public good has the simple linear form: $z = \beta\Sigma_i q_i$, where q_i stands for each individual's contribution. Consider the special case in which all n people have identical preferences, $u_i = u_i(q_i,z)$, $i = (1, \ldots, n)$. Let $h_i(q_i,z)$ be the marginal rate of substitution (MRS) between z and q_i:

$$h_i(q_i,z) = -\frac{\partial u_i/\partial q_i}{\partial u_i/\partial z}, \quad i=(1,\cdots,n), \quad \text{with} \frac{\partial u_i}{\partial q_i} < 0, \quad \frac{\partial u_i}{\partial z} > 0.$$

The partial derivatives of $h_i(q_i,z)$ with respect to q_i and z are assumed to be both positive. It follows from the symmetry of the problem that each person's obligations must be the same as everyone else's, so that in equilibrium everyone must make the same contribution. Therefore, the quantity of the public good produced will be given by $z = \beta n q_i$, where i is any individual. Each agent maximizes his utility level subject to the technological constraint and to the reciprocity principle:

$$\max_{q_i} u_i = u_i(q_i, z), \text{ subject to } z = \beta\left(q_i + \sum_{j \neq i} q_i\right) \text{ and } q_i \geq q_j,\ \forall j \neq i.$$

This problem yields a continuum of solutions comprised between two limit-values of q_i. The upper bound corresponds to the Pareto-optimal solution $h_i(q_i^o,z) = \beta n$, where q_i^o is the contribution that i would most prefer that everyone should make. This solution follows from the maximization problem: $\max_{q_i} \Sigma_i u_i(q_i, \beta n q_i)$. The lower bound is actually the Nash equilibrium solution. In the latter, the principle of reciprocity is actually not operating and self-interest dictates a contribution, q_i^*, which solves the following maximization problem:

$$\max_{q_i} u_i = u_i(q_i, z), \text{ subject to } z = \beta\left(q_i + \sum_{j \neq i} q_j\right).$$

We then have $h_i(q_i^*,z) = \beta$ and the fact that the *MRS* is continuously increasing ensures that q_i^o always exceeds q_i^*. If $q_i < q_i^*$, 'every individual would find that self-interest dictated a larger contribution, even if he had no expectation that others would reciprocate.' If $q_i > qi^o$, every individual would be contributing more than he was obliged to, but if $q_i^* \leq q_i \leq qi^o$, 'everyone is obliged to reciprocate everyone else's contribution, while neither reciprocity nor self-interest dictates that anyone should contribute more than he actually does' (Sugden, 1984: 778).

There are therefore a multiplicity of equilibria one of which is Pareto-optimal, while all the others involve undersupply of the public good. The problem is clearly an assurance game problem: 'even for a society of identical individuals, the theory of reciprocity does not predict that the free–rider problem *will* be solved. Because of the assurance problem, a society of moral citizens can get locked into an equilibrium' in which everyone contributes much less than what he would prefer that everyone, including himself, contributed (Sugden, 1984: 781).

Things get more complex when the homogeneity assumption is relaxed and one assumes instead that preferences may differ between agents and subgroups coexist in which the members' moral obligations are circumscribed to one another. In other words, the principle of reciprocity applies only to subgroups and not to the 'society' at large. In such conditions, the problem associated with the provision of public goods by moral agents is made even more serious. Indeed, Pareto-efficiency is possible in a very special case only, namely if 'everyone were to be asked to choose a single contribution for everyone in the community, they would all opt for the same contribution' (Sugden, 1984: 781). This is obviously a circumstance that the heterogeneity of preferences makes very unlikely.

As is evident from the above characterization of equilibrium, even when everybody in a 'society' abides by the reciprocity principle, the Pareto-efficient equilibrium is almost impossible as soon as there is some heterogeneity (in the sense of segmentation) in this 'society'. In the words of Sugden: 'the more homogeneous a community is in respect of incomes and tastes, the more closely it can approach Pareto efficiency, and the greater will be its success in producing public good through voluntary activities. . . . People in heterogeneous communities may be just as willing to meet their moral obligations to one another as people in homogeneous ones, and yet the heterogeneous communities may still be less capable of supplying public goods through voluntary co-operation' (Sugden, 1984: 783).

6.2 Norms as Social Devices Shaping Preferences and Expectations*

Norms and co-operation

In Chapter 5, we have described a number of unfortunate situations in which co-operation does not get established or is not sustainable even though there are agents who would like to co-operate in the group. In particular, situations can arise in which people who are relatively strongly interested in co-operation start by co-operating but thereafter defect when they realize that there are not enough people around to join them. Or, they may continue to co-operate but other agents who are less interested in co-operation or are free-riders do not participate in the collective action. Now, it may be argued that collective actions are more likely to be successful if:

1. there are more agents with an AG pay-off structure in the group, and less of them with a PD structure;
2. the interest in co-operation among AG players is greater to start with;
3. the interest in co-operation increases among AG players with a comparatively low initial interest or even among PD players as they are subject to guilt feelings when they have repeatedly defected while a significant proportion of members in the group have actually co-operated;
4. agents with an interest in co-operation are vengeful enough to be ready to sanction free-riding even though this activity does not bring them any direct reward;
5. co-operation-inclined people are not easily discouraged by bad experiences while they are easily comforted by good ones: in other words, their expectations are asymmetric, being rather rigid with respect to bad experiences and highly flexible with respect to good experiences;
6. the members of the group, even if they are all PD players interacting continuously, have stronger expectations and more trust in the others' predisposition to act co-operatively or to choose a brave reciprocity strategy.

The following discussion is based on the idea that the fulfilment of the aforementioned conditions largely depends on the prevalence of moral norms in the society.

* This section is largely inspired by Platteau (1994).

This is because moral norms have several positive effects. They structure individual expectations and foster mutual trust thanks to the development of group identity. They also modify the preferences or the pay-off structures of the agents. This should not be taken to mean that norms necessarily transform individual preferences in the framework of a *particular* CPR problem. Indeed, especially when groups are relatively small, moral norms, by articulating the society together, may have the effect of connecting various situations in which the same individuals interact. As a result, actors do not view a given CPR problem in isolation of other collective action domains. They instead tend to consider them as various parts of the 'total' situation of the group to which they belong. In this 'total' situation, individual contributions must be roughly in balance, lest the stability or the survival of the group should be threatened. Viewed in this light, *the main role of moral norms is that it leads people to perceive the 'game' of social life as a kind of generalized assurance game*: by contributing to a particular public good, an individual manifests his willingness to share the life of the group and his understanding that everyone has to participate at some level in collective efforts to make the group viable.

On the other hand, an important possibility is that, under the pressure of emotions, moral agents may act without calculating whether their decision is optimal for them. In other words, they are no more rational agents in the sense of economic theory. True, emotional reactions can easily be interpreted as deliberate choices by a rational agent, provided that his utility function is redefined so as also to integrate emotional rewards and moral judgements in its arguments. Norms would then fit into the orthodox framework of economic theory. We do not, however, follow this approach here and, for reasons which will become clearer in the discussion, we instead argue that such an approach conceals too many important aspects of the issue at hand to be considered fruitful.

Norms as internalized rules of conduct

Norms are expectations about one's own action and/or that of others which express what action is right or what action is wrong (Coleman, 1987: 135). The concept suggests a standard of conduct which people believe they ought to follow lest they should expose themselves to some form of sanctioning or to some unpleasant experience. Obedience to the norm will occur when the sanctions or discomfort are sufficiently great and sufficiently certain to make disobedience less immediately attractive than obedience (ibid. 141–2). For patterns of behaviour to be sustained by norms, a society (and the underlying social consensus) must therefore exist to impose sanctions on norm violators. This can be done through a central agency acting as an external norm-enforcer, through agents inflicting sanctions upon one another in a decentralized manner, or via a self-policing mechanism. None the less, the first two solutions are fraught with serious problems. As far as the first one is concerned, it must be stressed that central monitoring can prove extremely costly because the central agency must collect a lot of information to avoid making errors in imposing punishments. As James Buchanan emphasized, life in society would be extremely costly and difficult if a great many aspects of social intercourse were not organized anarchistically (Buchanan, 1975: 118; see also Shott, 1979: 1329).

The practicability of the second solution is obviously much greater in small groups where interactions among individuals are somewhat close and continuous (and where reputation loss is an effective threat) than in many-person settings where relationships are largely anonymous and where private sanctioning activities are certain to bring no future reward to the punishing agent. Therefore, the third solution is all the more relevant as a practicable way of solving collective action problems in large groups. A self-policing mechanism obtains when external monitoring and sanctioning devices (whether formal or informal) can be actually dispensed with. *Moral* norms, understood as rules that are at least partly internalized by the agents (thereby forming, in Freudian terms, their *super ego*) and prompt them to take others' interests into account, provide such a mechanism.[1]

Internalization of standards may be said to arise when an individual actually conforms because of a personal attitude about the act itself, that is, when conformity becomes a motive of its own because it is *intrinsically* rewarding or because deviation is *intrinsically* costly (Weber, 1971: 22–3; Opp, 1979: 777, 792; 1982: 146; Jones, 1984: 89; Taylor, 1987: 13). Hence 'internalization refers to the aspect of the process of socialization through which attitudes, values, and behaviour patterns come to be maintained even in the absence of external rewards or punishments' (Jones, 1984: 89–90; see also Aronfreed, 1968, 1969, 1970: 104; Bergsten, 1985: 115). As a result, moral norms are followed even when violation would be undetected, and therefore unsanctioned, because the moral act—which appears to be in conflict with the immediate or direct interests of the actor himself—is valued for its own sake (Griffith and Goldfarb, 1988: 22; Elster, 1989*a*: 131; 1989*b*: 104).[2]

Now, an important lesson from developmental psychology is that moral behaviour and the ability to empathize emerge hand-in-hand with the maturation of specific emotional competencies.[3] In this maturation process, identification obviously plays a crucial role since a failure to follow the standards set (consciously or not) by reference persons is bound to generate the painful feeling that one is unable to meet their

[1] A person may be considered to face a moral decision whenever the welfare of one or several other persons potentially depends upon his actions (Schwartz, 1970: 128).

[2] Our approach to moral norms is thus radically different from the rational choice approach adopted by Vanberg. For him, indeed, if moral norms help solve PD problems, they are used strategically by the actors. More precisely, if people stick to such norms, it is only because it is difficult to identify situations in which it would not be detrimental to violate them (which happens when violation is undetected) or because of the risk of misidentifying such situations. Given imperfect information, moral routines are therefore rational and morality can be viewed as an 'efficient behavioral technology' (Vanberg, 1988: 3, 21–30). Quite revealingly, Vanberg has dismissed the true role of emotions in the process of internalization of moral norms, thereby negating the genuine nature of this process. Thus, he writes that 'internal sanctions cannot be considered an autonomous, independent source of moral enforcement. They are a source that ultimately derives from, and ultimately remains dependent on, the direct or indirect experience of external enforcement' (ibid. 31). For a general critique of the view that norms are merely *ex post* rationalizations of self-interest, see Elster, 1989*a*: 125–51; 1989*b*.

[3] In psychology, empathy denotes 'an individual's affective experience when it is elicited by social cues which transmit information about the corresponding affective experience of another person' (Aronfreed, 1970: 107). It refers to 'vicarious emotional experience' (Shott, 1979: 1328). As initially pointed out by

expectations and, thereby, to deserve their love or respect. Thus, the principal claim of Kagan (1984) is that moral norms are actually supported by a limited number of simple, highly uniform emotional capacities. According to him, the main motivating force behind moral behaviour is the desire to avoid feelings of guilt and shame which are themselves the combined outcome of unpleasant emotions (anxiety, empathy, responsibility, fatigue/ennui, uncertainty).[4] 'Bad' or unpleasant feelings stirred by violations of the prevailing moral norms are the ingredients of a 'tortured conscience' which tend to deter many people from breaking these norms. Such deterrence would not occur if violating norms was just felt as a mistake or a lapse from rationality (Elster, 1989*a*: 188). In addition, as found in numerous experiments, subjects induced to commit some transgression (or to believe that they have transgressed) are more likely than non-transgressors to engage in altruistic or compensatory behaviour. This is apparently because they are eager to repair their self-image so as to convince themselves as well as others of their moral worthiness (see Shott, 1979: 1327).

It is noteworthy that, in the above scheme of analysis, emotions or passions have a positive role to play in society. This is at variance with the position adopted by Adam Smith in *The Theory of Moral Sentiments*: there, we are told that passions (fear and anger on the one hand, and 'the love of ease, of pleasure, of applause, and of many other selfish gratifications' on the other hand) are so many drives that are apt to mislead man into mischievous actions while their control enables him 'upon all occasions to act according to the dictates of prudence, of justice, and of proper benevolence' (Smith, 1759: pt. VI, sect. III, 238). What Smith appears to believe is that, when man reasons coldly, he can think of the long-term or of the social consequences of his behaviour (at least if he is a 'wise' man) while, on the contrary, when he is given to the urgent drives of passions, he is unable to see beyond his immediate short-term interests and he may thus be sometimes seduced 'to violate all the rules which he himself, in all his sober and cool hours, approves of' (ibid. 237). What we argue instead, following a line suggested by Frank (1988), is just the opposite: emotions are susceptible of leading people, almost unconsciously, to overcome the temptation to give in to short-term considerations and to therefore act in accordance with their long-term interests.

From the above discussion, it is evident that inculcation of moral norms involves much more than purely cognitive learning. This is particularly true of primary socialization which an individual undergoes in childhood since it takes place in circumstances that are highly charged emotionally (Berger and Luckmann, 1967: 149–57). Note carefully that primary socialization (henceforth called PS) creates in the child's consciousness a progressive abstraction from the roles and attitudes of *concrete*

Adam Smith (1759), empathy (called sympathy) can be of two sorts according to whether one's emotion arises from the emotion one observes in another (it thus consists of feeling the emotion *the other person* feels) or from the emotion one would feel in another's situation (Shott, ibid.). In fact, the concept was defined for the first time by David Hume (1740). See below, for more precise references.

[4] 'When a person knows he is responsible for an action that harms others but no one else knows it, he feels guilt. If others do know, he feels both guilt and shame. If others wrongly believe he has harmed another, he feels only shame' (Frank, 1988: 153). The reader will find a good summary account of Kagan's theory in ch. 8 of the book of Robert Frank.

significant others (usually the parents) to roles and attitudes *in general*, implying that the child becomes able to identify 'with a generality of others, that is, with a society' (ibid. 152–3). This is an important aspect in so far as any moral rule includes an element of conceptual generality that involves the capacity to recognize the claims of others and to impose such rules both on oneself and on others similarly situated (Griffith and Goldfarb, 1988: 22–3). Moreover, since it is rooted in the idea that there exists a community of people linked by solidarity ties, a strong moral attitude is generally associated with the belief that most others are also behaving morally, *although the attitude itself is not formulated in conditional terms.*[5]

Now, it bears emphasis that the ability to put others on a similar footing with oneself can apply to groups of varying size. Generally, *limited-group morality* is understood as morals restricted to concrete people with whom one has a close identification while *generalized morality* is morals applicable to abstract people (to whom one is not necessarily tied through personal family or ethnic links) (see, e.g. Granovetter, 1985). The first concept clearly involves personal loyalty feelings. By contrast, generalized morality implies the ability to recognize the claim of a large *generality* of others and to identify oneself with a society of abstract individuals (refer to Weber's distinction between *Gemeinschaft* and *Gesellschaft*). This ability is clearly present in the ethical principle according to which we ought not to do to other people what we would not like them to do to us; or in the Kantian generalization principle according to which one ought to abstain from any action that would threaten to disrupt social order were everybody to undertake it or that one would not be prepared to see everyone else adopt (an action is morally possible only if it can be universalized without self-contradiction).

It would be wrong to assume that, once they have been properly internalized, moral norms are completely compelling with the result that decision outcomes are mechanically determined. In the words of Dasgupta, an individual's upbringing 'ensures that he has a disposition to obey the norm. When he does violate it, neither guilt nor shame is typically absent, but the act will have been rationalized by him' (Dasgupta, 1993: 209). As has been aptly noted by Elster, moral beings are usually outcome-insensitive with respect to benefits but not with respect to costs: the costs of co-operation may be so high as to offset the call of duty. Furthermore, they are somewhat sensitive to benefits in the following sense: if they do not consider the likely impact of their *own* co-operation, they pay attention to the impact of universal co-operation. It is plausible, Elster argues, that the strength of their feelings of duty depends on the difference between universal co-operation and universal non-co-operation: 'The smaller the difference, the lower the voice of conscience and the more likely it is to be offset by considerations of cost' (Elster, 1989*a*: 193).

Regarding the stronger propensity to co-operate in small groups (see Olson, 1965), we are now able to add the following point: in so far as moral norms arise more easily

[5] This statement differs from that made by some authors who consider that a strong moral attitude may be *caused* by the belief that few others are cheating: the citizen adopts a moral attitude of unconditional compliance if and only if he believes that most others comply, so that 'the behaviour of others is the cause of his moral stance, not an element of it' (Elster, 1989*a*: 213–14).

in small than in large groups and tend to represent the collectively rational outcome as morally desirable—norms of limited morality are easier to come by than those of generalized morality—co-operation is more likely to emerge and to be sustained in the former than in the latter. Why is it that moral norms are likely to arise more easily in small than in large groups? According to Homans (1950), repeated interactions among people give rise to 'friendliness' and the associated feelings tend to prompt them to establish informal codes of 'good' behaviour and to assign positive utility to compliance.

The need for reinforcement processes

We have seen above that primary socialization plays a crucial role in the norm-generation process. Nevertheless, moral norms are subject to erosion: they form a 'social capital' (Coleman, 1988) liable to depreciation, especially so if norm-abiding individuals come to realize that many people around them behave opportunistically. They therefore need more or less continuous reinforcement to be maintained. One such kind of reinforcement consists of what Berger and Luckmann have called secondary socialization. Secondary socialization is 'the acquisition of role-specific knowledge, the roles being directly or indirectly rooted in the division of labour' (Berger and Luckmann, 1966: 158). Contrary to primary socialization which cannot take place without an emotionally charged identification of the child with his significant others, most secondary socialization 'can dispense with this kind of identification and proceed effectively with only the amount of mutual identification that enters into any communication between human beings' (it is necessary to love one's mother, but not one's teacher).

In primary socialization, the child does not apprehend his significant others as institutional functionaries, but as mediators of the only conceivable reality: in other words, he internalizes the world of his parents not as one of many possible worlds, not as the world appertaining to a specific institutional context, but as *the* world *tout court* (Luckmann, 1966: 154, 161). This explains why the world internalized in primary socialization is 'so much more firmly entrenched in consciousness than worlds internalised in secondary socializations'. As a matter of fact, since the main function of secondary socialization is to transmit specific knowledge (in schools, in factories, etc.), the social interaction between teachers and learners can be formalized and the former are in principle interchangeable (ibid. 154, 162).

Note that reinforcement of moral norms is particularly effective when church attendance ensures that people are continuously exposed to a moral discourse which repeatedly emphasizes the same values as they were taught by their primary socialization agents during childhood. The Church (both Catholic and Protestant) obviously played a central role in the process of moral-norm generation and maintenance throughout modern Western history. Its impact was all the more significant as (1) it promised a considerable reward (an eternal life of absolute happiness) for all those who were ready to incur personal sacrifices by behaving in other-regarding ways; and

(2) monitoring costs could be brought to a minimum in so far as God was thought to act as an impartial and free-monitoring agent. In the words of Frank:

> Teaching moral values was once the nearly exclusive province of organised religion. The church was uniquely well equipped to perform this task because it had a ready answer to the question. 'Why shouldn't I cheat when no one is looking?' Indeed, for the religious person, this question does not even arise, for God is *always* looking. (Frank, 1988: 250)

Moral-norm reinforcement must also come from the State or the rulers. As noted by Kenneth Arrow, 'it is not adequate to argue that there are enforcement mechanisms, such as police and the courts; . . . it has to be asked why they will in fact do what they have contracted to do' (Arrow, 1973: 24, quoted from Williamson, 1985: 405). In actual fact, morality and a high sense of public purpose among the rulers are important not only because they ensure that rules will be properly enforced but also because of the positive demonstration effect exercised by leaders with whom people have perhaps come to strongly identify. Indeed, other-regarding norms are more easily followed by the people when they can observe a broad consistency between those culture-determined norms and the actual behaviour displayed by the élite in everyday life.

Morality and legitimacy

In deciding how to act, people do not look only at the way their leaders behave but they also assess the degree of legitimacy of rules and institutions. As emphasized by Tyler (1990), compliance with a rule is indeed strongly influenced by the extent to which individuals think that the rule and the enforcing agency are legitimate. The idea is that people are more willing to comply when they perceive the rule and the enforcing agency as appropriate and consistent with their internalized norms of fairness. In the words of Sutinen and Kuperan, 'legitimacy depends in large part on the authority's ability to provide favourable outcomes. That is, people perceive as legitimate and obey the institutions that produce positive outcomes for them. However, there is considerable evidence that people place great importance on procedural issues' (Sutinen and Kuperan, 1994: 14). Tyler has actually demonstrated that the people he studied abide more by the law if the procedures employed by the legal or political authority are deemed to be fair (Tyler, 1990). This implies, in particular, that rule violators are not only treated in acceptable ways (an outcome-related criterion), but also that they are effectively detected and consistently prosecuted. For instance, people may wish that freeriders are being punished, but they may not agree to have them thrown into jail at the first (minor) offence.

The relationship between morality and legitimacy is more complex still. As a matter of fact, that rules and procedures ought to be in conformity with cultural patterns and moral norms is only part of the picture. The other way round, it is also true that social perceptions of what are legitimate behaviours are *partly* influenced by the legality of the matter (see Kaufmann, 1970). In other words, when they are embodied in laws, rules can influence these cultural patterns and moral norms: they may thus shape people's sense of duty and what is right. Of course, for legal rules to be effective, it is important that the political élites follow them scrupulously. For example, in fisheries management, when government and industry leaders disparage management measures, 'the fishing community's sense of obligation to the management program is weakened, leading to more noncompliance' (Sutinen, Rieser, and Gauvin, 1990: 342).

In a pioneering attempt, Kuperan and Sutinen have tried to explain actual behaviour of compliance with management rules in fisheries not only as a function of deterrence variables (probability of detection of violators, severity of the sanctions imposed, etc.) but also through variables that capture the effect of moral obligation and the impact of legitimacy (Kuperan and Sutinen, 1994). They conclude, in an econometric study measuring the determinants of compliance with zoning regulations in Malaysian fisheries, that the latter variables have a significant effect. Nevertheless, their results are to be treated with caution in so far as the different effects which we have highlighted above are not clearly distinguished in their estimates. In particular, their index of moral development is constructed in such a way that it can be interpreted as an index of law-abidingness. There is admittedly no easy way to disentangle empirically the various relationships between law-abidingness, morality, and legitimacy.

Conclusion

To summarize, the prevalence of moral norms in a society tends to favour the emergence of co-operation through better realization of the conditions (1)–(6) stated above. Thus, when such norms are well established and effectively sustained through appropriate secondary socialization processes, people tend (*a*) to adopt the others' viewpoint when making decisions that may harm others' interests and to feel internally rewarded when behaving in other-regarding ways; (*b*) to be confident that others will abide by the same code of good behaviour as themselves; (*c*) to cling to this code even when they had unpleasant experiences in which they were 'suckers'; (*d*) to feel guilty after they have (perhaps mistakenly) deviated from the moral rule; and (*e*) to feel vengeful and willing to punish detectable free–riders (and perhaps also people who refuse to do so and continue to entertain good relations with the freeriders).

The fact that moral norms are typically inculcated in early childhood when they are strongly associated with the maturation of specific emotional competencies is important with respect to almost all the aforementioned points. In particular, this fact helps resolve the problem of punishment incentive (Elster, 1989*b*: 41; Taylor, 1987: 30): what incentives individuals have to monitor and sanction defectors when these activities are clearly public goods involving a new, second-order free–rider problem. In effect, such a problem may vanish as soon as one assumes, in the tradition of Smith's *Theory of the Moral Sentiments* (1759) that rational assessment is merely one of many inputs into the psychological reward mechanism and 'rational calculations often lose out to other, more basic forms of reinforcement' (Frank, 1988: 197). Thus, vengefulness is an *emotion* that may easily drive persons to punish defectors even at a significant positive (short-term) cost to themselves, particularly so if they are deeply (morally) shocked. Emotions can indeed be viewed as commitment devices which have the effect of breaking the tight link between utility-yielding goals and the choice of action (Sen, 1985; Frank, 1988).

It is also useful to recall that the monitoring problem does not even arise if moral rules are backed by religious beliefs according to which God knows everything about all our actions (and thoughts). In these circumstances, co-operation can be sustained even in the presence of high costs of fraud detection since a free-monitoring device is actually available. It may be further noted that, in so far as religious beliefs imply the hope that eternal life (or a better future life) will be accorded to all righteous people, the latter not only tend to feel guilty when they defect (especially so if others co-operate), but also they are not easily discouraged by bad experiences. In other words, believers continue to adhere to the moral code (co-operate) even though they have possibly been 'suckers' on repeated occasions. By continuing to behave morally despite unpleasant experiences, they may even be convinced that they deserve special attention from God.[6] When such religious beliefs do not exist or are not shared by a significant majority of people, it is all the more important that moral norms should be regularly reinforced by other agents of secondary socialization or by role models (such as political leaders) lest they should gradually erode leading to a vicious circle of unravelling co-operation.

6.3 Considerations about the Emergence and Erosion of Moral Norms

It has been argued that moral norms have a decisive role to play in establishing and sustaining co-operation in large groups. These norms fulfil the function of imposing ' "impartial" constraints on the pursuit of individual interests, constraints which are socially desirable in serving interests that individuals share as members of a social community' (Vanberg, 1988: 3). Now, to have a theory of norms, we should know how they arise, how they are maintained, how they change over time (how they vanish and how they are displaced by other norms), and whether and how they can be manipulated, all questions which are essentially unanswered to this date. Clearly, these are questions of considerable complexity and around which there are likely to be enduring debate and heated controversies for a long time to come. Depending on the type of answer provided, different approaches will be suggested to central problems such as the one raised in this chapter.

Emergence of moral norms

Insights from eighteenth-century philosophy

The enormous stake involved in the choice of approach to the dynamics of norms can be illustrated by considering the issue of norm emergence. Two radically opposite

[6] There is an obvious analogy between this argument and that put forward by Kant according to which ingratitude can stimulate giving, because the benefactor 'may well be convinced that the very disdain of any such reward as gratitude only adds to the moral worth of his benefaction' (Schoeck, 1987: 204, quoted from Elster, 1989*a*: 259).

views are possible. The first of these views is profoundly optimistic and is grounded in the well-known evolutionary approach to institutional change. In a pioneer attempt made over two centuries ago, David Hume proposed a remarkably articulate formulation of the evolutionary theory when he tried to explain the process of emergence of social order in a market economy.

Hume actually believed that public good cannot be established unless individuals are driven not only by selfish passions but also by a 'moral sense' (a view inherited from Hutcheson). Yet moral behaviour depends upon rational considerations and, in an age of cultural and scientific progress, individuals cannot fail to see the necessity for private property, law, and government. Far from contributing to corruption and degeneracy, the development of 'commercial society' can be expected to pave the way for morality, justice, and good government in so far as it goes hand in hand with moral and political progress (McNally, 1988: 167–8). At this point, Hume's ideas as contained in his *Treatise of Human Nature* (1740) deserve to be detailed more fully. This is done below by quoting at some length the paraphrasing description recently proposed by McNally:

> In the *Treatise* Hume accepts that self-love is the origin of law and government. Nevertheless, since 'the self-love of one person is naturally contrary to that of another', competing and conflicting self-interested passions must 'adjust themselves after such a manner as to concur in some system of conduct and behaviour'. After individuals discover that unbridled selfishness incapacitates them for society, 'they are naturally induc'd to lay themselves under the restraint of such rules, as may render their commerce more safe and commodious'. As rules of social regulation are developed, they become customary and are passed on to future generations. Eventually people come to cherish the rules which hold society together. They develop a sense of *sympathy* for those who observe social norms. Moreover, they come to model their behaviour in such a way as to be worthy of the sympathy and approval of others. Through custom and education, then, individuals develop a love of praise and a fear of blame. For Hume, moral principles are not innate or providentially inspired. They are practical rules developed in the course of living in society; morality refers to the norms and conventions which prevail there. These norms and conventions can be said to enter into the commonsense view of the world most individuals acquire . . . [Sympathy] is a capacity derived from experience and modified as the customary rules of social life change. Sympathy has a rational dimension; it derives from the individual's understanding of the necessity for norms of conduct and behaviour. Thus, although 'self-interest is the original motive to the establishment of justice', as society develops it becomes the case that 'a sympathy with public interest is the source of the moral approbation, which attends that virtue' (McNally, 1988: 168–9)

For Hume, property, law, and government are therefore the outcome of the evolution of human society.[7] Through the experience derived from their mutual interac-

[7] The following excerpt from Hume's *Treatise* shows how much articulate his evolutionary argument was: 'and when each individual perceives the same sense of interest in all his fellows, he immediately performs his part of any contract, as being assur'd that they will not be wanting in theirs. All of them, by concert, enter into a scheme of actions, calculated for common benefit, and agree to be true to their words; nor is there anything requisite to form this concert or convention, but that every one have a sense of interest in the faithful fulfilling of engagements, and express that sense to other members of the society. This immediately causes that interest to operate upon them; and interest is the *first* obligation to the performance of promises. Afterwards a sentiment of morals concurs with interest, and becomes a new obligation upon mankind' (Hume, 1740: Bk. III, pt. II, sect. V, 522–3).

tions in the (nascent) market economy, individuals come to see the necessity of, and to accept the constraints imposed by, those institutions and conventions which preserve the social order. Men 'cannot change their natures. All they can do is to change their situation' and 'lay themselves under the necessity of observing the laws of justice and equity, notwithstanding their violent propensity to prefer contiguous [short-term] to remote [gains]' (Hume, 1740: Bk. III, pt. II, sect. VII, 537). 'Public utility' becomes the basis of moral decision and, as Hume put it in his *Enquiry Concerning the Principles of Morals*, 'everything which contributes to the happiness of society recommends itself directly to our approbation and good will' (quoted from McNally, 1988: 169). That moral norms serve not only to shape individual preferences but also to structure individual expectations did not escape Hume's attention. As attested by the following excerpt, norms can serve as an assurance device: 'this experience assures us still more, that the sense of interest has become common to all our fellows, and gives us a confidence of the future regularity of their conduct: And 'tis only on the expectation of this, that our moderation and abstinence are founded' (Hume, 1740: Bk. III, pt. II, sect. II, 490). It may be further noted that Hume's analysis allows for internalized norms in so far as he holds that social rules are passed on to successive generations through education and customs.

Applied to the problem of CPR management, the position of Hume can be stated thus: through experience, individuals progressively realize that, in order to avoid being trapped in PD-structured situations, they have a long-term interest not only in laying down rules and building up rule-enforcing agencies but also in *spontaneously* submitting themselves to the rules or norms thereby established (with the result that enforcement costs will be reduced to a minimum). This may hold true at any level. At the level of the State, for example, individuals will spontaneously help to create and then support the laws and enforcing machinery required to ensure a sustainable development of the CPR which cannot be effectively managed without at least some degree of state intervention. Supporting behaviour is supposed naturally to arise from the people's abiding respect for all legal rules which they have contributed to establish.

The same willingness to lay down, and to comply with, socially desirable rules manifests itself in the context of large—or small—group settings whose members are concerned with the management of a given CPR. As all or most people gradually come to have a full understanding of their long-term interest and of the need to co-operate towards promoting these interests, they are again ready to participate in the necessary collective actions and to constrain their own behaviours so as to make this co-operation a sustainable venture over time. It is noteworthy that Hume appears to have explicitly assumed that people have a preference structure resembling that of an AG, which explains why co-operation may be possible even in a large-group setting.

In a radically opposed and much less optimistic view than the one expressed by Hume, moral norms appear not as something which may gradually and unconsciously evolve when the need arises, but as a precondition that must be established before any action requiring trust can take place. Thus, for example, Edmund Burke held the opinion that 'the expansion of commerce depended itself on the *prior* existence of "manners" and "civilisation" and on what he called "natural protecting principles" grounded in the ' "spirit of a gentleman" and "the spirit of religion"' (Hirschman, 1987: 160, referring to Burke, 1790: 115).

Adam Smith had a more ambivalent attitude even though, on the whole, he inclined to think in the way of his friend David Hume. That is, he essentially shared the doctrine which can be traced back to Montesquieu and which Hirschman has dubbed 'the Doux-commerce thesis' (Hirschman, 1977; 1982). According to Smith, for instance, the spread of commerce and industry enhances virtues such as industriousness, assiduity, frugality, punctuality, and probity (Rosenberg, 1964; Hirschman, 1982: 1465; Young, 1992: 80).[8] As is well known, in his *Theory of Moral Sentiments* (1759), Smith laid much stress on the fact that all individuals have a capacity for sympathy with others, that is, they are all able, by an act of imagination, to adopt the others' viewpoint and to understand their reactions (see, in particular, pt. III, ch. I; see also Hume, 1740: Bk. II, pt. II, sect. VII and pt. III, sect. VI). This capacity of sympathetic identification which enables actors to adopt the standpoint of an *impartial spectator* who observes situations of human interactions dispassionately is the fundamental basis of society: it supplies a system of cultural restraints in which moral checks upon the passion of self-love can be embedded (McNally, 1988: 182; Brown, 1988: 61–2, 67; Young, 1992: 73–7). Note that Smith actually believed that the capacity to sympathize was especially noticeable among those occupying 'the inferior and middling stations of life'. This is because, being obliged to be prudent, *they had to learn* that the pursuit of self-interest must be held within socially acceptable bounds (McNally, 1988: 186).

See from this angle, Smith shared the belief that

> a society where the market assumes a central position for the satisfaction of human wants will produce not only considerable new wealth because of the division of labour and consequent technical progress, but would generate as a by-product, or external economy, a more 'polished' human type—more honest, reliable, orderly, and disciplined, as well as more friendly and helpful, ever ready to find solutions to conflicts and a middle ground for opposed opinions. (Hirschman, 1982: 1465)

On the other hand, there is no doubt that Smith stressed the serious limitations of the self-regulating capacity of human societies. There is therefore a political task—the constitution and preservation of the moral basis of society—that should be undertaken by a select group of virtuous men capable of following the moral ideals of conscience and embodying the civic habits necessary to political stability (Hirschman, 1982: 192–208). In contrast to Hume, Smith believed that there are natural standards of human conduct which are not simply the result of human convention (Young, 1992: 76). For him, therefore, social order must be 'fabricated' within the body politic so as to lay down the rules and set up the institutions susceptible of directing self-centred econ-

[8] In the words of Smith, 'Nothing tends so much to corrupt mankind as dependency, while independency still increases the honesty of the people. The establishment of commerce and manufactures, which brings about this independency, is the best policy for preventing crimes' (cited from Young, 1992: 80).

omic appetites into socially desirable channels. Also worth noting is the fact that Smith stressed the role of the Church in producing and strengthening morality (Colclough, 1991).

Insights from game theory

There is a clear affiliation between most contemporary authors writing on the subject and either of the above two strands of eighteenth-century political thought. Thus, on the one hand, Hayek (1948, 1979)—for whom rules of good conduct emerge naturally and get reflected in evolving common law—neatly belongs to Hume's descent, like many other scholars more or less closely related to him, such as Nelson and Winter (1982), Gauthier (1986), Mueller (1986), Ellickson (1991), McKinnon (1992), and Murrell (1992). Perhaps closest to Hume is the philosopher Gauthier who asserts that an individual 'reasoning from nonmoral premises would accept the constraints of morality on his choices' (Gauthier, 1986: 5).[9] On the other hand, the sociologist Talcott Parsons—for whom a society is 'prior to and regulates utilitarian contracts between individuals' (Mayhew, 1984: 1289)—and the economist Field (Field, 1981: 193; see also 1984)—have their thinking anchored in the other realm where no spontaneous order exists. As we have shown above, game theory offers some insights into the question of the emergence of rules or norms of co-operation. A well-known group of them have adopted the (Hayekian) evolutionary perspective according to which rules and (moral) beliefs of a free society are the unintended outcome of a process of evolution occurring in the absence of any conscious human design. Thus, for Sugden, the conventions, or established patterns of behaviour, which create order in a market society are supported by moral beliefs (people believe that they ought to keep to these conventions). Yet 'there is no independent principle of justice that provides a rational basis for these beliefs' because 'the belief that one ought to follow a convention is the product of the same process of evolution as the convention itself' (Sugden, 1989: 87; see also Schotter, 1981, 1983, 1986). Trust would thus come out, as it were naturally, everyone having understood that all have an interest in behaving honestly and being thereby led to expect that they will actually behave so.

As has already been argued in Chapter 4, there are nevertheless serious limitations and difficulties with the kinds of proofs adduced in support of the hypothesis that evolutionary processes are at work to produce conventions, rules, and (moral) norms conducive to co-operative outcomes. As a matter of fact, the most intriguing result of game theory is that many different outcomes can be sustained as equilibria by rational actors. The question as to how a particular equilibrium becomes selected is therefore at the heart of the game theorists' research programme. The problem is really complex, and some outstanding authors actually believe that: 'What evolution produces will largely be a matter of historical accident' (Binmore, 1992: 434). The path-dependence approach also stresses the point that culture and history matter (see, e.g.,

[9] Janos, a political scientist, also implicitly adheres to Hume's approach when he writes that, in the historical experiences of the West, 'the market economy served as a school for impersonal modes of conduct that are indispensable for the effective functioning of complex societies and large-scale polities' (Janos, 1982: 314).

Brian Arthur, 1988; David, 1988, 1992*a*, 1992*b*; North, 1990). The underlying idea is that 'the process by which we arrive at today's institutions is relevant and constrains future choices' (North, 1990: 93; see also Matthews, 1986: 915; Basu *et al.*, 1987: 13). Rather than being 'a story of inevitability in which the past neatly predicts the future', it is 'a way to narrow conceptually the choice set and link decision making through time' (North, 1990: 98–9). The source from which path dependence stems lies in increasing returns which comprise several self-reinforcing mechanisms: large initial set-up costs at the time of institutional innovation; learning effects; co-ordination effects (via contracts with other institutions or with the polity in complementary activities); and adaptive expectations which occur because increased prevalence of contracting based on a specific institution enhances beliefs of further prevalence (ibid. 94–5; see also Bardhan, 1989).

For Dasgupta, repeated games need some form of 'friction' to generate predictable outcomes, and a form of 'friction' is precisely provided by moral codes (there are certain things that are 'not done' although they are feasible) (Dasgupta, 1988: 70–1). These moral codes are left unexplained but could be interpreted as the product of a particular history or the ingredient of a particular culture. Gambetta draws attention to the same point when he insists that, in repeated PD games, the tit-for-tat strategy is inconceivable without at least some predisposition to trust:

> when the game has no history a cooperative first move is essential to set it on the right track, and *unconditional distrust could never be conceived as conducive to this*. . . . This problem may be circumvented by assuming the presence of uncertain beliefs and a random distribution which accommodates the probability of the right initial move being made and being 'correctly' interpreted. Yet there is no reason why the appropriate conditional beliefs should typically be the case, and the optimal move may be hard to come upon by accident (while we may not want to have to wait for it to come upon us). If it is true that humans are characterised by a lack of fine-tuning and a tendency to go to extremes, the assumption that trust will emerge naturally is singularly unjustified . . . tit-for-tat can be an equilibrium only if both players believe the other will abide by it, otherwise other equilibria are just as possible and self-confirming. To show that trust is really not at stake, Axelrod should have shown that whatever the initial move and the succession of further moves, the game tends to converge on tit-for-tat. What he does do is express a powerful set of reasons why, *under certain conditions*, . . . *a basic predisposition to trust can be perceived and adopted as a rational pursuit* even by moderately forward-looking egoists. (Gambetta, 1988*b*: 227–8, emphasis added)

At this stage, it is also useful to bear in mind the 'satisficing' model to strategy learning explored by Bendor *et al.* (1994) (see above, Chapter 4, sect. 2). Indeed, a noticeable feature of this model is its 'self-fulfilling' property: a human group with low initial aspirations due to, say, a disappointing experience in the past, will tend to reproduce the same outcome in the present and in the future. It must be remembered that the underlying behavioural assumptions involve a low degree of rationality in some well-defined sense.

Some game theorists believe that a rational basis can be given to explain the emergence of a particular norm understood as an established behavioural pattern. Most of their efforts, however, take place within the framework of repeated games of the co-ordination or of the chicken kinds (Lewis, 1969; Ullmann-Margalit, 1977; Schotter, 1981, 1983, 1986; Sugden, 1989).[10] These works are of interest because an AG can be considered as a co-ordination game largely defined. Indeed, co-ordination games are typically games in which there are several equilibria. Yet, while in pure co-ordination games (as defined by Lewis), players are more or less indifferent between these various equilibria, in co-ordination games *sensu lato*, such as the assurance game analysed in Chapter 5, the multiple equilibria are strictly Pareto-ranked. Now, a convention[11] can start to evolve as soon as some people believe that other people are following it, thereby providing a *focal or salient point*. The crucial question is of course what gives rise to this initial belief. One important possibility is that some forms of co-ordination are more prominent than others, and people have a prior expectation of finding the most prominent ones. But, as emphasized by Sugden, 'prominence is largely a matter of common experience' with the implication that 'conventions may spread by analogy from one context to another' and one should expect 'to find family relationships among conventions, and not just a chaos of arbitrary and unrelated rules' (Sugden, 1989: 93–4). In the words of North: 'Conventions are culture specific, as indeed are norms' (North, 1990: 42).

An interesting implication of Sugden's way of posing the co-ordination problem is the following: inasmuch as conventions arise in an evolutionary way through common experience, the culture of the people concerned matters a great deal and it is impossible to understand their rules without knowing their particular history. The focus is no more on universal truths or rationally deduced unique equilibrium institutions (as in classical game theory), but on rules that can *work* in a given cultural setting.[12] In fact, as stressed by Myerson, 'from a game-theoretic perspective, *cultural norms* can be defined to be the rules that a society uses to determine focal equilibria in game situations' (Myerson, 1991: 114).[13] Clearly, conventions or norms do not emerge spontaneously from the free interactions of independent non-socialized individuals. For a game to be played, actors must be in total agreement not only about the rules of the game but also about a way to interpret them unambiguously. While the former

[10] Co-ordination games describe situations in which the players' main concern is to co-ordinate their behaviour in some way, and in which their interests coincide but not in an a priori obvious way (Bianchi, 1990: 10). The important feature of a two-person chicken game is that there are two equilibria and in each of these one player co-operates while the other defects. For a description of the chicken game, see Taylor (1987: 35–49); Sugden (1989: 85).

[11] A convention is defined by Sugden as an *evolutionarily stable strategy* (ESS) in a game that has several ESS's (Sugden, 1989: 91).

[12] As a matter of fact, deductive equilibrium analysis does not explain the process by which decision-makers acquire equilibrium beliefs. It is both the strength and the limitation of the deductive equilibrium method that it is able to abstract from the complicated dynamic process that induces equilibrium and from the historical accident that initiated the process. On the contrary, inductive selection principles select equilibrium points based on the history of some pre-game, hence these principles are not independent of accident and process (Van Huyck *et al.*, 1990: 234–6).

[13] To quote Myerson again, the importance of culture emerges as soon as one deals with situations where there is a relatively large set of equilibria. The very necessity to refer to a focal-point effect reveals 'an essential limit on the ability of mathematical game theory to predict people's behavior in real conflict situations'. Clearly, 'game theory cannot provide a complete theory of human behavior without complementary theories from other disciplines', such as social psychology and cultural anthropology (Myerson, 1991: 113–14).

condition refers to the existence of a social fabric prior to the unfolding of the game, the latter condition points to the existence of a common cultural patrimony. To put it in another way, what evolve are essentially operational rules of conduct which are embedded in a society's set of 'fundamental constitutive rules' (Field, 1984: 702) or 'foundational entitlements' (Ellickson, 1991: 284), not themselves subject to spontaneous evolution.

Another feature of Sugden's analysis that deserves to be emphasized is that, since an inefficient convention may be more prominent than an efficient one, rules that emerge are not necessarily Pareto-efficient (Ellickson, 1991: 94). The evolution of norms can not be explained by the aggregate social benefits they engender (Elster, 1989*b*; Bowles and Gintis, 1993).[14] Further, if a less than efficient solution prevails, the shift to a more efficient one cannot happen spontaneously because of the presumably great stability of a convention (any violator stands to lose from not abiding by it). Bianchi has thus pointed out that some active intervention from an external agency may be needed to effect a shift from a less to a more efficient rule or convention (Bianchi, 1990: 11; in the same vein, see also Steuer, 1989). Note that experimental results confirm that the first-best outcome (the pay-off-dominant equilibrium) of a co-ordination game is an extremely unlikely outcome either initially or in repeated play (Cooper *et al.*, 1990; Van Huyck *et al.*, 1990).

The meaning of the above implications for the problem of trust is rather straightforward. In particular, one vexed issue is the question as to how one can expect trust to arise in a society that has a long experience of distrust (that is, in what eighteenth-century thinkers call a 'corrupt' society).[15] Assuming that many people aspire to co-operative conventions and just need to be reassured about others' preferences, an active intervention from an external agency (e.g. from the State) could apparently solve the problem as suggested by Bianchi. Things may not be so simple, however. Indeed, to succeed such a solution requires that people have enough trust in the external agency, and this will in turn depend on the historical experience of their relation with it and the way they have interpreted that experience.

A fascinating case illustrating the long-lasting influence of trust-destroying events is that of southern Italy which has been recently studied and contrasted with the

[14] It is perhaps puzzling to note that present-day sociologists who are interested in the topic of norms seem to be strongly influenced by the economic model. Thus, one of them observes that 'if one hopes to find an alternative to the economic theory of norm formation in the sociological and social psychological literature, one is disappointed . . . sociologists and also social psychologists, either explicitly or implicitly, propose that the emergence of norms depends on the costs and benefits which are associated with them' (Opp, 1982: 141). This certainly applies to the work of Opp himself who does not hesitate to use the self-interest paradigm in ways that many economists would actually disapprove (there is no room for moral norms in Opp's scheme of thought) (in the same vein, see Coleman, 1990). On the other hand, despite his willingness to escape the grip of the 'economic model', Etzioni (1988) has not really succeeded in articulating an alternative scheme of analysis.

[15] In a recent paper, Tirole has thus argued that the persistence of corruption in a society may partly be explained by the (bad) reputation of previous generations. More precisely, younger generations may inherit the reputation of their elders with the consequence that they have no incentive to be honest themselves even though they would perhaps like to behave honestly (Tirole, 1993). As pointed out by Seabright, this means that trust acts as a state variable whose value influences the probability of future co-operation (honesty) independently of the direct pay-offs associated with such co-operation (Seabright, 1993: 123).

altogether different historical trajectory of the northern part of the country (Banfield, 1958; Gambetta, 1988*a*; Putnam, 1993). In the Mezzogiorno, the language used by the people actually testifies to the deep-rooted tradition of distrust that is plainly traceable from early medieval times to today.[16] Thus, to be a sucker is known as *fesso*, an Italian term which also means 'cuckolded' (Putnam, 1993: 111–12). Proverbs likewise point to the pervasive culture of diffidence not just towards the outsider but also within the community, even in small villages. In Calabria, for example, there is the saying that '*chi ara diritto, muore disperato*' (he who behaves honestly comes to a miserable end). Other proverbs are: 'Damned is he who trusts another'; 'Don't make loans, don't give gifts, don't do good, for it will turn out bad for you'; 'Everyone thinks of his own good and cheats his companion'; 'When you see the house of your neighbour on fire, carry water to your own' (quoted from Putnam, 1993: 143–4). It is therefore not surprising that, as a result, southern Italy is permeated by 'defection, distrust, shirking, exploitation, isolation, disorder, and stagnation', all negative features that 'intensify one another in a suffocating miasma of vicious circles' (ibid. 177). The same 'culture of distrust' seems to permeate a society like the Philippines where, even within rural communities, people are bent upon cheating or free–riding upon one another for fear of being oneself the victim of others' opportunism. As a result, many social workers complain, collective action is very difficult to achieve at local level. Yet, when living abroad, Philippine workers are usually noticeable for their trustworthiness.

Erosion of moral norms

The problem of norm erosion is especially important: indeed, contrary to conventions that solve pure co-ordination problems, norms that overcome assurance problems are likely to be less stable since moral rules or preferences for co-operation may be subject to erosion. Recently, a number of scholars have drawn attention to the fact that the social capital constituted by a society of trustful and trustworthy individuals can be gradually 'eaten up' (Buchanan, 1975: 16; Hirsch, 1976; Bergsten, 1985; Mishan, 1986: chapter 8; Vanberg, 1988: 33; Bowles and Gintis, 1993). According to Hirsch, for example, social virtues such as 'truth, trust, acceptance, restraint, obligation' that are needed for the proper functioning of the market economy tend to be undermined by 'the individualistic and rationalistic base' of that system (Hirsch, 1976: 141–3). As for Bergsten, he believes, contrary to Durkheim (1893), that a high degree of division of labour contributes 'to reduce the shared experiences from which mutual understanding and tolerance stem' (Bergsten, 1985: 122). This may threaten the moral fabric of the market society by fragmenting the social space within which sympathetic interaction takes place.[17]

Adopting the same starting-point as Bergsten (the determining role of labour

[16] In those times an autocratic regime and vertical networks of patron–client bonds were established as a response to the violence and anarchy endemic in the whole of Europe. In northern Italy, by contrast, the solution invented was quite different, relying less on vertical hierarchy and more on horizontal collaboration networks that were to give rise to the famous communal republics (Putnam, 1993: ch. 5).

[17] For McNally, this doctrine can be traced back to Adam Smith himself (McNally, 1988: 188–9).

division), it is actually possible to construct another hypothesis that leads to an identical conclusion even though it treads a somewhat different route. Thus, with increasing division of labour and specialization of knowledge in the Western world, the family is more and more confined to the role of a consumption unit (Becker, 1981) and the secondary socialization that takes place under the auspices of specialized agencies tends to supersede the family with regard to this second phase of socialization (Berger and Luckmann, 1967: 166). Moreover, in so far as parents find themselves increasingly less able to devote enough time and energy to teaching moral values to their children—since both parents often work full-time outside their home or many children spend some portion of their childhood in single-parent homes—the intensity of the parent–child relationship is reduced, thereby making primary socialization less effective (Frank, 1988: 250). In addition, grandparents tend to live in distant places (Coleman, 1988: S111) and, if this is not the case, their interactions with their grandchildren are much less intense than they were before. Loss of primary socialization's effectiveness may also result (*a*) from reduced durability of family relationship (because members of the family are less indispensable to each other or are indispensable for a shorter period of time) and (*b*) from restricted family size (it is more difficult to teach other-regarding norms to single children than to children who continuously interact with brothers and sisters in what often turn out to be conflictual situations). Finally, to the extent that secondary socialization depends on the depth of primary socialization, it also tends to be affected (Berger and Luckmann, 1967: 160; Bergsten, 1985: 128). All these effects are likely to make the maintenance of moral norms more and more problematic. It is true that secondary socialization agencies (such as the school) might partly take over from the family the role of moral-norm supplier. Yet, unless high-powered ideological messages are diffused though their channels on a sustained basis, norm transmission will be considerably less effective than before. Indeed, as Etzioni has observed: 'Values that have lost their affective elements become empty shells, fragments of intellectual tracts or phrases to which people pay lip service but do not heed much in their choices' (Etzioni, 1988: 105).

There is another powerful reason to expect a gradual erosion of moral norms in market societies. The idea that capitalism's emphasis on self-interest tends gradually to erode the norms without which this system cannot function is part of an old doctrine (see Hirschman, 1982) to which twentieth-century economists have been sometimes attracted (Schumpeter, 1942; Mishan, 1986). This idea can be elaborated as follows. A central feature of recent evolution in capitalist societies may be seen as the rise of individualism, a phenomenon directly associated with the development of a materialist society based upon mass consumption. This development has been accompanied and promoted by active marketing policies that have largely succeeded in conveying the deceptive message that happiness or removal of pain can be achieved through *individual* consumption of *things* (goods and services). In the process, the problem of death and human suffering has been essentially obliterated by creating the illusion of man's immortality or eternal youth. This is an especially significant evolution for the following reason: when the inescapability of death and suffering is erased from people's conscience through their constant immersion in a ceaseless stream of consumption (market's ingenuity has actually succeeded in supplying powerful means of calming or suppressing pain and even grief), the need for a symbolic universe that legitimizes these painful experiments by explicit reference to an ever-living *community* of beings tends to disappear. In the words of Berger and Luckmann:

> A strategic legitimating function of symbolic universes for individual biography is the 'location' of death. . . . Whether it is done with or without recourse to mythological, religious or metaphysical interpretations of reality is not the essential question here. The modern atheist, for instance, who bestows meaning upon death in terms of a *Weltanschauung* of progressive evolution or of revolutionary history also does so by integrating death with a reality-spanning symbolic universe. All legitimations of death must carry out the same essential task—they must enable the individual to go on living in society after the death of significant others and to anticipate his own death with, at the very least, terror sufficiently mitigated so as not to paralyse the continued performance of the routines of everyday life. . . . The symbolic universe also orders history. It locates all collective events in a cohesive unity that includes past, present and future. . . . Thus the symbolic universe links men with their predecessors and their successors in a meaningful totality, *serving to transcend the finitude of individual existence* and bestowing meaning upon the individual's death. *All the members of a society can now conceive of themselves as belonging to a meaningful universe*, which was there before they were born and will be there after they die. (Berger and Luckmann, 1966: 118–21, emphasis added)

Thus, when people are exclusively concerned with enjoying their present life and preoccupied with suppressing any pain or grief that may befall them, they do not feel any more the need to belong to a totality that transcends them and imparts a meaning to their life and sufferings. Now, it is precisely the belief that they belong to such an entity that breeds sympathetic feelings in human beings and drives them to take the situation of others into account when they make their behavioural choices. We may therefore expect morality to gradually fall into decay and the role of religion to be correspondingly reduced as the market proves increasingly able to create the illusion that it can fill up man's deep existential wants (under the deceiving appearances of ever-changing artefacts).[18] The outcome of this evolution is the pervasive influence of what has been called a 'doctrine of self-preoccupation', that is, a doctrine that urges 'the individual to search for self-actualisation, i.e. to pursue his self interests with little regard for the wishes and opinions of other persons' (Berkowitz, 1970: 149; see also Hirsch, 1976: 141–3 and ch. 11). The problem is actually compounded by the fact that mass communication media that are largely responsible for the propagation of indi-

[18] In a recent article, Vaclav Havel, the present president of Czechoslovakia, laments on the pervasive presence of fraud and deceit which has characterized his country since its 'freeing' from totalitarianism. To save the country from potential chaos, he calls for a revival of a sense of 'superior responsibility' that would take into account the interests of the community and of the future generations. According to him, this 'superior responsibility' springs from the certainty that nothing ends up with our individual death 'because everything survives us somewhere above us', in what he calls the 'memory of the being', that is, 'in this part inseparable from the mysterious order of the cosmos, nature and life, which believers call God, and to whose judgement everything is subject'. In other words, 'authentic conscience and genuine responsibility are always the eventual reflection of the implicit postulate according to which we are observed "from above" where everything is considered and nothing forgotten' (Havel, 1991). A possible interpretation of the above solution to the freerider problem is that people obey moral norms when they imagine that sanctions will be inflicted upon them from some transcendental deity were they to violate them (see e.g. Vanberg, 1988: 4).

vidualistic consumption-centred values in contemporary market societies have come to play such an important role in the shaping of people's preferences and aspirations. The function of the family as a supplier of moral norms is therefore eroded on a double ground. On the one hand, the intensity of the parent–child relationship is reduced due to constant interference of media messages: in this case, instead of being reinforced, primary socialization is actually weakened by secondary socialization processes. On the other hand, the parents themselves are exposed to the new materialistic values so that primary socialization is itself being transformed in the sense that it increasingly neglects the teaching of other-regarding norms.

To adopt norm-guided behaviour, an individual should first recognize the dependence of others on him by becoming aware that his (potential) action has consequences for them. He must then have knowledge of the relevant moral norms and, finally, he must ascribe some responsibility to himself for the action. At each of these steps moral norms may be prevented from influencing his behaviour (Schwartz, 1970: 132).[19] Unfortunately, the effect of the above-described changes is precisely to make each of these three conditions increasingly hard to meet: individuals are less and less concerned with what happens to their fellow citizens (or the society at large) when they behave in a certain way; they are little interested in norms or standards of behaviour that set constraints on their 'freedom' (the ideology of the 'free' society has worked beyond expectation); and they tend to shift responsibilities to other potential actors, on the system as a whole, on chance factors, etc.

The foregoing discussion thus suggests a working hypothesis that is quite in line with the dialectic approach followed by Marx and Schumpeter (the Schumpeter of *Capitalism, Socialism, and Democracy*) to analyse the evolution of market societies. More specifically, capitalist development being based upon a high degree of division of labour and upon continuous processes of competitive innovation that call for ever-avid consumers, it tends to cause a gradual erosion of the moral norms on which the effective functioning of a market economy rests. Such a situation may lead to a state of things where a growing number of problems which the capitalist civilization itself creates or increases (in particular, the destruction of the ecological patrimony) are left unattended. As a consequence, not only the people's quality of life may be reduced but also the future basis of their material prosperity may be jeopardized. An alternative outcome is resource-preservation at the price of increased centralization of social life, the State substituting itself increasingly for a deficient private initiative. However, as we have already pointed out, state interventions are likely to be costly (with the consequence that people's incomes net of taxes will be impaired) and to lack effectiveness in so far as they are not backed by moral norms inducing people to respect the legal rules and to co-operate with the resource-preserving agencies.

[19] Moreover, the deactivation of moral norms may occur spontaneously—the individual may not take note of consequences, he may not know the relevant norms, he may not see himself as a responsible agent—or it may arise from a defensive redefinition of the situation once a moral norm arouses inhibiting emotions (Schwartz, 1970: 131–2).

7

The Possibility of Co-operation: Lessons from Experimental Social Psychology

A host of experimental studies in social psychology have been conducted during the last decades with a view to testing the behavioural assumptions of economists. A large number of these studies have been actually concerned with examining the relevance of the freerider problem in the provision of public goods as well as the validity of the conclusions derived from the prisoner's dilemma. It is not our intention to offer a detailed review of the results contained in this burgeoning literature. What we purport to do is more modestly to call attention to some significant results that are particularly relevant to the issues raised in the preceding three chapters.

7.1 Co-operation in Repeated Games

Do experiments tend to bear out the hypothesis that, when actors interact closely on a recurrent basis within a PD payoff structure, co-operation is a distinct possibility? The theory predicts that co-operation might emerge throughout most of the game when it is being repeated infinitely—an hypothesis that is obviously impossible to test strictly in laboratory conditions—or when the game horizon is finite but indefinite (players know that the game will stop one day, but they ignore when exactly this will happen). In the latter circumstances, the subjective probabilities that a given period might be the last, such as they are assessed by the actors, play a critical role in determining whether co-operation is an equilibrium outcome.

As a matter of fact, results from one study designing PD experiments appear to show that significantly more co-operative choices tend to be made when the subjects of the experiment are led into thinking that there is a higher chance of the game continuing after each play (Roth and Murnighan, 1978), thereby confirming a major result of game theory. However, Roth considers that the results are equivocal because, even when this chance is sufficiently high to make co-operation an equilibrium outcome, a majority of first-period choices were found to be non-co-operative in the same study (Roth, 1988: 999). What must be borne in mind here is that, in computing the minimum probability of continuing (after each play) required to make co-operation an equilibrium outcome, Roth and Murnighan did not allow for the possibility that subjects might well entertain doubts about which strategy the others are following. Yet we know that when such a possibility exists, even with a high probability that the game continues, players may choose not to co-operate if they strongly believe that their opponent(s) will follow a 'nasty' strategy. Seen in this perspective, the results obtained by Roth and Murnighan need not appear as 'equivocal' any more.

Another interesting experiment has been designed by Selten and Stoecker (1986). In this experiment, the subjects were invited to play a series of twenty-five successive ten-period repeated PD: in other words, they were proposed to participate in a repeated play of a repeated game. The underlying idea of the researchers was to give subjects the opportunity to learn from previous experience. The findings indicate that the typical outcome was initial periods of mutual co-operation, followed by an initial defection, followed by non-co-operation in the remaining periods. Recall that, on the basis of the theory, we would have expected generalized free–riding to take place from the very beginning of each repeated game. This is all the more so as the number of periods in each game is not only finite but also rather small. The problem with the theory here is perhaps that it unrealistically assumes that people are able to calculate the strategic implications of their present choices by using the sophisticated chain of reasoning implied by the backwards induction argument.

Interestingly, the same study shows that the first defection occurs earlier and earlier in subsequent repeated games. The explanation advanced by Selten and Stoecker is that players actually learn from their experiences. This explanation has been summarized by Roth in the following way: 'in the initial rounds players learned to co-operate (and consequently exhibited more periods of mutual co-operation starting from the very beginning and breaking down only near the end). In the later rounds, players learned about the dangers of not defecting first, and co-operation began to unravel. There is a sense in which this observed behaviour mirrors the game-theoretical observation that the equilibrium recommendation is not a good one, but that all other patterns of play are unstable' (Roth, 1988: 1000). The findings of Selten and Stoecker are essentially consistent with many other observations of finitely repeated games in which co-operation obtains for some periods, but breaks down near the end (ibid.).

To sum up, evidence from experimental studies does not systematically invalidate the predictions of the theory of repeated or extended games. Yet, these studies also show that co-operation is possible even in repeated PD games that are played only a limited number of times (the game horizon is finite and rather short). This may be due to two different reasons. First, as pointed out above, people probably do not use such a sophisticated device as the backwards induction argument when they reason about their strategic choices. This interpretation is actually confirmed by a series of recent experiments conducted by Ostrom *et al.* (1994). In these experiments (about which more will be said soon), it was found that the subjects frequently debated which strategy to adopt despite the high levels of information that were given to them. In particular, subjects found the task of determining optimal strategies difficult. As a result, 'many individuals utilize heuristics learned from childhood experiences. On playgrounds around the world, children arguing about the allocation of toys, space, use of facilities, etc., are taught, depending on the situation, to use principles such as: share and share alike (equal division); first in time, first in right; take turns; share on the basis of need; and flip a coin (use a randomizing device)' (Ostrom *et al.*, 1994: 217–18). Second, it must be borne in mind that, as demonstrated by Kreps and his associates, people may well co-operate until near the end of finitely repeated games if they entertain some slight doubts about the type of strategy followed by their opponent(s). What the two explanations call into question is people's ability to behave in perfectly rational ways: in the first case, it is in fact argued that people have limited computing abilities while, in the second, they suspect that their opponent(s) may genuinely behave 'irrationally' (that is, in a way that does not maximize his (their) payoffs) by following a tit-for-tat strategy instead of the dominant strategy of defection.

Axelrod's computer tournament may be recalled here since it suggests that behaviour will eventually converge towards co-operation, a finding even more favourable to co-operation than those obtained in experiments with human subjects. What needs to be stressed is that the length of the repeated game in Axelrod's exercise was much longer (200 periods) than in all experimental studies: his tournament therefore mirrors more closely a repeated game with an infinite or indefinite time-horizon than a finitely repeated game. Furthermore, Roth is probably right when he suspects that the difference in results may have something to do with the difference between computer simulations and actual experiments: even though the computer simulations designed by Axelrod were conducted 'with an element of experimental flavour' (tournament entries were solicited from invited players), the point remains that 'experiments with human subjects introduce a certain amount of open-ended complexity in the form of human behaviour, that is absent from a tournament in which individuals are represented by short (or even moderately long) computer programs' (Roth, 1988: 1001).

7.2 Co-operation in Games with Communication

To assess the impact of communication on the predisposition of individuals to co-operate, let us consider a series of one-shot experiments conducted by Dawes *et al.* (1977).[1] Subjects were asked to give one of two responses, 'co-operate' or 'defect', which resulted in payoffs in the form of a multiperson PD: by defecting one gets a benefit at the expense of the other parties. Four different versions of this basic experiment were run by the authors. In the first place, subjects were not allowed to talk to one another before deciding whether to co-operate or to defect. In the second place, talk was permitted provided it was not related to the experiment itself. In the third place, subjects were allowed to discuss the experiment but any explicit declaration about their choices was forbidden. In the fourth and last version, all restrictions were lifted, implying that it became possible for the subjects to make promises about their choices.

An essential feature of all four versions of the experiment is that choices were confidential (subjects were required to mark their choices in private and they were promised that their decisions would never be disclosed to the other players) so that a defector had no reason to fear retaliation, and there was therefore no practical way to

[1] Our account is based upon Frank (1988: 223–5).

enforce promises to co-operate. As emphasized by Frank, since confidentiality meant that promises were not binding, communication should have made no difference (Frank, 1988: 224). Contrary to this prediction, however, unanimous defection did not occur in any of the four versions. Yet, the more people were allowed to communicate, the less often they defected: in version 1 (no communication), 73 per cent of the subjects defected; in version 2 (irrelevant communication), 65 per cent did; in version 3 (open communication) and in version 4 (open communication + promises), only 26 and 16 per cent, respectively, of the subjects chose to defect.

There are thus two striking results in this experiment. First, even in the polar case of complete anonymity (version 1), more than one-fourth of the subjects chose to co-operate at a positive cost to themselves, a cost of which they were obviously fully aware. This is a really surprising outcome given that the game is played during only one period, so that co-operation cannot serve to build one's reputation. Second, co-operation appears to increase with communication. Commenting on this last result, Frank remarked that 'decisions about co-operation are based not on reason but on emotion':

> To cheat a stranger and to cheat someone you have met personally amount to precisely the same thing in rational terms. Yet in emotional terms, they are clearly very different. Face-to-face discussion, even if not directly relevant to the game itself, transforms the other players from mere strangers into real people. (Frank, 1988: 224)

The authors of the study actually pointed out that the affect level was very high among the subjects (particularly when explicit promises to co-operate were made). Thus, we are told that comments such as, 'If you defect on the rest of us you're going to have to live with it the rest of your life', were not at all uncommon. Moreover, the mere knowledge that *someone* defected, even without knowing the identity of the defector, often poisoned the atmosphere of the entire group. And when, in a preliminary version of their experiment, Dawes *et al.* told one group their choices would later be revealed, the three subjects who defected were the target of a great deal of hostility: they were, literally speaking, considered as genuine betrayers of the group.

Another series of laboratory experiments has led to the conclusion that discussion raises the co-operation rate by a significant margin but only in so far as the subjects believe their effort is going to benefit members of their *own* group. In other words, 'group identity appears to be a crucial factor in eschewing the dominating [non-co-operative] strategy' (Dawes and Thaler, 1988: 194–5). Moreover, when discussion is permitted, it is very common for people to make promises to contribute. Are these promises important in generating co-operation? Evidence seems to indicate that promise making is related to co-operation only when every member of the group promises to co-operate. Indeed, in systematic experiments designed to test the impact of promises on co-operation, it was found that in such groups with universal promising, the rate of co-operation was substantially higher than in other groups. In other groups where promising was not universal, there was no relationship between each subject's choice to co-operate or defect and (*a*) whether or not a subject made a promise to co-operate, or (*b*) the number of other people who promised to co-operate. According to

Robyn Dawes and Richard Thaler, 'these data are consistent with the importance of group identity if (as seems reasonable) universal promising creates—or reflects—group identity' (ibid.: 195). To put it another way, discussion followed by universal promising has the effect of establishing trust among the members of the group, thereby transforming a collection of people into a collective being with a specific (group) identity. People become willing to co-operate because direct communication leading to universal promise-making has given them the assurance that they will not be 'suckers' if they co-operate. One way of interpreting the change that has taken place is to say that discussion together with universal promising transforms the players' payoffs from a PD to an AG structure while instilling in them confidence that other people will co-operate from the beginning of the game.

In a recent series of aforementioned controlled experiments at Indiana University, Ostrom *et al.* (1994) have attempted to reproduce the decision problem of an agent in a CPR situation. The produce is allocated between the agents according to the amount of individual contribution. In other words, the return from the CPR for individual i is given by:

$$\left(x_i / \sum_j x_j\right) \times F\left(\sum_j x_j\right), \text{ where } F\left(\sum_j x_j\right) = a\sum_j x_j - b\left(\sum_j x_j\right)^2 \text{ is the}$$

total output of the CPR. As b is positive, it is assumed that there are decreasing returns to scale (a negative externality) in the exploitation of the CPR (see Chapter 5).

In the experiments carried out, each subject received information about the values of the parameters a and b, and was given an initial endowment in the form of tokens susceptible of being invested in the CPR. In such a problem, the level of group investment that is collectively rational is equal to $a/2b$, while the Nash symmetric equilibrium level is given by:

$$\sum_j x_j = \frac{na}{(n-1)b}.$$

Typically, in the different experiments, eight subjects interacted during thirty rounds. The main results (see Chapters 5, 6, and 7) are as follows:

1. The individual actions do not correspond to a Nash equilibrium.
2. An increase in the initial endowment tends to promote overexploitation of the CPR.
3. Communication fosters co-operation.

In the present context, it is this last result that we want to emphasize. In situations where the individual actions of each subject are kept secret, but communication is possible at certain points of the experiment, the actions tend to be more co-operative than when communication is forbidden. It is noteworthy that the impact of communication is rather short-lived. As a result, an increase in the frequency of communication has the effect of getting the total investment level nearer to the collectively rational outcome. Therefore, in the words of the authors, 'these experiments provide strong evidence for the power of face-to-face communication in a repeated CPR dilemma where decisions are made privately' (Ostrom *et al.*, 1994: 167).

Another important result that comes out of this experimental work is that, when the opportunity to communicate is costly (someone has to invest time and effort to create and maintain arenas for face-to-face communication), the problem of providing the institution for communication is not trivial. Indeed, it reduces the speed with which an agreement can be reached and the efficacy of dealing with players who break an agreement. Yet, it is striking that all groups eventually succeeded in providing the communication mechanisms (but only once) and in dealing (to some degree) with the CPR dilemma. According to the authors, the advantage of communication is that it provides 'an opportunity for individuals to offer and extract promises of co-operation for non-enforceable contracts'. They even go so far as saying that 'keeping promises appears to be a more fundamental, shared norm than "co-operation *per se*"', an interpretation that rests on the fact that, when actions are observable, people make violent reproaches when someone is breaking a promise, is being uncooperative or is taking advantage of others who are keeping a promise (Ostrom *et al.*: 168).

As we have already pointed out in connection with the first series of experiments reported above, emotions seem to play an important role as soon as communication and promise-making become possible. This is again borne out by yet another result achieved by Ostrom *et al.*, namely that when offered the opportunity to do so subjects are even willing to pay a fee to place a fine on another subject far more than predicted: in other words, they overuse sanctioning mechanisms (ibid.: 192). In net terms, this overreaction to defections may lead to a worse collective outcome than could be obtained under less informed situations (in which only the collective outcome is known to the participants).

It is important to note that communication need not always be explicit. As a matter of fact, in (small) groups whose members are in close and more or less continuous interaction with one another, explicit discussion and promise-making can often be dispensed with in routine decision problems. People know each other well enough and their mutual expectations are sufficiently structured to enable them to make their decisions straightaway. In this regard, mention ought to be made of experimental work which took place within a small group setting. This study was conducted in a Nepalese village by Bromley and Chapagain (1984) and it essentially consisted of asking the 140 sampled household heads about their intentions with respect to a willingness to contribute toward the enhancement of a village asset. A first conclusion reached by the authors is that freeriding is *not* a dominant feature in the village studied: indeed, they found a substantial interest on the part of their respondents to contribute to a collective village asset and to refrain from exploitative behaviour with respect to a village forest or a village grazing area. A second important conclusion is that a majority of the same respondents indicated that their behaviour was not much affected by the likely behaviour of others: 'A clear majority do not free–ride, nor would they if they thought others would' (ibid.: 872). In fact, across the various experiments conducted by the authors, approximately one-third of the respondents only considered the likely actions of others to be decisive in their own resource-use decisions. One should nevertheless be wary of jumping to the conclusion that many Nepalese villagers are unconditional (and therefore irrational) co-operators and that the above-reported evidence offers only weak support for the AG model. As has been aptly pointed out by Bromley and Chapagain themselves:

> while the villagers seem to imply that they do not much care about what others intend to do, we believe it is reasonable to assume that the villagers know what is expected of them, and that others know likewise. Hence, while claiming that the actions of others are not generally of concern to them, they may be secure in the knowledge that the resource-use decisions of the others will not be greatly out of line with some accepted norm. We hypothesize the presence of a 'background ethic' or norm that influences collective resource use decisions. This norm has evolved over time as the members of a village struggle with the daily task of making a living. The majority care about the collective welfare, a minority will take more than is 'safe or fair', and both will do so irrespective of what they think others will do. (Bromley and Chapagain, 1984: 872)

In other words, we have here a mixed situation in which a majority of AG players interact with a minority of PD players and where not only the proportion of the former but also the degree of trust among themselves are high enough to induce them to co-operate. In the interpretation of Bromley and Chapagain, norms establish trust without the need for any explicit communication.

7.3 Co-operation in One-Shot Games

Do we have evidence that people can co-operate when their relationships are anonymous and when they play the equivalent of a one-period game? The answer is 'yes': individuals do not seem to exploit free-riding opportunities in the manner predicted by the PD paradigm. As a matter of fact, reciprocal altruism (altruistic acts performed in the expectation of a future personal gain—that is, in a more exact parlance, selfishness with foresight) and tit for tat cannot explain co-operation in many experiments because the games are played only once or defection simply cannot be detected.

Such findings tend to indicate that people do not necessarily have the preference structure characteristic of the PD, and that normative considerations play an important role in Western societies where the experiments have been conducted (see, in particular, Rapoport and Chammah, 1965; Darley and Latané, 1970; Eiser, 1978).

One of the most well-known studies here is that made by Marwell and Ames (1979). What these authors show is that the free-rider problem rarely prevented groups from making substantial investments in a public good consisting of a group exchange where cash earnings from invested tokens were returned to all the members of the group by a pre-set formula, regardless of who had done the investing. It would seem that normative factors such as fairness influence contribution decisions. Indeed, most of the subjects appear to believe that there is a 'fair' contribution to be made to the public good and this belief influences their decision regarding how much to invest. In the words of the authors, 'what does make a difference in investment seems to be whether subjects are "concerned with being fair" in making their investments' (Marwell and Ames, 1979: 1357).[2]

In the same study, Marwell and Ames have also confirmed Olson's prediction that public goods are more likely to be provided by groups in which some individual member has an interest in the good that is greater than its cost. Their results indeed show that the groups containing such a member invest substantially more in public goods than do other groups. Yet, even though a single member has an interest in providing the public good alone, the other members with a lower interest in this good have also been found to contribute significantly. In other words, in contrast to Olson's notion that 'the weak will exploit the strong', 'these individuals do not particularly take advantage of the fact that they have a high-interest member in the group by reducing their own investments' (Marwell and Ames, 1979: 1355).

Finally, it is worth mentioning that the amounts of individual contributions are not much higher when the group is small (four persons) than when it is large (eighty persons). The 'incentive dilution' argument does not seem to significantly affect the investment decision. Note that the players never interacted with one another so that it was possible to tell them in various experiments that there were any number of members in their group and have them make their investment decisions in terms of this assumption.

Victim-in-distress experiments are interesting in that they test the people's ability to help in situations akin to the chicken game (doing nothing is worse than anything

[2] Some authors tend to dismiss the explanation of co-operation anomalies in terms of fairness considerations. For example, Weg and Zwick ran a series of experiments simulating a sort of ultimatum game that allows a null-valued quit move and reached the conclusion that moderate demands by the player who makes the offer arise from strategic as opposed to fairness considerations (Weg and Zwick, 1994). Bear in mind that, in an ultimatum game, two players are given an infinitely divisible sum (the 'pie') to be shared between them. Player 1 makes an offer—in which case the game terminates and the player receives the agreed upon shares—or chooses to reject the offer and the game terminates with both players receiving nothing. In theory, since player 2 prefers any positive amount to nothing, the unique subgame perfect partition for such a game assigns zero to player 2 and the whole sum to player 1. Yet, experiments have consistently shown that player 1 refrains from taking full advantage of his privileged position. Almost always, indeed, his offers are significantly larger than zero, averaging about 3 per cent of the pie with 50 per cent the most common offer (ibid.: 20–1).

To give an account of this violation of theoretical predictions, the authors use an infinite horizon sequential fixed-cost bargaining game. Two players, bearing costs c_1 and c_2, alternate in making offers concerning how to divide a pie and, if the proposal made by one player is rejected by the other player, the game proceeds to the next period with the roles of the two players being reversed. The game terminates only when agreement is reached, at which point the players receive their agreed upon shares minus the accumulated costs. By broadening the response repertoire to an offer allowing a quit move that terminates the game with both players receiving nothing (but still liable for any accumulated cost) and by comparing behaviour in no-quit bargaining games to behaviour in games with null quit moves, Weg and Zwick show that if player 1 does not take full advantage of the situation in ultimatum games, it is not for the sake of fairness but from the fear of loss. In other words, 'those who are first to move in ultimatum games are almost invariably intimidated by player 2's veto option'. The reason why intimidation exists is that player 2 is envious of player 1's larger share and therefore willing to reject insignificant amounts for the sake of eliminating the source of envy. It is only when a rejection is not too costly to himself that player 2 is actually willing to reject player's 1 offer (ibid.: 28). It must be pointed out that the interpretation proposed by Weg and Zwick, while quite interesting in the context of ultimatum games, cannot be used to explain other violations of the outcomes predicted by the rational egoist's model of the economists (see the description of some experiments still left unexplained by such theories in the text).

else). Thus, in one study, a team of psychologists staged a mock distress scene in a New York subway in order to discover whether people would come to the aid of a fellow passenger who had suddenly collapsed (Piliavin *et al.*, 1969, quoted from Frank, 1988: 217). In one version of the experiment the victim was made to appear as seriously ill while, in a second version, the intent was to make him appear drunk. The authors found that, in the first version, the victim received help from at least one passenger in 95 per cent of the cases while, in the second version, he was assisted in as many as 50 per cent of the cases (a good result given that the victim was made to appear as being clearly responsible for his state of distress).

An interesting fact about this experiment is the following: in the stage distress scenes, there were, on the average, more than eight other passengers present in the end of the car where the victim fell. And yet in almost all of the cases reported under the first version of the experiment, at least one person quickly helped. Moreover, it was found that the likelihood of assistance did not go down as the number of bystanders increased. Therefore, the diffusion-of-responsibility explanation—when there are several observers present, the pressures to intervene do not focus on anyone and the responsibility is shared among all the onlookers, as a result of which each may be less likely to help—does not seem to be valid here (Frank, 1988: 218–19).

What makes the subway experiment resemble the chicken game is that, since bystanders were at short distance from one another, each could easily know that no one else had come to the victim's aid. And, as Robert Frank observed, 'each person might want very much of *someone* to help the victim, and yet at the same time not want to be the one to do it. If none of the subway bystanders acted, each would know immediately that the victim was still in jeopardy' (ibid.: 219). This is precisely what differentiates the subway experiment from the tragic story of Kitty Genovese who could scream for more than half an hour as she was brutally stabbed and raped (in New York City) without any of her thirty-eight neighbours coming to her rescue.

There is another series of experiments that deserve to be mentioned in the present context. They have been conducted by Hornstein *et al.* (1968).[3] In what is typically a one-shot game, it has been found that an astonishingly high 45 per cent of 'lost' wallets were returned completely intact to their owners in New York City (during the spring of 1968). In large groups, co-operation may therefore arise in spite of the fact that explicit communication and promise-making are impossible. This presumably happens when moral norms serve as a substitute for such processes of direct exchange of words and promises, such as is the case when people adhere to a Kantian ethics. It is precisely the function of moral norms to unite together, without the mediation of words, people who do not directly interact with one another.

In addition, Hornstein and his associates were able to show that the return rate was significantly higher when the subjects of the experiments were exposed to a positive attitude of benevolence on the part of a third party. The interpretation offered by the authors is that the third party served as a role model for the subjects. A related lesson is that feelings or sentiments, not reason, motivate human decisions in situations

[3] See Frank (1988: 213–16) for a summary account of these experiments.

where our own acts have a significant influence on others' well-being: exposure to different kinds of persons or acts (benevolent or malevolent) evokes particular emotions which drive people to behave in certain ways (Frank, 1988: 216). Another experiment which confirms the important function of role models (or the fact that altruism or morality is encouraged by the observation of it) is that reported by Singer (1973). A helpless-looking woman was standing near a car with a flat tyre. It was found that drivers passing this woman were more likely to come to her rescue when they previously had the opportunity to observe helping behaviour in a similar type of situation.

Such experiments would seem to suggest that role models serve as a signalling device reminding people that there are honest people around. The result would be to enhance people's trust in others' predisposition towards fair dealing. Yet, this is to neglect the emotional dimension rightly emphasized by Frank. It is actually more satisfactory to view role models as privileged agents who reactivate emotional capacities associated with primary socialization processes. Moreover, if one still wants to cling to the rational egoist's model of the economists, one may consider that role models have the effect of increasing—or restoring to previous levels—the values of the payoffs attached by people to the outcome of joint co-operation. Note carefully, however, that contrary to a well-established tradition in economic theorizing, this latter interpretation assumes that individual preferences are *not* stable. It also enables us to better understand the potential role of political leaders in diffusing or reinforcing co-operation-fostering norms. Political leaders now appear as norm reactivators. When they publicly behave in co-operative ways, they naturally arouse in people the emotions associated with that type of behaviour provided, of course, that people have sufficiently strong feelings of identification with them. Of course, political leaders as role models fulfil other functions than simply reactivating inclinations to co-operate among the people. As we have discussed in Chapter 6 (Sect. 2), they may thus play powerful roles in *shaping* people's sense of duty and what is right.

8

The Regulated Common Property

In its discussion of the solution to the 'problems of the commons', the property rights school does not only overemphasize the efficiency gains which can be expected from privatization, but it also overlooks the potentialities displayed by common property arrangements. Indeed, in the arguments proposed, it is as though the group, or the community, were able to control access to the resource but not to control its use by the members of the community. In other words, it is assumed that common ownership systematically fails to satisfy the 'authority axiom' following which the well-defined group acts with a unified purpose. 'The inability of groups to act in a socially responsible manner . . . is usually blamed on the impossibility of groups to co-ordinate and co-operate on a pattern of resource use . . . . Thus . . . the authority axiom is violated because members of the group are always presumed to have the incentive to cheat on any co-operative agreement' (Larson and Bromley, 1990: 239).

The case for or against the property rights school's view can be decided only on empirical grounds. Part II—more particularly Chapters 10 and 12—will help us better assess the claims of this school. As we shall then see, the question raised is much too complex to receive a yes/no type of answer. A convincing and credible answer must allow for subtle distinctions and carefully worded nuances so as to avoid the two opposed pitfalls of cynicism and romanticism, or of undue pessimism and excessive optimism. At this stage, what needs to be borne in mind—and this is sufficient to vindicate the kind of approach followed in the present chapter—is the following: there exist empirically significant circumstances in which rural groups or communities with an exclusive right of access to a particular resource may succeed in designing and enforcing rules or arrangements that allow them to control the use of the resource in a systematic and effective manner. In other words, human groups (of restricted size) can impose enough discipline upon their members to save common property resources from destruction or degradation: in such instances, the authority axiom is thus satisfied. We will henceforth call this property regime a regulated common property, in opposition to the unregulated common property which does not satisfy the authority axiom.

8.1 The Efficiency of Regulated Common Property

Let us first analyse the means at the disposal of the community regarding the use of the resource by its members. In economic theory, an important way of correcting externalities, such as those associated with common property, has been suggested by Pigou, and consists of taxes, subsidies, and quotas. We shall examine this approach in some detail before pointing to a number of other aspects of the efficiency issue under common property.

Taxes and quotas

Let us re-examine the example of the fishery given in Chapter 2. Total catches, Y, were given by the following expression:

$$Y = a\left(\sum_{i}^{m} n_i\right) - b\left(\sum_{i}^{m} n_i\right)^2,$$

where m indicates the number of fishermen in the community and n_i the number of boats fisherman i operates. By letting P_N stand for the rental price of a boat, as shown in Chapter 2, the profit-maximizing number of boats per fisherman, in the Nash equilibrium of the unregulated common property, is:

$$n_N = (a - p_N)/(b(m + 1)). \tag{1}$$

This is the generalization of the formula obtained for two fishermen: $(a - p_N)/3b$. The total number of boats in this equilibrium, N_N, is therefore equal to:

$$N_N = mn_N. \tag{2}$$

The optimal (efficient) number of boats is given by setting $m = 1$ in these two equations. One obtains:

$$N^* = (a - p_N)/2b. \tag{3}$$

Let us now introduce a tax scheme such that the new Nash equilibrium supports the Pareto-optimal solution described in (3). To have such a property, the tax scheme must imply the imposition of a tax rate on the variable factor, so that the agents will have an incentive to reduce its amount in use. Let us impose a tax rate, t, per boat. Equations (1) and (2) become:

$$n_T = (a - p_N - t)/(m + 1)b \tag{4}$$

$$N_T = n_T m. \tag{5}$$

The tax per boat must be such that $N_T = N^*$ for the new equilibrium to be Pareto-optimal. Let us call such a tax rate, t^*. It is standard algebra to show that:

$$t^* = (m - 1)(a - p_N)/(2m). \tag{6}$$

The tax rate so calculated has an interesting interpretation. Indeed, assuming that $(m - 1)$ fishermen operate the optimal number of boats, n^*, what is the impact (the 'externality') fisherman i causes on them by operating one more boat? Total profit of the $(m - 1)$ fishermen is given by:

$$P(m-1) = \frac{[m-1]n^*}{[m-1]n^* + n_i}\{a[[m-1]n^* + n_i] - b[[m-1]n^* + n_i]^2\} - p_N[m-1]n^*. \tag{7}$$

The externality imposed by fisherman i on all other fishermen is therefore equal to:

$$dP(m-1)/dn_i = -[m-1]n^*b = -\frac{m-1}{2m}[a-p_N] = -t^*, \quad (8)$$

where use is made of equation (3). Therefore, the optimal tax is that which obliges agent i to fully internalize the externality he imposes on others by not behaving in an optimal manner.

This simple example shows how, through an adequate tax scheme, the community or the State is able to achieve efficiency in a common property resource. One should note that the community could have alternatively imposed a quota, q^*, on the number of boats each fisherman is allowed to operate and also achieve efficiency. In that case,

$$q^* = N^*/m = (a - p_N)/(2bm), \text{ from equation (3).} \quad (9)$$

The above example can be generalized so that, in general, Pareto-efficiency is achieved through quotas or taxes which allow agents to internalize fully the externalities which their own decisions are bound to cause. Therefore, the State (or the community) need not necessarily resort to privatization to solve the commons problem. It can achieve the same efficient equilibrium through an appropriate tax policy. Moreover, the following can be shown (for more details, see Dasgupta and Heal, 1979: ch. 3):

1. Any Lindahl equilibrium with markets for externalities can be established as an appropriate tax equilibrium.
2. There are cases, such as the foregoing example examined above, where, even though a Lindahl equilibrium does not exist, a Pareto-efficient tax equilibrium can be established.

Since, through taxes, virtually any externality can be correctly internalized by the agents, one can surmise that an open-access equilibrium can also be made Pareto-optimal through an appropriate tax scheme. Let us illustrate this by way of the above example. We know that, in the open-access equilibrium, the total number of boats, N_0, is such that profits are nil:

$$N_0 = (a - p_N)/b. \quad (10)$$

For the open access equilibrium to be Pareto-optimal, the tax per boat, t, must be such that: $N_0 = N^*$. One gets:

$$t = (a - p_N)/2. \quad (11)$$

This has interesting implications. Indeed, by taxing appropriately, the State is able to correct the externality caused by open access. The problem is nevertheless that, *in many cases, open access itself results from the impossibility to control the access to the resource*. In these conditions, one cannot see how the State will be able to impose a tax on the use of the resource.

As illustrated above, quotas can be used in place of taxes to increase the efficiency of the common property equilibrium. However, this does not imply that taxes and quotas are always equivalent. For example, when there are some uncertainties associ-

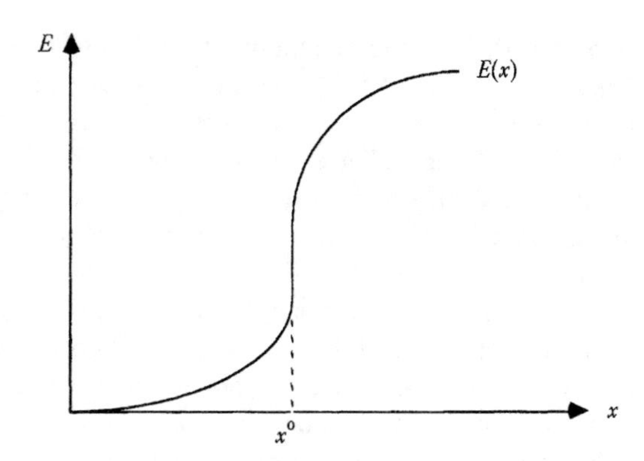

FIG. 8.1. Taxes versus quotas and threshold phenomena

ated with threshold phenomena (as is the case for many environmental problems), quantity controls may be more appropriate. To illustrate this, let us assume that the size of the externality, E, grows with the amount of the variable factor used, x, as described in Figure 8.1.

Through quotas, the regulatory agency can ensure that the amount of variable factor, x, will always remain below x°, while, if the impact of taxes on the chosen amount of x is stochastic, or is not known with certainty by the regulating agency, the only way to ensure that $x \leq x^\circ$ is to impose a high tax rate on x, which can be undesirable because it is likely to be inefficient. In this case, quotas are preferable to taxes. However, in many instances (e.g. pollution or energy-saving), taxes may be preferred to quotas because they provide incentives to technological progress aimed at reducing externalities still further. From the point of view of dynamic efficiency, taxes are often superior to quotas (see Dasgupta and Heal, 1979: ch. 13; Schokkaert, 1991; Fisher, 1981: 199–203; Baumol and Oates, 1971).

It is worth emphasizing that the amount of the tax that needs to be imposed on the users to achieve the Pareto-optimal outcome is not necessarily feasible. As a matter of fact, if these users have valuable exit options, they will threaten to leave the user group in case the tax reduces the expected benefits from their participation in the collective resource's exploitation below what they can get in their best alternative occupation. Such a threat of withdrawal may be a cause of worry for the group in so far as losing one of its members means that it is going to be less effective, for example, because the presence of everybody is desirable for certain actions (CPR maintenance or protection, risk-sharing) requiring co-ordinated efforts. In these circumstances, exit possibilities have the effect of reducing the amount of the taxes which a group can impose on deviant members. In technical terms, the threat to impose the optimal tax (in the above-defined sense) may not be credible since the group is willing to renegotiate the initial punishment scheme and the defector is well aware of it (the punishment scheme is not 'renegotiation-proof'). It is possible, however, to impose lower tax amounts or punishments that are self-enforcing, yet, precisely because they are less harsh, the amount of co-operation they can support is reduced. In that case, as pointed out by

Fafchamps, 'deviants will not be able to renegotiate themselves out of their own punishment' (Fafchamps, 1992: 163). We will return to this point in Chapter 12 when we will attempt to understand the rationale of non-decentralized sanction systems.

An oft-used mechanism for regulating common property consists of *temporarily* excluding a rule violator. Hirshleifer and Rasmusen have shown that this mechanism can actually correspond to a subgame-perfect equilibrium strategy in a particular kind of game. The game they describe is based on the following assumptions: (i) a defector gets a higher payoff than a co-operator in the round in which he defects; (ii) payoffs per member are an increasing function of the number of members who co-operate; (iii) the payoffs per member when everyone defects do not depend on the size of the group; (iv) a member always prefers to be in the group than being ostracized; (v) the voting procedure used by the group to exclude a violator does not entail any direct or indirect benefit; (vi) for a violator to be excluded (ostracized), it suffices that one member votes for his exclusion; and (vii) ostracism lasts only one round.

Under these assumptions, they then prove that, even in a finite repetition of this game, the following strategy, supporting co-operation till the penultimate period, is a subgame-perfect equilibrium: (*a*) co-operate until the last round, (*b*) defect in the last round, (*c*) vote for excluding anyone who deviates from the above strategy, including players who fail to vote for excluding defectors, those who have wrongly voted for excluding a co-operator, those who fail to ostracize those who fail to ostracize violators, and so forth. The crux of the argument lies in the fact that players can credibly threaten to exclude a defector in the last round since such a move does not entail any cost for them. The possibility to inflict a real punishment at no cost to the punisher has the effect of breaking the logic of the backward-induction argument underlying the non-co-operative outcome of the finitely repeated PD game.

If it is moreover assumed, in violation of assumption (v), that players gain a little bit of pleasure from excluding a violator, that is if they have 'a little morality', the above strategy is the unique subgame-perfect equilibrium of the game. As pointed out by the authors, 'the strategy "Always Defect, Never Ostracize", for example, is no longer an equilibrium because players would raise their payoffs by ostracizing defectors in the next-to-last round'. In this case, 'Morality achieves co-operation because some players want to reduce the welfare of others, if those others behave wrongfully' (Hirshleifer and Rasmusen, 1989: 100–1).

The logic highlighted in the above game can be extended to a wide class of problems including social dilemmas such as co-ordination games or appropriation problems with respect to a common property. This means that assumptions (i) and (ii) are not essential to reach the aforementioned result. As a matter of fact, the important assumption is assumption (iii) according to which, if everyone defects, there is no benefit from a larger group size. Note that, in the commons problem, every remaining participant necessarily gains from the temporary exclusion of a violator, even when everyone 'defects', so that this assumption holds *a fortiori*. On the other hand, the voting procedure for exclusion is not important. Thus, the result that ostracism can enforce co-operation can also be derived if exclusion is decided on the basis of majority. Moreover, ostracism works in much the same way if it is irrevocable.

However, for obvious reasons, this last extension is permitted only if the gain derived from a larger group is not too high.

There is another point which is worth making: punishment is generally more effective when it can be made escalating through a suitable design mechanism. This is particularly evident if information is imperfect since, in these circumstances, there is always a risk of imposing an unjustified sanction on a resource user who did not actually break the rule. If, however, the same individual is presumed to be a rule breaker on several occasions, then the probability that he actually behaved co-operatively becomes very low. As a result, harsher and harsher punishments can be meted out to him without incurring too much risk of misapplying sanctions. Graduated sanctions can also be justified when information is perfect. As a matter of fact, it is probably not very effective to impose harsh punishments on someone who is caught for the first time violating the rule. By imposing a small fine on him, the society wants to send him a warning (or, to reactivate the ruling norms) rather than actually punish him. As pointed out by Ostrom, a small penalty may be quite sufficient to remind the infractor of the importance of compliance. Such an approach is especially advisable when resource users may make 'mistakes', since a large fine or harsh punishment imposed on a person facing an unusual problem may produce resentment and unwillingness to conform to the rules in the future (Ostrom, 1990: 97–8). Consequently,

> Graduated punishments ranging from insignificant fines all the way to banishment, applied in settings in which the sanctioners know a great deal about the personal circumstances of the other appropriators and the potential harm that could be created by excessive sanctions, may be far more effective than a major fine imposed on a first offender. (Ostrom, 1990: 98)

External authority and imperfect monitorability

As hinted at above, in many field settings detection of free–riding is difficult and costs have to be incurred to make it possible. It can, however, be argued that imperfect monitorability as such is not an unsurmountable impediment to the intervention of an external authority which would be entrusted with the task of imposing sanctions to punish non-compliance with resource-preserving rules. This theoretical result is important in the context of large groups in which the intervention of such an authority may be needed to provide the appropriate 'selective incentives' to the resource users. In the words of Olson, 'unless the number of individuals is quite small, or unless there is coercion or some other special device to make individuals act in their common interest, rational, self-interested individuals will not act to achieve their common or group interests' (Olson, 1965: 2; see also Taylor, 1987: 9). To demonstrate our point, we proceed in several steps. First, consider the PD game described in Figure 8.2.

Suppose an external authority enters the picture and decides to sanction defection in such a way as to transform the above PD game into another game where mutual co-operation would become a unique equilibrium outcome (see Figure 8.3).

Thus, by inflicting a punishment of 2 payoff units on each defector (whether he is found to defect singly or to defect simultaneously with the other player), the external

		Player B	
		C	D
Player A	C	10, 10	–1, 11
	D	11, –1	0, 0

FIG. 8.2. A 2 × 2 prisoner's dilemma game

		Player B	
		C	D
Player A	C	10, 10	–1, 9
	D	9, –1	–2, –2

FIG. 8.3. A 2 × 2 external-authority game with complete information (adapted from Ostrom, 1990: 10)

authority has been able radically to modify the situation: the dominant strategy of each player is now to co-operate instead of free–riding as in the initial game.

However, things are apparently more difficult when the external authority possesses only incomplete information about the relevant parameters. Indeed, it can then be shown, with the help of an example drawn from a recent book by Ostrom (1990), that its intervention may turn out to be an outright failure *for a given level of punishment*. If the information about the particular actions of the resource users is incomplete, the external authority cannot avoid making errors in imposing punishments. Let y^d be the probability with which the agency punishes defections (a correct response) and, y^c, the probability with which it punishes co-operative actions (an erroneous response). Note incidentally that $(1 - y^d)$ represents the probability with which it fails to punish defections (an erroneous response) and $(1 - y^c)$ the probability with which it does not punish co-operative actions (a correct response). The fine imposed on a defector amounts to 2 payoff units. The payoff structure of the game is thus as described in Figure 8.4.

Notice that there is complete information when $y^d = 1$ and $y^c = 0$, in which case the game displayed in Figure 8.4 is strictly the same as that shown in Figure 8.3. Information is incomplete when both y^d and y^c lie (strictly) between zero and one. Assume, for example, that the external agency imposes sanctions correctly with a probability of only 0.7 ($y^d = 0.7$ and $y^c = 0.3$): in other words, there is a 30 per cent chance that a defector escapes punishment and that a co-operator is being imposed an unjustified sanction. We then have the specific payoff matrix shown in Figure 8.5.

		Player B	
		C	D
Player A	C	$10-2y^c$, $10-2y^c$	$-1-2y^c$, $11-2y^d$
	D	$11-2y^d$, $-1-2y^c$	$-2y^d$, $-2y^d$

FIG. 8.4. A 2 × 2 external-authority game with incomplete information: a general form (adapted from Ostrom, 1990: 11)

		Player B	
		C	D
Player A	C	9.4, 9.4	–1.6, 9.6
	D	9.6, –1.6	–1.4, –1.4

FIG. 8.5. A 2 × 2 external-authority game with incomplete information: an example (adapted from Ostrom, 1992: 12)

It is easy to verify that, given this payoff structure, the resource users again face a PD game: their dominant strategy is to violate the resource-preserving rules.

For the Pareto-superior outcome to materialize, it suffices that the payoff obtained by a player when he free-rides while the other co-operates is smaller than the payoff he would receive by co-operating with a co-operator. We therefore require that the following condition be satisfied:

$$10 - 2y^c > 11 - 2y^d.$$

In more general terms, if C and D stand for the payoffs, respectively, of co-operation and defection in conditions where the other player co-operates and before any sanction has been imposed, and if F stands for the fine imposed by the external authority, efficient monitoring requires that

$$F > (D - C)/(y^d - y^c).$$

In other words, the higher the incentive to defect, and the more imperfect the monitoring (the less likely a correct punishment is meted out to the agents), the higher the amount of the fine must be in order to make monitoring activities effective.[1] In small

[1] It has been argued that one of the main reasons for the low rate of compliance with fishery regulations in the USA is the fact that the severity of sanctions is modest in comparison to the gains realized from illegal landings (Sutinen, Rieser, and Gauvin, 1990: 353–4). On the other hand, it has been shown econometrically that in the inshore lobster fishery of Massachusetts (USA), the fishermen's perceived probability of detection and conviction affects their violation rate (Sutinen and Gauvin, 1989).

groups, since the difficulty of monitoring is obviously much less than in large groups, the probability of incorrect punishments is correspondingly lower. Therefore, the amount of the fine to be imposed to induce compliance is also lower. To take advantage of group size, it is clearly advisable that monitoring and sanctioning responsibilities be delegated to local or community-based authorities.

Monitoring costs can also be reduced by shifting to methods of resource conservation that are relatively easy to check out. Indeed, monitoring being less imperfect, it could become effective with a lower amount of fines. The point can be made as follows. Difficult-to-monitor conservation methods imply that lengthy investigation procedures are necessary to provide adequate evidence that a suspected violation has actually occurred. These lengthy procedures have the effect of reducing the number of cases that can be investigated and, as a result, the perceived risk of detection by violators is low (y^d is low so that the right-hand term of the above equation is high) (Sutinen, Rieser, and Gauvin, 1990: 360–1).

In fishing, for example, gear restrictions are typically viewed as inefficient regulatory measures because they increase the costs of production (Crutchfield, 1961). However, since they may be less costly to enforce than other measures, gear restrictions could turn out to be the most efficient method of regulation when enforcement costs are taken into account (Sutinen and Andersen, 1985: 384). In particular, gear restrictions are less costly to monitor than the control of individual vessel quotas or minimum-size or minimum-weight restrictions. In the case of the latter, indeed, the alleged violator can challenge the techniques used by enforcement agents in sampling and measuring the size of the catch (Sutinen, Rieser, and Gauvin, 1990: 360). Alternative methods of monitoring are particularly advisable when the amount of the fine required is too high to be practically feasible: if the penalty meted out by enforcement authorities is perceived as too severe (i.e. unfair) by the community of users, the latter are likely to resist and social pressure against violators will be weakened (ibid.: 341).

Decentralized taxes and imperfect monitorability: an illustration

Monitoring activities can also be carried out in a completely decentralized way by the user groups concerned. In a recent paper, Weissing and Ostrom (1991) have analysed this issue in the context of water management systems. Towards that purpose, they have constructed an $(N + 1)$-agent 'irrigation game' in which, at each period, there is one turn-taker who pumps water out of the collective channel and N turn-waiters. There is a predetermined set of rules which regulate access of each agent to a turn-taking position according to a rotating pattern. Potential conflict exists between these two types of agent since the turn-taker can steal water and the turn-waiters are negatively affected by this event. Also, sanctioning activities are assumed to be performed by the users themselves without the intervention of any external authority (there are transfers of payoffs from agent to agent), even though we are not told how the participants come to agree on the amount of the (uniform) fine to be imposed and why the rule-breakers agree to pay the fine under conditions where it is not evident that punishment is self-enforcing. Something essential is obviously left out of the

TW / TT	–M	M
–S	0 / 0	0 / $-C$
S	B / $-B$	$\alpha(-P)+(1-\alpha)B$ / $\alpha(P)+(1-\alpha)(-B)-C$

FIG. 8.6. Normal form of the two-person irrigation game

model (the punishment mechanism is not made explicit) and we have therefore to conclude that, implicit in the irrigation management system modelled by Weissing and Ostrom, a regulating agency is at work.

In the following, we shall present a modified version of their most basic model. We assume that there is one turn-waiter (TW) and one turn-taker (TT). TT has two possible actions, 'stealing' (S) or 'not stealing' (–S), and TW, without knowing TT's decision, has to decide between 'monitoring' (M) and 'not monitoring' (–M). Stealing can only be detected by monitoring, but monitoring is not completely efficient. Assume that the probability of detection is equal to α and μ is the 'monitoring tendency', that is, the probability with which TW monitors TT. Accordingly, the probability for TT to remain undetected is given by: $\eta(\mu, \alpha) = (1 - \alpha\mu)$, which the authors call the *monitoring deficiency* of the system. The payoff matrix associated with this game is given in Figure 8.6.

As can be seen above, when TT does not steal and TW does not monitor, their payoffs are equal to zero, reflecting a *status quo* situation. When TT does not steal and TW monitors, the latter incurs the fixed monitoring cost C. If TT steals and TW does not monitor, the former gets a payoff of $+B$ (the value of the water stolen), and the latter gets $-B$ (the value of the water lost). Now, when TT steals and TW monitors, TT earns $\alpha(-P) + (1 - \alpha)B$, where P represents the fine paid by TT to TW if his stealing is detected. The payoff accruing to TW is $\alpha(P) + (1 - \alpha)(-B) - C$. In such a game, the characterization of equilibria obviously depends on the values of the parameters. Here, we shall assume that, when TT steals, it cannot be TW's best response to abstain from monitoring, which implies $\alpha > C/(P + B)$.

Two cases must be distinguished. First, consider the situation in which $\alpha < B/(P + B)$, meaning that, when TW monitors, TT's best reply is to steal. In such a situation, there is a unique Nash equilibrium: TT always steals (it is a dominant strategy) and TW monitors. Second, we have the situation in which $\alpha > B/(P + B)$. In this case, it is no more rewarding to steal if the other monitors. As a result, there is no equilibrium in pure strategies in the above game. There is a Nash equilibrium in mixed strategies, in which TT steals with probability $\sigma^* = C/(\alpha P + \alpha B)$ and TW monitors with probability $\mu^* = B/(\alpha P + \alpha B)$.

At the equilibrium, the stealing probability of TT is a positive function of the relative cost of monitoring with respect to the expected benefits. Conversely, the monitoring probability of TW is a positive function of the benefit of stealing water relative to its expected cost. The striking result is that, at equilibrium, stealing always occurs with positive probability, and, yet the turn-taker is not fully monitored. This derives from two key assumptions of the model. 'On the one hand, monitoring is only profitable if there is a positive chance to prevent a stealing event. If no stealing occurs, the costs of monitoring outweigh its benefits. On the other hand, stealing is always profitable if no monitoring occurs. . . . A strategy combination without stealing cannot be in equilibrium since a zero stealing rate induces the turn-waiters not to monitor, and a zero monitoring rate in turn gives the turn-taker a positive incentive to steal' (Weissing and Ostrom, 1991: 240).

Weissing and Ostrom show that the above result (some stealing occurs at equilibrium) also obtains when there are many turn-waiters. There are two different kinds of equilibria. In the asymmetric case, some agents are relatively specialized in monitoring activities. An interesting finding derived by the authors in a companion paper (1992) is the following: the introduction of a specialized guard will sometimes *but not always* make an irrigation system more efficient in the sense of reducing both the stealing and the monitoring rates. (Note that, in their corresponding model, the rewards of the guard consist not only of the value to him of the avoided water loss, but also of a special reward obtained in the case where he himself has detected the stealing event.) This suggests that the relative specialization of one agent in monitoring activities may reduce the turn-waiters' incentive to monitor the turn-taker's behaviour. Between the turn-waiters, the structure of the monitoring game being played is that of a chicken game.

In the symmetric case, all turn-waiters monitor at the same equilibrium rate. It is then possible to demonstrate that the equilibrium rate of stealing increases with the number of turn-waiters. This is because the total benefit of detection of a stealing event is evenly spread among all turn-takers, whether they monitor or not. As a consequence, the individual benefit from monitoring and detection decreases with the number of turn-waiters (Weissing and Ostrom, 1991: 227). Other comparative-static results) obtained are rather straightforward: for example, the equilibrium stealing rate increases with a decrease in the detection probability of monitoring (α), in the size of the fine, (P) or in the loss of water due to undetected stealing, (B), and with an increase in the cost of monitoring, (C).

Since rule violation occurs at equilibrium when enforcement is imperfect, one must expect the optimal steady-state size of the stock of a renewable resource to be all the smaller as enforcement is more costly. This has been formally demonstrated by Sutinen and Andersen for a fishery. When enforcement is imperfect, the optimal steady-state stock size lies between the smaller open-access stock size and the larger stock size where catch rates are assumed to be perfectly controlled at zero cost (Sutinen and Andersen, 1985).

Enforcement costs of a regulated common property

As has been explained above, common property, whether regulated or not, differs from open access because the community detains an exclusive right of use on the resource, and is therefore entitled to *exclude* non-members. The enforcement of common property rights therefore entails costs, similar in nature to those resulting from the establishment of private property. However, it should be noted that, on the one hand, common property may be more effectively established than private property. It has indeed been argued by Bruce and Fortmann that 'the combined social and physical force of a community may be better able than single individuals to protect a resource against incursions by outsiders' (Bruce and Fortmann, 1989: 9). On the other hand, enforcement costs of common property are likely to be lower than those of private property, since, in most instances, former users of the resource simply get their rights recognized through common property. In other words, recognizing common property amounts in many cases to enacting an *état de fait*. Furthermore, in those situations where the privatization process has resulted in a parcelling out of the resource, the costs of enforcing privated property rights (such as the costs of fencing, or those involved in surveillance activities) may be high relative to those incurred under common property.

This being said, regulation of common property may also entail significant transaction costs since a centralized decision unit, namely a *political authority*, has to be established. Demsetz (1967) thus argues that: 'negotiation costs will be large because it is difficult for many persons to reach a mutually satisfactory agreement. . . . But even if an agreement among all can be reached, one must yet take account of the costs of policing the agreement, and these may be large also' (Demsetz, 1967: 354–5). There are many aspects to this issue and many of them will be addressed in Chapter 12 in the light of empirical evidence. At this stage, it is sufficient to say that the costs involved will be lower if there is adequate leadership to create the necessary consensus or, at least, to drive enough resource users to adopt co-operative behaviour. Traditional leadership seems to be particularly welcome in so far as, since it is already in existence, it entails no set-up costs. Yet, as will be seen in Chapter 12, this solution may also present important shortcomings. Furthermore, if there are costs associated with the enforcement of political authority to regulate common property, once established, this authority will be in a better position than private owners to cope with 'residual' externalities and with the new externalities which may later emerge (see above, Chapter 3).

In the above, we have assumed that the regulation task under the common property regime is entrusted with the user community. This need not be so since the State is also a potential candidate for such a responsibility. The question as to whether the State or the community (or any intermediate agency) is more effective as regulating agency is, of course, a crucial question that deserves careful consideration. It has actually many facets which will be discussed throughout Part II, more specifically in Chapters 11 (sect. 1) and 13.

At this stage, suffice it to say that information is a central dimension of any choice of the appropriate level and method of regulation. As demonstrated above, by imposing Pigovian taxes, a regulating agency equipped with the necessary powers can achieve efficiency in a common property resource. What is worth bearing in mind is that this solution is feasible only if the regulating agency possesses satisfactory information about the state of the resource (e.g. the stock of a fishing population), the flow of its current use, and the identity of its users. Only then can the right fee be levied on the right people. Yet, the more centralized this agency the more difficult the task of collecting the relevant information and, therefore, the more serious the problem of implementation of Pigovian taxes (or quotas). As pointed out by Deacon (1992) in his discussion of the means of controlling tropical deforestation, such a difficulty is likely to preclude the State from *directly* managing common property resources.[2] Being closer to the resources to be managed, user communities possess an informational advantage compared with any centralized agency. Yet, on the other hand, the information-processing ability of the latter is typically higher than that of the former. Hence the need for a co-management approach as further explained and illustrated in Chapter 13.

8.2 The Distributive Effects of Regulating Common Property

In this section, we investigate the distributive impact of regulating common property. We assume that regulation enhances income through the increased efficiency it is supposed to bring about in the management of the resource. We assume furthermore that this is correctly perceived by the agents concerned: they fully anticipate the gains associated with regulation. Otherwise, they may (wrongly) expect that regulation will decrease their expected income and they will oppose it.

Regulation with heterogeneous resource users

A well-known statement of the problem of heterogeneity in regard to collective action potential is due to Johnson and Libecap (1982) who analysed the cause of failure of co-operative mechanisms for catch restriction in the overcapitalized shrimp industry of Texas, USA:

> Contracting costs are high among heterogeneous fishermen, who vary principally with regard to fishing skill. The differential yields that result from heterogeneity affect the willingness to organize with others for specific regulations . . . regulations that pose disproportionate constraints on certain classes of fishermen will be opposed by those adversely affected . . . Indeed, if fishermen had equal abilities and yields, the net gains from effort controls would be evenly spread, and given the large estimates of rent dissipation in many fisheries, rules governing effort or catch would be quickly adopted . . . For example, total effort could be restricted through uniform quotas for eligible fishermen. But if fishermen are heterogeneous, uniform quotas will be costly to assign and enforce because of opposition from more productive fishermen. Without side payments (which are difficult to administer), uniform quotas could leave more productive fishermen worse off' (Johnson and Libecap, 1982: 1006, 1010).

Treading the same way as Johnson and Libecap, Kanbur (1992) has recently attempted to demonstrate formally that, when agents are not identical and their differ-

[2] There are thus numerous experiences (in Canada, Western Europe, Japan, and, most recently, in New Zealand) where overfishing under a regulated regime has (partly) occurred as a result of the excessive fishing quotas set by the State.

ences get reflected in their assigning divergent (marginal) values to a natural resource, the income increment achieved through a co-operative agreement maximizing the sum of their payoffs will differ among them. Moreover, for some individuals there might even not be an increment at all: under certain conditions, co-operation will require some users to restrict exploitation and the others to intensify exploitation relative to the Nash equilibrium.

Since the example constructed by Kanbur is faulty, we present an alternative formulation of the problem from which it comes out that at the optimum the 'small' users (those with a lower level of exploitation of the CPR in the unregulated situation) may be worse off than in the decentralized, inefficient equilibrium. (In Kanbur's example, the opposite conclusion was attained: rather paradoxically, the technically more efficient (and large) users were losing when the optimal regulation without transfers was followed.) Consider two individuals, indexed 1 and 2, choosing harvesting efforts y_1 and y_2, that yield payoffs R_1 and R_2, as given below:

$$R_1 = a_1\left(y_1 - \frac{1}{2}y_1^{\,2}\right) - \frac{1}{2}\left(y_1 + y_2\right)^2 \tag{1}$$

$$R_2 = a_2\left(y_2 - \frac{1}{2}y_2^{\,2}\right) - \frac{1}{2}\left(y_1 + y_2\right)^2 \tag{2}$$

The payoff functions embody a negative externality: each individual's action affects the payoffs of the other individual adversely. They also contain an asymmetry in the parameters a_1 and a_2 to indicate that the marginal value of the action differs between the two individuals. One way to interpret the above equations is to construe the first term as private net benefits and the second term as a common social cost that depends on joint exploitation of a given natural resource. The Nash equilibrium values, superscripted by N, are thus:

$$y_1^{\,N} = \frac{a_1 - a_2 + a_1a_2}{a_1 + a_2 + a_1a_2} \tag{3}$$

$$y_2^{\,N} = \frac{a_2 - a_1 + a_1a_2}{a_1 + a_2 + a_1a_2} \tag{4}$$

Assuming that $a_1 = 2$ and $a_2 = 1$, we obtain the following individual levels of exploitation and corresponding payoffs: $y_1^N = 0.6$, $y_2^N = 0.2$, $R_1^N = 0.52$, $R_2^N = 0.06$.

By contrast, the efficient solution requires that $(R_1 + R_2)$ is maximized. With the above parameter values, it turns out that y_2 must be equal to zero ($y_2^C = 0$): in other words, efficiency would require user 2 to be prevented from access to the resource. In that case, the efficient solution is obtained by maximizing R_1 alone. Setting both y_2 and R_2 to zero, we then get: $y_1^C = 1$, and $R_1^C = 1$. A comparison of these two sets of results shows that individual 1 gains from regulation and that the total level of resource exploitation is actually increased. This apparently paradoxical outcome obtains because the comparative inefficiency of user 2 is so high (at the Nash equilibrium, the net income of user 2 is only 11% of that of user 1 while his comparative level of resource use is 1/3) that joint exploitation of the resource imposes considerable sacrifices on the more efficient user. Evidently, if heterogeneity in resource use efficiency is less, the room for conflict regarding regulation is considerably narrowed down. For instance, if all users are identical, they will all benefit from regulation. Or, if $a_1 = 2$, and $a_2 = 1.8$, $y_1^N = 0.51$, $y_2^N = 0.46$, $R_1^N = 0.29$, $R_2^N = 0.17$, while $y_1^C = 0.36$, $y_2^C = 0.29$, $R_1^C = 0.38$ and $R_2^C = 0.23$. In the latter case, therefore, both users increase their payoffs by moving from Nash to regulated equilibrium.

With regard to the illustration provided by Johnson and Libecap, an interesting question in the above analytical framework is what happens if regulation takes the form of a uniform quota imposed on all users. Such a solution may be appealing because of its inherent simplicity. In our example, when $a_1 = 2$ and $a_2 = 1$, we find that, at the regulated equilibrium, the uniform quota maximizing the sum of the two individual payoffs is equal to 0.27. The corresponding payoffs are, respectively, 0.32 and 0.09. Clearly, the most efficient user is worse off and the less efficient user is better off than under the Nash equilibrium situation (and, consequently, than under the unconstrained regulated equilibrium). This result also holds when $a_1 = 2$, and $a_2 = 1.5$ (the uniform quota is equal to 0.30, and the payoffs are respectively 0.33 and 0.20), yet there is some minimum level of heterogeneity in resource use efficiency below which it ceases to be true.

To conclude, the main implication one can draw from the analysis proposed here is that, where agents are heterogeneous, regulating the commons efficiently may cause conflicts of interest to erupt. Following the analysis proposed by Fernandez and Rodrik (1991), we now show that regulations that, once adopted, would be supported by a majority of users may in fact be opposed by a majority of the same users before it is implemented. Conversely, reforms that are detrimental to many *ex post* may appear *ex ante* as beneficial to a majority of voters. These will be adopted, but, once implemented, will be rejected and a return to the initial situation will occur. As a consequence, *majority voting leads to a* status quo *bias*. The rationale which underlies this counter-intuitive result is the following: in all reforms, there are losers and winners, some may know that they will win, but an important number of voters do not know what their own individual situation will look like after the reform. If their expected income is negative, they will vote against it. In other words, *ex ante* uncertainty about the *identity* of the winners from the reform may lead to its rejection, even though, if adopted, the reform would have benefited a large majority of people.

Regulation with uncertainty about the identity of the winners

Let us consider a simple example (for a fuller analysis, see Fernandez and Rodrik, 1991), in which all agents are risk-neutral and identical, except that a fraction of them anticipate that they will win, while the others are uncertain about their future, post-reform situation. Suppose, for instance, that regulation is achieved through (randomly) excluding some members, say n, from the collective ownership over the resource, increasing the collective income from Y to Y' with $Y' > Y$. (Other ways of regulating the resource can be easily imagined to fit in with the example below.) Let M stand for the minority of agents who know that they will not be excluded, with $M < N - n$, where N stands for the initial number of agents sharing collective ownership over the resource. It is evident that $(n/N-M)$ represents the probability for an uninformed agent to be excluded by the regulation measures. His expected gain in income resulting from regulation is therefore equal to $(Y'/N-n)\cdot(N-M-n/N-M)-Y/N$ which may be positive or negative. If it is positive, the regulation is adopted, n users get excluded, and the $(N-n)$ remaining users support the reform. If it is negative, then a majority of users oppose the regulation proposed, even if, *ex post*, $(N-n)>N/2$ (that is, even if, were the reform implemented against the will of a majority of users, *ex post*, a majority would vote for its continuation). In other words, 'there are reforms which, once implemented, will receive adequate political support but would have failed to carry the day *ex ante*. The argument does not rely on risk-aversion, irrationality, or histeresis due to sunk costs' (Fernandez and Rodrik, 1991: 1146).

To give a numerical example, suppose that the regulation considered reduces the number of users from 100 to 60, while the income per user increases from 10 to 20 units. Total income therefore rises from 1,000 to 1,200 units. Suppose also that thirty users know in advance that they will not be excluded. *Ex ante*, if such a reform is proposed to the users, seventy among them will oppose it since their expected gain associated with it is negative: $(30/70)\times 20-10=-10/7<0$. However, if the reform is implemented, the remaining users will oppose a return to the initial situation. Graphically, we have the situation represented in Figure 8.7.

The question may now be asked as to whether it is possible, when regulation increases the expected income of *each* user, that it will still be opposed by a majority of users and, therefore, be blocked. There are two different kinds of argument pointing to a positive answer to this question. The first one is based on risk-aversion, the other, on private information problems. In the following, we will develop these two arguments successively by first analysing the case where regulation takes place through the exclusion of some agents. Thereafter, we will analyse the case where regulation is achieved through appropriate taxation or through remuneration of the variable factor at its marginal productivity ('as if' the resource was managed by a capitalist).

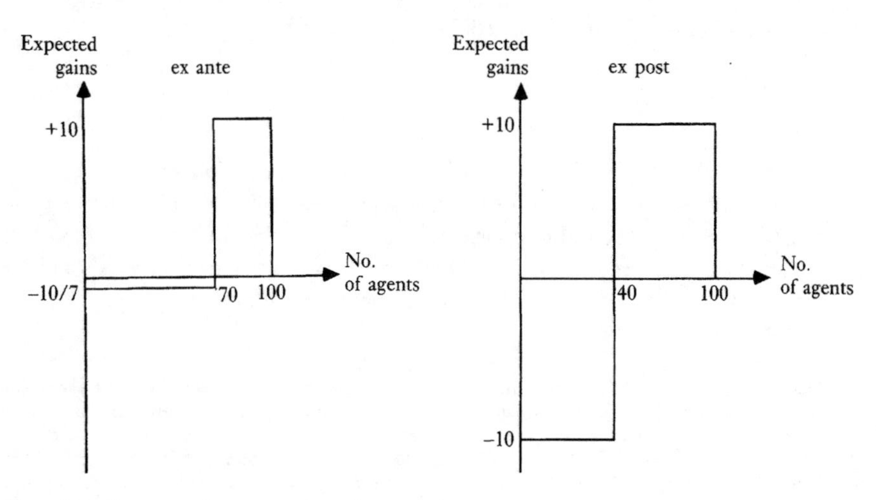

FIG. 8.7. *Ex ante* and *ex post* gains of a regulation

Regulation with risk-aversion

In many instances, regulation through the individual reduction of each agent's level of effort alone, e.g. through the imposition of an appropriate tax scheme, is not possible. In those cases, regulation must take place through the exclusion of some former users, as in the example presented above. (Note that exclusion *per se* does not necessarily lead to the efficient level of exploitation. But exclusion may well be a necessary step before any other efficiency-improving measure is contemplated.)

In a first situation, let us assume that regulation does not increase (nor decrease) total income. Take the example of a fishery, and assume that each fisherman is entitled to operate only one boat. Suppose furthermore that the number of boats operated exceeds the efficient number, and that no taxes nor any side-payment can be made. In these circumstances, the only way to regulate the use of the resource is to exclude some fishermen, the remaining ones being then in a position to reap and share amongst themselves the benefits of such a measure through the increasing productivity of their boat.

Under these assumptions, one may ask the following question: will the fishermen agree to regulate the fishery by excluding some of them, if the selection of those to be excluded is uniformly random? The answer is negative[3] if the fishermen are risk-averse. Total output is equal to Y and the total number of fishermen is equal to N. If, say, K agents are randomly selected for exclusion, each fisherman has a probability K/N of being excluded and a probability $(N - K)/N$ of staying in the fishery. If he is excluded, he gets nothing, while if he stays in the fishery, he gets $Y/(N - K)$. His present income is equal to Y/N. If his utility function, $U(.)$, is concave, so that $U'' < 0$, the utility attached to a certain income of Y/N is, by definition, greater than the utility associated with any lottery yielding an expected income of the same amount, for example, a lottery giving an income of zero with probability K/N and an income of $Y/(N - K)$, with probability $(N - K)/N$. We can thus write:

$$U\left(\frac{Y}{N}\right) > E(U) = \frac{K}{N}(0) + \frac{N-K}{N}U\left(\frac{Y}{N-k}\right)$$

$$\Leftrightarrow U\left(\frac{Y}{N}\right) > \frac{N-k}{N}U\left(\frac{Y}{N-k}\right).$$

The expected utility each fisherman gets from the exclusion scheme is always smaller than the current level of utility. This result is easy to check from Figure 8.8 in which $E(U)$, the expected utility associated with the lottery involving the exclusion of K individuals, is measured by the vertical distance between the horizontal axis and the straight line OR at the initial (pre-exclusion) level of income Y/N.[4]

[3] For a more general analysis, see Steinherr and Thisse (1979).

[4] This is because the ratio of the initial, pre-exclusion average income to the income earned by the remaining individuals after the exclusion of k individuals from the group is exactly equal to the ratio which the expected individual utility of the lottery bears to the utility associated with the above post-exclusion income, $U[Y/(N - k)]$. This relation directly follows from the algebraic definition of $E(U)$ given in the text.

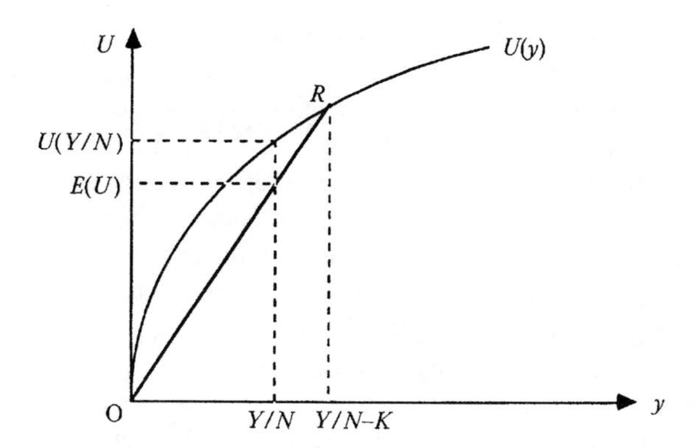

FIG. 8.8. Impact of a random exclusion process on utility levels

Note that this result also holds even if the excluded fisherman is able to get some outside employment, provided his alternative income is sufficiently lower than his current income in the fishery. This is also true if the remaining fishermen would actually give him some side-payment to compensate for his being excluded, provided that the total sum of these side-payments is less than his current income (if equal, he will of course be indifferent, assuming no work disutility).

We have thus far examined the case where the expected gains from regulation are minimum since total income remains constant. If regulation implies an increase in total output, each agent will have to compare the increased productivity brought about by the regulation scheme with his degree of risk aversion and to choose whether or not to support the regulation scheme.

From the above analysis, we may conclude that the amount of support of a regulation scheme based on the random exclusion of some former users depends crucially on (*a*) the 'productive' effect of regulation, that is, the expected total increase in total output such a scheme is likely to lead to, (*b*) the possibility for the excluded former users to find some outside employment, and (*c*) the degree of risk-aversion displayed by the users group. In some cases, any regulation scheme based on random exclusion will be opposed by all fishermen, *even if some side-payments are permitted.* (The side-payment issue will be analysed in more depth in the following section.) Therefore, one may expect that, when regulation through exclusion must take place, exclusion will not be random but will be invariably directed towards a definite subgroup of members of the community. One may also expect that, when the group is homogeneous, exclusion will not always be resorted to and, as a result, overpopulation of productive units is likely.

Regulation with private information

As has already been hinted at above, *if everything relevant to the problem is known to everybody*, one can easily design a tax schedule such that exploitation of the commons is Pareto-optimal. In the case where the proceeds of the taxes[5] are siphoned off, say, by the central state, then every productive member of the community will be worse off. This is the result obtained by Martin Weitzman in his model described in Chapter 3. If, however, the proceeds are redistributed, one can always find a scheme of transfers such that every member of the community is better off, since the new situation Pareto-dominates the initial situation. One such scheme obtains when members receive a share of the tax proceeds proportional to the amount of variable factor they were applying in the initial situation (characterized by overexploitation).

In the following, we will follow John Roemer's terminology and call such an allocation a *Nash-dominator equilibrium*,[6] in the sense that it dominates the Nash equilibrium. On the other hand, the *proportional equilibrium*, in which tax proceeds are distributed proportionately to the amount of variable factor each member operates in the new (efficient) equilibrium, does not always Pareto-dominate the initial situation: under this distribution rule, some former users may be worse off and prefer the unregulated commons to the efficient proportional allocation. (This result actually follows from our modified version of Kanbur's model.) This also holds true for the *equal-sharing equilibrium* where tax revenues are distributed equally among the members, that is, on a per head basis. Of course, the three sharing rules described above differ only when the agents themselves are different. Otherwise, the three rules result in an identical outcome. One should also note that quotas (instead of taxes) support the proportional equilibrium: if agents agree upon individual quotas and these quotas are efficient, then the proportional equilibrium obtains.

Finally, these allocations can also be decentralized as a competitive equilibrium, in which the community establishes a firm which owns the commons, and runs them competitively by hiring labour and maximizing profits. Each agent supplies his own labour force, l_i, and owns a share θ_i of the firm. The difference between the three equilibria bears upon the distribution of the shares: in the equal-sharing equilibrium, $\theta_i = l/N$, in the proportional equilibrium, $\theta_i = l_i/\Sigma_i l_i$, and, in the Nash dominator equilibrium, θ_i is equal to the proportion of labour spent under the unregulated common property regime. In all these cases, the final allocation is Pareto-optimal (but does not necessarily Pareto-dominate the initial situation).

However, in many instances, the community or the traditional authority is not in a position to have all the information relevant to the problem: here again, phenomena of 'private information' may be encountered. Typically, preferences and private endowments are likely to be private information: only the agent concerned knows 'exactly' his preferences, skills, and endowments. The central authority will then ask the agents to announce their preferences and endowments, process these informations, and propose an allocation. The question is whether or not there exists some way of 'passing from the announced preference and endowments to an allocation that provides the

[5] It is important to note that, in the present context, the problem of distribution of tax proceeds is strictly equivalent to that of distribution of profits among former users who have become wage-labourers in a profit-maximizing enterprise exploiting the common resource. One can reformulate all the results below in the latter way. Therefore, the results arrived at here also apply to a privatization process where private property rights on the resource are divided among former users.

[6] This section is based on John Roemer (1988). More details and proofs are provided there.

proper incentives for agents to tell the truth and with the property that a Nash equilibrium for the game involves a vector of announcements for the fisherfolk that implements' (Roemer, 1988: 19) an equilibrium with some desirable properties, such as Pareto-efficiency. In such a case, the proposed allocation is said to be 'implementable in Nash equilibrium'. Under private information, John Roemer (1988) reaches two important results:

1. 'There is no allocation mechanism that is Pareto-efficient, Pareto-dominates the common ownership equilibrium, and can be implemented in Nash equilibrium' (Roemer, 1988: 21).
2. The proportional allocation is not implementable in Nash equilibrium.

Hence, in the presence of private information, if an efficient allocation has to be achieved,[7] then, some agents will be hurt, and were they allowed to do so, they would veto the regulation scheme. Furthermore, whatever the agreed-upon allocation scheme, it cannot be achieved without a high degree of centralization. A central, neutral, and credible authority is needed to achieve an efficient allocation in the presence of private information. Or, agents have to be identical, in which case the private information problem disappears.

8.3 Common Property Resources in the Context of Pervasive Factor-Market Imperfections

In the applied research literature dealing with CPRs, attention is not infrequently called to various factor-market imperfections that are pervasive in rural areas of many developing countries. These imperfections are purported to lend a crucial justification to the CPR institution at village level. It is therefore important to take cognizance of the underlying arguments in order to have a more complete view of the possible advantages of common over private property. The imperfections mentioned usually concern three rural markets: those of labour, insurance, and credit. We will examine each of these in turn even though the corresponding arguments often come down to stressing that CPRs play an essential social role by helping to prevent marginalization of people.

Labour-market imperfections

The point here is that perhaps the most important role played by CPRs in developing countries nowadays is that of an *employer of last resort* and as a vital source of income for the rural poor. Thus, for example, in an in-depth analysis of eighty Indian villages located in semi-arid areas, Jodha has found that as much as 20 per cent or more of the incomes of poor families are directly generated out of use of local CPRs in seven out of twelve districts examined on this count (Jodha, 1986: 1177; see also Jodha, 1992: 10–

[7] Strictly speaking, one should replace 'achieved' by 'Nash implementable'. Other concepts of implementation exist (see Roemer, 1988: 29).

19). Moreover, in five semi-arid districts located in four different states, CPRs were estimated (at the beginning of the 1980s) to provide to the poor exclusive employment for 43–49 days per household or 18–31 days per adult worker during the year, that is, marginally more than the days worked on their own farms (this is in addition to part-time employment when CPR-based activity was undertaken casually while performing other jobs). Note also that, in most districts, CPRs were the only source of employment for 23–30 per cent of the total days for which the adults of poor households would otherwise have been involuntary unemployed (Jodha, 1986: 1174–7).

Other authors like Das Gupta (1987), Agarwal (1991), and Beck (1994) have also laid emphasis on the fact that in many parts of the Indian subcontinent, access to a wide range of communal (natural) resources is still a critical informal security mechanism whereby the deprived sections of rural populations can survive when they are recognized members of the village community where these resources are located (see Table 8.1 adapted from Das Gupta's intensive study of two Indian villages and from which it can be seen that free collection of products from local CPRs is more widespread in the village less advanced in terms of adoption of the new agricultural technology). The existence of this informal security mechanism is actually considered by Das Gupta as a major reason behind the high rate of population retention in India's

TABLE 8.1. Incidence of community-support mechanisms based on free collection of products from local CPRs in two Indian villages, 1984

	Rampur (a modern village located on the Delhi-Haryana border)	Azamgarh (a comparatively backward village in Eastern UP)
Percentage of households		
Green fodder	67.3	81.8
Food		
Leafy vegetables	95.9	98.2
Fish	—	41.8
Fruit	—	25.5
Buttermilk	57.1	—
Fuel		
Agricultural waste	67.3	98.2
Firewood	—	96.4
Dung	—	21.8
Dry leaves	—	7.3
Other		
Clay	77.6	96.4
Thatching	—	94.5
Bamboo	—	20.0

Note: Adapted from Das Gupta (1987: tables 2 and 4).

rural areas or, what comes down to the same thing, behind the comparatively low incidence of distress migration in the country.

The range of products available from village CPRs and required for current subsistence needs is often much larger than that indicated in the table. Communal resources may thus serve 'as a source of various types of food, medicinal herbs, fuel, fodder, water, manure, silt, small timber, fibre, house-building with handicraft material, resin, gum, spices, and so on for personal use and sale' (Agarwal, 1991: 182).

In the rural areas of East and South-east Asia community mechanisms for redistributing access to productive resources appear to be stronger than in India (Hayami and Kikuchi, 1981; Hayami, 1981) and this certainly holds true for Sub-Saharan Africa, where access of community members to local CPRs as a mechanism of last-resort employment is perhaps more dominant than anywhere else (see Freudenberger and Mathieu, 1993: 12). In contrast, the rural poor in Latin America appear to have few community support mechanisms available to them: in many areas, village communities 'have not developed deep-rooted rights of members to live in and partake of the available economic opportunities the community offers' (Das Gupta, 1987: 117).

As will be amply illustrated at a later stage (Chapter 10), absorption of additional resource operators may or may not be achieved through a greater intensity of use of the CPR. In the latter case, a given level of resource flow is shared among a growing number of people, usually through some rotation system. In the former case, accommodation of new operators is liable to give rise to a 'tragedy of the commons' although, placed in this perspective, the situation hardly appears as a genuine tragedy. Indeed, as explained by Bromley:

> The problem quite often, is that these resource systems are asked to absorb the very people who cannot be absorbed by the more conventional agricultural regimes found on private lands . . . the marginal ecosystems are asked to take on those slaughed off from the highly commercialised lands, the exclusion rights that run with fee-simple land redirect people to the marginal ecosystems. It hardly seems fair to condemn those resource complexes for failing to do what the commercialised ecosystems cannot do. (Bromley, 1986: 594)

Note that, in the example referred to here by Bromley, the privatization process has not been complete and overexploitation of the remaining common lands has resulted.

In conclusion, there is abundant evidence to show that village-level CPRs often assume critical importance for the livelihood of the rural poor in developing countries. To these people, they may indeed serve as a indispensable source of part-time or full-time employment and income.[8] In a context of severe shortage of employment opportunities, any attempt to establish or restore efficiency in CPR management through a privatization programme may therefore have socially catastrophic consequences. The problem obviously arises because 'overexploitation' also means overemployment, and, in the absence of any other employment opportunities and of a smoothly running

[8] The literature abounds in examples where collection of products from local CPRs is complementary with other, privately run productive activities, the complementarity being of a seasonal or a physical nature. Among tribals in central India, for example, during normal pre-harvest seasonal shortages, gathered food provides 12% of energy intake compared with 2% in the post-harvest period. In Bihar, forests are the only means of tribals' survival in the lean seasons, when the undergrowth of trees is picked for edible herbs, mushrooms, tubers, and so on (Agarwal, 1991: 184).

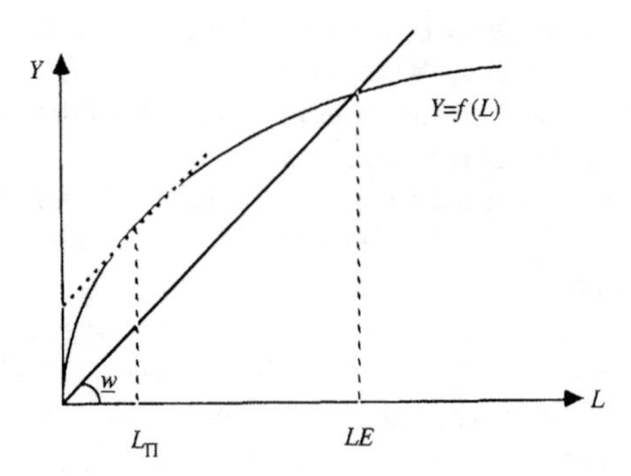

FIG. 8.9. Comparing the employment generated under a profit-maximizing and an employment-maximizing management

labour-market, it should not be blamed or even corrected, except in those instances where it leads to a degradation of the resource base. Figure 8.9 illustrates the differential employment opportunities created by a profit-maximizing strategy (L_P) on the one hand and an employment-maximizing strategy (L_E) on the other hand.[9] We assume the wage rate to be fixed at the subsistence level $\underline{w}$.

Against the above background, it is easy to grasp the strong relevance of the aforementioned result concerning the difficulty for a group or community to regulate CPRs through exclusion of some of its members. To recall, risk-averse resource users may never agree to a scheme in which regulation of a CPR is achieved through the exclusion of randomly selected members of the user group. True, the most well-to-do people in the village may voluntarily waive their customary use rights because they have now obtained access to more productive employment opportunities. Yet, the problem is likely to remain to the extent that new employment opportunities do not expand as rapidly as rural population so that the absolute number of villagers dependent on local CPRs for subsistence increases inexorably.

Insurance-market imperfections

The insurance role of CPRs is stressed by some authors. According to this view, in the absence of properly functioning insurance markets, CPRs enable agents performing a similar productive activity to pool risks. This is noted to be a particularly important function where the resource itself is subject to wide spatial variations in yields, such as grazelands.

For example, in the tropical and subtropical rangelands of the Sahel and East Africa rainfall varies considerably from year to year. But, more importantly, rainfall is unevenly distributed over an area in any given year. Rain is usually produced in this region by individual storms creating narrow rainfall paths with inter-storm areas remaining quite dry. Wallen and Guvynne

[9] For an excellent analysis of this issue under the efficiency-wage hypothesis, see Stiglitz (1976).

(1988: 27) note that in parts of Kenya, these storms rarely exceed five kilometres in width and are normally less than one kilometre wide. As a result of this pattern of rainfall, a traveller on horseback during a single day in the rainy season can easily pass through several spots that are saturated with water and full of grass and others that have not received any rainfall. The proper utilization of such pastures requires that livestock producers have the freedom to move animals over a large area in order to efficiently use available forage resources. Masai herders in East Africa must have access to between 120,000 and 200,000 hectares of rangeland to be able to cope with this situation. (Gilles and Jamtgaard, 1981: 132–3; see also Wiessner, 1982; Cashdan, 1985; Wilson and Thompson, 1993: 305–6)

The risk-pooling function of CPRs can be captured more formally in the following way. Suppose that the commons can be divided into n grazing areas within which rainfall is evenly distributed. Across each of these n grazing areas, rainfall would vary substantially. Assume also that the variability in rainfall is the same in each area (i.e. $\sigma_1 = \sigma_2 = \ldots = \sigma_n$). Standard calculus yields the following expression for the total variability of precipitation over the whole area:

$$\sigma_T^2 = n\sigma^2[1 + \rho(n - 1)],$$

where ρ is the arithmetic mean of all the correlation coefficients, ρ_{ij}, for any pair (i,j) of a share $1/n$ of the commons of grazing areas. Individual variability is therefore:

$$\sigma_i^2 = \frac{\sigma^2}{n}[1+\rho(n-1)].$$

It is evident from the above last equation that σ_i^2 falls as n increases or ρ decreases.

However, contrary to a view commonly held, risk considerations alone are not sufficient to explain why private property should be inferior to common ownership. For instance, one could think of parcelling out the entire grazeland into small, appropriately scattered pastures so that, by possessing a large enough portfolio of them, each herdsman can be effectively protected against the risk of income shortfalls. If such an alternative is not feasible, it must necessarily be because costs of enforcing private property rights are too high relative to the land yields. In other words, it is only in so far as they are combined with high enforcement costs and low resource productivity that insurance motives can make common ownership more desirable than private property. Alternatively, one could think of bringing the entire grazeland under the private ownership of a single owner who would then lease out grazing rights to the herdsmen. In this case, the comparative inefficiency of private property is to be explained by the combination of the monopoly argument and risk-pooling considerations (risk minimization implies the creation of a monopoly).

CPRs also play an important insurance function in so far as they guarantee the people's livelihood in emergencies. They 'provide the rural poor with partial protection in times of unusual economic stress. For landless people, they may be the only non-human asset at their disposal' (Dasgupta and Mäler, 1991: 19). By allowing other members in a situation of distress to make use of the resource (which is then used only for that purpose), every member of the community ensures himself against complete destitution, it being understood that use rights are temporary and may be opposed once the cause of distress has disappeared. It is interesting to note that, in most instances, the CPR performing that function is of very low economic value, so that a profit-maximizer would judge its exploitation non-profitable in normal circumstances.

Lastly, the point is often made that CPR overexploitation may not necessarily result from an incentive structure which drives people to behave in a socially irrational way. It may also be caused by the absence of insurance markets. This is particularly evident in the case of herders who tend to maintain flocks of considerable size but relatively poor quality as a way of hedging against the risk of animal loss. As pointed out by Dasgupta and Mäler, in Sub-Saharan Africa, 'herds are larger than they would be were capital and insurance markets open to the rural poor. This imposes an additional strain on grazing lands, most especially during periods of drought' (Dasgupta and Mäler, 1993: 6).

Credit-market imperfections

An advantage of village-level CPRs which is sometimes pinpointed by anthropologists is their role as an informal credit source. Thus, for example, in the case of the Yoruba community studied by Lloyd (1962), we are told that people can use the forests as an asset to meet community needs: oil palm is then harvested communally and used towards some collective purpose agreed upon by the community (Bruce and Fortmann, 1989: 9). Or, in an interesting analysis of privatization in a village of Karnataka carried out by Karanth (1992), we are told that:

> The (village) garden served in the past as a source of 'oil money' for the two temples in the village, which was the proceeds of the sale of produce (mango, tamarind, jack and soap nuts) by auction. The temple priests now (at the end of a gradual privatisation process) grumble over the deprivation of oil money, which they have now to meet out of their own earnings in the temple or by the way of sale of produce. (Karanth, 1992: 1685)

Moreover, in particular circumstances also defined by the community, individuals may be allowed an extraordinary access to the CPR in order to use the income thus generated for an economic or social activity; or, else, the community itself exploits the CPR but reserves the product collected for helping one of its members to meet a particular expenditure such as that involved in a wedding or a funeral ceremony. We have personally encountered the same kind of arrangement in many Senegalese coastal villages where collective fishing expeditions are periodically organized by the community or a social group with a view to financing a communal project (such as the construction of a mosque or a school) or to supporting a particular member so as to enable him to meet a given expenditure.

In many cases, the CPR thus performs the role of a sort of communal bank upon which the community or its members individually may draw in certain predetermined circumstances. To that extent, it appears as a substitute for non-existent or imperfect credit markets. As for the previous point, it must nevertheless be asked whether or in what sense common property is really superior to private property in performing that function. After all, it could be contended that, at least for those CPRs which are liable to be privatized at reasonable costs, the division of the CPR into small individually held patches might also enable community members to have a bank substitute available to them. Thus, in the same way as villagers raise pigs, goats, or sheep for the purpose of constituting an easy-to-mobilize and moderately divisible asset fund, they can grow or monitor trees on a private basis for the same purpose.

What is then the rationale of common ownership? There are two elements in the answer to that question. First, collectively held resources enable a community to meet collective needs at comparatively low transaction costs. In other words, the alternative of collecting private contributions from each individual would prove more costly, in many cases, than the solution that consists of organizing a collective harvesting operation where everyone can easily monitor others' actions. Second, equity considerations militate against privatizing village-level CPRs for the above purpose. As a matter of fact, inasmuch as it is bound to give rise to increased socio-economic differentiation (if only because people differ in their individual abilities to manage the resource), privatization is problematic. This is all the more so as the needs to be fulfilled from the incomes generated from the resource have an essentially social character, since they usually serve to establish social identity and respectability. A community or social group may understandably be eager to allow all its members to incur a minimum amount of expenditure towards performing inportant social functions (ceremonies or rituals), or to prevent excessive competition from arising in the symbolic sphere of social life. And, for the same reason as that mentioned above (lower transaction costs), holding a kind of communal bank in the form of a CPR may well be the most effective way to achieve this objective (as compared to the alternative of organizing a system of transfers with all the attendant moral hazard problems).

8.4 Conclusion

When the common property is regulated, efficient use can be achieved through appropriate taxes and subsidies aimed at correcting all the existing externalities. Yet, depending on the level of centralization of the regulating agency, the informational requirement of such a solution will be more or less stringent. In particular, it is unlikely that a state agency will possess sufficient knowledge about the state of the resource, its flow of use, and the identity of its users to be able to manage it directly in an efficient manner. Even assuming that the characteristics of the resource and its users are perfectly known, there still is the problem that monitorability of the users' behaviour may be imperfect. As a consequence, to discourage rule-breaking, the State will have to impose heavy fines which may well give rise to corruption and more openly obstructive practices. For these reasons, decentralized regulation appears less problematic although the ability of user communities to effectively process the available information ought not to be overestimated. Moreover, even when regulation is decentralized, perfect monitoring is the exception rather than the rule and it is therefore to be expected that rule violations will always occur at equilibrium.

When considering the possibility of common property regulation, distributive effects should never be ignored. Several situations can actually arise in which agreement about resource management is difficult to reach. Thus, when users are heterogeneous in the sense that they have different endowments, a co-operative solution may be so detrimental to the interests of the least-skilled users that, given the difficulty of implementing compensatory transfers, they will strongly oppose it. Furthermore, if regulation implies that some users should be deprived of access to the resource, uncertainty about the identity of those to be excluded will entail resistance against reduction of the user group's size. This is all the more likely to happen if users are risk-averse, an expected behavioural characteristic of poor users facing tight subsistence constraints in a context of highly imperfect credit and insurance markets. Note in this respect that common property is *de facto* a method of pooling the users' risks and thereby serves the essential function of a substitute for missing insurance markets.

If regulation takes the form of a taxation scheme and the tax proceeds are siphoned off by an agency (like the State) located above the user groups, the latter will be worse off than under the unregulated regime and they will therefore exercise all their leverage to prevent such a management scheme from being implemented. It would then seem logical to remit these proceeds to the users in proportion to the amount of variable factors which they were applying in the initial situation. Nevertheless, owing to private information problems, an efficient allocation will not be achieved without hurting some agents: the efficient situation cannot be Pareto-ranked when compared with the unregulated situation.

Finally, in any discussion concerning the relative merits of various regimes of CPR ownership, the fact must be borne in mind that overexploitation of village-level natural resources is often tantamount to overemployment: stress on the CPR directly results from a lack of alternative employment opportunities. For this reason, as long as these alternative opportunities are not created in sufficient numbers and the State does not intervene to alleviate the predicament of the worst-affected users, private property or strongly regulated common property will appear less desirable than a regime where access rights and rules of use take explicitly into account the subsistence constraints of poor villagers.

9

Some Concluding Reflections on the Privatization of Common Property Resources

In many discussions about the overexploitation of natural resources, the blame is often put on the presumed absence of a well-defined set of property rights. In this perspective, privatization appears as the logical prerequisite to an efficient use of these resources.

In the preceding chapters, we have attempted at a theoretical level to assess how far such a claim is justified. This was done by carrying out an in-depth economic analysis of three alternative property regimes: open access, private property, and common property. In the latter property regime, a distinction was made between the unregulated and the regulated common property depending on whether a political authority is able to design and enforce different constraining rules for the resource use by the members of a well-defined community.

It has been shown that the core argument advanced by the champions of the privatization programme rests on the comparison between an idealized fully efficient private property system and the anarchical situation created by open access (or, to a lesser extent, an unregulated common property). What has been argued in those chapters is that such a comparison is not only unfair to many traditional property regimes, but also scientifically illegitimate if used as an argument in favour of private property over natural resources. What a private property regime really needs to be compared to is a situation of regulated common property. When this is done, a rather surprising result emerges. Indeed, if (1) information is perfect and (2) there are no transaction costs, *regulated common property and private property are equivalent from the standpoint of the efficiency of resource use*. In other words, a common property regime has no structural trait which makes it inherently inefficient. Both the above property regimes can therefore support a Pareto-optimal equilibrium.

In other words, the property right school is guilty of confusing property regimes in which a resource is free for the taking with other regimes where access to, and use of, the resources are subject to strong internal regulations. As has been rightly emphasized by all the authors adhering to what may be called the 'collective action' school, a sound discussion about the relative advantages and disadvantages of various modes of CPR management cannot take place as long as situations of no property (*res nullius*) or open access are not carefully distinguished from situations of common property (*res communis*) in which a joint ownership unit exists and rules of restrained access to CPR are implemented.[1] Note that what often appears to the outside observer to be open

[1] See Ciriacy-Wantrup and Bishop, 1975; Klee, 1980; Runge, 1986; Wade, 1988; Berkes, 1989; Bromley, 1989*a* and 1989*b*; Acheson, 1989; Bromley and Cernea, 1989; Ostrom, 1990.

access may really involve implicit co-operation by individual users according to a series of rules.

In a second step, the possible sources of inefficiency of a privatization programme has been analysed by identifying the conditions under which the establishment of private property would automatically constitute an efficiency-increasing move compared with a regime of unregulated common property. More specifically, property rights have to be well defined, all markets in the economy must exist and, moreover, be perfect and competitive, and there are no costs entailed in the enforcement of private property rights. In the real world, however, none of these conditions is likely to be satisfied and, therefore, it cannot be predicted a priori whether the establishment of private property over natural resources enhances efficiency or not.

Before privatizing common property resources, considerable attention should be paid to two advantages of traditional common property systems. First, these systems embody a variety of implicit entitlements that enable the resource users to make up for deficient markets in such crucial areas as employment, credit, insurance, and social security. Second, they also correspond to a complex set of rights and obligations embedded in long-term personal relationships that promote informal co-operation. Establishing private property rights is therefore tantamount to dissociating the economic use of the resource from all elements of personalized relationships and this, contrary to a widely held view based on the restrictive assumption of complete and perfect market, is liable to impair efficiency. As far as income distribution is concerned, what is worth stressing is that, historically, traditional users seldom get their rights of use recognized when privatization occurs. As a result, despite the increased efficiency private property is presumed to bring about, their welfare must fall. This holds true even if they now exploit the resource as wage-earners.

In a third step, attention has been shifted to the problems inherent in a common property management system. Without denying the relevance of the tragedy of the commons' story to explain degradation of natural resources in important circumstances, the fact must be reckoned that problems of resource management may well entail co-ordination or chicken game-like problems or a mixture of different payoff structures. In this new perspective, the focus of the analysis is no more on the irresistible tendency of individuals to overexploit the commons, as in the simple one-short PD game, but on human encounters involving problems of trust, leadership, co-ordination, group identity, and homogeneity. The role of moral norms in backing trust, creating an aversion for freeriding on others' efforts, and linking all individuals together in a kind of generalized assurance game needs to be underlined. These beneficial effects of moral norms are more likely to take place within the framework of small group settings. This advantage of small groups is compounded by the fact that interactions among resource users are continuous and that their actions are easily observed and memorized. It is in fact in large groups that moral norms are most necessary since there is no internal mechanism to induce and sustain collective action in an anonymous environment. Unfortunately, this is where they are the most difficult to establish.

Recent findings from experimental social psychology point to a more optimistic conclusion even regarding large groups. This is because communication among actors and the possibility of promise-making induced by it tend to generate emotions which deter people from exploiting others. It is as though the feelings of some kind of proximity thus created, even for a limited period of time, would carry with them a sense of fairness which permeates their actions. To put it in another way, communication, when it can take place, may make people change their minds, thereby modifying the structure of their preferences and the payoff matrix of the game that is being played.

There is apparently an insurmountable limit to the questions that game theory can answer and it is related to the aforementioned problem of trust. Ultimately, indeed, co-operation may not emerge in a group whether large or small, if enough trust does not prevail among a sufficient number of people. There must exist a sufficient proportion of people who have both an inclination towards co-operation and optimistic expectations regarding others' willingness to join the collective action. Given these initial conditions for co-operation, it is difficult to adhere (completely) to the evolutionary doctrine according to which co-operation may emerge spontaneously from the mutual interactions of the people.

We have clearly reached a point where the assistance of historical knowledge is absolutely needed. Why is it that a reasonable amount of trust exists in this particular group while complete distrust is the rule in another one? Why is it that a large number of people have a predisposition towards co-operation in this particular society or community while inveterate opportunists dominate in another one, making collective actions well-nigh impossible there? These are the kinds of questions which can be highlighted only by inquiring into the specific history of concrete societies, which often implies that the role of cultural and political factors is explicitly brought into the picture. Indeed, our analysis points to the importance of these *cultural beliefs* which capture individuals' expectations with respect to actions that will be taken by others in various situations involving the production of public goods.[2]

In a fourth step, the possibility of making up for deficient spontaneous (decentralized) co-operation by resorting to purposeful regulation of common property has retained our attention. The use of 'selective incentives', such as taxes, may in principle solve all the externality problems generated by common ownership. Upon second look, however, there are a number of serious difficulties associated with this solution.

[2] In so far as they are concerned with expectations, cultural beliefs can be given a precise economic meaning and game-theoretical representation. Indeed, since they are identical and commonly known among the people partaking of a particular culture (or belonging to a particular cultural group), when each person plays his best response to his cultural beliefs, 'the set of permissible cultural beliefs is restricted to those that are self-enforcing. Hence, this specific subset of cultural beliefs can be formalized as a set of probability distributions over an equilibrium strategy combination. Each probability distribution reflects the expectation of a player with respect to the actions that would be taken on- and off-the-path-of-play' (Greif, 1992: 4). It is important to emphasize that cultural beliefs differ from strategies because they are qualities of individuals and not games. In the words of Greif again, cultural beliefs are qualities of individuals in the sense that those 'that were crystallized at some point in time with respect to a specific game impact decisions in historically subsequent strategic situations. Past cultural beliefs provide focal points and co-ordinate expectations, thereby influencing equilibrium selection and society's enforcement institutions', with the latter being composed of cultural beliefs as well as the rules of the game (ibid.).

In particular, besides the well-known issue of the acceptability of a regulation scheme and the required enforcing authority, there are the problems of private information and imperfect monitorability. These problems are difficult to overcome, especially so if resource users are heterogeneous. Nevertheless, what needs to be emphasized is that, once they are established, regulatory schemes may well be less vulnerable to mistakes and small deviations than decentralized solutions. This is essentially because they provide a stable framework of unambiguous incentives that helps to structure expectations and to direct actions towards a well-defined goal.

In view of the foregoing considerations, none of the property regimes appears intrinsically efficient and, whether or not privatization of natural resources is advisable on the grounds of pure economic efficiency depends crucially on the specific situation considered. In many situations where regulated common property is criticized for being inefficient, private property would indeed pose similar problems. For instance, in those cases where agents are not fully aware of the ecological processes at work, or where protection of the resource against intruders cannot be guaranteed, or where the poverty of the agents drives them to overexploit their resources, state intervention is in fact needed to support common property, and it would also be needed if the resource were privatized. In other words, in those cases where common property is patently inefficient, the cause of that inefficiency should be thoroughly investigated before formulating any policy recommendation. Also, the kind of state intervention and the degree of decentralization advisable are matters that deserve careful scrutiny and, before opting for particular formulae, the glaring failures of state appropriation of village commons should be borne in mind.

An important issue which is bypassed in our analysis is that of technical progress. It is often alleged that the main gain to be expected from the privatization of natural resources consists of the increasing rate at which innovations ('technical progress') are produced and adopted. It is presumed that the economic inducements to innovate are much more powerful under private property than under common property. Unfortunately, on this particular issue, so little is known that it is almost impossible to give a balanced account of the different arguments in support of or against a particular property regime. In general, private property appears as much more responsive to innovation than common property. For instance, in his remarkable analysis of English enclosures, Allen (1992) concludes that:

> the diffusion of new techniques bears out the fundamentalist claim that enclosure led to agricultural improvement. . . . the open field villages were far less innovative than the enclosed. It is a far cry from that conclusion, however, to establishing that the enclosure movement made a substantial contribution to productivity growth in early modern England. Crop yields and labour productivity (not crop rotations) were the two critical factors of advance. Both about doubled between the middle ages and the nineteenth century. Enclosure, however, made only a minor contribution to these increases. (Allen, 1992: 15)

In more recent experiences such as the green revolution in Asia and Latin America, it is also patent that public agencies have played a major role in both the production and the diffusion of agricultural innovations (see, e.g., Hayami and Ruttan, 1971).

At a theoretical level, the innovative superiority of private property is difficult to assess. First, free competition is of course important in the adoption of innovations, since one is forced to keep up with competitors. Yet this argument applies to common property as well as to private property. Second, it might be argued that the private owner who experiments and innovates is alone responsible for his own acts: does he not concentrate all the gains of innovation? What must be said however is that he also bears all the risks attendant on his own experiments. In a common property, the risks as well as the gains of a localized experimentation can be spread over the whole community of users. Therefore, under common property, innovative behaviour should tend to be less risk-averse than that under private property. (Notice incidentally that this is distinct from the social security function of traditional rights of access: people are more induced to incur risks in their activities when they have the assurance of such rights.) Third, under competitive private property, many people experiment with different things, while under common property, the ideas are screened by a political authority or by a collective decision-making process. This of course tends to reduce the diversity of new ideas and innovations but, at the same time, where the adoption of the innovation requires much co-ordination (e.g. in the case of anti-erosive barriers, or for weed-control in agricultural activities), a common property of sufficient size may prove more adequate. Fourth, if, as has been argued, privatization tends to increase socio-economic differentiation and to exclude part of the former users from access to the resource, it may well be that common property, by enabling more people to ensure basic subsistence *and* to participate in economic decision-making, also allows more ideas and innovations to be produced and diffused. Fifth, as is well known in public good literature, for many innovations, the externalities involved are such that only the State is able to carry them out at a socially efficient level.

As can be seen, at a theoretical level, no decisive arguments can be found in support of a particular property regime. More scientific thinking is obviously required to develop and refine the different arguments that we have merely sketched above regarding the impact of a particular property regime on the nature and forms of innovative activities, and regarding the role of the State. Furthermore, a thorough analysis of different historical experiences is called upon in order to assess more carefully the relevance and relative importance of those arguments as well as to uncover new influencing factors that a purely conceptual approach may have missed.

PART II

The Feasibility of Local-Level Resource Management: An Empirical Assessment

Introduction

There is a more or less explicit conclusion that lies behind many popular discussions of environmental degradation (particularly among ecologist militants) and that emerges from a whole current of anthropological thinking. This conclusion can be stated under the form of a three-pronged proposition: (*a*) traditional management systems (which have been designated as regulated CPRs in Part I) have been the rule rather than the exception in much of the developing world; (*b*) as long as they have held together, they have been fairly successful in conserving the natural resources at stake; and (*c*) unfortunately, many of these systems have broken down under the disruptive impact of external forces (see, e.g., Panayotou, 1988: 91).

Are these ideas part of a 'persisting myth' that tends to 'romanticize' human communities and their abilities to apply wisdom and foresight in their relationships with their resources and each other (McCay and Acheson, 1987: 10; see also McNicoll, 1990: 152)? Or, on the contrary, are they a rather correct reflection of the genuine potential of traditional village societies for managing their localized CPRs as long as their internal social order is not disturbed by government policies, population growth, and broad market forces? Also, once traditional management systems have been eroded under the impact of these external factors, is there any hope that they can be somehow rejuvenated or adapted to modern challenges provided, of course, that a suitable environment is created around them? Finally, to the extent that socio-anthropological research points to diverse experiences of both success and failure in collective actions for the management of local-level CPRs, what are the main determinants of the eventual outcome of such actions and what factors can account for their presence or absence? These are the central questions which are addressed in Part II of our work.

Let us now give a brief sketch of how it is organized. In Chapter 10, we attempt to assess the claim that members of traditional village societies were able to manage their CPRs effectively. Then, in Chapter 11, we examine whether, in what sense and how local-level institutions for managing the commons have been adversely affected or even destroyed by exogenous forces or external factors. This chapter comprises two parts. In the first part, the impact of state interventions and regulations as they have taken place in many Third World countries during recent decades is evaluated while in the second one attention is focused on the influence of population growth, market integration, technological change, and some other factors. The basic idea is (1) to make up our mind about the practical effectiveness of systems of public ownership and centralized management of CPRs, particularly in the context of developing countries; and (2) to gauge the vulnerability of traditional local arrangements to sudden or significant changes in their background environment. In Chapter 12, learning from numerous positive as well as negative localized experiences with common property management, an effort is made to identify the main factors that can simultaneously account for the effectiveness and long-term viability of CPR management schemes in some observed cases, and for the absence or failure of such arrangements in other recorded instances. In Chapter 13, broad policy implications are drawn from the results achieved in the previous chapters and special attention is devoted to examining the possibility for both the State and the local communities to play a role in the management of CPRs, acting in concert and adding up their respective strengths while making up for their respective weaknesses.

We end this introduction with a caveat. The empirical material used in this chapter is essentially derived from socio-anthropological research in which participant behaviour within the confines of in-depth case-studies is the dominant form of investigation. Such a methodological approach is appropriate given that the precise identification of the characteristics of local-level institutions for CPR management requires deep knowledge of the society concerned as well as varied insights into its global working. Nevertheless, leaving aside the well-known vexed problem of whether case-studies pertaining to localized areas widely scattered throughout the world can lead to generalizable results, due mention must be made of the following difficulty stressed by Kanbur. Many, if not most, socio-anthropological studies were undertaken not necessarily to elucidate the mechanisms of CPR management. It therefore takes a certain interpretation and interpolation to fit the observations reported in the case-study into a coherent picture of resource management. 'In these situations we are often twice removed from the basic phenomenon—relying firstly on the interpretations of the participant observers and secondly on the interpretations of the case study oriented common property analyst' (Kanbur, 1992: 12).

10

Were People Traditionally Conservationists?

10.1 The Romantic View: A First Appraisal

A widespread view among students of traditional, precapitalist societies is that members of these societies were efficient managers of their natural resources, meaning that they followed rules and patterns of behaviour geared towards self-sustainability. Unfortunately, as we have already pointed out in Chapter 1, the concept of sustainability is problematic because it is often used in a loose way which lends itself to several interpretations. Statements such as: a resource is managed in a sustainable way when over the long term it is 'maintained *at some optimal level*' (Lawry, 1989*a*: 8, emphasis added) bear witness to this difficulty. In such circumstances, the hypothesis that traditional societies effectively managed their resources becomes unfalsifiable due to lack of rigour in the definition of the key concept supposed to characterize the behaviour of the people concerned. There is then a high risk that the conclusion reached by the researcher reflects his a priori belief about the ecological soundness of traditional practices.

For the sake of illustration, consider the following account of the traditional organization and behaviour of Californian Indians with respect to their natural resources (more particularly their salmon estuary fisheries):

> Like all hunter-gatherers, California Indians were intimately familiar with the ecology of their food resources and actively manipulated their environment in order to enhance its stability and productivity. . . . The Indians seem to have harvested as much from their environment as it could predictably yield. . . . Native Californian hunter-gatherers . . . took pains to control their use of resources so as to sustain their way of life . . . the Indians managed their fisheries successfully over the long run, and at sustained levels of harvest that might well incite the envy of twentieth-century fishers and lawmakers. (McEvoy, 1986: 28, 38–9)

How are we to interpret this series of statements? First, what does the concept of 'predictable' yield refer to? Second, the first part of the text suggests that efficient management is tantamount to conserving the resource ('enhancing its stability'), that is, to maintaining over time its regenerative or reproductive capacity. However, the subsequent idea that 'Indians managed their resource so as to sustain their way of life' points to a much larger (and, as we have argued in Chapter 1, more meaningful) notion of sustainability understood as the safeguarding of the consumption capacity of future generations. Third, the latter part of the text speaks of 'sustained levels of harvest' without giving any clue to the meaning to be attached to this expression.

This being said, it is probably fair to reckon that, when the context of the whole argument is considered, many authors seem to adhere to the narrow definition of resource sustainability, namely that of resource conservation or maintenance: members of traditional village societies, according to this opinion, are seen as harvesting the maximum yield from their resources as they can safely extract without endangering the regenerative capacity of these resources.

Now, there are several problems with the view that traditional societies were efficient resource managers in the above restricted sense. The first problem arises from the fact that, with such a narrow definition of resource management, a society in which population pressure has made slash-and-burn cultivation non-sustainable (forest resources are being gradually degraded due to overexploitation) and which has subsequently converted forests into permanent agricultural fields cannot be considered as managing its resources efficiently. To meet the conservationist criterion, such a society would have, for example, to limit its population size so as to match the available forest resources *within the confines of the existing technology* (slash-and-burn cultivation). Clearly, the conservationist criterion is problematic as soon as changes in technology and social organization are brought into the picture. Some authors explicitly acknowledge this difficulty. Thus, in the particular case of forestry exploitation in East Kalimantan, Indonesia, Jessup and Peluso have noted the following: when in the past villagers were led by such circumstances as warfare, demographic changes, and fluctuations in the long-established trade in minor forest products to deplete certain resources and switch to others, the switch was not necessarily made at a point that would conserve the resources. Hence their conclusion that so-called 'traditional' forest-dwelling people were not necessarily more conservative users of resources before the modern boom in tropical forest exploitation (Jessup and Peluso, 1986: 508–9).

The societies with which the upholders of the conservationist thesis seem to be mostly concerned are those which operate—or are supposed to operate—in a more or less static environment: peace reigns, population is stationary or is implicitly assumed to be duly controlled to match the resources; there is no technical change; economic activities are not disturbed by radically new trade opportunities; etc. Moreover, the livelihood of their members depends to a large extent upon a single resource the conservation of which therefore constitutes a crucial determinant of their present and future survival capacity.

A second issue worth raising is that traditional management practices may be coincidental rather than intentional, a fact which is stressed by several authors even though the evidence to decide whether a practice is intentional is in most cases tenuous (see, e.g., Cordell and McKean, 1986: 101; Ruddle, 1988: 81; Verdeaux, 1990: 192; Johannes, 1982; Scudder and Conelly, 1985). Leaving aside the problem that natural resources do not remain in unaltered condition even when unused (Brookfield, 1991: 48–9), a situation in which conservation is clearly unintentional arises when the technology is so primitive that it cannot enable the people to affect the level of the stock through their productive efforts (this happens when, beyond a point, the costs of exploiting a resource become infinite), and/or when population is sufficiently low compared to the amount of resource as to make overexploitation impossible. The case of taboos is more difficult to handle because, if it is true that many taboos have the effect of conserving resources, one cannot be certain that they have been especially designed for that purpose.

A society may be said to be conservationist if resource conservation has been (purposely) achieved through the operation of ecologically oriented motives. When this is not the case, because such an outcome has resulted either from motives unrelated to the ecological concern or from exogenous, uncontrollable events, the society is not conservationist although resources have been actually maintained. Thus, for example, if a community controls its size so as to adjust it to the stock of available resources in such a way that this stock is maintained over time, it is conservation-oriented whereas, if restricted population size (not only of human beings but also of animals) is the result of epidemics and intergroup conflicts, it may not be thus characterized. Likewise, if a community makes conscious technological choices with a view to preventing resource destruction, it can be legitimately described as conservationist whereas, if an environmentally harmless ('soft') technology is used that has not been selected with such a purpose in mind, this description is not appropriate.

The above distinction between intentional and non-intentional conservation practices is not a purely academic matter. Indeed, the potential for village- or group-level resource management in today's circumstances partly depends upon the people being sufficiently *aware* of the impact of their own actions on the state of the surrounding resources.

Now, it must be admitted that the proponents of the 'romantic' view of traditional ecological conservationism are not content with pointing to the *outcome* of conservation: resources were not degraded or depleted in traditional village environments. Most of their efforts have been actually devoted to showing that in many instances precapitalist societies have evolved sets of *rules* explicitly destined to conserve resources. The rules are basically of two kinds: on the one hand, there are those controlling access to the CPRs by outsiders, so as to prevent open-access situations from arising (these rules are essential to systems of territoriality) and, on the other hand, we find rules regulating allocation and use of the resource. In fact, even the authors who are ready to concede the existence of some unintentional resource-conserving devices frequently point to the simultaneous existence of restrictions or measures clearly designed to conserve stocks (see, e.g., Cordell and McKean, 1986: 101; Ruddle, 1988: 81–3). The standard position can thus be expressed in the terms used by Carrier with specific reference to fishing in Oceania:

> The notion that traditional marine tenure systems are linked to the conservation of fish stocks in Oceania is partly supported by the assumption that since native people are intimately familiar with the ecological systems they exploit and upon which they have depended, they have learned the necessity and techniques of conservation. (Carrier, 1987: 144)

There is a third problem which deserves to be mentioned at this preliminary stage of our discussion. The problem emerges from the confusion which is often made between two analytically distinct issues, namely that of open-access situations and that of resource management proper. Indeed, as has been stressed in Chapter 1, the management of resources is a dynamic issue to which the concepts of maximum sustainable yield or optimum economic yield are clearly related whereas open access gives rise to a static problem which involves non-separable externalities and in connection with which the concept of rent dissipation takes on its meaning.

In many cases, unfortunately, the authors make statements which mix up the two issues. A clear illustration of this tendency is provided by the following excerpt of a paper written by Cordell and McKean: 'Perceptions of what constitutes a "safe" number of people on fishing grounds are primarily based on acceptable levels of boat crowding rather than on estimates of the reproductive reserves of fish that are necessary to sustain certain levels of production' (Cordell and McKean, 1986: 101). In other cases, ambiguity is created by the fact that authors use the concept 'traditional management systems' to refer to the ability of traditional communities to control the open-access problem rather than to solve that of resource conservation, thereby adding considerably to the terminological confusion around the concept of resource management on which we have lamented at the beginning of this section. To illustrate this second possibility, we may quote Panayotou when he writes that 'a possible test of the performance of the traditional *management systems* would be in terms of their capacity to forestall the dissipation of economic rents, which is the theoretically predicted and empirically observed outcome of *open-access* fisheries' (Panayotou, 1988: 88, emphasis added; in the same vein, see also Levieil, 1987). From his own as well as other empirical investigations, he then concludes that in a country like Sri Lanka, where even in modern times many coastal villages have remained 'closed' communities, fisheries are 'successfully managed' because fishermen there are earning incomes above their opportunity costs (which can be approximated by what comparable socio-economic groups earn in the rest of the economy). By contrast, traditional management systems in Malaysia (east coast), the Philippines, and Thailand 'have disintegrated' because in these latter countries 'small-scale fishermen were found to earn incomes far below their opportunity costs and to depend on a variety of non-fishing occupations to make a living' (Panayotou, 1988: 88–9).

The fact of the matter is that the stock of a resource *may* be conserved even in situations where rents have been dissipated as a result of open access (see above, Chapter 1): this would be the case if the numerous users of the resource follow strict conservation rules or if the users' harvesting behaviour is not susceptible of affecting the resource stock. If management is taken to imply the conservation of the resource, it is therefore not true that traditional management systems in South-East Asian fisheries have disintegrated simply because rents have vanished.

10.2 An Interpretative Analysis of the Available Evidence

A simple typology of traditional village societies

So much for general considerations and preliminary comments on what we have called the romantic view of traditional conservationism. It is now the time to evaluate it more closely and to attempt to provide more precise answers to questions such as: did rules exist in traditional village societies in connection with the management of their collective resources; to what extent rules of access to these resources have been consciously designed to conserve resources; and to what extent have they achieved their objective?

Degree of flexibility of access rules	Existence of conservation rules	
	Conservation rules do not exist	Conservation rules do exist
Access rules are quite flexible	I	IV
Access rules are quite strict	II	III

FIG. 10.1. A typology of traditional village societies with respect to resource management

To make significant progress in this inquiry and to organize the empirical material at hand in a systematic way, it is important to avoid general statements supposed to apply to all traditional societies at the same time. After all, village societies that are relatively closed, are not permeated by a market logic (or are only superficially so), and are to a large extent insulated from the rule of a centralized state machinery are still so diverse that it is hardly possible to assess their performance or situation *vis-à-vis* resource conservation without classifying them into at least a few basic types. Two discriminatory criteria seem to be particularly appropriate and will serve as guidelines for the following discussion. They actually rest upon the distinction which we have just re-emphasized between the issue of open access on the one hand and that of resource management (or conservation) on the other hand. The first criterion thus refers to the degree of flexibility of rules of access to CPRs while the second criterion concerns the presence or absence of resource conservation rules strictly conceived (that is, excluding access rules). We then have the four possibilities indicated in Figure 10.1.

Each one of the above four situations will be examined in turn, starting with type-I societies, and then proceeding to analyse those of type-II, -III, and -IV.

A point of departure: the case of type-I societies

According to the above typology, type-I societies are characterized simultaneously by the presence of flexible access rules and the absence of conservation mechanisms. This first category ideally corresponds to societies which live amidst abundant natural resources defined as resources for which there is no competition (they are therefore not subtractable since all users can jointly benefit from exploiting them) and which cannot be threatened with the risk of degradation/depletion even when they are openly accessible. A state of resource abundance may be related to three main kinds of circumstances:

1. population size is restricted compared to the amount of available resources;

2. technology is primitive with the result that labour productivity is quite low and/or the cost of exploiting a certain range of the available resources (particularly those portions of the resources which are not easily accessible) tends to infinity; and
3. people are not profit-maximizers, say, because they produce mainly for subsistence purposes and have a marked preference for leisure or leisurely activities (in the terminology of the new household economics, they have a preference for the kind of Z-goods which are highly time-intensive).

Now, it can be argued that the third condition is automatically satisfied in traditional societies which are by definition relatively well insulated against the stimulus of external economic opportunities or against the drive of newly created wants. Given that, the first condition (restricted population size) is normally sufficient to cause resources to be and remain abundant in the aforedescribed sense. Indeed, even if people know highly efficient techniques to exploit their natural environment, they are not interested in applying them on an extended scale because they prefer to use the resulting gains in the form of increased leisure. The same may not, however, be said of the second condition: as a matter of fact, the existence of simple technologies may not suffice to prevent competition from arising around a resource if population is large enough to strain it. Therefore, Berkes's statement that a subsistence fishery has a built-in self-limiting principle that protects it from degradation (Berkes, 1988: 85) would be valid only if it could be shown that because people are subsistence-oriented they have a built-in tendency to hold their numbers in check.

There is admittedly one circumstance in which primitive technology is a sufficient condition to avoid the risk of an open-access resource being degraded or depleted: this case occurs when the marginal cost of exploiting the resource becomes infinite beyond a certain threshold point. The most obvious example which comes to mind is that of marine fisheries: in the past, fishermen did not have the technical ability to harvest many of the resources lying in the open sea. Under such conditions, densely populated communities may possibly destroy species of fish living in the inshore waters but not those dwelling at some distance from the shoreline. This is not a clean case, however, since 'inshore' species of fish may then be considered as a scarce resource while fish in general remain plentiful, much in the same way as well-located lands or lands of comparatively high fertility may be scarce while land in general is abundant (if lands of high fertility are privately owned, this corresponds to the well-known Ricardian case where rents are zero at the extensive and intensive margins).

In societies where resources are abundant, people typically do not see their finite nature. Thus, Berkes observes that James Bay Cree fishermen believe that fish is an inexhaustible resource (Berkes, 1988: 84) and Kurien notes in the same vein that, to fishermen in Kerala (South India), marine resources appeared as limitless before modernization took place in the inshore fishery (Kurien, 1991: 3). In Botswana (Eastern Central District), to take an example pertaining to another sector, we are told that even today villagers do not see their grazing areas as a finite resource, a perception which results from the fact that those areas are still fairly extensive and not well demarcated (Zufferey, 1986: 90). Traditionally, local chiefs found solutions to overgrazing problems by requesting farmers to move to different areas (ibid. 67, 70). According to the same author, 'the stocking rate and grazing capacity of the land were/are rather marginal considerations in managing grazing resources. Permission for or prohibition of outsiders in those grazing areas was rather based on the degree of relationships they had with village wards or community residents' (ibid. 67).

Around Zinder, Niger, we learn that before woodstock abundance gave way to scarcity, 'trees were managed "passively": people simply allowed natural regeneration to reclaim fallowed fields'. 'Though their usefulness was recognised, trees were generally taken for granted because supplies more than met demand. Trees on village lands (typically one to two square miles in all) were apparently dealt with as a CPR, but access and use rules were probably very loose, given the abundance of wood at that time' (Thomson *et al.*, 1986: 395).

As noted before, we cannot be sure, when people move from one area to another in a context of general resource abundance, that the resource in the abandoned area has not been depleted in an irreversible way. If it has been actually destroyed, however, it must be borne in mind that it is only a localized fraction of the resource and not the resource as a whole which has been depleted, which nevertheless implies that the stock of the resource is not maintained. Yet, in many instances, as suggested by the above example about Zinder and by the system of slash-and-burn shifting cultivation, no threshold of irreversible depletion is reached and the resource located in an abandoned area may gradually regenerate or recover, possibly over a long or very long time-span. Of course, in so far as the resource is abundant, the fact that the period needed for its regeneration is long or very long does not really matter.

That communities endowed with plentiful resources, perceived as limitless, do not develop conservation rules or devices is easy to understand. What is less obvious is the well-substantiated fact that, whenever control of access to localized resources is feasible at a reasonable cost, traditional communities tend to devise rules towards that purpose irrespective of the degree of pressure on those resources. In other words, the *existence* of rules of access does not depend upon whether the resource at stake is under strain but upon whether it can be controlled at a non-prohibitive cost by the community which has established itself on it (*proposition 1*). None the less, *the degree of flexibility* of such rules is very much a function of the extent of resource availability: they tend to be highly flexible and to be applied in a liberal way when pressure on the resource is low while they tend to be more narrowly interpreted and more strictly applied when pressure is higher (*proposition 2*).

Let us first try to account for proposition 1 that is the most problematic. The question to be addressed can be put thus: why is it that villagers do not leave access to resources completely open when this cannot affect their incomes negatively nor cause such resources to be overexploited or threatened in any way? The answer to that question seems to be that in traditional societies rules of access were not *primarily* or *originally* intended for safeguarding the incomes of community members let alone for conserving the local resources. They had another, still more essential or vital function that is not strictly economic or ecological but symbolic. In effect, rules of access to local resources truly manifest and symbolize the social identity of the group which first colonized the area where these resources are located. They simultaneously serve to articulate its corporate ownership structure as well as to establish political intergroup boundaries. As this point is often missed in the literature dealing specifically with resource management issues, it is useful to delve somewhat further into it (see Platteau, 1992: 72–4).

One fundamental characteristic of (lineage) societies inhabiting resource-abundant areas is that they are grounded in people and not in land since it is people and not land that are a scarce resource. Typically, territorial boundaries between lineage-dominated groups are not precisely defined; they are 'in a state of flux'. Also, *no man's land* areas exist which serve as protection zones or reserve land for any possible future expansion due to demographic growth, migratory movements, etc. (Biebuyck, 1963: 15; Coquery-Vidrovitch, 1982: 67; Noronha, 1985: 7, 57). It is true that the group which first occupied an area is always keen to put a mark on it, often by setting fire to the bush and considering that the territory ends up where the fire stops. However, this operation does not correspond to a precise demarcation of the territory which is thus taken possession of. Rather, it is a symbolic gesture by which the head of the founding lineage signifies that a privileged association begins between this portion of land area and the social group which he represents.

The symbolism of this gesture is actually twofold. For one thing, an organic link is created with the land which imparts a specific identity and emotional feeling to the residents. Such an event is memorized, in the form of a 'founding myth', as the starting-point of a people's history. Indeed, 'to say that the ancestors' land cannot belong to everybody is to refer to that particular history of the social group that is attested by the demarcation of a portion of land'. (Gruenais, 1986: 293, our translation). It may also be noted that what is often known as the 'bush' (a loosely defined part of the territory) plays an active role in the social reproduction of the group or lineage (ibid. 294). In actual fact, the 'bush' is believed to be inhabited by supernatural beings which have a strong influence on the life of the people living in the surrounding area. It is therefore a sacred portion of the territory where most rituals take place which serve to strengthen the harmony between the living people and the supernatural powers (acting on behalf of the dead ancestors) on the one hand and the unity among these people themselves on the other hand (Godelier, 1974: 342–3; Raynaut, 1976: 281–2).

Holding a share in a corporate property reinforces feelings of having identifiable social roots and of belonging to a supportive and united human entity. As Marx understood it long ago, since within the tribal social structure 'the relation to property is mediated through membership in the group, property appears as a relationship signifying social identification'. This idea actually fits into his historical scheme according to which the initial emergence of property (which must by necessity be tribal) 'depends on a prior existence of group cohesion, i.e. some kind of social, tribal organization' (Avineri, 1968: 112).

For another thing, a political act is accomplished whereby a chief establishes himself as an indispensable mediator between a loosely delimited land area and all the people who are going to live in it. In the words of Gruenais:

In this dialectics of the relation between man and his environment which takes us to the very heart of the political sphere, what is at stake is less the land itself than the link tying the people to a local authority. . . . As a matter of fact, land in itself, or its expanse, has no real meaning for the powerful. The 'original' demarcation of a territory expresses the establishment of a privileged relation between the physical environment and a particular political figure. This relation becomes meaningful only in so far as it is being recognised. And land is a pertinent object for those in power only when it is peopled by individuals who accept the same relation, which may then become the means through which authority is exercised. It is thus on the basis of a threefold relation—land environment/authority/social group—that a particular territory is formed. (Gruenais, 1986: 290–1, our translation)

Corporate ownership is not only manifested in the existence of CPRs such as forests, bushes, and pastures, but also in the fact that all physical subdivisions or partitions (such as individual or collective fields, residential plots, village granaries, etc.) are conceived of as superficial territorial and residential realities that are superimposed on an immutable and essential 'land' entity (Gruenais, 1986: 287). Given the above, it is not surprising that the main responsibility of the political authority is to guarantee the perpetuation of the group through the inalienability of its land and other assets (Minvielle, 1977: 22–4). The principle of inalienability of the lineage land patrimony is all the more strongly adhered to as an important symbolic meaning is attached to it. Indeed, in so far as the land is emotionally identified with the ancestors to whom it is believed to provide an everlasting shelter—land is a 'sacred trust' in the holding of the ancestors who are buried in it and who need to be continuously addressed to through appropriate rituals (Caldwell and Caldwell, 1987: 422)—the objective of keeping it under the control of the community is viewed as an inescapable way of maintaining the latter's social integrity. Even if the lineage territory comprises more land than can be cultivated by its members, the surplus land is entrusted to the chief who has to keep it on behalf of the whole social group (Crousse, 1986: 202).

It is worth noting that what applies to land resources also applies to water resources (irrigation canals, ponds, rivers, lakes, estuaries, backwaters, inshore maritime areas, etc.) in so far as the latter are simply treated as an extension of the former. In the specific case of inshore fisheries in the Pacific islands, we are thus told that 'Many Oceanian societies do not have the concept of dividing natural resources and the space that they occupy into aquatic and terrestrial components' (Ruddle, 1988: 76). In effect, the lateral or coastwise boundaries of a community's exclusive fishing area were generally a seawards extension of the community's terrestrial boundaries (Ruddle, 1988: 78; see also Hviding and Baines, 1994). As a consequence of this lack of differentiation between aquatic and terrestrial boundaries, 'the principles of sea tenure and the rights to exploit marine resources tend to differ little from those that govern land tenure'. Furthermore, the same symbolic function is attached to sea and land tenure systems. In the Fiji islands, for example, the word *vanua* 'refers to a social unit that is associated with an identifiable physical territory. This social unit is regarded as the human manifestation of the physical environment . . . Land-water is seen as the extension of the self, and, similarly, its human occupants are the personification of the land-water' (Ruddle, 1988: 76). There is no doubt that Ruddle's analysis with respect to the Pacific marine fisheries is also valid for many other fisheries (whether inland or maritime) all over the traditional world.

To sum up: provided that they are excludable, resources tend to be somehow demarcated[1] and placed under the corporate custody of a given community even when they are abundant relative to the members' needs. None the less, the degree of internal control exercised over local users as well as the tightness of rules of access for outsiders are conspicuously low in these circumstances. To illustrate the first aspect, we can quote a study conducted in a Javanese sea fishery:

> Fishermen and local leaders can remember no time at all when any traditional controls were exercised. This no doubt is largely due to the Javanese lack of recent contact with the sea, and the extremely rich soil on the island, which allowed them a relatively easy living without venturing near it. (Sya'rani and Willoughby, 1987: 4)

It was likewise observed in San Miguel Bay, Philippines, that when fish resources were abundant relative to the demands of a small population, 'the degree of specific institutional controls on decision making and interaction was quite limited' (Cruz, 1986: 123).

As for the second aspect, we know from proposition 2 above that when a resource is plentiful, rules tend to be quite flexible. This implies that outsiders can be more or less easily granted use rights over localized CPRs through acquiring the status of member of the relevant corporate ownership group. In most cases, however, they may not quickly accede to the rank of 'ordinary' or first-rate citizen, especially if they have been incorporated in the community as slaves or indentured servants. Traditionally, access to land and other resources was thus not necessarily predicated upon kinship or descent-based ties but could also be grounded upon loyalty and patronage relations which were often associated with ascriptive forms of status or social identity (Berry, 1984: 91).

There are several ways for an outsider to gain access to a group-controlled resource. All of them rest upon the basic principle that to gain such access a non-community member must agree to enter into the local network of personal interrelationships and he must accept the political authority of the local chief (or group of elders). One common method of meeting this exigency consists of paying regular fees or dues to the local political authority acting on behalf of the whole resource-controlling group. Such was, for instance, the condition to be fulfilled by non-community members in order to be able to use village forests and pasture lands in Nepal when population was small relative to the available resources and when no commercial exploitation had yet begun to take place (Arnold and Campbell, 1986: 428). On Etal atoll in the Mortlock Islands

[1] In Marovo, Solomon Islands, for example, boundaries are marked and validated by ancient shrines which are stone chambers in the mainland forest, on lagoon seashores, or on islands in the lagoon and barrier reef, and which contain the skulls of named ancestors, together with heirlooms such as sacred clamshell artefacts. In most cases, the boundary of the territory of a given lineage group does not extend from coast to reef in a straight line, 'instead veering between points marked by small islands, deep-water channels and other important features of the lagoon seascape. Surface guides to the location of marine boundaries include water colour, wave patterns, and turbulent flow over submerged reefs. Though often not discernible to outsiders' eyes, the location and surface manifestations of the marine boundaries of Marovo are an integral part of the everyday practical knowledge on which fishing is based' (Hviding and Baines, 1994: 19, 22).

(Pacific), the waters are divided into those areas adjacent to the reef, and the open sea, the latter being relatively unimportant to the islanders. Both areas are divided among the clans and sub-clans, which have exclusive rights to their tracts. Note that all clans are ranked by their order of arrival on the island with the head of the first being regarded as the 'paramount chief' of the atoll ('he holds proprietary rights over all land and sea, which forms the basis of the clan's suzerainty over all later-coming clans'): as a consequence, rights over land and sea are essentially use rights. 'Members of other clans must seek prior permission to fish in a clan's rights area, for which they must pay by presenting 25 per cent to 50 per cent of their catch to the exclusive rights holders whose waters they work' (Ruddle, 1988: 80–1).

In the laguna of Aby in the Ivory Coast, lineages which could claim 'ownership' or custodian rights over a particular channel used to put up weirs known as *atere* in the water: an *atere* was a reed-made structure designed as a labyrinth for the purpose of ensnaring passing fish. Till the nineteenth century, we are told, 'everybody, whether or not a member of the *atere*-owning lineage, was allowed to participate in the fish harvest, yet when people were not members of this lineage, they were required to pay a fee (calculated as a share of the catch) to its chief' (Perrot, 1990: 181; see also Weigel, 1985*a*). In Mali, similar practices were observed in the Niger delta among the *Bozo* fishermen (Fay, 1990*b*: 216–26). Thus, for instance, traditionally, when fishing consisted of catching fish on their way through a given territory, all neighbouring communities were entitled to join the harvesting operations provided that they abided by the priority order set by the local lineage under the leadership of the 'master of the waters' (the latter being the living figure symbolizing the pact struck between the water-owning lineage and the local spirit of the waters) (ibid. 224; see also Weigel, 1985*b* and Cormier-Salem, 1986 for the description of similar practices in Benin and Senegal).

In the traditional logic of socio-political functioning, the regular dues paid by outsiders, whenever they exist, are to be interpreted as symbolic gifts manifesting an act of political allegiance and social identification that needs to be continuously renewed (or that, at least, needs to be renewed until the outsiders are integrated as full-fledged members into the local community). In actual fact, it does not make sense to treat these dues as an 'economic' (scarcity) price since the resource whose access is preconditioned upon their payment is typically abundant. This is true even when, as in the last aforementioned examples, access to the abundant resource is mediated by the use of a fixed capital structure. In these circumstances, indeed, the fee imposed upon the outsiders is not to be conceived of as a rent for the use of this capital good since the amount of the fee is significantly influenced by non-economic factors such as the degree of closeness of the relationship between the outsiders and at least some members (more particularly the chief) of the host community.

Another common way for an outsider to gain access to localized CPRs is to establish personal links of friendship or godparenthood with some resident family. This mechanism can be illustrated with respect to (informal) sea tenure arrangements found to prevail among small-scale fishermen on the southern Bahian coast (Brazil). There, becoming a godparent is a widely used strategy to gain access to a new fishing territory when the willing entrant does not already have some kind of kinship or friendship relationship with one or several local residents. Cordell and McKean (1986) provide the following details about the mechanism of entry into the territory of an established fishing community:

> The first step is to arrange to sell a catch to hawkers in neighbouring territories, to make gifts of fish all around, and if the catch is good, to pay for a beer-drinking session. After initially displaying good will, the visiting captain may either volunteer or be asked to be a godparent to another fisherman's child. These relationships are frequently established after only a brief acquaintance, and a major benefit is to confer summer fishing rights. These ongoing rights may endure for many years, reinforced by other types of cooperation. Alternatively, a captain planning to fish close to another community's sea space will arrange to take along a crew member who has a local friend . . . Some people will venture into interstitial areas to fish only when they have a network of friends or actual kin in adjoining villages. (Cordell and McKean, 1986: 95–6)

As a consequence of such practices, a large number of informal contracts are entered into with a view to establishing sea rights and they result in wide-ranging circles of fishermen bound by a same ethical code of good conduct. These 'huge personal networks with many godparent connections' often run through a series of villages and make for a ritualized extension of sea rights that 'restores an element of flexibility in fishing opportunities where waters are otherwise exclusively used and claimed by single villages' (Cordell and McKean, 1986: 96). Similar arrangements have been actually observed in Lake Titicaca where fictive kinship ties and coparenthood ties are established to gain access to aquatic resources (Levieil, 1987: 74–85); or among the Yolngu of Northern Australia where it is impossible to enter a fishing territory if one does not have 'a friend' in the local community (Davis, 1983). For activities involving several people, an effective strategy to gain access to a diversified set of resource grounds consists of building up teams that comprise individuals belonging to different communities. Thus, in Marovo, Solomon Islands, when a fishing group intends to go to a fishing ground of another corporate kin group, an attempt is usually made to include in the canoe crew at least one person with strong kinship links to that other kin group. By adopting such a strategy, the captain is saved the trouble of asking permission to the guardian of the fishing territory which he wants to enter: 'This is a way of legitimating *vis-à-vis* others, and to the group members themselves, the fact that entry permission has not formally been asked.' Indeed, 'to bring along a fellow fisherman with recognised, strong blood ties to the group in possession of those other reefs is in fact a "moral safeguard", and the "outsiders" forming the remainder of the crew draw on his "power to speak about" his own group's prime fishing grounds' (Hviding and Baines, 1994: 25).

These informal rules have sometimes been carried on into recent times even within industrialized countries. Thus, in the Maine lobster fishery (USA), every fisherman must be accepted by the local 'harbour gang' to gain access to a given fishing territory, hence the importance for any outsider to accumulate a sufficient capital of family or friendly relationships with the local community. If the acceptance procedure has not been followed according to the informal ruling code, a considerable amount of social pressure will be used to force the intruder to leave and, if needed, his fishing equipment will be destroyed (Acheson, 1987, 1988).

A final remark is in order. There is evidence that access of outsiders or semi-outsiders to a resource area may be easier for subsistence products that, by definition, are not harvested in big quantities than for commercial products that have a rapidly expanding market. Thus, for example, fishermen of Marovo, Solomon Islands, typically rely on a multitude of primary, secondary, and tertiary use rights in (land and) sea resources through wide-ranging kinship privileges. Their rights of access are more restricted as the distance of their family ties with the local communities and their resource guardians increases. In particular, except in areas for which close ties exist, these rights do not include commercial harvesting of resources especially when commercial fishing is very intensive. This said, in areas where rights of access are the weakest (there are, of course, areas where fishermen have no rights at all given total absence of any sort of family relationships), no one would object to the 'outsider' taking fish for his own family's daily food needs (Hviding and Baines, 1994: 23–4).

Strict access rules but no conservation: the case of type-II societies

General considerations

Let us now shift our attention away from resource-abundant societies to consider situations in which resources have become scarce in the sense that they are now the object of potential competition among users. This is taken to mean that the number of users is sufficiently high relative to the resource flows for any additional entry to cause the average product to fall or the average cost of extraction to rise. In other words, the resource is now subtractible in the sense that each individual user is potentially capable of subtracting from the welfare of other users. For the sake of illustration, consider the case of maritime fishing. When the resource is abundant—implying that the average product or cost is constant—there are numerous beaches from which fishing operations can be launched, fish can be caught in sufficient quantities near the shore, and anyone who so desires can therefore start to fish without hurting the interests of the existing fishermen. When the resource has ceased to be abundant, all the most productive beaches have already been occupied and additional fishermen have either to settle on less productive or more risky beaches (for example, those where the sea bottom is not as smooth or desirable for beachseine operations, or where the launching and landing operations are fraught with danger), or to get access to a high-quality beach through acceptance by the local community. In the former case, the new entrants have to bear the whole burden of the decreasing returns to fishing (or of the increased risk) while in the latter whether it is so will depend upon how they are integrated into the local community and, particularly, upon the nature of the access rights granted them. The burden of decreasing returns is shared among both new entrants and existing fishermen if no discrimination is practised *vis-à-vis* the former which is typically the case when they come from the natural growth of the resident population.

Now, it must be borne in mind that the decline in the average product (the increase in the average cost) resulting from the pressure of a growing number of resource harvesters (assuming constant technology) may be due (1) *only* to the enhanced competition for the resource that this growing pressure entails, or (2) both to this enhanced competition *and* to the erosion of the environmental capital stock. The first situation points to a purely distributive problem caused by the very scarcity of the resource: since the resource is increasingly difficult or costly to harvest, there arises the question as to how the cost of extracting it is to be shared among the various claimants. Such a situation therefore requires well-defined sharing rules which are obviously tantamount to access rules (it being understood that exclusion is the obverse of access). The second situation involves both a distribution problem *and* a genuine resource management problem. (In the socio-anthropological literature, unfortunately, the expression resource management is generally used to denote the ways and methods applied to solve both types of problems indiscriminately, thereby creating a lot of unnecessary confusion.)[2] Consequently, it calls not only for sharing rules but also for conservation mechanisms lest the pressure on the resource, other things being equal, should be stronger in the future than in the present.

If we were to follow the logic of the romantic view, we would argue that societies confronting situations of the first aforementioned type tend to adopt well-defined sharing or access rules while those confronting situations of the second type tend to devise both sharing rules and conservation mechanisms. Our own position is different, however, because we do not believe that societies optimally and instantaneously adjust their rules or institutions to the evolving challenges which they meet. In the new institutional economics (NIE)—a new and rather eclectic branch of economics which deals explicitly with issues of institutional change—when such change is slow or hard to come (societies do not evolve the optimal rules which they need as soon or as effectively as they would need), it is necessarily because of some sort of collective action problem which prevents the new rule or institution from being supplied, thus frustrating the individual actors' demand for institutional change. In other words, people are assumed to be wise, lucid, and rational and the problem arises only from the fact that individually rational actors do not necessarily produce collectively rational outcomes as is epitomized in the PD story (bear in mind that any rule or institution is a public good and that its production is therefore vulnerable to the freerider problem).

Our thesis is at variance with that of the NIE inasmuch as we believe with McNicoll that, contrary to the assumption commonly made in the social sciences (including, to an increasing extent, in sociology), people are actually 'error prone, partially informed, culturally blinkered to varying degrees, and somewhat arbitrarily mixing short- and long-run considerations in their decisions' (McNicoll, 1990: 148–9; see also Lane, 1991: 52 for evidence from cognitive psychology). To put it in another way, societies may not optimally adjust to the evolving challenges which they face, not only because interactions among their members give rise to collective action problems, but also because the nature of the problem at stake is not correctly perceived or is simply misunderstood by the actors concerned. In the context of the present discussion, our

[2] e.g. the concept of 'appropriation externalities' used by Schlager (1990, 1994) is confusing because it does not clearly distinguish between the static and dynamic problems resulting from increased pressure on CPR (fish) resources. On the other hand, her distinction between 'appropriation externalities' and 'assignment problems' (to be defined later) is unfortunate as an 'assignment problem' can be considered as the outcome of an 'appropriation externality'.

hypothesis can be formulated as follows: people in traditional societies are naturally inclined to think that, when their income derived from the exploitation of CPRs happens to fall, this must be *entirely* caused by the encroachments of new producers (especially so, of course, if the latter are strangers endowed with superior techniques) whose activities have the effect of diminishing the share of the current resource flows available to the existing operators. The idea that decreasing incomes can also follow from a reduced stock of the resource as a result of overexploitation and mismanagement by *all* the producers involved (that is, as a result of their own harvesting behaviour as well as that of new entrants) does not readily come to people's mind.

When these conditions obtain, societies therefore tend to adopt strict access rules while neglecting to evolve conservation devices: they thus correspond to type-II societies in our basic typology. Note that another possible situation is that in which a stock is depleted owing to the more intensive harvesting efforts made by a *constant* number of existing producers (either because the latter use more effective harvesting techniques than before, or because they have increased their working time). In these circumstances, and following the same logic as that described above, people are unlikely to attribute to their own behaviour any decline in the number of resource units which they are able to currently appropriate or use from their natural resource system. If this is the case, they do not respond to the worsening of their incomes by trying to halt the process of resource degradation so as to maintain their long-term income-earning capacity. (Bear in mind that resources have been assumed to be scarce—people cannot easily move to other areas or start harvesting new resource stocks—and that people's livelihood crucially depends on what they are able to harvest from their natural environment.) In terms of our typology, what we encounter here is a variant of type-I or type-II society depending upon whether rules of access are relatively flexible or relatively strict, that is, depending upon whether there is a threat from potential users who do not belong to the local community.

We are thus faced with a set of three distinct situations which need to be elucidated. To recall, there is first the situation in which the sheer pressure of a growing number of users creates a problem of distribution of the resource flow currently available from the natural system concerned. To this situation, people react by developing stricter rules of access. Second, there is the situation where the above distributive problem is compounded by a problem of stock depletion/degradation, yet people react as though there were no management problem and the only issue were that involved in sharing the current flow from a given resource stock. Third, we have the situation in which stock depletion/degradation takes place with a constant number of users who exploit their natural environment in a rather intensive way. In such a case, people remain passive and there is continuous erosion of the environmental capital stock.

Regulating access to CPRs

How can we account for the above reactions and, in particular, how are we to explain the difficulty of traditional societies' members in admitting the possibility of resource destruction as a result of man-made efforts or human intervention or, at least, how are we to explain their unwillingness or inability to take active steps to remedy such kinds of situation?

The first thing to note is that, in a number of significant cases, the fact that new entrants directly compete with existing producers for the use of a resource is patent and it is just to be expected that the people concerned respond to the newly created problem as essentially one of pure distribution. Two striking illustrations of this phenomenon of straightforward competition are those of village woods on the one hand, and of fishing spots on the other hand, that is, situations in which the resource is well localized and either directly visible (like in the first example) or within almost tangible reach (like in the latter example). Now, when a CPR is manifestly strained by increasing population pressure, the spontaneous reaction of the local community is (*a*) to tighten the rules of access so as to make it more and more difficult for outsiders to use the CPR; and (*b*) to design more precise rules for the sharing of access and the avoidance of conflicts among the growing number of insiders. The latter process may involve *de facto* privatization of use rights or some sort of rotation.

Let us consider the problem of access to choice fishing spots in some detail. This is an instructive illustration since a recent study based on a sample of thirty fisheries concludes that fishing groups are usually quite effective in solving 'assignment problems' of the aforementioned kind while they systematically fail to overcome externalities that arise from competition for scarce fish in the open sea (Schlager, 1990, 1994).[3] Depending on the resource available in a particular spot and on the level of labour productivity, a smaller or greater number of fishermen will be able to operate from this spot without impairing each other's catching capacity. Moreover, the fishing technology used may involve labour indivisibilities. This implies that the minimum number of fishermen required to exploit the targeted stock may sometimes be rather high (say, up to twenty-five to thirty-five people), as evidenced by the beachseining technique in which a large bag-shaped net (called a beachseine) with coir-wings of extensive length is slowly dragged from the shore after having been put out at sea with the help of a boat.

Let us assume that (*a*) there are *m* suitable fishing-spots available in a given community's territory (in a beachseining community, for example, this means that there are *m* separate near-shore areas of sufficient size where the sea bottom is sandy and free from rocks and other obstructions so that the net can be dragged smoothly); (*b*) on each

[3] Interestingly, although fishermen do sometimes succeed in devising and enforcing quotas in order to affect market prices, they prove unable to use the same method towards conserving their resource (Schlager, 1994: 264–5). At the time of writing, a challenging experiment is taking place in the coastal fishery of Senegal. In Kayar and in Joal, fishermen, under the initiative of their nationwide union (the CNPS, or Collectif National des Pêcheurs Sénégalais), attempted to impose quantitative restrictions upon the harvesting of exportable species (the rose daurade for Kayar and the octopus for Joal) so as to cause prices to increase. After a few months, due to rather localized supply of these species and strong collective discipline supported by severe sanctions, this objective was attained. The question nevertheless remains as to whether such a system can be maintained for a long time. What deserves to be emphasized, however, is that, in the same movement, attempts are being made to restrict the operation of purse-seine nets handled by motorized (artisanal) canoes since there are clear signs of overfishing of pelagic species caught by this technique. Note carefully that, although a genuine people's organization, the CNPS has benefited from the support of the ICSF (the International Collective in Support of Fishworkers), an international NGO that defends the cause of small-scale fishermen and fishworkers.

day, a particular fishing spot can be worked by h shifts of fishermen, assuming that each shift works to its maximum capacity (to stick to the above example, the laying of a beachseine and its subsequent operation takes about two or three hours and, as the net must be dried after use, it can be operated only once in a day, thus allowing two or three other nets to be operated from the same beach site), and (*c*) n fishermen make up a shift. Then, a situation of resource abundance obtains if the number of fishermen willing to operate from the fishing territory of that community (N) is smaller than or equal to $m \times h \times n$. If, on the contrary, N has become greater than $m \times h \times n$, a potential for conflicts arises because accommodation of the ($N - m \times h \times n$) excess fishermen would necessarily cause a reduction in the catches of the fishermen who were working before fishing space became scarce. In these circumstances, local fishermen immediately understand the threat to their incomes posed by the excessive number of operators in the area. As a result, they typically respond to the new situation by restraining and eventually stopping access of outsiders to their fishing grounds much in the same way as was observed in agriculture when pressure on land became to be felt by local residents. Thus, while in Africa up until recently strangers could easily obtain rights to clear virgin forest lands against the payment of a share of their crop to the customary custodian of the (unoccupied) land, as the land frontier became gradually exhausted, indigenous ideology began to reassert with vigour 'the inalienable rights of the native custodians of the land, and the inalienable rights of individual usufruct' (Robertson, 1987: 77).

Note that, as theoretically argued in Chapter 8 (Sect. 2), it is important, in order that exclusion can actually occur, that the identity of the winners and losers be well known before exclusion takes place. This is amply verified on the ground since 'outsiders' tend to be excluded while 'insiders' continue to have their customary rights of access protected.

The enforcement of increasingly exclusionary arrangements in the form of barriers to entry into the local fishery may not, however, be sufficient to prevent the multiplication of conflicts if population pressure also arises from the natural growth of the resident community. This is why many fishing communities have taken steps to regulate access to the available fishing spots even among community members. One method adopted towards this end consists of assigning long-term exclusive use rights to particular groups or families. It often favours groups or families which were the first to settle down in the area and therefore occupy the top of the social hierarchy. Thus, for example, on Ulul atoll in the Pacific, 'islanders can fish freely anywhere in the island's sea territory, apart from one particularly wide and fish-rich tract of reef flat near a large reef passage, which is reserved for the exclusive use of the chief's clan' (Ruddle, 1988: 80). In the more egalitarian Indian societies of the Lower Klamath area in California, a social group was just a loose aggregation of individuals and nuclear families clustered together in small villages along the rivers and coast. Among the Yurok, the Hupa, and the Karok, 'individual men claimed exclusive use of fishing sites, improved game yards, or gathering sites for themselves and their families. Good fishing-spots were the property of individuals or partners and were transferable. Others could not fish at or immediately below a private spot, although a few good pools or rapids were open to common access' (McEvoy, 1986: 34). There were none the less other exceptions to the privatization rule. For one thing, 'resources gradually lost their private character away from the center of the area and back from the rivers and coast, where land was of less economic value'. For another thing, important exceptions to the same rule 'occurred when people of one village or several together cooperated in building seagoing boats or salmon weirs' (ibid.).

In San Miguel Bay, Philippines, even in times of general abundance of fishery resources, 'near-shore areas were allocated to specific families for exclusive use for fixed gear, due to the limited availability of such sites' (Cruz, 1986: 123). In Bahia, Brazil, long-term private claims are assigned over brackish water spawning-grounds, reefs, and net fishing spots defined by the lunar-tide cycle (Cordell and McKean, 1986: 92). In Japan, in the small-scale fixed-net fishery individual operators are assigned fishing spots based on their traditional usage patterns, a practice vindicated on the grounds that these nets must be individually tailored to the topography of the sea bottom in each spot fished. In some areas, moreover, octopus holes within a joint rights area are owned and inherited as personal property (Ruddle, 1987: 46).

Our last example is taken from a much more sophisticated fishery and illustrates the fact that regulatory efforts can emerge in new areas from traditional practices brought about by strongly knit immigrant ethnic groups. Thus, during the last quarter of the previous century, in the Bay Area shrimp fishery (California), we are told that, without any formal authority to do so, Chinese shrimp companies (after they had won control over this fishery by virtue of their comparatively low production costs) recognized each other's proprietorship over certain fishing areas and each company thus possessed two or more grounds that it worked at different times of the year. This regulatory system was devised with a view to protecting the substantial investment each company made in fishing assets. So strong was the system that it still functioned as late as the 1930s, long after most of the industry had been legislated away at Sacramento (McEvoy, 1986: 96–7).

As a result of the granting of long-term exclusive rights, some groups or families may be excluded from access to the available (scarce) fishing sites and be forced to outmigrate and, perhaps, to settle in less productive fishing grounds. For the sake of illustration, let us consider the recent evolution of the situation obtaining in the Niger delta (Mali). According to Bozo fishermen's customs, group control over the water channels and group rights over particular spots on the weirs built across these channels were easily transferable to families with which original settlers united by marriage: they could thus be given over by a father (or a brother) to a marrying daughter (or sister) and the latter's descendants would be entitled to inherit them; or they could be transferred as a betrothal gift to seal the alliance with the family into which the daughter was to marry. However, when competition arose during the last decades around the available fishing sites, it became usual for the descendants of a native woman who are geographically or genealogically distant to waive their traditional use rights (Fay, 1990*b*: 2245).

It is worth noting that secrecy often operates as an effective mechanism that assigns choice fishing spots, thereby minimizing competition among fishermen (White, 1977;

Forman, 1980: 20–2; Carrier, 1987: 147; Ruddle, 1987: 53–4; Acheson, 1989: 362–3). Secrecy is possible simply because knowledge and skill for locating dense concentrations of fish or choice fishing sites are difficult to acquire. Thus, for example, Ruddle remarks that in Japan 'by far the commonest way in which temporary private tenure to communal sea space arises is through the exclusive use of fishing spots as a result of closely guarded personal knowledge' (Ruddle, 1987: 53–4).

Another method of regulating access to scarce fishing sites inside a local community—a method which is probably more widespread than the *de facto* privatization of these sites—is to lay down or recognize use rights by rotation so as to promote equitable access to resources and to minimize interpersonal conflicts between fishing units. Under such circumstances, all the members of the community are expected to share in the costs of its natural growth in terms of loss of individual welfare. Rotating access to scarce fishing spots naturally implies that only temporary use rights are assigned to individual fishing units. The period of time for which these rights are granted may vary significantly yet in most recorded cases it does not exceed one day and can even be as short as a few hours. Note that, when the period is relatively long, it is presumably because, rather than a scarcity of fishing locations relative to the number of fishing units, there prevails a scarcity of productive locations or a strong disparity in the productivity of different available locations. In these conditions, rotation can be slower because the objective pursued is to equalize expected incomes over the medium or the long term rather than to share a limited number of spots among the fishermen so as to enable all of them to earn a minimum income in the short term.

On the other hand, it is a common practice in many fishing communities to let the firstcomer's priority principle decide who will be assigned a given fishing spot on a particular day. In Yaeyama and off the main island of Okinawa (Japan), for example, 'the priority right to a fishing spot by a firstcomer is absolutely sacrosanct . . . it is ironclad in customary law' (Ruddle, 1987: 56). It is thus important to emphasize that acknowledgement of the rights of a firstcomer to a fishing location may involve well-established informal tactics or codes of conduct. This can be vividly illustrated with the system of sea tenure discovered by Cordell and McKean in southern Bahia in the Brazilian north-east:

> When a captain wishes to fish in a particular spot outside the system of lunar-tide property rights, he announces his intention—including what tide level or series he will use in casting nets—several days in advance at a local bar where fishermen like to congregate. All that is required is for another fisherman to be present as a witness. To ensure the claim, the captain must follow his proclamation by going to the chosen spot the day before fishing to leave a canoe anchored with paddles sticking up in the air. This forewarns competitors that the casting space has been taken. Fishing captains go to considerable lengths to support each other in this routine, which is part of the sea tenure politics that shore up the entire fishing system. (Cordell and McKean, 1986: 96)

There is another widespread system of allocating fishing spots for temporary use and it seems to be all the more predominant as locations are more productive and therefore more intensely sought after. This system consists of predetermining a complete sequence of net-laying rights for regulating access to fish resources during a whole fishing season or even during only a single day's fishing operations. In many cases, the mechanism used for determining the sequence of rights is a simple lottery, a mechanism which is still in force nowadays in some advanced countries' fisheries, as in some mussel fisheries of southern France. In other cases, however, the order of (rotating) access to a particular fishing spot is set by a local customary authority: thus, among the Somono fishermen of West Africa, it was the responsibility of the so-called river's master (the *Ba Tigi* in local parlance) to decide the fishing turns (which lasted twenty-four hours each) by taking into account the intensity of demand, the abundance of fish, and the principle of equality between lineages (Jeay, 1984: 5).

The literature provides solid evidence of the ability of traditional communities to devise sometimes ingenious systems for allotting fishing sites to their members on a rotating basis. One such system has been observed by Taylor in the small estuarine salmon fishery of Teelin Bay (on the Glen River) in Ireland where it was still in operation in the early 1970s. Taylor's description is as follows:

> Seven eighteen-foot open boats sat motionless around the perimeter of Teelin Bay, half a mile across at its widest. Each boat was manned by four or five men sitting quite still and staring in various directions over the water. A seine net lay in the stern of each boat, from which a single line led to another crew member standing on shore. After a while a salmon leaped just downriver from one of the boats, the crew of which immediately began to row furiously upriver and around the leaping fish, paying out the net as they went. The shore man held the line taut, holding one end of the net stationary as the crew rowed and brought the other end of the net around to complete the circle. All boat hands then pulled the bag thus formed, and its contents, aboard. Having stowed their salmon in one end of the boat and neatly piled their net for the next *dol* (as each casting of the net is called in Gaelic), the crew looked up and around toward the other boats scattered about the estuary. One of these boats was in fact rowing toward the crew that had just taken a *dol* and yet another vessel was heading for the position vacated by the second boat. Within a few minutes, about half of the boats had thus exchanged positions, and all with no words other than a polite greeting. The same system operated upriver in the illegal channel, where each boat, after taking a *dol*, would simply row upstream to the end of a virtual queue. (Taylor, 1987: 296–7)

The sea tenure system discovered by Alexander (1980, 1982) and by Amarasinghe (1988, 1989) in the beachseine fishing communities of southern Sri Lanka clearly involves an initial assignment of fishing spots through a lottery and then rotating these among the fishermen in a predetermined manner so that all of them get equal chances not only to fish but also to fish in the best spots (Hannesson, 1988: 9).

As we have already mentioned, beachseining is a fishing technique that requires a rather large water space (since it is intended for catching a whole school of fish) located close to the shore and with a smooth sea bottom. Furthermore, the laying of a beachseine and its subsequent hauling takes only a few hours so that, on a particular day, only a maximum of four nets can be operated on each suitable location. It must also be borne in mind that the probability distribution of incomes from beachseining is significantly affected by the timing of fishing operations, within a daytime as well as across seasons. For one thing, expected incomes are always higher when the net is laid in the (early) morning both because big catches tend to occur early in the day and because the earlier fish is brought to the market the higher its price. For another thing, there are considerable inter-seasonal variations in fish catches and, in particular, a sizeable portion of yearly incomes from beachseining are obtained during a flush season which lasts only one month and the exact occurrence of which can never be safely predicted.

From Alexander's account (1980: 97–102; 1982; ch. 7), we can infer the following set of social rules that determine the local sea tenure system as a non-market organization ensuring equal access to productive resources:

1. Membership in the village community, whether hereditary or acquired in a lifetime, involves a right of access to the community-controlled sea area (local fishermen belong to the same kinship group).
2. Behaviour of the rentier-capitalist type is not allowed, which implies that ownership of a net carries the obligation to work it when required.
3. There is no labour market and, since a beachseine normally requires eight fishermen to operate, joint ownership of nets is the rule and the usual ownership share in a net is 1/8. In fact, each net is divided into eight sections or shares but 'once the net is in operation individuals have no particular rights to the sections they have contributed' (Alexander, 1982: 142).
4. Access to the sea is preconditioned upon the ownership of a net share. Nevertheless, this does not lead to exclusion of a fraction of the community in so far as all members, rich or poor, have access to capital. Indeed, a common way for a poor fisherman to acquire a share in a net is to receive it on credit (payment being postponed until after a good catch) from other shareholders in need of an additional partner (ibid.: 143).
5. There is no market for net shares which can be transferred only through inheritance. The importance of such share transfers lies in the fact that the heir thus acquires the right to fish at the local beach: a net share therefore plays the role of an entry ticket into the local fishery (ibid.: 203).

Notice, incidentally, that when families grow in size, they may choose between either maintaining joint family ownership of their fishing assets—in which case all the siblings get fractions of one-eighth shares in old and newly constructed nets—or giving over one-eighth shares in the existing nets to some sons and one-eighth shares in newly constructed nets to others. While the former method has the advantage of spreading production risk over several nets (Alexander, 1982: 143), the latter enables the heirs to be more independent of each other for the management of fishing assets.

Now, given the comparatively high productivity of early-day fishing operations, there arises an intense competition for taking the first turn on each available spot as soon as the total number of nets (k) exceeds the number of spots (m). Designing rules to regulate access to the sea *within daytime* is then necessary to avoid serious conflict over the use of the suitable water space. In addition, rules governing rights of access *across days* will be required when the number of existing nets exceeds the maximum number of hauls per day, that is, the number of fishing spots (m) times the maximum number of daily hauls on each spot (h). To sum up:

> regulation within days must occur if $k > m$; regulation within and across days must occur if $k > hm = 4m$.

The sea tenure system in south Sri Lanka's beachseine fishery is based upon the principle of equal access: every net should have equal chances not only in terms of access to the water but also in terms of access to catch and income opportunities. And when new individuals enter into the fishery and new nets are being constructed beyond the point where $k = 4m$, access to the available water space for existing nets will be proportionately reduced. Equal access is guaranteed through a turnover system that determines turns in a sequence of net-hauling rights. Thus, in Gahavälla—the village where Alexander conducted his in-depth study—the fishing area is divided into two stations: the harbour side (from which most big catches come) and the rock side. The net cycle begins on the harbour side and, after a net has had the dawn turn on that side, it is entitled to the dawn turn on the rock side on the next day. Subsequently, it may be used on the rock side each day once the net immediately following it in the sequence has been used. The sequence of net use over a period of five days is shown in Table 10.1.

As can be seen from the table, twelve nets have been used at least once in a period of five days. Furthermore, nets 5–8 have been worked a maximum number of five times during this period; nets 4 and 9 have been used four times; nets 3 and 10 three times; nets 2 and 11 twice; and, finally, nets 1 and 12 only once. If the total number of nets is twelve, net 1 will reappear in the harbour site on the sixth day (where it will have the last turn) and in the rock site on the tenth day (where it will have the first turn). As for net 5, it will have a new dawn turn in the harbour site on the thirteenth day: a complete net cycle lasts twelve days. Over the full net cycle, each net will have been operated eight times (the total number of possible turns per day in all the existing fishing stations), that is, for two out of three days on an average: the intensity of use of

TABLE 10.1. Sequence of net use in the village of Gahavälla

Day	Harbour				Rock			
	Dawn		Night		Dawn		Night	
One	5	6	7	8	4	3	2	1
Two	6	7	8	9	5	4	3	2
Three	7	8	9	10	6	5	4	3
Four	8	9	10	11	7	6	5	4
Five	9	10	11	12	8	7	6	5

Note: Adapted from Alexander (1982: 145).

each net is thus equal to hm/k. It is worth noting that, for each net, the period of use is strictly continuous: in the above example, once its first turn has come, a net will be worked during eight days in succession and, thereafter, it will be left idle for four days.

Now, it is important to notice that the interseasonal variability of catches does not create major problems in the above procedure as long as the total number of nets does not exceed by too large a margin the total number of possible turns (or hauls) per day (in all fishing stations): this should be evident from the foregoing example. However, if the total number of beachseines increases significantly due to population pressure, increasing market integration, and rising fish prices, or any other reason, as the period of net use is strictly continuous, the annual returns of any beachseine will be governed mainly by its position in the net cycle: most incomes will accrue to the nets which happen to have many turns during the flush period.[4] This is exactly the situation which was observed in Southern Sri Lanka from 1940 onwards: in Alexander's area of study, for example, only twenty-five of the ninety-nine nets received turns during the flush period in 1970–1 (Alexander, 1980: 105–7; 1982: 147, 203–8).

The aforementioned problem must nevertheless be viewed in its right perspective. Indeed, it is over a single year that the customary means of regulating access to the sea tend to make the distribution of the catch more and more unequal as the number of nets increases: over a longer period, returns should be expected to even out. Thus, Alexander writes: 'a particular net's turn is not tied to any point in the year, and over a four-year period each net will be used in each month. As the fishermen are unable to predict the flush period with any great accuracy, each net has an equal chance of good catches each year' (Alexander, 1982: 147). Yet, this clarification should not be taken to mean that the multiplication of nets does not raise problems. Even assuming that the economic pie is sufficient to provide for the livelihood of all households, there remains the question as to how year-to-year fluctuations in income will be buffered by them. Clearly, risk-pooling and intertemporal redistribution mechanisms become increasingly necessary to compensate for the partial failure of the traditional method of risk management.

In the case of the Alanya fishery (Turkey) studied by Berkes (1986), the devising of a rotating system of access to the sea is of much more recent origin than that found in Sri Lanka. Here, indeed, it is only in the early 1970s that the local fishermen began experimenting, on a trial-and-error basis, with a mechanism for regulating the use of the available fishing sites in an equitable manner. This institutional innovation was actually motivated by the need to reduce the incidence of conflicts that had become increasingly frequent and violent due to enhanced competition among fishermen for the better sites, as well as by the need to decrease the costs resulting from more difficult search for, and more intense fighting over, a fishing spot. The guiding principles of the system eventually adopted are the following. First, within the area normally used by Alanya fishermen, all suitable fishing locations are named and listed.

[4] In the earlier example, if the number of nets is doubled (from 12 to 24), each net will be used only one out of three days; and if it is quadrupled, it will be used one out of six days. In the latter case, each net will be idle during forty days in succession after each eight-day period of use, thus implying that it may not be used even once during the whole flush season (which lasts approximately one month).

Note that the adjacent sites are defined in such a way that no externality is created: the nets set in one spot cannot block the fish that should be available at the adjacent sites. Second, a list of all eligible fishermen is laid down and in the beginning of the fishing season the eligible fishermen meet in the coffee house to draw lots and are thus assigned to a given fishing site except those who draw blanks because the number of candidates exceeds that of the available sites. Third, once the season has started, each fisherman makes a daily move eastward to the next site and, after the middle of the season has been reached, each fisherman moves west so as to give all participants equal opportunities at the stocks that migrate from east to west during the first half and from west to east during the second half of the season. We are also told that Alanya fishermen are so pleased with this system that some of them set up similar arrangements for other activities (for example, in the case of chartering boats to tourists during the summer).

In a lagoon fishery located near Sète in southern France, mussel fishermen use a similar system. Here, however, despite the scarcity of fishing sites, rights of use are assigned for a full year. If rotation is thus much lower than in southern Sri Lanka or in Alanya, it is because mussels are cultivated in the sea and they have a long crop cycle making a fishing site akin to a land plot. As for the losers in the lottery—the lottery decides not only how the best sites are to be allotted but also who is going to be denied access to the lagoon—as in the Alanya fishery they have to fall back on other activities and wait till the next year's registration process to try their chance again (personal observation of Platteau).

It may be noted that, since there may exist substantial interseasonal variations in the abundance of fish or in the availability of fishing locations (due, for example, to tidal fluctuations), the system of fishing turns may be organized only during the low season when the chance of conflict over water space is great: fish is scarcer and consequently the better spots are more intensely sought after or the suitable fishing spots are fewer (see, e.g., Cordell and McKean, 1986: 94–5; Levieil, 1987: 115). Also worth mentioning is the fact that rotation-based spatial access codes may serve to regulate access to the water among different fishing communities. Thus, for example, in southern Bahia, competitive encounters may easily arise in the intervillage buffer zones if several boats arrive simultaneously, sometimes from different ports, running after a sizeable school of fish whereas the tide offers room and time for only one net cast. To cope with this kind of situation, 'net bosses follow a standard procedure of drawing lots to decide who will cast first. Once an order is established, a tide marker, usually a pole stuck in the bank, dictates a sequence of net-shooting rights. Not more than one tide-level change is allowed each boat. On this basis, captains decide whether to remain' (Cordell and McKean, 1986: 96–7). When conflicts break out, it is usually because a boat does not close its seine and draw in the catch in the specified time, thereby disturbing the queuing pattern. If the next boat in line decides to begin its operations regardless, the two nets can become fouled (ibid.: 97).

Another interesting illustration of rotating access to fish resources between neighbouring communities is found among the Indian river fishermen of California. It is easy to understand why salmon weirs built over the entire width of a river formed a potential cause of serious quarrel among bands inhabiting different parts of that river. It is precisely to avoid such conflicts that an understanding existed for the timely dismantling of weirs, or the opening of portions of them so that upstream tribes could take their shares of the run. None the less, given the extreme importance of the stake involved, this type of understanding is inherently unstable. Yet, in California, legitimization through myth apparently helped to make it sustainable over the long term (McEvoy, 1986: 37–8).

Notice finally that examples of rotation systems to regulate access to scarce resources abound in other sectors than fishing. Thus, in Uttarakhand (Uttar Pradesh, India), we learn that, traditionally, many villages had fuel reserves even on common land measured by the government, which the villagers cut over in regular rotation by common consent (Guha, 1985: 1940). In Nepal, systems of spatial control adopted by some communities in the middle hills of the country have ensured equal access to both nearby and more distant areas to all members of the community (Arnold and Campbell, 1986: 436). In Japan, rotational access was traditionally provided—possibly by lottery—when forest resources showed variability in spatial or temporal productivity. Thus, grass varied enormously in quality according to how thickly it grew in different spots and how much extraneous undesirable plant matter was included. Therefore, since the grass in the fodder commons was collected by all households together and then tied up into equal bundles, a lottery system was used to assign the bundles randomly to the different member households (McKean, 1986: 556–7).

It is also possible to refer to traditional grazing-control systems which aimed at ensuring fair access to the available pastures for different herders or groups of herders. For instance, the *dina* system, which was established in 1818 by a powerful Fulani leader assisted by a council of eighty territorially based chiefs, served the purpose of regulating the sequence in which various pastures in the Niger river delta (Mali) were grazed along with the grazing rights of different groups. Rules of access to grazing were defined and livestock movements were co-ordinated throughout the delta, in such a way that grazing pressure was fairly evenly distributed (Lawry, 1989*a*: 4). This being said, the sector for which rotation procedures are best documented is certainly that of irrigation or water distribution. Just to give one example, in Marpha village (Mustang District) in Nepal, an ancient local custom ensured that irrigation water was distributed in an equitable manner over the course of the year among all the villagers. It thus enjoined that the barley crop be watered from the top of the north fields downward; that is, the fields closest to the head received first water. Then, for buckwheat, the second crop cultivated in Marpha, the order was reversed so that the tail-end fields were watered first (Messerschmidt, 1986: 463; for other examples, see Ostrom, 1992; Tang, 1992). As noted above for fishing locations, schemes for rotating water may be enforced only periodically if there is wide variability in the level of the resource availability: thus, in the Erguita mountain tribe of Morocco, in a year with good rains, 'there are no water allotments to distribute, and no rotations to observe' (Mahdi, 1986: 181).

Failing to manage CPRs

One thing that comes out of the above presentation is that sharing arrangements devised for regulating access to a scarce resource in a more or less equitable manner (at least within the local community) are more likely to be observed when the physical and technical attributes of the resource tend to create many opportunities for conflict. This is particularly evident in the case of surface irrigation systems since they pose an inherent conflict between farmers upstream and those downstream: if upstreamers take too much water, downstreamers may end up with agricultural failure. The case of inland fishermen using weirs crossing over the entire width of a river is basically similar in that it also creates opportunities for serious externalities now imposed by downstreamers on upstreamers. Conflicts are likewise very probable when resource users have to compete for scarce locations, whether they be fishing spots, pastures, or woodlands, in which cases assignment problems unavoidably arise. In all these circumstances, rules are badly needed not only to reduce transaction costs but also to avoid repeated outbursts of sheer violence. In a study based on thirty case-studies of fisheries, Schlager has thus found that the existence of assignment externalities is significantly related to whether or not fishermen have adopted systematic procedures for fishing operations (Schlager, 1990). In the case of irrigation in India, a high correlation has been found between the degree of water scarcity on the one hand and the level of activity of informal water users' organizations and the incidence of rules for tank-water rotation on the other hand (Easter and Palanisami, 1986).

What needs to be recalled at this stage is that rules solving assignment problems do not, by themselves, help to conserve resources: as a matter of fact, management of a resource implies restraint in its use and there is nothing in sharing rules to ensure that users control the extent of pressure on the natural environment or the mode of exploiting it. It could be argued that exclusionary arrangements directed against outsiders have the (unintended) effect of limiting the pressure brought to bear on a resource, thereby helping to maintain its viability. This, however, misses the main point in so far as tightening the access to a resource by outsiders only postpones the problem if this is not accompanied by measures of restraint impinging on the insiders themselves. If the latter kind of measures are not enforced, the threat on the resource posed by outsiders is likely to be just replaced by the increasing pressure exercised by the insiders, because they grow in numbers and/or they are more and more willing to respond to market opportunities. Admittedly, it may be the case that a scarce resource is not liable to be depleted as a result of the users' behaviour, in which circumstances distributive measures are really the only ones required. Beachseine fishing (a technique that has no destructive potential) is a good illustration of such a possibility.

In the first part of this section, we have suggested that traditional societies may possibly fail to adopt rules other than those answering the rather immediate need to regulate access to the local CPR, and this failure may possibly take place even when vital resources are threatened with depletion or degradation. In other words, such societies do not necessarily take steps to conserve resources although the latter are obviously finite. To understand why it is so, the following fact must be borne in mind:

rural people, particularly so in hunter-gatherer societies, are traditionally inclined to view the flow product of a resource system as a given. When an excessive number of claims are laid to this given flow product—so that the number of resource units harvested per unit of time by individual claimants tends to diminish—the need is felt to sort them out and, as we have seen, this is always done by referring to the basic principle according to which priority access must be reserved for members of the local community. What is therefore important to realize is that rural dwellers are *not* used to see the flow of harvested natural products as yielded by a resource system or stock on which they may themselves impinge through their own harvesting behaviour. If they do not adopt conservation measures, it is because they do not perceive the relationship that exists between the stock and the flow of a resource nor the causal link between their own actions and the level of this stock. Consequently, they are not aware that they can increase the availability of appropriable resource units (to use Ostrom's language) in the future by harvesting in a restrained and selective fashion in the present. In other words, they are not aware of the existence of the sustainable yield curve since they do not clearly perceive the fact that today's choices may constrain the set of future choice possibilities. This comes down to saying that the concept of resource management is alien to them.

How is it that members of traditional societies consider natural products as a given on which they have no hold? The answer lies in the fact that they share a magical pre-rationalist view of the world. They thus conceive of surrounding resources as being provided by some supernatural agencies (deities or cosmic forces) which are in charge of catering to human needs. If at all resources have to be conserved, it is a task for the gods, not for the humans. Humans must only be careful to please the gods so that the latter do not stop caring for them by supplying regular sources of livelihood for day-to-day subsistence. Thus, for example, in the minds of the Mbuti pygmy tribe of Equatorial Africa, 'it is not the hunters who catch the game, it is the Forest which gives the game to the hunters so that they can catch it and subsist and reproduce by consuming it'. In this worldview, the forest is seen as 'the collection of all the animate and inanimate beings that live in it'. It is a personalized deity which is figured out 'at once as the father, the mother, the friend, and even the lover' of the Mbuti (Godelier, 1974: 340–1).

Among North American Indians, there was a 'probably universal' belief in active, watchful, and potentially vengeful animal spirits. 'The Indians had to use them carefully and propitiate them for their sacrifice if they were to rely on their continued abundance. Animism was the way in which the Indians, like most hunter-gatherers, expressed their awareness of the fact that their lives and those of their food resources were ecologically intertwined' (McEvoy, 1986: 31).

This kind of belief is still alive today, at least among the older generations: to take just one example, the Bakusu in Zaïre remain convinced that animals and certain types of food are released or supplied to the living by the ancestors who act as the custodians of the food resources upon which man's livelihood crucially depends (personal communication of Mr Masaki). Likewise, artisanal fishermen of Kerala (India) view 'Mother ocean as a life-giving system rather than a hunting ground' (Kurien, 1991: 3).

In West African inland fisheries, local water spirits are thought to be the sources which activate or withdraw fish. In Nepal, according to Messerschmidt, there is a nearly universal belief that certain resources have supernatural characteristics. Thus, various gods and godlings 'are commonly believed to dwell in or be otherwise closely associated with water sources, forests, pasture sites, and other resources or natural objects' (Messerschmidt, 1986: 468). At a village called Muktinath in the Upper Kali Gandaki, for example, 'the springs that serve as a principal source of irrigation and drinking water are elaborately enshrined near the source within a sacred forest of considerable antiquity. This water and forest place is, furthermore, considered a source of spiritual power and authority.' (ibid.).

The idea that natural resources are under the responsibility, or are even the concrete manifestation, of supernatural agents which continuously and actively intervene in human affairs so as to allow men to survive is also a typical feature of traditional agricultural societies. Thus, it is in the hope that the bush will recover from a period of (shifting) cultivation that Mende tribesmen in the Gola Forest (Sierra Leone), when they are about to fell trees to make a farm, or burn dried vegetation, invoke the patient understanding of the ancestors and spirits of the land for the necessary damage they must inflict on the bush (Richards, forthcoming: 150). Speaking about the systems of belief among traditional peasantries of Europe, Badouin has noted that land is conceived of as an active agent that 'carries the crops much in the same way as it serves as a basis for all sorts of buildings' (Badouin, 1971: 25, our translation). Another French rural sociologist, Barthez, has similarly remarked that the peasant traditionally perceives himself as a collaborator or a partner of nature. The isomorphism between man and land can be taken very far: like man, land must be fed to be capable of producing (Barthez, 1982: 32–5; see also Bourdieu, 1980: 197–9). As aptly summarized by Bourdieu: 'Convinced as he is that he does not have any effective means of influencing his own future and the level of his future production, the peasant does feel responsible only for the actions undertaken, not for their failure or success which depend on natural and supernatural powers' (Bourdieu, 1977: 39, our translation).

Now, the point has often been made that, in so far as they personify and deify nature in the above-described way, people in traditional rural societies are naturally inclined to show a deep and abiding respect for their environment, which starkly contrasts with the Promethean attitude of people in modern, rationalist societies. Furthermore, since the cult of ancestors—which is tightly enmeshed in, or associated with, the cult of nature—manifests an unremitting concern for the continuity of generations, past, present, and future, they are naturally predisposed to take account of the interests of succeeding generations while making their decisions (their discount rate of the future is close to zero). For example, Guha is deeply impressed by the attitude of deep respect displayed by villagers in Uttarakhand (Uttar Pradesh, India) towards their local forests, as well as by their concern for future generations, two intermingled attitudes to which he tends to ascribe much of their presumed success in managing forest resources. According to him, indeed, many of the myths and legends emphasize the deep sense of identity of tribal people with the forest: 'In tribal forest areas, not only did the forests have a tremendous influence in moulding religious and spiritual life, but the inhabitants exhibited a deep love of vegetation, often acting entirely from a sense of responsibility towards future generations by planting species whose span of maturity exceeded a human lifetime' (Guha, 1985: 1940). The same kind of analysis is made by Messerschmidt when he writes:

> Belief systems in which nature is sanctified often function to hold resource abuse in check through some combination of respect and fear that disturbance or neglect of the supernatural may cause more harm than good to the resource and to the people associated with it. At various levels, these beliefs serve to remind people of the miraculous (hence fragile) nature of the resource and of the people's own responsibilities to manage it for the sustained public good. (Messerschmidt, 1986: 469)

It is no doubt true that people in traditional societies are acutely aware of the immense fragility of the ecological systems in which they live, and that they are consequently very much willing to adopt the kind of behaviour required to maintain the long-term viability of these systems. None the less, this is not sufficient to make them effective resource managers. In effect, it is not because people are both respectful of nature and concerned with the well-being of future generations that they are able to view resource systems as partly man-made and to have a clear analytical perception of the relationship between the intensity of exploitation and the level of yields. Thus, Richards notes that, although living from the forest, Mende farmers of Sierra Leone 'do not see themselves as standing over it, either to exploit or to conserve it. In local eyes the relationship is the other way round—the community is under the protection of the forest' (Richards, forthcoming: 139). In actual fact, the adaptive attitude of people *vis-à-vis* nature in traditional societies may lead them, in a perfectly consistent manner, even to accept the disappearance of a resource on the simple ground that this is the will of some supernatural force. Worse still, they may actually behave in a resource-destructive way if this type of behaviour accords well with their idea as to how resource systems reproduce themselves. It is useful, at this stage, to illustrate these possibilities and to gain precise understanding of the underlying ecological conceptions.

To begin with, we may refer to a fascinating article by Carrier (1987) in which the author attempts to elucidate the ecological practices and beliefs of the Ponams fishermen of Papua New Guinea. According to Carrier, the Ponams believed that 'substantial changes in the marine environment such as the extinction of species were not necessarily undesirable, though they may be inconvenient in practice' (Carrier, 1987: 153). Thus, even though sea turtles were extremely important in Ponam life (they played a central role in weddings and other feasts and were enjoyed as a regular part of the diet), Ponams actually objected to the government's plan aimed at the conservation of this resource because they felt that the cost of the restraint required from them could not be possibly balanced by any real benefit. After all, 'if sea turtles were going to die out, as the government said, it would be because God wanted them to. A halt on hunting sea turtles would not change God's mind but would be very costly to the Ponams' (ibid. 154). Interestingly, Ponams islanders were quite aware that areas could be overfished: they actually said that 'this had happened on some of the small islands off the northeast Manus coast' where rapacious fishermen 'were said to have fished their lagoons so much that it became much more difficult to catch fish than before'. Yet they refused to ascribe the declining catches to a decrease in fish population and they instead held that catches fell because fish became wary. 'Fish, many Ponams explained, are like people: confronted with danger, they move.' Thus, at this pragmatic level of knowledge, 'fish themselves are the agents of ecological change and the cause of decreased catches'. Islanders used this explanation to account for the presence of Japanese and Korean fishing vessels in their waters: 'the vessels were following fish that had fled waters closer to Japan and Korea' (ibid. 154–5). To take a last example, although Ponams could agree, as a matter of principle, that too much shell gathering would lead to failure of the beds—a failure which they themselves experienced around the middle of this century—they typically located the ultimate cause of shell depletion in the supernatural sphere: growing disrespect among islanders for the group that controlled the production of shell money led God or perhaps the ancestors to move the beds elsewhere (ibid. 156).

One characteristic feature of the ecological model adhered to by the islanders of Papua New Guinea is therefore that men are not the crucial agents of environmental change even though they may possibly be instrumental in bringing it about. The latter part of this proposition explains the fact noted by Carrier that some conceptions of the environment held by these people had functional aspects which meshed with Western understanding. Yet the former part makes it plainly clear that 'the fundamental way they viewed the environment was alien to Western thought' (Carrier, 1987: 156). The crux of the matter is that 'they did not organize the facts that they knew about marine life into the same models that Westerners have produced': as a result, their practical conclusions were derived from a completely different 'cultural superstructure' (ibid. 150, 156). Contrary to the Western view which tends to see human action as the principal agency of ecological disruption, their view was based on the belief that external agencies are at the heart of environmental phenomena. To quote Carrier again: 'Contrary to the materialist view of a self-ordering and self-sustaining natural environment, Ponams held that the ordering and operation of the world was dictated by God. God and fish themselves were the critical agents of change in natural resources' (ibid. 153). Revealingly, when they converted to Catholicism in the 1920s, they interpreted their new religion in a syncretic way in which their traditional core belief that God (the supernatural powers) acts continually in the world could be maintained. They also ensured the continuity between the old and new world-views by seeing God as an ultimate ancestor (ibid.).

Let us now turn our attention to a second illustration taken from another original study, this time by Brightman (1987), concerning the Boreal forest Algonquians. What makes the case of these Indian hunting tribes particularly worth exploring is the existence of a considerable body of evidence pointing to the lack of conservation and intentional management among them as well as to 'a proclivity to kill animals indiscriminately in numbers beyond what were needed for exchange or domestic use' (Brightman, 1987: 123). For instance, by the late 1700s or early 1800s, 'the Crees in the

Northern Department had overhunted beaver and big game to the point that reliance on hare and fish, migration south onto the plains, and starvation became humiliating and tragic consequences' (ibid. 125). Still more puzzling are reports about the apparently purposeless slaughters of certain species such as the deer or the beaver, and reports about non-selective killings of all animals, great and small, male and female, belonging to given species.

How can one account not only for the absence of resource management but also for the aforementioned acts of indiscriminate and non-selective hunting among American Indians? The first thing to note is that, like islanders in Papua New Guinea, Indian hunters of North America did not understand their own role as determinants of ecological change in general and of resource depletion in particular. Consequently, they were unaware that animals can be managed, that is they were unaware of their ability to influence the availability of animals in the future by harvesting in a restrained and selective fashion in the present: 'the conviction that hunters can reliably manipulate the quantities of animals subsequently available to them cannot . . . be ascribed to prehistoric and early-contact-period Algonquians' (Brightman, 1987: 132). Again like with Ponams, although Algonquians—or at least some of them—could recognize their *proximate* role as agents in the destruction of animals (most notably, the beaver), they would never admit final responsibility, the *ultimate* cause of any ecological change being necessarily located in decisions of supernatural beings: if the beaver disappears, it is ultimately because the creator and the trickster-transformer intended to destroy it (ibid. 133). Yet the idea that hunting pressure could reduce species populations *in the long term and on a large scale* was all the more absent in Algonquian culture that game animals killed by hunters were thought to spontaneously regenerate after death or reincarnate as foetal animals (ibid. 131). Thus, Cree trappers could well imagine that 'an adult, trapped animal was "the same one" that had been killed the previous winter', and modern Crees followed ritual procedures in which animal bones and blood were disposed in such a way as to prefigure and influence animal regeneration and reincarnation (ibid.). This last belief points to a central element of the Algonquian culture, namely that their environment was one of primordial abundance. This ecological optimism was actually reinforced by the feeling that 'game could not be destroyed but only temporarily displaced' (in the same way as depleted shell beds were thought by Ponams to have been relocated elsewhere), and that 'animals were "given" to hunters when they were needed' (ibid. 132).

The above ecological model can no doubt account for the absence of effective management among Boreal forest Indians, yet it is probably not sufficient to explain the kind of overkilling that has been reported in the literature dealing with the old hunting practices of these people. Acts of indiscriminate killing, at least among certain American Indian tribes, may be understood by reference to a specific belief concerning the mode of operation of their resource systems. This belief—widespread among the Iroquoians in the Great Lakes area—is the idea that animals are able to communicate with each other and to share their experiences. More precisely, Iroquoians believed that they had to kill all the animals which they encountered because, if they did not do it, the animals would go and tell the others how they had been hunted. The result, the Iroquoians thought, was that they would not find any more animals in times of want (Brightman, 1987: 125).

In another study, Berkes has described the life of Cree Indian fishermen in the James Bay. He reached the same conclusion as Brightman and Carrier, namely that those fishermen believed, at least until recently, that 'fish is an inexhaustible resource, and that the numbers available are independent of the size of the previous harvest' (Berkes, 1987: 84). Berkes's contribution is especially interesting because he deals with the ecological attitudes and practices of a presently living traditional group. It is therefore worth quoting him at some length:

> Cree fishermen use the most effective gear available to them and the mesh sizes that give the highest return in a given situation, . . . the Cree are not conservationists because, among other things, they do not know and do not seem to care about animal population numbers, they never throw back undersized fish, and they concentrate their efforts on vulnerable aggregations of fish . . . Cree practices violate nearly every conservation-oriented, indirect-effort control measure in the repertory of contemporary scientific fisheries management. Furthermore, the Cree abhor catch-and-release practices currently fashionable in North American sport fishery management, disapprove of population surveys, and oppose tagging experiments . . . many groups of northern Indians and . . . Canadian Inuit (Eskimo) think that animals will go away if you count them or otherwise show disrespect. In many of these groups, as with the Cree, *it is the animals who are considered to be making the decisions; hunters are passive*. Any management system claiming to maximize productivity by manipulating the animals is considered arrogant. Thus, not only does the Cree ideology differ from Western scientific management, but it also opposes it. (Berkes, 1987: 85–6, emphasis added)

Much the same can be said of the observation made by Martin regarding the cod fishermen of Fermeuse, Newfoundland (Canada):

> *Until very recently*, Fermeuse fishermen have seldom thought of anyone's fishing activities, perhaps least of all their own, as having an appreciable effect upon fish populations. 'Queer things' happen, as in years when fish does not appear, but this is explained in terms of natural factors (e.g. a change in water temperature) over which man has no control. (Martin, 1979: 285; cited from Schlager, 1994: 247, emphasis added)

In the same vein, Wilson and Thompson partly trace present overgrazing in Mexican pastoral *ejidos* to the *ejidatorios'* limited technical understanding 'regarding the complex interdependence of individual grazing decisions and the impact these choices have on the range resource and, ultimately, on livestock productivity and human welfare'. In particular, 'local understanding of elementary soil–water–plant–animal relationships is rudimentary' (Wilson and Thompson, 1993: 314).

Strict access rules and conservation: the case of type-III societies

A few illustrations

In the previous sections, we have referred to traditional societies in which conservation rules are conspicuously absent either because resources are abundant (an objective factor which makes these rules useless) or because the people concerned do not perceive themselves as important determinants of ecological change when resources are liable to depletion/degradation (a subjective factor that prevents people from adopting the 'right' kind of behaviour). We are now considering the case of societies in which competition over a scarce CPR that is at the same time liable to depletion/degradation has led the corporate custodian community to adopt not only strict access rules but also conservation procedures or management mechanisms. (Bear in mind that a scarce CPR is one that has become subtractible due to pressure of human exploitation.) There is actually plenty of evidence that these type-III societies may exist or have existed both in the Third World and in today's advanced countries. To make things clearer, it is worth illustrating this new possibility by quoting a number of striking examples from the literature.

Let us first have a look at the fishing sector. It is not difficult to find instances where management rules have been effectively enforced together with strict access rules with the apparent effect of ensuring the long-term viability of local fisheries once threatened with depletion/degradation. For example, in feudal Japan during the Edo Period (1603–1867), 'strict regulations were drawn-up by the Uwajima fief to ensure the conservation of resources. The use of bottom gill nets for the benthos catch was prohibited, and fishing with a small mesh trawl net ("with a mesh like a mosquito net") was forbidden. Pesticides were not permitted and night fishing with torches was regulated by season and sometimes prohibited. Seaweed harvesting was also banned during the spawning season because the eggs of some species of fish attach to the weeds. Similar regulations obtained in other fiefs, such as Fukuoka' (Ruddle, 1987: 21).

Turning now to a more egalitarian type of society, we may refer to local systems of fisheries management in Sahelian West Africa. Thus, among the three main fishing groups operating in the Niger River delta (the Bozo, Somono, and Sorko), regulation was based on village control over local fish resources. The timing of fishing, the spots where fishing was allowed or prohibited, the size of specimens kept, and the technology used were regulated by a local 'water master' who was also in charge of enforcing exclusionary rules against outsiders (Lawry, 1989*a*: 4; Fay, 1990*a*: 170–4, Verdeaux, 1990: 209 n. 8; Jeay, 1984). Since the 'water master' always symbolized a treaty of alliance with the spirit(s) believed to inhabit the local waters ('the water and the fish belong only to the spirits'), his authority was great among the fishermen and it was actually supported by a series of myths describing in a typically symbolic way the various rules and agreements in force within the local group as well as *vis-à-vis* neighbouring communities. The role of 'water-masters' was especially important in connection with the partitioning of waters among various groups of claimants or with the succession of fishing operations by different groups using different techniques, not a surprising fact given the high conflict potential involved in these situations. 'The conflicts presented by those [Bozo] myths often lead to conclusions backed by the strength of the water spirits: such spirits emasculate the Somono enemy, cause the appearance of hordes of crocodiles in order to repel bambara fishermen, or it is the water master himself who is a spirit, knows how to spoil the fishing party, and can transform himself into an offensive fish' (Fay, 1990*a*: 169, our translation). Yet, ideological intimidation was also a powerful means of sanctioning breaches against conservation rules. In the laguna Aby in the Ivory Coast, the fisherman who operated during the closed season exposed himself to the reprisals of the local spirit which could inoculate him with one or several diseases or even make him mad (Perrot, 1990: 184).

In the Pacific islands, a wide range of restrictions on fishing have been used for centuries which, according to Ruddle, 'were clearly designed to conserve stocks' (Ruddle, 1988: 81). This is confirmed by Johannes, a biologist, who goes so far as saying that Pacific islanders 'devised and practised almost every basic form of modern marine fisheries conservation measure centuries ago, long before the need for marine conservation was even recognized in Western countries' (Johannes, 1982: 259, cited from Acheson, 1989: 362; see also Hviding and Baines, 1994: 25). This wide range of conservation measures included: the use of closed seasons (particularly during spawning), size limitations (bans on taking small fish), bans on destroying eggs, taboos on certain fishing areas, instructions to allow some proportion of the fish (or turtles) to escape so as to maintain the breeding stock, and, more recently, limitations on numbers and amount of gear that could be used.

In the Molucca Islands (in the eastern part of Indonesia), the people have inherited a system of traditional regulation called *sasi*. *Sasi* literally means 'prohibition'. It is a customary law that prevents the people from degrading their natural resources according to a communal agreement. *Sasi* actually applies both on the mainland and in coastal areas. On the mainland, it regulates the protection of forests and staple foods like *sago* plants. At sea, it regulates the harvesting of certain kinds of marine resources such as sea cucumber, pearl shells (in Aru islands), a sardine-like fish (in Haruku islands), etc. Closing *sasi* means that for a certain period determined by communal agreement people are prohibited from taking out certain natural resources (Marut, 1994: 6).

What needs to be stressed, however, is that if communities of inshore fishermen are frequently found to have regulations regarding fishing gear, fishing seasons, and the rotation or assignment of favoured fishing locations, they typically fail to regulate the total pressure on the stock of fish by restricting harvesting efforts in the open season (Schlager, 1990; Scott, 1993). This failure can be ascribed to both informational problems (it is easier to monitor a vessel's gear and location or whether a closed-season regulation is violated than to monitor the individual catches of many vessels in ordinary times) and to the heterogeneity of fishermen communities regarding endowments (see above, Chapter 8, Sect. 2 and below, Chapter 12, Sect. 3).

One of the most widely cited example of self-managed CPR is that of a collectively-run system of meadows and forests in the Swiss Alps, described by Netting (1972, 1976, 1981) on the basis of the case-study of Törbel village. This study is instructive because the system emerged at a time when agrarian pressure on the alpine ecosystem was much higher than it now appears under low fertility and net population exodus. Indeed, from the sixteenth to the late nineteenth centuries, 'the Swiss highlands resembled very much the overcrowded mountain ecosystems of the developing countries today'. More precisely, new crops and cultivation techniques had permitted denser settlement, as a result of which both humans and livestock overstressed the natural environment. Ecological consequences are well known: 'The increase in the number of goats, and the greater fuel demands of the larger population caused serious degradation of the mountain forests' with consequent floods, avalanches, and topsoil loss (Pfister, 1983: 293–4, 297, quoted from McNicoll, 1989: 150).[5]

It is in the last quarter of the fifteenth century that the inhabitants of Törbel signed a convention establishing an association to achieve collective regulation over the use of the alp, the forests, and the waste lands. According to the articles stipulated in that convention, access to well-defined common property was strictly limited to citizens. Moreover, rules regulating access to CPRs within the village community and intensity of use for the whole village, as well as rules providing for the protection of these resources from destruction, were carefully designed and effectively enforced. For example, it was decided that no citizen could send more cows to the summer grazing grounds than he could feed during the winter. Substantial fines were (and, apparently, still are) imposed on any villager found guilty of appropriating a larger share of grazing rights. This so-called 'wintering' rule is used by many other Swiss villages as a means for allocating appropriation rights to the commons. An alp association is specifically in charge of arranging for distribution of manure on the summer pastures, and organizing the annual maintenance work, such as building and maintaining roads and paths to and on the alp, and rebuilding avalanche-damaged corrals or huts. As for trees that provide timber for construction and wood for heating, they are marked by village officials and assigned by lot to groups of households, whose members are then authorized to enter the forests and harvest the allotted trees. The various measures taken—particularly the tight controls aimed at preventing overgrazing and the investments in weeding and manuring the summer grazing areas—have allowed Törbel villagers not only to maintain but even to enhance the productivity of their CPRs for many centuries. And it would seem that Netting's major findings are consistent with experience in many Swiss locations (Ostrom, 1990: 64).

We are also very fortunate to have at our disposal a remarkably well-detailed study by McKean (1986) on the experience of Japan in the management of traditional common lands. The author estimates that about 125 million hectares of forests and uncultivated mountain meadows were held and managed in common by rural villages during the Tokugawa period (1600–1867)—this represented approximately half of the surface of this category of land, the other half being under imperial or private property—and that more than 3 million hectares are still managed in this way today (McKean, 1986: 538). According to her, thousands of Japanese villages have actually succeeded in developing 'management techniques to protect their common lands for centuries without experiencing the tragedy of the commons'. Even as late as the 1950s, the remaining common lands continued to be managed on a sound ecological basis (ibid. 534).

McKean collected materials on three villages—Hirano, Nagaike, and Yamanaka—with a view to assessing the way commons were regulated on a micro-basis in Tokugawa Japan. From her account, it is plainly evident that Japanese villages used

[5] For a good summary of Netting's major findings, see Ostrom, 1990: 61–5 (on which our own account has been based).

extremely detailed rules of access and conservation procedures in connection with these local-level commons. For example, in order to prevent the *kaya*—a grass grown to produce thatch for roofs—from being cut at an immature stage for horse fodder, villagers usually designated an area with *kaya* as 'closed' during the growing season. On the other hand, to ensure that daily cutting of fresh fodder for draught animals and pack-horses did not deplete the supply available for winter, villagers of Hirano designated one open area for daily cutting of fresh grass and another closed area as a source of grass to be dried into fodder for the winter' (McKean, 1986: 553–4).

Village forests were essentially divided into two zones: open patches of forest and closed reserves. Villagers could enter the first zone at any time 'as long as they obeyed rules about taking fallen wood first, cutting only certain kinds of trees and then only those that were smaller than a certain diameter, and only with cutting tools of limited strength (to guarantee that no tree of really substantial size could be cut)': or 'about leaving so much height on a cut plant so that it could regenerate, or taking only a certain portion of a cluster of similar plants to make sure the parent plant could propagate itself, or collecting a certain species only after flowering and fruiting, and so on'. Also, to limit the quantity of plants collected, village authorities could prescribe the size of the sack or container used towards that purpose. To control access to the first zone in a tighter way, the same authorities could also issue entry permits 'carved on a little wooden ticket and marked "entrance permit for one person"' (McKean, 1986: 554–5).

As for the closed reserves, they were set aside 'for items that had to be left undisturbed until maturity and harvested all at once at just the right time, or that the commons supplied in only adequate, not abundant, amounts'. The time for collection and the rules to be followed by each collector were decided by the village headman. For example, if the supply of a given natural product was limited, 'the reserve might be declared open for a brief period (two or three days) and households allowed to send in only one able-bodied adult to collect only what could be cut in that time'. Precise rules for harvesting varied from product to product and from village to village, yet, as a matter of principle, they 'appeared to be a judicious combination that rewarded strength and hard work but also severely limited the circumstances in which cutting was allowed, which ensured that the total supply was not threatened and no extreme inequality appeared among households in a given year or among *kumi* [groups of households] over time' (McKean, 1986: 555–6). The latter requirement, as we have seen in the previous section, could drive the local authorities to devise fixed rotational sequences so that each household or group of households had access to patches of varying quality.

Finally, it is important to note that there were written rules about the obligation of each household to contribute a share to collective work intended for maintaining the commons, such as systematic programmes of harvesting and weeding of certain plants in a particular sequence to increase the natural production of the plants they wanted; or the burning of the common meadow lands which was conducted each year to burn off hard and woody grasses and thorny plants (and kill pests), and which involved 'cutting nine-foot firebreaks ahead of time, carefully monitoring the blaze, and occasional fire-fighting when the flames jumped the firebreak' (McKean, 1986: 558–9).

There is solid evidence of effective traditional forest management systems pertaining to Third World countries as well. In Table 10.2, taken from Arnold and Campbell (1986), various types of rules and procedures used to conserve forest resources in traditional Asian village societies have been listed. In their study of traditional management systems of hill forests in Nepal, these authors have noted that there was a tendency for these systems to be very conservative, allowing access only to a few products: if the amount of a resource was too small to be adequately shared, or if it was difficult to control an open harvest, communities preferred to stop collection of the resource altogether. Thus, for example, in an oak forest managed for leaf litter, all fuelwood cutting was banned, even though some trees were overmature or unproductive' (Arnold and Campbell, 1986: 438). As a matter of principle, the length of time during which the forest was open to member villagers for specified product collection, the number of times in the year when collection was permitted, and the timing of the periods of access were determined in such a way that the plants exploited could grow before they were again harvested (ibid. 436). A study conducted in two districts along the upper Kali Gandaki river watershed in north-central Nepal confirms the existence of traditional community forest management systems in this country (Messerschmidt, 1986). It however brings out the fact that these systems may be of quite recent origin, dating back to only a few generations or even a few decades. For instance, in Ghasa (Lete *panchayat*) forest access to sheep and goats has been strictly forbidden since 1974 (yet cattle, water buffalos, horses, and pack-mules are allowed to graze). In this village, moreover, cutting fuelwood and building materials by individuals is prohibited, although cutting poles and timber for public use is allowed on request. Also, every winter, each Ghasa household is required to collect debris and litter within the forest in order to reduce the risk of forest fires. Note that, if the district forest controller's staff intervenes to regulate permits for thinning the forest, the system basically remains under local control: access is controlled and the forest is patrolled by members of a panchayat forest committee following an old-style dating to pre-panchayat times (ibid. 461–2).

Traditional community forest management systems have also been reported for India. Thus, in the hill districts of Uttar Pradesh, in a vast area known as Uttarakhand, informal practices used to regulate the utilization of forest produce by local communities. We are thus told that old customary restrictions on the use of the forests operated 'over large areas': the grass cut by each family was strictly regulated and branches or trees could be cut only at specified times, and with the approval of the entire village community. Successful management of the village forests 'was facilitated by the near-total control exercised by villages over their forest habitat' (Guha, 1985: 1940). A recent survey of six villages in the Almora district (Agrawal, 1994) shows that, in most of them, there still exist rules prescribing how fodder is to be extracted from the village forest (e.g. when cutting leaves from trees for fodder, villagers must leave behind at least two-thirds of the leaf cover on the tree) and prohibiting animal grazing for most of the year. In some cases, also, in ways very similar to those observed in Japan, it is specified how much fodder can be extracted from the village forest by each (resident) rights-holder and how many animals can be grazed, and these

TABLE 10.2. Control systems used in traditional forest management

Basis of group rules	Examples
1. Harvesting only selected products and species	Trees: timber, fuelwood, food (fruit, nuts, seeds, honey), leaf fodder, fibre, leaf mulch, other minor forest products (gums, resins, dyes, liquor, plate leaves, etc.) Grass: fodder, thatching, rope Other wild plants: medicinal herbs, food (tubers, etc.), bamboos, etc. Other cultivated plants: upland crops (maize, millet, wheat, potatoes, vegetables), fruit, etc. Wildlife: animals, birds, bees, other insects, etc.
2. Harvesting according to condition of product	Stage of growth, maturity, alive or dead Size, shape Plant density, spacing Season (flowering, leaves fallen, etc.) Part: branch, stem, shoot, flower
3. Limiting amount of product	By time: by season, by days, by year, by several years By quantity: number of trees, headloads, baskets, number of animals By tool: sickles, saws, axes By area: zoning, blocks, types of terrain, altitude By payment: cash, kind, food or liquor to watchers or village, manure By agency: women, children, hired labour, contractor, type of animal
4. Using social means for protecting area	By watcher: paid in grains or cash By rotational guard duty By voluntary group action By making use of herders mandatory

Source: Arnold and Campbell (1986: 437).

quantities can vary from year to year depending on an assessment of the state of the resource made by panchayat officials who inspect it before opening it to villagers. Simple measures are often used to meter the amount of grass withdrawn from the forest area. For example, 'passes entitle holders to cut a specified number of fodder bundles' and 'users are provided with a rope that they must use to make a bundle out of the grass they have cut' (ibid. 272). In two of the six villages surveyed, the grass in the village forest is sold primarily through auctions. The auction winner is free to cut grass from that section of the community forest for which he has successfully bid during the time set for that purpose (ibid.).

Our last example is taken from South America. The Huastec Indians of north-eastern Mexico manage their forests in an indigenous system based on communal or individually owned forest plots called *te'lom* (Alcorn, 1984). In these forest patches, arboriculture and natural forest management are integrated to produce elements of primary and secondary vegetation as well as introduced species. A great diversity of species—typically over 300 species—are found in a *te'lom* plot, some used for construction purposes, others for utilization in and around the farmstead, still others as medicinal plants, as fruits and leaves fed to domestic livestock, or as human foods. Most of the *te'lom* are managed in a way that causes little disturbance of the forest ecosystems. 'Useful plants that arise naturally are selectively allowed to mature to productive size. If a desired species does not, or cannot volunteer, or does not volunteer where it is desired, a person will plant or transplant it into the *te'lom*. Thus, the number of useful species in a *te'lom* increases slowly as some are planted or transplanted and others arise spontaneously and are spared. Unwanted plants [are] irregularly removed.' (ibid. 394).

Some interpretative comments

How are we to account for the conservationist attitude displayed in the aforementioned societies and, above all, how are we to reconcile such evidence with the one adduced in the previous section and with the interpretative analysis offered in the same? There are apparently two ways of explaining conservation-mindedness in type-III societies that are consistent with our interpretation of the case of type-II societies. First, it can be contended that type-III societies differ in nature from type-II societies, more specifically, the latter are hunter-gatherer societies while the former are agricultural societies in which people's perceptions of their relationships with the surrounding environment are much more conducive to resource management practices. Second, it may be pointed out that societies can learn over time the need to conserve their resources when these become scarce. Or else, the two explanations can be combined by stressing that some kinds of society learn better or more quickly than others how to adjust to a changing environment.

Authors of many of the case-studies referred to above have actually expressed the opinion that a learning process has clearly been at work in the societies concerned. Yet, there is significant variation in the way these authors have characterized the learning process. Some seem to suggest that societies learn quite quickly about the changing nature of their environment and about the kind of response required of them, implying that, contrary to what we have argued in the previous section, they may optimally adjust to evolving environmental challenges confronting them. For example, Messerschmidt writes that, in Nepal, the villagers of Ghasa 'recognised in the 1960s that their local Ramjung pine forest was rapidly being depleted by overcutting, indiscriminate grazing, and general abuse'. As a result, they decided to close off approximately five hectares to allow regeneration; other measures quickly followed (Messerschmidt, 1986: 461). Unfortunately, we are not told in this case how villagers became aware of their new environmental problems and how they came to effectively respond to them.

Other authors appear to think that, if village communities learn quickly about new challenges emerging from increased pressure on natural resources, they may possibly fail to respond practically in the appropriate way because of some sort of collective action problem. Thus, again with reference to Nepal, Arnold and Campbell remark: 'Awareness of the problems created by deforestation is widespread and well understood. However, there is considerable variation in villagers' conviction that remedial action could be successful' (Arnold and Campbell, 1986: 438). The same authors nevertheless also observe that effective forest management responses are unlikely to be forthcoming where shortages of fuel and fodder have become 'so severe that they could no longer be remedied by using the remaining resource, even if it were more effectively managed'. On the contrary, 'management systems have developed in areas where small shortages of fuel and fodder had emerged' (ibid. 434; see also 436). A pertinent question to ask is then why, in some cases, management responses have failed to arise *in time*, that is, when they could still be productive. A possibility is clearly that, awareness building only slowly, it may come out when appropriate incentives to conservation measures have disappeared. To conserve local resources, users need special incentives provided by an external agency (see below Chapter 12).

Revealingly, authors who have gone more deeply into the history of the societies studied usually propose an analysis in which the learning process explicitly appears as much more lengthy and hazardous than in the above-quoted works. At this stage, it is useful to return to McKean's outstanding study of traditional common lands in Japan (1986). On the one hand, McKean clearly suggests that critical pressure on natural resources may induce the people concerned to adopt management measures to protect these resources from depletion/degradation. Thus, according to her, an important conclusion emerging from her case-study of three villages during the Tokugawa era is that 'as demand for the products of the commons—whether that demand reflected wealth or poverty—approached the maximum sustainable yield of the commons, portions of the commons would be set aside as reserves and the rules would be progressively tightened' (McKean, 1986: 558). This conclusion no doubt rings like a straightforward application of the theory of induced institutional innovation: new rules or institutions tend to evolve whenever changes of factor endowments and/or technical change create discernible disequilibria between the marginal returns and the marginal costs of factor inputs (see, e.g., North and Thomas, 1973; North, 1981, 1989; Kikuchi and Hayami, 1980; Hayami and Kikuchi, 1981; Ruttan and Hayami, 1984; Hayami and Ruttan, 1985). Here, increasing scarcity of (forest) land induces village communities to tighten the rules regulating access to, and use of, the land.

When seen in perspective, McKean's analysis is actually much more subtle. As a matter of fact, before turning to her village case-studies, she has been careful enough to sketch the historical context in which conservation of common lands has taken place in Tokugawa Japan. Here, we learn that throughout Japan in the seventeenth century considerable deforestation occurred due to a sudden surge in the demand for timber caused by the rapid construction of cities and castles after the return of peace conditions (during the sixteenth century the country had been devastated by a widespread civil war). On the one hand, the appetite of *daimyo* (feudal lords) for timber led them to get hold of the best village forests and to deplete them in a short time (after a while, the *daimyo* realized the extent of the ecological crisis and started experimenting with conservation). On the other hand, there was increased environmental pressure on remaining common lands which caused serious degradation of village forests. In fact, 'this encounter with environmental degradation may be the reason that so much common land today turns out to be grassland and meadow—this land was probably prime forest before the 17th century' (McKean, 1986: 547). It is the opinion of McKean that this traumatic experience of ecological crisis actually induced village communities to take active steps to prevent it from occurring again:

For our purposes, the significance of this episode of deforestation during the 17th century is threefold: visible deforestation seems to have made villagers aware of the very real risks of overuse and enabled them to develop and enforce stricter rules for conservation on their own initiative to save their forests and commons from the same fate. Rather than destroying the commons, deforestation resulted in increased institutionalization of village rights to common land. And it promoted the development of literally thousands of highly codified sets of regulations for the conservation of forests and the use of all commons. (McKean, 1986: 549)

It is particularly interesting to note that, in response to this visible experience of deforestation, Japanese villages have chosen not only to adopt strict conservation measures but also to regulate access to common lands in such a way as to discourage population growth. Thus, households and not individuals were the unit of accounting and villages possessed the power to determine which households could be granted rights of access to the commons. Moreover, large households had no advantage over small ones and, in particular, they could not claim an enlarged share of benefits from the commons: such benefits were accorded irrespective of the household size. In addition, large households could not obtain advantages by splitting into several households since permission to form a branch household from the main household had to be obtained from village authorities and the latter 'recognised that creating an additional household would enlarge the number of claimants on the commons without enlarging the commons' and were therefore reluctant to grant such permission. Records from some villages actually show that, about midway through the Tokugawa period, the number of formally constituted households did not increase 'because no new households were permitted unless an old one died out for lack of heirs'. Consequently, 'users of the commons did not try to increase their numbers in order to increase their share of the commons, nor did anyone count on the benefits from the commons to bail them out after a period of irresponsible procreation'. 'Slow judicious' population growth was the rule during the Tokugawa period. In actual fact, it is clear from the contents of village and domain legal codes that 'everyone was conscious of a sense of "limits"' (McKean, 1986: 551–3). And if awareness of ecological stress could lead to effective collective response, it was because the historical evolution of villages 'gave each village a sturdy internal structure and a strong sense of identity by the early Tokugawa period' (ibid. 549).

In the same vein, a recent study about forest management in Imperial China points out that in the region of Nanping (Fujian province), people realized in the middle of the nineteenth century that their forests had been depleted by indiscriminate cutting. As revealed by an inscription on a stone stele discovered in the city of Nanping, the people then decided to carefully regulate cutting of timber in the surrounding mountains and to impose fines on all offenders (Menzies, 1994: 78). The same idea that learning is a time-consuming and hazardous process also comes out of the already-cited study by Brightman on the ecological attitudes and practices among Boreal forest Algonquians (1987). In this study, we are informed that, following intensified exploitation, limited-access land tenure and conservation eventually appeared as adjustments to depleted environments. Conservation was actually 'a postcontact innovation that did not develop on any scale prior to game depletions in the early 1800s' (Brightman, 1987: 126). Contrary to what was observed in Japan, it does not seem to have generated from within the hunters' groups but as a result of the exogenous intervention of the Hudson's Bay Company. Still, the question remains as to why Crees and other groups eventually accepted the Company's conservation policies whereas, before, they circumvented them 'when and how they could' (ibid. 137–8).

The answer provided by Brightman is that continuous and visible experiences of game shortages slowly led Algonquians to question their traditional beliefs and, after a certain point, to reinterpret them in a way more consistent with the changed circumstances. When old beliefs could obviously no more account for what was there for everybody to see, they had to be adapted so as to acknowledge an explicit link between overhunting and game depletion, and to make (fur-bearing) animals appear as manageable. In the works of Brightman, 'Crees encountered in the game shortages a contradiction of cosmic proportions: despite conventional ritual treatment, animals were not renewing themselves but were disappearing'. Game shortages therefore 'motivated a reinterpretation of indiscriminate or "wasteful" hunting and trapping as offensive to animals and to the spirit entities regulating each species'. These spirit entities—the 'Great Moose', the 'Great Beaver', the 'Great Lynx', etc.—were now imagined to interfere with the harvests of hunters who trapped unselectively or wasted the products of animals. For example, among Labrador Naskapi, when in 1914 the main herd of caribou failed to migrate south along its usual route, the ensuing famine was attributed to the anger of the caribou spirit at prior waste and overhunting (Brightman, 1987: 136–8). Conservation was thus redefined as a religious obligation the violation of which caused severe punishment by the game spirits or the animals themselves in the form of game shortages. In conformity with an ancient belief, depletion of animals was understood 'less as an objective decrease in the numbers of animals present than as a limitation on their visibility to the hunter and on his access to them' (ibid. 139).

It therefore appears that in traditional village societies *awareness of ecological stress* under increasing human pressure on natural resources *grows only slowly and typically requires concrete, visible experiences of depletion or degradation to be stimulated.*[6] Effects must be highly visible before people realize what is happening. In other words, abstract reasoning and explanations do not have much impact here. This finding is quite in agreement with Bourdieu's analysis of the structure of time consciousness in such societies. According to Bourdieu, indeed, villagers are well capable of setting

[6] For a discussion of some policy implications of this fact, see Broad (1994).

their sights on a distant future provided that this future is susceptible of being bound up or connected with the present and the past through organic links directly suggested by daily experience. What proves much more difficult for them is to conceive of the future as a point in time where an infinite number of abstract and indeterminate possibilities can occur, that is, where humans can project things which they believe could come true if they only decided to make them arise. This is so because such a concept of the future presupposes that people are able to suspend their routine adherence to the customary data of day-to-day experiences, that is, to distance themselves from how they live in the present and how they or their ancestors have lived in the past (Bourdieu, 1963).

If the above analysis is correct, rural people can obviously destroy their future sources of subsistence whenever new circumstances have emerged to which they have not been accustomed through a long-established experience. The problem is then that the right level of ecological awareness may arise late and even too late. This point has been recently emphasized in a report issued by the World Bank:

> Rural people deplete their forest and soil capital, often unaware that they are destroying their future source of fuel, fodder, and soil protection. The people do not realize the danger until the local forest is nearly gone and they must go farther into the countryside to find fuelwood. When the stock is eventually used up, . . . the extent of the crisis becomes evident . . . There is no 'fast fix' when this happens . . . Deforestation by local people using wood for local uses can be a slow and largely unnoticed process; realization of the damage may come too late for them to do anything about it without significant outside intervention. (Gregersen, Draper, and Elz, 1989: 9, 144)

In the same vein, Arnold and Campbell have noted that in Nepal: 'People are only now seeing the consequences of these pressures on a scale sufficient to persuade them to evolve new methods of resource conservation in common lands' (Arnold and Campbell, 1986: 429–30; see also Cernea, 1989: 30).

The same lack of, or delayed, awareness accounts for the oft-noted difficulty in establishing village woodlots in rural communities whose tradition has been long centred on the priority of (communal) pasturage. In some of these communities woodlots are established in the face of considerable opposition which can occasionally lead to the purposeful destruction of fencing and of young trees, but will most commonly manifest itself in the current damage caused by 'individual stock owners and herdboys seeking grazing for their animals and unimpressed by the need to protect the woodlot' (Bruce, 1986: 166).

This being said, and given the importance of visibility in triggering off awareness of ecological stress, we may expect this awareness to develop more rapidly in those societies in which 'a sense of limits' has already entered people's minds due to previous experiences of scarcity. Thus, other things being equal, awareness of newly arising stress in the commons is more likely to develop in agricultural societies, especially so if intensive or semi-intensive agricultural practices are being used. In the circumstances, indeed, villagers know by experience that to remain productive land must be either allowed to rest some time or replenished with organic manure or chemical fertilizers. Presumably, they should then be able to use this body of experience to understand by analogy the risks of depletion/degradation and the need for conservation in village forests, meadows, or rivers. At least, they are apparently in a better position to reach such an understanding than, say, hunter-gatherers who cannot draw on a store of analogous experiences to help them assess correctly ongoing processes of game or fruit depletion. Thus, for example, Arnold and Campbell note: 'when a small number of highly desirable or visible seedlings are planted in a forest area, the need to restrict grazing until the seedlings are established is apparent to all the villagers in the area. Once planted, the existing natural forest is transformed from an area that did not depend on humans for its reproduction to a "cultivated" area needing protection from livestock, and management becomes meaningful to people who for generations were accustomed to alternative land use patterns' (Arnold and Campbell, 1986: 447).

In the same connection, like Ostrom (1990), Cernea lays stress on the fact that an important condition for success of group farm forestry schemes is that a clear link is created 'between a well-defined small group and a well-defined tract of forest land that is to be protected or planted', so that the impact of efforts can be measured and a clear correlation between people's contributions and the returns they get can easily emerge (Cernea, 1989: 61). Also, it is perhaps significant that Mende tribesmen in the Gola Forest (Sierra Leone), who are deemed by Davies and Richards to be 'accurately aware of the major changes taking place with the passing of the forest frontier and subsequent population increase' (Davies and Richards, 1991: 63; see also Richards, forthcoming: 152), have been (shifting) rice cultivators for generations, well-accustomed to the complex ecology of rotational bush-fallowing.

Also, we may safely predict, again for the same reason—ease of visibility—that awareness of ecological stress will build up more easily when the impact of over-exploitation on the resource stock is more visible and when the connection between use behaviour and the level of this stock is more evident and more predictable. This is why the emergence of such awareness depends on the physical and geographical nature of the resource. It will thus more easily emerge with respect to a localized, visible, and predictable resource than in the case of a resource that stretches over vast and seasonally changing geographic areas, is largely unpredictable, and hardly visible. For example, inland fishermen may more easily understand their role as determinant of ecological change than maritime fishermen who operate in the open sea. Through experience and observation, the former easily come to know, say, that fish spawn in the tributaries that feed into the river's main stem and that they must therefore avoid fishing in these zones to let the resource grow and reach maturity. By converting the spawning areas into sacred places considered to be defended by local water spirits, they may then ensure that nobody is tempted into entering them and transmit their knowledge to future generations.

Marine fishing is a much more complex affair, especially in tropical areas where there are innumerable fish species whose biological habits and movements are still poorly known and whose mutual interactions are infinitely intricate. When fish stocks fluctuate unpredictably and their population dynamics is not well understood, it is obviously difficult, even for scientists, to establish clear and predictable connections between fishermen's harvesting behaviour and the state of the resource. Also, while setting aggregate quotas for a whole fishery, they are liable to make gross mistakes which may have disastrous consequences if estimates of the maximum sustainable yield have been too optimistic (such as recently happened in New Zealand).

Clearly, signs of depletion may be very hard to interpret and causes of depletion may be very difficult to determine. How could we expect fishermen to form a correct idea about their own responsibilities for a decline of fish catches when climatic factors beyond their control might well account for it? In Kerala, for instance, a marked decrease in total fish landings occurred in the mid-1970s and persisted throughout the 1980s. Small-scale fishermen's organizations and activists put the blame for such decline on the rapacious operations of a sizeable fleet of trawlers which entered the sector by the late 1960s and the early 1970s. Their lobbying action even led the government eventually to decide on a seasonal ban on trawling in the early 1990s. Yet, in 1991, due to the abundant presence of pelagic fish species off the coast of Kerala, there has been a sudden and unexpected increase in the aggregate catch which more or less equalled the peak average level attained in 1971–75. Obviously, since the upsurge of fish landings took place so quickly after the ban had been brought into effect, this conservation measure cannot account for the fishery's recovery.

In the same way, and to the complete surprise of the scientific community, the lobster resource has tripled over the last two decades in Eastern Canada's waters despite the fact that exploitation rates on legal-size lobsters is estimated to be as high as 90 per cent (Belliveau, 1994: 3). In the other direction, in the North Atlantic there is a natural phenomenon known as the 'Northern oscillation' which caused a cooling down of the Canadian seas in the early 1980s and led to a significant decline of fish stock levels in coastal fisheries. However, the most well-known climatic disturbance that occurred during recent decades, the 'El Nino' phenomenon, had the opposite effect of heating up waters through the abnormal invasion of warm waters low in salt content (as a consequence of fluctuations of atmospheric pressure and wind systems). It struck the south-east Pacific during the years 1982–3 and caused a sudden collapse of the anchovetta fishery in Peru (which was then the world's top producer of fish with a yearly total catch of 12 million tons) and severe depression in the Equatorian fishery as well. The previous occurrence of a similar event was probably more than 18 million years ago!

This being said, there is enough solid evidence to show that in many fisheries the disastrous experience of resource depletion during the post-war era has largely been caused by overfishing (see above, Chapter 2). Present trends in developing countries are unfortunately pointing to similar disasters also caused by human overexploitation, as exemplified by the degradation of many inshore fisheries under the impact of rapid technological modernization (including that of artisanal techniques), widespread use of ecologically harmful fishing methods, and high growth rates of the fishing workforce. (This certainly applies to the above-mentioned case of Kerala with respect to prawn resources.)

Hence the emphasis of some economists upon the necessity 'to get fishermen to understand the need for fishery-management measures, and to understand the long-term effects on fish stocks of not complying with the management measures in place' (Sutinen, Rieser, and Gauvin, 1990: 366).

Fishery is not the only natural-resource sector in which erroneous analyses of environmental change are possible. Thus, in a recent piece of research, Melissa Leach and James Fairhead have argued that, in part of Guinea, environmental policy has been misinformed by the erroneous idea of an ongoing savannization of tropical forest. According to the authors, this misinformation has resulted from the fact that 'observers have been tempted to see each zone as the anthropogenically degraded derivate of a vegetation type not found further south' (Leach and Fairhead, 1994: 81). By thus analysing the forest-savanna mosaic in the Kissidougou region as the degraded outcome of a prior natural forest formation, botanists did not consider the possibility that 'transition woodland could represent a stable intermediate form, the establishment of forest in savanna, or the complex outcome of local management strategies' (ibid.: 82). Preconceived ideas of vegetation change and a prejudiced view of local users as environment destroyers have led both national and international experts to pay too much attention to apparent processes of degradation readily observable in the short term (for example, the clearing and burning of wooded lands for farming, and the setting on fire by hunters and herders) and too little attention to processes of regeneration and the impact of local practice on them (ibid.: 85). This tendency, Leach and Fairhead note, is actually reinforced by the unhappy fact that 'presenting a degrading or threatened environment has become an imperative to gain access to donors' funds' and that, often, 'the environmental problem is built into the very terms of reference of consultants who have neither the time nor the social position to investigate village natural-resource management and its changes on any other terms' (ibid.: 84, 86).

Note carefully that in the analysis of Leach and Fairhead, misinformation about the causes of environmental change is attributed to experts while peasants are considered to be perfectly informed. This is not necessarily true, as we have already illustrated, and one must always be wary about the romantic bias which consists in systematically placing the burden of responsibility for mistakes on experts and bureaucrats (a bias which also characterizes the peasant view of the outside world). A striking case where local users are typically misinformed about ecological stress and the mechanism of resource overexploitation is that of groundwater resources. As rightly pointed out by Moench, in this case it is hard to know who is using the resource, how much water users are extracting, and what is the relationship between actions and consequences. The problem is again exacerbated by the fact that wells and pumps tend to be located on private lands and individually owned. In this context, 'it is extremely difficult for an understanding of resource dynamics to emerge at a community level. Individuals may understand the behaviour of their own wells but they are rarely able to put this behaviour in the context of other's use patterns at least until major disruptions have already occurred.' As a consequence, 'few communities are aware of the potential for overdevelopment until it occurs and, when it does occur, they tend to resist any management actions which would infringe on established patterns of individual use' (Moench, 1992: A-7-8). Together with inappropriate state policies—pricing of electricity at subsidized rates for irrigation pumping; electricity pricing structure conducive to overexploitation (the use of a flat horsepower-based annual fee makes the marginal cost of pumping water nil); subsidized credit programmes for well development by individuals—the above difficulty helps account for the dangerous processes of falling water-tables, saline intrusion, and depletion of economically accessible groundwater reserves in several parts of the Indian subcontinent, most notably in the districts of Mehsana (Gujarat) (Bhatia and Drèze, 1992; Moench, 1992).

Flexible access rules and conservation: the case of type-IV societies

Here is no doubt a problematic case in so far as, in the absence of strict access rules, it may prove difficult to ensure that conservation measures will be followed by resource users: for example, if people can freely enter into a forest (or in the sea) without being checked at any point, it will be *a fortiori* difficult to control their use behaviour when they are in the forest (at sea). None the less, if resource users adhere to a moral code and if they have properly internalized it—each user abides by a set of rules enjoining certain modes of using the resource and he (she) does so because of a personal attitude about the act itself—type-IV combination can actually occur. This is the result of the fact that moral norms may serve as a substitute for monitoring devices inasmuch as they are followed even though violation would be undetected (see above, Chapter 6).

This kind of situation is perhaps not as exceptional as it may appear at first sight. Thus, it is well known that in the open sea—a resource domain the access to which is particularly costly to regulate—fishermen often obey a moral, gentlemen's code of behaviour not only in the case of emergencies (when certain forms of helping behaviour are prescribed) but also with respect to voyage routes, choice of fishing spots, and fishing practices (see, e.g., White, 1977). Such professional codes, which are inculcated through secondary socialization processes and sometimes even during (early) childhood, are typical examples of generalized or abstract morality as we have defined it in Chapter 6. Adherence to generalized moral values has the effect of binding users together even in the absence of any formal organization to monitor and regulate their behaviour.

It is worth stressing that type-IV combination points to a solution to complex problems of environmental management in the context of non-excludable resources or resource domains. Think, for example, of the risks represented by the dumping of toxic products or the release of obnoxious effluents into the sea (on these environmental risks, see Ruddle, 1982), or the use of environmentally destructive methods such as dynamite to catch fish. Here are clearly harmful acts which are extremely difficult to monitor effectively. If people could be convinced to behave out of a moral sense while they use resources or while they are in a position to affect a resource stock by producing externalities, resources would be better preserved despite the lack of external control. It is thus evident that type-IV situations are unlikely to arise at the level of well-localized village commons where, as we have seen, access rights are usually defined by local communities (see type-I, -II, and -III situations). This explains why we could not find any convincing examples of this kind of situation in the socio-anthropological literature dealing with village CPRs.

10.3 Conclusion

There are a number of important lessons to draw from the foregoing extensive discussion. These lessons can be summarized as follows:

1. When trying to assess the collective behaviour of traditional rural communities *vis-à-vis* the environment, it is essential to make a clear distinction between two sorts of problem: one of pure distribution and one of resource management. While the first problem is static, the second one involves a time dimension. While the first problem refers to the question as to how access to a resource is to be defined—that is, who are to be accorded the right to appropriate part of the current resource *flow* and who are to be denied such a right; or how is this flow to be shared among competing claimants?—the second problem implies that attention is given to the way current levels of harvesting effort and modes of appropriating the resource affect the resource *stock* over time.

2. From our survey of the socio-anthropological literature, it can be concluded that, if members of traditional rural communities are relatively good at perceiving and solving distributive problems arising in connection with the use of natural resources (they can even design ingenious systems of rotation to regulate access among 'insiders' in an equitable way)—especially so when the resource is highly visible and well localized—they are not inherently conservationists as they are often portrayed in popular accounts and even—though perhaps to a lesser extent than before—in socio-anthropological writings.

3. It is common practice to ascribe mismanagement of village commons to collective action problems. These problems are no doubt a critical hurdle on the way to better conservation of natural resources, and we shall return to them in Chapter 12. What is worth noticing, however, is that, as pointed out above, traditional rural societies were apparently able, at least in certain circumstances, to make effective collective arrangements to solve distributive problems. Why should they then have been less efficient in organizing to prevent depletion/degradation of CPRs? The answer to this question in the present chapter is that members of such societies do not conceive of their natural environment nor of their own relations with it in the same way as people in modern, rationalist societies do.

In point of fact, they perceive surrounding natural resources as a kindness provided by some supernatural agents which constantly look after basic needs of the people placed under their protection. Consequently, they have a proclivity to think that these resources are infinite or limitless. And if experience shows too patently that such is not the case, they may still refuse to come to the view that their own harvesting behaviour is liable to seriously affect resource stocks. On the contrary, to reconcile their system of beliefs with the newly emerging reality, they tend to imagine that resources have not been actually destroyed but simply moved or relocated elsewhere (or made invisible) by an act of will of some god or spirit. Besides saving the essentials of their old beliefs, a reinterpretation of this kind has the advantage of presenting a shortage of resource as a temporary phenomenon which can (perhaps) be easily reversed. What bears emphasis is that magical beliefs prevent rural people from drawing a conceptual distinction between resource stock and resource flow and, *a fortiori*, from understanding the link between current rates of resource appropriation and the level of the stock. The very notion of resource management remains alien to them, which, after all, is not surprising given the intellectual sophistication required to grasp it.

4. Given the complexity of some ecological processes (such as the determinants of fishing stocks in many tropical maritime fisheries), there may be a genuine uncertainty about the exact influence of human harvesting efforts on the level of a resource stock, not only among users but also among experts and scientists. In such circumstances, the (sudden) depletion of a resource may be *correctly* perceived as a reversible process that is essentially determined by exogenous forces. Highly intensive harvesting efforts, when such uncertainty exists, are obviously not understandable in terms of the tragedy of the commons or the prisoner's dilemma. In this case, however, the government may be perfectly justified in setting rules of restraint in order to reduce the risk of irreversible depletion of a resource that is or may turn out to be essential in the future (see Chapter 1).

5. Traditional rural societies are far from static, however. Awareness of ecological stress under conditions of increasing and continuous human pressure on the environment may grow even if only slowly and even if it typically requires visible signs of depletion/degradation to be stimulated. This awareness is therefore likely to develop more rapidly in those societies in which 'a sense of limits' has already pervaded people's minds due to previous experiences of scarcity. Moreover, it emerges more easily with respect to localized, visible, and predictable resources than with respect to resources showing the opposite characteristics. Such a movement towards increased causal understanding of natural phenomena is bound to imply radical revisions of old systems of beliefs so that man can now appear, at least in a roundabout way, as an important agent of ecological change.

6. The fact nevertheless remains that, since awareness-building is in this case a time-consuming and hazardous process, people may realize the need for conservation measures too late, that is, when a resource is already irretrievably depleted, or when it has been destroyed to such an extent that incentives to conserve the remaining portion have vanished. The possibility of resource destruction resulting from slow or imperfect understanding of what is going on and what to do points to the essential role of grass roots education in preserving village-level CPRs. It is too easily assumed, by economists in particular, that lack of incentive is the main constraint that prevents villagers from conserving their commons. In still numerous contemporary situations, knowledge of local-level ecological processes and of people's responsibilities for environmental destruction is inadequate. Therefore, *especially when ecological change is rapid*, outside assistance is needed to help villagers to analyse their own situation and

its inner dynamics as well as to design effective management solutions. As shown by varied experiences of patient work with rural groups, great progress towards achieving the first objective can actually be made by helping them to draw together a number of critical on-the-field observations which have so far remained unconnected, and to articulate these observations in meaningful causal sequences.

11

Recent Changes Affecting Collective Action at Village Level

In the previous chapter, we have attempted to characterize traditional rural societies in terms of their relations with the surrounding environment. By traditional societies we mean societies that are relatively closed to external influences, in particular to those forces which bring in their wake the market mechanism, significant and more or less continuous technological change, new sets of values and aspirations centred on consumption and individual development, as well as a centralized state system bent on organizing and regulating economic and social life over an unified national space, in a formal legalistic way, and on the basis of rational principles. Since the colonial period in most Third World rural societies and even before in some of them, the above forces have affected village life in such a marked way that it is no more possible to consider these societies as traditional. In this chapter, it is therefore important to assess the nature of the changes involved and the extent of vulnerability to such changes of village-level arrangements with respect to CPR use. Only then will we be able to gauge the ability of village communities to manage natural resources in present circumstances and to identify the conditions under which their resource management initiatives are more or less likely to be successful, a task which will be accomplished in Chapter 12.

This chapter is divided into two sections. In the first section, we essentially draw the lessons from the centralized approach to environmental management that has been followed by many governments in the Third World. In the second section, it is argued that village arrangements for solving problems of access to, and/or conservation of, local-level CPRs have evolved under the joint impact of several aforementioned factors.

11.1 State Regulations of Resource Use: Their Nature and Drawbacks

A centralized approach to resource management: a review of some experiences

In most developing countries, governments have chosen to centralize management of local-level natural resources, vesting it in administrative bodies and possibly granting medium- or long-term leases to private agents or companies. State assumption of resource ownership has usually been predicated upon the preconceived idea that private and communal tenure pose a serious threat to resource conservation and sound exploitation, or that an equally serious threat arises from the simple absence of any local control over the resources (that is, from an open-access situation). Or again, as pointed out by Lawry, the State's principal objective in centralizing control could be 'to assert its political authority over local interests, not to impose a new resource-management regime' (Lawry, 1989*a*: 5). The latter possibility probably applies with special force to Sub-Saharan Africa. In this region, indeed, national States are young and fragile structures which have been established in a fluid political set-up where it was deemed important by the new rulers to weaken local organizations and to break the independent power of local customary chieftains (see, e.g., Coquery-Vidrovitch, 1985; Young, 1986; Bayart, 1989). In any event, by assuming ownership of village-level, natural resources, governments have dismantled rights of local customary authorities over village commons, thereby sometimes perpetuating the colonial policy legacy.

Thus, for example, the State of Mali took over control of all resources at independence in 1960 and 'in the process supplanted the authority of local groups to regulate access to and use of local resources' (Lawry, 1989*a*: 4). In the Niger River delta, this has actually meant that the traditional grazing-control system known as the *dina* (see above Chapter 10)—whose political basis had already been eroded under French colonial rule—came to an end and, together with it, Fulani hegemony in the area on which it was based (ibid.). A similar shift in the locus of resource control took place in the fishing sector since fishing groups were divested of their traditional rights over local fisheries. All waters entered the national domain of state property and customary dues received by local water masters were replaced by state taxes imposed on all operating fishermen irrespective of their ethnic origin and place of residence. Outsiders thus obtained legal free access to the waters of the Niger River delta provided that they met their fiscal duties *vis-à-vis* the new independent State (Jeay, 1984*b*; Kone, 1985). It may be noted that, in this case, the Malian State has gone farther in the way towards centralization than French colonial rulers since the latter recognized customary rights of local communities and tribes over well-delimited, small water bodies. What they ignored, and sometimes actively opposed, by contrast, were rights over large and more or less open water spaces. They indeed adhered to the so-called Grotius doctrine according to which the sea may not be the object of any appropriation because it is inalienable by nature and because the abundance of fish resources actually deprives exclusive access rights of any positive value (see, e.g., Christy, 1983).

In the Sahelian countries, in general, forestry management under independent governments has been more in line with colonial policy than inland water management. The French West Africa forest service was established in 1935 and charged with overall responsibility for managing the woodstock. Following metropolitan French forestry tradition, the forestry department in West Africa was granted relatively extensive controls over the exploitation of the woodstock not only inside but also outside national domain lands. Accordingly, 'small forestry agencies were set up by French administrators in each colony to implement central policies elaborated through a bureaucratic process and imposed through the colonial administrative hierarchy' (Thomson *et al.*, 1986: 399). The new legislation introduced far-reaching changes in the regulation of woodstock use. First, state forests were created which were subject to exclusive forest service control concerning woodstock and land use. Second, and much more importantly, 'this legislation centralised the forestry service's authority to regulate the exploitation of the 15 most valuable species of trees outside, as well as inside, the state forests'. For example, cutting live specimens, or lopping off branches above the height of 10 ft. was prohibited without prior authorization (which could however be obtained free from the forestry service if trees were destined for personal use) or without a cutting permit (which was sold to holders if the wood was to be harvested for sale).

Essentially, independent governments of West Africa inherited the centralized approach of their colonial predecessor by maintaining the institutional framework contained in the French forestry code (Thomson *et al.*, 1986: 399–400). As pointed out by Toulmin, current forestry legislation in the Sahel relies heavily on direct state regulation of how trees and their products can be used by local people and forest codes 'consist largely of lists of restrictions or prohibitions on forest use, with permits issued by the forest service for certain allowable activities' (Toulmin, 1991: 27). Moreover, 'Even trees on farms are subject to such restrictions and farmers must pay for a permit before cutting or using a tree that they themselves have planted. Community-based management of forest resources is also not allowed for within these codes, or is permitted only in terms of increased restrictions on use' (ibid.).

Just consider the case of Mali whose Forest Code is typical of forestry legislation in the Sahel and is not markedly different from the first code promulgated by the French in 1935. The area of general jurisdiction of the Forest Code is the 'forest domain' which actually comprises as much as 90 per cent of the total land area of Mali. (Cultivated land which has been left fallow for more than five years is considered part of the forest domain.) Moreover, all protected species listed in the code (including *Acacia albida*, nere, and karite, three of the most common and economically important tree species in Mali) are protected wherever they occur in the country, even within cultivated fields (Lawry, 1989*a*: 13–14). In the Sahelian zone, uprooting or cutting of trees or bushes in order to provide animal feed is forbidden while cutting of branches less than 1.5 m. from the ground is prohibited. 'These restrictions apply to all species of tree, native and exotic, and all trees occurring on individual holdings' (ibid. 13).

Subsistence cultivation and grazing are permitted within the so-called 'protected forests' (a territorial unit defined within the forest domain) while they are strictly forbidden in the 'périmètres de restauration' (another territorial unit corresponding to areas undergoing planned reforestation or considered in need of special protection) and forbidden except in special circumstances and under controlled conditions in 'forest reserves' (a third territorial unit in the forest domain classification). Individuals collecting wood, including fuel wood, from the forest domain for commercial purposes must secure a permit from the forest service. On individual holdings, listed species may not be harvested unless the farmer has obtained a permit which is however free. By contrast, collecting deadwood in 'protected forests' for domestic use does not require any permit (Lawry, 1989*a*: 14).

'Those who violate rules, including those who fail to secure a free permit, are subject to citation by forest agents and payment of fines.' Permit fees and fines are important sources of forest service revenue, part of which is distributed as commissions to forest service personnel. Forest agents indeed receive a percentage of all fine revenue generated by their individual enforcement activities (Lawry, 1989*a*). Note that temptation to evade the permit obligation is all the greater as there is no guarantee that farmers would be issued permits upon request: forest agents are 'generally disdainful of farmer-management ability', being convinced that 'without their guidance, farmers would cut down trees before reaching maturity, would coppice trees improperly, and so forth' (ibid. 15).

In India, too, the State came to consider forests as resources to be protected against their former users. Since this experience is especially well documented from colonial times onwards, and since it is probably typical of forest policies followed elsewhere under British rule or influence, it is worth looking at carefully. As early as 1850, a commission mandated by the British colonial administration prepared a report one conclusion of which was that Indian forests were being destroyed mainly due to local people's mismanagement (Agarwala, 1985). Five years later, active steps were taken towards establishing a forestry department which would be in charge of elaborating and enforcing a scientific forest policy. A German botanist, D. Brandis, was called to lead the new department. The first forestry law dates back to 1865 when, for the first time, legal restrictions were imposed on the collection of forest products by a central authority. The same law also enabled the government to declare as government forest all lands covered with trees, shrubs, and bushes provided, however, that such a measure did not adversely affect the rights of individuals or communities (Fernandes and Kulkarni, 1986: 87). The 1865 law was revised a first time in 1878 when three forest categories were distinguished—protected forests, reserved forests, and village forests—with the former being the most strictly regulated from above and the latter being the locus of the largest local autonomy. Gradually, a shift nevertheless took place in the direction of increasing centralized control. Thus in 1894, an official report stated that:

> The sole object with which State Forests are administered is the public benefit. In some cases, the public is the whole body of tax-payers, in others, the people on the track within which the forest is situated: but in almost all cases the constitution and preservation of forests involve in greater or lesser degrees, the regulation of rights and restriction of privileges of users in the forest area which may have previously been enjoyed by the inhabitants of its immediate neighbourhood. This regulation is great and the cardinal principle to be observed is that the rights and privileges of individuals must be limited otherwise than for their own benefit, only in such degree as is absolutely necessary to secure that advantage. (Cited from Fernandes and Kulkarni, 1986: 86–7)

The idea that people must be 'protected against their own improvidence' gained growing acceptance. The tribals, in particular, were deemed to be incapable of managing surrounding forest resources themselves and it was therefore considered the duty of the government to regulate village forests and meadows so as to conserve them (Beck, 1994: 194). A second revision of the 1865 law occurred in 1927 under the Indian Forest Act, 1927. This Act essentially enlarged government's prerogatives to control forests (the government became empowered to acquire almost any land for the 'public benefit') and increased the role of the forestry department while simultaneously restricting further the rights of local people, thus giving rise to strong popular protest movements known as 'forest satyagrahas' (Bandyopadhyay and Shiva, 1987: 26–7). Partly as a response to these protests, the government of Madras made an interesting attempt, going in the opposite direction to that followed so far: as a matter of fact, it chose to give local people more responsibility in the management of their forests through an elected forest panchayat. In this, it was actually following the recommendation made by the Royal Commission on Agriculture (in its 1928 report) with respect to forest areas where woods are interspersed with cultivable patches of land (Shingi *et al.*, 1986: 7–11). Unfortunately, in the face of active opposition from forest officials, attempts to establish village forests on land not vested in government were implemented only in piecemeal fashion (Guha, 1985: 1947).

Another noticeable exception to the centralized tendency of colonial forest management policy, and one which has proved more successful and more lasting than the attempt made by the Madras presidency, is the Van Panchayat Act passed in 1931 following protracted resistance by the hill villagers in the middle Himalayan ranges of Uttar Pradesh (Uttarakhand). Under the provisions of this Act, villagers could create community-managed forests from the forests controlled by the Revenue Department. Any two villagers could thus apply to the deputy commissioner of the district to create a panchayat forest located within the village boundaries (Agrawal, 1994: 269–70). The Van Panchayat Act prescribes the formation of village forest councils and determines the frequency of their meetings as well as certain fundamental management tasks to be duly performed by them. More specifically, villagers must (*a*) demarcate the boundaries of their panchayat forest; (*b*) protect it from illegal tree-felling, fires, encroachments, and cultivation; and (*c*) close 20 per cent of the forest area to grazing every year. As for daily operation, it is chiefly governed by rules that village forest councils have themselves crafted, possibly aided by government officials. The above legislation, which represents a pioneering attempt at devising co-management arrangements with user communities (see Chapter 13 for further probing), is still in use nowadays and, according to Agrawal, it has 'facilitated the efforts by residents of nearly four thousand villages to create local institutions that would permit them to use and manage a significant proportion of local forests' (ibid. 270; see also Chapter 10, sect. 2).

At independence, however, the government of India was not to reverse the main trend of colonial forestry policy. On the contrary, it clearly opted for strengthening it through a series of legislative and other measures aimed at enhancing government's control over forest resources and multiplying restrictions imposed upon tribal populations in view of the continuous degradation of these resources. From the following excerpt of a governmental report published in 1960–1, it is evident that priority was given to national over local interests:

> Villages in the neighbourhood of a forest will naturally make greater use of its product for the satisfaction of their domestic and agricultural needs. Such use, however, should in no event be permitted at the cost of the national interests. The accident of a village being situated close to a forest does not prejudice the right of the country as a whole to receive the benefits of a national asset. The scientific conservation of a forest inevitably involves the regulation of rights and the

restriction of the privileges of users depending upon the value and importance of the forest, however irksome such restraint may be to the neighbouring areas. . . . While, therefore, the needs of the local population must be met to a reasonable extent, national interests should not be sacrificed because they are not directly discernible, nor should the rights and interests of future generations be subordinated to the improvidence of the present generation. (Government of India, 1960–1: 129)

A considerable degree of distrust in tribals' ability to manage local-level forest resources is apparent in the above statements: it is the tribals who bear full responsibility for depletion of these resources which must consequently be protected against their inhabitants. Such distrust was displayed in the actual policies followed on the field by forest department officers. The judgement was all the more unfair as the government did not make any serious effort at integrating the tribals into forest conservation endeavours, and as it did not show similar reservations about the private interests to which it often conceded exploitation rights with a view to extracting maximum revenue from the Indian forests. Later, in 1976, the position of the government was reasserted even more bluntly in the report of the National Commission on Agriculture (NCA). There, running counter to the conclusions of several other reports (such as the one issued by the Task Force on Development of Tribal Areas in 1973), the NCA recommended that the rights of tribal populations over the forest be significantly curtailed since they were obviously unable to maintain them in a proper state:

Free supply of forest produce to the rural population and their rights and privileges have brought destruction to the forests and so it is necessary to reverse the process. The rural people have not contributed much towards the maintenance or regeneration of the forests. Having overexploited the reserves they cannot in all fairness expect that somebody else will take the trouble of providing them forest produce free of charge. (Government of India, 1976: pt. IX, 25)

Such radicalization of the top-down control approach adopted by the government of India in matters of forestry finds its final expression in the Indian Forest Bill of 1980 which proved to be much more distrustful of local capabilities than any Forest Act passed by the British (see Kulkarni, 1986). The rigidity of the government's prejudices concerning these capabilities is particularly noteworthy in view of the fact that two reports issued in the meantime or almost simultaneously (one as a result of an Inter-State Conference of Forest and Tribal Welfare Ministries held in 1978, and the other issued in 1980 by the Task Force on Taking Forestry to the People created at the initiative of the Secretariat for Agriculture and Co-operation) in fact decided on the need for associating tribal communities in forest-related programmes, treating them as partners in benefits accruing to forest areas, granting them individual rights on the trees and their usufruct, and initiating broader development projects so as to diversify the employment and income-earning opportunities open to them (Government of India, 1981*a*: 40; Shingi *et al.*, 1986: 22–4).

Let us now look more closely at the Indian Forest Bill of 1980. This Bill increased still further the possibility of the government appropriating forest areas and, accordingly, it further reduced the tribals' rights over them, in so far as it provided that

'Forest includes any land containing trees and shrubs, pasture lands and any land whatsoever which the State Government may, by notification, declare to be forest for the purpose of this Act' (Government of India, 1981*b*, Indian Forest Bill, 1980: 2). Indeed, the Bill so much enlarged the scope of centralized forest administration as to make it almost boundless. On the other hand, the same division of forest areas into three zones (protected, reserved, and village forests) as that adopted under the British colonial administration is retained. Whenever a villager would like to claim a right over a product yielded by a protected or reserved forest, or meadow, he must address his demand to the competent forest officer who is free to grant or to deny that right. The chapter on village forests is very general so that it is difficult to make out precisely what rights local inhabitants have over these forests. In addition, the government is allowed by the Bill to transform village forests into protected or reserved forests through simple notification in the *Official Gazette* if, for example, it considers that the local population threatens the existence of the forest nearby (see Fernandes and Kulkarni, 1986; D'Abreo, 1982).

Moreover, the Bill lays down in a very detailed manner all the acts that are prohibited in protected and reserved areas, as well as the sanctions accompanying them. For instance, if a person is found using dried wood as fuel, or grazing cattle or collecting minor forest produce in these areas, he is liable to a fine amounting to as much as Rs 1,000 (a family earns a maximum income of Rs 20 per day!) and to a one-year imprisonment sentence! Administrative officers are thus vested with enormous powers over local people, and this is all the more disquieting as section 128 of the Bill provides that 'No suit or criminal prosecution or other legal proceedings shall lie against any public servant for anything done by him in good faith under this Act' (Government of India, 1981*b*, Indian Forest Bill, 1980: 64). Additional evidence of the repressive character of the new law as well as of the huge powers conferred upon forest officers is found in section 111: 'All offences under this Act shall be cognizable and any Forest Officer or Police Officer may, without a warrant, arrest any person against whom a reasonable suspicion exists of his having been concerned in any forest offence (ibid. 58). The orientation of the 1980 Bill has been confirmed in the Report of the National Committee on Development of Backward Areas (1981):

> 'It is clear that rights on the forests as were envisaged in the early days cannot be sustained in the same form. The situation has considerably changed and any effort to go back to the old form will be disastrous. . . . The broad approach outlined by the National Commission on Agriculture will have to be followed. (Government of India, 1981*a*: 40–1)

It is remarkable that, in 1982, still another committee, known this time as the Committee on Forest and Tribals in India and constituted by the Ministry of Home Affairs, took a view completely opposite to the hard-line centralized approach followed by the government. Instead of considering tribal people as destructive agents unable to take a long-term view about their resources, the report issued by this committee sees them as potentially active partners in the struggle against deforestation and as inhabitants in need of regular means of subsistence. A number of recommendations made in this report under the heading 'Forest Policy' are worth quoting here:

(i) Forest policy and forest system should be directed towards managing a renewable endowment of vast potential for subserving national, regional as well as local developmental goals. In fact, the individual tribal, the local tribal community and national interest should be regarded as three corners of a triangular forest policy.
(ii) Forest policy must fulfil three sets of needs (*a*) ecological security; (*b*) food, fruit, fuel, fodder, fibre, timber and other domestic needs of particularly the rural and tribal population; and (*c*) cottage, small, medium and large industries including the requirement of defence and communications.
(iii) A national forest policy should recognise the positive role of the people in maintaining forests and environment in unambiguous terms and not merely in its implication.
(iv) Wherever community rights exist on forest land, they should be recognised and adapted to serve the urgent needs of the soil and water management and re-afforestation of denuded tracts by suitable species.
(ix) A programme of large-scale plantation should be taken up with the help of tribals giving them rights on the trees planted by them in assigned areas and their usufruct. (Government of India, 1982: 63–5)

Given the above statements, it is not really surprising that the central government of India chose to somehow disown this report by preventing its widespread diffusion.

The government of Nepal followed an even more radical policy by nationalizing all (non-registered) forest and waste lands—including private and village-controlled forests—in 1957. Later, under the Forest Act of 1961, the definition of forest land was extended to include all land adjoining forest areas and left fallow for two years (Arnold and Campbell, 1986: 430). According to Bromley and Chapagain, this centralized bureaucratic approach to forest management 'upset centuries of traditional patterns of resource control and of the village governance structure over resource use; the existing political structure, with its attendant rights and duties, was rendered quite irrelevant' (Bromley and Chapagain, 1984: 869). In reaching the decision to nationalize all forest lands, the Nepalese government was led by several considerations and motives. First, alarmed at the rapid population growth rates, it was seriously concerned with curbing the process of forest depletion/degradation. Second, since malaria control programmes had made the lower hills and plains habitable, relatively pristine areas were being cleared for agriculture, a process which the government was anxious to hold in check. And, third, the conviction arose in government circles that the State was to be more effective at managing forest resources than a large number of isolated villagers (ibid.).

In Pakistan, we are told that the bureaucracy in the post-independence period has been unwilling to share control with the rights-holders in the areas of *guzara* (village) forests (which are demarcated from the state reserve forests). This was true even under the co-operative scheme (in the Punjab province) instituted during the 1940s as an alternative to the panchayat system. As a matter of fact, the *guzara* Co-operative Societies were placed under the general direction of the civil administration and they were 'completely disregarded' by this administration which eventually got rid of them in the early 1960s (Azhar, 1993: 121–3). True, a pilot programme to revive forestry co-operatives in the West Frontier province has recently been started on a modest basis. Under this scheme, each co-operative is in charge of the management of a specific forest area in accordance with a plan approved by the forest department. They receive technical assistance in preparing the management plan and have access to the services of field foresters paid by the provincial government. No other subsidies are given, and all other forestry costs (replanting felled areas, maintenance, extraction, and so on) are borne by the co-operatives which are entitled to retain at least 40 per cent of the revenues from the sale of trees. Yet, an evaluation study cited by Michael Cernea reveals that *guzara* farmers 'see government interference and the intrusion of party politics as a mortal threat to these cooperatives' (Cernea, 1989: 62–3).

In Botswana, in the 1960s the government introduced new institutions as part of a national development strategy. As a result, 'the traditional resource management pattern, very much "chief-community" centered, lost a great deal of its autonomy. Local chiefs, virtually stripped of their traditional jurisdiction, now have to come to terms with modern institutions, which although foreign to most rural dwellers, ultimately control their community resources' (Zufferey, 1986: 69). The central piece of the new system of land management is the Tribal Land Act of 1968 which gave to the Land Boards (LB) and the Subordinate Land Boards (SBL) the control and custody of the country's natural resources, mainly agricultural lands and pastures. Despite the intention of the government to integrate local participation into the land-planning and administration process (through the LBs and SLBs acting as the official representative bodies at the local level over land matters), the power and controls established under the Act have remained considerably centralized and local input into the formulation of land policies has been minimal (ibid. 82–3). Most important policy decisions are legal prerogatives of District Council and Land Board authorities, subject to ministerial or presidential approval (SLBs being essentially advisory bodies). Particularly noticeable is 'the extensive number of prerogatives directly attributed to the minister'. Thus, 'Grants of common law land rights and the conditions attaching to the grant of customary land rights require either the approval or the written consent of the minister. Transfer, change of user, prohibitions on grant of land, and appeals against transactions of common law land rights also are immediately subject to consideration or consent of the minister' (ibid. 84–5).

This kind of example could be multiplied *ad infinitum*. The aforementioned country case-studies are nevertheless sufficient to demonstrate that many Third World governments, under the influence of colonial rule or not, have adopted a centralized, top-down, and bureaucratic policy approach in order to improve the management of village-level natural resources.

What needs to be added, before looking more closely at the causes of government failures in resource management is that projects supported by foreign donors have often suffered from the same inadequacies as those mentioned with respect to projects undertaken by national governments. In particular, they have typically failed genuinely to involve village communities in the management of local resources and they have been typically conceived as essentially technical projects to be implemented by administrative and legal procedures (Jodha, 1992: 33). In Jodha's words, 'the key focus had been on techniques and funding rather than on resource *users*' (ibid. 72), thus ignoring the simple truth that 'participation in development cannot occur as just an add-on to technical programs' (Cernea, 1989: 1). Thus, for example, in India during the 1980s, the 'community woodlot' schemes supported by the government and the World Bank have produced disappointing results: because of their failure to rely on appropriate actors, they have ended up 'as administratively led interventions with little results other than diminishing the CPR lands left available to the poorest people' (ibid. 33; Cernea, 1991). Much the same can be said of so-called 'social forestry' projects since most of these projects are actually a far cry from the theoretical vision of social forestry which is 'to induce a large number of small farmers to plant fuelwood trees systematically for their own needs and on their own (and other available) lands' (Cernea, 1989: 4; see also Fortmann, 1988). At the root of the problem is the fact that 'the planners of financially induced social forestry programs often do not yet realise that consideration of [these] social factors has to be *woven into the very fabric* of such programs *from the outset*' (Cernea, 1989: 8). To take a last example, from two visits in a World Bank supported, pasture-centred project (during early 1970s) called 'drought proofing of drought prone areas' in the state of Rajasthan (India), Jodha drew the following account which is reminiscent of the conclusions reached by Bromley and Cernea (1989) with respect to similar projects in Africa:

The key decision makers about project activities were district officials from the soil conservation, planning and statistics departments, important officials of the district and village *panchayats*, and a few village influentials who managed to present their private land as CPRs in order to capture benefits from the project. Villagers in general were unhappy with the project as it not only reduced their usable resources but it provided no chance for their complaints and views. Shortly after the end of the project (during the second visit of the author), in 8 out of 13 cases, all the physical and institutional arrangements provided by the project had disappeared. Of the remaining five cases (that showed a visible impact from the project), three belonged to influential individuals as their private grazing cum fodder collection fields. (Jodha, 1992: 34)

Causes of government failures in resource management

Everybody seems to agree today that this centralized approach has been an outright failure in the sense that natural resources have not been better managed than before. Even though a rigorous demonstration is impossible, there are some grounds (to be made more explicit below) to believe that things have actually got worse than they would have been under an alternative management regime. Just consider the case of Indian forestry. In 1980, close to 23 per cent of the Indian territory was claimed to be covered with forests by the government since this was the proportion of Indian land controlled by the Forest Department. This figure compares unfavourably with the objective of 33 per cent stated in the report of the National Commission on Agriculture as the proportion of forests required to maintain the ecological balance of the country and at the same time meet the domestic demand for forest products. If data collected through observation by satellites are to be trusted, the situation is actually much worse than that conveyed by using the official figures. According to this new estimate, indeed, forests represented only 14 per cent of Indian territory during the years 1980–2 (Desai, 1988: 192), implying that a large part of the government-controlled forests are not forests at all. Comparing satellite data for 1972–5 and for 1980–2, we reach an estimated rate of deforestation of almost 19 per cent over a period of seven years. This represents an average annual loss of 1.3 million hectares of forest, that is, eight times as much as the loss admitted by the Forest Department (ibid.)!

Increasingly, acknowledgement of failure of centralized approaches to resource management is driving governments to reconsider, amend, and even reverse their previous policies. Perhaps the most glaring illustration of such a change is the complete reversal of forest land policy which occurred in Nepal in 1978 when the new National Forestry Plan entailed devolution of responsibility for forest protection and exploitation to the panchayat level and provision for long leases of forest areas (McNicoll, 1990: 163). It was only in 1983–4, however, that transfer of forests to local control began to take place on a substantial scale (Arnold and Campbell, 1986: 426). The categories of forest transferable to local community control under the new regulation included the Panchayat Forests (entrusted to village panchayats 'for reforestation in the interest of the village community') and the Panchayat Protected Forests (entrusted 'for the purpose of protection and proper management') (ibid. 431).

In forest policy matters, India made a much more prudent turn than Nepal. The Forest Department first embarked upon a so-called social forestry programme which also proved to be disappointingly ineffective, a result of the fact that, as it is conceived, it is 'merely an extension of the state's control and a further restriction upon the use of common property resources' (Blaikie *et al.*, 1986: 496). A more serious re-orientation was obviously called for. After the Committee on Forest and Tribals in India (1982) pleaded for a broad-based approach to forest management involving the active participation of local populations (see above), the Department of Environment soon followed suit by issuing a series of 'Recommendations Regarding the Revision of the National Forest Policy' (1983) that went in exactly the same direction. After having sounded the alarm about the high rate of depletion of India's forest resources and after having deplored the government's 'false sense of complacency' about this serious predicament—'areas which have long since been stripped of cover or have been diverted to non-forest uses continue to be reported as "forest" lands in statistical returns' (ibid. 3)—the report went to propose a number of basic changes in the national forest policy, including a more community development-orientated approach involving local development bodies such as village panchayats (see section 3.8 of the report). Soon after, the Forest Department made a move towards putting this recommendation into practice by starting community forestry programmes. Unfortunately, as evidence from large social forestry projects (many of which were assisted by the World Bank) in Uttar Pradesh, Gujarat, Himachal Pradesh, Rajasthan, and West Bengal attest, community woodlots or village woodlots soon turned out to be failures. 'On account of the little interest shown by community members', the model was then modified to give considerable management authority over village woodlots to the village panchayats (Cernea, 1989: 34–5). Again, 'the slippage of community woodlots into panchayat woodlots did not remedy anything', largely because communities were not really involved and panchayats were oversized (Cernea, 1989: 35–6; Colchester, 1994: 89). The next step, known as the Joint Forest Management Policy, started by the late 1980s in the states of Orissa and West Bengal. It will be commented on further in Chapters 12 and 13.

The government of India also acknowledges the failure of watershed projects (such as the River Valley Project in the Himalayan foothills) undertaken with a view to reducing accelerated siltation of dams located on rivers and to enhancing irrigation capacity. It recognizes explicitly that its failure to involve local people in the planning of such projects, and its failure to adopt a 'multidisciplinary and integrated approach to the planning and implementation of watershed rehabilitation and development', was a major cause of poor project performance (World Bank, 1983, cited from Bromley and Cernea, 1989: 32). In neighbouring Pakistan, the situation is strikingly similar. Thus, just to quote an example, in Azad Jammu and Kashmir where the Forest Department intervened to try to stop the area's alarming deforestation and environmental deterioration, it got into open conflict with many local inhabitants. By the late 1970s, over 50,000 prosecutions for forest offences were pending in the Azad Kashmir courts, amounting to about one family in six involved in an alleged forest offence (Cernea, 1989: 11).

The reasons behind the failure of many Third World governments to manage their natural resources are numerous and complex. In the following pages, we shall be content with pinpointing the most important of them which have usually the effect of lowering the morale and reducing the incentives of local populations for managing village-level resources in an ecologically sound manner.

1. A major difficulty with any centralized approach to resource management is a problem of information. Given the great diversity of resource types, it is difficult to establish straightforward management prescriptions that can be widely followed. No government agency can know local realities in sufficient detail to conceive of valid solutions to the highly differentiated ecological problems that arise at village level (Arnold and Campbell, 1986: 442; Dasgupta and Mäler, 1990: 24). This applies with special force to tropical areas where the number of species available (in the ocean, in the forest, etc.) is considerably larger than in temperate climatic zones. The government is clearly at a disadvantage compared to the historic users who can be expected to possess extensive knowledge of local resources and constraints (Zufferey, 1986: 86). In keeping with what we have argued in Chapter 10, it must however be added that, since the village environment has changed rapidly during recent decades, local inhabitants are likely to be imperfectly informed about ongoing processes of resource depletion and degradation. Consequently, the information gap between specialized government agencies and villagers has probably narrowed down and the latter may need external assistance to help them to better assess their resource problems and to conceive and put into effect viable solutions to them. What is required is thus a two-way process of information-sharing between rural people and the administration.

2. Another considerable difficulty which arises in connection with resource management by government agencies is of course that of enforcement of government rules

(see above, Chapter 8). Thus, for example, Arnold and Campbell have emphasized that in Nepal the nationalization of all forest lands (see above) led to an unsolvable problem of policy implementation: 'The desirable objectives of this new policy proved very difficult to achieve. Effective government supervision of thousands of patches of forest scattered through remote hill terrain, accessible only with extreme difficulty, proved impossible' (Arnold and Campbell, 1986: 430). This certainly holds true for fisheries as well. On the one hand, inland fisheries are often as highly scattered and inaccessible as patches of tropical forest while supervision measures need to be specified in great detail and tailored to the differentiated needs of each local situation. Just to give one example, it is extremely difficult to enforce mesh-size regulations when fishermen can avoid purchasing nets from central purchase points because they themselves make their nets or because they can buy smuggled nets from a neighbouring country (a common occurrence in many Third World countries with long and difficult-to-control borders). On the other hand, the monitoring of offshore fisheries is an especially arduous task given the extensive nature of the resource. This is particularly true in regard of small-scale fishermen (who form the great bulk of the marine fishing labour force in developing countries) since their fishing crafts are designed in such a way that they can be launched from, and landed on, the beaches where or near which their highly dispersed villages are usually located. As a result, the possibility for the administration to control them from harbour points is precluded.

To these considerations, one must add the constraint arising from the limited funds and staff available to enforce resource-preserving rules, a limitation typical of poor countries with many pressing priorities which may appear more important than the long-term conservation of natural resources. Thus, in Pakistan, since management of the *guzara* forests is only one of the myriad functions of the civil administration, there is a 'glaring absence of personnel specifically earmarked to look after these forests' and this has disastrous consequences for their future survival (Azhar, 1993: 122). Regarding fishery management, which coastal developing country can be expected to have an effective police fleet continuously patrolling the open sea to check the fishing practices of tens of thousands of small-scale fishing units or of foreign vessels?

There are at least two important consequences of this situation. First, given the absence or lack of effective supervision by state authorities, a large discrepancy has arisen between the formal decision-making system that is supposed to govern resource use and the actual pattern of interaction among resource users (Cruz, 1986: 126). More precisely, what state authorities have created in many resource domains is a *de facto* system of open access where, before, there often existed common property regimes regulated by local authorities or organizations. For example, one Malian official from Mopti characterized the situation in the Niger River delta 'as empty of any institutional or tenurial basis for resource management and control' (Lawry, 1989*a*: 5). From this perspective, the 'emasculation' of local organizations, wherever they existed, appears to be a tragic outcome. Thus, with reference to woodstock management in the Sahel, the following has been observed: 'As it happened, most villages had lost their power of independent activity as the result of efforts of both the colonial and independent regimes to establish controls over major forms of organisation in rural areas. Villages (or quarters within them) had no authority to enforce sanctions against violators of locally devised use rules. In practice, few such rules appear to have been made' (Thomson *et al.*, 1986: 399). A similar phenomenon has been noted with respect to fishing in the Niger River delta: 'Because of the limited extent of traditional village lands, the fisherman passed from a minuscule jurisdiction to a larger jurisdiction, with the resulting weakening of traditional control structures without the practical operation of a substitute control system' (Kone, 1985: 100).

In the latter instance, as in so many others, what the new rules have actually meant on the ground is the uneasy 'cohabitation of two power bodies' (traditional and modern) which may all too readily enter into conflict with each other. Thus, according to state formal rules, as we have already noted, outsiders are allowed free access to local fisheries. In practice, however, no outside fisherman, at least till recently, dared throw his net without the prior agreement of the local water master, which involved the regular making of small gifts during the period of his stay in the locality. (This is because an agreement with the water master symbolizes an agreement with the invisible powers believed to rule over the local water space.) At the same time, the ability of local water masters to impose conservation rules or restrictions, particularly on outsiders, is gradually eroded in so far as it is not legally backed by the State. Groups of outsiders equipped with modern gears are less and less ready to comply with local traditional rules (which often prohibit the use of new techniques) as the social prestige of local authorities is reduced and as they can refer to new rules more congenial to their interests (Jeay, 1984*b*; Kone, 1985; Fay, 1990*b*). We will return to this important point at a later stage of this chapter.

The problem is further exacerbated when administrative boundaries within which state management rules are supposed to apply cut across traditional social or natural ecological units. This has clearly happened in Mali where the redrawing of *cercle* and district boundaries throughout the delta region has obliterated the former rough correspondence between social and political units on the one hand and areas of resource use on the other (Lawry, 1989*a*: 5; see also Fay, 1990*b*: 233–4). Likewise, in Botswana, greater centralization at national and district levels has caused internal boundaries to become less important with the result that the movement of herd owners between groups and areas was greatly facilitated. This increased mobility across what had formerly been separate pasture areas as well as the erosion of the authority of local chiefs had the effect of increasingly transforming the country's pastures into an open-access resource (Peters, 1987: 187–8).

A second consequence of ineffective supervision of resource use by government agencies is the high incidence of field-officer discretion in imposing prohibitions or in levying fines (see, e.g., Blaikie *et al.*, 1986: 490; Toulmin, 1991: 28). The situation thus resembles the external-authority game with incomplete information described in Chapter 8: to recall, when the probability that the external authority makes errors in meting out punishments is sufficiently high and this imperfect monitorability effect is not compensated by sufficiently high fines or sufficiently severe sanctions, resource users may be confronted with a prisoner's dilemma situation and therefore be induced to free ride or violate state regulations. This effect actually concurs with the above conclusion that the extreme difficulty of supervising the users' actions very closely tends to create a *de facto* open-access situation. Rule violations are of two major types: (1) overuse or overextraction of a common resource over and above the limits set by the State, and (2) theft of state property (Blaikie *et al.*, 1986: 493). In Tamil Nadu, for example, the first type is mostly represented by overextraction of fuelwood and overuse of grazing land by goats while the theft of state property of timbers (such as sandalwood) clearly falls under the second type.

Concerning the latter, we are also told that illegal acts are not necessarily committed by local inhabitants—at least by poor or middle-income villagers—since most serious and blatant violations occur when 'a few private individuals, often backed by considerable capital and equipment, do mount raids on these trees' (Blaikie *et al.*, 1986: 494). In Senegal, to take another example, woodcutters are given permits by the forestry service that often let them enter into forest areas to cut down trees of vital importance to the survival of local communities (Bergeret and Ribot, 1990: 135–9, cited from Freudenberger and Mathieu, 1993: 22). In Guatemala, likewise, we learn that 'in any encounter between the police and the bark-strippers, it was usual for the latter to bribe their way out of trouble. This was but one aspect of the broader problem facing many Indian communities in Guatemala where the rule of law had only limited application and where the rights of Indian groups were not respected' (Utting, 1994: 241).

It may also happen that the state enforcing agency does not fulfil its duties simply because of a lack of proper incentives or poor understanding of the stakes involved. Thus, regarding a government-owned irrigation system in Sri Lanka, Harriss reports that: 'Prosecutions have to be carried out by the police, who have usually treated water offences as trivial, and who do not have the same incentives to tackle them as in other cases. Further, delays over court proceedings and the very light fines, which have been imposed on those who have been found guilty of irrigation offences, have made the legal sanctions ineffectual' (Harriss, 1984: 322).

3. It is equally important to notice that corruption often contributes to making resource conservation still more difficult. Corruption may be either supply- or demand-induced, or both. It is supply-induced when, owing to the low level of their salaries or to the irregularity with which they are paid, state agents (like forest guards) actively seek bribes from villagers who are caught in some rule-breaking, or get themselves involved in violations of the rules which they are supposed to enforce. For example, when the Ugandan State collapsed in chaos, forest guards' salaries were no longer paid and the former guards were directly implicated in the encroachment on the forest reserves (Bruce and Fortmann, 1989: 16).

Also, in a pioneering work, Wade has shown in great detail how, in India, the effectiveness of public service organizations, such as Irrigation, Agriculture, Forestry, and Soil Conservation Departments, is seriously impaired by well-institutionalized and predictable corruption practices. These practices are actually enmeshed in a special circuit of transactions—articulated around the mechanism of transfer of officials from less to more desirable posts—in which the bureaucracy channels illegally acquired funds upwards to higher ranks and politicians who use these funds for distributing short-term material inducements in exchange for electoral support

(Wade, 1982, 1985). The effects of such a politico-administrative system of corruption may be disastrous. For instance, agents of irrigation state departments who are in charge of canal management are 'under pressure to behave almost exactly contrary to the ostensible objectives of their job': instead of reducing water uncertainty, they artificially increase it so that users pay them bribes in order to get timely deliveries of water; instead of maintaining the canals in good condition, they leave large stretches of the canal unmaintained so as to save maintenance funds for other uses (Wade, 1985: 485).

Effects appear to be still more damaging in the case of soil conservation departments, given that topsoil is India's most precious resource. Thus, these departments commonly fail to solidify the newly constructed ridges, or to provide a structure for taking water from upper and lower terraces, as a result of which rainwater cuts through the unimpacted ridges at the weakest point, thereby causing gullies to form. The ensuing soil erosion can be very high since it has been reported that the rate of soil depletion from an area treated in this way is some ten times greater than from adjacent areas without the 'conservation' programme. The costs are as follows: '(1) permanent loss of production from the land on which the programme is situated; (2) semi-permanent loss of production from the alluvial fans lower down on which the sediment is deposited; and (3) increased sedimentation in lower rivers causing greater flood risk and reservoir siltation' (Wade, 1985: 485–6). According to Wade, a good part of these catastrophic effects arise from the need for officers to raise money in order to get—and then keep—decent postings. The effectiveness of India's public service organizations therefore suffers from the transfer mechanism on two counts: (1) officials do not stay long in their post if they are located in poor and remote areas and, if they do, they are obsessed with the prospect of moving; and (2) in so far as transfers can be purchased, they are incited to perform their job in ways contrary to the ostensible objectives of their departments.

On the other hand, corruption is demand-induced when the fines imposed on rule-breakers are so high compared to their current incomes that they are incited to persuade the monitoring agents who caught them to reach an (illegal) compromise acceptable to both parties; or when users are powerful enough to make these agents accept a (small) bribe rather than enforce state regulations. The first possibility is clearly encouraged by the heavy fines imposed on rule-breakers by India's Forest Department under the Indian Forest Bill (see above). It is also manifest in the common practice of Tamil Nadu's villagers to 'informally arrange an annual bribe to local forest guards to facilitate the grazing of goats, for example (by a capitation "fee" of about Rs5 per goat-owning family)'. Artisans using bamboo follow a similar arrangement (Blaikie *et al.*, 1986: 494; see also Karanth, 1992: 1687, for Karnataka, where the annual payment to the forest guard varies between Rs10–15 per sheep and goat that a farmer brings to the forest for illegal grazing). Also, when official fisheries inspectors are planted on motorized fishing boats to monitor the species of fish caught, it is usual for fishermen to offer them compensation in return for their turning a blind eye on their rule violations (personal observation of J.-Ph. Platteau). Official agents may of course find themselves in a much stronger power position—at least *vis-à-vis* common villagers—than what is implied in these examples. This is particularly true in the case of tribal populations which have usually no useful connection with powerful patrons or the political élite, and are therefore easily discriminated against. In such circumstances, resource users may have no other choice than to pay amounts actually exceeding the official fines. Again with reference to Tamil Nadu, we learn that

In one village, the collection of green manure from the more productive reserve forests attracts a standardized charge of Rs80, of which Rs36 is an unreceipted fine to forest guards. The forest guards (and perhaps forest rangers, too) have an informal organization for dividing this rent amongst themselves and for collecting it in a variety of ways. One tribal village, well-endowed with reserve forest, has forest guards who arrive two or three times a year with a lorry, make a spot-check on fuelwood stocks of households, and confiscate and remove any timber that they believe was cut green. The value of a lorryload is estimated to be at least Rs1,000. (Blaikie *et al.*, 1986: 494)

In many cases, of course, corruption seems to arise as much from demand as from supply pressures without it being possible to say whether one force or the other played a major role in getting it started. Such appears to be the case in the following example. In Mehsana district in Gujarat state (India), overexploitation of groundwater resources through electrical pumping led the government to lay down precise spacing norms for new wells and to refuse electricity connections to wells whose owners violated these norms. Yet, this regulation is systematically ignored in practice because electricity connections can easily be obtained with a fee (or a bribe) to the line man (Moench, 1992: A-11). Moreover, extensive tampering with meters was one of the reasons why the electricity boards initially moved to a flat-rate charge even though this pricing structure encourages water overextraction (ibid.). Commenting on this kind of practice, a well-known Indian expert in irrigation, Dhawan, reached the bitter conclusion that the 'eroded state of ethics' in India (a loss of the values of generalized morality preached by Gandhi and his followers?), together with an inadequate administrative set-up in the countryside and the difficulty of enforcement in the case of small landholdings, make effective implementation of state regulations of groundwater use simply impossible (quoted from Moench, 1992: A-11).

Finally, it deserves to be noted that, in some cases, corruption is actively encouraged by perverse pieces of legislation such as the 1974 Land Registration Ordinance in Pakistan, which bestowed legal recognition upon most of the unauthorized appropriation of traditional common (*shamilat*) lands. In the words of a former senior area official, this ordinance was

a legislative disaster (that) opened the floodgates of encroachments . . . The result was that brazen-faced encroachments were made into the very heart of forest lands. Here was an opportunity for unscrupulous revenue officers to oblige friends and relatives or make hay while the sun shone at the cost of rich forests and vegetative covering of hills. (Cited from Cernea, 1989: 20)

4. The incentive to rule violation or at least to non-co-operation on the part of resource users is almost always increased by the fact that relations between them and the state bureaucracy are usually distant and antagonistic and that, in many cases, state

regulations have had the effect of setting the government against the peasant when successful resource management precisely requires the opposite circumstances (Bromley and Cernea, 1989: 17). In Mali, for example, far from being regarded as benevolent extension agents, 'forest agents are seen generally by the public as para-military police agents' (Lawry, 1989*a*: 15). Various types of reaction may be expected from resource users placed in these conditions. First, state agents may live so far away from users that the latter do not consider them a reasonable source of authorization (Thomson *et al.*, 1986: 419). Second, and more critically, users tend to view local resources as government property rather than their own, an attitude that seriously erodes their motivation to protect them (Arnold and Campbell, 1986: 430; Azhar, 1993: 117–18), all the more so if the bureaucracy is strongly imbued with an ethic of regulation and control (Blaikie *et al.*, 1986: 501) and if it provides them very few economic incentives (as when they are asked to work on new plantations without being given even the right to collect the produce of the trees planted). Bromley and Chapagain have well described this disincentive effect:

> Such external influences are critical in the process of pitting villagers against themselves and of ultimately shifting resource stewardship away from the village. When resource responsibility is taken away from the village, so is the concern for the viability of the resource. It is the 'patron syndrome' turned on its head; villagers do not care much for things that the state gives to them, and the same thing would seem to apply to the things that the state takes away. (Bromley and Chapagain, 1984: 872; in the same vein, see Agarwal and Narain, 1989: 13, 27)

There is worse. Instead of being simply indifferent in the sense of losing responsibility towards the resource, users may react more aggressively against what they consider to be an illegitimate dispossession of their own wealth. These reactions may go much beyond spreading rumours maligning the integrity of certain officials and even local leaders (Messerschmidt, 1986: 473). In India, for example, this is attested by the explosive, 'quasi-insurrectional' situation of acute conflict between the Forest Department and the Adivasi in the Chotanagpur region of Bihar (Commander, 1986) or by the utterly negative reaction of Uttar Pradesh's forest-dwellers to India's national forest policy. In the former area, 'Ho tribespeople who have lost rights to forest lands have mobilised against official forestry programmes and developed a "forest cutting movement". Despite their ancient tradition of respect for forests, including the preservation of sacred groves for religious ceremonies, the Ho have turned to forest clearance as a means of asserting their rights to use the lands which forestry laws deny them' (Colchester, 1994: 83). Forest-dwellers in Uttar Pradesh manifested their anger in a similar way:

> in its extreme form alienation occasionally forced the peasant to degrade the surroundings he once lived in symbiosis with. The lack of interest that has, at times, been exhibited by forest communities in preserving vegetation on land that is no longer vested in them may be traced to the loss of community control consequent on state intervention . . . Today, in an ironical but entirely predictable development, villagers in parts of Garhwal look upon the reserved forest as their main enemy, harbouring the wild animals that destroy their crops. This is of course a classic form of alienation wherein the forest now appears as an entity *opposed* to the villager.

Above all, alienation signifies a mode of life in which circumstances distort man's innate qualities and compel him to act in a self-destructive fashion. (Guha, 1985: 1947)

All over Asia, the tensions between the government and the forest-dwellers are particularly acute because the latter have been considered for a long time by the former as marginal, backward people who need to be directed in a paternalistic way. (The problem is still more complicated when, as this often happens, forest people inhabit border areas and are perceived as a threat to national security.) In some countries, like Thailand and the Philippines, the government has not hesitated to treat those 'indigenous' people in a ruthless way involving forced resettlement (two and a half million of them are thus estimated to have been forcibly relocated in the Philippines) and sheer denial of national citizenship (in Thailand, 'hill tribes' have been denied Thai nationality and residence and even expelled into Burma by the army at gunpoint). It is a sad fact that, in countries like Bangladesh (in the Chittagong hill tracts) and India (in Assam State), progressive encroachment on tribal lands by lowland settlers and tea-planters has been actually supported by the government which refused to grant secure communal land rights to the tribal people (Colchester, 1994: 74–6).

Similar problems have sometimes been reported for Sub-Saharan Africa (Freudenberger and Mathieu, 1993: 13) and for Latin America. In Honduras, for example, a serious problem is the high incidence of illegal forest fires which appear to be 'set out of spite because the *campesino* believed that the Honduran Forestry Development Corporation has usurped his forest' (Utting, 1994: 252). More violent was the armed rebellion of several Miskito Indian organizations against the Sandinista government in Nicaragua during the 1980s. But the history of Europe is also instructive, as Guha aptly reminds us. There, too, the take-over of woodland for hunting or for timber production was deeply resented by the peasantry. For example, French peasants resorted to extensive forest fires at state incursion into their rights: in fact, they 'had come to hate the forests themselves, and hoped that if they ravaged them enough they would get rid of their oppressors' (Weber, 1976: 59–60, cited from Guha, 1985: 1947). The same kind of story repeated itself much later in the Asturias (Spain). Here, the Civil Guard had often to be sent to the villages in order to contain peasants' attempts to reassert local control over forests lost to the State. The tension mounted rapidly when, in the twentieth century, the government planted pine forests in selected uplands with a view to maximizing income from wastelands. These forests then became 'the object of local antagonism. Periodic attempts were made to burn them and return the *monte* to potential summer grazing for the community'. As late as the 1960s and 1970s, 'fires were set by unknown villagers or allowed to escape control by known villagers, destroying some mountain pine forest or scrub growth' (Fernandez, 1987: 272–3).

In many cases, non-violent resistance is the weapon most widely used by dispossessed villagers against the government: it can take on many forms including marching, rallying, setting up human barricades across the logging roads, ripping out seedlings, burning nurseries, chopping down eucalyptus trees, etc. These are the tactics adopted by the *Chipko* protest movement in Uttar Pradesh hills and the

Appikko movement in Andhra Pradesh (India) which have a long history of popular mobilization against government control of forests (Bandyopadhyay and Shiva, 1987; Guha, 1989; Gadgil and Guha, 1994). It is, to a large extent, because of the dogged determination of Indian villagers and activists that the forest management policies of the government were changed (Colchester, 1994: 82–3). It is also interesting to note that the Indian administration had to enrol local inhabitants almost by force to have them participate in its social forestry programmes (Fernandes and Kulkarni, 1986; Fernandes, Menon and Viegas, 1988). In Thailand, Sarawak (Malaysia), and other Asian countries, similar protest movements using strikingly identical methods have developed during recent times. In the Philippines, by contrast, organized armed resistance has been resorted to in certain areas where people were being denied other means of expressing their opposition (Colchester, 1994: 84–5).

It bears emphasis that misunderstandings about new resource policies (all the more frequent as official rules are often unclear and ambiguous) and sheer distrust of a government's sincerity or ability to hold on to its promises may also account for non-co-operative behaviour of rural dwellers even in contexts where they could apparently benefit from the official resource policy. If user groups have the same feeling as this ex-village chief in Antsalaka (Madagascar) who complained that officials 'ask us only to protect forests; for whose benefit they don't say' (Ghimire, 1994: 221), there is little chance that effective management of natural resources will ensue. In Niger, villagers' reluctance to participate in village woodlots is to be ascribed to their scepticism regarding the government's real intentions. As we are told, many of them 'assumed that the woodlots really belonged to the government or to the forest service, which they feared would claim the wood at will and without further compensation for villagers' efforts' (Thomson *et al.*, 1986: 404). As a result, they try to minimize their inputs: they kill off seedlings by benign neglect and, when a fence collapses, or when animals break through it, they do nothing to protect trees. A fundamental flaw in this experiment was in fact that the agents who established the woodlots gave no effective guarantees of property rights to the producer/users, nor did they provide any information about the distribution of trees or wood produced (ibid. 404–5).

In a reafforestation project in Azad Kashmir (Pakistan), the smaller farmers were reportedly 'fearful of losing possession or control over their land to the government once it was planted by the Forest Department, or of being deprived of rights to collect fodder and graze their cattle. Most of the smaller farmers interviewed indicated that they might offer small plots for project [tree] planting, provided they could be convinced that the Forest Department would not alienate their lands and that they would be able to cut grass for their cattle' (Cernea, 1989: 220). In Uttar Pradesh (India), to take an additional example, villagers sometimes deforested woodland because they were 'apprehensive that the demarcation of reserved forests would be followed by the government taking away other wooded areas from their control'. More specifically, 'forest reservation evoked the fear that if the villagers looked after the forests as of yore, a passing forest official will say—"here is a promising bit of forest—government ought to reserve it". If, on the other hand, they ruin their civil forest, they feel free from such reservation' (Guha, 1985: 1946–7). In Orissa state, likewise, an evaluation of the Social Forestry Project conducted in 1987 found that '82 per cent of the villagers did not know how the produce from village woodlots would be distributed; most of the people did not expect any share from the final output and looked upon such woodlots as another category of reserved forests' (Cernea, 1989: 36). Lessons from Central America—which has experienced one of the highest rates of deforestation in the world during the past three decades[1]—confirm the extreme importance of a clear mutual understanding as well as solid trust between state agents and user groups (Utting, 1994).

As pointed out earlier, lack of genuine involvement or participation of user communities is often at the root of failure of social forestry programmes, so much so that the very term 'community forestry' has become a 'buzzword' or a 'mere untrue slogan' (Cernea, 1989: 33, 36). Failure is thus bound to happen when, as is frequently the case, forestry departments take full responsibility for the setting up of village woodlots which they then hand over to specially constituted but unprepared village committees. In the words of Arnold and Stewart:

> Mechanisms for direct consultation by the Forest Department with villagers have generally not been put in practice . . . (Forest Committees) have been formed in an ad-hoc manner, without much if any prior consultation among the various groups in the village about their composition and in many cases were not functioning at all actively . . . The literature reports an almost universal failure to precede woodlot establishment with public discussion. Repeatedly reports record villagers being unaware that the woodlot had been established for the community; it was a 'government woodlot'. (Arnold and Stewart, 1989, cited from Cernea, 1989: 37)

5. We have pointed out above that governments are often found to allocate insufficient budgets to resource conservation because other, more pressing, priorities carry heavier political weight. It may now be added that the same considerations may drive them to try to extract maximum revenue from the nation's natural resources without due regard to the viability of the resource base. Thus, for example, in an already cited report, the Department of Environment of India has reached the conclusion that, among the major reasons behind the depletion of India's forest resources, there is not only the 'inadequate forest department staff and technical equipment' to practise scientific extraction methods and to monitor forest use, but also 'the tendency for the Government to look upon forests as a revenue-generating sector and the consequent pressures to maximise extraction even against technical advice' (Government of India, 1983: 2). In Pakistan, too, enthusiasm for scientific management of *guzara* forests under direct state responsibility quickly waned not only because of the slowness of administrative work but also because the forest department undertook heavy felling for sales from these forests (Azhar, 1993: 122).

The same criticism can also be levelled at India's fisheries policy which aimed at maximizing foreign exchange rather than state revenue. The sudden emergence in the 1960s of international markets (particularly in the USA and Japan) for luxury frozen fish (such as prawns, lobsters, and tuna) combined with pressure of strong balance-of-

[1] Since 1960, the extent of forest cover has declined from approximately 60% to just one-third of the total land area (Utting, 1994: 233).

payments constraints led the Indian government actively to support the growth of harvesting and processing capacities in Kerala state (in whose waters prawns and lobsters are highly concentrated) without considering its impact on the resource stock (Kurien, 1978). Such stories can be told for many other countries (in both advanced and developing countries)—in Vietnam, for example, 'a good part of deforestation is accounted by the felling of trees by the government itself for purposes of construction and for exports' (Rao, 1988: A-144)—and they clearly attest that it is risky to rely exclusively on the central government to manage and protect the nation's natural resources, especially so if such an objective demands substantial commitments of public financial resources. Given the proclivity of governments to subordinate environmental considerations to short-run economic or political interests, it is probably wiser, wherever possible, to economize on monitoring and information costs by directly involving user groups in resource protection programmes.

Besides or, more often, in conjunction with the above motivation, there is the well-known problem of the vulnerability or subservience of government agencies to business interests. In the aforementioned report by India's Department of Environment, the authors have found fault with 'the tendency of industry to use forest resources in an inefficient fashion because of the very low prices at which these are usually made available by the government'; as well as with the insufficient efforts of the government 'to prevent excessive felling by forest contractors' (Government of India, 1983: 2). That the government of India has made its forest policy too much reliant on private industrial interests has been a recurrent complaint voiced by the critics of its national forest policy (see, e.g., Fernandes and Kulkarni, 1983; Fernandes *et al.*, 1988). Evidence actually confirms that many forest areas in India have been leased out to private industry as logging concessions.

Of course, this is not typical of India only (see Repetto, 1988). In a country like the Philippines, the situation has reached the most extreme proportions. There, the now defunct government agency Panamin (Presidential Assistance to National Minorities), which was officially set up for the purpose of protecting the indigenous people's rights and interests, actually played a disastrous role amounting to sheer betrayal of its mission. In the words of Marcus Colchester, 'far from preventing the pillage of indigenous lands by mining companies, loggers and hydropower projects, Panamin collaborated with the armed forces in depriving the peoples of their ancestral lands' (Colchester, 1994: 74). The fact of the matter is that the majority of this agency's board members 'came from wealthy industrialist families, many of whom had direct financial interests in companies encroaching on indigenous lands'. This was certainly the case for Manuel Elizalde, a relative of President Marcos, who played the key role in Panamin. His political base and personal wealth, indeed, lay in extractive concerns such as mining, logging, and agribusiness. Moreover, he maintained his own private army in Cotobato in Mindanao to fight the insurgent indigenous peoples who, in despair, took up arms against the government by joining the communist insurgency group (ibid. 75). Clearly, the problem is not only that private agents or companies acting as concessionaires often overexploit or misuse natural resources, it is also that they may easily behave in harsh ways with local villagers, for example by depriving them of access to customary resources to which they are or are not legally entitled.

The first effect is particularly damaging when the state actually subsidizes destructive techniques used or activities performed by private individuals or companies: just think of the considerable public support afforded by the cattle industry in countries like Botswana, Brazil, Mexico, or Costa Rica;[2] or of the subsidization of imported trawlers in many Asian countries. With particular reference to Botswana, Zufferey went so far as saying that 'if one considers the amount of financial support allocated to the cattle industry in comparison to that allocated to planning and managing land resources it would not be entirely wrong to say that disaster is actually subsidised' (Zufferey, 1986: 89). In the case of Brazil, fiscal incentives to degrade forests include (i) the virtual exemption of agricultural income from income taxation that has the effect of adding to the demand for land (especially at the frontier where urban investors and corporations compete aggressively for land to establish livestock ranches); (ii) provisions contained in the progressive land tax that encourage the conversion of forest to crop land or pasture; and (iii) tax credit schemes aimed toward corporate livestock ranches that subsidize inefficient (extensive style) ranches established on cleared forest land[3] (Binswanger, 1991). According to the same source, an upper-bound estimate of the effect of the last measure is 4 million hectares of added deforestation, mostly in the subhumid forest zones of Mato Grosso and Tocantins (ibid.: 828). As an illustration of the second (distributive) effect, we may refer to the situation obtaining in East Kalimantan, Indonesia. In the early 1970s, the Indonesian government granted timber concessions to a large number of foreign and national companies, and, according to Jessup and Peluso, this had several detrimental effects on local communities. In particular, 'despite their legal right to collect minor forest products within timber concessions, villagers have at times been denied entry to those areas, and timber company personnel have otherwise infringed on the rights of local residents'. For instance, there is evidence of company guards confiscating rattan from collectors, of loggers raiding caves and selling the stolen birds' nests to unauthorized buyers, and of timber companies illegally cutting Borneo ironwood, a species reserved for local use; such acts sometimes led to violent confrontations between local inhabitants and company guards or loggers (Jessup and Peluso, 1986: 520–1).

In Sarawak, Malaysia, forest-dwellers feel equally helpless even if, as in the case of Indonesia, the process of dispossession is less brutal and open than in the Philippines. We are thus told that, in Sarawak, 'the corrupting influence of the timber trade has promoted the domination of the economy by nepotistic, patronage politics', with the consequence that rural peoples 'can no longer rely on their political representatives to defend their interests': as a matter of fact, 'the practice of dealing out logging licences to members of the state legislature to secure their allegiance is so commonplace in Sarawak that it has created a whole class of instant millionaires' (Colchester, 1994: 79). The consequences of this policy bias in Sarawak are particularly catastrophic. As a matter of fact, 'the World Bank has estimated that the country is logging its forests at

[2] In Central America, those who acquired security of tenure in the agrarian frontier areas in the 1960s and 1970s 'were often cattle ranchers who in the space of two or three decades destroyed much of the region's forest' (Utting, 1994: 243).

[3] For an account of alternative, more profitable and more environment-friendly ranching methods, see Mattos and Uhl (1994).

four times the sustainable rate, while the International Timber Organization predicts that the primary forests of Sarawak will be logged out by the turn of the century' (ibid.: 82). In such circumstances, it is not surprising that most popular protest movements in Asian forest areas have directed their main criticism at the logging licences generously distributed by too often corrupt governments.

It is worthy of note that the process of dispossession of small people need not be brutal. It can just take place through the ordinary play of market forces. Thus, in Brazil, tax exemption of agricultural income (see above) makes it attractive for wealthy individual farmers to buy land from small farmers in areas of well-established settlement. 'Because the income tax preference for agriculture, agricultural profits, and other factors are capitalized into the land price, small farmers and other poor individuals cannot buy land in areas of well-integrated land markets. If they want to acquire land, they have to squat on land at the frontier' (Binswanger, 1991: 827).

Sometimes, it must be pointed out, even members of village communities may give in to the temptation to grant licences of resource exploitation to commercial companies (for example, by selling logging rights to timber companies) in order to secure cash income for meeting pressing monetary needs. Thus, for example:

> Despite apparently secure land rights, New Guinean communities have frequently negotiated away rights over their lands, by leasing them to logging and mining companies in exchange for royalties. Only later have they come to regret the massive damage that their environments have sustained from such operations . . . many New Guineans are very inexperienced in the cash economy and even less aware of the social and environmental implications of inviting in foreign enterprises . . . many New Guineans have unreal expectations about what is achievable. Crucially, many no longer believe that their own future, much less that of their children, lies on the land. Taxation, schooling, labour saving technology, new fashions and consumerism have generated a demand for cash without the corresponding growth of a market for traditional produce. Cashing-in natural resources is thus the only ready option for most communities. (Colchester, 1994: 86–7)

6. When dealing with the issue of government intervention, especially in the context of young nations still in the making, one must always bear in mind that a paramount objective of the State is the maintenance of law and order and, possibly, the building up of some sort of national consensus. The importance assumed by other objectives such as long-term protection of the resource base depends to a large extent on the way they influence performances in regard to this paramount objective. A remarkable illustration of this essential fact[4] can be found in the process that has led to the total ban on trawl fishing, decided on in 1980, by President Suharto of Indonesia under presidential decree, PD 39/1980. This is a noticeable act because Indonesia is one of the few countries in the world where trawling is proscribed throughout the whole year in all areas where there is a preponderance of small-scale fishermen. Moreover, the ban has been hailed as a 'bold and innovative' step and as 'the most recent in a series of management policy measures designed to protect coastal fisheries resources' (Bailey *et al.*, 1987).

[4] Also bear in mind the aforementioned fact that forest-dwellers are often perceived as a threat to national security because they live in forest areas that are not easily controlled by national armies due to inaccessibility.

When the story behind it is carefully scrutinized, however, one inevitably comes to the conclusion that it was a political decision unmotivated by considerations of long-term resource management. Witness to it the fact that President Suharto apparently did not consult with the Fisheries Department before making his 'bold' move: there was never any suggestion from this department for the imposition of the ban which was a unilateral decision of the President (Mathew, 1990: 34). That resource management was not the objective pursued by Suharto is also evident from the fact that (i) only 3 per cent of the total expenditure of the director-general of fisheries is targeted for fisheries resource management and environmental protection; and (ii) complementary measures have not been taken to protect the resource. Regarding this last point, it is noteworthy that the pressure on the resource has not been actually reduced. For one thing, the government has actively encouraged the development of aquaculture to promote prawn production. Consequently, mangrove forests (where prawns breed) have been massively converted into brackish culture ponds and fry and gravid females have been intensively harvested for the culture-farms, two processes which threaten to reduce the natural populations of all shrimp. (There is actually a ban on conversion of mangroves in the 200-metre greenbelt, but it is not being observed.) For another thing, small-scale fishermen could successfully replace trawling gear with trammel-nets and produce the same quantity of prawns as was caught before the ban (ibid.: 21, 28–9, 32–3).

What was the real motive behind the ban? According to Sebastian Mathew, on whose work our account is based, 'a plausible objective of the ban is the resolution of physical conflicts between trawlers and gill-net fisheries which were exacerbating from the mid-1970s leading to destruction of property, bloodshed and loss of lives' (Mathew, 1990: 35). Maintenance of law and order in the archipelagic waters seems to be of paramount importance in Indonesia. Since the process of integrating all Indonesians into one nationality is still in progress, it is crucial to keep the waters separating the six thousand inhabited islands as peaceful as possible. In so far as the fishermen provide the effective communication links between these islands, such an objective cannot be reached as long as violence reigns on the sea. Now, to understand why the problem of violence at sea was resolved by banning trawl fishing, a covert motive of Suharto must be highlighted. To understand this motive, it must be kept in mind that the ethnic factor plays a very important role in the economy of Indonesia. Ethnic tensions were largely prevalent in the fishing sector where a neat divide existed between indigenous small-scale fishermen and Chinese entrepreneurs engaged in trawler fishing (and also in the entire range of medium- and large-scale operations). The decision to ban trawling was therefore an anti-Chinese measure inextricably linked with the political atmosphere prevailing in the country. Suharto was in fact all the more vulnerable to popular resentment against Chinese economic dominance, as zealot Muslims resented the fact that he did not declare Indonesia as an Islamic State, and as he himself was well connected with Chinese financial interests.

Suharto was forced to take sides when the conflicts that broke out on the fisheries front, and were largely a protraction of ethnic riots in the mainstream society, got the support of Muslim leaders. More and more people from the non-fishing community joined the struggle against (Chinese) trawlers mainly because of ethnic reasons and 'by the late 1970s it was threatening to acquire extremely grave dimensions'. Against this backdrop, the ban on trawling appeared to Suharto as a providential strategic weapon to use with a view to gaining political capital on the eve of 1982 elections (Mathew, 1990: 34–9). Beneath or behind the rhetoric used to provide a resource management rationale to the trawler ban, the real issues were one of distribution—to redistribute fishing incomes from (Chinese) trawlers to (indigenous) small-scale fishermen—and one of law and order—to put an end to the bloody conflicts on the sea which were threatening to aggravate racial tension and to disrupt the whole socio-political fabric of the country. Due to a specific combination of circumstances, Indonesian state power had a political interest in changing access rules in the fishing sector. In so far as trawling is an aggressive technique, it is true that a trawler ban could have been a good beginning for the development of an integrated resource management system. That it was not so is hardly a surprise since conservation was definitely not the prime mover in Suharto's decision.

Obviously, 'law and order' and other political considerations need not prompt a government to take environmentally positive measures as in the case of Indonesian fisheries. They may as well drive it to behave in the opposite way. Under the pressure of strong political bases, the government may indeed refrain from applying unpopular conservationist measures. In Costa Rica, for example, we learn that non-enforcement of forest regulations has become 'an explicit strategy of the state to avoid or reduce tensions' (Utting, 1994: 239). Sometimes, it is powerful local bosses or patrons who may force the government to retrace its steps or to abstain from implementing management schemes. Thus, in some areas of Uttar Pradesh (India), the administration does not dare to mete out legal punishments or impose (legal) fines for contravening regulations (e.g. to cut off electricity for well owners who ignored spacing regulations) for fear of violent reactions by the people concerned and their determined leaders or for fear that they may shift parties in the next elections. As an article in *The Economist* reports:

> Thousands of Mr Tikait's supporters bear guns. Mr Tikait tells farmers not to pay for canal water or electricity for their wells. No state government has dared cut off the farmer's electricity supply for fear of losing votes, or of tangling with Mr Tikait's gunmen. This erosion of the rule of law is happening, not in secessionist-minded Punjab Assam or Kashmir, but in Uttar Pradesh, the very heartland of India. (*The Economist*, 10–16 Aug. 1991: 23–4, quoted from Moench, 1992: A-11).

The 'softness' (Gunnar Myrdal) of many States in the developing world actually points to an insurmountable limit to a top-down approach in which the State has to resort to taxes and fines in conditions of highly imperfect monitorability of users' behaviour. As a matter of fact, we have offered a theoretical argument to the effect that severe punishment has to be imposed to make up for imperfect information about users' behaviour if centralized management schemes are to be effectively implemented. It has to be added now that this solution may well prove impracticable in so far as the imposition of heavy fines or severe sanctions (like prison sentences) may cause considerable resentment among the populations concerned and thereby threaten the stability of the ruling political order. Or, such a measure will be somehow circumvented, e.g., through active corruption of the state agents in charge of fine collection, and the scheme will not be properly enforced.

In the above, we have laid much stress on the fact that the paternalistic, bureaucratic, and top-down approach followed by most governments is largely responsible for repeated failures of village-level resource management. What needs to be added before considering other important factors in the evolving environment (physical and human) of many Third World rural communities is that this criticism does not only apply to state agencies. It is also valid for international organizations, especially those which have assisted state-engineered resource management programmes in developing countries, and even for some non-governmental organizations which have not paid sufficient attention to people's participation. Thus, according to Cernea, the experience with community woodlot projects which have been so much in vogue since the late 1970s amounts 'to an extraordinarily telling case of an international programme intended to capture popular participation, which nevertheless was launched and generously financed without having elementary understanding of the kind of social process and system it needs to put in motion'. As a matter of fact, 'investment in the technical process outpaced by far the investment in the human/institutional process' (Cernea, 1989: 37–8). More surprisingly, as a case-study of Zimbabwe has recently revealed, non-governmental organizations involved in conservation projects are not necessarily better than large, non-voluntary public agencies in promoting a participatory, people-centred approach (Vivian, 1994).

Note that lack of attention to the relevant units of social organization and their internal dynamics explains not only management failures and resource use inefficiencies but also increasing inequalities and socio-economic differentiation. A vivid illustration of the latter possibility is provided by the World Bank-assisted Azad Kashmir Hill Farming Technical Development Project (HFTDP) in Pakistan. As a mid-term evaluation revealed, the planting of trees for reafforestation purposes which was reported by project staff to be on communal lands turned out in fact to be on land under individual private control. In other words, 'the tracts of *shamilat* [communal] land that had been offered for planting—and assumed by the project staff to benefit the communities—had surreptitiously changed their tenurial status to become private land. The *de facto* owners hoped to get "their" *shamilat* lands planted at government expense, without making repayment commitments. No community decision-making was involved, and no community woodlot was established' (Cernea, 1989: 21).[5] The social polarization that ensued was not necessarily efficiency-promoting. In actual fact, the evaluator came to the conclusion that 'the wealthiest landowners, who have the resources to contribute to the costs of establishing and protecting tree stands, had not done so, nor did they intend to do so in the future. At one of the reforestation sites, I

[5] The fact of the matter is that, through an incremental appropriation process, land which was customarily held jointly by the village communities came to be increasingly operated and used by private individuals, the encroachers being often villagers located closer to one or another plot (or side) of the commons (Cernea, 1989: 16–19).

found that the main part of the 100 acres planted in the first year belonged to one influential family of six brothers, only one of whom was "almost" a full-time farmer, while the others were absentee landlords operating shops and small enterprises in Muzaffarabad' (ibid.).

Unexpected disequalizing effects have been reported for numerous other resource development projects at village level, yet it is not clear in many cases whether the processes yielding these effects have also been detrimental to efficiency. Thus, in the Ferlo of northern Senegal, wealthy Fulbe nobles have manipulated a donor project to fence off vast acreages of pastures around deep boreholes and, as a result, these parcels have become the private grazing areas of a few individuals (Freudenberger and Mathieu, 1993: 16).

11.2 Other Recent Changes on the Rural Scene

Massive intervention of central authorities in environmental matters is only one of the factors that have deeply affected rural life and villagers' ability to self-organize for resource protection during recent times. Among the other important factors at work is, of course, population growth.

Population growth

In Chapter 10, two population-related processes have been brought to light. First, population growth tends to drive resource users to tighten rules of access in two ways. On the one hand, increasingly exclusionary arrangements are adopted so as to make entry into CPR domains more and more difficult for outsiders or non-community members. The identity of the losers is thus well known before exclusion takes place and only the insiders have the right to vote about whom to exclude, thereby overcoming the dilemma posed by Fernandez and Rodrik (see Chapter 8). On the other hand, rules tend to be devised to regulate access among the insiders or community members if the latter (continue to) grow in numbers. In many cases, as we have seen, these rules involve individual restraint in use of the CPR so as to equalize expected benefits for all participants. They are particularly strict when the use of the CPR creates many opportunities for serious conflicts, which is likely to be the case when the resource is highly visible and well localized.

Second, for population growth to lead users to adopt genuinely conservationist practices—for example, to show restraint in harvesting not only or necessarily with a view to sharing the resource flow with other users but also with a view to ensuring the long-term viability of the resource base—a time-consuming process of awareness-building is needed. In the most successful case, exemplified by Japan, it is remarkable that resource protection measures have been accompanied by population control measures and have been adopted before the entire resource base was depleted/degraded in an irreversible way. Yet, it is worthy of note that, even in this very successful case, Japanese villagers had gone through a traumatic and highly visible experience of deforestation before learning to manage the remaining forests in an effective way. In the worst case, by contrast, awareness of the problem comes too late when the resource stock has been depleted to such an extent that incentives to protect it do not exist any more.

At this point, we need to re-emphasize that the induced institutional innovation hypothesis rules out cases of the latter kind. Two of the most articulate exponents of this view have thus hypothesized that 'the social structure becomes tighter and more cohesive in response to a greater need to coordinate and control the use of resources as they become increasingly more scarce . . .' (Hayami and Kikuchi, 1981: 22). So long as a (non-labour) resource is abundant, there is no need to co-ordinate its use among community members (or, we may add, to exclude outsiders). The need arises only when, the resource becoming scarce, 'people begin to compete for or cooperate in its use'. Then, 'Efficient coordination requires rules defining rights and obligations among people on the use of the resource as well as rules to settle possible conflicts. As scarcity increases and the competition is intensified, it becomes necessary to define the rules more clearly and to enforce them more rigorously' (ibid. 21). Now, the solution consisting of developing a market to handle the problem of scarce resource allocations is not possible if property rights cannot be clearly specified and transaction costs are prohibitively high. When this is the case, non-market institutions tend to develop to regulate villagers' behaviour directly. Inasmuch as environment determines which resources are scarce, which are relatively difficult to privatize and which are relatively easy to handle at village level, environmental conditions are 'a critical variable in the formation of village structure' (ibid. 21–2).

Hayami and Kikuchi have used their hypothesis to explain the significant difference in tightness of rural societies as between Japan and many South-East Asian countries (Malaysia, Thailand, and the Philippines in particular). Thus, compared with Japan, South-East Asia (with the major exception of Java) was characterized by an abundant supply of land, at least until the middle of the nineteenth century. It is therefore 'natural to expect that the farming communities molded under such land-surplus conditions would be loosely structured, compared with Japanese villages that have been molded under strong population pressure for a long time' (Hayami and Kikuchi, 1981: 22). Likewise, water is a critical resource limiting rice production throughout the world. Yet, contrary to what obtains in countries such as Thailand where the flooding water is not a scarce economic resource for which the peasants compete or co-operate among themselves (since water control of a major river delta cannot be handled at village level), the mountainous topography in Japan renders local co-operation effective in controlling a water supply based on small streams. According to the authors: 'The need for collective action to construct and maintain irrigation systems and to settle conflicts over the use of water at local community level can be identified as a major force in the development of the tightly structured social system in Japanese villages' (ibid. 22–3). Again as expected, in the Ilocos region of the Philippines, characterized by mountainous topography and high population density, we find tightly structured villages with efficient irrigation organizations.

Regarding the problem of *how* collective organizations actually emerge in response to growing resource scarcity—or, in game-theoretical terms, how one can establish the initial trust required to make co-operation possible in what looks like an infinitely repeated game—the authors point to two distinct kinds of argument. The first one explicitly refers to biological evolutionist theory by resorting to a Darwinian selection mechanism: 'the villages without mechanisms to provide for irrigation would be unviable and some more cooperative group would take over' (Hayami and Kikuchi, 1981: 23 n. 10). As for the second one, it uses Olson's vindication of collective action in 'privileged' or 'intermediate' groups (see above, Chapter 5). This being said, the authors are keen to draw attention to the importance of the time required for social change:

> The cohesion and solidarity of the village community are based on the norms and moral principles sanctioned by tradition and ingrained in the minds of the villagers. They do change in response to change in the relative scarcity of resources, but the change takes a very long time, often several generations. (Hayami and Kikuchi, 1981: 23)

Although appealing and illuminating, the above hypothesis still begs a number of important questions. One of its essential weaknesses obviously lies in its being too simple and schematic: there are too few explanatory variables used to account for variations in tightness of village social structure. In particular, considering the case of resources that (*a*) can be handled at village level and (*b*) cannot be easily privatized, it is difficult to accept the view that only population density acts as a determinant of tightness or cohesiveness of social structure in rural communities. As we shall see in the next subsection and again in the following chapter, other dynamic factors are at play which are liable to prevent population pressure from inducing the functionally needed non-market institutions. And to the extent that most of these factors are typical of modern times, the thesis put forward by Hayami and Kikuchi can be blamed for ignoring the role of time in the sense of the historical context in which population pressure takes place.

In their final comment, however, these two authors acknowledge the importance of time in the sense of the (dynamic) time-flow required for a process to work out its effects. This is extremely apposite, yet one may want its implications to be drawn in more detail. If Hayami and Kikuchi have not done so, it is probably because they have in fact made two *implicit* assumptions which are critical for their central conclusion to hold (social structure is tighter when population density is higher). The first assumption is that population growth is not too rapid so that people can adjust to the intervening changes in resource scarcity levels. Indeed, if population growth rates are high, as they have been and still are in many developing countries since the Second World War, the fact that institutional innovation can take 'a very long time, often several generations' to come by becomes quite troublesome. This is evidently because, before people have become aware of the new challenge confronting them and/or before they have proved able to develop the collective action capability required to meet it, the scarce resource may well have vanished, leaving nothing behind for which villagers can 'compete or cooperate among themselves' (see above, Chapter 10).

The second implicit assumption underlying Hayami and Kikuchi's piece of reasoning is that population growth can be somehow brought under control (as it has actually been in Tokugawa Japan). In other words, as we have already pointed out, villagers should respond to the newly arising scarcity not only by evolving new rules for allocating and conserving the resource, but also by designing mechanisms intended for penalizing high fertility. Let us assume away the first above-mentioned difficulty by considering a situation where village communities have actually succeeded in *bringing about* the rules or institutional mechanisms required to allocate the resource in an orderly manner and to conserve it in the long run. There then remains the critical question, untouched by Hayami and Kikuchi presumably because of their second implicit assumption, as to whether these rules or mechanisms are *viable* under conditions of continuous population pressure however slow the pace of population growth: obviously, besides the question of *emergence* of institutions, there is the question of their *persistence*.

The answer to such a question is obviously negative when the population of access rights-holders is allowed to grow and eventually reach a point where individual incomes extracted from the resource fall below the subsistence level, while alternative sources of income are not available. The temptation to violate conservation rules (to catch juvenile fish, to cut shrubs or let goats feed on them, to clear new fields in the forest, etc.) is then likely to be irresistible since, owing to the survival constraint, the discount rate of future incomes becomes infinite and free riding behaviour appears as a natural weapon in the struggle of each against each for sheer subsistence. In the Langson province (northernmost hilly region) of Vietnam, for example, 'despite the collectively imposed discipline on the peasants for the protection of environment and 100 per cent literacy rate, large-scale deforestation comparable to that in the Indian Himalayas has been witnessed': the area under forest has been reduced from 36 per cent to 17 per cent of geographical area of the district in the course of only six years (in the 1980s). According to Rao who reports this finding, this destructive process cannot be entirely ascribed to the felling of trees by the government for purposes of construction and for exports. It also results from rapid conversion of forest areas into arable lands as a consequence of the local peasants' noticeable impoverishment (Rao, 1988: A-144).

It is true that Hayami and Kikuchi do not make any explicit mention of the problem of renewable resources in their argument about the role of population. The rules they therefore consider are meant for allocating—not for conserving—resources that have become scarce. It must nevertheless be emphasized that community rules are liable to dissolve under the continuous pressure of population growth not only when they serve to ensure the long-run viability of the resource base but also when they specify ways of allocating resource flows or benefits among the different claimants. The idea is that, when the individual share of a resource flow accruing to each community member becomes so low that a livelihood can no more be sustained from it, people are strongly inclined to violate the sharing rules so as to appropriate a larger share for themselves at the expense of the other rights-holders. This last outcome can be vividly illustrated by referring to the degeneracy of the system of rotating access to the sea observed in Southern Sri Lanka by Alexander and Amarasinghe (the first in the village of

Gahavälla and the second in that of Tangalle). The example is particularly appropriate since we have already had the opportunity to describe in detail how this system worked (see Chapter 10). The studies of both Alexander (1980, 1982) and Amarasinghe (1988, 1989) converge to show that once population growth (and market integration) reach a critical level, traditional income-sharing and work-spreading arrangements tend to degenerate or to disappear altogether.

Following the account given by Alexander (1982, chs. 9–11), the dynamics of this degeneracy process in Gahavälla can be described as follows. In the beginning (before 1914), the beachseiners were a prosperous community as the pressure on employment within the fishing industry was still low and as the fishery was not fully exploited (by that time, many fishermen used to supplement their incomes from small-scale agriculture and cottage industries). In the following decades, however, the situation was fundamentally altered when economic opportunities in agriculture (and ancillary industries) were dramatically reduced due to both population growth and changes in cultivation patterns. Beachseining was soon to become the main source of income in the area and, noticeably, 'all of the men engaged in beachseining before 1940 held rights of access, either by descent or marriage'. As a result, average household incomes started to fall and 'sons from large families had to construct additional nets if they wished to continue beachseining'. The adding of new nets whose marginal productivity was nil from the standpoint of the community was not opposed because 'the function of the rights of access concept was not to limit the number of nets, but to ensure that outsiders did not construct nets for use on Gahavälla beach and thus accelerate the fragmentation process' (ibid.: 203–4, 206).

A point was eventually reached, however, where this process began to threaten the livelihood of beachseiners and 'ownership of a single share was insufficient to sustain life' (Alexander, 1982: 206). A cumulative kind of involution resembling a 'tragedy of the commons' was initiated from then on since, to protect their income, existing participants had to construct additional nets. This was with a view to preventing the number of their turns per unit of time and their chance of participating in the flush period from declining too much. Note that fishermen could not use the same net more than once during a particular net sequence in so far as each net was given a number, represented a different team of partners, and was an individualized ticket of entry into the local fishery. Increased socio-economic differentiation was the inevitable outcome of the above evolution: as a matter of fact, many fishermen who could not afford to finance new shares were driven out of the beach and forced to sell their shares to more affluent participants. An active market for net shares thus developed—in violation of customary rule (5) (see Chapter 10)—as access rights became an increasingly scarce asset. (For understandable reasons, none the less, other shareholders had a strong practical veto over prospective sales of a share.) It became plainly evident that by guaranteeing equal access to all *nets* registered in the village, the community was less and less able to ensure equality of access to all village members.

From 1933 onwards, the government attempted to limit the number of nets allowed to operate and, moreover, the legislation it provided permitted sales of shares to fishermen without hereditary rights of access to the fishery. The customary system of rights of access was thus effectively destroyed and, after 1940, many of the share sales were to outsiders (Alexander, 1982). However, in so far as limitations on the number of nets were not very effective, a quasi-open-access situation developed and, on the eve of the Second World War, local inhabitants were confronted with apparently insuperable problems of survival. Fortunately, the new economic opportunities created by the war radically changed the prospects for the fishing industry while at the same time giving a new impulse to the differentiation process under way. Indeed, the dramatic increase in fish prices which resulted from important developments in fish marketing and from the growing integration of Gahavälla into the national economy brought a new prosperity to this area. Most of the fish catches were now sold in fresh (and no more in dried) form and the new lucrative avenue of investment thus opened could not fail to attract a class of wealthy capitalists and traders who usually belonged to the landed élite and had tight connections with the political establishment and strong positions in local state institutions (Amarasinghe, 1988: 168–9). To enter the field, these non-fishermen capitalists had recourse to several strategies: (*a*) construction of new nets; (*b*) purchase of net shares on the local share market; and (*c*) appropriation of existing net shares through the use of violence (Alexander, 1982: 226–39 and Amarasinghe, 1988: 164–5). Strategy (*c*) was often resorted to when strategies (*a*) and (*b*) proved difficult, that is, when the government and/or the existing beachseiners endeavoured to limit the number of new nets allowed to be constructed, and when net owners were reluctant to sell shares whose economic value had suddenly appreciated.

Nothing could eventually prevent this aggressive new élite from enhancing its hold over the fishery and from concentrating an increasing share of the fishing assets and the corresponding rights of access to the resource. The cumulative involution process described earlier took on a new momentum as small individual shareholders 'were forced to join in the construction of new nets, for otherwise their equity in the total catch would diminish' (Alexander, 1982: 211). As a result, the incomes of these small owners started again to fall to precarious levels and many of them were obliged to sell their shares to men 'who were not descendants of the original owners': 'the final nails were hammered into the coffin of the "rights of access" and the kinship basis of the shareholder's group was destroyed' (ibid. 212). At that time, the large shareholders realized that they did not need any more to construct new nets since strategy (*b*) now proved to be amply effective for them to increase their control of the catch. Interestingly, when the government proposed to solve the problem of overmultiplication of nets by reducing the total number of nets but increasing the number of shares in each net to twenty-four, it met with the strong opposition of the small shareholders. Apparently, the latter felt that it would be difficult to reach an agreement on procedures for amalgamation (the transaction cost of changing the ownership structure was high) and, above all, that a crew of twenty-four was too large to be efficient (ibid. 214).

An expected concomitant of the foregoing rise of a small entrepreneur élite was the rapid development of a labour market—in violation of aforementioned rules (2) and (3) above (see above, Chapter 10). Whereas before complementary labour was always provided by the owners' children when needed (for example, when an owner happened to own more than one share in a net, or became sick or old), large shareholders began to hire crew labour on an increasing scale to operate their nets and it was not rare to find proletarianized fishermen working as wage labourers on shares they once owned (Alexander, 1982: 151, 246). Note incidentally that, in an understandable manner, displaced local beachseiners resented more the attempts by small outsider owners to work their own shares than the capitalist strategy of big owner-investors who at least supplied them with employment (ibid. 245).

In many areas suitable for beachseining in Sri Lanka, the fishing industry actually ended up being controlled by one or two big owners whose position was confirmed through the system of net licensing introduced by the government to stabilize the situation (Alexander, 1982: 214). In some other areas like Gahavälla and Tangalle, where access to the resource was not monopolized to such an extent, accumulation of nets and labour force growth proceeded much farther and the resulting poverty drove many crew labourers to leave their owner-employers in order to form fishing co-operatives or seek alternative employment in other fisheries and other industries (Alexander, 1982: 212–14; Amarasinghe, 1988: 170). If their economic lot eventually improved, it was only because beachseining was eventually supplanted by much more efficient harvesting technologies which dramatically increased the productivity of fishing efforts (Amarasinghe, 1988: chs. 10–14; 1989). Incidentally, the above comparison testifies to the efficiency advantage of monopoly whenever collective ownership of rights of access to a resource collapses to the point of degenerating into an open-access situation.

The aforetold story, like all real-world stories, is obviously complex, much more complex than can easily be captured with the help of a simple model. Population growth has obviously been a critical determinant of the evolution of the system of access to the sea, but it has not been the only one. Government intervention and market integration have been two other crucial forces in the process. We shall soon have the opportunity to discuss the significance of the latter factor but it is patent that it had a corrosive effect on the system under concern. As for the government, it has contributed to worsen the situation by intervening in an untoward manner when it attempted to legislate a limitation of the number of the permitted beachseines without giving itself the means to enforce it, and when it ran counter to the local customary rules by allowing outsiders to make their way into the fishery.

A central lesson to draw from the story of Gahavälla and Tangalle remains that, if population pressure continues unabated while the economic environment is constant, rights-holders are inevitably led to adopt defensive strategies that threaten the viability of the community-based, direct allocation system. The adding of new nets is of course legitimate in so far as it comes from new entrants into the local workforce, but it is not so when it is the outcome of attempts by existing operators to avoid a decline in their individual share of the total product of the fishery. That local communities have gradually lost their power of control over the rotation system is evident from the fact that they were unwilling and/or unable to stop this process of illegitimate construction of new nets. It is clear that rapid socio-economic differentiation is the inevitable outcome of such an anarchy and that it can be ultimately held in check only if population growth is slowed down and/or new income and employment opportunities are created (or if fortunate exogenous circumstances, such as a rise in the price of the product sold by the villagers, do occur). It must be borne in mind that degeneracy of the rotation system did not threaten the viability of the resource base simply because the prevailing technology (beachseining) was not susceptible of causing biological overfishing.

A last remark is in order. In the same way as the negative effect of population growth on both allocation and management rules can be cancelled by newly emerging income and employment opportunities, the positive effect of population control can be annihilated by the sudden disappearance of regular opportunities for income and employment that existed in the past. For example, villagers may be outcompeted by external producers as when local craftsmanship is rendered unprofitable by the growth of modern manufacturing units in the towns. As a result, local artisans become jobless or peasants lose an important source of complementary income to supplement their regular agricultural earnings or to fall back on in times of crisis. Or, to take another example, more labour-saving techniques, crops, or activities may be introduced in the village with the consequence that the poor are driven out of agricultural employment. In both these cases as well as in similar circumstances, the affected people will tend to make up for the loss of income by exploiting village CPRs more intensively. This means that there will be an increasing strain on community support systems and increasing risks of degradation of the underlying resource base.

For instance, Rao has observed that, in India, the rapid development of commercial tree-farming, especially in large farms, although in itself resource-conserving, may ultimately contribute to a further degradation of the rural environment. This is so because substitution of commercial trees for field crops (following the steep rise in the prices of timber and fuelwood relative to those of field crops) and the accompanying conversion of wheat and rice fields into commercial tree plantations entail a considerable loss of employment and incomes for the rural poor who have been depending on wage employment for the cultivation of field crops. As a result of this shift from labour-intensive field agriculture to highly capital-intensive plantation farming, the poor may be driven to the unregulated exploitation of natural resources, thus increasing the pressure on the forests which the development of commercial tree-farming has helped reduce (Rao, 1988: A-143). This kind of effect is all the more likely to occur since, in India, as we have seen earlier (see above, Chapter 4), access to a wide range of communal (natural) resources is still an important informal security mechanism whereby the rural poor survive. The price to be paid for this fortunate result—fortunate given the lack of alternative employment opportunities—is the progressive degradation of village CPRs due to overcrowding: (*a*) fewer and fewer resources are available per person, and (*b*) the quality and quantity of the overall resources deteriorate (ibid. 108). In his analysis of the situation obtaining in semi-arid districts, Jodha found that the productivity of CPRs has been falling rapidly during recent decades, thereby resulting in shortening periods of supplies of fuel, food, fodder, and timber, a deterioration in the botanical composition of vegetation, the silting of water sources, and other detrimental effects (Jodha, 1985). The problem is further compounded by the fact that the total area under CPRs as a proportion of total village area has dramatically declined from 15–42 per cent (depending on the semi-arid district considered) in 1950–2 to 9–28 per cent in 1982–4 (Jodha, 1986: 1177). This decline, according to Jodha, is to be attributed partly to population growth and to the physical submersion of land under large-scale irrigation projects, but mainly to land privatization moves that, unfortunately, have largely favoured the bigger farmers who received disproportionately large tracts of comparatively high-quality land.

The intervention of other factors than population growth is actually reflected in the fact that, in the dry tropical parts of India, there are groups of villages with high population growth rates and yet limited decline in CPR area while, conversely, high rates of CPR decline are sometimes associated with limited population increases (Jodha, 1992: 61).

Before turning to these other factors, it is of interest to note that in some circumstances population reduction can actually threaten ecological equilibria by weakening the indigenous institutions (such as collective labour arrangements) that regulate collective action in resource management. Thus, in a study about rural Mexico, it has been argued that emigration of a large number of people has caused local farming to suffer from chronic environmental degradation and productivity stagnation. The reason put forward by the authors is that landscape transformation for agricultural sustainability (involving steep-slope management and erosion control done with landscape levelling, terraces, and land containers) requires the pooling of a sufficient amount of labour and the smooth working of the institution that organizes it. Such requirements have been wiped out following the departure of a sizeable portion of the local labour force (Garcia-Barrios and Garcia-Barrios, 1990).

Market integration, technological change, transformation of value and belief systems

Market integration is a catch-all expression which denotes all the processes that have the effect of linking up village economies with the broader world via sale of output, purchase of inputs, labour, financial and other markets. Such processes have been dramatically promoted by the rapid development of communication networks and transportation means, especially during recent decades, as well as by rising urbanization rates and the consequent growth of market demand for agricultural products. For obvious reasons, the rural areas located near urban concentrations have been more deeply affected by these changes than remote areas, particularly so if the latter are not easily accessible.

The role of economic factors

What are the effects of market integration on villagers' collective action capabilities with respect to local-level CPRs? The answer provided by the literature on this question leans on the negative side: market integration erodes the ability of rural communities to manage their CPRs successfully. The following examples illustrate the main trend highlighted in most studies dealing with the dynamics of rural change in regard of CPR management. In the hill districts of Uttar Pradesh, we are told that the *panchayat* forests, though small in extent as a consequence of government policy, were often well maintained in both the colonial and post-colonial periods. A recent survey even concluded that 'while some of the *panchayat* forests there [in Tehri Garhwal] are in better condition than the reserved forests in the area, they are uniformly better maintained than forests under the jurisdiction of the civil administration' (Guha, 1985: 1947). Yet, in some areas, traditional mechanisms of allocation and control have broken down as 'a consequence of the commercial penetration of hill economy and society that followed in the wake of state forestry'. Thus, in the Kumaon Hills where commercialization had penetrated earlier, the experience of forest *panchayats* is 'a mixed one' compared to other regions where extraction is still 'carefully regulated, with monetary fines being levied on offenders' and where parts of *panchayat* lands are closed to grazing by common consent (ibid.).

With respect to the same hilly region (Kumaon), another author has contended that, if employment opportunities did not exist in the plains, human and draught animal populations would not have been allowed to continue to expand since remittances from emigrant family members would not have been available to support these increases. Arguing in a way reminding us of the induced institutional innovation hypothesis, he speculates that, without these opportunities, 'the natural consequences of over-exploitation of the environment would have, in the long run, pinned down population density at a level where the recuperative capacity of the environment balanced the amount of exploitation'. It is therefore because of the possibility of migration and the resulting inflow of cash that 'there are no forces inherent in the situation today to jolt local people into an awareness of what is happening' (Ashish, 1979: 1060). As will be argued in the concluding section of this chapter, however, as a general story the account provided by Ashish is unduly pessimistic: other effects can be at work that mitigate the risk of resource overexploitation.

Local-level management is much more certain to be problematic when, as attested by the Nepalese experience, a market develops for forest products thus giving rise to increased production for sale by insiders as well as by outsiders. It has indeed been observed that proximity to markets for forest fuel products 'tends to undermine forest management: where firewood can be sold nearby at high prices, it is hard to prevent poaching in *panchayats* near market centers' (Arnold and Campbell, 1986: 438). In the Myagdi district in the Upper Kali Gandaki, for example, as urban growth increases the demand for fuelwood products and building materials, outsiders begin cutting wood in the forests or 'buying it from indiscriminate and uncaring (or unknowing) others, *including locals who have abandoned traditional management custom*' (Messerschmidt, 1986: 467, emphasis added; see also 458–9). For most of the Nepalese hills, according to one view, the main factor which limited the amount of deforestation till recently was 'the relatively small population *and the lack of any commercial exploitation*' (Arnold and Campbell, 1986: 438, emphasis added). As for India, Jodha has noted that improved accessibility and market integration of hitherto isolated, fragile areas into the mainstream economy have led to overexploitation of CPRs (Jodha, 1992: 37). In the Sahelian countries, too, forest degradation often follows excessive cutting of live firewood for urban consumption, the articulation with urban markets being made by businessmen residing in the cities (Gannon *et al.*, 1993; Cline-Cole *et al.*, 1990). It is a well-known fact that the best way to destroy forests in these countries is to build up roads linking big cities with villages surrounded by forested areas.

The same holds true for many other countries as well. Thus, if commercial logging is virtually non-existent in upland Nepal, although it is common in the Terai, it is because Nepal's minimal road system provides access to only a small percentage of the nation (Metz, 1991: 809). Finally, it is of interest to note that in the monastic forest of Imperial China, 'neither religious discipline, nor prohibitions imposed by the State, were always adequate to face the pressures of land scarcity and high prices for timber outside the monastery itself. It is quite common to read of monks, or of the abbot himself, working in collusion with timber merchants to sell timber, despite official ban on cutting . . . At times, economic links could outweigh the normative values protecting the monastery's environment' (Menzies, 1994: 68–70).

Another example comes from Japanese fisheries, a sector in which Japan has a long tradition of community-based management of sea resources. What bears emphasis here is that, in areas like the Inland Sea that have undergone massive economic structural change during the last forty years, traditional systems of coastal management and access rights have been gradually perverted. Thus, in this now heavily industrialized area, 'the synergistic impacts of environmental pollution and overfishing have put a premium on the diminishing aquatic resources. This, in turn, has led to the emergence of the illicit transfer of fishing rights' (Ruddle, 1987: 51). Such an outcome has not been observed in regions more protected from the impact of industrialization and the 'vastly enlarged range of employment opportunities' that is brought in its wake.

On the other hand, we have seen above that, in Sri Lanka, traditional systems of rotating access to the sea have gradually disintegrated, first under the continuous pressure of population growth, and later, after the Second World War, under the impact of increased market penetration. As a matter of fact, significant rises in fish prices resulting from growing demand from urban well-to-do households together with the rapid development of transport and communications created new incentives for fishing investment which did not fail to attract equally powerful interests in the sector. Under this new pressure, the customary rotation system, already made fragile by population growth, became completely distorted in favour of an aggressive capitalist élite which succeeded in pre-empting control of an increasing share of traditional access rights. Defensive reactions by impoverished rights-holders could only contribute to make the system still weaker (see above).

The situation in fisheries is indeed highly instructive: species for which traditional systems of resource management are under most severe stress and which are currently overfished are all species (such as prawn, squid, cuttlefish, and lobster) which have high commercial value. By contrast, customary rules of access and traditional management practices are relatively well followed for species that are harvested only or mainly for subsistence purposes (personal communication of Sebastian Mathew). This observation certainly applies to other natural resource sectors as well.

Let us pause for a moment in order to ponder over the meaning of the above observations. As a matter of fact, it may perhaps appear surprising that the increased value of common property assets brought about by market integration does not systematically lead to a more orderly or conservative use of the resources concerned. To address this question in the light of the aforementioned examples, it is necessary to distinguish clearly between the case of Sri Lanka's beachseine fishery on the one hand, and the examples referring to forestry and open-sea fisheries, on the other hand. In the former instance, the regulatory system which dealt exclusively with an allocation problem was already under severe stress when the price rise caused by better market integration occurred. In actual fact, this system had almost degenerated into an open-access situation and, in these circumstances, by causing a perceptible increase in the average income earned from participation in the (fixed-space) fishery, the price rise had the effect of attracting new entrants. Under conditions of a more or less perfectly competitive labour market (and more or less open access to the fishery), this process had to continue till individual labour incomes became equalized across the various sectors.

More delicate is the problem raised by the other examples, since they tend to suggest that market integration causes resource depletion. This is a puzzling effect: indeed, we would have expected price rises to induce rural dwellers to better conserve their local natural resources with a view to having a sustainable flow of future CPR products to sell on the market at later dates. A first explanation for this unexpected outcome has been already pointed out in Chapter 1 (sect. 4). The effect of an increase in output price is ambiguous: on the one hand, as hinted at above, it increases the incentive to conserve the resource by enhancing the future value of production but, on the other hand, it also increases the incentive for use of production inputs and reduces incentives for use of conservation inputs in the current period (to the extent that there is competition between these two uses, such as happens when labour is scarce). A second factor which may account for resource overexploitation when prices rise is the existence of considerable uncertainty about future prices. This uncertainty tends to induce producers to seize upon present opportunities to the largest possible extent without much concern for the future state of the resources.

In addition, it must be emphasized that increased market integration yields other effects than output price increases. Other things do not remain equal and, even when the net effect of a rise of the price of CPR products is to encourage conservation, other forces may work in the opposite direction. Three such forces are worth mentioning. First, increased market integration often means that rural dwellers are exposed to new attractive consumption possibilities. This has the effect of altering their intertemporal preferences in such a way that their future incomes are more heavily discounted than before. Second, by opening up new income-earning opportunities that are more rewarding than those previously available, market integration increases the likelihood that it will not any more be optimal for individual producers to conserve local natural resources (see Chapter 1, sect. 4). They may instead be induced to deplete them to a shut-down point and plough back the profits thereby earned in other, more promising enterprises. Third, market integration may enable villagers to commercialize CPR products that were used essentially for subsistence purposes in the previous situation. In such circumstances, these villagers may suddenly realize that there is a risk for a local resource to be depleted owing to the emergence of new uses for its product(s). They may fear that, if they do not exploit it intensively, other villagers or outsiders will do it and thereby prevent them from benefiting from the new windfall income opportunities.

It deserves to be stressed that it is only in the last case, where an open-access situation must be presumed to exist (either because it originally existed or because collective regulation has collapsed under the impact of market opening), that we can speak of a genuine tragedy of the commons. Indeed, all the other above-described factors will also operate if the villagers have private property rights over the resource. Careful empirical research of a kind that is unfortunately not yet available is required to determine which explanation or combination of explanations is the most plausible to account for the rapid depletion of local resources following market integration, whenever it is observed.

The role of non-economic factors

We have just hinted at the possibility that increased market integration will lead to resource degradation due to the collapse of CPR management schemes. In the following pages, we probe into the non-economic consequences of market integration that may undermine such schemes. As a matter of fact, market integration is an all-encompassing process involving numerous interdependent changes most of which seem to be rather uncongenial to collective resource conservation mechanisms. Among those changes, attention is focused below on the following indirect effects of market integration: erosion of traditional authority patterns, of village solidarity and social cohesion, and of old systems of magical beliefs.

1. Erosion of traditional authority patterns is often considered a major factor sapping the vitality of village-level organizations for CPR management and allocation. Interestingly, there appears to be a link between the extent of isolation of villages from market centres on the one hand, and the degree of social cohesion or effectiveness of social sanctions, on the other hand. Thus, from an empirical study covering India's dry regions, the following relations come out (Jodha, 1992: 41–2):

(*a*) In smaller and isolated villages, where traditional social sanctions are still respected, the decline of CPR area is less.

(*b*) Protection of CPR area is better in the villages relatively further from market centres, where market forces are less effective in eroding traditional values *vis-à-vis* CPRs.

(*c*) The decline in CPR areas is less pronounced in villages with a lower degree of commercialization, because there is less erosion of social sanctions and informal arrangements protecting CPRs.

(*d*) Such decline is also less in villages which are relatively independent of state patronage for resource transfers, which implies fewer opportunities for interference in village affairs from above and reduced pressure for privatization of CPRs as part of populist programmes.

One important cause behind the erosion of traditional authority is the well-known fact (which we have partly documented in the first section of this chapter) that the functions of village leadership have been gradually usurped by government administration, thereby creating a situation in which traditional power-holders inexorably lose a good deal of their erstwhile legitimacy. In addition, the spread of 'modern' Western education and the growing exposure to market values, both centred on the idea of abstract or *a priori* equality (all individuals ought to be treated in the same way and, in particular, they all should have a chance to accede to political power) increasingly lead the new generations to question old forms of authority and power. The tension of change is particularly high when the older generations continue to strictly adhere to the erstwhile principle of age-based division of work and prerogatives, all the more so because the younger generations are increasingly (formally) educated and therefore more competent to assume responsibilities in the newly emerging world.

In many cases, the two above-described effects are at work, yet in parts of Sub-Saharan Africa, it seems that the first effect is predominant, especially in countries (like Muslim countries) where the impact of 'modern' Western education is still limited. For example, in the region of Kordofan (Sudan) traditional systems of forest management have failed during recent decades and desertification resulted from indiscriminate fuelwood cutting. One important cause behind this resource depletion process is apparently that the powers of the village sheikhs to control tree-cutting went into decline following the 1970 legislation which claimed title to most rural land for the government (Bruce and Fortmann, 1989: 14). The replacement of traditional 'native authorities' with less effective 'people's councils' by the post-independence governments (a process similar to that observed in India with the introduction of the new *panchayat* system) was another reason accounting for the breakdown of social control in all land matters. Existing control mechanisms thus became unable to withstand the pressure of a growing market for charcoal (replacing the declining market for gum arabic) and vast areas of gum trees were cut for fuelwood. Furthermore, 'even where *Acacia Senegal* survived, population pressure forced the telescoping of the traditional cultivation cycle from 17 to 9 years, resulting in declining fertility and increasing wind erosion' (ibid. 15).

2. A second impact of market penetration is best understood when it is borne in mind that the phenomenon of occupational, geographic, and social mobility which is so important a feature of market development is actually rooted in two main ideas: the aforementioned idea of abstract equality on the one hand, and that of apportionment of material wealth according to personal achievements on the other. By opening up new and varied avenues for social and economic mobility and by propagating the view that anyone with the required will and competence can achieve such mobility, the market tends to encourage the overt expression of individualistic propensities among the people, to dissolve old co-operative ties, and to disentangle the individual's interests from those of the social group. Deeper and deeper penetration of market values has the effect of loosening the web of traditional social relations: people become more and more free of group pressure to conform and less and less concerned about the well-being of the family or the social group.

Rising individualism can undermine the strength of informal village organizations in two ways depending on which generation actuates it. For one thing, the older generation can contribute to the weakening of these organizations if its members give in to the temptation of using their position of political and social pre-eminence to gain illicit personal material advantages. This is what has apparently happened in the laguna of Aby (Ivory Coast) where the traditional regulation system for access to and use of the waters has gradually dissolved due to the 'corruption' of the elders responsible for the good functioning of the system. Increasingly lured by the new consumption possibilities opened by the market, local elders have indeed chosen to make more money on the basis of their erstwhile social prerogatives.

For example, they have been more and more liberal in allowing outsiders to lay their nets (beachseines) in their locality because they can thereby collect substantial underhand dues on their own account. This has had the effect of infuriating the younger generations whose fishing incomes have been consequently reduced (Verdeaux, 1990: 203; see also Hviding and Baines, 1994: 27, 29–30, for similar observations regarding Solomon Islands). In the Niger River delta (Mali) the expression 'profiteer water master' has recently gained currency in certain areas where there are mounting tensions about access rights and management practices (Fay, 1990*b*: 232–3). It is true, as Fay has remarked, that accusations of profiteering may not necessarily be well grounded, yet their growing incidence attests that the adjustment of customary resource regulation systems to rapidly evolving realities gives rise to serious tensions and suspicions which are liable to thwart their effectiveness and vitality. In Marovo (Solomon Islands) some young people are dissatisfied with the way elders handle matters of resource management, arguing that they 'too readily succumb to the blandishments of the proponents of large scale commercial activities which involve deforestation and soil erosion'. Furthermore, there is widespread resentment at the commercial activities of commercial catcher-boats during most of the year in the lagoon and frequent complaints about inequities in the distribution of cash 'royalties' within the corporate kin group. These grievances and misgivings are a constant source of dispute in the area (Hviding and Baines, 1994: 27, 29–30). In Sarawak (Malaysia), to take a last example of a rapidly spreading phenomenon, the indigenous élite very often sides with loggers against the local people (Colchester, 1994: 87).

For another thing, younger generations tend to be less and less interested in village affairs in general, and in the regulation of local CPRs in particular, when they have alternative income sources in the village (e.g. by growing cash crops in individual fields) or, above all, when they have got an employment in a distant place. For example, in the Eastern Central district of Botswana, Zufferey tells us that 'traditionally, the village *kgotla* was the only representative institution at village level ruled by the unquestioned final decision of the chief'. Nowadays, the *kgotla* is still recognized as the official focus of rural communities and as the main village body dealing with customary law and general community issues: 'It is the acknowledged public place where information is disseminated and violators disciplined' (Zufferey, 1986: 13). Nevertheless, in spite of the high legitimacy it has been able to maintain (*kgotla* decisions or resolutions 'represent' the community), the *kgotla* is gradually losing part of its vitality because many villagers, primarily young men and women often with higher formal education, were forced to seek employment in South Africa or towns and major villages in Botswana. As a consequence, 'a good proportion of the most able-bodied segment of the population lives outside the villages and at any time is not represented at the village *kgotla*' (ibid.). True, these migrant workers periodically return to their extended family and still belong to their village. Unfortunately, upon their return they do not show much interest in participating in discussions of local problems. Because they spend a large proportion of their time at beer parties, 'the village *kgotla* has become the preserve of older residents' and 'no means has yet been found for incorporating the migrant labor force into the community consultation and decision processes' (ibid.).

There are several reasons why young people may shun involving themselves in village affairs. Two are worth mentioning here. First, they may not wish to submit themselves any more to an authority structure which they have come to dislike (see above). Second, they may not feel motivated to participate in collective discussions or activities in which their personal interest is no more evident. In this connection, it must be borne in mind that an essential role of kinship is customarily to ensure the continuity of traditional activities and to organize the succession of traditional rights of access to local CPRs (Ruddle, 1987: 51). When children take up new occupations—an inevitable outcome of job diversification accompanying the development of the market—especially so when they work outside the native place, kinship ties become less necessary than hitherto and therefore tend to be less attended to by the new generations. Now, to the extent that kinship is a critical component of the village social structure and a crucial determinant of the underlying social discipline, the erosion of kinship ties translates itself into a weakening of such discipline.

3. A third aspect of market development which has been well highlighted by Schumpeter is the fact that a market is an institution grounded in a rationalistic world-view. More precisely, market development is preconditioned on the activities of agents willing and able to apply cost-benefit calculus to their economic enterprises and, ultimately, to many other spheres of their entire life experience (Schumpeter, 1942: ch. 11). This kind of attitude tends inexorably to foster a scientific predisposition to query all social institutions and practices until their rationale is clearly demonstrated. The immediate consequence is that younger generations which are particularly exposed to market experiences and to the 'modern' education values which have accompanied its development in the West, are inevitably led to question the old magical beliefs and taboos that were held by their fathers and forefathers.

The problem here is that the erosion of magical beliefs in the existence of supernatural powers and in a sort of fusion between Man and Nature—'man, culture and society are commonly seen as integral parts of nature, and vice versa' (Ruddle, 1988: 76)—has the effect of removing an inbuilt check on the overexploitation of village-level CPRs. This effect has been noted on several occasions. For instance, Jessup and Peluso have observed that in East Kalimantan (Indonesia) raiding caves to steal birds' nests has become more common not only because the number of outsiders (loggers, immigrants, and itinerant traders) has increased in recent years but also because 'the threat of magical protection has become less of a deterrent to thieves' (Jessup and Peluso, 1986: 522–3). On the other hand, in West African inland fisheries where fishermen traditionally believe that waters are an extended reality peopled by local (water) spirits—'entering the water is equivalent to entering the abode of the spirits and these creatures are dangerous but also potentially helpful once they have been properly coaxed' (Fay, 1990*b*: 223, our translation)—things are changing to such an extent that in the laguna of Aby, for example, fishermen now say that 'today it is Abidjan and no more the spirit which gives orders' (Verdeaux, 1990: 208). In an aforementioned study examining the case histories of 176 CPR units in the dry tropical parts of India, Jodha has come to the conclusion that adherence to certain rituals and religious sanctions helps in a significant number of cases to sustain CPR management schemes at village level (Jodha, 1992: 51–3; see also Lansing, 1987 regarding irrigation management in Bali).

The role of technological change

That market development brings technological change in its wake hardly needs emphasis. The impact of such change that is most relevant to our topic has already been pointed out in Chapter 10 (sect. 2): to the extent that technical progress allows much more intensive exploitation of CPRs, the risk of resource degradation is considerably greater than it ever was before. Nowhere is this more evident than in the fishing sector where the development of seaworthy boats, powerful harvesting techniques (such as bottom-trawling and purse-seining), and sophisticated navigational (satellite) and fish-finding (echo sounders) equipment empowers man virtually to catch all fish living in the sea with amazing precision and effectiveness. This is contrary to traditional (artisanal) techniques which were characterized by minimum wastage of by-catches due to the selectivity of fishing gears (an important aspect in tropical fisheries where there are large numbers of species occurring in relatively small quantities); the seasonally diverse range of fishing activities which allowed for stocks and habitats to recover during closed seasons; and relatively low harvesting capacities owing to the passive nature of fishing methods (which implied low-energy requirements) (O'Riordan, 1994: 10).

Attention needs also to be drawn to more indirect possible effects of technological change while continuing to refer to the case of fisheries. First, technical progress often results in a significant *enlargement* of available techniques which may all possibly be technically efficient. For example, different groups of fishermen confronting varying sets of relative factor availabilities and prices may choose to operate distinct harvesting techniques. In the presence of severe market imperfections, some groups may even retain techniques that have been rendered technically obsolete by recent technological advances. The problem is then that the sector is characterized by growing heterogeneity down to the village level, as a consequence of which opportunities for conflict increase and collective action is made more difficult, especially so if pressure on the resource has become high (see below, Chapter 12, sect. 3).

Second, technical change is liable to affect the users' ability to self-monitor their CPRs. In theory, this impact is ambiguous since there are several effects which do not work in the same direction. In practice, however, the net impact tends to be negative. The first thing to note is that technical change has often meant that equipment is introduced which can be handled by individuals or by small groups of people and can therefore more easily escape traditional surveillance and control. This is so because monitoring costs increase significantly (possibly even more than proportionately) when the number of harvesting units rises. Verdeaux has thus laid considerable stress on the fact that the above kind of technical innovation—the gradual displacement of collectively operated large nets by individual gears such as small gill-nets—has been a major factor behind the growing failure of traditional management systems in West African lake fisheries (Verdeaux, 1990: 126, 203–4).

The difficulty of monitoring is further considerably increased when the new equipment is much more mobile than that traditionally employed. This is particularly so in the case of maritime fisheries where most small-scale fishermen now use motorized fishing crafts (usually equipped with outboard engines) which move quickly and can consequently reach distant fishing grounds, thus extending the zone of operations to a dramatic extent (see, e.g. Christy, 1983: 7). The difference with the previous situation is all the more striking as, in the past, most fishing activities were based on the use of easy-to-monitor stationary gear (such as stake-nets, set-nets, bottom-fixed nets, weirs, fish-traps, etc.) or on large-size enclosing nets (such as the beachseines) handled from the beach by large teams of operators. To these considerations, one must oppose the fact that improvements in the technology of surveillance itself could allow rural communities to better monitor the use of their natural resources. Unfortunately, these new technologies of surveillance (such as helicopters or quickly moving coastguard vessels) are very expensive and obviously beyond the reach of many such communities. On the whole, at least as far as fishing is concerned, there is no doubt that recent technical changes have contributed to render monitoring of resource use much more costly than ever before. In other words, whereas detection of rule violations was comparatively easy in the past, it now requires costly equipment and complex operations.

11.3 Conclusion: A Tentative Appraisal of Ongoing Processes

The aforedescribed changes in the economic and social environment with which village societies are confronted are of utmost importance from the standpoint of the present study. Unfortunately, they tend to undermine rather than to strengthen the collective action capabilities of these societies. Let us now summarize the most significant of these deleterious effects and, whenever possible, to interpret them in a meaningful way in the light of the theoretical insights provided in Part I.

First, in many countries state intervention in the management of village-level natural resources has had the effect of threatening traditional sources of subsistence livelihood; making customary rights highly insecure and thereby destroying informal co-operation mechanisms; bypassing traditional regulatory authorities and, by doing so, undermining their power and social prestige; and allowing large-scale intrusion of business interests in the domain of these resources. A puzzling question here is why this intrusion has in the majority of cases led to a rapid degradation of natural resources. A possible answer is that, in many instances, the concessions granted by the State contain no restrictive clause regarding the preservation of the resource, and therefore, the licensee feels under no obligation to return the resource in a fairly good state.

This may explain degradation, but the very rapidity of the degradation process remains to be accounted for. A plausible explanation lies in the short-term nature of many logging concessions. In Sumatra (Indonesia), for example, environmental destruction has a lot to do with the fact that such concessions are usually granted for twenty years while hardwood takes thirty-five years to grow (*The Economist*, 24 Sept. 1994: 68). Moreover, even when lease contracts are long term, the incentives of the licensees may not be much improved in so far as the credibility of the government is often doubted. There are indeed frequent changes of policy or political regime which lead licensees to feel insecure about the future state of their rights. Note that, even if private rights are secure, markets where rights over natural resources are traded are imperfect enough to prevent an efficient pattern of exploitation. In addition, rights-holders may truly wish to exploit the resource as intensively as possible because they feel uncertain about its future price and/or because they want to plough back the profits thereby earned in other investment avenues that look more promising, more secure, or fit better with the investor's preference structure (for example, a preference for urban over rural assets). Regarding the effect of price increases, it may be recalled that a rise in the price of CPR products does not necessarily have the effect of increasing the users' incentive to conserve the resource (see Chapter 1).

Second, there is apparently an insurmountable limit to a top-down approach in which the State has to resort to taxes and fines in conditions of highly imperfect monitorability of users' behaviour. This is essentially because, in conditions of costly monitorability of users' behaviour, a central agency has to impose severe punishment to deter rule-violation and make a centralized management scheme effective. Unfortunately, this solution is likely to be difficult to implement in many countries since the imposition of heavy fines may cause considerable resentment among the populations concerned and thereby threaten the stability of the ruling political order. Or, such a measure will induce perverse behaviour in the form of active corruption of state agents with the result that the scheme will not be properly enforced. The latter problem is particularly worrying because it involves obvious equity problems: indeed, the ability actively to corrupt the law-enforcers varies considerably among individuals and groups according to their wealth and political leverage.

Third, one of the most glaring effects of market integration is that it enhances economic, social, and geographical mobility. This produces numerous effects that affect collective action capabilities at the village level. The most important effect, in the context of this study, is that it gradually detaches individuals from their traditional community settings. There are several aspects involved here:

1. People no longer believe that their own future, less that of their children, lies with the natural resources surrounding their native village. Since their traditional

rights and obligations are not tradable on a perfect market, they are led to neglect or overexploit the resource (see above, the last motive mentioned under the first point to explain resource overexploitation by business interests). In game-theoretical terms, the exploitation game in which they play is no more of infinite duration.

2. The frequency of their interactions with other rights-holders over local-level resources diminishes, with the result that the degree of their involvement in community affairs is lower and their information about the resource is reduced. On both counts, their incentives to adopt co-operative behaviour are impaired.

3. By offering alternative opportunities to meet increasingly specialized needs, market integration has the effect of separating the various spheres of economic and social life at the level of the village, the family, or the clan. Hence, it reduces the scope for interlinked long-term relationships and the size of the social units within which informal co-operation mechanisms take place. As a result, the global assurance game which the members of the rural community were playing gradually dissolves to leave room for a series of restricted PD games.

4. The diffusion of urban values and the spreading of formal Western-type education erode traditional patterns of authority and loyalty networks that often play an important role in the enforcement of CPR management schemes. They also tend to instil in the youth negative images of hard manual work and rural-based occupations.

Fourth, market integration causes dramatic shifts in individual preferences through the demonstration of new consumption patterns and modes of living. This profound change creates in people a pressing need for cash, i.e. it modifies their rate of time preference in favour of present consumption. As a result, they may be tempted, whenever possible, to overexploit their resources, to grant exploitation licences, or even to sell out their productive assets in order to obtain the needed liquidities. The pressure of new consumption needs may be actually so strong as to push even poor people to take sale decisions the pros and cons of which are not sufficiently weighed, so that these decisions are likely to be regretted at a later stage. There are several ways through which the pressure of needs drives people to adopt such irrational behaviour: myopia and imperfect knowledge or foresight about their long-term income prospects or the long-term consequences of their present decisions in conditions of rapidly changing ecological and socio-economic environments, or even obedience to social norms prescribing costly consumption patterns aimed at preserving or enhancing social status.

The intrusion of business ventures into the traditional resource domain is therefore not to be ascribed only to collusion between the State and powerful private interests. It may also sometimes result from voluntary sales by customary rights-holders who are possibly inexperienced in the cash economy or, more often, by rapacious chiefs and rural élites who are eager to make easy profits regardless of their responsibilities as traditional trustees of the village commons. In this last regard, market integration (together with national political integration) has a potentially vicious effect in that it vastly increases the power of customary authorities by making available new sources of privilege and wealth that are independent of their traditional, rural-based constituencies. In particular, the emergence of privatizable rights over erstwhile village commons leaves ample room for surreptitiously transforming traditional custodianship prerogatives into tradable exclusive rights.

This last point shows that, even in the absence of mobility, traditional users may be prompted to degrade their local resources. It bears emphasis that resource degradation consequent upon increased market integration need not take the form of depletion of the whole resource. Indeed, market integration may also result in a modification of the resource composition, with some species being replaced by other species which are more commercially profitable but less interesting from an ecological viewpoint. The example which springs to mind is that of forestry since producers who are eager to extract forest products as intensively as possible are likely to fell primary forests and replace them by quick-maturing tree species (such as eucalyptus). Clearly, environmental degradation is to be measured in qualitative as well as in quantitative terms and, once this is done, there may appear to be much more ground for state intervention in order to prevent negative external effects from occurring.

The foregoing conclusions may sound too pessimistic, however. And, to some extent, this impression is true. As a matter of fact, market integration may yield positive effects that are to be weighed against the negative outcomes highlighted above and that may turn out to be decisive in certain circumstances. More notably, by creating new income-earning opportunities unrelated to the exploitation of land and other natural resources, it may help relieve pressure on village-level CPRs, especially if the CPR products do not have a high commercial value. If the latter condition is not satisfied, as we know, there is a risk that, in order to invest their savings in other avenues deemed more attractive, rural dwellers will follow a shut-down path of resource exploitation. Yet, in this case, *provided that there are no externalities*, CPR degradation ought not to be a cause of worry since villagers do not depend any more on them for their subsistence. It may also be borne in mind that, when pressure on local CPRs is made less intense, there is a better chance that traditional users will become fully aware of the threat to their environment and will be able to take effective steps towards countering it before it is too late (see Chapter 10).

Besides relieving pressure on local CPRs, the emergence of alternative economic opportunities which follows increasing market integration may put an end to resource degradation processes. Indeed, remittances from relatives who have found a regular job in urban areas may alleviate subsistence constraints on those who have stayed in the village and enable them to build up their resource to a level where it is optimal to conserve it (the steady-state level). In other words, remittances may allow poor rural dwellers to get out of the vicious trap in which the resource is gradually degraded down to the (shut-down) point where production is no longer possible (see Chapter 1, sect. 4).

Despite the above qualifications, the tone of this chapter remains rather pessimistic. In so far as many writings analyse the conditions of successful village-level CPR regulation in developing countries—the object of our next chapter—outside of the macro-context in which rural communities actually evolve, we thought it important to draw attention to a number of broad-level changes that tend to make this collective regulation more difficult. More precisely, we wanted to emphasize that development of the market logic in the context of a modern nation-State gradually and deeply affects the mode of functioning of these communities at the same time as it alters the world-view and consequently the behaviour of the actors in the countryside. In Chapter 12, we largely abstract from the above changes and attempt to look at the determinants of success or failure of CPR regulation from an empirical perspective grounded in village case-studies. The conclusions that are reached in Chapter 12 will therefore have to be qualified by the considerations put forward in this chapter but the more optimistic view presented in the next chapter should mitigate the more pessimistic tone of the foregoing analysis.

12

Conditions for Successful Collective Action: Insights from Field Experiences

12.1 A General Overview

The previous chapter has highlighted a number of important changing circumstances that tend to make village-based schemes for resource management increasingly difficult. As aptly summarized by Lawry:

> the 'modernisation process' itself has reduced incentives for individuals to participate in localised collective arrangements, has undercut the economic viability of common property institutions, and has reduced the political legitimacy of local management authorities. Population growth and technological change have increased pressures on natural resources to the extent that 'minimum' common property rules do not provide effective regulation. Local institutions, weakened by far-reaching economic and political changes, are unlikely to impose intensive controls, especially where there is little precedent for direct regulation. Local common property management will not emerge simply by giving greater official rein to local action. (Lawry, 1989*b*: 4)

In the same vein, Wade has noted that:

> Indeed, some of the large-scale and long-term changes occurring in the rural areas of developing countries may be lowering the average probability of cooperative solutions. Rapidly rising person/land pressures may increase the dangers of trusting people and increase the number of people to be trusted; migration may reduce 'recurrence and noticeability'; state penetration of rural areas may only undermine old systems of authority without permitting or establishing new ones, resulting in a hiatus of confidence. (Wade, 1988*a*: 216)

This being said, Wade also insists that 'a sweeping pessimism is ill-founded, both empirically and analytically'. According to him, there are sufficient examples of success of locally devised rule systems or resource management schemes 'to negate the necessity of full private property rights or for control by a central authority in order to protect common-pool resources' (Wade, 1988*a*: 199). None the less, there is no denying at the same time that there are also numerous—even 'many more'—examples of failed attempts by villagers to manage local CPRs and of degenerating commons in the absence of state regulation or private property (ibid. 208).

The following accounts offer striking illustrations of failures of group management in the specific cases, first, of an irrigation scheme in Nepal and, second, of a village forestry in Pakistan:

> Water allocation is primarily first come, first served. Thus, farmers at the head . . . tend to get all the water they need, while farmers at the tail often receive inadequate and unreliable amounts

of water. This situation has often led to conflict between head and tail farmers. Sometimes hundreds of farmers from the area near the middle village of Parshai will take spears and large sticks and go together to the head village of Baramajhia to demand that water be released. At Baramajhia farmers are often guarding their water with weapons. If water is released, Parshai farmers have had to maintain armed guards to assure that the . . . canal remains open. (Laitos *et al.*, 1986: 147, cited from Ostrom and Gardner, 1993: 105)

Increasing demand for fuelwood and timber had caused large-scale deforestation in Azad Kashmir over the preceding 30 years . . . Both the formal and customary systems allowed and regulated wood gathering . . . In practice, however, customary user rights have been very liberally interpreted and broadened, while the use-limits set through formal regulations have been transgressed. Within a radius of several miles from many human settlements, virtually all trees were debranched beyond the limits set by sylvicultural recommendations . . . Outright topping has also occurred and prematurely killed the trees. Roadside trees are similarly molested. On community lands, open access practices *in the absence of community management* have fully consumed the tree cover. Forest resources have also been devastated by local livestock that graze without adequate controls. (Cernea, 1989: 10–11)

It is perhaps too simplistic to view the experiences of common-property management in terms of outright failure or success. It is likely that a good number of these experiences are only partially successful. A recent study by Lopez (1992) has precisely attempted to measure the degree of success of common property management practices in the tropical fallow agriculture of Western Ivory Coast. His measurement method is based on a comparison between the amount of land actually left fallow by the villagers on the one hand, and the amount which would be left fallow under an open-access regime or a perfectly regulated common property, on the other hand. Success of collective action for soil conservation is captured by a unique coefficient which measures the relative position of actual practices compared to the above two reference situations. The main conclusion of the author is that communities do exert some control on the utilization of their (communal) land resources, yet the extent of this control is far from being sufficient to ensure their optimal exploitation, implying that, under the current institutional arrangements, the level of land left fallow is substantially lower than the socially optimal level. More precisely, 'the estimates suggest that for reasonable discount rates, the community controls force individual farmers to act "as if" about 20 per cent of the true social shadow price were charged to them as a user fee for the use of land' (Lopez, 1992: 19). The lost benefits resulting from such regulation failure are all the more important as, even in the short run, there are no real output trade-offs when overexploitation of land is reduced via restricted use. Indeed, under some reasonable assumptions, the positive effect of reducing the contemporaneous externality more than offsets the negative direct effect of reducing the cultivated area (ibid. 20).

In view of the mixed results of village-level management of natural resources, it is essential to examine as many field experiences of success and failure as possible with a view to identifying the conditions or circumstances that are more conducive to effective local-level management of CPRs. This is precisely the kind of approach which many researchers have followed since the publication of the well-known

Proceedings of the Conference on Common Property Resource Management under the initiative of the US National Research Council (1986).

In a recent book, Ostrom has offered us a detailed review of a good sample of meaningful experiences where villagers have attempted, successfully or not, to organize collective action related to providing local public goods (Ostrom, 1990). Her explicit aim was to understand the factors that can enhance or detract from the capabilities of individuals so to organize. A similar intent underlies other recent attempts, such as the one made by Schlager (1990) to systematize the findings of quite a number of carefully selected case-studies of fishery management, or those made by Tang (1992), or by Ostrom again (1992) with respect to irrigation systems. At this preliminary stage, it is interesting to cite the factors which condition the success of local-level resource management schemes according to three already quoted authors who have based their conclusions on either a specific case-study or a series of experiences chosen across a wide spectrum of sectors and countries. The latter applies to Ostrom (1990) while the former holds true for Wade (1988*a*)—who relies on his own first-hand study of village-based irrigation and grazing systems in South India—and also for McKean (1986)—who has focused her attention on traditional CPR management systems in Japan.

Ostrom has formulated seven so-called 'design principles' that characterize all the robust CPR institutions which she has analysed, plus an eighth principle used in the larger, more complex cases. By design principle, she means 'an essential element or condition that helps to account for the success of these institutions in sustaining the CPRs and gaining the compliance of generation after generation of appropriators to the rules in use' (Ostrom, 1990: 90). These design principles play an important role because 'they can affect incentives in such a way that appropriators will be willing to commit themselves to conform to operational rules devised in such systems, to monitor each other's conformance, and to replicate the CPR institutions across generational boundaries' (ibid. 91). The author's conviction is that they form a core of necessary conditions for achieving institutional robustness in CPR settings. Table 12.1 summarizes them.

Let us now turn to the contribution of Wade. His basic conclusion is summarized as follows:

> My argument suggests that, as an extreme case, we could *not* expect to find effective rules of restrained access organised by the users themselves when there are many users, when the boundaries of the common-pool resources are unclear, when the users live in groups scattered over a large area, when undiscovered rule-breaking is easy, and so on. In these circumstances a degradation of the commons can confidently be expected, and privatisation or state regulation may be the only options. The further an actual case deviates from this extreme the more likely will the people who face the problem be able to organise a solution. (Wade, 1988*a*: 215)

In a more detailed manner, the likelihood of successful collective action is seen to depend on:

1. *The resources*

The smaller and more clearly defined the boundaries of the common-pool resources the greater the chances of success.

TABLE 12.1. Design principles illustrated by long-enduring CPR institutions

1. Clearly defined boundaries. Individuals or households who have rights to withdraw resource units from the CPR must be clearly defined, as must the boundaries of the CPR itself.
2. Congruence between appropriation and provision rules and local conditions. Appropriation rules restricting time, place, technology, and/or quantity of resource units are related to local conditions and to provision rules requiring labour, material, and/or money.
3. Collective-choice arrangements. Most individuals affected by the operational rules can participate in modifying the operational rules.
4. Monitoring. Monitors, who actively audit CPR conditions and appropriator behaviour, are accountable to the appropriators or are the appropriators.
5. Graduated sanctions. Appropriators who violate operational rules are likely to be assessed graduated sanctions (depending on the seriousness and context of the offence) by other appropriators, by officials accountable to these appropriators, or by both.
6. Conflict-resolution mechanisms. Appropriators and their officials have rapid access to low-cost local arenas to resolve conflicts among appropriators or between appropriators and officials.
7. Minimal recognition of rights to organize. The rights of appropriators to devise their own institutions are not challenged by external governmental authorities.

For CPRs that are parts of larger systems

8. Nested enterprises. Appropriation, provision, monitoring, enforcement, conflict resolution, and governance activities are organized in multiple layers of nested enterprises.

Source: Ostrom (1990: 90).

2. *The technology*

The higher the costs of exclusion technology (such as fencing) the better the chances of success.

3. *Relationship between resources and user group*

(i) Location: the greater the overlap between the location of the common-pool resources and the residence of the users the greater the chances of success.

(ii) Users' demands: the greater the demands (up to a limit) and the more vital the resource for survival the greater the chances of success.

(iii) Users' knowledge: the better their knowledge of sustainable yields the greater the chances of success.

4. *User group*

(i) Size: the smaller the number of users the better the chances of success, down to a minimum below which the tasks able to be performed by such a small group cease to be meaningful (perhaps because, for reasons to do with the nature of the resource, action to mitigate common property problems must be done, if at all, by a larger group).

(ii) Boundaries: the more clearly defined are the boundaries of the group, the better the chances of success.

(iii) Relative power of sub-groups: the more powerful are those who benefit from retaining the commons, and the weaker are those who favour sub-group enclosure or private property, the better the chances of success.

(iv) Existing arrangements for discussion of common problems: the better developed are such arrangements among the users the greater the chances of success.

(v) Extent to which users are bound by mutual obligations: the more concerned people are about their social reputation the better the chances of success.
(vi) Punishments against rule-breaking: the more the users already have joint rules for purposes other than common-pool resource use, and the more bite behind those rules, the better the chances of success.

5. *Noticeability*
Ease of detection of rule-breaking free riders: the more noticeable is cheating on agreements the better the chances of success. Noticeability is a function partly of 1, 3(i), and 4(i).

6. *Relationship between users and the state*
(i) Ability of state to penetrate to rural localities, and state tolerance of locally based authorities: the less the state can, or wishes to, undermine locally based authorities, and the less the state can enforce private property rights effectively, the better the chances of success. (ibid. 215–16; see also Wade, 1987: 231–2)

Although they are presented in a more discursive way, McKean's conclusions are especially worth quoting in view not only of the great precision and subtlety of her analysis but also of the importance of the Japanese historical experience with respect to village-based resource management. From her study, several factors come out as crucial determinants of the success achieved by Japanese villages in management of local-level CPRs. First, 'their small size, their very strong community identity and a sense of mutual interdependence that was reinforced by a formal structure of collective responsibility . . . almost certainly enhanced their ability to make *any* regulatory scheme work, even a very badly designed one' (McKean, 1986: 567). Second, Japanese villagers were acutely aware of the risk of resource overuse as well as of the relationship between use behaviour and the state of the resource: for instance, they 'knew how much forest they had to leave intact to produce the fertilizer they needed for their cultivated plots' (ibid. 568).

A third essential condition for success is that the rules laid down by the village community were clear and simple so as to be easily understood by the people concerned. 'Every time I asked about the reason for a particular rule', writes McKean, 'my informants gave a sophisticated and sensible explanation in terms of the environmental protection and fair treatment of all the villagers'. In addition, 'even if the village elders were the prime repositories of accumulated scientific knowledge, this information circulated regularly through the village' (McKean, 1986: 563). As hinted at above, rules were also fair enough to carry legitimacy:

Japanese villagers were deeply concerned with some notion of fairness . . . Fairness was not synonymous with equality in material possessions . . . But there was an overriding sense that access to the commons should be distributed according to some principle of fairness that ignored existing maldistributions in private wealth. Hence the frequent use of random distributions, assignment to parcels or products of the commons by lottery, frequent rotations to move the good and the bad around, and scrupulous attention to bookkeeping to keep track of contributions and exchanges and offsetting aid offered by one household to another. Such methods provided assurance to each co-owner that the sacrifices and gains of other co-owners would be similar, and offered the additional advantage of removing the competitive impulse (which is very dangerous when it becomes a race to see who can deplete the commons first) and thus relieving pressure on the commons . . . Nor did this notion of fairness mean that entitlement was automatic for all comers . . .; a household had to earn its eligibility through some period of established residence in the village, and casual drifters were ignored. (McKean, 1986: 568–9)

Moreover, rules were flexible so as to allow adjustment to changing circumstances. Thus, 'when villagers felt that the rules were too lax, or when they began to fear the environmental consequences of too many violations, they modified their management techniques in the direction of still greater caution in order to save the commons' (McKean, 1986: 566, see also 568).

Finally, the Japanese experience demonstrates that *rules are not self-enforcing*. This is because, although Japanese villagers 'internalised the preservation of the commons as a vital goal' and had a long tradition of co-operative organization, they were 'vulnerable to temptations to bend, evade, and violate the rules governing the commons' (McKean, 1986: 569). A fourth factor underlying successful CPR management in Japan is therefore that there existed effective schemes of penalties aimed directly at controlling free riding. There are apparently at least three conditions that must be fulfilled for a punishment system to be effective: (1) sanctions must be escalating (Japanese villages had 'an escalating scale of penalties'); (2) they must be flexible enough to allow for exceptional circumstances; and (3) special devices must be built into the system to watch the watchers (ibid. 564–70).

In conclusion, McKean notes,

the [Japanese] villagers themselves invented the regulations, enforced them, and meted out punishments, indicating that it is not necessary for regulation of the commons to be imposed coercively or from the outside. This, along with the fact that villagers could change their own rules through a process of consultation and consensus that was democratic in form if not always in fact, almost certainly increased the legitimacy of the regulations. Although the Tokugawa social order was very oppressive toward individuals whom it classified as 'deviant', the village itself was largely self-regulating in this regard, and did not require intervention by an autocratic state to protect the commons. (ibid. 571)

As is evident from the above excerpts as well as from the conclusions reached by many other authors, there is wide consensus on the fact that local management of CPRs may only work adequately under a limited range of conditions. There is also wide agreement on the nature of a large number of such conditions. Thus, for example, most authors emphasize that user groups must be small, live close to the CPRs, and be free to set access and management rules in their own way; the CPRs must be clearly defined and people must have a high level of dependence on them; rules as well techniques of calculation and control must be simple and fair; there must be well-established schemes of punishment and these work best when they are graduated to fit the offence; costs of monitoring must not be too high; well-known and low-cost conflict-resolution mechanisms must be available; crucial decisions must be taken publicly; and some record-keeping and accountability must be provided for.

Beyond this apparently massive consensus there are however a number of important 'shadow zones' either because authors may not all agree on the exact meaning to be attached to the foregoing propositions or concepts, or because they (implicitly or explicitly) diverge on some of the conditions under which local management of CPRs is likely to have a reasonable degree of success. Furthermore, there are certain crucial issues which are left unresolved or are inadequately dealt with in the existing literature. The subsequent sections are devoted to highlighting these 'shadow zones' and discussing some of the problems involved. Also, a special effort is made in the course of the discussion to relate crucial empirical findings or observations to theoretical insights developed at length in Part I.

12.2 The Problem of Economic Incentives

The role of external financial assistance

We have already strongly emphasized that, for corporate management of CPRs to be effective, an essential prerequisite is that resource users correctly perceive the potential benefits of collective action, which requires that they are well informed not only about the state of the resource but also about the possible impact of use behaviour on its stock (see above, Chapter 10). When this is not the case—bear in mind that deforestation or overexploitation of fish stocks by local users can be a slow and largely unnoticed process with the result that realization of the damage done may come too late—ignorance and not material incentives is the real culprit for degradation of the resource.

As hinted at in Part I, another important reason which may account for collective action failure irrespective of any free rider problem is high discount rates of future incomes by people subject to the pressure of survival constraints or other needs. (Remember that this argument is valid only if markets for credit and for use rights over the resource are highly imperfect or absent.) A clear illustration of this phenomenon is provided in Jodha's study of India's dry regions. As a matter of fact, the critical importance of CPR resources for the poor is reflected in the fact that, since these resources were privatized, they have been exploited with increased intensity compared to the pre-privatization period. More specifically, CPRs in these areas typically consist of submarginal lands that can be sustained only under low-intensity uses (e.g. natural vegetation as against annual cropping). However, in most cases, these submarginal or fragile lands have been shifted to crops following privatization with the result that not only their sustainability is jeopardized but also their ecological function in the total dryland system is undermined (Jodha, 1992: 62–3).

The observation is often made that rural inhabitants need special economic incentives to protect the environment. These incentives must be designed in such a way as to compensate resource users for temporary losses of income by providing them new sources of regular employment and income. The central role of economic incentives has been especially stressed in the literature dealing with community forest management. Thus, for instance, in her study of the Honduran resin tappers, Stanley has emphasized that 'income generation from the forests serves as a crucial incentive to mobilise community protection of the environment' (Stanley, 1991: 768). With respect to reafforestation programmes in Haiti, Murray noted in the same vein that 'ecological protection and restoration will occur only as secondary effects to activities which generate income' (Murray, 1986: 200, cited from Stanley, 1991: 769).

Precisely the same theme recurs throughout a World Bank report on the role of social forestry in sustainable development. Here, the authors repeatedly argue for a comprehensive approach that integrates conservation and production objectives: people seldom accept environmental or conservation measures that are not accompanied by income-maintaining or enhancing strategies. In the words of the authors, 'earning income is one of the stronger incentives in eliciting widespread local participation in social forestry activity', as attested by project experiences in as diverse countries as Haiti, India, Indonesia, Kenya, the Philippines, the Republic of Korea, and many others (Gregersen *et al.*, 1989: 142; see also Cernea, 1989: 30; World Bank, 1992: 141–2; Freudenberger and Mathieu, 1993: 20; Utting, 1994: 240–3). The approach used in an Indonesian programme is particularly interesting: it provides hill farmers with grants to compensate them for the loss of production during the initial improvement activities of soil conservation, tree-planting, and fodder establishment. In this way, we are told, 'family incomes are not reduced during the crucial period of introducing changes in land use'. Embodied in this practice is 'the judgment that the initial grants paid to the farmers are not subsidies, but rather payments for the offsite or downstream benefits that will arise as a consequence of the improvement work on upland farms' (Gregersen *et al.*, 1989: 27–8).

In West Bengal, to take another example, there has been an interesting experience with group-farm forestry schemes targeted on landless people. Under such schemes, marginal public land is leased on a long-term basis by the government to clusters of landless people with a view to enabling them to grow trees. If the ownership of the trees and the responsibility for their maintenance as well as for the use of the products are vested in the individual leaseholders, collective action is expected to take place for the planting and the protection (such as taking turns in watching activities) of the trees. Now, and this is what interests us here, since the target group is made of landless who are highly dependent on the immediate income from their labour for their daily subsistence, the scheme has provided for labour payments to help meet consumption requirements of the families during the early stages of the plantation (Cernea, 1989: 57). Furthermore:

> The area allotted and the number of trees to be planted guarantee enough wood from lops, tops, dead trees, and branches to meet a substantial part of a family's domestic requirements. The stem volume is then available for sale, and the total output ensures participant interest. The group strategy thus not only maximises land use for forestry but also provides the users with fuel or construction materials, as well as with cash income. These plantations generated good revenues which some families invested in purchasing land, planting potatoes, and other such gains. Overall, some 20,000 ha. have been successfully planted under group farm forestry arrangements in West Bengal during the last six-seven years. (Cernea, 1989: 57–8).

Success of such group-farm forestry schemes is testified by the experience of a programme implemented around Nagina village (in Arabari forest range). There, indeed, participant families which are mainly landless scheduled caste and aborigine families which have traditionally drawn their livelihood from forest and farm labour, were granted ownership rights over low-quality land (known as *patta* land) unsuitable for agricultural production. The aim of the farm forestry programme (started in 1981) was to motivate clusters of farm families to plant trees on a contiguous plant of 20 ha. or more land in the laterite areas where these *patta* lands are located. The Forest Department provided free seedlings, and one dose each of fertilizer and pesticides. Moreover, *in the initial years*, it also offered incentives in the form of small grants of cash money for each surviving plant at the end of the first and second years (with a higher rate for plants remaining after two years). However, 'digging of pits, planting, fertiliser application, replacement of dead trees, etc. were the responsibility of participating families and no remuneration was paid for these tasks' (Shah, 1988: 4–5).

More important subsidies were not required to make the programme work because the real cost to the participant families of establishing the plantation was very low: the land planted with trees had no alternative use; pits were dug in summer months when farmwork was difficult to come by; and protection did not pose much of a problem. In better-endowed areas like in the alluvial tracts of West Bengal, 'farm forestry did not—and is unlikely to—make as much progress as in the laterite districts, if only because land as well as labour have considerable opportunity costs there' (Shah, 1988: 6).

The reforestation experiment known as the Arabari experiment is one of the most successful stories in village-based CPR management. It started as early as in 1970 in the Midnapore district (West Bengal) and, in many ways, it can be considered as a pioneer attempt which inspired many subsequent reafforestation projects. The idea was to stop forest depletion 'by providing villagers with an amount of employment in forest protection-cum-replanting work which in monetary terms would be equivalent to what villagers earned by sale of stolen forest products' (Cernea, 1989: 58–9). Several features of this project are worth emphasizing, most of which point to the crucial importance of establishing the right incentives and making sure that the people concerned have well understood that they are to be the primary beneficiaries of the project. First, not only has employment been created in the planting of trees but employment creation has been spread and phased over the year so as to provide regular incomes to the inhabitants of the eleven villages involved in the experiment. Second, supply of fuelwood to them has been ensured at a nominal, low price. Third, a revenue-sharing arrangement has been put into use under which the Forest Department pays the villagers 25 per cent of the selling price of the mature trees in cash. Fourth, the responsibility for the protection of plantations has been entrusted to villagers with minimum official interference.[1] Fifth, an intensive communication effort has been made to explain the incentives and the experiment rationale to the villagers. Sixth, institutional arrangements have been provided to the effect that

[1] In fact, it has become a common feature of the new Joint Forest Management Policy adopted by many Indian states (Orissa, West Bengal, Bihar, Gujarat, Haryana, Jammu and Kashmir, Andhra Pradesh, Maharashtra, Rajasthan, and Tripura) that economic benefits under the form of grasses, lops and tops of branches and minor forest produce, as well as a portion of the proceeds from the sale of trees are provided to villagers who get organized specifically for forest protection and regeneration (Arora, 1994: 692).

rotating representatives are elected to monitor work attendance and to collect/distribute payments. According to Cernea, the results achieved in this set-up are impressive:

the villagers enforced total protection of the forest, primarily by desisting from making illegal cuttings, while their employment in replanting generated revenue for them and for the project as well. The self-imposed and self-enforced reduction in firewood cutting and the watching and patrolling by villagers acted as a 'social fencing' around the state forest. The tensions between the villagers and the Forest Department eased. The upshot of this successful experiment was that the once degraded forests were rehabilitated spectacularly within 3–5 years and have continued to grow since. Moreover, other villages joined and the experiment soon expanded from 11 to 16 villages, covering 1506 ha. by 1978; some of the newly included blank areas were planted with cashew nuts, which in a few years provided a cash crop sold on the open market, with part of the sale proceeds going to the villagers.

Recent (1989) assessment confirmed not only the sustainability of the initial Arabari model but also its rapid spread in the mid and late 1980s to many more areas. While the experiment started without formal group formation in each of the small villages involved, the subsequent follow up took on stronger characteristics of group creation, with the establishment of Village Protection Committees . . . some 700–800 such groups were formed in the southwest zone of West Bengal, protecting over 70,000 ha. of degraded/replanted forests: . . . The will to do so developed as these groups believed in the assurance of sustained benefits. (Cernea, 1989: 60–1)

To shift attention to another continent, mention may be made of the USAID-funded project of management of the Guesselbodi forest reserve, Niger. This 5,000-ha. forest was extremely degraded and overgrazed when the project began there in 1981. A management plan was put in place in September 1983 which combines promotion of ecological objectives with generation of economic benefits for the local population through marketing of fuelwood in Niamey (Lawry, 1989*a*: 6–7). When, on the contrary, there is no provisioning of tangible, compensatory benefits, users remain the agents of vicious cumulative processes of resource degradation. Thus, how tempting it is to deplete nearby forests rather than cultivate trees for fuelwood, animal fodder, anti-erosion, and other purposes? In Malawi, for example, the returns to labour invested in gathering fuelwood have been estimated to be fifteen times higher than the returns to labour invested in growing fuelwood and over five times higher than to labour invested in growing trees for poles (Cernea, 1989: 51).

In India, when special economic incentives are not provided, the rural poor tend to adopt measures manifesting a high degree of desperation: premature harvesting of CPR products (such as the catching of immature fish), increased frequency and unseasonal lopping of trees, removal of plant/bush roots, overcrowding of CPR areas, and the use of hitherto unusable or inferior products that are possibly health-damaging (Jodha, 1992: 46–8). In Azad Kashmir (Pakistan), under the impact of several factors analysed in the previous chapter, customary rules governing the use of local forest resources have become more and more liberally interpreted and broadened with disastrous ecological consequences:

Within a radius of several miles from many human settlements, virtually all trees were debranched . . . In many locations only the top 10 to 20 per cent of the crown of trees remains. Outright topping has also occurred and prematurely killed the trees. In the Chir pine areas, long thin vertical slices of the bole of the tree are removed at stump level for home lighting. Roadside trees are similarly molested. On community lands, open access practices in the absence of community management have fully consumed the tree cover. (Cernea, 1989: 11).

It is sometimes believed that, to be effective, subsidies to users confronted by subsistence constraints in conditions of highly imperfect credit markets should be sufficient to cover not only the direct cost entailed by the conservation strategy (tree-planting, for instance) but also the opportunity costs of the production factors (mostly land and labour) used towards that purpose. Subsidies need not be so large, however. As can be argued on the basis of a dynamic analysis of the conservation problem proposed by Pagiola (1993) and summarized in Chapter 1 (sect. 4), what poor CPR users require is an assistance that allows them to overcome their inability to bear the cost of profitable conservation investments (whether under the form of temporary restraint in using the resource or of investment in resource-preserving infrastructure). In other words, this category of users is caught in a vicious circle because it must meet its subsistence needs *in every period* in circumstances where the existing level of the available resource is too low to yield a sufficient flow of extractable produce without being gradually but inexorably degraded. The external help must therefore be calculated in such a way as to enable them to build up the resource to a level compatible with a conservation strategy in the long run (that is, the steady-state level).

Clearly, the amount of assistance needed will depend on the biophysical characteristics of the resource and, more particularly, on its level of productivity at the beginning of the incentive scheme. It is a priori possible that users require only a small trigger in order to move from a shut-down to a conservation path. At the other extreme, as pointed out in Chapter 1, the possibility also exists that biophysical conditions are initially so bad and/or conservation practices so ineffective that no conservation strategy is going to be profitable in the long run: production will never be sustainable, whatever the conservation efforts undertaken. In this case, there is no other solution than creating alternative income-earning opportunities for the rural poor and, if the natural resources on which their subsistence presently depends have a value for the society, the sooner these new opportunities are created, the better it is (since the resources may be completely degraded if they come too late). Yet, if conservation is a feasible strategy, it bears emphasis that a policy of assistance to poor CPR users is likely to be all the more effective as they have in general great incentives to seek to conserve their resource base precisely because they have limited alternative income sources (see Chapter 1).

Now, to the extent that villagers have high alternative income opportunities, their incentive to follow a shut-down path of resource exploitation is great and the amount of the incentives required to make them shift to a conservation path may be much higher than in the case of poor users. In this respect, bear in mind the above-noted difference between the degree of success of farm forestry schemes between laterite and better-endowed districts in northern India. In Chapter 11, we made the point that there is no reason to feel concerned about people degrading local natural resources when they have available to them better income opportunities and when the resources do not yield external effects. If the latter condition is not satisfied, concern is of course fully justified and an active policy may have to be pursued with a view to inducing resource users to adopt a conservation strategy. This will require the amount of the subsidy to be equal to the difference between the best alternative income and the income that can be derived from the resource when it is conserved in the long run. Or, the State could buy the resource from its customary owners, an alternative that is likely to be less costly than the above policy which implies continuous subsidizing. In the same logic, if the objective is improved management of resources which have important ecological functions yet are of low commercial value, and if this objective conflicts with use of resources which are of high commercial value but generate negative externalities (for instance, when wildlife and forest resources compete with land for agricultural and pastoral use), it is important that the subsidies granted cover the opportunity costs of land and labour (Lawry, 1989*b*: 17–18).[2]

A last remark concerns the attitude of the rural rich and their consequences for the poor's access to customary CPRs. The former people tend to alleviate the problems of the latter inasmuch as they stop using CPR products which they consider as inferior goods. In the dry tropical parts of India, for example, rich villagers resort to their own supplies of biomass or substitute non-renewable and/or external products for renewable CPR products (e.g. stone fencing for thorn fencing, rubber tyres for wooden tyres for bullock carts, iron tools for locally made wooden ones). Unfortunately, this is only one side of the coin. As a matter of fact, the behaviour of the rich may also worsen the predicament of the poor: this clearly happens when they try to grab CPR lands, to prevent others from using their private land during off-season, or to enrich their own soil by mining silt and topsoil from CPR lands and bring it on private fields. In addition, their attitude is indirectly detrimental to the poor's interests if, as an élite, they show indifference to CPR degradation and avoid committing their authority and mobilization ability to CPR rehabilitation (Jodha, 1992: 46–7). Similar evidence exists for other areas, such as the coastal Niayes of Senegal, where 'the uplands once used as reserves for field crop cultivation as well as pastures for village livestock have been sold by the village elders to well-off "Sunday farmers" who wall off the plots and plant fruit orchards and gardens' (Freudenberger and Mathieu, 1993: 16).

To summarize, even assuming that they are aware of the ongoing processes of resource depletion and of the extent of damage done, rural dwellers are likely to be reluctant to participate in local conservation efforts if they do not receive external assistance to tide over the critical period during which they must build up their resource to the steady-state level where it can be optimally maintained (if this level actually exists). This conclusion makes sense of Jodha's finding that higher productivity and yields of CPRs play an important role in inducing better CPR management or, conversely, people show little interest in protecting local CPRs if incomes derivable from them are negligible. It also tallies with our finding in Chapter 10 that rural communities tend to resist CPR management if depletion is so advanced that there is an acute shortage of CPR produce needed for bare survival.

[2] e.g. villagers could be given hunting-rights or a percentage of the revenues generated by state leases of hunting concession rights (Lawry, 1989*b*: 17–18).

Such findings suggest the possibility of two distinct situations, one virtuous and the other vicious. The first situation corresponds to a steady-state equilibrium in which a resource stock is constant in the long run while it produces every year the highest income that users can hope for. The second situation is unstable since the resource is inexorably degraded under the pressure of continuous extraction efforts. Note that these efforts may come not only from poor people facing hard subsistence constraints but also from rich people who have available to them attractive alternative income opportunities. Since conservation is not ensured, the productivity of the resource is reduced every year and the shut-down point is gradually approached. Regarding poor CPR users, Jodha is therefore right in pointing out that an external intervention is needed in order to restore or augment the productivity of village-level natural resources when these are seriously degraded (e.g. through new technologies susceptible to enhancing regeneration, increasing the flow of biomass, and improving the physical status of CPRs) so that these users can be motivated again to use them in a sustainable manner (Jodha, 1992: 53, 68).

An intriguing question

One trivial implication which can be drawn from the above analysis is that villagers may well let their CPRs degrade to such a point that it is no more possible to conserve them in the long run without the support of external assistance. It is noteworthy that this observation is hardly compatible with the 'induced institutional innovation' hypothesis or with the central thesis defended by Wade in his book *Village Republics* (see also our discussion of McKean's study of CPR management in Japanese villages in Chapter 10).

In this book, Wade indeed contends that 'villagers will deliberately concert their actions only to achieve intensely felt needs which could not be met by individual responses' (Wade, 1988*a*: 211). On the basis of the evidence from his sample of irrigated and dry villages in South India, he draws the conclusion that deliberately concerted action 'arises only when the net material benefits to be provided to all or most cultivators are high—when without it all or most cultivators would face continual collision and substantial risk of crop loss'. More precisely, 'where risks associated with irrigation and common grazing are high cultivators will straightforwardly come together to follow corporate arrangements designed to reduce those risks' (ibid. 186–8). Thus, in villages where the risks of both grazing and irrigation are high—that is, in villages fed from near the tail-end of an irrigation channel more than several miles long, with fine, water-retentive soils—one tends to find a corporate response in the form of local organizations geared towards ensuring the reliability and adequacy of water supply. In dry villages with fine, water-retentive soils, there are high grazing risks, which tend to generate only an intermediate level of corporate organization. Finally, in top-end irrigated villages, the risks of both irrigation and grazing are relatively low, and the level of corporate organization tends to be less than that of many dry villages (ibid. 185; see also Wade, 1986*a*, 1986*b*, 1987).

The basic idea of Wade is that it is *prima-facie* silly to think, as in the conventional picture of Hardin's tragedy of the commons, that people facing congestion or depletion of their CPRs will do nothing to alleviate it for themselves (Wade, 1988*a*: 208). On the other hand, Wade can certainly not be accused of ignoring or even downplaying moral hazard problems commonly associated with collective action. As he puts it, 'the concerting of action is itself something in need of explanation even once the incentives or "needs of capital" have been identified'. In other words, it is not because all or most villagers could benefit from joint action that such action will necessarily be forthcoming (ibid. 188). This being said, and even though precise propositions to that effect are nowhere to be found, Wade's work on irrigation and grazing groups in South India leaves one with the strong impression that moral hazard and other collective organization problems get eventually solved whenever corporate forms of action are badly needed to solve survival problems.[3]

This last kind of statement is encountered in other works as well. Thus, for instance, Lawry points out that 'economic incentives are often insufficient to stimulate individuals to participate in or sanction local-level resource management' and this tends to happen when the resource is of minor importance in relation to other sources of income, when substitutes exist, etc. (Lawry, 1989*b*: 6). Not surprisingly, Lawry reaches the same conclusion as Wade that 'collective action is more likely to result where the common resource is critical to local incomes and is scarce', and when its privatization appears to be unfeasible or too costly (ibid. 7–9).

Since there is so much contradictory evidence, an interesting question is why in some cases (such as those studied by Wade) common property management is developed while in some others privatization or degradation occurs. What is worth emphasizing is that Wade pays a good deal of attention to the case of (surface) irrigation water, a CPR the regulation of which does not require present-day sacrifices to secure future incomes. Indeed, irrigation typically raises an allocation, not a conservation problem (that is, a problem in which absence of restraint harms the interests of other users but not one's own and others' interests in the future) and, as argued in Chapter 10, rural communities are much more successful in solving allocation than conservation problems. Equally important is another feature of the case, namely that there is no technically feasible alternative to co-ordination, at least in the short or medium run. Furthermore, the canal irrigation system has well-defined boundaries, is highly visible and the social group of users has clear spatial boundaries, is relatively small in size, and resides in the middle of the resources it exploits. Finally, most members share the same perception of risk of congestion and wish to use the resource in basically the same way (Wade, 1988*a*: 189).

It is true that Wade also bases his conclusion on his observations regarding regulation of common village pastures, a CPR which raises both conservation and allocation problems. This is a more intriguing finding since, in other countries like Rwanda,

[3] If he did not believe so, he could not have written e.g. that 'the *main* factor explaining the presence or absence of collective organization in these villages is the net collective benefit of that action' (Wade, 1988*a*: 206, emphasis added). Nor could he have made this strange statement: 'It is more likely that Hardin's relentless logic will operate where the resource is not vital than where it is. *Where survival is at stake, the rational individual will exercise restraint at some point*' (Wade, 1988*a*: 205, emphasis added).

pressure on land has led to the opposite outcome: full privatization of communal pastures. A plausible explanation of this divergence is to do with factors that will draw our attention at a later stage in this chapter. Just note here that the absolute need to act collectively for regulating irrigation in South India may have yielded positive external effects for other sectors where joint use is only one among several possibilities: once a community has acquired some experience of co-operation in one sector, it is easier for her to develop it in other sectors as well. This argument cannot be applied to Rwanda which has very different topographical conditions and opportunities for joint action: farms tend to be highly scattered over hilly areas and farmers are consequently used to rely largely on their own efforts. The same actually holds true for many rural settings in other parts of the world, too: in Central America, for instance, highly dispersed settlement patterns exist and there is little social cohesion outside of the family unit (Utting, 1994: 256).

It is worth noting that Wade has actually reckoned quite explicitly with the possibility that villagers confronting crisis conditions tend to indulge in opportunistic behaviour: they can show no concern for their future incomes and ignore the effects of their own behaviour on their social reputation in the local community. According to him, indeed, the main exception to the argument that rational individuals can (subject to some conditions) voluntarily comply with rules of restrained access occurs when some people in the community become desperate. As a matter of fact, 'they may then contemplate short-run strategies which they would not contemplate in normal times' and transform themselves into cheaters (Wade, 1988*a*: 204). Wade has come across such a case in his study of Kottapalle village. Yet no disruption took place because the organization was already firmly established and could adapt itself to the crisis situation by tightening the rules and increasing the fines to a significant extent. What needs to be underlined, however, is that the crisis was essentially of a temporary nature since it was caused by a shortage of surface water resulting from erratic climatic factors.

Our central point is precisely that, under the *continuous* (and not passing) pressure of crisis conditions, collective action may be prevented from arising or from being sustained when anarchistic solutions are available and sacrifices have to be incurred today in order to preserve future incomes.

12.3 The Twin Issues of Group Size and Homogeneity

Small is beautiful

One of the conditions for successful collective action most tirelessly and unanimously emphasized in the empirical literature is that user groups must have a small size. In Chapters 4, 5, and 6, we have offered strong theoretical reasons why small size may be such an important determinant of co-operative success and these reasons are strikingly similar to those advanced by social scientists. When groups are small, members tend to have frequent and highly personalized relationships and they have therefore a strong incentive to consider the more indirect and long-term consequences of their choices instead of paying exclusive attention to immediate costs and benefits. Moreover, the close, face-to-face nature of these relationships guarantees that people are well informed about each other's actions and preferences. Identity feelings are also likely to be strong with the result that emotions easily come into play to sustain co-operative behaviour. This effect, however, may not be as decisive as is too often implied. As a matter of fact, personal antagonisms and rivalries are also very much pervasive in village life, and they are probably less disruptive when diluted over a large group than when concentrated in a small one. Lastly, a point on which economic theory has laid much emphasis is that the smaller the group, the less diluted are the incentives to behave in a socially efficient way since the externality is correspondingly reduced.

The important question to ask is how small is small supposed to be. An opinion that is frequently encountered is that user groups ought to have a size much smaller than that of a village community. For example, in attempting to understand the causes of widespread failure with village woodlots experiments, an already-cited report has laid stress on the fact that 'the community was not effective as a social unit in tree-growing programs', except in China and the Republic of Korea where community forestry has been supported authoritatively by the government (Gregersen *et al.*, 1989: 133; Cernea, 1989: 33, 62). A similar conclusion is reached by Wilson and Thompson in their account of the breakdown in *ejido* productivity on extensive, livestock-herding areas in Mexico. According to them, indeed, pastoral management at community level (the level of the *ejido*) has proved a failure, presumably owing to the excessive size of the groups concerned. In a revealing manner, indeed, this failure of group management has led in a significant number of cases to the formation of grazing coalitions within smaller groups 'where cooperation is assured and benefits are enjoyed under very severe ecological conditions' (Wilson and Thompson, 1993: 300). The most effective of these (smaller) grazing associations are based upon the extended family. They practise intensive grazing management with short grazing periods and hoof action contributing to a more sustainable and productive range resource. Outside these short periods, multiple families combine their livestock into one large herd (200–600 animals) and move the entire grazing operation to range camps situated in remote areas less subject to population pressure (ibid. 310–12).

In the field of irrigation, to take yet another example, empirical evidence tends to show that successful irrigation systems usually operate in relatively small communities (Tang, 1992). Some sociologists consider that water-users' associations should correspond to hydrologically defined outlet units such as blocks of field neighbours under canal irrigation. Coward thus writes that 'for purposes of irrigation organization the critical unit is the "irrigation community", composed of field neighbours, and not the village community, composed of residential neighbours' (Coward, 1980: 208, quoted from Wade, 1988*a*: 214). There is a good ground, therefore, for subdividing an irrigation system into relatively separable units so that the actual number of farmers whose actions directly affect one another is kept quite small and it is relatively easy for each farmer to monitor other farmers (Weissing and Ostrom, 1991: 244–5). Wade has expressed strong dissent with this view arguing that in the villages he studied in Andra Pradesh the only corporate water organization is based on the village rather than the outlet, and the effectiveness of this pattern of collective action has been amply demonstrated by experience. Why it is so is explained by him in terms of features of social organization and in terms of economies of organizational scale achieved by combining water and grazing (Wade, 1988*a*: 213–14). Essentially, Wade's position—to which we shall soon revert—is that existing social ties and authority structure assume greater importance than strictly ecologically defined parameters in determining the optimal size of user groups (in this case, irrigation groups).

Other examples confirm Wade's intuition that small size is not a necessary condition of success in collective action. Thus, in Panama, the *Kuna* Indians have succeeded in systematically administering their own natural resources on a large scale, and this success included the setting up, during the early 1980s, of a wildland park and botanical sanctuary in an area covering 600 sq. km. (Utting, 1994: 251–2). The strong authority structure underlying this Indian society and the sharing of common norms by all its members probably go a long way towards explaining their remarkable performance. Another interesting illustration comes from the Gambian German Forestry Project (GGFP) in the Foni Brefet district. There, indeed, we are told that village leaders refused to divide a forest customarily shared among several villages on the ground that a clear delineation of the forest space could easily ignite intervillage conflicts. As a result of this opposition, it was decided to create a multivillage association that would 'enforce measures to exclude nonresident woodcutters from the use of the entire forest and to set up mechanisms to encourage controlled commercial woodcutting by resident villagers' (Freudenberger and Mathieu, 1993: 17). In this case, a tradition of good neighbourliness and, presumably, the need to unite against a common outside threat (represented by commercial woodcutters) have helped foster co-operation within a large group. The last point can also be derived from the experience of the Sehlabathebe Grazing Association in Lesotho. Indeed, if this large association covering eleven villages has been quite successful in enforcing exclusive use by local residents of pasture lands over which they have been granted exclusive grazing rights by the State, it has been far less effective in enforcing internal management rules among these local rightholders (Swallow and Bromley, 1994*b*: 7, 18). The lesson from these examples seems to be that there is some sense in saying that large groups are made more like small groups when their members share common norms possibly enforced by a well-recognized authority, or when they are confronted by a common challenge arising from without and they need to protect themselves against outsider encroachments. Note that the proposition according to which users are much more prone to take action to enforce a CPR boundary against outsiders than to enforce rules among themselves has been a central conclusion from Chapter 10. Clearly, as explained below, this discussion raises the issue of group homogeneity.

What bears emphasis, indeed, is that proponents of the view that small groups are more likely to be successful in collective actions do not base their argument entirely on considerations related to the closeness and frequency of relationships among members of such groups nor on the problem of incentive dilution with large groups. Another justification they often resort to is that small groups are more homogeneous than large groups. For example, the basic reason why Gregersen *et al.* think the village community is an ineffective social unit for tree-growing programmes is that, in their own words, 'the interests of community members often differ to such an extent that unified action is impossible'. The most important source of failure with the community approach to resource management lies in the large size and internal stratification of communities as social units. A small group is likely to be less diverse and less subject to internal strife (see, however, the aforementioned proviso regarding this effect); it is also better able to enforce rules about equal contributions by its members through peer pressures. Therefore, as in the case of a water-user association formed around a small branch of an irrigation system, a small group may succeed in operating a woodlot without the conflicts that surround community woodlots (Gregersen *et al.*, 1989: 133, 135). A similar position is adopted by Lawry: 'where interests are heterogeneous and views toward appropriate resource-use standards vary, sufficiently strong support for enforcement of many kinds of rules will not emerge' (Lawry, 1989*b*: 7).

A few empirical studies have tried to test systematically the relationship between group homogeneity and success in collective action. In an aforementioned research about the determinants of effective CPR management in the dry regions of India, Jodha notes that the decline of CPR areas is less in villages with lower socio-economic differentiation, that is, in villages where access and benefits from CPRs are relatively equitable (Jodha, 1992: 41). Most authors concerned with village-level collective action for CPR management actually reach similar conclusions. This is especially so with field studies concerned with local water management and conflict resolution in water use. Thus, from a study of twenty-three community irrigation systems in different countries, Tang has reached the conclusion that a high degree of rule conformance and good maintenance tend to be associated with a low variance of the average annual family income among irrigators (Tang, 1991, 1992). That co-operation to form water-user organizations is easier to come by when the group involved is relatively egalitarian (as measured, for example, by the variation in farm size among the member farmers) is also evident from empirical studies conducted in the Indian states of Gujarat and Tamil Nadu (Jayaraman, 1981; Easter and Palanisami, 1986).

Unfortunately, the oft-heard argument about the comparative effectiveness of (small) homogeneous groups is not tight enough to be fully satisfactory.[4] Too often, heterogeneity is blamed as a matter of principle without enough effort being devoted to spelling out the precise conditions under which it undermines collective action. In

[4] The discussion about the virtues of small homogeneous groups is often conducted as though the problem of heterogeneity could be avoided. That this needs not be so is attested by the following example. Watershed rehabilitation and management unmistakably call for group action: rehabilitation of deforested watersheds demands much more than massive planting of trees; it involves flood control and soil-conservation measures requiring the building of bench terraces, the levelling and refilling of soils, etc. The point is often made that it is the people inhabiting a given watershed landscape and who have adjusted their activities to it over long periods of time who should form the social unit suitable for meeting this challenge. Yet, the fact has also to be reckoned that 'a single watershed may contain a broad diversity of tenurial arrangements, stratified social groups, and various farming systems and land use patterns, evolved as forms of adaptation to the various physical segments of the watershed' (Cernea, 1989: 67). Moreover, watershed rehabilitation and management may require changes in the land-use rights, in the rules of land transmittal, in settlement patterns and the number of inhabitants (ibid.: 67–8). To succeed, collective action by groups that are not really small nor homogeneous in all respects is therefore necessary.

the following, we make an attempt to clarify the issue by considering various possible sources of heterogeneity in a group and the way they can possibly bear upon collective action capabilities. This will enable us to show that, contrary to what the above view implies, but in accordance to some of our theoretical findings in Chapter 5, there is no *systematic* link between group homogeneity and success in collective action.

Heterogeneity is not necessarily bad

There are three main sources of heterogeneity which bear upon the capability or the motivation of resource users to participate in collective action. First, heterogeneity may result from ethnic, race, or other kinds of cultural divisions. Second, it may arise from differences in the *nature* of the interests various individuals may have in a particular collective action. Third, it may originate in inter-individual variations in some critical endowments, that are reflected in varying *intensities* of interest. While the first two causes of heterogeneity are a strong impediment (especially the second one) to collective action, the same cannot be said of the third cause. The discussion below substantiates this proposition.

1. Regarding the first-mentioned source of heterogeneity, the important thing to note is that *cultural differences* may have a negative impact on collective action in so far as they leave room for different interpretations of the rules of the game being played,[5] for different views about who should enforce them, and for different perceptions of social conventions and norms supporting co-operation. The fact must indeed be reckoned that the game-theoretical models reviewed in Chapters 4 and 5 are grounded in a restrictive assumption, namely that all players have a perfectly similar understanding of the world. It is unfortunate that such an assumption is frequently violated in field settings since important collective challenges arise in contexts involving people from very different backgrounds. In many cases, the troubles created by migrants can actually be interpreted as belonging to this first category of problems. For instance, in the higher rainfall areas of southern Burkina Faso, villagers complain that they cannot control what they consider the abusive practices of migrants fleeing the drought-prone northern parts of the country because these new arrivals will not respect traditional authorities of the host community (Freudenberger and Mathieu, 1993: 20; Laurent *et al.*, 1994). In Senegalese coastal fisheries, to take another example, conflicts often arise from the uneasy cohabitation of local fishermen on the Petite Côte with migrant fishermen native of the northern part of the country (Saint-Louis).

2. The second source of heterogeneity is no doubt implicit in almost all statements about the disadvantages of heterogeneous groups. When users have different interests in the management of a resource, defining a common objective for regulating the commons is problematic. Here, examples abound. Many of them are quite significant and worth mentioning.

Heterogeneity of interests or objectives is particularly threatening for collective action aimed at resource management when a fraction of the resource users have alternative

[5] On this point, see Hechter (1987).

income-earning opportunities and, more seriously still, when they also reside outside the area where the resource is located. In Mali, for example, the predominance of absentee herd-ownership which resulted from the great Sahelian droughts in the 1970s (when pastoralists were forced to sell their livestock to farmers or, more generally, to town-dwellers like traders and civil servants) appears to be a major stumbling-block on the way towards pastoral institution-building for sustainable rangeland management. According to a recent evaluation study of the Mopti Area Development Project:

Absentee herd owners favour open access rangelands so that their herds can graze anywhere. They may even use their political influence to prevent pastoral associations receiving legally defensible land rights. Their herders, on the other hand, working for a wage, are fully engaged in herding. The pressure of work, their low social status, and the fact that the animals they are herding are not their own demotivate them from becoming involved in natural resource management. (Shanmugaratnam *et al.*, 1992: 20)

Similar difficulties are encountered in Mauritania where, although recently authorized by law to deny outsiders access to their demarcated rangelands when pasture is scarce and overgrazed, pastoral associations seem to continue to apply Islamic law and to follow local customs, implying that the stock of absentee herd-owners still graze on their commons (Shanmugaratnam *et al.,* 1992: 25). Given that the extent of herd dispossession is considerable (like in Mali), the problems created by absentee ownership for pastoral management are not to be underestimated:

Both Moor and Peul pastoralists have lost large shares of their livestock through sale to absentee herd owners. . . . The abolition of animal taxes since the droughts of 1984–85 and the introduction of property taxes have given further impetus to absentee ownership. Many richer people in the towns prefer to invest in cattle instead of in real estate. Absentee herd owners in Mauritania are mainly concentrated in Nouakchott and a few other towns. They prefer to keep their herds as close as possible to their towns; for instance, the bulk of the herds belonging to owners living in Nouakchott are found within a radius of 100 kilometers around the city. Such concentration of herds in limited areas contributes to over-grazing and exacerbates land-use conflicts around the towns. (Shanmugaratnam *et al.*, 1992: 25–6)

Note in passing that the above description also fits well with other country experiences in Sub-Saharan Africa, for instance in Burundi (many cattle herds grazing around the capital city of Bujumbura belong to city-dwellers).

Marine fishing is another sector where resource management is seriously undermined by the existence of different interests, most notably between small-scale (artisanal) fishermen and industrial fishing companies. Contrary to the former, the latter have indeed many exit possibilities, not the least because they can easily move their fleets to other, possibly distant fishing-grounds[6] or even switch to other economic sectors if fish resources have become too degraded to make their investments in fisheries economically attractive. An immediate consequence of this situation is that industrial operators feel much less concerned about conservation of fish resources in a

[6] Just think of the present redeployment of industrial fleets of European (both Western and Eastern) and Far Eastern origin along the Western coasts of Africa.

given harvesting ground, or perhaps even in general, than artisanal fishermen whose subsistence crucially depends upon the state of these resources owing to a lack of alternative income opportunities.

A vivid illustration of this contradiction of interests is the conflict which arose during recent decades around mackerel fishing between hook-and-line artisanal fishermen and industrial seiners in the coastal waters of Katsuura in Japan (Chiba prefecture). While the former have been taught from their childhood that catching young fish is a bad thing that jeopardizes the future of the resource (a fisherman found guilty of such an act gets a bad name), the latter have systematically caught all the mackerel regardless of their size. This indiscriminate fishing on the part of industrial companies eventually caused the depletion of mackerel stocks not only in Chiba prefecture but in the whole coastal area where these fish migrate (from Izu islands south of Tokyo to the offshore of Hokkaido Island, northern Japan) resulting in tremendous hardship for small-scale fishermen. The same story has been actually repeated for sardines and tuna and, today, it seems to hold true for skipjacks as well (oral communication of Masao Suzuki and Yoshiaki Aziki at the 10th Anniversary Conference of the International Collective for Support of Fishworkers (ICSF), Cebu, Philippines, 2–7 June 1994). Unfortunately, examples such as these are very easy to find all over the developing world.

Conflicts between men and women regarding the use of village commons can also be regarded as conflicts of interests. For instance, in many parts of Africa, men want to clear forests to open new fields for cultivation while women want to preserve them as a permanent source of firewood (Freudenberger and Mathieu, 1993: 14). Furthermore, socio-economic differentiation can easily lead to collective action problems if the pressure of survival constraints among the poor translates into high discount rates of future incomes while the rich have low discount rates (see above the crisis situation in Kottapalle mentioned by Wade).

It must be stressed that the difficulties associated with heterogeneity of interests are often compounded by the problem of cultural heterogeneity. An example which immediately springs to mind is the well-documented failures of herders and agriculturalists to reach joint agreements about how to regulate the use of common lands (see, for example, Bassett, 1993 about the conflicts between the Senufo peasants and the Fulani herders in Côte d'Ivoire). Another illustration is provided by the conflicts existing in many parts of the world between fishermen and agriculturalists or aquaculturists when the latter encroach upon mangrove areas that are so crucial for prawn reproduction.

When heterogeneity of interests is present, a negotiated agreement is clearly required to the effect that each interest group enjoys well-delimited rights and faces well-defined constraints. This often implies that the physical domain of the CPR is subdivided into several sections corresponding to the different interest groups. Thus, for example, in Valença (Brazil), following the introduction of new harvesting techniques which created heterogeneous interests and consequently gave rise to bitter conflicts (involving many acts of physical violence), the local fishermen 'divided their estuary into various areas and assigned a different technology to each area' (Cordell, 1972, cited from Schlager, 1994: 248). More precisely:

> The mangrove fence and barricade net are always located highest on the shore, succeeded by the dragged nets, encircling nets, and tidal flat fish corrals. Finally, moving out to the channel are positioned the fish traps, trotlines and gillnets. In any case, the distribution of techniques in a wedge of water is always such that they do not overlap. (Cordell, 1972: 42, cited from Schlager, 1994: 249)[7]

Unfortunately, there is no guarantee that different interest groups will be actually able to reach an agreement. Just to quote one example, in the Bay of Izmir (Turkey), there are many co-operatives yet each co-operative seems to represent the narrow interest of a particular gear type competing for access to the resource. None is apparently able 'to tackle the larger problems of managing a crowded fishery in the proximity of a large urban centre, or protecting the collective interests of fishermen against resource degradation' (Berkes, 1986: 223).

3. The third source of heterogeneity lies in *differential endowments*. In such situations, different resource users may have a common interest in regulating the use of the resource. Therefore, as a matter of principle, they can be expected to participate in collective action. It is only in exceptional circumstances when transfers are needed to compensate potential losers that heterogeneity in endowments may inhibit collective action due to difficulties in effecting those payments. The above proposition is borne out by the model of Ravi Kanbur reviewed in Chapter 8. In the latter, indeed, the people least endowed with skills, knowledge, assets, etc., are those who oppose a resource management scheme due to the intractability or costliness of side payments. Exactly the same problem arises in the example referred to by Johnson and Libecap in which, because fishermen are equipped with different techniques, their willingness to organize with others is made difficult (see above, Chapter 8). In the Nova Scotia lobster fishery (Canada), fishermen have well understood the need for resource conservation yet they have never agreed on how to share the control effort. There has always been a wide divergence between their own desired number of traps and the average number of traps they believed should be the standard (Scott, 1993: 194).

It is equally possible to think of situations in which people disadvantaged with respect to some endowments are unlikely to contribute to resource regulation. This happens when they are excluded from its benefits because they do not have access to some key factor. (Note incidentally that, in such circumstances, heterogeneity in endowments is tantamount to an heterogeneity of interest.) For instance, behind the failure of a grazing association established in Lesotho within the framework of a pilot range-management project apparently lay a considerable diversity of endowments in livestock production and livestock management practices in the local population (Lawry, 1989*b*: 10–11). In particular, smallholders and households short on herding labour and management skills (households headed by women or by men absent for

[7] See also Davis, 1984: 141–3, regarding division of fishing areas among different techniques in Port Lameroon Harbour, Nova Scotia (Canada).

work, mainly in South Africa) were less able to adopt many of the more intensive range-management and livestock-production practices promoted by the project's management plan. Furthermore, households which did not own cattle posts in the mountain pastures sought to avoid incurring the cost of gaining access to the posts belonging to others by keeping their livestock in the village year-round, in clear violation of the plan.

The idea that economic inequality is not necessarily an obstacle to resource regulation emerges from the already quoted study by Wade. In the South Indian villages he studied, there are indeed marked inter-household differences in landholdings and wealth. Yet, big landowners who also form the village's élite are not powerful enough to control all the land located near the irrigation channel. Holdings are typically scattered about the village area in small parcels, partly to diversify production risks and partly as a result of inheritance practices. Landowners, whether big or small, may have a plot close to one irrigation outlet and another plot close to the tail-end of a block fed from another outlet. For this reason, all landowners have *a common interest* in establishing and enforcing a system regulating access to water (Wade, 1988*a*: 185). In the words of Kanbur, fragmentation of holdings *vis-à-vis* the irrigation channel under conditions of inequality of landholding has caused 'a "homogenization" of the returns from co-operation when compared to the non-co-operative outcome' (Kanbur, 1992: 20).

In the *Zanjera* irrigation communities of the Philippines, to take another example, land along a lateral canal is divided into several blocks or sections perpendicular to the source of water so that blocks are at different distances from this source. Each of the blocks is further divided into several parcels and each share in the irrigation system corresponds to one parcel in each block, so that each shareholder has to cultivate parcels of various distances from the water source. As a result, all the farmers have some land in the most advantageous location near the head of the system, and some near the tail. This arrangement has the effect of equalizing income-earning opportunities and providing insurance to the farmers. It has also the important advantage of motivating them to deliver water throughout the entire watercourse and 'to contribute many hours of physically exhausting labor in times of emergency, when control structures have been washed out, and for routine maintenance' (Ostrom, 1990: 83).[8]

A similar system has been found operating in Sri Lanka and is known as the *Bethna* system. According to Quiggin, the rice areas are divided into a number of sections at varying distances from the dam, and each of the villagers is entitled to cultivate a portion of each section proportionate to their overall landholding (Quiggin, 1993: 1133–4). A positive aspect of this system where total landholdings are divided into a number of separate parts is that in periods of water shortage participants in the water-sharing scheme may decide to restrict the area irrigated to the sections nearest to the dam. In this way, output per unit of water is higher than if water were spread over the entire field (ibid.).

It is interesting to note that the scattering of landholdings which 'may arise from a

[8] Moreover, 'in years when rainfall is not sufficient to irrigate all the fields, a decision about sharing the burden of scarcity can be made rapidly and equitably by simply deciding not to irrigate the bottom section of land' (Ostrom, 1990: 83).

desire to reduce intragroup conflict' also characterized European agriculture in early medieval times, as attested by the open-field system found in thirteenth-century England (Homans, 1970: 90; see also Quiggin, 1988).

When economic inequality *does not thus prevent uniformity of interest* in a collective agreement, it can even be a favourable factor if the rich can assume a leadership role. Such a situation in which economic inequality generates the necessary incentives for playing a leadership role has been apparently encountered by Wade in the above study. The reasoning is as follows: since benefits of unified action are positively related to land area, the élite have a disproportionately great interest in the effective regulation of water resources and this helps ensure that the required corporate organization is started and effectively run. In the words of Wade, 'the effectiveness of a council depends on its councillors all having a substantial private interest in seeing that it works, and that interest is greater the larger a person's landholding (provided holdings are in scattered parcels)' (Wade, 1987: 230). The claims that big landowners can make 'are sufficiently large for some of them to be motivated to pay a major share of the organisational costs' (Wade, 1988*a*: 190). To tie up this observation with our discussion in Chapter 5, it must be noted that the game of irrigation implicit in Wade's example typically raises a co-ordination problem and, given their high stake in proper co-ordination, the élite have a particular interest in initiating it.

The same explanation underlies the story of the success of a village grazing scheme in Lesotho. In Ha Nchele, a lowland village in this country, rotational grazing has been introduced on village-grazing lands as an alternative to taking animals to a cattle post in the mountains. According to Sharp (1987), success was obtained in spite of very little external assistance partly because the village chief held the greatest number of livestock, thus enhancing his personal interest in the project. Of course, an important feature of the whole experiment is that he did not abuse his power as chief (cited from Swallow and Bromley, 1994*b*: 5).

Besides their leadership role, the élite may provide the authority structure that is required for proper enforcement of regulatory rules. Wade has clearly this latter function in mind when he writes: 'Many who might be tempted to free ride are socially subordinate to others in the user group, and are checked from doing so by sanctions which derive from the wider order of caste and property without the [irrigation] council having to use its own authority' (Wade, 1988*a*: 193). The same basic position is asserted elsewhere, even in stronger terms:

> corporate organisations, to be effective, should be based on existing structures of authority. In practice, this means that the council will be dominated by the local élite which is a disturbing conclusion for democrats and egalitarians. But rules made by the majority of villagers would carry little legitimacy in the eyes of the powerful. (Wade, 1987: 230)

The very fact that Japanese rural societies—a model case of successful village-based collective action for CPR management—had a deeply asymmetrical social structure provides a significant confirmation of Wade's thesis. The same can be said of lineage-based societies in Imperial China. The representatives of dominant lineages had a great deal of influence in the selection of the forest manager and in the setting and enforcement of all the rules regulating the access to and the use of the local forests and wildlands. Acting as an élite who controlled a large portion of the land and the benefits it yielded, clans generally applied a combination of appeals to moral norms (Confucian appeals to order, respect for the ancestor, and family loyalty) and coercive enforcement (fines and punishment) (Menzies, 1994: 80–5). Still another illustration is provided by rural Mexico where the Indian *caciques* (rich Indians acting as patrons) used to mobilize labour and assume leadership for the management of common lands, including important conservation measures such as steep-slope management and erosion control (Garcia-Barrios and Garcia-Barrios, 1990). As Bardhan puts it: 'In many local communities some rudimentary forms of cooperation have been sustained and enforced over the years by traditional authority structures. While there may have been some bit of a sharing ethic, the predominant social norm was often that of an unequal patron-client system, in which the powerful who might enjoy disproportionate benefits from the institution of cooperation enforced the rules of the game and gave leadership to solidaristic efforts' (Bardhan, 1993*b*: 638). In the Pithuwa irrigation system in Nepal, for example, it so happens that many of the large landowners have their lands located near the tail of the system (which is also near to the east–west highway and thus low-cost transportation of produce to markets). Even though the area was not organized prior to canal construction, thanks to the initiative of some prominent farmers, the whole irrigation project became self-managed through evolution from organization on one branch at the tail of the system to the organization of the entire system (Laitos *et al.*, 1986: 126–7, quoted from Ostrom and Gardner, 1993: 105).

It is interesting to note that, in the literature about co-operatives as in the literature dealing with CPR self-management, the importance of social homogeneity has often been stressed. Here also, however, some dissent begins to be voiced, grounded on solid field experiences. For instance, in a recent report issued by the World Bank, we are aptly reminded that 'the idea that cooperatives can function only if members have the same background can be refuted by the examples of successful ones in both developed and developing nations' (Braverman *et al.*, 1991: 13). Thus, rural co-operatives in the Netherlands were often created by groups 'of influential, better-off farmers who took the initiative to start a service or credit co-op and to contribute the bulk of initial share capital. Smaller producers would join at a later stage, contributing smaller shares' (ibid. 6).

After having stressed the potential positive role of economic inequality for collective action, we must add the caution that there obviously exist certain limits beyond which social heterogeneity becomes harmful for this purpose. Again, this point has not escaped Wade's attention: 'where stratification breeds class antagonism, . . . the bite of reputation loss may be reduced, because the reference group is confined to the subordinate class and collective free riding by members of the subordinate group might be encouraged' (Wade, 1988*a*: 193). Factional antagonisms are a constant threat for corporate village organizations. In Kottapalle village, Wade notes, the problem has been overcome 'by giving these antagonisms and suspicions an institutionalised expression': the composition of the irrigation council is carefully balanced between the two existing factions, decisions are taken by consensus, not majority vote, etc. (ibid. 195).

In fact, it is not only the objective economic situation of various users and the technical conditions characterizing the CPRs (such as, for example, whether the lands of the rich are located near the head-end or the tail-end of an irrigation system) that matter. The personalities of the village élite as well as the general social atmosphere prevailing in the society are also crucial factors influencing the possibility of co-operation. This seems to be the main lesson to draw from the following account of various field experiences with hill irrigation systems in Himachal Pradesh (Chand, 1994). These systems, known as *kuhls*, consist of small gravity channels constructed along mountainsides and they typically deliver water to several villages. In one case, heterogeneity promoted orderly and equitable distribution of water by supplying the necessary leadership. Thus, in Kalowan *kuhl*, till 1960 no set timings were observed for inter- and intra-village distribution of water and this situation of quasi-anarchy led to frequent disputes. In 1960, however, a local landowner who is also the village revenue collector mobilized farmers of the command area to frame a set of norms for water distribution. The agreement reached among the water users concerned was recorded in a document which contains elaborate information on days and timings of water supply to each of the six villages served by Kalowan *kuhl* and to all beneficiaries. Everyone has full knowledge of this information.

In Gandhori *kuhl*, in contrast, no such co-ordinated move happened to the great profit of the local élite. Indeed, high-caste farmers have frequent access to water even though a majority of them have their fields at the tail-end of the system. The opposite is true of low-caste members who do not get water frequently despite the fact that the fields of many of them are located nearer to the channel. Revealingly, about 86 per cent of low-caste farmers stated that they would prefer government control of the *kuhl*, while only 30 per cent of high-caste members expressed this preference. The lower-caste farmers understandably felt that under government control they would get their due share of *kuhl* water, whereas high-caste farmers prefer local control to keep their hold of the irrigation system and thereby get a larger share of the available water (ibid.). Of course, if the village élite have their irrigable lands more favourably located than in Gandhori *kuhl*, it is still easier for them to enhance their interests at the expense of poorer CPR users. As pointed out by Pranab Bardhan, where the rich farmers are able to get enough water for their land without having to organize corporately and without having to incur large additional expenditures themselves since they own the land immediately below the canal outlets, they are highly likely even to block the formation of a co-operative water control committee at the expense of the small cultivators lower down. This is because such a committee might curtail their own irrigation freedom (Bardhan, 1993*b*: 637).

Of course, the more hierarchical the social structure, the more important the personal qualities of the leadership. Thus, in the monastic forests of Imperial China to which we have already referred, we learn that 'under a weak or unscrupulous abbot, wood might be illegally felled and sold'. In contrast, there are examples of 'strong, devoted monks, who not only protected the land under their care, but led their community in restoring degraded lands' (Menzies, 1994: 69). Some time during the twelfth century for example, the abbot of the Fu Yan Chan (Zen) monastery at Heng Shan (Hunan province) stated: 'There are remote places on this peak where none of the *Cunninghamia* (a tree species) is in good condition. This means that we cannot be sure of the flow of the water and the supply of firewood to our retreat. We must not be remiss in our mission and foolishly fail to make provision for them' (cited from Menzies, 1994: 69). It must be added that, under the leadership of such enlightened abbots, not only the monk community but also the entire population of villagers depending upon the monastery (usually as tenants) were driven to better management of local forests.

The importance of a more or less harmonious social atmosphere (even in the presence of significant wealth differentials and inequalities in socio-political status) for efficient intra-village economic transactions may actually drive the upper strata to behave like good patrons and to accept a situation in which a relatively egalitarian access to local CPRs is guaranteed to everyone in the village, especially so if they are essential for the survival of the lower strata. In such a case, co-operation in the management of these CPRs under the leadership of the upper strata arises not because the richest people in the village have a greater interest in the CPRs as in Wade's example above, but because their natural leadership position enables them to ensure the success of CPR management schemes. In this context, it is useful to bear in mind some of the results achieved in Chapter 5. Indeed, assuming that the upper-class people have an AG payoff structure, or a CG payoff structure, or even a PD payoff structure, while the lower-class people have an AG payoff structure—given relatively harmonious social relations, they are willing to co-operate if the upper-class people show a good example, yet will behave non-co-operatively otherwise—we know that co-operation will get established if the upper-class people assume a leadership role.

That egalitarian access to village CPRs can exist in differentiated societies is actually testified by several important examples. Thus, in situations where irrigation allows new land to be brought under cultivation, communities which have a highly asymmetrical social structure are sometimes observed to ensure fair distribution of the new lands to all members, possibly as a result of external pressures (exercised by donor or state agencies). For instance, in the strongly differentiated communities inhabiting the Senegal River valley (on the Senegalese bank), methods of alloting irrigation plots do not discriminate according to the social identity of the members. The assignment of plots through a lottery system tends to be favoured because, when some plots are better located than others, it is the only system that is considered legitimate by the villagers. In several village irrigation schemes, it has been found that, on the one hand, members of the minorities or lowest castes (including previous slaves) were not barred from access to irrigated land and, on the other hand, members of the highest castes did not arrogate to themselves more than one parcel or larger parcels than those assigned to the other participants in the scheme (Boutillier, 1982: 303–4; Diemer and van der Laan, 1987: 133). However, previous slaves are not entitled to hold significant positions in the irrigation group's committee since they may only be appointed as messengers or public criers (Diemer and van der Laan, 1987: 136, 141; see also Bloch, 1993;

Shanmugaratnam *et al.*, 1992: 27, 36, for similar observations about both Senegal and Mauritania; see also Tang, 1992, reporting evidence based on a large sample of irrigation systems).

Situations where social heterogeneity is combined with a relatively egalitarian treatment of all villagers with respect to use of local CPRs have been clearly pointed to by McKean in the case of Japan. In Japanese villages, indeed, inequality in private landholdings and political power went hand in hand with equal access to CPRs. Random distributions, assignment to parcels or products of the commons by lottery, and rotation systems were thus frequently used to avoid unfair allocation of use rights regarding these resources considered as vital to all people, rich and poor.

There thus exist a variety of situations that can arise when heterogeneity takes on the form of unequal endowments. As we have just noted, unequal endowments in private landholdings and social and political status can go together with a relatively egalitarian access to local CPRs. In such circumstances, the village élite can possibly provide the leadership required for collective action in the CPR domain. This is all the more likely if agrarian relations are of the patron–client type. When unequal endowments in private wealth are also reflected in unequal shares in the local CPRs, several possibilities present themselves that are more or less conducive to collective action. To begin with, the élite can enjoy a strategic position in their access to the CPRs and they may have no need for any kind of corporate organization. This corresponds to the case referred to by Bardhan in which landlords have all their irrigable lands located immediately below the canal outlets. This is the worst case since no collective action will take place and the poorer resource users will be at the losing end (see Chapter 5 for the corresponding game-theoretical model).

Alternatively, the strategic position of the rich may not enable them to dispense with the collaboration of the other users: for example, their lands are favourably located (near the head-end of the water control infrastructure), yet the maintenance of the infrastructure on which they depend requires more labour efforts than they can supply themselves. Under such conditions, they may want to play a leadership role to ensure that the necessary public goods are provided. Their dependence on the labour of the poorer sections of the village community may confer on the latter a certain bargaining strength which can be used to ensure a co-operative solution in the allocation of the resource flows (similarly, the distribution of the water will not be monopolized by the landlords). The situation is still more favourable to co-operation if the élite have a disproportionately high interest in the CPRs but they do not hold any kind of strategic position: this is the case mentioned by Wade in which the lands of the rich are scattered all along the irrigation system. Here, again, one can expect them to assume leadership and, moreover, to be particularly attentive that water is equitably distributed throughout the whole system.

This typology is not exhaustive. It should nevertheless be sufficient to convey the point that social, political, and economic heterogeneity is not necessarily dooming co-operation in CPRs to failure. In important circumstances, heterogeneity may even promote co-operation compared with a situation in which there is more homogeneity in wealth and other kinds of endowments. Moreover, implicit in the above discussion are a number of criteria that must be taken into consideration when one wants to assess the impact of heterogeneity on collective action potential in specific field situations. In particular, the following questions have to be raised to delineate the problem:

1. Does the main source of heterogeneity lay in cultural differences, in varying interests in the CPR under concern, or in different wealth endowments?
2. If heterogeneity arises from the last source, do the rights of access to the CPR reflect unequal endowments in private wealth, or are they defined on a more egalitarian basis?
3. Are the élite holding strategic positions in the CPR domain (irrespective of whether they can claim a disproportionate share of it or not)?
4. Do the élite need the collaboration of lower-class users to build up and maintain the infrastructures required to efficiently exploit the CPR or to enforce exclusion and use-restraining rules?
5. Are the relations between the élite and the rest of the resource users structured by patron–client exchanges of services or are they less personalized, less multi-stranded, and perhaps more antagonistic?

12.4 The Rationale and Characteristics of Sanction Systems

The rationale of local sanction systems

In the first section of this chapter, the existence of an effective sanction system has been listed as a major determinant of success in CPR regulation schemes. In the literature, there is unanimous agreement on this crucial point. Yet the question is to be asked as to why sanctions are required to enforce CPR regulation. Indeed, one important result of the theory of non-co-operative repeated PD games is that co-operation *may* evolve without the support of *external* sanctions if actors follow strategies of brave reciprocity understood as strategies of conditional co-operation. This requires, for example, that the actors' horizon is infinite or finite but indefinite, an assumption that is a good approximation to reality in many cases of local-level resource use. The basic reason why co-operation is then possible lies in the simple fact that strategies of conditional co-operation are obviously strategies of punishment and reparation (see above, Chapter 4).

Such a mechanism of purely decentralized punishment embodied in the actors' strategies is not without important shortcomings, however. In particular, even assuming that actors are all willing to follow strategies of brave reciprocity, the fact that the set of possible punishments is highly restricted creates serious problems. This is evident in N-player repeated PD games. Assume thus that there are N users of a given resource. Rule-breaking is common knowledge and, in a given round or period, one of the N actors violates management rules in front of the $(N-1)$ other actors who have abided by them. Why should the latter choose to retaliate by also breaking the rules during the next period, when such retaliation clearly jeopardizes the whole management scheme with disastrous long-term consequences for everybody? Rather than punishing oneself in order to effectively punish the rule-breaker, is it not more rational to inflict selective punishment on him?

It can be argued that, since no punishment occurs at equilibrium, there is no need to worry about the destructive nature of punishments: on the contrary, the severity of punishments is precisely aimed at making the threat sufficiently effective that nobody is incited to defect. Yet, this is to forget that players can make 'mistakes', that is, they may happen to deviate from their rational strategy of co-operation. And if these 'mistakes' are too frequent, there is a serious risk of a 'Nash equilibrium reversion' (Abreu, 1986), implying that players revert to single-period Nash-equilibrium behaviour. This is a serious limitation inasmuch as rural people are typically confronted with natural and other hazards which may easily drive them, from time to time, inadvertently to violate access or conservation rules. To allow for 'irrational' moves or stressful conditions, punishment mechanisms must be flexible and tolerant enough. Such flexibility is hard to achieve with simple decentralized punishment strategies that rest on a restricted set of actions: thus, in the repeated Prisoner's Dilemma, punishment can only consist of a sequence of two possible actions—co-operate or defect. Subtle, gradual, and relatively costless responses, such as enquiries, warnings, mild threats, etc., are thereby ruled out.

It bears emphasis that inflicting selective punishment on deviant players is a sensible strategy not only on rational but also on emotional grounds. As a matter of fact, people who have been cheated may strongly resent it and wish to relieve their emotional stress by punishing the cheater 'just to teach him a lesson', or by denouncing the fraud so as to bring sanction from the competent agency. Of course, the emotional drive to punish deviant behaviour will be all the more powerful if norms of fairness exist to back up the prevailing code of conduct. In game-theoretic terms, the positive role of emotions can be conceptualized as follows. Because of the vengeful reaction of co-operative players, the payoff of a deviant player is much less than the material gain from free riding on others' efforts. This may be so much so that the total payoff from defecting while others co-operate is actually less than the payoff obtained by co-operating with the other players. Under these conditions, emotions have the effect of transforming a PD game into a virtuous game in which universal co-operation is the only Nash equilibrium. Notice carefully that, when emotions perform the above function, the difficult 'public good' problem of sanctioning is automatically solved: the cheated agents do not really ponder over the private cost of sanctioning and it is actually refraining from punishing or denouncing that appears to them as a painful experience.

Now, it is important to recognize that equilibrium strategies may possibly exist that use selective *self-enforcing* punishments in the form of payoff transfers among agents. Note incidentally that these transfers need not correspond to material exchanges but may possibly consist of symbolic sanctions such as apologies. It is evident that this type of equilibrium strategy is inconceivable without some degree of collective regulation (about the amount of the transfers, the circumstances in which it must be applied, etc.), yet an essential feature is that it does not require a central enforcing agency. The self-enforcing character of punishment strategies results from the fact that the stream of future incomes the deviant player can earn by leaving the group and earning the best alternative income is lower than the stream he can obtain by remaining in the group and co-operating with the other members even after he has paid the fine. Clearly, the maximum punishment that can be imposed on individuals who deviate from the co-operative path yields the expected autarkic payoff (Fafchamps, 1992: 162–3).

Things may not be so easy, however. More precisely, the punishment path may not be 'renegotiation-proof' if the threat to impose sanctions on the deviant player is not credible because the group would be less well-off after the departure of the deviant player (see above, Chapter 8). In the words of Fudenberg and Tirole, 'equilibria that enforce "good" outcomes by the threat that deviations will trigger a "punishment equilibrium" may be suspect, as a player might deviate and then propose abandoning the punishment equilibrium for another equilibrium in which all players are better off' (Fudenberg and Tirole, 1993: 175). To put it in another way, the group would be ready to renegotiate the original agreement because it would lose from the departure of the deviant player and, since the latter knows it, he may use this bargaining strength to force the group to forgive him for his defection.

It must nevertheless be reckoned that, regarding the types of situation considered in this book, the above problem of punishments that do not satisfy the 'renegotiation-proofness' test is probably limited. Indeed, to the extent that co-operation among the players is needed because there is dangerous pressure on the CPR, one may expect them to feel relieved rather than worried by the departure of deviant users. Even in this case, however, there are two circumstances in which this problem may remain significant. First, as pinpointed in the conclusion to Chapter 4, the use of the CPR may not be an isolated game, that is, there may be interlinkages between what is being played here and what is being played in other sectors of the CPR users' social life. Second, collective action in the group may require the co-ordinated efforts of all the members, say, for maintenance or surveillance activities (see Chapter 5).

Leaving aside the above difficulty arising from 'renegotiation-proofness', decentralized mechanisms resting on self-enforcing punishments are far from being satisfactory. There are two main reasons for this. First, as we have stressed in Chapters 4 and 5, in most non-co-operative games there exist a plethora of possible equilibria, some of which are Pareto-dominated. A society may therefore be justified in attempting to design a system of collective sanctions which transforms the game in such a way that the Pareto-optimal outcome is the unique equilibrium. Second, under conditions of imperfect information, decentralized punishment mechanisms provide the agents with considerable opportunities for all sorts of information manipulation that can easily lead to partial and arbitrary outcomes. For instance, an individual may be tempted to take revenge on another participant by wrongly accusing him of trespassing the rules and claiming the corresponding transfer.

This shortcoming is to be taken very seriously in the light of an aforementioned disadvantage of small groups, namely that highly personalized relationships create a fertile ground for strong negative feelings, such as envy and rivalry, which can lead to group implosion if not properly checked. In such a context, the temptation to fraudulently manipulate decentralized monitoring and punishment mechanisms is likely to be strong. The implication of this diagnosis is that, *even in relatively small groups* such as village communities, collective regulation through a central authority may be desirable. Obviously, such a central authority must be considered fair and legitimate by the people concerned lest it should be very costly to enforce.

Reckoning with the need for such a centralized system of sanctioning does not mean, however, that all decentralized mechanisms and procedures have to be done away with. As a matter of fact, to be effective, a collective sanction system must consist not only of formal procedures but also of informal conventions and rules that are commonly understood and accepted by the members. This is because situations on the ground are typically fraught with so many uncertainties and contingencies that no formal rule or contract could ever specify all the relevant conditions. Only general principles such as those embodied in moral norms and codes of honour allow the unpredictable to be approached with appropriate flexibility. Formal sanction systems cannot alone be expected to cover satisfactorily all the possible contingencies and room must therefore be left for complementary mechanisms grounded in the ethics of the society. Clearly, the effectiveness of a collective sanction system depends on the balance that is struck between these two inevitable components, and the more uncertain and complex the circumstances surrounding the members' decisions the larger should be the role of informal rules.

Organized versus decentralized monitoring

In conditions of imperfect observability of individual actions, monitoring activities are an essential component of a village control system aimed at preventing freeriding. Indeed, when monitoring is lax or observation errors are frequent, sanctions may not be applied in the way required to deter rule violation. This raises the question as to whether monitoring can be left completely decentralized or whether it is better organized at the group level. The most obvious problem with a decentralized system of monitoring is that it may not be sufficiently reliable. Monitoring is a public good and there is therefore no guarantee that someone who detects rule-violation will incur the cost of reporting it to the relevant authority. This is all the more so if he may fear incurring the wrath of the presumed violator while he cannot be sure that his denunciation will lead to actual punishment. On the other hand, a fraud detector may show partiality in his reporting, protecting his friends or allies and harassing his rivals or enemies. These considerations go a long way towards explaining why in field settings monitoring activities are often organized in a collective way.

Ease of monitoring depends on the characteristics of the natural resource considered and on the size of the user group. Thus, regarding the first factor, monitoring is particularly easy with respect to certain resources which are highly visible and/or well localized, and when users reside in close proximity to these resources. In the case of surface irrigation systems, for example, poaching of water is relatively easily observable as each irrigator keeps a constant eye on his neighbour's actions. When water rotation turns are organized, monitoring is thus costless: 'the presence of the first irrigator deters the second from an early start, the presence of the second irrigator deters the first from a late ending' (Ostrom, 1990: 95). And likewise in fishing-site rotation systems. On the other hand, the use of some resources such as open sea fisheries,[9] forestries, and groundwater, is considerably more difficult to monitor even when user groups are rather small.

Regarding the second factor, since monitoring is a public good, it is subject to the 'incentive dilution' problem and, consequently, the need to organize monitoring activities collectively should increase with the size of the user group. Thus, for a given resource such as irrigation water, one expects a significant relationship between the existence of formal monitoring mechanisms as measured by the presence of guards accountable to the water users, on the one hand, and the size of the resource system, on the other hand. This prediction seems to be confirmed by a systematic study conducted in the Philippines. It was indeed found that 80 per cent of small irrigation systems (less than 50 h.) operate without formal guards, while the proportion declines to 55 per cent for medium-scale systems (from 50 to 100 h.) and to 30 per cent for large systems (more than 100 h.) Furthermore, it is interesting to note that farmers tend to patrol their own canals even when some of them are also patrolled by appointed guards (de Los Reyes, 1980, cited from Weissing and Ostrom, 1991: 238–9, 246–7).

That the presence of monitors is an important factor affecting the level of rule conformance comes out of the survey by Tang (1992, 1994) of a large sample of irrigation systems (mostly located in Asia). This is especially true of farmer-owned systems since routine rule conformance is reported in thirteen out of the fourteen farmer-owned systems *with* guards in the sample, but in only five out of eleven farmer-owned systems *without* guards. The same relationship holds true in government-owned systems although it is less significant than for farmer-owned systems: four out of the eleven government-owned systems *with* guards are characterized by a lack of routine rule conformance. Interestingly, this follows from the fact that local guards in farmer-owned systems 'are more likely to impose sanctions on rule violations than guards hired by the government-owned irrigation systems' (Tang, 1994: 240–2), a difference which is probably to be ascribed to the relatively poor incentives provided to guards in the latter as compared to the former systems (see above, Chapter 11, sect. 1). Unfortunately, while attempting to assess the effectiveness of formal monitoring systems, Tang does not control for the size of the irrigation systems.

Do we have to infer from the above considerations about the importance of collective organization of monitoring and sanctioning activities that results from non-co-operative game theory are of little relevance for assessing the potential of village communities to manage their natural resources? The answer is negative. As we have just seen above, there is a positive relationship between the size of a user group and the probability that it regulates CPRs through a formal monitoring and sanctioning system. In so far as in many such formal systems are nested (very) small and typically homogeneous groups comprising only a few families that operate in a fully decentral-

[9] Even in open-sea fisheries, the monitoring of some rules about the use of the resource may sometimes be rather easy, as when by looking at a boat even from a distance one can determine the type of gear utilized and whether it operates in a forbidden fishing zone (Schlager, 1994: 253).

ized way, the theory remains valid: by demonstrating that co-operation is a possible outcome within the framework of repeated interactions in small groups, it contributes to establish the feasibility of management systems resting on multiple layers of nested user groups.

Examples of such 'federated' systems include irrigation, fishery, and pastoral management. Thus, most of the large, self-organized irrigation systems that have successfully survived for long periods of time are organized in three or four different tiers. This allows for clear and unambiguous rules for allocating water among relatively separable units, an absolute prerequisite for the effectiveness of any such subdivision of the system into management micro-units (Weissing and Ostrom, 1991: 259 n. 31). Likewise, in pastoral management, it has been noted that, if water points can be more effectively managed by small cohesive groups, management of viable units of rangeland requires larger groups formed by combining several such small groups (Shanmugaratnam *et al.*, 1992: 6). As for fisheries, it will be seen in Chapter 13 that the Japanese system of coastal fishery management—one of the most impressive achievements in CPR management to date—devolves substantial responsibilities to fishermen communities constituted as fishing co-operatives (known as fishermen associations) which are themselves often organized into smaller units. These small units, whether they are fishing squads or residential groups, appear to be the main agencies for the allocation of fishing rights in coastal waters.

In the following, we consider a number of case-studies which provides us with rather detailed information about monitoring and sanctioning activities in village communities. As is evident from these examples, there can be significant variations in the degree of collective organization regarding these two activities. In the first case-study, observability of individual actions is perfect and the entire sanctioning system rests upon decentralized, informal mechanisms of social opprobrium and gossip: there is thus no organizational structure to monitor people's behaviour and to impose punishment upon deviant actors (monitoring and punishment are self-enforcing). In the other four case-studies, observability is imperfect and monitoring and sanctioning activities are collectively organized.

Sanctioning in Teelin Bay, Ireland

In Teelin Bay (Ireland), the estuarine salmon fishermen use a rotation system of access to the most valuable fishing-spots. Only exceptional and slight violations of the underlying code of conduct are observed. Abidance by the rules of the salmon rotation system within the restricted space of the local community 'is perceived as merely the "natural" expression of local behavior' and rests 'only on the egalitarian ethos of communal reciprocity, which is, in turn, understood as natural' (Taylor, 1987: 299, 302). Few would or do try to violate these rules and, when a violation takes place, communal punishment does not have to be organized because the opprobrium of informal social control that follows, under the form of 'an enormous amount of pointed whispering gossip in pub and household', is apparently sufficient to deter deviants from cheating again. The egalitarian ethos of the community is thus preserved since no one 'is perceived as having the authority to directly reprimand or punish the offender' (ibid. 299, 303).

What needs to be emphasized is that non-compliance with the rotation rule is effectively sanctioned through informal social pressure, which has the effect of transforming the original repeated PD game into an assurance game, or into a PD game with self-enforcing punishments in the form of payoff transfers. There remains, however, the second-order public good problem of who will have the incentive to punish by exerting such social pressure. Such punishment decisions must be analysed within the framework of another repeated prisoner's dilemma, since no collective sanctioning system exists to drive the agents to apply first-order punishment. The co-operative outcome corresponds here to a situation where everybody exerts social pressure on any member found to break the rotation rules.

Monitoring and sanctioning in rural Japan

In McKean's already-quoted survey of village CPR-related practices in rural Japan, we are offered exceptionally precise information about monitoring and sanctioning mechanisms and it is therefore useful to describe them in detail by closely following McKean's illuminating account.

Apparently, Japanese villages widely resorted to selective inducements and punishments in order to ensure due respect for the written codes which most of them had to govern their CPRs. Regarding inducements, we are thus told that 'there was an intrinsic pride in the importance of doing one's duty by the commons and in preserving the village's well-being; a young man brought credit to his family and future by doing the job properly' (McKean, 1986: 564). Regarding punishments, the evidence is that 'violating rules that protected the commons was viewed as one of the most terrible offences a villager could commit against his peers, and the penalties were very serious' (ibid. 561). In order to detect rule infractions, purposeful monitoring was practised in the form of groups of detectives destined to constantly patrol the commons: 'the detectives would patrol the commons on horseback every day looking for intruders, in effect enforcing exclusionary rules'. Their job was considered 'one of the most prestigious and responsible available to a young man' (ibid. 560–1). According to villages, these positions changed hands more or less frequently and, in some of them, all eligible males had to take a turn, so that no family was without its full labour supply for very long. In the poorest villages, specialized but rotating detectives did not exist (probably because people were too poor to spare the required labour), yet anyone could report violations (ibid. 561).

As we have mentioned in the first section of this chapter, sanctions obeyed a number of principles which can be summarized under three main headings. First, the specific punishments stipulated in the village written codes for specific violations followed a built-in scheme of escalating penalties for non-co-operation. This escalating scale of penalties began with confiscation of the contraband taken from the CPRs, as well as the equipment and horse, which a violator could retrieve only after having paid a fine and apologized to the detectives who apprehended him (interestingly, the *sake* given as payment of a fine was referred to by special terms indicating the humility of the rule-breaker). The contraband harvest was of course retained by the village. If the offence was relatively great or the apology unsatisfactory, the head of the culprit's household or his *kumi* (an intermediate grouping comprising several households and constituting a very important unit of accounting and distribution of responsibilities and benefits connected with the CPRs) or temple priest was called to make the apology on his behalf and offer a larger fine in his stead (McKean, 1986: 550, 561–2).

When necessary, Japanese villages did not hesitate to threaten to use their more powerful sanctions: 'ostracism in increasingly severe stages, followed by banishment'. Ostracism—which implies that the village community 'cuts off all contact with the offender except for assistance at funerals and fire-fighting'—was thus resorted to in gradual stages, 'starting with social contact and only escalating to economic relations if the offender did not express remorse and modify his behavior'. Moreover, 'to ensure that the villagers would remember to shun contact with someone subjected to ostracism, that person might be expected to wear distinctive clothing (a flashy red belt or pair of unmatched socks)' (McKean, 1986: 562). McKean reckons that this was 'a horrible punishment for the Japanese villager, not only because it cut him off from a highly group-oriented society and made daily life unpleasant, but because it actually deprived the villager of tangible services essential to daily living', including access to the CPRs. It is therefore not surprising that ostracism was an effective deterrent to repeated and serious rule infractions, especially for ordinary villagers who would never jeopardize the survival of their household and their family's reputation for many generations when a simple apology could extinguish the controversy (ibid. 562).

It is worth stressing the obvious fact that the effectiveness of social ostracism as a weapon against rule-breaking hinges very much on the degree of physical immobility of CPR users. In present-day circumstances where mobility is much higher than before, this effectiveness has no doubt been significantly reduced (see above, Chapter 11, sect. 2).

A second basic feature of sanction mechanisms in rural Japan is their flexibility or tolerance. According to McKean, there were two kinds of circumstance in which inspectors or village leadership were inclined to manifest a good deal of tolerance towards detected rule-breakers: (*a*) when violation followed an obvious error on the part of CPR managers or village leaders which could have damaging consequences for the rule-breakers (for instance, the village chief set the day of mountain-opening too late, thereby preventing some people from cutting in time the poles needed to support garden vegetables raised on private plots); (*b*) when the rule violators stole from the CPRs only out of desperation. In the former case, tolerance arose from awareness of the fact that rule-breaking was an act of understandable protest against a mistaken decision. In the latter case, 'inspectors or other witnesses who saw violations maintained silence out of sympathy for the violators' desperation and out of confidence that the problem was temporary and could not really hurt the commons' (McKean, 1986: 566). When a collective disaster occurred, as in the village of Yamanaka during the Depression of the 1930s, tolerance *vis-à-vis* widespread rule-breaking was generalized for the same reason. There was no fear of an irreversible collapse of the whole CPR conservation system: indeed, 'instead of regarding the general breakdown of the rules as an opportunity to become full-time free riders and cast caution to the winds, the violators themselves tried to exercise self-discipline out of deference to the preservation of the commons' (ibid.).

The third and last feature of Japanese rural sanction systems to which we wish to draw attention concerns the reliability of CPR monitors or inspectors. This issue involves the question of the monitors' incentive to perform their job adequately and the related question as to who will watch the watchers. Monitors had two kinds of incentives both of which have already been mentioned: on the one hand, they gained social prestige and, on the other hand, they derived material advantages since they were entitled to keep the small fines paid by detected rule-breakers (in the form of cash and *sake*). Regarding the second issue, three observations deserve to be made. First, as we have pointed out earlier, the duty of watching usually rotated through the body of male members of the community so that everyone got his turn to exercise the monitoring power and to obtain the advantages associated with it. Second, the monitors or detectives patrolled in teams and were collectively responsible for their actions. Third, whenever exceptional circumstances arose which significantly increased the temptation to break the rules on the part of both users and monitors, mutual monitoring by all users replaced specialized monitoring by appointed guards. For example, we are told the following story. 'When the village of Shiwa suffered a drought, farmers at the downstream end of the irrigation system, including the water guards on patrol, were sorely tempted to alter the dikes so as to receive more than their allocated share of water. During such times, the collective response was for all adult males to patrol the dikes all night long in mutual surveillance' (McKean, 1986: 565). The above arrangements were apparently effective. The most important abuse of power by the (young) detectives consisted of ignoring repeated offences in exchange for sexual favours from attractive girls whom their fathers purposefully sent to collect grass (ibid. 564).

Let us now turn to three other case-studies. The first of these studies confirms the effectiveness of social opprobrium as a sanctioning device in rural communities and, moreover, it explicitly points to an intergroup punishment mechanism that makes social excommunication extremely costly. The second study provides valuable details about monitors' incentives and it lays stress on the importance of accountability for the effectiveness of any sanction system, especially in times of crisis. Finally, the third study is especially interesting because it supplies information not only about monitoring and sanctioning mechanisms but also about the incidence of rule-breaking, the effectiveness of monitoring, and the state of the CPR.

Monitoring and sanctioning in the Solomon Islands

In Marovo (Solomon Islands) as in traditional Japanese villages, banishment is also the ultimate and most serious step along the punishment scale for free riders. According to a recent study:

> When people not so entitled are observed to enter certain fishing grounds, use certain restricted fishing methods or harvest protected species, a response usually follows from the guardians of the area or resource in question. In addition to receiving communications of a more or less

heavily rhetorical nature, habitual trespassers are often subjected to wider social pressures aimed at creating personal shame. This is a serious measure in Marovo society, where there is generally a strong wish to avoid open conflict and public criticism. In some instances, chiefs demand compensation from offenders, in the form of cash or the resource 'stolen'. In certain serious cases, most notably dynamite-fishing, offenders may even be reported to the local police, resulting in court cases and heavy fines. The most serious measure applied towards really notorious poachers and trespassers is a form of social excommunication through which the offended group effectively revokes the poacher's status as a kinsman. This punishment may be meted out on a joint basis by several groups and may have grave consequences for Marovo individuals, who typically rely on a multitude of primary, secondary and tertiary use rights in land and sea resources through wide-ranging kinship privileges. (Hviding and Baines, 1994: 24)

In the above example, excommunication is a particularly tough measure because the sanction is applied multilaterally, leaving practically no chance of survival to the unrepentant free rider. For another thing, if the management responsibility (the so-called *nginira*, or 'power to speak about' fishing resources) is vested in the elders who are each kin group's spokesmen and guardians of the territory, their decisions are often directly enforced by men in their twenties and thirties. As a matter of fact, 'since these younger men are more often out on the fishing grounds they are better informed about shifts in resource availability and environmental change, and most likely to detect any trespassers' (Hviding and Baines, 1994: 26). Subsequently, elders take up trespassing cases through traditional procedures of consultation.

Monitoring and sanctioning in Andhra Pradesh

In the village of Kottapalle (Andhra Pradesh) studied in detail by Wade, monitors like common irrigators or field guards are appointed by and responsible to the village council. The common irrigators' job is to distribute water between the paddy-fields, apply it to each field, and help bring more water down the distributary to the village. The role of field guards is to enforce village regulations intended for minimizing losses to standing crops in unfenced fields, and to guard against crop thefts. They are hired for a period extending from a few months (common irrigators) to most of the year (field guards) and the procedure of appointment is repeated every year; this enables the council to rotate the monitoring groups (if demand for this job exceeds the supply) and to get rid of agents whose work was deemed unsatisfactory in the past. A reputation for being hard-working and conscientious is important in their selection while faction allegiance is probably not. Monitors are paid by the farmers or herders at a rate set by the village council. In addition, they work in small groups, partly because violating the procedures, say for equitable distribution of water, is more difficult with more than one monitor present. Field guards are empowered to take straying animals to the village pound, from which the owner has to pay a standard fine set in cash by the council to get them back. However, where many animals are involved, the case is brought before the council, which fixes the fine (Wade, 1988*a*: 63–8, 75–86). The fines are of non-trivial amounts—a day's field wages for an animal caught at night, and much more for water infringements (ibid. 193).

Incentive considerations clearly underlie the system of monitors' payment. For example, 'the field guards' salaries are set at less than the daily wage of an agricultural labourer so as to give them a strong incentive to collect the fines, for they keep all of the small fines and a fixed percentage of the larger ones' (Wade, 1988*a*: 193). As for common irrigators, they are paid from acreage levies. Free riding on their services, Wade observes, is held in check by knowledge that termination of these, when water is scarce, would produce an immediate crisis for everyone with land in a tail-end location within the village (ibid. 194). In other words, abidance by the rules is more forthcoming here than it tends to be in the case of CPRs whose mismanagement produces only long-term consequences. For another thing, people know that non-payment of the common irrigators (which is done after the first harvest and in kind) can be penalized the following year; it is indeed possible for common irrigators to interrupt a non-payer's water supply until his crops suffer yield-reducing stress (ibid.).

Another interesting feature of sanction mechanisms highlighted by Wade is that, as in the Japanese villages studied by McKean, the effects of fines are reinforced by the threat of reputation loss:

> Whether because the desire for social acceptance by a group is a fundamental principle of social behaviour or because reputation loss has material consequences for an individual in terms of contracts foregone, reputation in a small agricultural community is not lightly exposed to attack. We have seen the council deliberately seeking to activate reputation sanctions, as in its strategy of bringing the maximum number of 'influentials' to council meetings at times of crises to signify by their presence and non-disagreement their acceptance of the decision. . . . Council meetings are in a public place, so that anyone with the confidence to do so can monitor the proceedings from the sidelines and even take part in the discussions . . . council meetings on contentious issues often turn into *de facto* general meetings. . . . In these various ways . . . accountability is maintained. (Wade, 1988*a*: 193, 195)

Monitoring and sanctioning in Uttar Pradesh

A recent aforementioned study by Agrawal (1994) provides us with interesting information about monitoring and sanctioning mechanisms in a sample of community-managed forests in Almora district which belongs to the middle Himalayan ranges north of Uttar Pradesh, known as Uttarakhand (India). The sample comprises six villages. In three of them, the village forest is in excellent, or excellent-to-good condition, while in the other three the resource condition is poor to fair. Note that all six villages have elected village forest councils so as to be able to take advantage of the Van Panchayat Act (1931) which provides for the creation of community-managed forests from the forests controlled by the Revenue Department (see above, Chapter 11, sect. 1).

Bear in mind that most of these villages have adopted rather precise rules prescribing how the forest is to be used (see above, Chapter 10, sect. 2). Yet there are considerable variations in the extent to which villages resort to monitoring and sanctioning to enforce these rules. In some villages, such activities are well organized. Guards are assigned different compartments of the forest and their rewards are made dependent on their performance. The panchayat may pay the guards a lower salary when many rule violations occur and it may even dismiss them and refuse to pay their salary if the levels of these violations are too high. (To detect lax behaviour on the part of the guards is relatively easy in so far as freshly cut grass or tree branches provide evidence that the guard concerned has not been guarding properly the section of the forest for which he is responsible) (Agrawal, 1994: 275).

The panchayats have recourse to various sanction mechanisms and, in this context, the effectiveness of apologies is not to be underestimated:

They ask offenders to render written or public apologies, confiscate cutting implements such as scythes, strip villagers of use rights, impose fines, report villagers to government officials, and sometimes, seek redress in courts. The sanctions they impose depend on a number of factors: the severity and nature of the offense, the economic status of the offender, whether the person is known to be a troublemaker, the attitude that the rule breaker displays towards the panchayat and its authority, and so forth. . . . the panchayats often excuse even repeat violators from paying fines imposed on them, if the offender is willing to render a written or public apology. Such an apology reinforces the authority of the panchayat to manage the forest and to punish other individuals who commit rule infractions. (Agrawal, 1994: 278)

In the villages where such sanction mechanisms exist and are impartially applied, they tend to be effective in the sense that 'many of the users pay their fines, appear before the *panchayat* when summoned, render apologies, and promise not to break rules in the future' (Agrawal, 1994: 280). Agrawal explains that: 'Even if the panchayat does not have formal legal powers to extract fines from rule breakers, in courts of law its word carries greater weight than that of an ordinary villager. Since it has been created by a statute of law, its mere existence has the support of law' (ibid.). To this explanation must be added the presence of informal retaliation mechanisms that threaten any unrepentant rule infractor with a variety of more or less subtle ostracization responses.

One of the central conclusions reached by Agrawal is that, as expected, 'a significant relationship exists between enforcement and resource condition': villages that commit substantial resources to monitor and sanction rule-breakers are more likely to prevent degradation of their local CPRs (Agrawal, 1994: 281–2). However, as the same study shows, a comparatively high incidence of rule-breaking may also occur irrespective of the resources devoted to monitoring. Thus, the characteristics of the CPR may make a given amount of monitoring comparatively ineffective, such as when the panchayat forest compartments are highly dispersed. Or, caste prejudice may lead to biased reporting of rule-breaking, as a result of which dominant castes 'get a licence to break rules' and 'the resentment against the Brahmins would goad Harijans to break rules as often as possible' (ibid. 276–7).

Another important finding of Agrawal's study is that rule violations occur routinely even in villages with relatively high levels of monitoring and sanctioning:

Villagers illegally entered the panchayat forests, cut grass and leaf fodder from trees, grazed their animals, collected twigs and branches, and in some instances even felled trees. Their activities occurred in violation of the rules, and in spite of the presence of guards who could discover and report them to the panchayat, which would then try to force them to pay fines. The records, while documenting high levels of abuse, underestimate the extent of illegal grazing and cutting. (Agrawal, 1994: 274)

It has been proved in Chapter 8 (sect. 1) that, if monitoring is imperfect, it is possible that rule-breaking always occurs at equilibrium (there is a Nash equilibrium in mixed strategy in which the resource user violates the rule with positive probability and the guard monitors also with positive probability). To recall, this situation happens when the payoffs are such that a resource user has no incentive to violate the rule if his behaviour is monitored (since, otherwise, rule-breaking would be a dominant strategy and would therefore occur systematically rather than probabilistically). That this equilibrium in mixed strategy provides a good description of the situation observed in the villages surveyed by Agrawal can be inferred from the fact that he mentions not only the imperfect monitoring ability of the guards (due to dispersion of community forests) but also the possibility for them to evade their duties: 'The guards are often absent from the forest and even when at their posts cannot monitor all compartments of the panchayat forest simultaneously' (Agrawal, 1994: 274). While opting for occasional rule violations, forest users therefore know that guards have a monitoring tendency smaller than one and that, when they actually monitor, the probability of detection of rule-breaking is also smaller than unity.

Of course, violations of the prevailing rules are less frequent or are of relatively minor importance in villages where more resources have been devoted to monitoring (for given CPR characteristics) and, as a consequence, community forests are less subject to degradation in these villages.

12.5 The Role of Tradition

Tradition can play two central roles to support village-based CPR management: (*a*) via norms of social behaviour and (*b*) via well-established patterns of authority and leadership. These two effects are in fact tightly linked in so far as one of the functions of traditional authorities is precisely to activate and reinforce social or moral norms.

Where history enters the scene

General considerations

Historical experience as embodied in tradition and mores helps not only to shape people's preferences but also to determine the degree of trust in their mutual reliability with respect to actions involving the possibility of free riding. Thus, when a particular society had repeated experiences of successful collective action experiences in the past, positive attitudes towards co-operation tend to be conveyed to its members through myths, customs, sayings, and norms, which are all elements of their specific cultural endowment. Since culture is 'acquired knowledge that people use to interpret experience and to generate social behaviour' (Spradley and McCurdy, 1980: 2), the saying 'nothing succeeds like success' is especially relevant in this context. In Sugden's language, past experience is encapsulated in a convention of co-operation with prior success in collective action providing a focal or salient point from which such a convention may spread by analogy (see above, Chapter 6). In actual fact, a history of co-operative success makes people highly trustful of others' willingness to co-operate. Being more prominent than the non-co-operative equilibrium largely as a result of common experience of past success in co-operation, the co-operative equilibrium is established and has a great deal of stability (bear in mind that an AG is a co-ordination game).

Success in collective action tends to breed success in collective action because it helps establish a reputation for co-operation that has the effect of making other co-operative ventures easier to undertake and to sustain. This virtuous process may proceed by analogy, spreading from one domain of social life to another (*co-operative equilibrium is reached through analogy*), or else, it may reinforce itself in one particular such domain (*co-operative equilibrium is stable*). Seabright has clearly the first possibility in mind when he writes that 'many voluntary organisations working in poor countries concern themselves with promoting plays, festivals and sporting activities among disadvantaged groups, not only because of the activities' intrinsic value but because they know of their value in "building trust" ' (Seabright, 1993: 122). Thus, in a revealing manner, the presence of a prior history of co-operative institutions in Indian communities with successful producers' co-operative societies has turned to be a positive predictor of co-operative society success (ibid.). On the other hand, when Messerschmidt expresses the opinion that the strength of village-based resource regulation systems in Nepal is due to their being rooted in tradition (Messerschmidt, 1986: 473), it is not quite clear whether he thinks of the first or the second effect, or of both of them.

Co-operative equilibria may, however, not be as stable as the theory of co-ordination games suggests. Indeed, as noted by Mary Douglas, any institution (and a convention is an institution, at least in a minimal sense) needs some stabilizing principle to stop its premature demise. In other words, contrary to the view of economists like Schotter or Sugden, conventions have to be grounded in something else than themselves, that is, on a justifying or legitimizing principle that makes them appear as something more than a mere social contrivance. In the words of Douglas:

> That stabilising principle is the naturalisation of social classifications. There needs to be an analogy by which the formal structure of a crucial set of social relations is found in the physical world, or in the supernatural world, or in eternity, anywhere, so long as it is not seen as a socially contrived arrangement. When the analogy is applied back and forth from one set of social relations to another and from these back to nature, its recurring formal structure becomes easily recognised and endowed with self-validating truth . . . The favorite analogy generalises everyone's preferred convention. (Douglas, 1986: 48, 50)

Thus, in many Third World societies and particularly in Sub-Saharan Africa, the cult of ancestors provides the stabilizing principle in which many conventions (high fertility, solidarity arrangements) are grounded: 'Ancestors operating from the other side of life provide the naturalising analogy that seals the social conventions' (Douglas, 1986: 50; see also Caldwell and Caldwell, 1987). In Asturia (Spain), to take another example, we are told that traditional co-operative institutions created 'a superordinate allegiance to something that transcended people's immediate and everyday sense of reality' (McCay and Acheson, 1987: 24). Until recently, this superordinate allegiance was constantly reactivated during moments of intense conviviality and commensality which were revitalizing experiences destined to create psychophysiological states of social euphoria (Fernandez, 1987: 284). As long as Douglas's stabilizing principle or naturalizing analogy exists, members of a community can co-operate in a rather non-calculated way as though to co-operate were the normal thing to do. This perhaps explains the observation made by Bromley and Chapagain in a Nepalese village: there, people do not explicitly or consciously condition their co-operative behaviour on that of others, presumably because of 'the presence of a "background ethic" or norm that influences collective resource use decisions' (Bromley and Chapagain, 1984: 872, see also above, Chapter 7).

Co-operation norms in sedentary and immigrant communities

A common way in which norms of co-operative behaviour are expressed in rural communities is through codes of honour. A remarkable illustration of this solution to the freerider problem is provided in Cordell and McKean's study of the mechanisms of enforcement of water-access rules in Bahia (Brazil). There, the central enforcement mechanism is the ethical code associated with *respeito* deemed by the authors to be 'far more binding on individual conscience than any government regulations could ever be' (Cordell and McKean, 1986: 94). In their words again:

> It is impossible to fish for long in a given community without receiving and showing *respeito*. People honor each other's claims because of *respeito*, which is created, bestowed, and reaffirmed through sometimes trivial and sometimes substantial acts of benevolence bordering on self-sacrifice. . . . Failure to cooperate in these practices can be much more devastating for a fisherman than would be breaking a government law. *Respeito is a cognitive reference point to the community conscience.* It influences how fishermen evaluate each other's actions on and off the fishing grounds. It is a yardstick for measuring the justice of individual acts, especially in conflicts. Collective social pressure to conform to the ethics of fishing is reflected in the *ôlho do povo* (watchfulness of the community's eye, or sense of justice), reminiscent of the forceful moral and ethical standard in Palauan fishing, 'words of the lagoon'. Reputations rise and fall in terms of the *ôlho do povo*. The *ôlho do povo* determines whether territorial competition in fishing is deliberate or accidental, and whether it is antagonistic enough to require counteraction. (Cordell and McKean, 1986: 94, 98, emphasis added)

Moral norms embodied in the *respeito* code of ethics are not completely internalized and therefore require to be supported by external sanctions. The community symbolically manifested as the *ôlho do povo* confers rewards on those who follow *respeito* and withdraws the benefits of exchange and reciprocity from those who violate it. In the best cases, reputation effects (enhancement or loss of reputation) are sufficient to grind rule-breaking to a halt. In the worst cases, external sanctions consist of more directly coercive measures (such as when an entire network of captains decides to deny territorial use rights to a troublemaker by sabotaging his equipment, booby-trapping net-casting spaces, engaging in deliberate net-crossing, etc.) aimed at forcing renegade fishermen to mend their ways or leave the community (Cordell and McKean, 1986: 98).

When serious rifts occur between different families or factions within the same community, the situation is of course more threatening. In these circumstances, certain individuals (usually retired fishing captains) are called upon as mediators who are people to be emulated and who 'epitomize *respeito* in all they do'. The conflict-resolution mechanism—which must be all the more powerful as conflicts of this sort usually reach across several generations and are marked by vengeful acts—then works in the following way:

Mediators must be able to comprehend and soothe social relationships that have fluctuated and festered over a long period of time . . . *To promote reconciliation, the mediator must invoke respeito*, the cooperative ethic, as it is reflected in the *ôlho do povo, and bring it to bear on individual consciences*. Thus, the way out of a dispute is not to fix blame and then to punish the wrongdoer, but to negotiate reunion (by appealing to the sense of justice) and to restore equality. A simple face-saving gesture by either one of the parties will suffice for openers. This involves humbling oneself and showing that one no longer wishes to carry a grudge. If successful, this strategy will lead to an exchange of favors or kindness. . . . Through an exchange of just such small favors and concessions, fishermen are frequently able to come to terms, reestablish *respeito*, renew cooperative relations, and reaffirm the value of honor and deference in avoiding water space challenges. (Cordell and McKean, 1986: 99–100, emphasis added)

It is interesting to note that, in the foregoing illustration, mediators serve both as role models (they 'epitomize *respeito* in all they do') and as norm reactivators (they 'invoke *respeito*' and 'bring it to bear on individual consciences').

The situation observed in the Molucca Islands (Indonesia) where a system of traditional CPR management known as *sasi* does still exist (see Chapter 10, sect. 2) bears a good deal of similarity to the system described above. As a matter of fact, management measures are enforced by a council of elders made up of representatives of extended families and in which the chair position is occupied by certain families by inheritance. Even though punishments are explicitly designed to ensure enforcement, people obey the law because they are keen to uphold the dignity of their families (as a single person's faults are regarded as the faults of the family) and also because they are aware of the advantages of regulation (Marut, 1994: 6).

Patterns of co-operative behaviour that are sustained by a long historical experience encapsulated in a body of traditions can be found not only in sedentary societies but also in immigrant communities. Thus, for example, it is well known that old ways were very powerful in shaping immigrant life in nineteenth-century America, including all matters related to resource access and use. This was a fact of considerable importance given that immigrants moved into new areas before the law could establish public order. In reality, the informal procedures employed by them to protect their investments and ensure the orderly development of their resource showed a high degree of continuity with traditional practices in their countries of origin. In areas peopled by different communities, this contributed to establish strongly segmented exclusive resource domains as well as highly diversified and colourful sets of practices and codes of informal law. To illustrate, fishermen who migrated to California 'did not lack traditions from which to build such ad hoc, quasi-legal systems for ordering their working lives' and, as they lived in close proximity to one another and in near isolation from everyone else, they 'proved more tenacious than other occupational groups in resisting the substitution of market relations for customary ones in their communities' (McEvoy, 1986: 95–6).

The fishermen's first task was of course to establish some form of tenancy over their resources, which implied laying down exclusionary rules. It is not surprising in this context that informal or quasi-legal boundaries for the fish resource followed ethnic lines and that, within each resource domain, fishing communities tended to organize along traditional patterns brought all the way from their native countries. For instance, on the Sacramento river the salmon business was entirely controlled by whites and any attempt on the part of the Chinese, to engage in salmon-fishing would have met with a summary and probably fatal retaliation. Within the 'white' waters, clear ethnic demarcations were also in force: 'Greek fishers marked the upper ends of their "drifts" with makeshift Greek flags. From this point boats set out at fifteen-to-twenty minute intervals on their downstream courses, and Italian or other gill-netters who intruded on the ground did so at their peril' (McEvoy, 1986: 96). Furthermore, once their claims to particular fishing grounds were well established, fishing communities started to regulate their business as they wished. Thus, in 1880, the salmon-fishing gill-netters allocated each boat a quota of forty fish per day for sale on the fresh market so as to maintain prices (ibid.).

As for the Chinese shrimpers and abalone hunters, they eventually succeeded in winning control over the Bay Area largely at the end of a long competitive struggle with Italians. Once in control of these waters, the Chinese organized an exclusively Chinese regulatory system which covered all the spheres related to their activities. Yet the Chinese were not allowed to catch crabs since this was the preserve of a strongly organized Italian association (which, later on, divided internally when Sicilians decided to protect themselves against the increasing power of northern Italian fish wholesalers). As a local newspaper put it: 'if anyone imagines that it is possible for a Chinese or member of any other nationality than an Italian to catch crabs in this bay for the market let him try it' (quoted from McEvoy, 1986: 97).

Japan and India: a contrast

The case of Japan has already drawn our attention on repeated occasions because it is a kind of model case for village-based resource management. It is instructive in the present context in so far as management and other co-operative practices in this country have a long history which is reflected in well-entrenched norms of co-operation. McKean has thus stressed than in Japanese villages CPR conservation has been internalized as a goal of vital importance over several centuries (McKean, 1986: 569). On the other hand, Ruddle has remarked that an understanding of the operation of the present-day system of sea tenure in Japanese inshore waters (about which more will be said in the next chapter) 'requires a good grasp of its historical context, since the degree of continuity of traditional management practices is an outstanding characteristic' (Ruddle, 1987: 2).

A fascinating but immensely complex question is of course that of the origin of the remarkable ability of Japanese rural communities for collective action, a question which is germane to the perplexing and more general question of how institutions get started. Different explanations have been put forward. Thus, Ruddle makes the well-known point that values of harmony together with community or group orientation had long been in existence in Japanese society. More particularly, they had been reinforced 'during the long feudal era, when Confucian values [imported from China] and a national ideology put down deep roots in a Japan that was firmly closed to outside influences' (Ruddle, 1987: 3; see also Ishikawa, 1975: 464–6; Morishima, 1982: ch. 1). Even after the Second World War when traditional values based on the key notions of loyalty and self-sacrifice were shattered at the national level, collective unity for the attainment of group goals remained predominant at the village, small group, and small organization level. At those lower social levels, 'the concept of harmony and conflict avoidance remain idealised norms', and the group or community continues to be 'a constant source of emotional and other support': 'Coupled with group orientation is the abhorrence of isolation and the extreme psychological trauma suffered by members pushed out of their group as a consequence of persistent anti-social behaviour' (Ruddle, 1987: 3–5). There has no doubt been a clear tendency to exaggerate the social harmony and collective unity virtues of Japanese society, particularly among Japanese social scientists. Conflicts have always been present at the core of Japanese societal life, including village life. None the less, it is fair to say that, compared to many other societies in the world, harmony and related qualities have been a major force in Japanese society at least until very recent times (ibid. 4).

Another, more materialistic explanation can be derived from the fact that a decisive event in Japanese history occurred around the middle of the sixteenth century when an advanced form of feudalism replaced the hereditary manorial system under Oda Nobunaga (Morishima, 1982: 41–4). On that occasion, indeed, 'the warriors had been removed from the countryside to the castle town in order to eliminate the danger to the lord of armed retainers directly in control of land and subjects' (Smith, 1959: 202). In this way, an administrative and government system emerged which made possible 'an extraordinary economy of force and officialdom' and was essentially based on the competence and reliability of local government. The only official between the village and the castle town was the district magistrate who usually had no military force at his command 'except a handful of armed men for guard duty'; he was charged with governing thousands of peasant families on behalf of the lord, which implied collecting taxes, administering justice, maintaining public order, etc. The fact of the matter was that these burdensome tasks were delegated to village communities because no alternative solution was available once the lord's armed retainers were requested to reside with him in the castle town. This forced such communities to assume new responsibilities and to settle almost all local affairs and problems on their own:

> Nowhere, for instance, did the lord undertake to levy taxes on individual peasants; rather, he laid taxes on villages as units, leaving each to allocate and collect its own, and to make up any deficit that might occur in the payments of individual families. This was but one of many administrative functions performed by villages in all parts of the country. Villages maintained their own roads and irrigation works, policed their territories, administered common land and

irrigation rights; validated legal transactions among members, mediated disputes, and passed sentence and imposed punishment in petty criminal cases; enforced the lord's law *and their own*, stood responsible as a whole for a crime by any of their members, borrowed money, made contracts, sued and were sued. Aside from transmitting the lord's instructions to the villages, the magistrate normally did little more than help assess villages for taxes and receive their payments and hear the more serious civil and criminal cases they referred to him. (Smith, 1959: 202–3, emphasis added)

The above two explanations might be considered complementary. The argument would run as follows: if Japanese rural communities could successfully undertake all the aforementioned functions when they had to, it is in part because of the pervasive presence of group-oriented values in their cultural patrimony. In other words, if success of these communities in a large range of collective actions appears to confirm the above-discussed thesis that 'necessity is the mother of all inventions'—that is, when co-ordination of individual actions is of vital importance to people's survival, it tends to take place in one way or another—it must be added that effective response to the considerable challenge which confronted them during the sixteenth century could not have been brought about had they not possessed a cultural endowment adequate to the task. After all, under the pressure of this challenge, village communities could well have broken asunder, a possibility all the more serious as fiscal and judiciary responsibilities were entrusted to them.

Still, the question remains as to whether the possession of group-oriented values by Japanese rural communities must be ultimately traced back to ideological factors or to some material determinants that appear to have played a crucial role in their history. While the former possibility has been suggested by Ruddle (see above), the latter is apparently the preference of Hayami and Kikuchi for whom, as we have seen in Chapter 11, tightly structured social systems emerged in Japan because of the critical need for effective community-level irrigation systems and for the proper resolution of conflicts over the use of water. In game-theoretical terms, the critical character of the need for collective action determines a payoff structure in which non-co-operative behaviour, whether unilateral or multilateral, entails such a high cost (the corresponding payoffs are infinitely negative) that co-operation is the only equilibrium strategy.

The above evolutionary hypothesis can actually be refined by arguing that, since local irrigation systems were well localized and visible, since users could easily assess the impact of their own actions upon other users, and since there was no conservation issue involved, collective action was rather easily induced by the felt need for it. Later, fed by such a positive experience, co-operation successfully spread (by analogy) to other domains where collective action was a priori more problematic. An important and testable implication of this amended evolutionary theory is that co-operation is more likely to be established in communities which, at some point in their history, were happy enough to meet relatively easy challenges *before* being confronted with more difficult ones in the sense of challenges requiring more trust to be successfully addressed. Note the similarity between such a view and the argument developed earlier (see above, sect. 2) to account for the persistence of common village pastures in South India and their disappearance in Rwanda.

Obviously, the foregoing considerations are to be related to our previous discussions about the role of economic incentives in the second section of this chapter and about the effects of population pressure in the second section of Chapter 11. When this is done, one understands that village societies can find themselves in more or less favourable situations from the standpoint of their collective action capabilities. Prospects are the brightest in societies which have developed a long tradition of co-operation starting from relatively non-problematic challenges and benefiting from a rather stable environment. On the other hand, prospects are the dimmest in societies which did not enjoy such favourable circumstances and are suddenly confronted with hard challenges under rapidly changing conditions that prevent them from gradually learning to find the adequate institutional responses. In these societies, external intervention in the form of external provision of specially designed economic incentives and/or specific organizational assistance (on which we shall soon say more) is absolutely required.

Returning to our Japanese example, there is a final point that needs to be made. On the basis of McKean's study, we have earlier emphasized that enforcement of resource management schemes in Japan was strongly supported by well-designed, rigorously applied, and possibly harsh sanctions or penalties. Built-in punishment mechanisms also existed to a considerable extent in a society where loss of reputation acts as a powerful deterrent to misdeeds: in Japan, as is well known, the notion of pride, 'often veiled by humbleness', is all-pervasive and assumes critical importance in any life circumstance (Ruddle, 1987: 5). This undeniably testifies that even strong co-operation norms are typically not sufficient to sustain collective action: a hardly surprising fact given that rural dwellers are likely to deviate from such norms in times of crisis when trust may unravel and payoffs may change in such a dramatic way as to transform an AG into a PD game (since future incomes are then heavily discounted). In present-day circumstances, moreover, sanctions have become all the more necessary as, along with the massive changes that have occurred in Japanese society during recent decades, many of the traditional norms of peasants' behaviour have begun to erode and 'litigation has become an increasingly common, if not still totally acceptable, means of settling disputes' (ibid. 3).

India offers a striking contrast to Japan. In many parts of the Indian subcontinent, indeed, collective action at village level is highly difficult due to the absence of any tradition of collective responsibility (e.g. there was no collective responsibility for payment of taxes) and to the strongly polarized structure of rural society. As long as people in the lower castes accepted the dominant ideology vindicating the strongly inegalitarian social system, collective action under the authority and leadership of upper-caste people did not create too many problems. Not to obey and not to render faithful service to their masters would have been considered as a grave violation of their life duty (*dharma*) by low-caste people and, in any event, the former could easily wreak all sorts of punishment on the latter whenever they deemed fit. Today, things have changed and lower-caste people no longer accept their status as an inexorable fate. They have actually learned to assert themselves against the upper castes (Harper, 1968; Breman, 1974; Hayami and Kikuchi, 1981: 236; see also Béteille, 1965). When social relations are thus ingrained by caste prejudice and a good deal of accumulated tension, they become explosive, thereby making collective action extremely difficult to start and to sustain.

In this context, it is not surprising that many village panchayats do not work as collective bodies: in Kottapalle, Wade notes, the panchayat 'has been moribund for as long as anyone can remember' and people take it for granted, 'with resignation rather than approval', that each successive president will use its income as more or less his own (Wade, 1988*a*: 56). Furthermore, all kinds of village committees—such as the village social forestry committees initiated under the social forestry programme of the government—'are often "paper" organisations characterised by indifference and ignorance on the part of the majority of their members' (Blaikie *et al.*, 1986: 490). In Indian villages generally, 'the ideas of loyalty to the territorially-defined community, of public-spirited concern for the village welfare as the touchstone of public virtue, have hardly developed' (Wade, 1988*a*: 57), in stark contrast to what is observed not only in Japan but also in South-East Asia, Sub-Saharan Africa, and other countries (including in Western Europe). Close to India, in Nepal, the Indian panchayat system was introduced in the 1960s and superimposed on pre-existing forms of local and ethnic (i.e. non-caste) communal governance and village leadership. Yet, in spite of the disruptions that ensued especially in traditionally non-caste-oriented communities, customary village organizations have remained very much alive. Regarding local CPR regulation, it has thus been pointed out that 'in some instances, newly organised local systems of management have sprung up, and in others, older, pre-existing systems have been rejuvenated or strengthened despite nationalisation and similar disruptive circumstances' (Messerschmidt, 1986: 459).

In the light of the above considerations, the fact that in the South Indian villages studied by Wade effective corporate organizations for regulating access to water could develop and work satisfactorily (think also of the above-documented success of the Arabari reafforestation experiment in West Bengal) may perhaps seem astonishing. Two things stressed by Wade are worth bearing in mind here. First, an important factor that apparently determined the success of these organizations lay in the pattern of ownership of irrigable lands: to the extent that the village élite have scattered holdings, externalities of water use are not 'unidirectional' and this élite has an interest in establishing and maintaining an adequate system of water access regulation (see above, sect. 3). Second, contrary to what we have noted in the case of Japan, moral norms of co-operative behaviour are noticeably absent in Indian villages, except perhaps when concerted action is directed against other collectivities. Thus, in the case of Kottapalle, Wade reached the following conclusion:

> Village-based organisation, even after several decades or more, has only a weak claim to morally motivated obedience. If the village council were seen as the village personified or as the embodiment of the ideal of cooperative ways of doing things, one would expect to see some symbolism by which this representation is achieved; but there is none. The village public realm is about getting things done rather than about ceremony and symbolism . . . The farmers' involvement remains calculative rather than moral . . . the council and its work groups are seen as a functionally-specific machine, to be judged according to its ability to control and support

the individual's search for his own advantage . . . This, in a word, is why there is a fairly steady pattern of corporate organisation, even though it lacks a strong underpinning of normative understanding that people *ought* to behave in a corporate kind of way. However, . . . a general sense of reciprocity, of doing to others as you would have them do to you . . . is present to some degree. It is reinforced by experience of past behaviour showing that (most) others *can* be trusted to do their share, to abide by the rules. Conversely, the 'ought' rapidly loses force if that trust is lost . . . for many in the population whatever sense of obligation they feel is probably secondary to the sanctions they would face as a result of their general social subordination. (Wade, 1988*a*: 196–7).

The impression which one gets from the foregoing analysis is therefore that trust is rather precarious because it is not supported by any kind of community-oriented values. Effective enforcement of CPR management schemes crucially depends on punishment mechanisms that must be rigorous and equitable enough not to arouse continuous suspicions and complaints. Consequently, such schemes are vulnerable to slight perturbations in the social context in which they operate, as when factional rivalries or caste prejudices suddenly arise. In addition, collective action would presumably be much more problematic than Wade actually observed if CPR management were to involve high monitoring costs: in this case, indeed, the existence of largely internalized norms of co-operative behaviour are particularly helpful in solving the free–rider problem.

Where analogy did not work: the case of Teelin Bay again

It is interesting to return for a while to Taylor's study of the Teelin Bay's fishermen community (Taylor, 1987). As we have seen earlier, Teeliners have successfully maintained an old rotation system of access to a small estuary of the Glen River in order to make salmon harvesting orderly and equitable. Co-operation under this system is deemed by the local fishermen so 'natural' that no formal sanction system exists to enforce it: norms of co-operative behaviour are well established and reputation effects are quite sufficient to deter free-riding. On the basis of the 'analogy doctrine', one would thus have expected that, when a priest came to the village in 1973 to convince its inhabitants to extend co-operation to the whole Glen River, he would have met with a positive response. In actual fact, things turned out differently: not only was the opposite reaction observed but Teeliners even displayed an attitude of resolute resistance to the priest's project.

Such an attitude cannot apparently be entirely or even chiefly explained by the fact that the realization of the project required the collective purchase by the community of Teelin's Glen River's fishing rights from a non-profit organization based in Dublin (known as Gael-Linn). The main reason for their paradoxical unwillingness to undertake concerted action about the water area concerned is apparently the lack of a tradition of co-operation in this portion of the customary fishing grounds. As a matter of fact, riverine salmon fisheries have long been a privately or institutionally owned and managed resource. In post-medieval times, landlords claimed such fisheries as adjoined their estates and they did not open them to the peasantry: 'locals might be employed to tend the landlord's weir or crew his net-boats, but unauthorised fishing was theft' (Taylor, 1987: 295). From this time onwards, there developed a tradition of poaching—'there were even a few individuals who would venture out at night and stretch a net across the entire width of the narrowest part of the river' (ibid.)—which came to be regarded by local fishermen as a sort of sport run at the expense of the landlord towards whom latent hostile feelings were thereby manifested. When the government took over ownership, this local cultural significance of poaching as an expression of hostility and opposition to outside authority persisted. In Taylor's words:

> Poaching, however, was also a valued tradition. Just as the landlord's role was to police his holdings, the tenant's role was to poach. Old men spoke with undisguised relish about the good old days, when close watch over the waters made poaching a true challenge. Otherwise law-abiding men would wink and smile at their own reminiscences of successful expeditions and even of capture and confinement. Today, small fines and the lack of effective enforcement seem to have made poaching a somewhat less challenging sport, but sport it remains. Evidently the fact that the landlords are gone and Irish government or Gael-Linn's bailiffs are now the regulators makes little difference in the local perception of the 'sides'; it is still locals versus outside authorities. (Taylor, 1987: 300)

Given the above culturally rooted perception, Teelin fishermen have absolutely no trust in one another's readiness to put an end to poaching practices. 'The problem, as they see it, is that poaching, as long as it does not violate local rights of access as defined in the rotation system, is a "natural" local characteristic. No one could imagine giving it up' (Taylor, 1987: 300–1). They are none the less willing to admit that it would be better if everyone would stop poaching, yet, since lack of trust is pervasive, the only way they consider it feasible to establish co-operation consists of involving an *external* authority able to impose punishment in an unyielding manner. The situation therefore resembles an AG where a non-co-operative equilibrium prevails due to generalized absence of trust. To establish trust and move to a co-operative equilibrium, actors believe than an external agency must enter the scene.

Taylor's story of Teelin fishermen is fascinating because it shows how tradition can shape the conditions in which one would like to see people co-operate. In a portion of the water space which has long been open to locals, a long tradition of co-operation regarding access to fishing sites has imparted a kind of 'naturalness' to the co-operative behaviour displayed by the fishermen. But where there has been a long tradition of inveterate poaching for historical reasons, the minimum trust does not exist among the same fishermen to get concerted action started. In these circumstances, creating a new convention (institution) by analogy cannot work simply because different cultural norms prevail in the two resource domains exploited by them. History clearly matters.

Trust can be built: lessons from two success stories

It would actually be wrong to infer from the above account that collective action is impossible unless it is rooted in a long tradition of co-operation. There is enough evidence to show that trust can sometimes be built over short periods of time provided that general surrounding conditions are favourable. Thus, for example, in her study of the Villa Santa co-operative of Honduran resin-tappers, Stanley argues that one of the chief factors behind the cohesion of the group which enabled it to successfully control a local forestry was the shared experience of migrating together from southern Honduras and participating in a strike to stop sawmill expansion. This collective action of forest protection—which involved the blocking of a road leading to local pine forests—'gave the co-operative an initial purpose, and served to bind members together' (Stanley, 1991: 765, 774).

The story of the Kirindi Oya and Gal Oya irrigation projects in Sri Lanka (started by the British in 1920) also deserves to be told in the present context. The factors responsible for water-poaching and the disintegration of the whole control system in the Kirindi Oya project are quite complex, yet they result largely from the large size of the group involved and from its social heterogeneity along several dimensions. Thus, according to Ostrom, among the internal factors accounting for Kirindi Oya farmers' inability to develop an effective set of management rules, the following are particularly worth singling out:

1. the very large number of farmers involved,
2. the fact that most farmers are poor settlers who have recently been recruited to the project and have little attachment to their land or to one another,
3. the extreme diversity of ethnic and cultural backgrounds,
4. the opportunity for wealthier farmers to control water through illegal or questionable strategies (potential leaders thus being able to take care of themselves without having to exert leadership to solve larger communal problems), and
5. the lack of physical control structures in the irrigation system itself. (Ostrom, 1990: 166)

To remedy the above deficiencies, a new experiment was tried on the left bank of the Gal Oya irrigation project which, by the late 1970s, was considered as a 'hydrological nightmare' characterized by widespread social and ethnic tensions (between Sinhalese and Tamil farmers); pervasive water thefts; large-scale corruption exacerbated by the clientelistic politics of a central regime unwilling to enforce rules impartially; and deep distrust and continuous recriminations (Ostrom, 1990: 167). The new project scheme, designed by a team of experts from the Agrarian Research and Training Institute (ARTI) and Cornell University, was based on the central idea that, as far as possible, rules have to be laid down by the resource users themselves, organized in small, socially homogeneous groups in which confidence is first to be re-established. To achieve that result, the ARTI–Cornell team chose to introduce 'human catalysts' in the form of institutional organizers (usually unemployed college graduates willing to live in the remote project area) who were to work directly with farmers and officials *at the field-channel level* with a view to facilitating their problem-solving capabilities. Once the few farmers (about twelve to fifteen) operating at that level are used to working together and have achieved concrete benefits from group action (e.g. repairing a broken control gate or desilting a field channel), the institutional organizers (IOs) would then help form a local organization and select, through consensus, a farmer representative. 'This representative could articulate the interests of the other farmers on his field channel at larger meetings and report back to the others what had happened in larger arenas' (ibid. 169).

The guiding principle followed by the ARTI–Cornell team was therefore that of building bottom-up organizations but only after having obtained the assurance that groups at the lowest level can effectively work together and have met with some initial success in collective action. In Ostrom's words: 'Mutual trust and reciprocity were nourished on a face-to-face basis prior to attempts to organize farmers into larger groups' (Ostrom, 1990: 172). The 'field-channel organization' (FCO) is the basic organizational unit of the Gal Oya project. FCOs are problem-solving units that operate mainly on an informal basis. A second tier of organization was built on top of the FCO at the level of the distributory channel. Named the 'distributory channel organization' (DCO), it involves between 100 and 300 farmers. A DCO's general assembly typically encompasses all farmers and committees made up of the farmer-representatives from the FCOs. As for officials, they are selected by consensus and are non-partisan. The third tier of organization, at the branch-canal or area level, followed after FCOs and DCOs had been established and linked. The fourth tier—a project-level committee playing the role of a forum in which farmers can directly participate in policy discussions—was initiated by the farmer representatives and the IOs.

In the opinion of Ostrom on whose work the foregoing account is based, the achievements of the Gal Oya project have been really impressive. Not only are water rotation procedures quite generally attended, but rotations frequently involve deliberate efforts by those located higher in the system to make water available to tail-enders, a noteworthy achievement in view of the fact that head-enders tend to be Sinhalese and tail-enders tend to be Tamils. Moreover, farmers began to work on clearing out the channels within a few months of the creation of an FCO and, at times, they have even participated in the clearing of distributory channels that were not cleared by officials because of lack of funding. Also, the level of conflict among farmers declined at the same time as better understanding and trust developed between farmers and officials of the Irrigation Department. Finally, the initial opposition of powerful farmers gradually disappeared and the day-to-day problem-solving regarding irrigation and agricultural problems could be taken away from politicized channels, an extremely important step given the spoils systems that had evolved in Sri Lanka (Ostrom, 1990: 169–72).

One of the most interesting lessons from this project is indeed that mutual trust can be gradually built up within the framework of small groups geared towards solving concrete problems of vital importance to members. If the Gal Oya irrigation scheme achieved the degree of success it did after so many years of disastrous failure in the whole region, it is undoubtedly because of its progressive bottom-up approach in which irrigators were initially placed in trust-enhancing conditions (small groups formed at the most decentralized level of the field channel where a number of crucial but rather easy-to-solve problems continuously arise) with 'human catalysts' to help them overcome initial distrust.

In other Asian countries, like the Philippines, Thailand, and Indonesia, field facilitators have become widely used in irrigation projects (Bruns, 1993). The role of such outsider catalysts seems to have been equally determining in other circumstances, for example in successful forestry programmes (e.g. in West Bengal, Jammu and Kashmir, and Haryana States in India) or in grazing schemes (such as the World Bank-funded Eastern Senegal Livestock Development Project) which have employed 'special change agents' who, by acting as motivators in the field, would favour the emergence of strong local user-organizations (Cernea, 1989: 51; Swallow and Bromley, 1994*b*: 8).

There is obviously a crucial difference between the two above stories. In the story of the Villa Santa co-operative, trust has arisen from within the group itself, largely as a result of the sharing of positive experiences. It must be noted that the decisive experience of the strike also needs to be explained since the strike is evidently a collective action. It is a well-known fact, though, that it is much easier to unite against some external enemy (in this instance, a sawmill company) than to establish co-operation among individuals in the absence of any outside threat. Trust-building in Villa Santa co-operative has thus been a two-step endogenous process. First, an opportunity presented itself which enabled people to get together rather easily (all the more easily as they had a common background of migratory experience). Then, during a second stage, banking on the trust thereby established, they could undertake constructive (rather than purely defensive) actions aimed at managing a whole forest area. In the second story, that of the Gal Oya irrigation project, external agents have played a critical role both in educating irrigators ('human catalysts' have helped them to learn in the field how to build up trust through carefully monitored concrete actions) and in ensuring a high degree of participation of the beneficiaries in the whole project set-up.

Clearly, when mutual distrust prevails, outside intervention is inevitable (a point which Teelin's fishermen have well understood). It is not sure, however, that it is going to succeed. There are circumstances—such as in Indian villages ridden with caste prejudices—in which the initial conditions for village-level unified action are so unfavourable that attempts at fostering them are doomed to failure.

This being said, there is at least a common thread which unites the two above-mentioned stories and ties them up in an interesting way with other theoretical considerations made before. As a matter of fact, the two experiences suggest that co-operation has more chance to get established when it is developed in a gradual way, starting with rather easy-to-meet challenges and then moving to more complex situations requiring more trust and collective discipline. This approach may have been followed spontaneously in the history of a particular community or it may have been purposefully pursued by some external agency as in the Gal Oya project. Note also that the above idea underlies efforts at promoting plays, festivals, and sporting activities before embarking upon more demanding collective enterprises (see above).

Leadership pattern: traditional or modern?

It is an often-stressed fact that success of collective action is frequently associated with effective, charismatic local leadership. Thus, for example, differences among Nepalese panchayats in terms of reafforestation achievements are 'quite largely attributable to the qualities of particular leaders' who are effective in organizing protection and in negotiating agreements with government agencies (McNicoll, 1990: 158, citing Mahot *et al.*, 1987). Good leaders are needed to perform a number of pivotal functions which can be straightforwardly derived from the foregoing analysis in this and previous chapters: (*a*) to help people become aware of the real challenges confronting them; (*b*) to convince them that they can ultimately benefit from concerted action; (*c*) to show them the good example (see Chapter 5); (*d*) to mobilize a sufficient number of them for enterprises requiring co-ordinated efforts (see Chapter 5 again); and (*e*) to ensure impartiality and fairness in the designing and enforcing of rules and sanction mechanisms. Bear in mind that, in game-theoretical terms, the presence of leadership ensures that the game is played sequentially and, as we have argued in Chapter 5 and recalled in the third section above, co-operation is more likely to occur when sequential moves are possible.

Now, to be an effective leader, a person must have at least two basic qualities: first, he must be competent and able to understand the main stakes of what is going on, and, second, he must evoke trust in his good intentions, 'that his use of power should be seen not to be predatory and self-interested, but concerned with the welfare of the larger whole' of which both he and his followers are part (Wade, 1988*b*: 491). Many experiences tend to show that the existence of well-recognized traditional leaders is an important factor of success in village-based management schemes or in concerted actions in general. This is apparently due to the fact that they possess the above two qualities or, in case they lack some technical competence required for the effective working of the schemes, they delegate the related tasks to someone more competent (and generally younger) than they are.

In many cases, therefore, we can observe that traditional authority patterns continue to play a dominant role in CPR management schemes or projects, often behind the new formal institutional façades imposed from outside. For instance, among the Thakali and Bhotia communities of mountainous Nepal, common assets like irrigation water and communal forests are still run under the guidance of traditional systems of community governance and local leadership. Over the past few decades, writes Messerschmidt, the ethnic Bhotia communities have succeeded in preserving the ancient and customary role of headman (who is chosen from among the most influential in the village, by the consensus of all household heads) despite imposition of the caste-based panchayat system. 'The Bhotia consider the panchayat to be a foreign concept, but pay lip service to its requirements. They elect a chairman and a panchayat council, but beneath this façade the village headman remains in charge. He manages by consensus and is backed by strong tradition . . . the panchayat system serves only as the community mouthpiece to the outside' (Messerschmidt, 1986: 464).

In Botswana, likewise, 'the traditional ward structure with its chiefs and headmen still remains the recognised forum for community consultation and the central motor of community mobilization and organization from which even modern institutions derive their authority' (Zufferey, 1986: 14). Thus, the village *kgotla* is still the main village body dealing with customary law and general community issues; moreover, its decisions continue to be considered to 'represent' the community (see above, Chapter 11). On the other hand, it is not rare to see the major executives of the village development committee (the official planning and co-ordinating body in the village community, introduced by the government in the late 1960s) to be close relatives of the chief. This is regarded by Zufferey as a positive feature in so far as the chief's relatives are found to command greater authority and respect in the community (ibid.: 36).

In general, traditional organizations rarely correspond in coverage and membership with modern community organizations imposed by central governments. The representatives on the councils, committees, and associations are usually not elected by a formal voting process but become members due to their social, economic, and lineage position in the community, clan, or tribe (Willmann, 1993). This is clearly the case in the South Indian villages studied by Wade where, as we have seen, local councils are typically controlled by members from the dominant castes and the wealthier landowners. Frequently also, an important election criterion is experience and knowledge, tantamount to age (ibid.). In most areas, elders have an overriding weight and tend to make decisions on behalf of the assembly. The age criterion is often combined with the economic/social status criterion inasmuch as the elders sitting on village councils come themselves from the wealthiest and more important families (see McKean, 1986: 551 for Japan).

Traditional authority and leadership patterns present considerable advantages for village-based collective action in general and for CPR management in particular. The prestige which customary leaders carry and the trust which they evoke may impart a great deal of legitimacy to their initiatives and decisions. In addition, the very fact that their (natural) authority is rooted in tradition tends to guarantee the continuity of the schemes based on it. Thus, for example, one of the main reasons why pastoral associations in eastern Senegal are more efficient among the Wolof and the Mandingo than among the Peul is that leaders of the former have more power and influence in matters of common concern besides the fact that they can rely on stricter and stronger traditional organizations, particularly above village level (Shanmugaratnam *et al.*, 1992: 38). Among the Boran pastoralists of northern Kenya, on the other hand, the elected clan leaders (known as the *jalaba*) have limited decision-making powers and all herd owners can speak in the traditional assemblies concerned with questions of natural resource use and management. Yet, the leaders have 'an extensive capacity for mediation and conciliation' (Swift, 1991: 36), which appears crucial for reaching viable compromises in societies accustomed to the unanimity rule.

There are nevertheless serious potential shortcomings in this solution, too. The first and most obvious one is personal inadequacy (incompetence, partiality, self-interestedness, corruption, laziness, etc.) of traditional leaders. Thus, in the above-cited study of Botswana, Zufferey has observed that in some communities where CPR management schemes have fared poorly, lapses on the part of the traditional headman or his close associates are often at fault. In Moshopa, for example: 'The chief was reported to be a major problem in the community because of his basic lack of knowledge about the role and objectives of modern institutions, his failure to hold meetings as promised, and his lack of determination in defending community interests' (Zufferey, 1986: 38). In Kgagodi, the village development committee which was elected on the basis of traditional influences and status has been blamed for selecting projects 'that improve its own "self-image" rather than the living standards of the community' (ibid.: 46).

The situation is still more uncertain when, as documented in Chapter 11, corruption of the traditional élite is mounting. As has been appositely remarked by Colchester, 'as local leadership becomes less accountable and less responsive to community needs and rights, the opportunities for making land use decisions that increase personal gain at the expense of community security, both social and environmental, are widening' (Colchester, 1994: 87). Thus, traditional leaders often cannot resist the temptation of quick and easy rents when there arises the possibility of intensive commercial exploitation of local natural resources which were so far harvested only or mainly for subsistence needs.

Traditional leaders need not always be incompetent or mischievous, yet the customary source of their legitimacy or their tribal affinities may be at the root of special difficulties. In particular, they may be hesitant to call into question erstwhile rules of access that now prove too lax for an effective management of natural resources. This fact has actually been mentioned earlier while discussing the problems arising from absentee herd ownership in several African countries. Another striking illustration comes from Niger. In this country, with the assistance of foreign donors (including the World Bank), the government has embarked upon a project of pastoral development in response to the disastrous consequences of the 1969 and 1972–3 droughts. The so-called *Projet de Développement de l'Elevage au Niger Centre-Est* is based on a pastoral organization consisting of three levels. The lowest of these tiers is the GMP (*Groupement Mutualiste Pastoral*) which is the unit for water management and collective water rights to GMP wells which were formerly public. We are told that the most important problem with these GMPs is 'the lack of a clear concept of membership by which to distinguish a member from a non-member, or to identify advantages exclusive to a member'. More precisely:

> In a typical case, a GMP is formed on the basis of a tribal sub-group, but not all the members of the sub-group need to become members of the GMP for it to be assigned collective water rights. Nevertheless, all of them, members and non-members alike, enjoy the collective right to the well. A GMP member is said to be entitled to a card. However, there is no prescribed membership fee although a few GMPs have collected a contribution of 500 CFA each from some of their members. (Shanmugaratnam *et al.*, 1992: 30)

Regarding outsiders, the customary principle of allowing them free access to the well and the surrounding pastures for a few days after which they have to make some payment to the well-owner to continue to enjoy the rights of access, is still followed by the management committees of the GMPs.[10] The problem is actually made more

[10] Recall that traditional wells are owned and managed by pastoral families and clans, and these private rights are recognized and respected by the community. The ownership of wells 'gives their owners some degree of indirect control over the surrounding pastures, although custom and the ecology of Sahelian pastoralism preclude monopolistic control'. The most important point to note is that members of the local community enjoy priority over outsiders in access to private wells. In return, the well-owner receives from the community the labour required for ensuring maintenance of the well infrastructure. Outsiders' access is regulated as explained in the text. What needs to be stressed, however, is the following: 'Rigid manage-

complicated still because many outsiders 'do not respect the authority of the GMP and attempt to by-pass it and use the well'. And this is in spite of the fact that the GMPs are dominated by traditional chiefs and their families (ibid. 31–3). This last observation takes us straight to the next potential problem associated with traditional leadership. Since it has already been discussed at some length (see above, Chapter 11), it needs only to be briefly mentioned here. Under the influence of rapidly occurring changes in macro-political structures—such as the introduction of the new village panchayat system (elected village councils) in India—the economic and technological environment, and values or beliefs, traditional authority of village elders or erstwhile feudal landlords is being increasingly questioned by at least certain segments of the rural population, most notably outsiders (as above), migrant workers, young age-groups, educated people, low social strata, and frustrated rival factions. In many cases, what tends to become more and more unacceptable are the old-fashioned, hierarchical, non-democratic, and rather secret mode of functioning of customary village institutions as well as their unbalanced membership.

There is apparently increasing evidence to show that, when traditional authorities are no longer performing or are deeply questioned, and/or when collective action is better taken at a lower-than-village level, co-operation has a better chance to succeed if group leaders are relatively young, educated persons who have preferably been exposed to modern values and ways through migration or similar experiences. Thus, from a study conducted in Tanzania, Putterman has concluded that 'there is mild support for a "modernisation" type hypothesis whereby "modernising" influences, rather than traditional ones, are considered to be conducive to collective labor participation. Education, migration, and previous participation in wage labor showed positive relationships with collective labor participation. These influences are also borne out at the village level' (Putterman, 1981: 393). The author ascribes this finding to the fact that education, migration, and wage employment history—which, incidentally, have the effect of *increasing* the village's social heterogeneity—tend to generate 'less parochial outlooks' (ibid.: 398). Similar results have been obtained by Sadan and Weintraub (1980) on the basis of their study of the factors of economic performance in Israeli co-operative settlements (which are composed of many immigrants with a traditional background). And Indian co-operative societies with relatively educated officers appear to be more successful than others (Seabright, 1993: 123).

The question as to why educated persons (typically with a history of exposure to the external world) turn out to be good initiators of co-operation deserves some attention. There are several possible explanations for this situation. In particular, educated persons may be better able to understand the advantages of co-operation, especially so if these advantages are long-term or not easily perceptible for some reason. Another possibility is that educated persons are comparatively good at designing effective mechanisms for initiating and sustaining co-operation. More importantly, education is

ment of private wells is limited by the tradition of reciprocity among pastoral communities and the ecological determinants of pastoral production in the Sahel. Given the low, erratic and unevenly distributed rainfall and the uncertainties it poses to livestock production, a private well-owner needs to transhume like any other pastoralist to find pasture and water' (Shanmugaratnam *et al.*, 1992: 31).

essential for the mastery of critical skills like bookkeeping and accounting, legal knowledge, correspondence in the official language, and so on. It also provides self-confidence in dealing with the government and the outside world (Shanmugaratnam *et al.*, 1992: 10), which is especially useful when government agents behave in an arrogant or ruthless fashion. This ability to address authorities or external agents on a more or less equal footing, using their own language and modes of thinking, may go a long way towards explaining why educated leaders enjoy increasing legitimacy and prestige among rural dwellers.

Many case histories could also be cited in support of the above set of explanations. For example, in Ronkh village on the Senegal River, successful collective action has been undertaken by a group of rural youth which could rely on the effective leadership of an educated person who decided to put an end to his teaching career in town in order to settle back in his native village (Gentil, 1986: 206–16). Note carefully that this case is quite different from the one described earlier (in Chapter 11) in which migrant workers return to their native village in Botswana but only for short periods of time. Having no stake any more in the collective affairs of their community, they show a natural inclination to feel unconcerned by them and to withdraw from the village's public forum. For another thing, it is worth pointing out that, in the aforementioned experience of the Villa Santa co-operative of resin-tappers in Honduras, the idea of the co-operative actually took hold with the guidance of lawyers and university students from the capital city of Tegucigalpa (Stanley, 1991: 772).

The main lesson to be drawn from the foregoing discussion seems to be the following. Given the rapid changes that have transformed the Third World country-side during recent decades, the ideal case presents itself when collective action takes place under the impulse and leadership of dynamic persons who (*a*) have been exposed to the outside world in one way or another, and (*b*) do not squarely confront or antagonize traditional structures and authority patterns but find a tactful way to collaborate with them, at least where they have remained alive. The first condition guarantees not only that these new leaders have developed non-parochial outlooks, but also that they have acquired knowledge about the nature of present-day challenges and about ways of dealing with official authorities at the national or regional levels and, possibly, with external donor agencies (an almost indispensable prerequisite of successful collective action in the modern context). As for the second condition, it ensures that unnecessary tensions are avoided and that the social prestige of customary rulers and institutions is mobilized in support of the new co-operative ventures. (Failure to achieve this could actually result in the deliberate blocking of any new initiative by resentful and vindictive traditional rulers.)

Thus, referring to the leadership structure of Senegalese pastoral associations (called *Groupements d'Intérêt Economique* or GIE) which have achieved some success in improving the management of rangelands and in reducing the frequency of resource-use conflicts both within and between pastoral communities of eastern Senegal, an above-cited study notes the following. In many GIEs, younger educated men are replacing traditional leaders, but these younger leaders still consult the elders in important decisions. This is a positive feature since 'the participation of the elders in the decision-making lends authority to GIE boards ensuring that decisions are followed up at the village level' (Shanmugaratnam *et al.*, 1992: 36). In the Pacific Islands, to take another example, we are told that many traditional leaders now accept the idea that their customary decision-making role must be given a stronger footing through the support of advisory groups of younger kin members with more formal education and wider experience of development matters. This evolution is apparently an important factor accounting for the success of local-level, community-centred organizations for resource management in meeting new challenges from the wider world through institutional innovations (Hviding and Baines, 1994: 35–6).

In the worst case, customary institutions may have eroded to the point of disintegration, giving way to bitter and uncontrollable rivalries of a personal, factional, or class nature. In such circumstances, rural communities need to radically transform their social and political institutions to undertake the required collective actions. Fortunately, there are encouraging signs that 'communities can manage to recreate open, accountable and, crucially, equitable forums for making decisions about resource management' (Colchester, 1994: 88). If these possibilities do not materialize, local-level, spontaneous collective action cannot be relied upon, at least for the near future, and only outside intervention—such as supervision of CPR management schemes by expatriate staff perceived to be not only technically competent but also socially neutral (Lawry, 1989*b*: 10)—can help to start it again on necessarily fragile grounds. The situation may not be much brighter if traditional leaders are so corrupt that they have lost all legitimacy (see above), or if they have little personal interest in CPR management and are mainly keen to avoid unpopular steps like enforcing rules governing CPR use, such has happened with so many new village panchayats in India (Jodha, 1992: 35). According to Jodha, this is because the legal and formal status of panchayats makes them 'a small scale replica of state authority' rather than a representative body of CPR users, particularly the poor villagers who crucially depend on CPRs for their daily livelihood (ibid. 69). The problem is, of course, seriously compounded when the government or other external agencies are only too willing to respond to the demands of opportunistic leaders for grants and relief that exempt their communities from genuine mobilization for the upkeep of village-level CPRs.

12.6 Conclusion

Below are listed the main conclusions which can be derived from the examination of empirical evidence in this chapter.

1. In situations involving conservation problems, villagers are usually reluctant to participate in local CPR management efforts if they do not receive *immediate* and adequate compensation for the sacrifices entailed, whether these sacrifices take the form of restraint in using the resource or of investment in resource-preserving infrastructure. External provision of appropriate economic incentives is therefore required. The transfers in favour of resource users willing to enter into a management scheme must not be so large as to make them opportunistically dependent on external assist-

ance. Yet, when resource users are hard-pressed by survival constraints and rehabilitation of the CPR entails a long gestation period, subsidies must be sufficient to allow them to build up the resource to the level where it can be optimally conserved over an indefinite time-horizon. On the other hand, when the resource to be conserved has alternative, highly valued uses that generate negative externalities, it is important that subsidies cover the opportunity costs of land and labour. The agents responsible for destructive practices are not necessarily subsistence-constrained users who are eager to draw as much income as they can from the CPR, but may also be rich users who find it optimal to follow a shut-down path of resource exploitation because they have available to them better alternative economic opportunities.

2. As expected from the theoretical insights provided in Chapters 4 and 5, collective action is more successful with small user groups. When the characteristics of the resource are such that co-operation must occur on a scale that involves large groups, the advantages of small groups formally demonstrated by the theory of non-co-operative repeated games need not be lost. Indeed, small units operating at a decentralized level can often be fitted into more complex co-operative structures that are endowed with rules and explicitly designed enforcement mechanisms.

3. Co-operation is enhanced when small groups live close to well-delineated CPRs and when they are able to lay down access and management rules in their own way. It is especially important that rules are kept as simple as possible (so as to be easily understandable and enforceable) and that they are perceived as fair by the people concerned. The latter requirement *may* imply that there is a relatively egalitarian access to local CPRs even when inequality in private landholdings and political power prevails within the village society. Its fulfilment may actually result from the fact that the social structure is articulated around patron–client relationships. If the village élite behave as natural leaders, they may then determine the success of collective action in these egalitarian zones of the village resource domain.

4. Large groups may sometimes succeed in carrying out CPR-management schemes. This tends to arise when a large group is made more like a small group because members share common norms possibly enforced by a well-recognized authority, or because they are confronted by a common challenge arising from without.

5. Homogeneous groups are often more conducive to collective action than heterogeneous groups. This is especially true when heterogeneity has its source in cultural differences and in varying interests in the CPR among the users. Yet, as has been shown in Chapter 5, there is no systematic relationship between group homogeneity and success in collective action. As a matter of fact, when heterogeneity originates in differential endowments of the users, co-operation may possibly be enhanced by the heterogeneous structure of the group. The latter result tends to occur when economic inequality does not prevent uniformity of interest in a collective agreement and when the privileged users can assume a leadership role and provide the authority structure required for proper enforcement of regulatory rules. As we know from Chapter 5, if these users have a high interest in a CPR and its management involves co-ordination problems, it is highly likely that they will take the initiative of collective action. By contrast, the worst case presents itself when the élite hold a strategic position in the

CPRs that enables them to dispense with a corporate organization and with the labour contributions of the rest of the resource users (for a recent treatment of the relationship between inequality and collective action in the case of common property resources, see Baland and Platteau, 1997, 1998, 1999).

6. External sanction systems are often needed to make up for several deficiencies of decentralized punishment mechanisms, whether the latter are embodied in strategies of conditional co-operation or involve payoff transfers among agents. In order to be effective, these systems must be escalating, flexible, and tolerant; moreover, monitors must have the right incentives to do their work seriously and be accountable to the group. Crucial decisions must be taken publicly and there is a critical role for well-accepted mediators to settle conflicts and serve as role models and norm-reactivators.

7. Past experience of successful collective action is an important 'social capital' for a village society since it becomes encapsulated in a convention of co-operation that provides a focal point from which it may spread by analogy. Rural communities with the best prospects for co-operation are probably those which were lucky enough to meet relatively easy collective challenges at some point in their history and could therefore build the trust required for confronting more complex situations. Those with the worst prospects, by contrast, are the communities which did not benefit from such a happy coincidence of historical events and became suddenly confronted with hard challenges without any preparation for collective enterprises. In the latter societies, collective action may nevertheless be possible even though it cannot be rooted in a long tradition of co-operation. Yet, success will then crucially depend on external assistance and it is important that the external agency uses a gradual approach starting with concrete, relatively easy-to-solve problems at the most decentralized level, preferably under conditions where social relations are not too distant or antagonistic.

8. Good leaders are essential to perform several critical functions: to help people become aware of the real challenges confronting them; to convince them that they can ultimately benefit from concerted action; to show to others the good example; to mobilize a sufficient number of them for enterprises requiring co-ordinated efforts; and to ensure impartiality and fairness in the designing and enforcing of rules and sanction mechanisms. Traditional authority and leadership patterns offer considerable advantages as long as they carry social prestige and legitimacy. However, customary leaders do not necessarily possess all the required qualities for effective leadership in present-day management schemes. Collective action is probably most satisfactory when it is led by relatively young, literate persons who have been exposed to the outside world and who can find some way of collaborating with traditional structures of authority and leadership.

13

Co-Management as a New Approach to Regulation of Common Property Resources

13.1 Enlarging the Range of Regulation Modes

The previous chapters have not led us to any definite, clear-cut conclusion. In Part I, some important shortcomings of private property of natural resources have been emphasized (Chapter 3). In Part II, attention has been drawn to the considerable problems raised by public ownership and centralized management of such resources (Chapter 11, sect. 1) while communal property has simultaneously been shown, on both empirical and theoretical grounds, to be problematic in some circumstances and promising in others (Chapters 10 and 12). Moreover, recent changes in the context in which rural communities operate tend to make village-level resource regulation more difficult than it was before (Chapter 11, sect. 2). Certainly, these results demonstrate that dogmatic attitudes based on the presumed absolute superiority of one form of resource regulation over the others are unjustified and damaging. Careful analysis of each particular case is required before any conclusion can be reached about the appropriateness of this or that form.

A more troublesome apparent implication of the analysis is that situations may be expected to arise where no viable solution is available. Thus, private ownership may be prohibitively costly (due to very high costs of fencing in the resource domain) and/or inequitable (if perceived as illegitimate, this solution may actually increase the attendant transaction costs). Direct state control may prove ineffectual for a variety of reasons including high information costs, lack of adequate monitoring devices, trained personnel, or financial resources, and subordination of environmental to shorter-term economic or political interests. In addition, the alternative approach of community-based management may be unrealistic because local conditions do not provide sufficient guarantee for effective CPR-related collective action, owing to recent changes in the rural scene and new challenges from the wider world, and/or to deep-rooted features of the social structure or to resource characteristics (the resource may spread over a large area; the evolution of its stock may not be visible; users may be highly scattered and reside far away from the resource, etc.).

Fortunately, the problem may be less intractable than it appears at first sight. This is because the distinction used so far between three well-defined resource property/regulation regimes is far too simplistic to serve as a useful guideline for policy-making. In effect, the state-based and community-based modes of regulation can be combined in numerous and imaginative ways which open the door to many more solutions than the three standard approaches usually referred to in the literature. As observed by

Lawry, 'it may be useful to think in terms of policies for shoring up the respective weaknesses of states and communities in managing collective resources' (Lawry, 1989*b*: 15), an approach which points to 'co-management' arrangements between government and rural communities. Under this new approach, rural communities or user groups tend to be regarded as 'the primary base for resource management' (Zufferey, 1986: 91), yet this does not imply that they acquire complete or near-complete autonomy towards that purpose. Rather than the more conservative plea for the preservation of—or return to—traditional systems of resource management, the basic message of many socio-anthropological studies seems to be that people have to be involved in the development of their resources in some way or other. Decentralization of controls and active participation of rural residents are the key elements in the approach advocated by most social researchers but, to repeat, adhesion to such principles does not by itself preclude a critical role for the State in view of the limitations of local-level collective action.

To argue for a (user) group- or community-centred approach is therefore not tantamount to asking for a drastic retrenchment of state responsibilities in resource management. The basic concern is actually with reshaping state interventions so as to institutionalize collaboration between administration and resource users and end those unproductive situations where they are pitted against one another as antagonistic actors in the process of resource regulation. Enough evidence has indeed been accumulated to show that, when rural inhabitants come to view state agents with hostility and distrust, all state efforts are doomed to yield disappointing results. This is partly because villagers are bent on violating rules and resist programmes the rationale of which they do not understand, all the more so if they have the impression that those rules or programmes are clumsy or do not reflect a proper understanding of the specific problems and constraints confronting them. Given pervasive informational asymmetries and the high cost of centralized monitoring of highly scattered activities, the sanctions are bound to be imposed in an arbitrary way and they must be severe to effectively deter rule-breaking. Yet, as has been emphasized in Chapter 11, heavy fines and severe sanctions are likely either to cause a lot of social resentment which many governments are keen to avoid, or to breed active corruption of state agents with the result that rule-breaking continues unabated.

Clearly, to be successful, co-management must operate within a framework where the state integrates the populations concerned early on in the design stages of the resource-preserving strategy. Also, considerable effort must be devoted to explaining to them the objectives pursued and the benefits they will gain from restricted and careful use of the resource involved. Most importantly, trust has to be built between the two partners. In this respect, given the deep-rooted 'culture of distrust' that permeates relationships between the State and local resource users, development projects initiated by local or foreign donor agencies can play a useful role within a co-management framework of action. They may not only help user communities to gain confidence in their collective action ability and to build up or adapt local institutional arrangements for the management of their natural resources, but they may also help in gradually overcoming the 'trust' gap that exists between these communities and the state authorities. It is important to stress that this gap is more likely to be reduced and local institutions are more likely to be effective if traditional arrangements or mechanisms already operating in rural communities are supported than if they are ignored (see, e.g., Cernea, 1989; Bromley and Cernea, 1989; Swift, 1991; Colchester, 1994; Utting, 1994). At least, this is true as long as these traditional arrangements carry enough legitimacy for a majority of the resource users concerned.

13.2 The Broad Nature of Co-Management Arrangements or Contracts

We have argued above that, if more attention is given to the possibilities inherent in the co-management approach, the range of situations in which direct involvement of user groups could be expected to increase effectiveness of resource regulation would presumably widen by a large margin. The question has now to be asked as to what is exactly the nature of complementarity between government and user groups or communities which could serve as a base for co-management arrangements. The answer to this question is derived from the analysis presented in previous chapters and can be summarized in the following way:

1. To the extent that the State is comparatively efficient in processing (rather than collecting) crucial information on village-level resources and the external effects they may produce as well as in designing efficiency-improving policies, it can provide technical assistance or guidance to user groups or communities. This is with a view to (*a*) helping them better assess the massive changes that have taken place in their environment during recent decades; (*b*) convincing them that effective remedial actions can be taken to redress ongoing ecological imbalances; (*c*) disseminating new practices aimed at ensuring preservation and sound exploitation of local resources; and (*d*) following up the application, and evaluating the appropriateness, of these new practices.

2. Economic incentives to resource users might be provided by the government so as to induce them to shift from a shut-down path to a conservation path of resource exploitation. Such a policy is particularly welcome if the resource generates significant positive externalities or if the users are subsistence-constrained villagers who lack the wherewithal to build them up to an optimal level compatible with conservation in the long run.

3. Government might help local systems of resource management by clarifying group territorial rights and by providing a legal framework which enables rural organizations 'to obtain legally enforceable recognition of their identity and rights and to call upon the state as an enforcer of last resort' (Wade, 1987: 232). This role is especially important given the fact that the viability of resource management projects may depend crucially on their receiving legal protection from encroachment by neighbouring groups or external intruders on the site of operation. In most cases, meeting the above requirement is obviously tantamount to giving customary users guarantees of exclusive group tenure and recognition of the importance of their traditional, limited-

entry recruitment procedures (see, e.g. Cordell and McKean, 1986: 105; World Bank, 1992: 142).[1] Moreover, rural communities sometimes need to be protected by the State against the damages caused by broad-level forces and other economic sectors, such as when coastal fishing communities suffer from industrial pollution, harbour siltation, or touristic encroachments (see, e.g., Soysa *et al.*, 1982). Such damage may actually do more harm to village-level resources than the harvesting efforts of the direct users themselves. The role of the State derives here from its ability to deal with externalities which, by their size or their nature, require a good deal of centralized intervention. Finally, the government might give support to the internal order of user groups by recognizing and enforcing their legal right to define resource-use rules and enforce sanctions on deviants (Swallow and Bromley, 1994*b*: 14).

4. Formal conflict-resolution mechanisms might be supplied by the State to be used whenever conflicts cannot be settled at the user group- or community-level, or whenever disputes between contending user groups have to be adjudicated. Such mechanisms may also be required to resolve intersectoral conflicts, particularly those arising from negative externalities such as pollution (like when prime fishing-grounds are being degraded by industrial and domestic effluents).[2]

5. The Government might provide financial and technical support to decentralized monitoring when monitoring activities necessitate the use of costly technologies and equipment to be effective (for instance, quickly moving patrol boats intended for inspecting industrial vessels that have encroached upon inshore waters assigned to small-scale coastal fishermen communities).

6 Efficiency could be improved by government promotion of competition among largely autonomous management units and by ensuring quick diffusion of information on best practices and working rules. This is an important role in so far as a major advantage of allowing considerable autonomy to design and reform rules in small units that are nested in larger (federal) systems is that more information may be generated from experience. Many more independent experiments can be carried out and, to the extent that self-organized units do not exist in physical and institutional isolation, they may learn a lot from one another by sharing their experiences (Weissing and Ostrom, 1992).

Of course, the above functions are a reflection of the weaknesses and limits of user groups or communities as resource regulators. On the other hand, the latter exhibit various strengths which ought to be advantageously exploited in co-management arrangements. In particular:

[1] Thus, e.g. if a group of pastoralists enter into the territory of a community and cut down young acacia trees for livestock forage in open violation of local conservation norms, the village authorities should be legally empowered to impose fines and even confiscate livestock. Government should come to the assistance of the community to assure that recalcitrant pastoralists pay the fines and, if contested by the latter, provide a forum for impartial review of the case (see the fourth function below) (Freudenberger and Mathieu, 1993: 27).

[2] As the experience of the District Tribunals in Gambia shows, local authorities can often resolve quite effectively rural conflicts around natural resources that are not easily settled at the level of the communities (Freudenberger and Mathieu, 1993: 24). In the lineage-managed forests of preindustrial China, the heads of various branches of a given (large) lineage used to have recourse to government authority when they could not effectively enforce the contracts drawn up for timber land-use (Menzies, 1994: 84).

1. They are well-informed about local ecological conditions even though they may possibly miss or misjudge recent evolutions of their environment or ascribe wrong causes to visible ecological processes under way (as when depletion of local fish stocks is systematically blamed on migrant fishermen who use different harvesting techniques; or even when a more or less prolonged decline in fish catches is a priori attributed to human overexploitation of fish resources).

2. They are well informed about local technical, economic, and social conditions, about problems or constraints that characterize their micro-society, as well as about the cultural patrimony on which they can draw to meet new challenges. Consequently, they are in a good position to devise well-adapted rules, procedures, and sanction mechanisms that are susceptible of gaining broad support among resource users, especially so if prestigious or effective local leaders are available to take the required initiatives. In particular, because they can make location- or community-specific rules, they are often better able to allow for fairness or equity considerations. In addition, rules developed locally often result from extensive trial and error by the users themselves, which ensures not only that they are well suited to local conditions but also that they are well understood by the people concerned.[3]

3. Because their size is relatively small, they can easily adjust their local rules and procedures to changing circumstances.

4. Not only do they often possess customary conflict-resolution mechanisms which can be used at low cost to solve numerous intra-community disputes on the spot, but they also have traditional techniques to minimize the incidence of interpersonal conflicts (for instance, simple warnings are frequently sufficient to deter rule-breaking).

5. Self-monitoring organized by users themselves is likely to be significantly less costly than centralized control exercised through formal administrative channels.

A simple and evident principle is then the following: the weaker the rural communities or groups in one or several of the above respects, the fewer should be the responsibilities devolved upon them by the State within the purview of co-management arrangements. Moreover, the stronger the suspicions that local groups or communities are under the sway of special powerful interests ready to sacrifice environmental considerations to short-run economic or political objectives, the less control of environmental outcomes ought to be surrendered to these groups or communities. In the borderline case where user groups offer almost no guarantee that they can effectively participate in resource management efforts, the range of actions they are legally empowered to take ought to be restricted to a minimum. If there are doubts about the user groups' ability to regulate local CPRs, sequential co-management designs might be experimented with to test this ability, possibly in several progressive stages.

[3] Regarding irrigation systems, it has thus been observed that 'operational rules handed down from bureaucratic agencies often turn out to be incompatible with the special circumstances of individual irrigated areas' (Tang, 1994: 239). This is a serious problem in so far as, to be effective, rules must match underlying physical domains. Thus, in many large irrigation systems, 'different watercourses vary in terms of such physical attributes as soil type, field topography, cropping pattern, and amount of water available. If there is only one collective-choice entity to create and enforce a single set of operational rules for an entire system, the set of rules is unlikely to match the physical domains of all appropriation areas equally well' (ibid. 238).

This being said, before concluding that local user groups have low ability to carry out the necessary collective actions, much caution is required. There have indeed been too many stories in which pessimistic conclusions have been hastily drawn without the support of sufficient knowledge regarding the priorities, social organization, decision-making structures, leadership, and survival constraints of these groups. Furthermore, such pessimistic conclusions are sometimes reached while the collective action ability of user groups has not been fairly tested because essential conditions for success that do not depend on them have not been fulfilled on the ground. In particular, one ought not to be surprised at the disappointing management performances of groups of intended beneficiaries when the State is reluctant to denationalize village-level natural resources and to clearly define and protect communal rights to rangeland, pastures, water, trees, and so on.

Local user communities must be given a fair chance to participate in the management of their natural resources. Yet, they ought not to be idealized as they tend to be nowadays in certain circles, journals, and conferences: just think of the present-day fashion about TURFs (Territorial Use Rights in Fisheries) considered by some individuals and organizations as the panacea for solving fishery management problems; or of the fad of many scientists and activists for community woodlot programmes conceived as the magic key to rehabilitate and conserve forests. Unfortunately, there is presently no conclusive evidence that user communities can be 'the solution' to problems of resource depletion and ecological destruction, *even within a co-management framework*. The best-documented case illustrating such an approach, that of Japanese fisheries described in detail below, only shows that user communities can be made effective partners for resource management in certain circumstances. Today, there are disquieting signs that even such a well-conceived scheme of co-management becomes seriously stressed as market opportunities expand and cause an intensive commercial exploitation of certain natural resources. The destructive pressures come from both outside economic interests and internal centrifugal tendencies.

A last point deserves to be made at this juncture. In many cases, it is unrealistic to expect the State to deal with each user group because this would entail considerable transaction costs. There is consequently a need for intermediate organizations that represent the interests of multiple user groups. These organizations have to be built up and cannot typically be derived from traditional institutions. Whether such a challenge can be met is a question of the utmost importance that cannot be answered today. One resource domain where attempts are currently being made at establishing broad-based organizations designed to mediate between the State and community-level user groups is that of fisheries. More will be said about these attempts in the next section.

13.3 Co-Management at Work

In order better to visualize the co-management approach, we would now like to refer to a few experiences which have been documented in the scant literature available on the subject. That the literature is poor ought not to surprise us inasmuch as co-management is a new idea that is just beginning to be tried on the field in a systematic way. Nevertheless, special attention should be paid to the system of coastal fishery management in Japan since this system has been thoroughly tested on the ground for a lengthy period of time, long before the concept of co-management arose in debates about resource conservation. In addition, a few other experiences which are still in an infancy stage will be considered so as to give the reader a rough impression of the kind of approach that is being presently experimented in various sectors and in various parts of the developing world. The spirit of experimentation and institutional innovation which accompanies all these attempts is probably the most promising sign of hope for those who dream about better conservation of the earth's resources for future generations. Failures should be accepted as the inevitable price to pay for the discovery of more effective ways of tackling this extremely complex problem.

Fisheries

The analysis of the aforementioned case of Japanese coastal fishery management forms the core of this survey of co-management in the fishing sector. After a rather detailed presentation of this unique case, a few localized experiences of co-management will be shortly reviewed. Finally, we will address the problem created by the need for intermediate organizations between the State and local user groups by referring to institutional experiments presently conducted in various parts of the world (more specifically, on the eastern coast of Canada).

Management in Japanese coastal waters: a long experience with co-management

Since the present system of coastal fishery management in Japan is deeply rooted in the history of sea tenure in this country, going back to feudal times (the Edo period), it is worth looking at it in a dynamic perspective to have a good grasp of the way it has evolved. Such an approach is made possible by the fact that several detailed studies are available on the subject. Our presentation is mainly inspired by the works of Asada *et al.* (1983) and Ruddle (1987) in which the interested reader will find additional references.

Antecedents in the feudal period. In feudal times, Japanese coastal villages were classified either as 'agricultural' or as 'fishing' villages. The purpose of this classification was to ensure that the rice-based feudal economy would not be threatened by farmers unduly switching to fishing with the attendant consequence that the scope of monetized transactions would increase (since fishing is a much more specialized occupation than agriculture). As a matter of fact, fishing operations were strictly prohibited in the adjacent waters of all 'agricultural' villages (except seaweeds harvesting for fertilizing purposes). Villages designated as fishing—where fishing operations were explicitly allowed by feudal authorities—were actually villages with small amounts of farmland, where fishing alone offered a viable livelihood. Resident communities were awarded fishing rights and, in order to limit the numbers entering the fishery from any particular community, fishermen's guilds came into existence (Asada *et al.*, 1983: 6). Membership in each guild was rigidly limited to persons born in a particular village and all members had to follow strictly the regulations of the guild, which established fishing zones, set seasonal limits and imposed restrictions on fishing gears and techniques (Ruddle, 1987: 25).

An institutionalized system of village or local sea tenure was thus born in which 'the generally acknowledged sea territory of each coastal village was simply a seaward extension of its terrestrial territory' (Ruddle, 1987: 13–14).[4] In 1719 this became codified, at least as far as Okinawa Island and other main islands were concerned. Since the 1719 law partook of a feudal logic, the performance of corvée and the payment of tributes (to both the fief government and to the village lord) on the one hand, and the confirmation of exclusive rights to a coastal sea territory on the other hand went hand in hand. Of course, the reckoning of these rights implied that the law upheld the customary practice whereby outsiders could not work a village's sea territory unless an agreed fee was first paid to the village officer responsible for village marine affairs. The boats and gear of outsiders apprehended working illegally were confiscated and were returned only after a fine had been paid.[5]

What deserves to be especially emphasized in the context of the present study is the following: 'despite an increasingly centralised and bureaucratised government during the Edo Period, coastal fisheries had only a local focus and were closely adapted to local physical, biological and socio-economic conditions', hence the noticeable 'lack of nationwide uniformity in the definition of coastal fisheries and their regulatory procedures'. This dominant feature of Japan's system of coastal fishery management, as we shall now see, has persisted to this day (Ruddle, 1987: 14–15). This is particularly in evidence in the case of conflict-resolution mechanisms since, much as we can observe nowadays, intra-village and intervillage disputes were essentially resolved in as decentralized a way as possible. Moreover, such mechanisms were sometimes very refined as when (monetary) compensations were required from fishermen found imposing negative externalities on others owing to the technologies used (ibid. 22). In the words of Ruddle, 'both the causes of conflicts and the processes employed to resolve them within and among villages during the Edo period differ little from those still mainly used at present. This constitutes an important part of the continuity of tradition fundamental to an understanding of present-day Japanese inshore fisheries' (ibid. 21).

The interim period (up to mid-twentieth century). As the feudal era drew to a close, in the middle of the nineteenth century, the above system came under increasing stress due to the conjoined operation of two irrepressible forces: population growth and

[4] Although village sea territories were formed mainly during the feudal era, in some cases at least their historical roots go much farther back. (Ruddle, 1987: 16).

[5] It may however be noted that fishing territories were sometimes used jointly by several villages—particularly so in bays which would have been difficult to divide among villages. Within the shared fishing territory 'the use of a given technology or the harvest of a particular species was reserved for one village, whereas other species could be taken using different gears, regardless of where the fisherman lived, provided that his residence was in one of the settlements having rights to the shared fishing grounds' (Ruddle, 1987: 17). Fishing communities thus had an analogue to the widespread practice of shared land in feudal Japan. (Shared lands were used jointly by several villages within a fief for the collection of fuelwood, thatching materials, and the like.)

commercialization of fisheries under the impetus of an enlarging cash economy. Serious disputes over fishing grounds consequently began to erupt, particularly between coastal 'agricultural' and 'fishing' villages. More precisely, 'agricultural' villages started to claim their own sea territories. Depending on the extent of pressure on the resource, these villages would still allow 'true fishermen' to retain *limited* rights of access to their local waters (for example, the right to harvest certain species of fish), or they would decide to strictly enforce exclusive rights thereby preventing former users from exercising their customary prerogatives. At the very end of Japan's feudal age, just prior to the Meiji Restoration, in 1868, the latter situation actually began to emerge in the most highly developed and productive fisheries (Ruddle, 1987: 18–19).

In 1876, after the dissolution of the fiefs, the ownership of all fisheries reverted to the central government. An open-access situation ensued, which led to intensified controversies and disputes over access and traditional rights, all the more so as new entries into coastal fisheries increased vastly, sometimes backed by powerful outside interests (like big merchants). The central government was obliged to abandon this system and to revive the traditional arrangement that had persisted throughout the feudal era. Thus, *de facto* ownership of existing fishing grounds reverted to each prefecture, the administrative division that replaced the fiefs after the Meiji Restoration (Ruddle, 1987: 24). In 1887, the Japanese government drew up regulations establishing fisheries co-operatives to co-ordinate the use of coastal fishing grounds and to maintain harmony within fishing communities following existing custom and practice. Repeated trial and error finally led to the enactment of a Fisheries Law (1901) which provided for the establishment of Fisheries Associations (henceforth denoted by FAs) in each fishing village and assigned fishing rights to them (Asada *et al.*, 1983: 6). The old guilds were thus revived as the local administrative agencies of the new system of fisheries management.

Unfortunately, implementation of the 1901 Fisheries Law seems to have done little or nothing to alleviate the economic plight of the small-scale fishermen, a fact which is much to do with the introduction of highly efficient offshore fishing crafts in coastal waters at the beginning of the 1920s. Serious conflicts with inshore fishermen ensued which intensified with the onset of the Depression of the 1930s. At this juncture, as a means of stabilizing the livelihood of coastal fishermen, common fishing rights were extended further offshore and a larger number of fishing rights were concentrated in the hands of the FAs. The intention was to keep large offshore vessels out of the grounds involved in order to conserve fishery resources and to strengthen FAs as the main agency of fishery management. Moreover, following the Second World War, a major revision of fishery legislation was carried out by the government with the purpose of expelling absentee owners from fishing villages and reserving fishing rights exclusively for working fishermen (Asada *et al.*, 1983: 7). This revision gave rise to the Fisheries Law of 1949 which was conceived of in direct continuity with the law of 1901. Since then, no major modification has been made to this legislation.

The current system: general considerations. The Fisheries Law of 1949 which, together with the Fisheries Co-operative Association Law of 1948, constitutes the cornerstone of the system of fishery management in post-war Japan, is comprised of measures relative to fishing rights, fishery licensing, and arrangements for fishery co-ordination (co-ordinating committees). Modifications to the 1901 Fisheries Law were based on three principles intended to eradicate the remaining elements of feudalism:

> (1) Henceforth fishery rights and licences were to be granted only to fishermen or fishing enterprises actually engaged in fishing, and leasing arrangements were prohibited;
> (2) The local administration of fishing rights was to be invested only in Fisheries Co-operative Associations (FCAs) or similar organisations; and
> (3) Sea Area Fishery Adjustment Committees, to be established for each sea area, were charged with preparing comprehensive plans for the full and rational use of coastal fishing grounds, and based on these plans fishing rights and licences were to be granted to FCAs, other bodies and individuals. (Ruddle, 1987: 35)

As for the Fisheries Co-operative Association Law, it 'restricted membership in FCAs to fishermen resident in the jurisdictional area of the Association and who were engaged in fishing for 90–120 days a year, the precise period being determined by each FCA' (Ruddle, 1987: 35). This new legislation obviously involved a significant reshuffling of fishing rights in favour of active fishermen and the cancellation of rights owned by 'big capitalists'. The move was undertaken on the grounds that 'active fishermen should be the beneficiaries of the fish resources in inshore waters' (Hannesson, 1988: 11). Whatever the intent, the local, community-based FCA has thus emerged 'as a vitally important intermediate organization that links the central and prefectural government with the individual fisherman. Although comprising the fundamental unit of government fisheries administration, and being the key organisation in the implementation of official fisheries projects, an FCA belongs entirely to the local community of fishermen' (Ruddle, 1987: 36).

It is important to emphasize that FCAs have developed as the natural outcome of a long tradition. Formed originally for the purpose of jointly managing coastal fishing grounds, fishermen's groups later had their functions extended into the economic area and they finally evolved into the present type of co-operative association. Note that, although adherence to and exit from an association is voluntary, almost all fishermen in fact belong to them. Moreover, every fishing village has such an association (Asada *et al.*, 1983: 9). As a consequence, all coastal waters, with the exception of ports, their adjacent tracts, and tracts reclaimed for industrial zones, are divided up among FCAs or Federations of FCAs (Ruddle, 1987: 36).

As hinted at above, the Japanese system of fisheries management relies on two kinds of regulatory device: fishing rights and fishing licences. Only pole and line fishing by small vessels in coastal waters is actually free of any regulation. In Table 13.1, the structure of Japanese fishing rights and licences is described in a summary way. Some comments are in order.[6]

The current system: fishing rights. The system of fishing rights, which is essentially a continuation of former practices, applies only to coastal fisheries. In these fisheries

[6] Our description of the Japanese system of fishing rights and licences is based on Asada *et al.* (1983: 9–14) and Ruddle (1987: 36–9).

TABLE 13.1. The structure of Japanese fishing-rights and licences

Categories	Granted to
RIGHTS	
(1) *Joint fishery rights*	
A. Gathering seaweed, shellfish and other benthos	
B. Specific small-scale net fisheries	Exclusively to FCAs.
C. Beachseines, unmotorized trawling, fish shelters	
(2) *Demarcated fishery rights*	
A. Special Demarcated Rights	Exclusively to FCAs.
B. Demarcated Rights	To FCAs, private organizations and individuals
(3) *Large-scale set-net fishery rights*	Ditto.
LICENCES	
(1) *Large-scale operations in distant waters*	Mostly to private organizations and individuals
(2) *Medium-scale operations in deep waters*	Ditto.
(3) *Small-scale nearshore operations*	FCAs or individuals

Source: Ruddle (1987: 37).

are found many fishing units using stationary gear, e.g. set-net, bottom-fixed net, etc., as well as aquacultural enterprises. The viability of such enterprises is preconditioned on their receiving legal protection from encroachment by others on the site of operation, so as to avoid damaging conflicts due to competition between fishermen (Asada *et al.*, 1983: 9). An important feature of these fishing rights is that they cannot be loaned, rented, or transferred to others, nor can they be mortgaged. They are indeed regarded as the exclusive and inalienable property of the fishermen to whom they have been granted (Ruddle, 1987: 36).

There are actually three kinds of fishing rights, viz. joint (or common), demarcated, and set-net rights. The most important are *joint rights*, which are awarded only to an FCA or to a Federation of FCAs, which in turn distributes them among the membership. These rights are established for four classes of fishery, visually: (*a*) fisheries for seaweeds, shellfish, crustaceans, and sedentary fin-fish species; (*b*) fisheries employing fixed gear, e.g. traps and the like; (*c*) beachseine, boatseine, and other fisheries which are relatively immobile or stationary on the fishing ground, and (*d*) inland-water fisheries.

The width of the zone governed by these rights varies considerably from one place to another, but the average is about 1 km. seaward from the shore. Moreover, the allocation of a fishing territory among these types of gear and the fishermen to be engaged in their operation is internally decided by a FCA.

Demarcated fishing rights are granted for aquaculture and are usually valid for five years. They are established within waters governed by joint fishing rights and are divided into two types. One type—known as 'special demarcated rights'—is held by FCAs and relates to aquaculture using sea-ponds, rafts, nets, and long-lines. In this case, since the operations involved are comparatively small in scale, the number of fishermen capable of participating is potentially large. In addition, the location of these harvesting operations being sheltered, it is relatively prone to pollution and, therefore, diverse activities with differing environmental quality requirements must be managed in a compatible and equitable manner. The other type—known as 'demarcated rights'—is granted for pearl culture and large-scale aquacultural projects involving the partitioning of sea inlets by dykes or nets. Rights for these projects which demand little co-ordination with other, potentially incompatible activities, are awarded not only to FCAs but also to private companies and individuals with the technical capability and investment capital required.

Set-net fishing rights apply to the use of large-scale nets of this type, fixed at depths of more than 27 metres (the concerned species are herring, migratory trout, and salmon). They are granted to private individuals and companies, as well as to FCAs. Since the high capital investment and large operating costs involved by this technique effectively limit the number of nets, the area and sites of operation can be easily restricted by the prefecture. Note that, because of a potentially substantial impact on other fishing operations in their vicinity, placement must be permanent. This is in contrast with small-scale set-nets which often require to be moved from place to place to secure a catch. Here, to equalize opportunity among participants, the FCA customarily reallocates the placement of these nets each year by means of a lottery.

It is noteworthy that in every instance joint rights embrace the entire sea territory of an FCA, whereas demarcated rights and those for set-nets are granted only for specific areas within the joint rights area. Furthermore, while all fishermen belonging to a specific FCA are entitled to fish in that FCA's joint rights area, only a limited number are granted demarcated and set-net rights. Because of the extent of capital investment and technical capacity required (see above), the restriction of these latter rights to FCAs might lead to the leasing of fishing rights, which would be contrary to the spirit of the Fisheries Law. In such cases, some criteria for qualification and the preferential ordering of allocations are used by the prefecture. Large fishing companies and persons who are not working fishermen, along with those who violate fishing and labour laws, are disqualified. The preferential order is somewhat complicated but generally follows the sequence of (*a*) FCAs, (*b*) organizations composed of many fishermen, (*c*) fishermen's organizations with a limited number of members, and (*d*) individuals and companies.

Fishing rights called 'co-operative-managed rights' refer to both joint or common fishing rights, and to demarcated rights owned by FCAs. Now, although the FCAs are awarded these rights, they seldom engage directly in fishing operations. 'Their function is to own the fishing rights and to administer use of the fishing grounds in the interest of optimal utilisation of fishery resources and of equal opportunity for their members. Equality of opportunity, however, is not always achieved. Within a co-operative, fishermen are apt to form groups based on type of fishery and fishing rights actually may be exercised by limited numbers. In any event, the rules for fishing ground utilisation are decided by a 2 to 3 majority vote at a general meeting of each association' (Asada *et al.*, 1983: 10). In fact, it is mainly to avoid controversy in the distribution and allocation of 'co-operative-managed rights' that practical implementation is left to the FCAs.

The current system: fishing licences. When it is necessary, for the purpose of resource conservation and/or the maintenance of orderly operations, to impose restrictions on effort in fisheries based on migratory fish stocks, a system of licensing is applied. Started in the trawl fisheries, this system has been gradually extended and, nowadays, it covers almost all Japanese fishing-vessel operations. In accordance with the size and operating conditions of the fishery concerned, licences are either granted by the Minister of Agriculture, Forestry, and Fisheries or by prefectural governors.

Fisheries requiring licences of the former type are called 'designated fisheries'. An overall allocation is established as deemed appropriate for the conservation or enhancement of resources and the maintenance of order in the fishery. The number of vessels to be licensed is then decided (by tonnage class, fishing area, and operating season). Applications for licence must be supported by proper credentials and licences are awarded on a priority basis to applicants with experience in the fishery involved. When there is an excess demand for such licences, criteria such as the applicant's previous operating history and his degree of dependence on that fishery are considered. No order of priority such as that applied in the case of fishing rights is taken into account, however. In principle, licences for all fisheries are renewable every five years, except for fisheries where catch quotas are decided annually on the basis of international agreements.

When resource conservation or fishery regulations require a strict control of the catch and/or effort in local fisheries (in which, for the most part, small-scale vessels are employed), prefectural governors are called for the issuance of licences. For administrative purposes, fisheries so licensed (called governor-licensed fisheries) are divided into two broad classes:

1. 'In the first class are those fisheries in which operations centre mainly in the coastal waters of a particular area, i.e. a prefecture or metropolitan district. When restrictive regulation is required, the prefectural governor, with the approval of the Minister of Agriculture, Forestry, and Fisheries, may establish his own fishery-adjustment regulations and institute a licensing procedure. The fisheries coming under this sort of arrangement are numerous and varied. In fact, nearly all major coastal fisheries are subject thereto.

2. The second class embraces coastal fisheries that, owing to a wide operational range and relatively high productive capability, require co-ordination across two or more prefectures. In such cases, according to the Fisheries Law, the prefectural governor concerned is required to declare the fishery a governor-licensed fishery and the Minister establishes a fixed allocation by area, restricting the number and type of fishing vessels that may be licensed. This class of fishery is termed a legislated governor-licensed fishery, i.e. a governor-licensed fishery as determined by statute. The class at present includes four fisheries, e.g. medium-sized seiners (five tons and over, but generally not exceeding 40 tons) and small trawlers (under 15 tons) (Asada *et al.*, 1983: 13)

For both classes of fishery, the method of licensing is almost the same as in the case of minister-licensed fisheries. Note however that licences issued by prefectures are granted to individual fishermen or to an FCA (when the number of applicants is large). In the latter case, the prefectural governor decides only the number of licences to be allotted per FCA (bear in mind that in Japan licences are always issued for vessels *and* fishermen), and each FCA is then expected to distribute them among its membership. Moreover, in order to impart maximum flexibility to the system, an FCA may receive several or more individual licences as a 'package', which then permits individual fishermen to switch activities in different years in accordance with technological change or altered family or personal circumstances, for example (Ruddle, 1987: 38–9).

In the interest of resource conservation, the Minister may decide outright bans on some fisheries, or else, annual renewal of permission to operate may be required. In many cases, however, licensing provisions contain restrictions of various kinds, such as closure of comparatively wide areas near shore to fishing operations (which applies in the case of fisheries having a highly productive capability, e.g. those using bottom trawls or purse-seines), closure of the fishing season (which applies to most fisheries, including offshore trawl, small-trawl, purse-seine fisheries, etc.), restrictions on vessels and gear (on the horsepower of the vessels, on the size of the net meshes, on the intensity of fish-collecting lights, etc.), restrictions on the body size of individuals of a species taken or landed, prohibition of landings at other than designated ports, and so on.

The current system: the sea-area adjustment commissions. Fisheries adjustment commissions were established to ensure the co-ordination of prefectural fisheries development within an overall national framework. According to Ruddle, 'these commissions form an essential intermediate link between the national and prefectural levels of Japanese fisheries administration' (Ruddle, 1987: 40). There are actually two kinds of such commissions. The first type (the Sea Area Fishery Adjustment Commission) has been established by the Ministry of Agriculture, Forestry, and Fisheries with a view to making, monitoring, and modifying fundamental management plans for sea areas under the control of local government. (Each of the sixty-five sea areas into which the marine waters of Japan have been divided corresponds to the maritime zone of one particular coastal prefecture). In principle, each commission is composed of fifteen members, nine of whom are officially elected by the fishermen and six appointed by the governor (four of whom are fisheries specialists and two represent the public interest). The functions of these commissions, in addition to the above-noted one of preparing management plans, consist of deciding on the eligibility of fishing rights and licences, resolving or mediating conflicts, and advising local governments on the management of living aquatic resources. 'Based on those plans and that advice, detailed regulations to control fishery operations and to ensure the conservation and rational exploitation of resources are established by the Fisheries Agency of each prefecture' while the prefectural regulations are supplemented and enforced by each FCA (ibid.).

The second kind of commissions are the United Sea Area Fishery Commissions which are established as a particular need arises. The control of the fishing of seasonally migratory stocks—which, by definition, cannot be regulated by any one prefecture alone—is one of their major functions. Permanent commissions of this kind, which are placed under the direct control of the Ministry, are established whenever recurrent and intense conflicts occur as a result of the fact that many fishermen from different FCAs and employing distinct and conflicting gears operate in a shared water space.

The current system: the Fisheries Co-operative Associations. The relatively high degree of local autonomy granted to fishermen under the Japanese system enables them, through their role on FCA committees and at general meetings, 'to determine the division of access rights among individual FCA members and to ensure that the interests of all parties involved are considered and accounted for. It also permits higher-level fishery regulations to be adapted to regional differences in ecology, target species, fishing effort, and level of industrialization or other impacts on local fisheries, among other things. Further, it guarantees that fishery management strategies, processes of conflict resolution and interpersonal and intergroup relationships will be, to a large extent, based on local customary law and codes of conduct' (Ruddle, 1987: 43). The continual process of interaction among the different levels of fisheries administration and the existence of intermediary bodies such as FCAs or Federations of FCAs allow for the incorporation of customary law within the regulations made at the higher levels. In the words of Ruddle again: 'The control of resources from within a fishing community as well as from above are two complementary and mutually reinforcing channels that constitute a viable system for the administration and management of coastal fisheries' (ibid. 44).

Basically, therefore, what FCAs do is to implement and enforce national and prefectural legislation and regulations which they supplement or complement, as local conditions require, by locally made rules and regulations. (For instance, the president of a FCA may at any time restrict the harvesting of any species to conserve resources and to control the fishery.) These local rules are then formalized in a FCA's special document to be submitted to, and approved by, the prefectural fisheries office. (As the need arises, this document is revised, necessitating reapproval by the same office.) A second important function of a FCA is to represent its membership's interests at higher administrative levels and *vis-à-vis* private organizations such as industrial corporations affecting local fishery operations (Ruddle, 1987: 44, 47).

Fishermen have a direct say in their FCA not only through their participation in the annual meeting of the general assembly (where issues arising from use rights are discussed, rules ensuring equitable use of the local fishing grounds are decided, and intergroup conflicts are settled) but also and mainly through their small-group decisions. Indeed, they are often organized into fishing squads (*han*) and residential groups (*ku*) which are the main entities in policy-making with respect to resource allocation. These small user groups are thus fitted into a larger structure and they are entrusted with monitoring and enforcing responsibilities (see above, Chapter 12). The opinions of these decentralized units are transmitted to the local FCA's board of directors, which is obliged to follow them as closely as possible. Thus, agreements made between the various squads and approved by the board can lead to the reservation of some waters within the FCA's fishing territory for the exclusive use of individuals or squads. Note carefully that such agreements do not necessarily guarantee equal access to an entire exclusive rights area for all local FCA's members in all types of fishing (Ruddle, 1987: 45–6).

It may be recalled here that membership in a FCA is strictly restricted to residents of the area covered by it and to persons engaged in fishing for a minimum of 90–120 days a year (the exact limit being determined by each FCA according to specific local conditions). Moreover, we know that fishing rights (and licences) cannot be loaned, rented, transferred, or mortgaged to others, yet rights can be inherited by a kinsman or a successor, provided that such a person is also a member of the same FCA. The rationale of these regulations has been described by Ruddle as follows:

> The restrictions . . . were intended to eliminate absentee ownership and the concentration of assets and profits in the hands of a few non-fishing capitalists, and thus once and for all to break the stranglehold over coastal fisheries by wealthy 'sealords' that in pre-war times not uncommonly kept the working fisherman permanently impoverished and beholden by an endless cycle of indebtedness. In their intent to control excesses it is unlikely that these laws ever really sought to prohibit all transfers of rights other than those based on succession or inheritance or to make access totally equitable nationwide, since clearly this would have been impossible given the great weight and variety of tradition and customary law throughout Japan. Further, . . . the transfer of rights (either permanently or temporarily) has historically been a major factor in the control of access to Japanese coastal fisheries. In earlier periods village rights were extended to other communities and individuals on the payment of fees, and government rights were similarly transferred in return for cash payments . . . Although both the letter and the spirit of the laws is upheld to exclude absentee capitalists from joint fishing rights areas, they are essentially of only secondary importance to unwritten, village customary laws. (Ruddle, 1987: 48)

Throughout Japan, it is birthright, followed by the requisite training and residence within the boundaries of a given FCA, that is the principal means by which FCA membership and fishing rights are obtained. (Marrying into a community and then working with the in-laws is another traditional way of gaining access to a fishery.) As most (coastal) fishing units are crewed by a father–son team or by two or more brothers, the senior person often owns the fishing rights and is a full voting member of the FCA, whereas the other(s) is (are) associate (non-voting) member(s). Rules governing access to joint fishing rights for new residents seem to vary significantly among FCAs and to be strongly influenced by local historical, economic, and socio-political factors. For example, in a village near Kyoto, new residents must live there for one generation before they become eligible to apply for membership and fishing rights. Furthermore, when a branch family is established by a son of a stem family of this village the new family must wait ten years before it can apply for membership and rights. We are told that 'tradition runs deep in this FCA, which maintains an exhaustive record of family lineage and succession to fishing rights' (Ruddle, 1987: 50). The importance of tradition also accounts for the fact that the history of social or class relations may bear upon the present pattern of allocation of fishing rights, sometimes with the effect of perpetuating former class privileges (in some communities, certain categories of fishing rights have been reserved for families of higher social status for many centuries), sometimes with the opposite effect of correcting previous inequities. The latter possibility arises when, for example, certain fishing rights remain allocated to just the descendants of the pre-war pauper class on the grounds that these people deserve to be compensated since they have been long discriminated against; or when descendants of former upper-class families who for centuries had discriminated against other social strata are considered to be involved in long-term reciprocity relations which require them to pay off the debts incurred by their ancestors (ibid. 49–51).

Finally, it must be pointed out that, in areas that have undergone massive economic structural change during the post-war period, traditional values and behavioural norms have become gradually less dominant. Thus, in the now heavily industrialized Inland Sea region, it is not rare to find illicit transfers of fishing rights. For example, in some FCAs, 'when a member retires from fishing he illegally sells his licence to another member, at a high price', a practice which tends to be sanctioned by the Association as long as it does not lead to excessive accumulation of rights and wealth by some individuals (Ruddle, 1987: 51–2).

The current system: management of conflicts. Conflicts at both local and supralocal levels are unavoidable. Important causes are disputes about access rights, gear conflicts (competition arising from the use by fishermen of different harvesting techniques), illegal fishing, and boundary jurisdiction. At the local level, the impact of interpersonal conflicts is nevertheless mitigated by 'the fully participatory consensus approach to decision-making that is characteristic of Japanese organisations' (Ruddle, 1987: 57). In traditional contexts, particularly in isolated areas, it is only rarely and in extreme cases that the customary technique for resolving conflicts through protracted negotiations made of concessions and counter-concessions proves ineffective, thereby necessitating a recourse to more formal channels (such as requiring the assistance of the Coast Guard to tame aggressive fishermen who repeatedly attempt to intimidate others into leaving a good fishing spot at which they have arrived first). In normal circumstances, according to Ruddle:

> First-comer's rights to a particular fishing spot, skill, knowledge and secrecy, pride of workmanship and community pressure to conform, all serve to balance excessive competitiveness and to ensure that all but the most intractable conflicts are resolved by informal mechanisms. Local community perceptions of social and 'owned' space are one of the keys to understanding the territorial and tenurial behaviour of Japanese coastal fishermen, since community norms are flouted at one's peril and the threat of social banishment is real and horrifying. (Ruddle, 1987: 87).

By contrast, in parts of Japan where customary mechanisms for conflict resolution and sanctioning have broken down as a result of modernization (see above, Chapter 11), 'competition is intense and the disregarding of official regulations and law-breaking more frequent and flagrant'. In such circumstances, litigation among fishermen is relatively high as are conflicts among FCAs, prefectures, and between the fishing and other sectors of the national economy. It is in these areas—such as the Inland Sea—that the resolution of conflicts by formal means assumes significant importance (Ruddle, 1987: 61).

An interesting illustration of the possibility of failure of traditional decentralized mechanisms of conflict-resolution relates to the serious problems which arose in Japan (as in so many other countries) from the entry of trawlers in coastal waters. For example, in the Essa Strait on Honshu Island, severe and often violent conflicts have erupted between trawler fishermen and traditional anglers and long-liners with the starting of a trawl fishery after the First World War. Mediation efforts of the Fishery Agency of the prefecture concerned repeatedly failed because of 'the diametrically opposed and tenaciously held views' of the representatives of both contending groups. As a consequence, the problem was turned over to the national Fishery Agency and, eventually, the Minister of Agriculture, Forestry, and Fisheries 'imposed an absolute ban on trawling in the Essa Strait until a mutually acceptable agreement could be concluded between the two sides'. Unfortunately, 'no such agreement has ever been reached' (Ruddle, 1987: 68–9).

For another thing, it is noteworthy that, since the late 1960s, judicial proceedings have been increasingly resorted to with a view to protecting inshore fishery rights within the context of growing negative externalities and loss of resource space imposed on fishing by the country's industrialization. If the traditional vehicles of conflict management have been supplemented by resort to the judiciary, it is because industrial companies tend to neglect the basic traditional behavioural norms of the rural sector. Now, it must be emphasized that 'to a large degree, traditional informal and formal methods of conflict management utilize the same methods: mediation, conciliation, arbitration, the use of go-betweens, protracted face-to-face contact and the payment of compensation, that result in concession, counter-concession and compromise to reach a mutually acceptable solution'. Moreover, a central lesson from the history of conflicts in Japanese fisheries is that 'general principles such as are codified into law must be applied flexibly and according to local conditions' (Ruddle, 1987: 82–3).

Particularly worth singling out is the ruling notion of livelihood rights which implies that the Japanese government recognizes fishing rights as having a value beyond economic worth, viz. that of ensuring the daily livelihood of (small-scale) fishermen. Thus, no fishing space belonging to FCAs can be used or acquired by private business interests unless the FCA concerned has agreed to sell its fishing rights. Furthermore, an important court's verdict has provided that fishing rights constitute 'a property protected by article 29 of the Constitution, which nobody could "buy" without the owner's consent'. The implication is that an *unanimous* agreement is required to sell fishing rights to a private company. In other words, any decision by a FCA which has the effect of depriving some members of their livelihood rights without their full agreement is unconstitutional. Therefore, even if only a minority of fishermen refuse to relinquish their rights, a private developer is forced to abandon his project since not even the central government is entitled to intervene when a FCA is resolutely opposed to such a transaction (Ruddle, 1987: 72, 80, 87).

Conclusion. What is interesting in the Japanese experiment is not only that (small-scale) fishermen enjoy legally guaranteed access rights to coastal waters but also that, through their own local organizations, they are in charge of establishing regulations for the internal distribution of these rights as well as for the control and operation of various types of fishery, as local conditions dictate. Sea tenure in Japan is actually a complex system which operates at various levels, 'ranging from the national government, through the prefecture and the local FCA, to the fishing squad and finally to the individual fisherman'. The FCA, in particular, is a vitally important intermediate organization that links the central and prefectural governments with the individual fisherman. It is at the core of the regulatory process (Ruddle, 1987: 85–6). Higher administrative levels intervene whenever (*a*) medium- or large-scale operations in distant or deep waters are concerned, especially so for migratory species; (*b*) problems arise within coastal communities which cannot be effectively solved by their local organization (the FCA); (*c*) problems arise among different fishing communities and prefectures, or else between fishermen and representatives of other sectors of the national economy; and (*d*) supralocal legislation is required to ensure proper management and conservation of fish resources.

In the latter circumstances, the government (or the prefecture) lays down a general framework of basic principles and fundamental rules to be implemented at community level after due adjustment has been made to local needs and conditions through locally designed complementary or supplementary measures. These adaptations are 'based on the empirical information provided either directly by the fishermen or indirectly by their fishing behaviour and performance' (Ruddle, 1987: 86). This procedure which consists of leaving the detailed application of basic ministerial or prefectural guidelines to the FCA and in many instances to the specialized fishing squads has thus the double effect of (*a*) imparting maximum flexibility to the system of sea resource management and, (*b*) exploiting the informational advantage of user groups and saving on transaction costs by relying on the fishermen's norm-abiding behaviour and by using their customary conflict-resolution mechanisms.

Has the Japanese system of fishing rights succeeded in enhancing conservation of resources? There is some evidence in the literature confirming this expectation. Thus, a detailed study reported by Hannesson shows that in Yubetsu (Hokkaido) efforts by the local FCA to limit the harvesting of scallop in the face of severe overfishing following the introduction of motorized vessels allowed the scallop fishery to recover. The recovery accelerated when the FCA decided to ban scallop fishing altogether and to oblige its members to gather scallop seedlings from an inshore lake and plant them in the area covered by its scallop fishing rights (Hannesson, 1988: 11). As we have mentioned earlier, there is also evidence that Japanese fishermen's associations put strong conservation measures into effect at the instigation of higher-level authorities or on their own initiative (as exemplified in the previously cited case of Yubetsu). More studies than are presently available are nevertheless required before one can safely conclude that FCAs are as effective in ensuring stock conservation as they are in regulating access to fishing grounds and in preventing or settling conflicts over fishing space. Oral reports from recent field visits (1993) actually point to the difficulty mentioned earlier that, if the system works rather well for species that have mainly a subsistence role, the same cannot be said with respect to the species which are subjected to intensive commercial exploitation due to their high value on the world market (personal communication of Sebastian Mathew).

As we have seen in Chapter 12 (sect. 3), the Japanese management system has not succeeded in preventing recent degradation of resources such as mackerel, sardines, tuna, and, perhaps, skipjacks. This is because too generous licences have been granted to industrial concerns by the Ministry of Agriculture, Forestry, and Fisheries. This being said, it must be reckoned that small-scale fishermen were able to use the existing institutionalized mechanisms to get the situation eventually redressed: under their pressure, the Fisheries Agency of the prefecture concerned decided drastically to curtail the number of licences issued (oral communication of Masao Suzuki).

It cannot be overemphasized that the above system 'has its origins in both customary law and in the formal legislation of the Japanese feudal era'. In many ways, 'the modern Japanese FCA is really only an elaborate variant of the traditional fishing village organisation that has persisted since feudal times'; and 'present-day regulations pertaining to entry rights and fishing grounds remain essentially the same as those of the Edo period as, in many areas, do those regarding size limitations and seasonal regulations on the species taken'. Even the tenured territories of the local FCAs 'have varied little, apart from a trend towards aggregation under consolidated FCAs, as have traditional concepts of the entry rights of outside fishermen' (Hannesson, 1988: 86). As we have already underlined (see above, Chapter 12), the fact that the organization of modern Japanese coastal fisheries is in many respects a continuation of a system developed during feudal times tends to make the Japanese experience hardly replicable in other countries where such a tradition of decentralized management through strong village communities does not exist or has largely been extinguished during recent centuries.

A few localized examples of co-management

In the late 1890s, the Norwegian government enacted special legislation for the Lofoten fishery (in the north of the country) where the Arctic cod has its spawning grounds. This was because, due to growing numbers of participating fishermen, this fishery had become seriously crowded. As in Japan, this legislation actually delegated responsibility for the regulation of the fishery to the fishermen themselves. Following one account, 'Special district committees of fishermen representing different gear groups were set up to make the rules for the fishery, such as: allowable fishing times; which gear is allowed on which fishing grounds; and how much space should be reserved for certain gears such as handlines, gillnets, longlines, seines. In addition to elected fishermen inspectors, a public enforcement agency was established to assure that the rules initiated by the fishermen were being obeyed' (Jentoft, 1989: 141). This system of co-management under which the fishermen of Lofoten have been given exclusive rights by the government still prevails today and, according to Svein Jentoft, it can be considered a success: it has worked well for a long period of time and the fishermen concerned take it for granted (ibid. 140–1, 153).

In the Alanya fishery in Turkey, as we have already pointed out (see above, Chapter 10), there are precise rules governing access to fishing sites and ensuring equitable rotation among the different rights-holders. The effectiveness of these rules is all the greater as they require extensive knowledge of local conditions which can be acquired only through prolonged experience. In the words of Ostrom: 'Mapping this set of fishing sites, such that one boat's fishing activities would not reduce the migration of fish to other locations, would have been a daunting challenge had it not been for the extensive time-and-place information provided by the fishers and their willingness to experiment for a decade with various maps and systems' (Ostrom, 1990: 20).

What needs to be noted in the context of the present discussion is that the Alanya co-operative claims a legal status on the basis of a broad interpretation of the Aquatic Resources Act which states that co-operatives have jurisdiction over 'local arrangements' (Berkes, 1986: 222). Such legal status, Ostrom thinks, adds legitimizing power to the authority of the Alanya fishermen's association to make and enforce local fishing regulations (Ostrom, 1990: 20). Yet, it should be emphasized that such legal status is noticeably looser than that enjoyed by the Japanese FCA and, therefore, the Alanya experience is only an imperfect illustration of what a co-management approach can achieve. In actual fact, and in contrast to coastal lagoon fisheries which are leased by the State and operated by private interests or co-operatives (in these fisheries, there is thus a sound legal basis for the regulation of access to the resource), other coastal fisheries are legally open-access territories. Consequently, the Alanya co-operative has no legal authority to restrict membership or to act as an exclusive organization gathering all of the fishermen under its umbrella (Berkes, 1986: 221–2). There is thus a profound ambiguity in the Turkish legislation which is hardly congenial to effective decentralized management of fish resources.

Located in Mindanao island in the southern Philippines, the Panguil Bay area is the source of some of the most valuable species of shrimp and crustaceans in the country. About forty-seven rivers and tributaries flow into the bay which has a coastline spanning 116 km. and a population of 450,000 inhabitants. Mangrove destruction and overfishing have contributed heavily to the decline of this abundant resource base during the past decade: less than one-third of the mangrove forests remain and, while fishing boats in the bay doubled between 1985 and 1991, the total catch dropped by 75 per cent (FAO, 1993: 146–7). In an attempt to combat problems resulting from environmental degradation, resource depletion, low productivity, and poverty, the Philippine government, supported by the Asian Development Bank and the Overseas Co-operation Fund of Japan, established the Fisheries Sector Programme (FSP) in 1989. Being one of the priority areas selected for improved coastal resource management, Panguil Bay has been made a testing ground for a new approach to CPR management based on site-specific planning and participation of local governments, NGOs and fishing associations. Note that, under the new Local Government Code, the management of municipal waters falls under the authority of the local government units and that the coverage of these waters has been expanded from 7 to 15 km. from the shoreline (Cura, 1994: 3).

The experience is apparently a success story. Thus, we hear that:

the decentralization, training and involvement of local law enforcement is credited with an impressive record in 1990: local forces confiscated or destroyed about 1,600 filter nets, apprehended more than 60 violators, seized 30 scissor nets and uprooted more than 200 net posts in Panguil Bay . . . In addition to communities enforcing regulations aimed at protecting their resources, local fishing associations are constructing, protecting and managing artificial reef sites in the mouth of the bay to replace coral reefs destroyed by dynamite fishing. Some municipalities and communities are developing territorial use rights in fisheries, delineating zones for specific fishing gears and establishing areas for seaweed, mussel and oyster cultivation. Coastal inhabitants are reforesting 600 ha. of open mud-flats through community-based contracts. Individual families are receiving certificates of stewardship to increase land tenure security and use rights to both these reforested mangrove forests and existing forests. At the same time, mangrove zoning is resulting in commercial production zones, buffer zones, limited use zones and strict nature reserves to improve management of the mangrove resources. (FAO, 1993: 47).

It needs to be pointed out, however, that the success achieved by this co-management project has probably much to do with the fact that, so far, the measures taken to protect local fish resources have been essentially directed against external intruders. A complete test of the ability of coastal communities to play their part in a co-management mechanism requires that they successfully participate in the *management*—and not only in allocation through exclusionary arrangements—of their resources, implying that they help design, monitor, and enforce rules of restraint to be applied to their own members (personal communication of Rolf Willmann).

Co-management prospects for broad-based user organizations

In the Canadian Atlantic fishery, the so-called Maritime Fishermen's Union (MFU) got started in the mid-1970s as a militant fishermen's organization that wanted to break the dominance of inshore fishermen by big commercial companies and to defend their way of life.[7] Made up of fishermen who mainly own and operate fishing vessels less than 13.7 metres in length, it covers a very long coastline comprising three maritime provinces on the east coast of Canada (Newfoundland where 70 per cent of the cod fishery is found is excluded, however). The fishermen concerned rely primarily on lobster fishing but they also catch other species. Their communities have usually been quite successful in regulating access to the fishing grounds for lobsters as well as in enforcing state-engineered conservation measures for that species (minimum legal size of lobsters allowed to be caught). Such a success, it seems, can be largely ascribed to the favourable characteristics of the resource (it is well localized) as well as to the fact that there is no competition from outsiders (in particular, from big commercial companies).

The MFU intends to strengthen itself with a view to co-managing other fish resources which are more problematic than lobsters. It appears that, after the complete failure of its management policy which resulted in the collapse of the cod and the herring fisheries (the latter of which has since recovered following the assignment of

[7] The following account is based on Belliveau (1994) and Cormier (1994) as well as on private conversations between Jean-Philippe Platteau and the above two authors who are, respectively, executive secretary and president of the MFU. Thanks are expressed to both of them for their willingness to share their experience with us.

a much lower share of the total quota to large industrial fleets), the Canadian government is now willing to deal with organizations such as MFU in order to delegate to them the tasks of distributing the fishing licences and enforcing specific regional quotas set on the basis of conservation considerations.[8]

It is a noteworthy feature of the present fishing scene that broad-based fishermen organizations have also arisen in developing countries such as Chile (Conapach, or the Confederacion Nacional de Pescadores Artesanales de Chile), India (the National Fishworkers Forum), Senegal (CNPS, or the Collectif National des Pêcheurs Sénégalais), and the Philippines (Kammppi, Bigkis-Lakas Pilipinas, Pamalakaya). These organizations are first and foremost concerned about the rapid degradation of the fish resources which are the mainstay of their members' livelihood. Their objectives are close to those pursued by the MFU in Canada. In the Philippines, for instance, the struggle of fishermen organizations is presently focused on the need for institutionalizing the participation of fishermen in coastal resource management through the creation of resource management councils in every municipality (Cura, 1994: 4). In the near future, it will be interesting to see to what extent they succeed in playing an effective role as co-managers of coastal fish resources, assuming of course that their respective governments agree to enter into co-management agreements with them.

Forestry

India: co-management as a beginning

In Chapter 11 (sect. 1), we offered the reader a rather detailed review of the forest policy of the government of India during both the colonial and the post-independence eras. At the end of this review, we quoted the so-called *Report of Committee on Forest and Tribals in India* (1982) in which the authors advocated a major turn towards a management strategy in which user groups were to play a much more active role than in the past. Article (xi) under the heading 'Forest Policy' (para. 5) thus reads:

> Tribal and local organisations, may be made use of if in good shape and after revitalisation if not in good shape, for management of protected and village forests for commercial, social and farm forestry purposes.

Further on, under the heading 'Management System' (para. 23), we find the following set of recommendations:

> (i) The crux of the problem of forest management lies in the need for integration of tribal and forest economies. The relationship between forest managers and tribals should be one of partnership. This will be possible if an identity-interest between the forest department and tribals is created.
>
> (ii) Forestry development programmes should aim at internalising its components into the rural production system as a whole.

[8] Clearly, this analysis is at variance with that proposed by Davis (1984) and Ostrom (1990: 175–7) with specific reference to the Newfoundland fishery. The latter puts too much blame on the government of Canada while it simultaneously exaggerates the self-regulatory abilities of local fishing communities.

(iii) The management should ensure strong backward and forward linkages between forestry and other development sectors on the local, regional, State and national levels.

(iv) Tribals should be inducted into a more constructive role of forestry. They should be employed in forest service at different levels by imparting specialised training.

(v) Forest management practices need to be modulated to be able to generate employment all the year round for prevention of migration and sustained supply of raw materials for the requirements of agriculture and industry.

(vi) The role of forester needs to be reappraised. The new emphasis should be on forester as an extension agent advising the owners or the management personnel of village, communal private and other forests for undertaking scientific forestry.

(vii) The transformation from conservation to development forestry should be induced through community forestry. Forestry activities should be carried out by many, often local institutions, rather than by a single forest department. In other words, a meta-management system should be applied rather than super-management.

(viii) The course from departmental production forestry to broad-based community forestry can be made smoother through public participation. At the State-level, a broad-based body comprised of officials, technical experts, academics, leaders of public (particularly tribals) opinion should be built up. At the forest, divisional and ITDP levels, advisory committees representing forest interests like government departments, statutory bodies and forest dwellers to review, formulate programmes and oversee their implementation should be set up. Similar committees should be set up at development block level.

(ix) The respective roles of the Forest Department, the Forest Development Corporations, the Tribal Development Corporations should be clearly spelt out. The Forest Department might be the apex agency for formulation of policies and programmes as well as for supervision of their implementation. Execution of programmes may be entrusted to field level corporate organisations like the Forest Development Corporations as well as local representative institutions.

Finally, under the final heading of the Report, 'Legislation', it is recommended that new laws be passed in order to 'strengthen the symbiotic relationship between forests and tribals' (para. 24). Under para. 25, more precise principles are laid down, in particular:

(i) The traditional rights, concessions and privileges of tribals in respect of all forest produce, grazing and hunting should not be abridged . . .

(ii) In the forest villages, they should be given heritable and inalienable right over the land which they cultivate.

(iii) There should be restriction on deforestation of the area vulnerable to soil erosion, landslide, desertification etc. Felling of fruit trees should, ordinarily, be prohibited.

(iv) Association of tribals should be ensured in a large scale plantation programme giving them the right to usufruct.

(v) Ownership right on the trees growing in the holding allotted to a tribal in a forest village should vest in him.

(vi) National parks, sanctuaries, bio-sphere should normally be not located close to the tribal villages. Persons displaced on account of their creation should be properly rehabilitated.

(vii) There should be an attempt at simplification of laws and procedures so that tribals can comprehend them.

(viii) Relevant law should be modified so that the village councils can obtain term-loan against standing tree-stock in forests.

(ix) If necessary, the State might assume the right to provide guidelines about land-use and resource-mobilisation on communal, clan and private lands.

After some hesitation—apparently due to deep-rooted mistrust of some officials in the users' ability to manage their resources effectively—the Government of India decided to experiment with at least some aspects of the new strategy suggested in the above report. Institutional structures similar to districts are thus currently being tested for forest management in many Indian states through joint forest management (JFM) projects. JFM typically involves user groups (generally villages) forming societies and reaching agreements with the Forest Department regarding the management of local forests (Moench, 1992: A-11). It is incumbent upon the Forest Department to set broad boundary conditions—for example, grazing and cutting limitations—and it is its commitment to turn over 25 per cent of the timber harvest and all minor forest products to the local society. In return, the latter body agrees to design and enforce a management system which meets its needs within the aforementioned boundary conditions.

According to Moench, the limited experiences that exist with JFM tend to suggest that it will only function well in certain circumstances. JFM appears to work successfully in West Bengal (bear in mind the successful Arabari experiment detailed in Chapter 12), in Orissa, while in Haryana, 'the greatest potential for success appears to be in situations where relatively small socially homogeneous villages are the primary users of clearly defined forest areas and have a high level of dependence on those forests' (Moench, 1992: A-11). It is apparently in the first of these states that the new policy has yielded the most convincing results and the fact that West Bengal has benefited from a longer period of experience with joint management than other Indian states no doubt accounts for this relative success. In the words of Dolly Arora: 'If JFM has been far more effective in West Bengal than in several other states, it is noteworthy that participation there preceded the adoption of JFM rules, and that too in a big way. There were no less than 1,200 protection committees already in operation in various parts of the state' (Arora, 1994: 696). (Note the striking similarity between these conditions of successful collective action and those mentioned in Chapter 12.) In other states (bear in mind, however, the noticeable exception of Uttarakhand in northern Uttar Pradesh which has been referred to in Chapter 11), the bureaucratization of the programme of participation seems to be a problem. As a matter of fact, the concern of forest officials for attaining high targets in terms of formation of forest protection committees has sometimes resulted in the formation of a large number of committees that either exist only on paper or are manipulated by a few powerful persons in the area (ibid. 694, 696).

In neighbouring Pakistan, in the West Frontier Province, a co-management experiment documented in Chapter 11 has also been started based on forestry co-operatives: to recall, these co-operatives manage a well-delimited forest area according to a management plan approved by the Forest Department and for the preparation of which technical assistance is provided to them. All costs related to maintenance and extraction of the trees are borne by the co-operatives that, in return, are authorized to retain at least 40 per cent of the revenue from the sale of trees. Unfortunately, the experiment does not seem to be promising owing to undue interference of the government and party politics which have the effect of demotivating the co-operative members.

Nepal: co-management as a new reality

In its forest management policy, the Nepalese Government has basically made the same mistakes as its Indian counterpart. Like the government of India, it has eventually come to question the premisses upon which its previous policy was grounded. However, it has shown quicker and stronger determination to reverse its previous policy (nationalization of all forest and waste lands, including village-controlled forests, in 1957) by making a radical shift towards people-based forest management. In 1978, indeed, the government of Nepal promulgated new regulations 'to enable substantial amounts of public forest land to be handed over to local communities to control and manage' (Arnold and Campbell, 1986: 431). As a matter of fact, it now became possible for the Forest Department to enter into agreements to transfer forest to village panchayats. The categories of forest that could be transferred to local community control are: (*a*) Panchayat Forests (PF), for the purpose of reafforestation in the interest of the village community; (*b*) Panchayat Protected Forests (PPF), for the purpose of protection and proper management; and (*c*) Contract Forests (CF), which could be awarded to either individuals or groups (ibid.).

During the early years, there was substantial resistance to authorizing the large-scale transfer of forest resources owing to the fears of many officials (who had been trained in the perspective of a centralized approach to resource management, as in so many other countries) that the local population would destroy them once government controls were lessened. In fact, the greatest barrier to community participation during the project's early years was the lack of widespread public knowledge of the purpose of the new strategy or of the details of managing a PPF (Arnold and Campbell, 1986: 444–5).

To help make the control transfer effective, the Community Forestry Development Project was established. This project was destined to support the three main elements of local management of forest resources: managed PPFs, planting of PFs, and production of seedlings for private planting. Forest nurseries were to be set up in all participating panchayats. Financing and training were to be provided for locally recruited panchayat forest foremen to run the nurseries and for panchayat forest watchers to protect the plantations and managed forests (in keeping with the tradition of forest watchers in former local forest management systems). Finally, a new cadre of forestry staff—the so-called Community Forestry Assistants (CFAs)—were to offer technical assistance and advice at the panchayat and village level. Special attention was lent to providing a system of information and extension materials for communication and training at the grass-roots level (Arnold and Campbell, 1986: 439–40).

The process of establishing and operationalizing a PPF involves three important steps. First, the panchayat requests the government to hand over an area as PPF and the transfer is effected. Second, a panchayat forest committee is created and made to function (experience shows that it is important that committee leadership is kept separate from panchayat leadership). And, third, a management plan is drawn up which constitutes the legal document attesting the agreement between the government, the panchayat, and the user groups involved. It is the responsibility of the CFA to engage 'in a continual dialogue with the users, panchayat officials, and forest committee to arrive at a management system that best meets their needs'. The expertise of the CFA is especially important given the fact that the great diversity of forest types makes it difficult to lay down general management prescriptions that can be widely followed. As for the committee, it must not only support and supervise all community forestry activities but also ensure equitable distribution of products from the PFs and PPFs to all households in the beneficiary group (Arnold and Campbell, 1986: 440–2).

As hinted above, officials' fears have not been vindicated. In the rare instances where PF plantations have been destroyed, the community's behaviour has always resulted from the belief that the government intended to usurp their forest. This suspicion actually followed from the fact that when the area was surveyed the local community did not know that the purpose of the survey was to transfer the area to the local people. These exceptional cases excepted, if we believe Arnold and Campbell, the co-management approach followed by the government of Nepal since the late 1970s has been largely successful even though too ambitious initial targets have often caused achievements to lag behind expectations. The response of villagers was particularly enthusiastic when information has been well diffused, public discussion of the issues involved has been widespread, and benefits as well as responsibilities have been well specified by product and beneficiary (Arnold and Campbell, 1986: 440, 444–6). According to Arnold and Campbell again, something remarkable was 'how quickly group consensus on the value of establishing a PPF usually materialised when the actual provisions of specific management plans (spelling out group rules for protection, harvesting, and benefit sharing) were brought under group discussion' (ibid. 446). For the same authors, perhaps the most important lesson from the whole experiment is that 'communities themselves will take the responsibility for devising methods for solving the common property problem *if they are given sufficient authority, information, and assistance* in doing so' (ibid. 449, emphasis added).

A more recent account by the World Bank is much less enthusiastic, however: panchayats 'gave the villages the most degraded lands, which required high investments for restoration and offered only delayed benefits'. According to this report, such an outcome is not surprising inasmuch as panchayats are 'large administrative units with little previous involvement in forestry' (World Bank, 1992: 143). Colchester has also recently expressed the opinion that the programme 'has not been without problems', particularly because the panchayat 'is too large a unit and too far removed from day to day decisions to effectively supervise and manage local forests' (Colchester, 1994: 90). As a consequence of this situation, the World Bank actually decided to support 'efforts to encourage management by smaller groups more closely associated with particular forest tracts and to give them responsibility for forests in good condition, as well as for degraded land' (World Bank, 1992: 143).

At this juncture, it is worth noting that co-management contracts can be struck between government and rural communities which are not focused on any single resource but encompass all of the resources located within the area of a given community. This more comprehensive approach has been adopted by the Government of Burkina Faso under its *Programme National de Gestion des Terroirs Villageois* (PNGTV).

The PNGTV operates in four stages described by Toulmin as follows:

(a) training and animation leading to the establishment of a *Commission pour la Gestion des Terroirs Villageois* (CGTV), with representatives from certain groups, such as men, women, young people, herders, inmigrants, etc.;
(b) work with the CGTV to define and mark the village's boundary and carry out an inventory of resources within the village lands;
(c) negotiation of a contract between the government and the CGTV regarding the investments to be made to improve the productivity and management of resources within the village lands;
(d) carrying out of the contract. (Toulmin, 1991: 28).

Unfortunately, it is too early to assess this Programme as most of the pilot villages are still in the first two stages. Toulmin is nevertheless of the opinion that 'as a whole, the programme seems well thought out and a reasonable starting point for establishing local systems of resource management', all the more so as it 'includes as an important element, a programme of investment and resource improvement aimed at raising the productivity and sustainability of resources within the village lands' (Toulmin, 1991: 28).

Irrigation

In Chapter 12 (sect. 3), we briefly described the extremely instructive experience of the Gal Oya irrigation project in southern Sri Lanka. As it has been designed by the ARTI–Cornell team, this project can actually be viewed, at least in part, as an experiment with a co-management approach. This said, it is again Japan that is the best example of the co-management approach in irrigation matters. The Land Improvement Districts (LIDs), which are 'the culmination of historical experience of irrigation and agricultural development through co-operation through different eras', are the central institution governing water management in this country (Mitra, 1992: A-78). True, the LIDs are a much more complex affair than the former water users' organizations mainly because they follow a comprehensive approach to land development (including irrigation and drainage projects) with the direct support and close assistance of national and prefectural governments. Yet, basically, they are nothing but farmers' organizations, constituted as juridical persons, with irrigation associations (each of which is organized on the basis of a village) as their substructure (ibid. A-78–80). In the following, we would nevertheless like to draw attention to another institutional approach to resource management which is much more centralized, yet does not fail to mobilize the efforts of resource users through various operational and organizational procedures.

To illustrate this *bureaucratic approach to participation* (this almost self-contradictory expression has been chosen to convey the rather paradoxical character of the organizations concerned), we refer below to two insightful and detailed studies of the management of irrigation systems in East Asia, particularly in Taiwan and South Korea (Wade, 1988*b*; 1990; Moore, 1989). These two countries are especially worth studying given their high rates of success in the management of irrigation water: Taiwan is thus considered a country possessing one of the world's most technically efficient irrigation systems, a remarkable achievement in view of the fact that most of its water control systems are gravity-flow systems without much storage (Levine, 1980).[9] Worth pointing out is that, in the first of the aforementioned studies, the author was actually motivated by the desire to understand the reasons for India's poor performance with respect to irrigation management. Comparative institutional analysis was considered a fruitful way to get an answer to that question. As is evident from the account given below, the exercise was indeed quite conclusive.

It must first be noted that, in countries like South Korea and Taiwan, management of irrigation water is in the hands of catchment-based parastatal agencies which, despite their pseudo-democratic labelling (irrigation associations in Taiwan and farmland improvement associations in South Korea), do not involve formal mechanisms of accountability. In the two countries, an element of authoritarianism is undoubtedly present. The following statement, made with respect to Taiwan, is sufficiently clear in this regard:

> Local Farmers' Associations and Irrigation Associations maintain, despite their formal non-government status, 'security' departments staffed by central Party or security personnel but financed by the Associations themselves. The utility of the Farmers' and Irrigation Associations as strategic institutions from which to maintain political surveillance at local level was enhanced by the policy towards 'private' associations pursued by the KMT in agriculture as in all spheres of public activity. Only officially recognised and registered associations may function. Those which are recognised—and closely controlled politically—are given *de facto* monopolies. Where organisations do not exist, they are created on state initiative as a preemptive measure. The only farmers' organisations officially tolerated are the Farmers' and Irrigation Associations and the marketing 'cooperatives' mentioned above. (Moore, 1988: 132)

Against this background, a central lesson from an analysis of the functioning of irrigation associations in both Taiwan and South Korea is that even centralized organizational structures can perform well if they follow appropriate operational and organizational procedures that have the effect of establishing trust between farmers and irrigation staff and within the irrigation hierarchy itself. This is precisely where, according to Wade, the East Asian type of organization has proved so much superior to that found in South Asia in general, and in India in particular.

A key feature of the East Asian type of organization for water management is that methods are used with a view to creating a sense of common purpose and corporate identity within each irrigation agency (IA). This result is achieved to a large extent by

[9] The success of both the Taiwanese and South Korean irrigation systems can also be measured in institutional terms. Worth noting is thus the fact that high levels of fee collection from water users have been achieved in the two countries.

obscuring the contractual nature of the employment relation between the IA and *individual* staff members, by setting objectives that can be shared by all members, by providing stable employment to officials, and by fixing pay scales which are not closely tied to hierarchical rank (so as to avoid 'the ingrained conflictualism' which is found between lower and higher staff in Indian irrigation departments).

A second feature, more directly relevant to our discussion in this chapter, is the high degree of staff involvement with farmers. In South Korea, for example, the lack of farmer participation in irrigation system management 'is partly offset by internalising farmers at the bottom of the formal management hierarchy itself, in the role of patroller'. At the same time as he is thus at the lowest level of the organizational structure, the patroller must be 'a farmer with land within the jurisdiction which he irrigates, so that he experiences irrigation problems at first hand' (Wade, 1988*b*: 495). Note that he is nominated each year by the headmen of the villages within his jurisdiction and that, if the latter are unsatisfied with his way of handling the task, they nominate someone else. Most staff of the IAs, even (male) clerks are expected and inclined to stop and chat with farmers whom they meet along the canals (for which rides they are provided with small motor cycles). In the words of Wade: 'The intensity of this local contact helps further to make up for the paucity of more formal channels of communication between farmers and staff, which is an expression of the authoritarian character of the South Korean political regime' (ibid.).

Recruitment and promotion procedures also play an important role inasmuch as they ensure that the senior-level staff are natives of the area in which they work. 'Hence the eyes of the irrigation staff are kept firmly on the locality, and identification between their interests and those of farmers is further encouraged' (Wade, 1988*b*: 495). Elaborating on this theme, Wade adds:

> Local affiliation of the staff is important because it gives both sides—staff and farmers—a set of shared experiences. This directly assists a sense of mutual obligation between them; and also provides a basis for a shared set of beliefs according to which the existing order is fair and just, and every betrayal is perverse and unjust—including betrayal of the irrigation agency's rules. This is a much more cost-effective method of avoiding free-rider problems than relying on a calculus of punishment. (Wade, 1988*b*: 495)

Much the same picture emerges from the situation in Taiwan where the staff of the irrigation associations are effectively linked to the local farmers on the one hand and to the national agencies on the other. For each rotation area, an irrigation group chief is elected to supervise water distribution and maintenance operations as well as to manage potential conflicts. In particular, they are in charge of closely monitoring the jointly hired common irrigators who have primary responsibility for the distribution of water and the guarding of the system against fraud and damage. As a matter of principle, these chiefs are local farmers and, to avoid undue interference of partisan politics, the process leading to their election is kept separate from elections for other offices. In addition, the irrigation staff themselves are typically recruited from local communities so as to ensure adequate incentives for effective management of the system. In the words of Moore:

The IAs are overwhelmingly staffed by people who were born in the locality, have lived there all their lives, and in many cases farm there. Further, IA staff are not sharply differentiated from their members in terms of education or income levels. I have a strong overall impression that IA staff are so much part of local society that they can neither easily escape uncomfortable censure if they are conspicuously seen to be performing poorly at their work, nor ignore representations made to them by members in the context of regular and frequent social interactions. (Moore, 1989: 1742)

There is obviously a direct parallel to be drawn between the above diagnosis and the finding reported in Chapter 6 according to which norms of reciprocity can be established by fostering communication in such a way as to transform other agents 'from mere strangers into real people'. The situation in India offers a striking contrast to that obtaining in East Asia since, in the former region, irrigation officers 'are normally rotated in and out of any one post every 18–24 months, and have no identification with the area of their responsibility' (Wade, 1988*b*: 495; see also 1982). Note that such high rates of mobility not only create low incentives for the effective management of irrigation systems, they also preclude any learning process since staff members are shifted to new assignments before they have become familiar with the setting in which they operate (Weissing and Ostrom, 1992). Moreover, the position of a 'guard' is usually held by a labourer who is directly supervised by an engineer, and both are part of the Operations and Management Division that holds a minor place in the (large) state-level irrigation department.

Equally worthy of note is the fact that in East Asia the staff have a direct sense of dependence on the prosperity of farmers under their own system because the IA has its own revenue base (the water fees collected from the farmers) from which it must meet most of its operating costs (Wade, 1988*b*: 494). Thus, in Taiwan, fees paid by farmers account for one-third to three-quarters of the financing of the IAs (Moore, 1989). In the same connection, another feature that deserves to be strongly emphasized is the importance attached, even by higher-level authorities, to expeditious payment of irrigation fees by water users and the interpretation of any delay as a sign that some problem has arisen that needs to be addressed. As Moore puts it:

During the two periods of the year when fees are due, most of the IAs' institutional machinery appears to be devoted to completing collections as expeditiously as possible. The same working station staff who provide farmers with irrigation services come to them to encourage them to part with their money if there is any sign of delayed payment. Each working station is required to make daily telephone reports to superiors about collections in their area. . . . And the headquarters are obliged to report regularly to the Provincial Water Conservancy Bureau. At each level, delays in fee payment are taken as *prima facie* evidence of a problem which requires attention. (Moore, 1989: 1743)

This interactive process is actually part of an institutional structure that makes all staff members at every level subject to detailed annual job performance evaluations. Great concern is shown about these evaluations as they result in ratings which directly or indirectly affect salary increments, promotions, and access to additional resources (Moore, 1989: 1743). Furthermore, by pressuring relatively autonomous irrigation associations to perform well (for instance, in terms of their speed of fee collection), the Provincial Water Conservancy Bureau tends to stimulate competition among them and to link them together by passing information on best practices and rules (Weissing and Ostrom, 1992). All this is a far cry from the situation obtaining in India where the field guards employed by the irrigation department are supervised by a staff that has practically no incentive to make the system work effectively. The water users' bargaining position is made low to the extent that they cannot affect the performance of the field guards by refusing to pay irrigation fees or by delaying payments. Indeed, since these fees go to a Revenue Department rather than to the division in charge of irrigation operations and maintenance, whether water users pay their fees or not does not make any difference to the material situation of the field guards.

Wade rightly lays stress on the fact that effective resource management by a bureaucratic agency depends on the perceived legitimacy of the irrigation staff's authority. In turn, this legitimacy 'depends on farmers' judgment of how competent the staff are and on how much they trust their good intentions'. To the extent that competence is difficult to assess—particularly so when the system is big—'trust becomes the crucial factor' (Wade, 1988*b*: 497). What needs to be added now is that the amount of required trust can be reduced by designing physical infrastructures in such a manner that farmers' dependence on the allocation decisions of officials is significantly diminished. One design feature which is advisable from this standpoint is the 'on-line' or 'break-point' reservoir since it provides 'a clear hand-over point where the officials' jurisdiction ends and the farmers' jurisdiction begins'. The important thing, here, is that the reservoir be 'at a low enough level for farmers to see the stock of water which is "theirs", for water to be able to reach all the fields within a few hours, and for farmers to have a large (legitimate) hand in how it is allocated'. Another promising system is that experimented in the state of Gujarat (India). Under this system bulk amounts of water are sold to a tertiary distributory—that is, to all the farmers dependent on this distributory as a unit—and the farmers themselves are entrusted with the responsibility of organizing the distribution of water and the collection of the fee (ibid. 496–7). This is in sharp contrast to many government-owned irrigation systems that have designed physical works without any concern as to how guards or farmers could observe activities at a low cost. Further, in most of these schemes (including those in India), the guards hired by a government agency are often given vast areas to cover and, for this purpose, they are not provided with even a bicycle, let alone a motorized vehicle, to travel to the canals themselves. (Weissing and Ostrom, 1992)

For a system of water management to work effectively, it is not only necessary that staff members have adequate incentives to perform their assigned tasks diligently, that user communities are made an integral part of the management system, and that physical infrastructures are properly designed so as to minimize the cost of fraud detection. It is also essential that a high degree of flexibility and autonomy be granted to decentralized management units so as to enable them to best adapt to local circumstances and variations. This is a point that Taiwanese authorities seem to have well understood. As a matter of fact, the Yun-Lin Irrigation Association which covers an area of 65,590 ha. of land has four regional management officers, forty-three working stations, 500 water groups, and 1,683 subwater subgroups based on rotational areas. What requires to be stressed is that each of the numerous (over thirty) systems in use in this command area has its own fee schedule (some systems have even more than one); 'each has a high degree of autonomy with respect to system operation, maintenance and improvement; each has specific water rights, usually based on historical development, which are respected in irrigation planning and operation, though they may be modified under emergency conditions' (Levine, 1978: 3, cited from Weissing and Ostrom, 1992).

In a recent paper in which the Indian and Japanese systems of water control and allocation have been compared, Mitra has argued that many efficiency losses and equity problems in the management of water in surface irrigation in India can be traced back to an administrative system 'devoid of organisational structure requiring people's participation' (Mitra, 1992: A-78). What is needed in India, and where India can learn from Japan, is a 'joint management' approach in which the Command Area Development Authorities (CADA)—an institutional innovation ushered in the mid-1970s with a view to improving farm-level irrigation water management—would involve farmers in their development and management programme. This approach is not feasible, however, unless the attitude and perception of the irrigation departments and other state agencies like CADA undergo 'a sea-change' in order to enlist the active and willing co-operation of farmers (ibid. A-82). As a matter of fact,

> The farmers' involvement and participation will not be forthcoming easily if the CADA is continued to be seen as a government programme imposed from the top. Under such circumstances farmers would not see CADA as a programme meant to benefit them or worthy of support. To ensure farmers' support, irrigation associations of the type of LIDs in Japan will have to be organised such that farmers are given the responsibility of irrigation management which brings about principle of equity as regard farmers' right to water. (Mitra, 1992: A-80)

The joint management approach envisioned by Mitra is one in which CADA would actually work as a liaison and catalytic agent between irrigation departments on the one hand and irrigation associations on the other. The latter would assume the responsibility for the distribution and utilization of the water at the tertiary level, maintain properly the distribution networks under their control, collect water dues from the members for payment to state authority, and adjudicate local disputes and resolve local conflicts. The effective working of such associations will admittedly take time since India does not have the background of Japan which has a very long history of water users' organizations (Mitra, 1992: A-81). In view of this lack of historical precedent in India, one may none the less wonder whether adoption of an organizational form more akin to the rather centralized pattern found in Taiwan and South Korea would not be more successful than emulation of the Japanese model in which people's participation has undoubtedly been more complete and the principles of co-management are more strictly or genuinely abided by.

Finally, it is of interest to note that a highly vulnerable point in many people-based irrigation projects is maintenance of the infrastructure: 'a pattern of neglect followed by repair and restoration is much more frequent than routine preventive maintenance'. This may come as a surprise since the conventional wisdom has it that if farmers feel they truly 'own' a system, they will take good care of it (Bruns, 1993: 1843). A plausible explanation is that irrigators have a strong incentive to delay maintenance action until there is a need for major repairs and rehabilitation. This is because they usually have to pay the full costs of routine repairs while the government pays fully for major repairs and rehabilitation. Current policies regarding government assistance thus create perverse incentives that do not encourage farmers to be diligent about maintenance. Requiring local cost-sharing, even for relatively large repairs and improvements, would be a major step towards solving this important problem (ibid.: 1844–5).

13.4 Conclusion

In selecting a form of resource regulation, a government is not confined to the spurious and simplistic 'State versus community' dichotomy. A wide range of intermediate options is actually available which will be more or less effective depending upon the strength and collective action potential of basic user groups. If these groups are not solid or autonomous enough to dispense with significant assistance from the State, if they need to be protected against the encroachments and the damage caused by broad-level forces and the powerful interests of other economic sectors, if there are severe intergroup conflicts which cannot be settled in a decentralized way, or if it is imperative that local action takes place within a national resource policy framework, some sort of co-management contract between government and user groups may appear as the most promising arrangement for management of local-level CPRs.

On the other hand, if user groups or rural communities are deemed to be totally incapable of sustainable collective action to manage such resources, co-management may look too ambitious an approach. In these circumstances, more authoritarian or bureaucratic methods are likely to be unavoidable. What is then important is to design operational and organizational procedures in such a way as to get resource users involved to the largest possible extent in management tasks and also gradually to develop—instead of stifling—whatever self-management abilities they may possess. As we have seen, this requires that the officials' jurisdiction be clearly demarcated from the users' jurisdiction.

Even assuming that rural communities have good potential for collective action, the challenge implicit in any genuine co-management approach ought not to be underestimated. It is indeed truly enormous, especially because political considerations can seriously threaten the viability of co-management schemes of village-level CPRs. As underlined in Chapter 11, government policies in many developing countries are often aimed at strengthening the hold of the State over the civic society. Unfortunately, this typically implies that state authorities have an interest in tightly controlling all significant attempts by local communities at organizing themselves, particularly so if these attempts result in the development of large-scale grass-roots movements or networks or in the assertion of claims for more autonomy. When strategies of political control (say, through more or less forced integration of these movements in dominant political parties or organizations) fail, every effort is generally made to break them or, at least, to undermine their strength by stirring up divisive tendencies within them. Such reactions can only have the effect of widening the trust gap between the State and the village communities.

Without a fundamental change in the state approach to the civic society, therefore, the prospects for genuine co-management look dim. But even admitting that such a change cannot be realistically expected to occur in the foreseeable future, depletion of local-level natural resources needs not occur if centralized state agencies set up for the purpose follow appropriate procedures that succeed in creating the right kind of incentives to prompt both state agents and local resource users to feel responsible and accountable for the management of village-level CPRs. The main lesson to be drawn from the successful East Asian type of organizational structure for irrigation management is precisely that resource management can be effective even within the framework of relatively centralized parastatal agencies, provided they are being granted considerable autonomy within their geographical juridiction.

General Conclusion

In this conclusion, we would like to bring into focus what we consider to be the most salient findings or propositions of our study and to draw the policy implications therefrom.

By concentrating their analysis on the impact of various property regimes on the pattern of resource use and generally assuming that information about resources is perfect or almost perfect, economists tend to overlook one of the most important causes of resource mismanagement. As a matter of fact, it appears that in many instances direct resource users and state authorities are not fully aware of the ecological processes at work, or, at least, they tend to underestimate the long-term negative effects of their present use on the future state of the resource.

As far as state authorities are concerned, their imperfect knowledge originates not only in limited expertise but also in the considerable complexity of the ongoing ecological processes. Unfortunately, these two factors tend to combine their effects in the case of developing countries. In effect, the aforementioned complexity is usually much greater in tropical than in temperate zones. For example, understanding fish behaviour is more complicated in tropical than in temperate waters, partly because the number of interacting fish species is considerably larger in the former than in the latter. In view of this comparatively great complexity, the lack of administrative, technical, and scientific expertise in poor countries is especially serious. Lack of financial means can only reinforce this handicap and is particularly difficult to remedy given that States in poor countries tend understandably to give priority to short-term objectives over long-term (including ecological) concerns. Here is clearly a field where outside assistance is fully justified. It must also be borne in mind that governments, especially so in the context of young nations, tend to give priority to distributive and political concerns (the two of which are usually intertwined) over efficiency considerations. Only wishful thinking can result from ignoring the basic facts that make up the political economy of the developing countries.

As far as user groups are concerned, one needs to call into question the romantic view according to which such groups are perfectly informed about the resource simply because of proximity. Confusion in the minds of researchers sometimes follows from the fact that in many village communities rules exist for regulating access to local CPRs in an equitable way. Yet from this, it cannot be inferred that these communities are able to devise rules for resource management proper (which is a more complex affair). If understanding of ecological phenomena or stock–flow relationships (which involve abstract concepts and causal reasoning) is inadequate among direct resource users, as seems to be attested by many field workers, education has obviously a central role to play in any approach aiming at improving CPR management. Here again, we find a clear case for outside assistance: villagers may need help to draw together a number of critical in-the-field observations which have so far remained unconnected, and to articulate these observations in meaningful causal sequences. Such assistance is likely to be called for especially when resources are not well localized, not easily visible, and rather unpredictable.

Things may be far more complicated still, as suggested by our above remark that ecological processes may be quite complex as in the case of many tropical maritime fisheries. If this is the case, one may have to reckon that there is genuine uncertainty about the impact of human harvesting efforts on the stock of a resource. And to the extent that exogenous factors (such as changes of currents) beyond man's control are possibly responsible for resource depletion (and, perhaps, at a later stage, for their sudden recovery), users may be perfectly justified in intensively exploiting their natural resources without getting too preoccupied about the ecological impact of their own harvesting behaviour. There is clearly no tragedy of the commons behind such kind of behaviour, yet the State may be justified in laying down rules of restraint to insure against the risk of irreversible degradation of an essential resource (whether for production or for consumption).

Economists have spent much effort on examining the question of the comparative efficiency of various resource management regimes. The insights provided by economic theory are extremely valuable, even though they do not point to a particular regime as 'the' best solution. Such a perspective of intellectual scepticism has been adopted in this book. Thus, privatization does not necessarily emerge as the appropriate solution in all situations where overexploitation of natural resources is under way. Private property on natural resources may be problematic both from an equity and an efficiency viewpoint. The equity problem is particularly worthy of attention in the context of poor countries where the livelihood of poor people crucially hinges upon their access to village-level CPRs. Efficiency problems are not to be underestimated in view of the pervasive market imperfections characterizing developing countries. On the other hand, state resource management, or any centralized mode of resource management, suffers from serious information gaps. Problems originate in the difficulty of collecting information not only about a huge variety of resource types and microclimatic constraints (for which general management prescriptions are of no avail) but also about the behaviour and the customs of the user groups themselves as well as the specific constraints confronting them.

What about the community-based approach to resource management? To the initial pessimism of the tragedy of the commons' doctrine, a more optimistic phase has succeeded characterized by the belief that village societies are able to use their resources efficiently provided that the State does not interfere. This change of mood and outlook is grounded in two significant intellectual events. For one thing, there has been an upsurge of in-depth field studies pointing to the considerable collective action potential of rural communities and, for another, non-co-operative game theory has shown that co-operation is a possible outcome in such communities, especially so if they are small and interactions among group users are frequent. Moreover, our game-theoretical analysis suggests that problems of the commons are not necessarily well depicted by the classic Prisoner's Dilemma. In actual fact, in many circumstances, co-ordination and leadership problems play a dominant role. In those cases, rural communities can effectively sustain co-operation even though users are numerous and do not interact frequently, provided that an effective authority structure exists to provide the required leadership and sufficient trust is established to countenance optimistic expectations regarding others' intended behaviour.

It is noteworthy that, if they lead to the same conclusion, these two strands of literature are grounded in different arguments or observations. While non-co-operative game theory suggests that purely decentralized (self-enforcing) and uncoordinated co-operation mechanisms are possible at (small) group level, socio-anthropological writings often bring to light collective arrangements that are backed by explicit rules of resource use as well as by formal and informal mechanisms to enforce them. Both contributions are clearly useful. By demonstrating that co-operation is a possible outcome within the framework of repeated interactions in small groups, non-co-operative game theory contributes in establishing the viability of small groups operating as the basic units of more complex management systems. On the other hand, by showing that village communities or relatively large user groups can succeed in devising and enforcing rules for complex local-level resource systems, socio-anthropologists point to the possibility of federated structures resting on multiple layers of nested user groups.

When they make their pro-community diagnosis, social scientists do not necessarily ignore the important changes that have affected village societies during recent decades. As a matter of fact, some of them clearly state that, as resource scarcity increases, those societies will be able to organize themselves to co-ordinate and control more tightly the use of village CPRs. In other words, co-operation tends to evolve and develop spontaneously whenever the need arises to impose restraints on the use of such resources. There are two main problems with these assumptions. The first problem has already been touched on above and consists of imperfect information about the state of the resources and the link between current rates of resource appropriation and the level of the stock. The second problem arises from the fact that, in stark contrast to the pessimism conveyed by the tragedy of the commons' view, the difficulties of successful co-operation tend to be underestimated. It bears emphasis that the above two problems are especially acute where the environment changes quickly as it has done in all developing countries during recent decades under the impulse of rapid population growth and rapid commercialization of CPR products.

The threat posed by market integration is to be taken very seriously. In the social science literature, rapid depletion of natural resources by the private sector is often represented as the outcome of a collusion between state authorities and business interests at the expense of traditional user communities. There is a good deal of truth in this way of picturing the situation. Yet, the question cannot be bypassed as to why private interests necessarily destroy the resource instead of preserving it. One plausible answer lies in the deficiencies and uncertainties characterizing the contracts struck between the State and private concerns. In particular, the inability of the State in many developing countries credibly to commit itself to granting secure use rights to private actors creates a perverse incentive to misuse natural resources and to overexploit them rapidly.

Another plausible answer that is almost systematically ignored in the empirical literature is simply that the actors concerned *rationally* degrade the natural resources on which they have acquired property rights. This rational behaviour may follow from the fact that they have available to them a number of alternative, more attractive income opportunities or investment avenues (they have many exit options) in which they can usefully plough back the profits earned in CPR exploitation. Such behaviour may also be a direct consequence of the fact that future prices of the CPR products are highly uncertain.

Furthermore, the complexity of the market integration process ought not to be overlooked. The expansion of market forces is an all-pervasive process which affects all actors, including the rural communities themselves. This is evident from the fact that traditional élites and, sometimes, even ordinary members of such communities do not withstand the pressure of these forces and grant concessions or even sell out property rights over natural resources to business ventures such as logging companies. In other cases, rural dwellers eagerly respond to new market opportunities by quickly increasing extraction of CPR products without apparent regard for long-term resource conservation. And it is not possible realistically to account for all these frequent failures by pointing to insecure rights over the resource concerned. In a revealing manner, irrespective of the nature of such rights, local management appears to be most effective for resources that have a subsistence function and least effective for those that have a high commercial value. To make matters more complicated still, market integration yields indirect effects that tend to undermine the collective action potential of customary user groups: the enhanced mobility of the people and the questioning of traditional values and patterns of authority are particularly noticeable effects.

There is good ground to believe that, when poor people overexploit local natural resources in situations where they are perfectly aware of the ecological impact of their actions, it is often because they face hard subsistence constraints which lead them to discount streams of future incomes. This interpretation is actually borne out by the fact that they generally need externally provided economic incentives to be induced to conserve these resources. Sometimes, also, their heavy discounting of future income arises from profound changes brought in their intertemporal preference structure by the demonstration of new consumption possibilities following increased market integration.

Especially in view of the above changes and behavioural responses to them, if natural resources are to be protected against the risk of destruction, it is essential that the State provides a clear framework of basic rights, rules, and objectives to serve as a guideline for a voluntarist resource management policy. If market forces have to be tamed for the purpose of resource conservation, it is at the national level that protective measures must first be taken. Indeed, the hope cannot be realistically entertained that rural communities alone will always be able to impose on themselves rules of restraint in the midst of powerful market pressures.

Now, given the disastrous failures of most governmental attempts at managing natural resources down to the village level, it is essential that user groups be integrated in the national resource-preserving strategy. This implies that they are granted clear and secure rights over local-level resources as well as unambiguous responsibilities, including monitoring and sanctioning prerogatives; that the rationale of any rule set at a higher level is being properly explained to them; that there is enough room left for user groups to adapt these rules to local circumstances; and that there exist procedures to change them in the light of evolving experiences at grass-roots level. At least, this must be so whenever village communities or smaller social units retain enough coherence and stability to be an effective partner of the State. Mutual trust plays a critical role for achieving successful collective action at village level. This requirement tends to favour societies which have a long and well-established tradition of co-operation in varied sectors of life (for example, Japanese village communities since the feudal Edo period). However, pessimism about co-operation potential in societies which do not have such a tradition is not necessarily warranted. As a matter of fact, some significant successes in the field attest that *trust can be created* under the impulse of catalytic agents who are often coming from outside the community. These experiences tend to confirm social psychology experiments in which communication about a common challenge has been shown to have the effect of instilling into people feelings of collective identity and group belonging.

There is obviously a wide range of organizational forms of co-management that run, at one extreme, from the paternalistic or rather authoritarian South Korean model (in which users are integrated at a low level of the administrative machinery) to, at the other extreme, devolution of significant responsibilities and granting of genuine autonomy to local communities or user groups, as testified by the Japanese experience of fishery management or, more recently, by reafforestation schemes in West Bengal (India). Whatever the precise mode of partnership chosen, there is no doubt that in many countries state intervention has to be reshaped to institutionalize collaboration between administration and resource users. Given the deep-rooted 'culture of distrust' that permeates relationships between the State and local resource users, development projects initiated by local or foreign donor agencies can help not only to strengthen trust within user groups but also to gradually overcome the trust gap that exists between these groups and the state authorities.

As is evident from some of the above conclusions and as suggested by game theory, a wide variety of situations can actually occur. It is the task of the field researcher to determine which theoretical model best suits the specific situation encountered on the ground. To answer that question, he must figure out what are the relevant characteristics of the resource (its location, its degree of visibility, the relationship between its stock and human harvesting efforts, the nature of the infrastructure required as well as the techniques available to exploit it, etc.), of the users (their wealth endowment, their rate of time preference, their interest in the resource and their perception of that interest, the available exit opportunities, etc.), and the social structure to which they belong (the class structure of the community, the pattern of local authority, the social norms prevailing, etc.). The illustrations provided in this book serve only to direct attention to a number of important possibilities and the way they are related to specific game forms.

In fact, empirical research that meets the aforedescribed intellectual challenge is badly needed. Socio-anthropological studies, in spite of highly instructive accounts and insightful observations, often lack the kind of analytical tightness that is so useful to organize empirical data in a meaningful way and to derive correct policy lessons from case-study materials. They may also be permeated by a 'romantic bias' that results in too much confidence in the self-governing ability of user communities and in too negative assessments of state performances. Our hope is that the present work will be able to stimulate systematic applied research evincing both the empirical thoroughness of many socio-anthropological studies and the economists' concern for conceptual clarity and generalization possibilities. Here is indeed a research topic calling for serious interdisciplinary collaboration.

It is only when this challenge is met that we shall have a better understanding of whether and why rural dwellers deplete their local natural resources. In particular, what is the exact responsibility of the type of strategic interactions subsumed in the tragedy of the commons' model as compared with other potential explanations, such as lack of awareness or knowledge about ecological effects of human efforts, heavy discounting of future income streams, uncertainty regarding future prices of CPR products, uncertainty about future property rights, ambiguous impact of output price increases on conservation practices, availability of more attractive income opportunities? This question needs to receive precise answers if we want to define the most appropriate solutions to end situations in which the lot of future generations is dangerously threatened. And since the state of our knowledge is at present so imperfect, the reader should consider many of the above statements as tentative conclusions or, better, as research hypotheses that require to be put to serious test.

References

Abreu, D., 1988, 'On the Theory of Infinitely Repeated Games with Discounting', *Econometrica*, 56/2: 383–96.

—— P. Milgrom, and D. Pearce, 1991, 'Information and Timing in Repeated Partnerships', *Econometrica*, 59/6: 1713–33.

Acheson, J. M., 1972, 'Territories of the Lobstermen', *Natural History*, 81: 60–9.

—— 1987, 'The Lobster Fiefs Revisited: Economic and Ecological Effects of Territoriality in the Maine Lobster Fishery', in B. J. McCay and J. M. Acheson (eds.), *The Question of the Commons—The Culture and Ecology of Communal Resources* (Tucson, Arizona: University of Arizona Press): 1–34.

—— 1988, *The Lobster Gangs of Maine* (Hanover, NH: University Press of New England).

—— 1989, 'Management of Common-Property Resources', in S. Plattner (ed.), *Economic Anthropology* (Stanford, Calif.: Stanford University Press): 351–78.

Agarwal, A., and S. Narain, 1989, *Towards Green Villages* (Delhi: Centre for Science and the Environment).

Agarwal, B., 1991, 'Social Security and the Family: Coping with Seasonality and Calamity in Rural India', in E. J. Ahmad, J. Drèze, J. Hills, and A. Sen (eds.), *Social Security in Developing Countries* (Oxford: Clarendon Press): 171–244.

Agarwala, V. P., 1985, *Forests in India* (New Delhi: Oxford University Press and IBH Publishing Co.).

Agrawal, A., 1994, 'Rules, Rule Making, and Rule Breaking: Examining the Fit between Rule Systems and Resource Use', in E. Ostrom, R. Gardner, and J. Walker, *Rules, Games, and Common-Pool Resources* (Ann Arbor, Mich.: University of Michigan Press): 267–82.

Akerlof, G., 1976, 'The Economics of Caste and of the Rat Race and Other Woeful Tales', *Quarterly Journal of Economics*, 90/4: 599–617.

Alcorn, J. B., 1984, 'Development Policy, Forests, and Peasant Farms: Reflections on Huastec-Managed Forests' Contributions to Commercial Production and Resource Conservation', *Economic Botany*, 38/4: 389–406.

Alexander, P., 1980, 'Sea Tenure in Southern Sri Lanka', in A. Spoehr (ed.), *Maritime Adaptations—Essays on Contemporary Fishing Communities* (Pittsburgh: University of Pittsburgh Press): 91–111.

—— 1982, *Sri Lankan Fishermen—Rural Capitalism and Peasant Society* (Canberra: Australian National University).

Allen, R., 1992, *Enclosures and the Yeomen* (Oxford: Oxford University Press).

Amarasinghe, O., 1988, 'The Impact of Market Penetration, Technological Change and State Intervention on Production Relations in Maritime Fishermen Communities: A Case Study of Southern Sri Lanka', unpublished Ph.D. thesis, Faculté des Sciences Economiques et Sociales, University of Namur (Belgium).

—— 1989, 'Technical Change, Transformation of Risks and Patronage Relations in a Fishing Community of South Sri Lanka', *Development and Change*, 20/4: 701–33.

Anderson, T. L., and P. J. Hill, 1977, 'From Free Grass to Fences: Transforming the Commons of the American West', in G. Hardin and J. Baden (eds.), *Managing the Commons* (San Francisco: W. H. Freeman & Co.): 200–16.

Arnold, J. E. M., and J. G. Campbell, 1986, 'Collective Management of Hill Forests in Nepal: The Community Forestry Development Project', in National Research Council, *Proceedings of the Conference on Common Property Resource Management* (Washington, DC.: National Academy Press): 425–54.

Aronfreed, J., 1968, *Conduct and Conscience: The Socialization of Internalized Control over Behavior* (New York: Academic Press).

Arora, D., 1994, 'From State Regulation to People's Participation—Case of Forest Management in India', *Economic and Political Weekly*, 29/12: 691–8.

Arrow, K., 1973, *Information and Economic Behavior* (Stockholm: Federation of Swedish Industries).

Asada, Y., Y. Hirasawa, and F. Nagasaki, 1983, 'Fishery Management in Japan', *FAO Fisheries Technical Paper*, No. 238 (Rome: FAO).

Ashish, S. M., 1979, 'Agricultural Economy Disaster', *Economic and Political Weekly*, 14/25: 1058–64.

Avineri, S., 1968, *The Social and Political Thought of Karl Marx* (Cambridge: Cambridge University Press).

Axelrod, R., 1981, 'The Emergence of Cooperation among Egoists', *American Political Science Review*, 75/1: 306–18.

—— 1984, *The Evolution of Cooperation* (New York: Basic Books).

—— 1986, 'An Evolutionary Approach to Norms', *American Political Science Review*, 80/4: 1095–111.

—— and W. D. Hamilton, 1981, 'The Evolution of Cooperation', *Science*, 211/4489: 1390–6.

Azhar, R. A., 1993, 'Commons, Regulation, and Rent-Seeking Behavior: The Dilemma of Pakistan's *Guzara* Forests', *Economic Development and Cultural Change*, 42/1: 115–28.

Badcock, C. R., 1986, *The Problem of Altruism-Freudian-Darwinian Solutions* (Oxford: Blackwell).

Badouin, R., 1971, *Economie rurale* (Paris: Armand Colin).

Bailey, C., A. Drviponggo, and F. Marahudin (eds.), 1987, *Indonesian Marine Capture Fisheries* (Manila and Jakarta: ICLARM).

Baland, J. M., and J. P. Platteau, 1997, 'Wealth Inequality and Efficiency in the Commons—Part I: the Unregulated Case', *Oxford Economic Papers*, 49/3: 451–82.

——, —— 1998, 'Wealth Inequality and Efficiency in the Commons—Part II: the Regulated Case', *Oxford Economic Papers*, 50/1: 1–22.

——, —— 1999, 'The Ambiguous Impact of Inequality on Local Resource Management', *World Development*, Vol. 27, N° 5.

Bandyopadhyay, J., and V. Shiva, 1987, 'Chipko: Rekindling India's Forest Culture', *The Ecologist*, 17/1: 26–34.

Banfield, E. C., 1958, *The Moral Basis of a Backward Society* (Chicago: The Free Press).

Barbier, E. B., 1989, 'The Contribution of Environmental and Resource Economics to an Economics of Sustainable Development', *Development and Change*, 20/3: 429–59.

Bardhan, P., 1993*a*, 'Symposium on Management of Local Commons', *Journal of Economic Perspectives*, 7/4: 87–92.

—— 1993*b*, 'Analytics of the Institutions of Informal Cooperation in Rural Development', *World Development*, 21/4: 633–9.

Barthez, A., 1982, *Famille, travail et agriculture* (Paris: Economica).

Bassett, T. J., 'Land Use Conflicts in Pastoral Development in Northern Côte d'Ivoire', in T. J. Bassett and D. E. Crummey (eds.), *Land in African Agrarian Systems* (Madison, Wis.: University of Wisconsin Press): 131–54.

Basu, K., 1986*a*, 'Markets, Power and Social Norms', *Economic and Political Weekly*, 21/43: 1893–6.

—— 1986*b*, 'One Kind of Power', *Oxford Economic Papers*, 38/2: 259–82.

Basu, K., E. Jones, and E. Schlicht, 1987, 'The Growth and Decay of Custom: The Role of the New Institutional Economics in Economic History', *Explorations in Economic History*, 24/1: 1–21.

Baumol, W. J., and W. E. Oates, 1971, 'The Use of Standards and Prices for Protection of the Environment', *Swedish Journal of Economics*, 73: 42–54.

Bayart, J. F., 1989, *L'Etat en Afrique: La politique du ventre* (Paris: Fayard).

Beck, T., 1994, 'Common Property Resource Access by Poor and Class Conflict in West Bengal', *Economic and Political Weekly*, 29/4: 187–97.

Becker, G. S., 1976, *The Economic Approach to Human Behavior* (Chicago and London: University of Chicago Press).

—— 1981, *A Treatise on the Family* (Cambridge, Mass.: Harvard University Press).

Belliveau, M., 1994, 'Fishworker Organisations: Comments from the Maritime Fishermen's Union Experience', *Tenth Anniversary Conference of the International Collective in Support of Fishworkers*, Cebu (Philippines).

Bendor, J., D. Mookherjee, and D. Ray, 1994, 'Aspirations, Adaptive Learning and Cooperation in Repeated Games', *Ruth Pollack Working Papers Series on Economics*, No. 27, Dept. of Economics, Boston University.

Benoit, J. P., and V. Krishna, 1985, 'Finitely Repeated Games', *Econometrica*, 53/4: 905–22.

Berdan, F. F., 1989, 'Trade and Markets in Precapitalist States', in S. Plattner, *Economic Anthropology* (Stanford, Calif.: Stanford University Press): 78–107.

Berger, P., and T. Luckmann, 1971, *The Social Construction of Reality* (Harmondsworth: Penguin Books).

Bergeret, A., and J. Ribot, 1990, *L'arbre nourricier en pays sahélien* (Paris: Editions de la Maison des Sciences de l'Homme).

Bergsten, G. S., 1985, 'On the Role of Social Norms in a Market Economy', *Public Choice*, 45/1: 113–37.

Berkes, F., 1986, 'Local-Level Management and the Commons Problem: A Comparative Study of Turkish Coastal Fisheries', *Marine Policy*, 10 (July): 215–29.

—— 1987, 'Common-Property Resource Management and Cree Indian Fisheries in Subarctic Canada', in B. J. McCay, and J. M. Acheson (eds.), *The Question of the Commons: The Culture and Ecology of Communal Resources* (Tucson, Ariz.: University of Arizona Press): 66–91.

—— (ed.), 1989, *Common Property Resources: Ecology and Community-Based Sustainable Development* (London and New York: Belhaven Press).

Berkowitz, L., 1970, 'The Self, Selfishness, and Altruism', in J. Macaulay and L. Berkowitz (eds.), *Altruism and Helping Behavior* (New York: Academic Press): 143–51.

Berry, S., 1984, 'The Food Crisis and Agrarian Change in Africa: A Review Essay', *African Studies Review*, 27/2: 59–112.

Beteille, A., 1965, *Caste, Class, and Power: Changing Patterns of Stratification in a Tanjore Village* (Berkeley, Calif.: University of California Press).

Bhatia, B., 1992, 'Lush Fields and Parched Throats: The Political Economy of Groundwater in Gujarat', *Economic and Political Weekly*, 27/51–2: A-142–170.

Bianchi, M., 1990, 'How to Learn Sociality: True and False Solutions to Mandeville's Problem', University of Rome, mimeo.

Biebuyck, D. (ed.), 1963, *African Agrarian Systems* (London: Oxford University Press).

Binmore, K., 1992, *Funs and Games: A Text on Game Theory* (Lexington, Mass.: D. C. Heath and Co.).

—— 1994, *Playing Fair: Game Theory and the Social Contracti*, (Cambridge, Mass.: The MIT Press).

Binswanger, H. P., 1991, 'Brazilian Policies that Encourage Deforestation in the Amazon', *World Development*, 19/7: 821–29.

Bish, R. L., 1977, 'Environmental Resource Management: Public or Private', in G. Hardin and J. Baden (eds.), *Managing the Commons* (San Francisco: W. H. Freeman & Co.): 217–28.

Blaikie, P. M., J. C. Harriss, and A. N. Pain, 1986, 'The Management and Use of Common Property Resources in Tamil Nadu, India', in National Research Council, *Proceedings of the Conference on Common Property Resource Management* (Washington, DC: National Academy Press): 481–504.

Bloch, P. C., 1993, 'An Egalitarian Project in a Stratified Society: Who Ends Up with the Land?', in T. J. Bassett and D. E. Crummey (eds.), *Land in African Agrarian Systems* (Madison, Wis.: University of Wisconsin Press): 222–43.

Bourdieu, P., 1963, 'La société traditionnelle: Attitude à l'égard du temps et conduite économique', *Sociologie du travail*, 5/1: 24–44.

—— 1977, *Algérie 60: Structures économiques et structures temporelles* (Paris: Les éditions de Minuit).

—— 1980, *Le sens pratique* (Paris: Les éditions de Minuit).

Boutillier, J. L., 1982, 'L'aménagement du fleuve Sénégal et ses implications foncières', in E. Le Bris, E. Le Roy, and F. Leimdorfer (eds.), *Enjeux fonciers en Afrique noire* (Paris: ORSTOM et Karthala): 301–8.

Bowles, S., and H. Gintis, 1993, 'The Revenge of Homo Economicus: Contested Exchange and the Revival of Political Economy', *Journal of Economic Perspectives*, 7/1: 83–102.

Braverman, A., J. L. Guasch, M. Huppi, and L. Pohlmeier, 1991, 'Promoting Rural Cooperatives in Developing Countries: The Case of Sub-Saharan Africa', *World Bank Discussion Papers*, No. 121 (Washington, DC: World Bank).

Breman, J., 1974, *Patronage and Exploitation: Changing Agrarian Relations in South Gujarat* (Berkeley, Calif.: University of California Press).

Brian Arthur, W., 1988, 'Self-Reinforcing Mechanisms in Economics', in P. W. Anderson, K. J. Arrow, and D. Pines (eds.), *The Economy as an Evolving Complex System* (Addison-Wesley Publishing Co.): 9–31.

Brightman, R. A., 1987, 'Conservation and Resource Depletion: The Case of the Boreal Forest Algonquians', in B. J. McCay and J. M. Acheson (eds.), *The Question of the Commons: The Culture and Ecology of Communal Resources* (Tucson, Ariz.: University of Arizona Press): 121–41.

Broad, R., 1994, 'The Poor and the Environment: Friends or Foes?', *World Development*, 22/6: 811–22.

Bromley, D. W., 1986, 'Closing Comments at the Conference on Common Property Resource Management', in National Research Council, *Proceedings of the Conference on Common Property Resource Management* (Washington, DC: National Academy Press): 593–8.

—— 1989*a*, *Economic Interests and Institutions: The Conceptual Foundation of Public Policy* (Oxford: Blackwell).

—— 1989*b*, 'Property Relations and Economic Development: The Other Land Reform', *World Development*, 17: 867–77.

—— and D. P. Chapagain, 1984, 'The Village Against the Center: Resource Depletion in South Asia', *American Journal of Agricultural Economics*, 66/5: 868–73.

—— and M. M. Cernea, 1989, 'The Management of Common Property Natural Resources: Some Conceptual and Operational Fallacies', *World Bank Discussion Papers*, No. 57 (Washington, DC: World Bank).

Brookfield, H., 1991, 'Environmental Sustainability with Development: What Prospects for a

Research Agenda?' in O. Stokke (ed.), *Sustainable Development* (London: Frank Cass): 42–66.

Brown, M., 1988, *Adam Smith's Economics: Its Place in the Development of Economic Thought* (London: Croom Helm).

Bruce, J. W., 1986, 'Land Tenure Issues in Project Design and Strategies for Agricultural Development in Sub-Saharan Africa', Land Tenure Center, LTC Paper 128, University of Wisconsin-Madison.

—— and L. Fortmann, 1989, 'Agroforestry: Tenure and Incentives', Land Tenure Center, Research Paper No. 135, University of Wisconsin-Madison.

Bruns, B., 1993, 'Promoting Participation in Irrigation: Reflections on Experience in Southeast Asia', *World Development*, 21/11: 1837–49.

Buchanan, J. M., 1975, *The Limits of Liberty: Between Anarchy and Leviathan* (Chicago: University of Chicago Press).

Burgess, M., 1992, 'Dangers of Environmental Extremism: Analysis of Debate over India's Social Forestry Programme', *Economic and Political Weekly*, 27/40: 2196–2200.

Burke, E., 1790, *Reflections on the Revolution in France* (Chicago: Regnery, 1955).

Caldwell, J. C., and P. Caldwell, 1987, 'The Cultural Context of High Fertility in Sub-Saharan Africa', *Population and Development Review*, 13/3: 409–37.

Carrier, J. G., 1987, 'Marine Tenure and Conservation in Papua New Guinea', in B. J. McCay and J. M. Acheson (eds.), *The Question of the Commons: The Culture and Ecology of Communal Resources* (Tucson, Arizona: University of Arizona Press): 142–67.

Cashdan, E., 1985, 'Coping with Risk: Reciprocity Among the Basarwa of Northern Botswana', *Man*, 20/3: 454–74.

Cernea, M. M., 1989, 'User Groups as Producers in Participatory Afforestation Strategies', *World Bank Discussion Papers*, No. 70 (Washington, DC: World Bank).

—— 1991, *Putting People First: Sociological Variables in Rural Development* (2nd edn., London: Oxford University Press).

Chakravarty, S., 1991, 'Sustainable Development', in O. Stokke (ed.), *Sustainable Development* (London: Frank Cass): 67–77.

Chand, R., 1994, 'Role of Water Rights in Farmer-Managed Hill Irrigation Systems', *Economic and Political Weekly*, 29/13: A-26–30.

Cheung, S. N. S., 1970, 'The Structure of a Contract and the Theory of a Non-Exclusive Resource', *Journal of Law and Economics*, 13/1: 49–70.

Christy, F., 1983, 'Territorial Use Rights in Maritime Fisheries: Definitions and Conditions', *FAO Technical Fisheries Paper*, No. 227 (Rome: FAO).

Ciriacy-Wantrup, S. V., and R. C. Bishop, 1975, 'Common Property as a Concept in Natural Resources Policy', *Natural Resources Journal*, 15: 713–27.

Cline-Cole, R. A., H. A. C. Main, and J. E. Nichol, 1990, 'On Fuelwood Consumption, Population Dynamics and Deforestation in Africa', *World Development*, 18/4: 513–27.

Coase, R. H., 1960, 'The Problem of Social Cost', *Journal of Law and Economics*, 3: 1–44.

Cohen, J., and M. Weitzman, 1975, 'A Marxian View of Enclosures', *Journal of Development Economics*, 1/4: 287–336.

Colchester, M., 1994, 'Sustaining the Forests: The Community-based Approach in South and South-East Asia', *Development and Change*, 25/1: 69–100.

Colclough, C., 1991, 'Structuralism Versus Neo-Liberalism: An Introduction', in C. Colclough and J. Manor (eds.), *States or Markets? Neo-Liberalism and the Development Policy Debate* (Oxford: Clarendon Press).

Cole, H. S. A., *et al.*, 1973, *Thinking about the Future: A Critique of the Limits to Growth* (Chatto & Windus, for Sussex University Press).

Coleman, J. S., 1987, 'Norms as a Social Capital', in G. Radnitzky and P. Bernholz (eds.), *Economic Imperialism. The Economic Method Applied Outside the Field of Economics* (New York: Paragon House Publishers): 133–53.

Collard, D., 1978, *Altruism and Economy: A Study in Non-Selfish Economics* (Oxford: Martin Robertson).

Cooper, R. W., D. V. Dejong, R. Forsythe, and T. W. Ross, 1990, 'Selection Criteria inCo-ordination Games: Some Experimental Results', *American Economic Review*, 80/1: 218–33.

Coquery-Vidrovitch, C., 1982, 'Le régime foncier rural en Afrique noire', in E. Le Bris, E. Le Roy, and F. Leimdorfer (eds.), *Enjeux fonciers en Afrique noire* (Paris: Orstom et Karthala): 65–84.

—— 1985, *Afrique noire: Permanences et ruptures* (Paris: Payot).

Cordell, J. C., 1972, *The Developmental Ecology of an Estuarine Canoe Fishing System in Northeast Brazil*, Ph.D. dissertation, Stanford University (mimeo).

—— and M. A. McKean, 1986, 'Sea Tenure in Bahia, Brazil', in National Research Council, *Proceedings of the Conference on Common Property Resource Management* (Washington, DC: National Academy Press): 85–112.

Cormier, G., 1994, 'Backgrounder to the Canadian Fishery', *Tenth Anniversary Conference of the International Collective in Support of Fishworkers*, Cebu (Philippines).

Cormier-Salem, M. C., 1986, 'La gestion de l'espace aquatique en Casamance', in *L'Estuaire de la Casamance: Environnement, Pêche, Socio-Economie*, Acta of the Seminar held at Ziguinchor, 19–24 June 1986 (Dakar: Centre de Recherches Océanographiques de Dakar-Thiaroye).

Cornes, R., and T. Sandler, 1983, 'On Commons and Tragedies', *American Economic Review*, 83/4: 787–92.

—— C. F. Mason, and T. Sandler, 1986, 'The Commons and the Optimal Number of Firms', *Quarterly Journal of Economics*, 101/3: 641–6.

Coward, E. W., 1979, 'Principles of Social Organization in an Indigenous Irrigation System', *Human Organization*, 38/1: 28–36.

—— 1980, *Irrigation and Agricultural Development in Asia: Perspectives from Social Sciences* (Ithaca, NY: Cornell University Press).

Crousse, B., 1986, 'Logique traditionnelle et logique d'Etat', in B. Crousse, E. Le Bris, and E. Le Roy (eds.), *Espaces disputés en Afrique noire* (Paris: Karthala): 199–215.

Crutchfield, J. A., 1961, 'An Economic Evaluation of Alternative Methods of Fishery Regulation', *Journal of Law and Economics*, 4: 131–43.

Cruz, W. D., 1986, 'Overfishing and Conflict in a Traditional Fishery: San Miguel Bay, Philippines', in National Research Council, *Proceedings of the Conference on Common Property Resource Management* (Washington, DC: National Academy Press): 115–33.

Cura, N., 1994, 'Fisheries and Fishworkers' Organisations: The Philippine Experience', *Tenth Anniversary Conference of the International Collective in Support of Fishworkers*, Cebu (Philippines).

Curtin, P. D., 1984, *Cross-Cultural Trade in World History* (Cambridge: Cambridge University Press).

D'Abreo, D., 1985, *People and Forests* (New Delhi: Indian Social Institute).

Darley, J. M., and B. Latane, 1970, 'Norms and Normative Behavior: Field Studies of Social Interdependence', in J. Macaulay and L. Berkowitz (eds.), *Altruism and Helping Behavior: Social Psychological Studies of Some Antecedents and Consequences* (New York: Academic Press): 83–101.

Das Gupta, M., 1987, 'Informal Security Mechanisms and Population Retention in Rural India', *Economic Development and Cultural Change*, 36/1: 101–20.

Dasgupta, P., 1988, 'Trust as a Commodity', in D. Gambetta (ed.), *Trust-Making and Breaking Cooperative Relations* (Oxford: Blackwell): 49–72.
—— 1993, *An Inquiry Into Well-Being and Destitution* (Oxford: Clarendon Press).
—— and G. Heal, 1974, 'The Optimal Depletion of Exhaustible Resources', *Review of Economic Studies*, Symposium on the Economics of Exhaustible Resources, 41: 3–28.
—— 1979, *Economic Theory and Exhaustible Resources* (Cambridge: Nisbet & Co. Ltd and Cambridge University Press).
—— and K.-G. Mäler, 1990, 'The Environment and Emerging Development Issues', STICERD, London School of Economics, Working Paper No. 28.
—— 1993, 'Poverty and the Environmental Resource Base', mimeo, University of Cambridge, forthcoming in J. Behrman and T. N. Srinivasan (eds.), *Handbook of Development Economics*, Vol. 3 (Amsterdam: North-Holland).
D'Aspremont, C., and L. A. Gérard Varet, 1976, 'Un modèle de négociation internationale pour certains problèmes de pollution', *Revue d'Economie Politique*, 86/4: 597–620.
—— 1979, 'Incentives and Incomplete Information', *Journal of Public Economics*, 11/1: 25–45.
David, P. A., 1988, 'The Future of Path-Dependent Equilibrium Economics: From the Economics of Technology to the Economics of Almost Everything?', Center for Economic Policy Research, Stanford University, California.
—— 1992*a*, 'Path Dependence and the Predictability in Dynamic Systems with Local Network Externalities: A Paradigm for Historical Economics', forthcoming in C. Freeman and D. Foray (eds.), *Technology and the Wealth of Nations* (London: Pinter Publishers).
—— 1992*b*, 'Why Are Institutions the "Carriers of History"?', Site Working Paper, Stanford University, California.
Davies, A. G., and P. Richards, 1991, 'Rain Forest in Mende Life: Resources and Subsistence Strategies in Rural Communities Around the Gola North Forest Reserve (Sierra Leone)', Report to ESCOR, UK Overseas Development Administration, London.
Davis, A., 1984, 'Property Rights and Access Management in the Small-Boat Fishery: A Case Study from Southwest Nova Scotia', in C. Lamson and A. J. Hanson (eds.), *Atlantic Fisheries and Coastal Communities: Fisheries Decision-Making Case Studies* (Halifax: Dalhousie Ocean Studies Programme): 133–64.
Davis, S., 1983, 'Traditional Management of the Littoral Zone among the Yolngu of North Australia', Seminar on Scientific Aspects of Traditional Management of Coastal Systems, Unesco, Jakarta.
Dawes, R., J. McTavish, and H. Shaklee, 1977, 'Behavior, Communication, and Assumptions About Other People's Behavior in a Commons Dilemma Situation', *Journal of Personality and Social Psychology*, 35/1: 1–11.
—— and R. H. Thaler, 1988, 'Anomalies Cooperation', *Journal of Economic Perspectives*, 2/3: 187–97.
Deacon, R. T., 1992, 'Controlling Tropical Deforestation: An Analysis of Alternative Policies', Policy Research Working Papers, WPS 1029 (Washington, DC: World Bank).
De Los Reyes, R. P., 1980, 'Managing Communal Gravity Systems: Farmers' Approaches and Implications for Program Planning' (Quezon: Institute of Philippine Culture).
Demsetz, H., 1967, 'Toward a Theory of Property Rights', *American Economic Review*, 57/2: 347–59.
Desai, V., 1988, *Rural Development* (New Delhi: Himalaya Publishing House).
Diemer, G., and E. Van Der Laan, 1987, *L'irrigation au Sahel: La crise des périmètres irrigués et la voie haalpulaar* (Paris & Wageningen: Karthala and CTA).
Douglas, M., 1986, *How Institutions Think* (Syracuse, NY: Syracuse University Press).

Durkheim, E., 1893, *The Division of Labour in Society* (ed. L. Closer, London: Macmillan, 1984).

Easter, K. W., and K. Palanisami, 1986, 'Tank Irrigation in India: An Example of Common Property Resource Management', in National Research Council, *Proceedings of the Conference on Common Property Resource Management* (Washington, DC: National Academy Press): 215–30.

Economist, 1992, 'Let Them Eat Pollution', 8 Feb.

Eiser, J. R., 1978, 'Cooperation and Conflict between Individuals', in H. Tajfel, and C. Fraser (eds.), *Introducing Social Psychology* (Harmondsworth: Penguin Books).

Ellickson, R. C., 1991, *Order Without Law: How Neighbors Settle Disputes* (Cambridge, Mass.: Harvard University Press).

Elster, J., 1989*a*, *The Cement of Society. A Study of Social Order* (Cambridge: Cambridge University Press).

——1989*b*, 'Social Norms and Economic Theory', *Journal of Economic Perspectives*, 3/4: 99–117.

Etzioni, A., 1988, *The Moral Dimension: Toward a New Economics* (New York: Free Press).

Fafchamps, M., 1992, 'Solidarity Networks in Preindustrial Societies: Rational Peasants with a Moral Economy', *Economic Development and Cultural Change*, 41/1, 147–74.

FAO, 1993, *Marine Fisheries and the Law of the Sea: A Decade of Change*, revised version of the special chapter of *The State of Food and Agriculture 1992* (Rome: FAO Fisheries Department).

Farrell, J., 1987, 'Information and the Coase Theorem', *Journal of Economic Perspectives*, 1/2: 113–29.

Fay, C., 1990*a*, 'Sacrifices, prix du sang, "eau du maître": fondation des territoires de pêche dans le delta central du Niger (Mali)', in F. Verdeaux (ed.), *La pêche-Enjeux de développement et objet de recherche* (Paris: Editions de l'ORSTOM): 159–76 [originally published in *Cahiers des Sciences Humaines*, 25/1–2, 1989].

——1990*b*, 'Systèmes halieutiques et espaces de pouvoirs: transformation des droits et des pratiques de pêche dans le delta central du Niger (Mali), 1920–1980', in F. Verdeaux (ed.), *La pêche: Enjeux de développement et objet de recherche* (Paris: Editions de l'ORSTOM): 213–36 [originally published in *Cahiers des Sciences Humaines*, 25/1–2, 1989].

Fernandes, W., and S. Kulkarni (eds.), 1983, *Towards a New Forest Policy: People's Rights and Environmental Needs* (New Delhi: Indian Social Institute).

——Menon, G., and P. Viegas, 1988, *Forests, Environment and Tribal Economy* (New Delhi: Indian Social Institute).

Fernandez, J. W., 1987, 'The Call to the Commons: Decline and Recommitment in Asturias, Spain', in B. J. McCay and J. M. Acheson (eds.), *The Question of the Commons: The Culture and Ecology of Communal Resources* (Tucson, Ariz.: University of Arizona Press): 266–89.

Fernandez, R., and D. Rodrik, 1991, 'Resistance to Reform: Status Quo Bias in the Presence of Individual Specific Uncertainty', *American Economic Review*, 81/5: 1146–55.

Field, A. J., 1981, 'The Problem with Neoclassical Institutional Economics: A Critique with Special Reference to the North/Thomas Model of Pre-1500 Europe', *Explorations in Economic History*, 18/2: 174–98.

——1984, 'Microeconomics, Norms, and Rationality', *Economic Development and Cultural Change*, 32/4: 683–711.

Fisher, A. C., 1981, *Resource and Environmental Economics* (Cambridge: Cambridge University Press).

Forman, S., 1980, 'Cognition and the Catch: The Location of Fishing Spots in a Brazilian

Coastal Village', in A. Spoehr (ed.), *Maritime Adaptations: Essays on Contemporary Fishing Communities* (Pittsburgh: University of Pittsburgh Press).

Forrester, J. W., 1971, *World Dynamics* (Cambridge, Mass.: Wright-Allen Press Inc).

Fortmann, L., 1988, 'Great Planting Disasters: Pitfalls in Technical Assistance in Forestry', *Agriculture and Human Values*, Winter–Spring.

Frank, R. H., 1988, *Passions Within Reason: The Strategic Role of the Emotions* (New York: W. W. Norton & Co.).

Friedman, J. W., 1990, *Game Theory with Applications to Economics*, 2nd edn. (New York: Oxford University Press).

Freudenberger, M. S., and P. Mathieu, 1993, 'The Question of the Commons in the Sahel', Land Tenure Center, University of Wisconsin-Madison (mimeo).

Fudenberg, D., and E. Maskin, 1986, 'The Folk Theorem in Repeated Games with Discounting and Imperfect Information', *Econometrica*, 54/3: 533–54.

—— and D. M. Kreps, 1992, *Lectures on Learning and Equilibrium in Strategic Form Games*, CORE Lecture Series (Louvain-la-Neuve: Université Catholique de Louvain).

—— and J. Tirole, 1993, *Game Theory* (Cambridge, Mass.: MIT Press).

Gadgil, M., and R. Guha, 1994, 'Ecological Conflicts and the Environmental Movement in India', *Development and Change*, 25/1: 101–36.

Gambetta, D., 1988, 'Can We Trust Trust?' in D. Gambetta (ed.), *Trust-Making and Breaking Cooperative Relations* (Oxford: Blackwell): 213–37.

Gannon, S., *et al.*, 1993, 'Tenure and Natural Resource Management in the Gambia: A Case Study of the Upper Baddibu District', Land Tenure Center, University of Wisconsin-Madison.

Garcia-Barrios, R., and L. Garcia-Barrios, 1990, 'Environmental and Technological Degradation in Peasant Agriculture: A Consequence of Development in Mexico', *World Development*, 18/11: 1569–85.

Gauthier, D., 1986, *Morals by Agreement* (Oxford: Oxford University Press).

Gentil, D., 1986, *Les mouvements coopératifs en Afrique de l'Ouest* (Paris: Editions l'Harmattan).

Ghimire, K. B., 1994, 'Parks and People: Livelihood Issues in National Parks Management in Thailand and Madagascar', *Development and Change*, 25/1: 195–229.

Gibbons, R., 1992, *Game Theory for Applied Economists* (Princeton, NJ: Princeton University Press).

Gilles, J. L., and K. Jamtgaard, 1981, 'Overgrazing Pastoral Areas: The Commons Reconsidered', *Sociologica Ruralis*, 21/2: 129–41.

Godelier, M., 1974, 'Anthropologie et économie. Une anthropologie économique est-elle possible?' in M. Godelier (ed.), *Un domaine contesté: l'anthropologie économique* (Paris: Mouton): 285–345.

Government of India, 1960–1, *Report of the Scheduled Areas and Scheduled Tribes Commission* (New Delhi).

—— 1976, *Report of the National Commission on Agriculture* (New Delhi).

—— 1981*a*, *Report on Development of the Tribal Areas* (National Committee on Development of Backward Areas: New Delhi).

—— 1981*b*, *Indian Forest Bill*, 1980 (New Delhi).

—— 1982, *Report of Committee on Forest and Tribals in India* (Ministry of Home Affairs: New Delhi).

—— 1983, *Recommendations Regarding the Revision of the National Forest Policy* (Dept. of Environment: New Delhi).

Granovetter, M., 1985, 'Economic Action and Social Structure: The Problem of Embeddedness', *American Journal of Sociology*, 91/3: 481–510.

Gregersen, H., Draper, S., and D. Elz (eds.), 1989, *People and Trees: The Role of Social Forestry in Sustainable Development* (Washington, DC: World Bank).

Greif, A., 1992, 'Cultural Beliefs and the Organization of Society: A Historical and Theoretical Reflection on Collectivist and Individualist Societies', Dept. of Economics, Stanford University (mimeo).

Griffith, W. B., and R. S. Goldfarb, 1988, 'Amending the Economist's "Rational Egoist" Model to Include Moral Values and Norms', Paper presented to the Conference on 'The Enforcement of Social Norms', Dept. of Economics, University of Delaware, Newark.

Gruenais, M.-E., 1986, 'Territoires autochtones et mise en valeur des terres', in B. Crousse, E. Le Bris, and E. Le Roy, *Espaces disputés en Afrique noire* (Paris: Karthala): 283–98.

Guha, R., 1985, 'Scientific Forestry and Social Change in Uttarakhand', *Economic and Political Weekly*, 20/45–7: 1932–52.

—— 1989, *The Unquiet Woods: Ecological Change and Peasant Resistance in the Himalayas* (Oxford: Oxford University Press).

Hannesson, R., 1988, 'Fishermen's Organizations and their Role in Fisheries Management: Theoretical Considerations and Experiences from Industrialized Countries', *FAO Fisheries Technical Paper*, No. 300 (Rome: FAO).

Hardin, G., 1968, 'The Tragedy of the Commons', *Science*, 162: 1243–48.

—— and J. Baden (eds.) (1977), *Managing the Commons* (San Francisco: W. H. Freeman & Co.): 8–15.

Harper, E. B., 1968, 'Social Consequences of an "Unsuccessful" Low Caste Movement', in J. Silverberg (ed.), *Social Mobility in the Caste System in India* (The Hague: Mouton): 36–65.

Harriss, J. C., 1984, 'Social Organisation and Irrigation: Ideology, Planning, and Practice in Sri Lanka's Settlement Schemes', in T. P. Bayliss-Smith, and S. Wanmali (eds.), *Understanding Green Revolutions* (Cambridge: Cambridge University Press): 315–38.

Havel, V., 1991, 'Méditation d'été', *Libération*, 7 Oct.

Hayami, Y., 1981, 'Agrarian Problems of India: An East and South Asian Perspective', *Economic and Political Weekly*, 16: 707–12.

—— and M. Kikuchi, 1981, *Asian Village Economy at the Crossroads: An Economic Approach to Institutional Change* (Tokyo: University of Tokyo Press).

—— and V. W. Ruttan, 1985, *Agricultural Development: An International Perspective* (Baltimore, Johns Hopkins University Press).

Hayek, F., 1960, *The Constitution of Liberty* (London: Routledge & Kegan Paul).

—— 1979, *Law, Legislation and Liberty* (London: Routledge & Kegan Paul).

Hechter, M., 1987, *Principles of Group Solidarity* (Berkeley, Calif.: University of California Press).

Henry, C., 1974*a*, 'Option Values in the Economics of Irreplaceable Assets', *Review of Economic Studies*, 41: Supplement, 89–104.

—— 1974*b*, 'Investment Decision under Uncertainty: The Irreversibility Effect', *American Economic Review*, 64/6: 1006–1012.

Hirsch, F., 1976, *Social Limits to Growth* (Cambridge, Mass.: Harvard University Press).

Hirschman, A. O., 1977, *The Passions and the Interests: Political Arguments for Capitalism Before its Triumph* (Princeton, NJ: Princeton University Press).

—— 1982, 'Rival Interpretations of Market Society: Civilizing, Destructive, or Feeble?', *Journal of Economic Literature*, 20/4: 1463–84.

—— 1987, 'Interests', in J. Eatwell, M. Milgate, and P. Newman (eds.), *The Invisible Hand* (London: Macmillan): 156–67.

Hirshleifer, D., and E. Rasmusen, 1989, 'Cooperation in a Repeated Prisoner's Dilemma with Ostracism', *Journal of Economic Behaviour and Organization*, 12/1: 87–106.

Homans, G. C., 1950, *The Human Group* (New York: Harcourt Brace & Co.).

—— 1970, *English Villagers in the Thirteenth Century* (Cambridge, Mass.: Harvard University Press).

Hornstein, H., E. Fisch, and M. Holmes, 1968, 'Influence of a Model's Feelings about his Behavior and his Relevance as a Comparison Other on Observers' Helping Behavior', *Journal of Personality and Social Psychology*, 10: 220–6.

Hume, D., 1740, *A Treatise of Human Nature* (ed. by L. A. Selby-Bigge, Oxford: Clarendon Press, 1888).

Hviding, E., and G. B. K. Baines, 1994, 'Community-based Fisheries Management, Tradition and the Challenges of Development in Marovo, Solomon Islands', *Development and Change*, 25/1: 13–39.

Ishikawa, S., 1975, 'Peasant Families and the Agrarian Community in the Process of Economic Development', in L. Reynolds (ed.), *Agriculture in Development Theory* (New Haven, Conn.: Yale University Press): 451–96.

Janos, A. C., 1982, *The Politics of Backwardness in Hungary, 1825–1945* (Princeton, NJ: Princeton University Press).

Jayaraman, T. K., 1981, 'Farmers' Organizations in Surface Irrigation Projects: Two Empirical Studies from Gujarat', *Economic and Political Weekly*, 16/39: A89–A98.

Jeay, A. M., 1984*a*, *Prédateurs de la nuit. Etude ethnosociologique d'une population de pêcheurs: les Somono (Mali)*, Ph.D. dissertation, University of Montpellier III.

—— 1984*b*, 'Droits traditionnels versus législation moderne et recommandations pour une gestion rationnelle des ressources de la pêche: le cas des Somono du Moyen Niger (Mali)', Université Montpellier III, France.

Jentoft, S., 1989, 'Fisheries Co-management: Delegating Government Responsibility to Fishermen's Organizations', *Marine Policy* (April): 137–54.

Jessup, T. C., and N. L. Peluso, 1986, 'Minor Forest Products as Common Property Resources in East Kalimantan, Indonesia', in National Research Council, *Proceedings of the Conference on Common Property Resource Management* (Washington, DC: National Academy Press): 501–31.

Jodha, N. S., 1985, 'Population Growth and the Decline of Common Property Resources in Rajasthan', *Population and Development Review*, 11/2: 247–64.

—— 1986, 'Common Property Resources and Rural Poor in Dry Regions of India', *Economic and Political Weekly*, 21/27: 1169–82.

—— 1992, 'Common Property Resources: A Missing Dimension of Development Strategies', *World Bank Discussion Papers*, No. 169 (Washington, DC: World Bank).

Johannes, R. E., 1982, 'Traditional Conservation Methods and Protected Marine Areas in Oceania', *Ambio*, 11/5: 258–61.

Johnson, R. N., and G. D. Libecap, 1982, 'Contracting Problems and Regulation: The Case of the Fishery', *American Economic Review*, 72/5: 1005–22.

Johri, A., and N. Krishnamukar, 1991, 'Poverty and Common Property Resource: Case Study of a Rope-Making Industry', *Economic and Political Weekly*, 26/50: 2897–2902.

Jones, S. R. G., 1984, *The Economics of Conformism* (Oxford: Blackwell).

Kahneman, D., J. L. Knetsch, and R. H. Thaler, 1990, 'Experimental Tests of the Endowment Effect and the Coase Theorem', *Journal of Political Economy*, 98/6: 1325–48.

Kalai, E., and E. Lehrer, 1993, 'Rational Learning Leads to Nash Equilibrium', *Econometrica*, 61/5: 1019–45.

Kanbur, R., 1992, 'Heterogeneity, Distribution, and Cooperation in Common Property Resource Management', Policy Research Working Papers, WPS 844 (Washington, DC: World Bank).

Karanth, G. K., 1992, 'Privatisation of Common Property Resources: Lessons from Rural Karnataka', *Economic and Political Weekly*, 27/31–2: 1680–8.

Kaufmann, H., 1970, 'Legality and Harmfulness of a Bystander's Failure to Intervene as Determinants of Moral Judgment', in J. Macaulay, and L. Berkowitz (eds.), *Altruism and Helping Behavior* (New York: Academic Press): 77–81.

Kikuchi, M., and Y. Hayami, 1980, 'Inducements to Institutional Innovation in an Agrarian Economy', *Economic Development and Cultural Change*, 29/1: 21–36.

Klee, G. (ed.), 1980, *World Systems of Traditional Resource Management* (London: Arnold).

Klein, P. A., 1984, 'Institutionalist Reflections on the Role of the Public Sector', *Journal of Economic Issues*, 18: 45–66.

Kone, F. A., 1985, 'Traditional Fishing Rights in the Central Delta of the Niger and the Lake Region: Conflicts and Recommendations With a View to Equitable and Rational Management of Fishery Resources', FAO Fisheries Report, No. 360 (Rome: FAO).

Kreps, D. M., 1990, *A Course in Microeconomic Theory* (New York: Harvester Wheatsheaf).

—— and R. Wilson, 1982, 'Reputation and Imperfect Information', *Journal of Economic Theory*, 27/2: 253–79.

—— P. Milgrom, J. Roberts, and R. Wilson, 1982, 'Rational Cooperation in the Finitely Repeated Prisoners' Dilemma', *Journal of Economic Theory*, 27/2: 245–52.

Krutilla, J. V., 1967, 'Conservation Reconsidered', *American Economic Review*, 57/4: 777–86.

—— and C. J. Cicchetti, 1972, 'Evaluating Benefits of Environmental Resources with Special Application to the Hell's Canyon', *Natural Resources Journal*, 12: 1–29.

Kulkarni, S., 1986, 'The Forest Policy and the Forest Bill: A Critique and Suggestions for Change', in *Towards a New Forest Policy* (New Delhi: Indian Social Institute): 84–101.

Kuperan, K., and J. G. Sutinen, 1994, 'Compliance with Zoning Regulations in Malaysian Fisheries', Dept. of Resource Economics, University of Rhode Island, USA (mimeo).

—— 1988, 'The Tenacious Past: Theories of Personal and Collective Conservation', *Journal of Economic Behavior and Organization*, 10/1: 143–71.

Kuran, T., 1990, 'Now out of Never: the Element of Surprise in the East European Revolution of 1989', Dept. of Economics, University of Southern California, Los Angeles (mimeo).

Kurien, J., 1978, 'Entry of Big Business into Fishing: Its Impact on Fish Economy', *Economic and Political Weekly*, 13/36: 1557–665.

—— 1991, 'Collective Action and Common Property Resource Rejunvenation: The Case of Peoples' Artificial Reefs (PAR's) in Kerala State, India', Centre for Development Studies, Trivandrum (mimeo).

Laffont, J.-J., 1975, 'Macroeconomic Constraints, Economic Efficiency and Ethics: An Introduction to Kantian Economics', *Economica*, 42/168: 430–7.

Laitos, R., *et al.*, 1986, 'Rapid Appraisal of Nepal Irrigation Systems', Water Management Synthesis Report No. 43, Fort Collins: Colorado State University.

Lane, R. E., 1991, *The Market Experience* (Cambridge: Cambridge University Press).

Lansing, J. S., 1987, 'Balinese "Water Temples" and the Management of Irrigation', *American Anthropologist*, 89: 326–41.

Larson, B. A., and D. W. Bromley, 1990, 'Property Rights, Externalities and Resource Degradation', *Journal of Development Economics*, 33/2: 235–62.

Laurent, P. J., P. Mathieu, and M. Totté 1994, 'Migrations et accés á la terse au Burkina Faso', Cahiers du CIDEP, No. 20, University of Louvain-la-Neuve', Belgium.

Lawry, S. W., 1989*a*, 'Tenure Policy and Natural Resource Management in Sahelian West Africa', Research Paper No. 130, Land Tenure Center, University of Wisconsin-Madison.

—— 1989*b*, 'Tenure Policy Toward Common Property Natural Resources', Research Paper No. 134, Land Tenure Center, University of Wisconsin-Madison.

Leach, M., and J. Fairhead, 1994, 'Natural Resource Management: The Reproduction and Use of Environmental Misinformation in Guinea's Forest-Savanna Transition Zone', *IDS Bulletin*, 25/2: 81–7.

Leadam, I. S., 1897, *Domesday of Inclosures*, 2 vols. (London: Royal Historical Society).

Levi, M., 1988, *Of Rule and Revenue* (Berkeley, Calif.: University of California Press).

Levieil, D. P., 1987, *Territorial Use-Rights in Fishing (TURFS) and the Management of Small-scale Fisheries: the Case of Lake Titicaca (Peru)*, Unpublished Ph.D. thesis, University of British Columbia, Vancouver.

Levine, G., 1978, 'Irrigation Association Response to Severe Water Shortage: The Case of the Yun-Lin Irrigation Association, Taiwan', Cornell University, Ithaca, NY (mimeo).

—— 1980, 'The Relationship of Design, Operation and Management', in E. W. Coward (ed.), *Irrigation and Agricultural Development in Asia: Perspectives from the Social Sciences* (New York: Cornell University Press): 51–62.

Lewis, D. K., 1969, *Convention: A Philosophical Study* (Cambridge, Mass.: Harvard University Press).

Lloyd, W. F., 1833, 'On the Checks to Population', in G. Hardin and J. Baden (eds.), (1977), *Managing the Commons* (San Francisco: W. H. Freeman & Co.): 8–15.

Lopez, R., 1992, 'Resource Degradation, Community Controls and Agricultural Productivity in Tropical Areas', University of Maryland, Washington, DC (mimeo).

McCay, B. J., and J. M. Acheson, 1987, 'Human Ecology of the Commons', in B. J. McCay, and J. M. Acheson (eds.), *The Question of the Commons: The Culture and Ecology of Communal Resources* (Tucson, Ariz.: University of Arizona Press): 1–34.

McEvoy, A. F., 1986, *The Fisherman's Problem: Ecology and Law in the California Fisheries, 1850–1980* (Cambridge: Cambridge University Press).

McKean, M. A., 1986, 'Management of Traditional Common Lands (Iriaichi) in Japan', in National Research Council, *Proceedings of the Conference on Common Property Resource Management* (Washington, DC: National Academy Press): 533–89.

McKinnon, R. I., 1992, 'Spontaneous Order on the Road Back from Socialism: An Asian Perspective', *American Economic Review, Papers and Proceedings*, 82/2: 31–6.

McMullen, R., 1988, *Corruption and the Decline of Rome* (New Haven, Conn.: Yale University Press).

McNally, D., 1988, *Political Economy and the Rise of Capitalism: A Reinterpretation* (Berkeley, Calif.: University of California Press).

McNicoll, G., 1990, 'Social Organization and Ecological Stability under Demographic Stress', in G. McNicoll, and M. Cain (eds.), *Rural Development and Population Institutions and Policy* (New York: Oxford University Press): 147–67 (initially published as a supplement to *Population and Development Review*, 15, 1989).

Mahat, T. B. S., D. M. Griffin, and K. R. Shepherd, 1987, 'Human Impact on Some Forests of the Middle Hills of Nepal, Part 4', *Mountain Research and Development*, 7/1: 111–34.

Mahdi, M., 1986, 'Private Rights and Collective Management of Water in a High Atlas Berber Tribe', in National Research Council, *Proceedings of the Conference on Common Property Resource Management* (Washington, DC: National Academy Press): 181–98.

Martin, K. O., 1979, 'Play by the Rules or Don't Play at All: Space Division and Resource Allocation in a Rural Newfoundland Fishing Community', in R. Andersen (ed.), *North*

Atlantic Maritime Cultures: Anthropological Essays on Changing Adaptations (The Hague: Mouton): 276–98.
Marut, Don K., 1994, 'Protecting Nature Means Protecting Ourselves', *Samudra*, 6: Special issue published on the occasion of the Tenth Anniversary Conference of the International Collective in Support of Fishworkers, 7 June, Madras.
Marwell, G., and R. Ames, 1979, 'Experiments on the Provision of Public Goods. I: Resources, Interests, Group Size, and the Free-Rider Problem', *American Journal of Sociology*, 84/6: 1335–60.
Mathew, S., 1990, *Fishing Legislation and Gear Conflicts in Asian Countries*, Samudra Monograph (Brussels: Samudra Publications).
Matthews, R. C. O., 1986, 'The Economics of Institutions and the Sources of Growth', *Economic Journal*, 96/384: 903–18.
Mattos, M. M., and C. Uhl, 1994, 'Economic and Ecological Perspectives on Ranching in the Eastern Amazon', *World Development*, 22/2: 145–58.
Mayhew, L., 1984, 'In Defense of Modernity: Talcott Parsons and the Utilitarian Tradition', *American Journal of Sociology*, 89/6: 1273–305.
Menzies, N. K., 1994, *Forest and Land Management in Imperial China* (London: St. Martin's Press).
Messerschmidt, D. A., 1986, 'People and Resources in Nepal: Customary Resource Management Systems of the Upper Kali Gandaki', in National Research Council, *Proceedings of the Conference on Common Property Resource Management* (Washington, DC: National Academy Press): 455–80.
Metz, J. J., 1991, 'A Reassessment of the Causes and Severity of Nepal's Environmental Crisis', *World Development*, 19/7: 805–20.
Mill, J. S., 1848, *Principles of Political Economy* (Harmondsworth: Penguin, 1985).
Minvielle, J. P., 1977, *La structure foncière du Waalo Fuutanke* (Paris: Orstom).
Mishan, E. J., 1986, *Economic Myths and the Mythology of Economics* (Brighton: Wheatsheaf Books).
Mitra, A. K., 1992, 'Joint Management of Irrigation Systems in India: Relevance of Japanese Experience', *Economic and Political Weekly*, 27/26: A-75–82.
Moench, M., 1992, 'Drawing Down the Buffer—Science and Politics of Ground Water Management in India', *Economic and Political Weekly*, 27/13: A-7–14.
Moore, M., 1988, 'Economic Growth and the Rise of Civil Society: Agriculture in Taiwan and South Korea', in G. White (ed.), *Developmental States in East Asia* (London: Macmillan): 113–52.
—— 1989, 'The Fruits and Fallacies of Neoliberalism: The Case of Irrigation Policy', *World Development*, 17/1: 733–50.
Morishima, M., 1982, *Why Has Japan 'Succeeded'? Western Technology and the Japanese Ethos* (Cambridge: Cambridge University Press).
Mueller, D., 1986, 'Rational Egoism Versus Adaptive Egoism as Fundamental Postulate for a Descriptive Theory of Human Behaviour', *Public Choice*, 51/1: 3–23.
Murray, G., 1986, 'Seeing the Forest while Planting the Trees: An Anthropological Approach to Agroforestry in Rural Haiti', in D. Brinkerhoff, and J. Zamor (eds.), *Politics, Projects, and People in Haiti* (New York: Praeger): 193–226.
Murrell, P., 1992, 'Evolution in Economics and in the Economic Reform of the Centrally Planned Economies', in C. Clague, and G. C. Rausser (eds.), *The Emergence of Market Economies in Eastern Europe* (Oxford: Blackwell): 35–53.
Myerson, R. B., 1985, 'Bayesian Equilibrium and Incentive-Compatibility: An Introduction', in

L. Hurwicz, D. Schmeidler, and H. Sonnenschein (eds.), *Social Goals and Social Organization* (Cambridge: Cambridge University Press): 229–59.

—— 1991, *Game Theory: Analysis of Conflict* (Cambridge, Mass.: Harvard University Press).

—— and M. A. Satterthwaite, 1983, 'Efficient Mechanisms for Bilateral Trading', *Journal of Economic Theory*, 29/2: 265–81.

Nabli, M. K., and J. B. Nugent (eds.), 1989, *The New Institutional Economics and Development: Theory and Applications to Tunisia* (Amsterdam: North-Holland).

Nadkarni, M. V., 1989, *The Political Economy of Forest Use and Management* (New Delhi: Sage).

Nelson, R. R., and S. G. Winter, 1982, *An Evolutionary Theory of Economic Change* (Cambridge, Mass.: Belknap Press of Harvard University Press).

Netting, R. McC., 1972, 'Of Men and Meadows: Strategies of Alpine Land Use', *Anthropological Quarterly*, 45: 132–44.

—— 1976, 'What Alpine Peasants Have in Common: Observations on Communal Tenure in a Swiss Village', *Human Ecology*, 4: 135–46.

—— 1981, *Balancing on an Alp* (Cambridge: Cambridge University Press).

Noronha, R., 1985, *A Review of the Literature on Land Tenure Systems in Sub-Saharan Africa*, Research Unit of the Agriculture and Rural Development Department, Report No. ARU 43 (Washington, DC: World Bank).

North, D., 1981, *Structure and Change in Economic History* (New York: W. W. Norton & Co.).

—— 1989, 'Institutions and Economic Growth: An Historical Introduction', *World Development*, 17/9: 1319–32.

—— 1990, *Institutions, Institutional Change and Economic Performance* (Cambridge: Cambridge University Press).

—— and R. Thomas, 1973, *The Rise of the Western World* (Cambridge: Cambridge University Press).

Olson, M., 1965, *The Logic of Collective Action* (Cambridge, Mass.: Harvard University Press).

—— 1982, *The Rise and Decline of Nations* (New Haven, Conn.: Yale University Press).

Opp, K. D., 1979, 'The Emergence and Effects of Social Norms. A Confrontation of Some Hypotheses of Sociology and Economics', *Kyklos*, 32/4: 775–801.

O'Riordan, B., 1994, 'Technology and Energy Use in Fisheries', *Tenth Anniversary Conference of the International Collective in Support of Fishworkers*, Cebu, Philippines.

Ostrom, E., 1990, *Governing the Commons: The Evolution of Institutions for Collective Action* (Cambridge: Cambridge University Press).

—— 1992, *Crafting Institutions: Self-Governing Irrigation Systems* (San Francisco: ICS Press).

—— and R. Gardner, 1993, 'Coping with Asymmetries in the Commons: Self-Governing Irrigation Systems Can Work', *Journal of Economic Perspectives*, 7/4: 93–112.

—— Gardner, R. and J. Walker, 1994, *Rules, Games, and Common-Pool Resources* (Ann Arbor, Mich.: University of Michigan Press).

Pagden, A., 1988, 'The Destruction of Trust and its Economic Consequences in the Case of Eighteenth-century Naples', in D. Gambetta (ed.), *Trust-Making and Breaking Co-operative Relations* (Oxford: Blackwell): 127–41.

Pagiola, S., 1993, *Soil Conservation and the Sustainability of Agricultural Production*, PhD Dissertation, Food Research Institute, Stanford University.

Panayotou, T., 1988, 'Comments on Kenneth Ruddle's "The Organization of Traditional Inshore Fishery Management Systems in the Pacific"', in P. Neher, R. Arnason, and N. Mollett (eds.), *Rights Based Fishing* (Dordrecht: Kluwer Academic Publishers): 86–93.

Perrings, C. P., 1989, 'Optimal Path to Extinction? Poverty and Resource Degradation in the Open Agrarian Economy', *Journal of Development Economics*, 30/1: 1–24.

Perrot, C. H., 1990, 'Le système de gestion de la pêche en lagune Aby au XIXème siècle', in F. Verdeaux (ed.), *La pêche: Enjeux de développement et objet de recherche* (Paris: Editions de l'ORSTOM): 117–88 [originally published in *Cahier des Sciences Humaines*, 25/1–2, 1989].

Peters, P. E., 1987, 'Embedded Systems and Rooted Models: The Grazing Lands of Botswana and the Commons Debate', in B. J. McCay and J. M. Acheson (eds.) *The Question of the Commons: The Culture and Ecology of Communal Resources* (Tucson, Ariz.: University of Arizona Press): 171–94.

Pfister, C., 1983, 'Changes in Stability and Carrying Capacity of Lowland and Highland Agro-Systems in Switzerland in the Historical Past', *Mountain Research and Development*, 3: 291–7.

Piliavin, I., J. Rodin, and J. Piliavin, 1969, 'Good Samaritanism: An Underground Phenomenon?', *Journal of Personality and Social Psychology*, 13.

Platteau, J.-Ph., 1992, *Land Reform and Structural Adjustment in Sub-Saharan Africa: Controversies and Guidelines* (Rome: FAO).

—— 1993, 'The Evolutionary Theory of Land Rights as Applied to Sub-Saharan Africa: A Critical Assessment', Faculty of Economics, University of Namur, Belgium (mimeo).

—— 1994, 'Behind the Market Stage Where Real Societies Exist: Part II, The Role of Moral Norms', *Journal of Development Studies*, 30/3: 753–815.

—— and J. M. Baland, 1989, 'Income-Sharing through Work-Spreading Arrangements: An Economic Analysis with Special Relevance to Small-Scale Fishing', Cahiers de la Faculté des Sciences Economiques et Sociales, No. 91, University of Namur, Belgium.

Posner, R., 1977, *Economic Analysis of Law* (Boston, Mass.: Little, Brown & Co.).

Putnam, R. D., 1993, *Making Democracy Work: Civic Traditions in Modern Italy* (Princeton, NJ: Princeton University Press).

Putterman, L., 1981, 'Is a Democratic Collective Agriculture Possible? Theoretical Considerations and Evidence from Tanzania', *Journal of Development Economics*, 9/3: 375–403.

Quiggin, J., 1988, 'Scattering in Common Property Systems', *Journal of Economic Behavior and Organization*, 9/2: 187–202.

—— 1993, 'Common Property, Equality and Development', *World Development*, 21/7: 1123–38.

Rao, C. H. H., 1988, 'Agricultural Development and Ecological Framework', *Economic and Political Weekly*, 23/52–3: A-142–6.

Rapoport, A., and A. Chammah, 1965, *Prisoner's Dilemma* (Ann Arbor, Mich.: University of Michigan Press).

Rasmusen, E., 1989, *Games and Information: An Introduction to Game Theory* (Oxford: Blackwell).

Rauscher, M., 1990, 'The Optimal Use of Environmental Resources by an Indebted Country', *Journal of Institutional and Theoretical Economics*, 146: 500–16.

Raynaut, C., 1976, 'Transformation du système de production et inégalité économique: le cas d'un village haoussa (Niger)', *Revue canadienne des études africaines*, 10/2: 279–306.

Repetto, R., 1988, *The Forests for the Trees? Government Policies and the Misuse of Forest Resources* (Washington, DC: World Resources Institute).

Richards, P., forthcoming, 'Saving the Rain Forest: Contested Futures in Conservation', in S. Wallman (ed.), *Contemporary Futures* (London: Routledge): 138–53.

Robertson, A. F., 1987, *The Dynamics of Productive Relationships: African Share Contracts in Comparative Perspective* (Cambridge: Cambridge University Press).

Roemer, J. E., 1988, 'A Public Ownership Resolution of the Tragedy of the Commons', Working Paper No. 295, Dept. of Economics, University of California, Davis.

Rosenberg, N., 1964, 'Neglected Dimensions in the Analysis of Economic Change', *Oxford Bulletin of Economics and Statistics*, 26/1: 59–77.

Roth, A. E., 1988, 'Laboratory Experimentation in Economics: A Methodological Overview', *Economic Journal*, 98/393: 974–1031.

—— and J. K. Murnighan, 1978, 'Equilibrium Behavior and Repeated Play of the Prisoner's Dilemma', *Journal of Mathematical Psychology*, 17: 189–98.

Ruddle, K., 1982, 'Environmental Pollution and Fishery Resources in Southeast Asian Coastal Waters', in C. Soysa, L. S. Chia, and W. L. Collier (eds.), *Man, Land and Sea: Coastal Zone Resources Use and Management in Asia and the Pacific* (Bangkok: Agricultural Development Council).

—— 1987, 'Administration and Conflict Management in Japanese Coastal Fisheries', *FAO Fisheries Technical Paper*, No. 273 (Rome: FAO).

—— 1988, 'The Organization of Traditional Inshore Fishery Management Systems in the Pacific', in P. Neher, R. Arnason, and N. Mollett (eds.), *Rights Based Fishing* (Dordrecht: Kluwer Academic Publishers): 73–85.

Runge, C. F., 1981, 'Common Property Externalities; Isolation, Assurance and Resource Depletion in a Traditional Grazing Context', *American Journal of Agricultural Economics*, 63/4: 595–606.

—— 1984*a*, 'Strategic Interdependence in Models of Property Rights', *American Journal of Agricultural Economics*, 66/5: 807–13.

—— 1984*b*, 'Institutions and the Free Rider: The Assurance Problem in Collective Action', *Journal of Politics*, 46/1: 154–75.

—— 1986, 'Common Property and Collective Action in Economic Development', *World Development*, 14/5: 623–35.

Ruttan, V., and Y. Hayami, 1984, 'Toward a Theory of Induced Institutional Innovation', *Journal of Development Studies*, 20/4: 203–23.

Sadan, E., and D. Weintraub, 1980, 'Ethnicity, Nativity, and Economic Performance of Cooperative Smallholding Farms in Israel', *Economic Development and Cultural Change*, 28/3: 487–507.

Schlager, E., 1990, 'Model Specification and Policy Analysis: The Governance of Coastal Fisheries' (Bloomington, Ind.: Indiana University, Workshop in Political Theory and Policy Analysis).

—— 1994, 'Fishers' Institutional Responses to Common-Pool Resource Dilemmas', in E. Ostrom, R. Gardner, and J. Walker, *Rules, Games, and Common-Pool Resources* (Ann Arbor, Mich.: University of Michigan Press): 247–65.

Schoeck, H., 1987, *Envy* (Indianapolis, Ind.: Liberty Press).

Schokkaert, E., 1992, 'Business Ethics and the Greenhouse Problem', in J. Mahoney and E. Vallance (eds.), *Business Ethics in a New Europe* (Dordrecht: Kluwer): 191–207.

Schotter, A., 1981, *The Economic Theory of Social Institutions* (New York: Cambridge University Press).

—— 1983, 'Why Take a Game Theoretical Approach to Economics? Institutions, Economics and Game Theory', *Economie Appliquée*, 36/4: 673–95.

—— 1986, 'The Evolution of Rules', in R. Langlois (ed.), *Economics as a Process: Essays in the New Institutional Economics* (Cambridge: Cambridge University Press): 117–33.

Schumpeter, J., 1942, *Capitalism, Socialism, and Democracy* (New York: Harper & Brothers).

Schwartz, S. H., 1970, 'Moral Decision Making and Behavior', in J. Macaulay and L. Berkowitz (eds.), *Altruism and Helping Behavior* (New York: Academic Press): 127–41.

Scott, A., 1993, 'Obstacles to Fishery Self-Government', *Marine Resource Economics*, 8: 187–99.

Scudder, T., and T. Conelly, 1985, 'Systèmes d'aménagement de la pêche fluviale', *FAO Fisheries Technical Paper*, No. 263 (Rome: FAO).

Seabright, P., 1993, 'Managing Local Commons: Theoretical Issues in Incentive Design', *Journal of Economic Perspectives*, 17/4: 113–34.

Selten, R., 1991, 'Evolution, Learning and Economic Behavior', *Games and Economic Behavior*, 3/1.

——and R. Stoecker, 1986, 'End Behavior in Sequences of Finite Prisoner's Dilemma Supergames: A Learning Theory Approach', *Journal of Economic Behavior and Organization*, 7/1: 47–70.

Sen, A. K., 1966, 'Labour Allocation in a Cooperative Enterprise', *Review of Economic Studies*, 33: 361–71.

——1967, 'Isolation, Assurance and the Social Rate of Discount', *Quarterly Journal of Economics*, 81/1: 112–24.

——1973, *On Economic Inequality* (Oxford: Clarendon Press).

——1985, 'Goals, Commitment, and Identity', *Journal of Law, Economics and Organization*, 1/2: 341–55.

Shah, T., 1988, 'Gains from Social Forestry: Lessons from West Bengal', IDS Discussion Paper, No. 243, Institute of Development Studies, University of Sussex.

Shanmugaratnam, N., T. Vedeld, A. Mossige, and M. Bovin, 1992, 'Resource Management and Pastoral Institution Building in the West African Sahel', *World Bank Discussion Papers*, No. 175 (Washington, DC: World Bank).

Shapley, L. S., and M. Shubik, 1969, 'On the Core of an Economic System with Externalities', *American Economic Review*, 59/4: 678–84.

Shingi, P. M., M. S. Patel, and S. Wadwalkar, 1986, *Development of Social Forestry in India* (Ahmedabad: Indian Institute of Management).

Shott, S., 1979, 'Emotion and Social Life: A Symbolic Interactionist Analysis', *American Journal of Sociology*, 84/6: 1335–360.

Shoup, J., 1987, *Transhumant Pastoralism in Lesotho: Case Study of the Mapoteng Ward* (Museru, Lesotho: Land Conservation and Range Development Project).

Shubik, M., 1982, *Game Theory in the Social Sciences: Concepts and Solutions* (Cambridge, Mass.: MIT Press).

Singer, P., 1973, 'Altruism and Commerce: A Defence of Titmuss against Arrow', *Philosophy and Public Affairs*, 2: 312–20.

Skinner, Q., 1974, 'Some Problems in the Analysis of Political Thought and Action', *Political Theory*, 2/1: 277–303.

Smith, A., 1759, *The Theory of the Moral Sentiments* (ed. by D. D. Raphael and A. L. Macfie, Indianapolis: Liberty Classics, 1982).

Smith, T. C., 1959, *The Agrarian Origins of Modern Japan* (Stanford, Calif.: Stanford University Press).

Solow, R. M., 1974, 'Intergenerational Equity and Exhaustible Resources', *Review of Economic Studies*, Symposium on the Economics of Exhaustible Resources, 41: 29–45.

Southgate, D., 1990, 'The Causes of Land Degradation along Expanding Agricultural Frontiers in the Third World', *Land Economics*, 66/1: 93–101.

——R. Sierra, and L. Brown, 1991, 'The Causes of Tropical Deforestation in Ecuador: A Statistical Analysis', *World Development*, 19/9: 1145–51.

Soysa, C., L. S. Chia, and W. L. Collier (eds.), 1982, *Man, Land and Sea: Coastal Resource Use and Management in Asia and the Pacific* (Bangkok: Agricultural Development Council).

Spence, A. M., and D. A. Starrett, 1975, 'Most Rapid Approach Paths in Accumulation Problems', *International Economic Review*, 16/2: 388–403.

Spradley, J. P., and D. W. McCurdy, 1980, *Anthropology: The Cultural Perspective* (New York: John Wiley & Sons).

Stanley, D. L., 1991, 'Communal Forest Management: The Honduran Resin Tappers', *Development and Change*, 22/4: 757–79.

Steinherr, A., and J. Thisse, 1979, 'Are Labor-Managers Really Perverse', *Economic Letters*, 2/2: 137–41.

Steuer, M., 1989, 'Culture and Optimality', London School of Economics, STICERD Discussion Paper No. TE/89/206.

Stiglitz, J., 1974, 'Growth with Exhaustible Natural Resources: The Competitive Economy', *Review of Economic Studies*, Symposium on the Economics of Exhaustible Resources, 41: 123–38.

—— 1976, 'The Efficiency Wage Hypothesis, Surplus Labour and the Distribution of Income in LDCs', *Oxford Economic Papers*, 28/2: 185–207.

Strand, J., 1992, 'Foreign Aid, Capital Accumulation, and Developing Country Resource Extraction', *Journal of Development Economics*, 38/1: 147–63.

—— 1994*a*, 'Developing Country Resource Extraction with Sovereign Debt', Dept. of Economics, Stanford University (mimeo).

—— 1994*b*, 'Developing Country Resource Extraction with Asymmetric Information and Sovereign Debt: A Theoretical Analysis', Dept. of Economics, Stanford University (mimeo).

Sugden, R., 1984, 'Reciprocity: The Supply of Public Goods Through Voluntary Contributions', *Economic Journal*, 94: 772–87.

—— 1986, *The Economics of Rights, Co-operation and Welfare* (Oxford: Blackwell).

—— 1989, 'Spontaneous Order', *Journal of Economic Perspectives*, 3/4: 85–97.

Sutinen, J. G., and P. Andersen, 1985, 'The Economics of Fisheries Law Enforcement', *Land Economics* 61/4: 387–97.

—— and J. R. Gauvin, 1989, 'An Econometric Study of Regulatory Enforcement and Compliance in the Commercial Inshore Lobster Fishery of Massachusetts', in P. A. Neher, R. Arnason, and N. Mollett (eds.), *Right Based Fishing* (New York: Kluwer): 415–28.

—— and K. Kuperan, 1994, 'A Socioeconomic Theory of Regulatory Compliance in Fisheries', Dept. of Resource Economics, University of Rhode Island, USA (mimeo).

—— A. Rieser, and J. P. Gauvin, 1990, 'Measuring and Explaining Noncompliance in Federally Managed Fisheries', *Ocean Development and International Law*, 21: 335–72.

Swallow, B. M., and D. Bromley, 1994*a*, 'Co-management or No Management: The Prospects for Internal Governance of Common Property Regimes through Dynamic Contracts', *Oxford Agrarian Studies*, 22/1: 3–16.

—— —— 1994*b*, 'Institutions, Governance and Incentives in Common Property Regimes for African Rangelands', *Environmental and Resource Economics* (forthcoming).

Swift, J., 1991, 'Local Customary Institutions as the Basis for Natural Resource Management Among Boran Pastoralists in Northern Kenya', *IDS Bulletin*, 22/4: 34–7.

Sya'rani, L., and N. G. Willoughby, 1987, 'The Traditional Management of Marine Resources in Indonesia', University Diponegoro, Java, Indonesia.

Tang, S. Y., 1991, 'Institutional Arrangements and the Management of Common-Pool Resources', *Public Administration Review*, 51/1: 42–51.

—— 1992, *Institutions and Collective Action: Self-Governance in Irrigation Systems* (San Francisco: ICS Press).

Tang, S. Y., 1994, 'Institutions and Performance in Irrigation Systems', in E. Ostrom, R. Gardner, and J. Walker, *Rules, Games, and Common-Pool Resources* (Ann Arbor, Mich.: University of Michigan Press): 225–45.

Taylor, L., 1987, '"The River Would Run Red with Blood": Community and Common Property in an Irish Fishing Settlement', in B. J. McCay and J. M. Acheson (eds.), *The Question of the Commons: The Culture and Ecology of Communal Resources* (Tucson, Ariz.: University of Arizona Press): 290–307.

Taylor, M., 1987, *The Possibility of Cooperation* (Cambridge: Cambridge University Press).

Thomson, J. T., D. H. Feeny, and R. J. Oakerson, 1986, 'Institutional Dynamics: The Evolution and Dissolution of Common Property Resource Management', in National Research Council, *Proceedings of the Conference on Common Property Resource Management* (Washington, DC: National Academy Press): 391–424.

Tirole, J., 1993, 'A Theory of Collective Reputations, with Applications to the Persistence of Corruption and to Firm Quality', IDEI, University of Toulouse (mimeo).

Toulmin, C., 1991, 'Natural Resource Management at the Local Level: Will This Bring Food Security to the Sahel?', *IDS Bulletin*, 22/3: 22–30.

Ullmann-Margalit, E., 1977, *The Emergence of Norms* (Oxford: Clarendon Press).

Utting, P., 1994, 'Social and Political Dimensions of Environmental Protection in Central America', *Development and Change*, 25/1: 231–59.

Vanberg, V., 1988, *Morality and Economics: De Moribus Est Disputandum*, The Social Philosophy and Policy Center, Original Papers No. 7 (New Brunswick: Transaction Books).

Van Huyck, J. B., R. C. Battalio, and R. O. Beil, 1990, 'Tacit Coordination Games, Strategic Uncertainty, and Coordination Failure', *American Economic Review*, 80/1: 234–48.

Verdeaux, F., 1990, 'Généalogie d'un phénomène de surexploitation: lagune Aby (Côte d'Ivoire) 1935–1982', in F. Verdeaux (ed.), *La pêche: Enjeux de développement et objet de recherche* (Paris: Editions de l'ORSTOM): 191–211 [originally published in *Cahier des Sciences Humaines*, 25/1–2 1989].

Viscusi, W. K., 1985, 'Environmental Policy Choice with an Uncertain Chance of Irreversibility', *Journal of Environmental Economics and Management*, 12: 28–44.

Vivian, J., 1994, 'NGOs and Sustainable Development in Zimbabwe: No Magic Bullets', *Development and Change*, 25/1: 167–93.

Wade, R., 1982, 'The System of Administration and Political Corruption: Canal Irrigation in South India', *Journal of Development Studies*, 18/2: 287–327.

—— 1985, 'The Market for Public Office: Why the Indian State is Not Better at Development?', *World Development*, 13/4: 467–97.

—— 1986*a*, 'Common Property Resource Management in South Indian Villages', in National Research Council, *Proceedings of the Conference on Common Property Resource Management* (Washington, DC: National Academy Press): 231–57.

—— 1986*b*, 'The Management of Common Property Resources: Collective Action as an Alternative to Privatization or State Regulation', Discussion Paper No. 54, Agriculture and Rural Development Department (Washington, DC: World Bank).

—— 1987, 'The Management of Common Property Resources: Finding a Cooperative Solution', *World Bank Research Observer*, 2/2: 219–34.

—— 1988*a*, *Village Republics: Economic Conditions for Collective Action in South India* (Cambridge: Cambridge University Press).

—— 1988*b*, 'The Management of Irrigation Systems: How to Evoke Trust and Avoid Prisoners' Dilemma', *World Development*, 16/4: 489–500.

—— 1990, 'Employment, Water Control and Water Supply Institutions: India and South

Korea', in W. Gooneratne and S. Hirashima (eds.), *Irrigation and Water Management in Asia* (New Delhi: Sterling Publishers).
Weber, E., 1976, *Peasants into Frenchmen* (Stanford, Calif.: Stanford University Press).
Weber, M., 1951, *The Religion of China: Confucianism and Taoism* (Glencoe: Free Press).
—— 1970, *The Protestant Ethic* (London: Allen & Unwin).
—— 1971, *Economie et société* (Paris: Plon).
Weg, E., and R. Zwick, 1994, 'Towards the Settlement of the Fairness Issues in Ultimatum Games—A Bargaining Approach', *Journal of Economic Behavior and Organization*, 24/1: 19–34.
Weigel, J. Y., 1985*a*, 'Contexte, évolution et perspectives d'aménagement des pêcheries lagunaires Ivoiriennes', Paper presented at the COPACE–FAO meeting, Lomé (Rome: FAO).
—— 1985*b*, 'L'aménagement traditionnel de quelques lagunes du Golfe de Guinée', *Circulaire Pêches*, 790 (Rome: FAO).
Weissing, F., and E. Ostrom, 1991, 'Irrigation Institutions and the Games Irrigators Play: Rule Enforcement Without Guards', in R. Selten (ed.), *Game Equilibrium Models II: Methods, Morals, and Markets* (Berlin: Springer-Verlag): 188–262.
—— —— 1992, 'Irrigation Institutions and the Games Irrigators Play: Rule Enforcement on Government- and Farmer-Managed Systems', in F. W. Scharpf (ed.), *Games in Hierarchies and Networks: Analytical and Empirical Approaches to the Study of Governance Institutions* (Frankfurt: Campus).
Weitzman, M., 1974, 'Free Access vs. Private Ownership as Alternative Systems for Managing Common Property', *Journal of Economic Theory*, 8/2: 225–34.
White, D. M., 1977, *Social Organization and the Sea: A Gulf Coast Shrimp Fishery*, unpublished Ph.D. thesis, Southern Methodist University (USA).
Wiessner, P., 1982, 'Risk, Reciprocity and Social Influences on Kung San Economics', in E. Leacock and R. B. Lee (eds.), *Politics and History in Band Societies* (Cambridge: Cambridge University Press): 61–84.
Williamson, O., 1985, *The Economic Institutions of Capitalism* (New York: Free Press).
Willmann, R., 1993, 'Community-Based Resources Management: Experiences with Forestry, Water and Land Resources', *FAO Fisheries Report*, No. 474, Suppl. (Rome: FAO): 317–36.
Wilson, P. N., and G. D. Thompson, 1993, 'Common Property and Uncertainty: Compensating Coalitions by Mexico's Pastoral *Ejidatorios*', *Economic Development and Cultural Change*, 41/2: 299–318.
World Bank, 1983, *India: Himalayan Watershed Management Project (Uttar Pradesh)*, Staff Appraisal Report (Washington, DC: World Bank).
—— 1992, *World Development Report 1992: Development and the Environment* (Washington, DC: World Bank).
Yoder, R. D., 1986, 'The Performance of Farmer-Managed Irrigation Systems in the Hills of Nepal', Ph.D. dissertation, Cornell University.
Young, C., 1986, 'Africa's Colonial Legacy', in R. J. Berg and J. S. Whitaker (eds.), *Strategies for African Development* (Berkeley, Calif.: University of California Press): 25–51.
Young, J. T., 1992, 'Natural Morality and the Ideal Impartial Spectator in Adam Smith', *International Journal of Social Economics*, 19/10-12: 71–82.
Zufferey, F. S., 1986, 'A Study of Local Institutions and Resource Management Inquiry in Eastern Central District', Research Paper No. 88, Land Tenure Center, University of Wisconsin-Madison.

Index